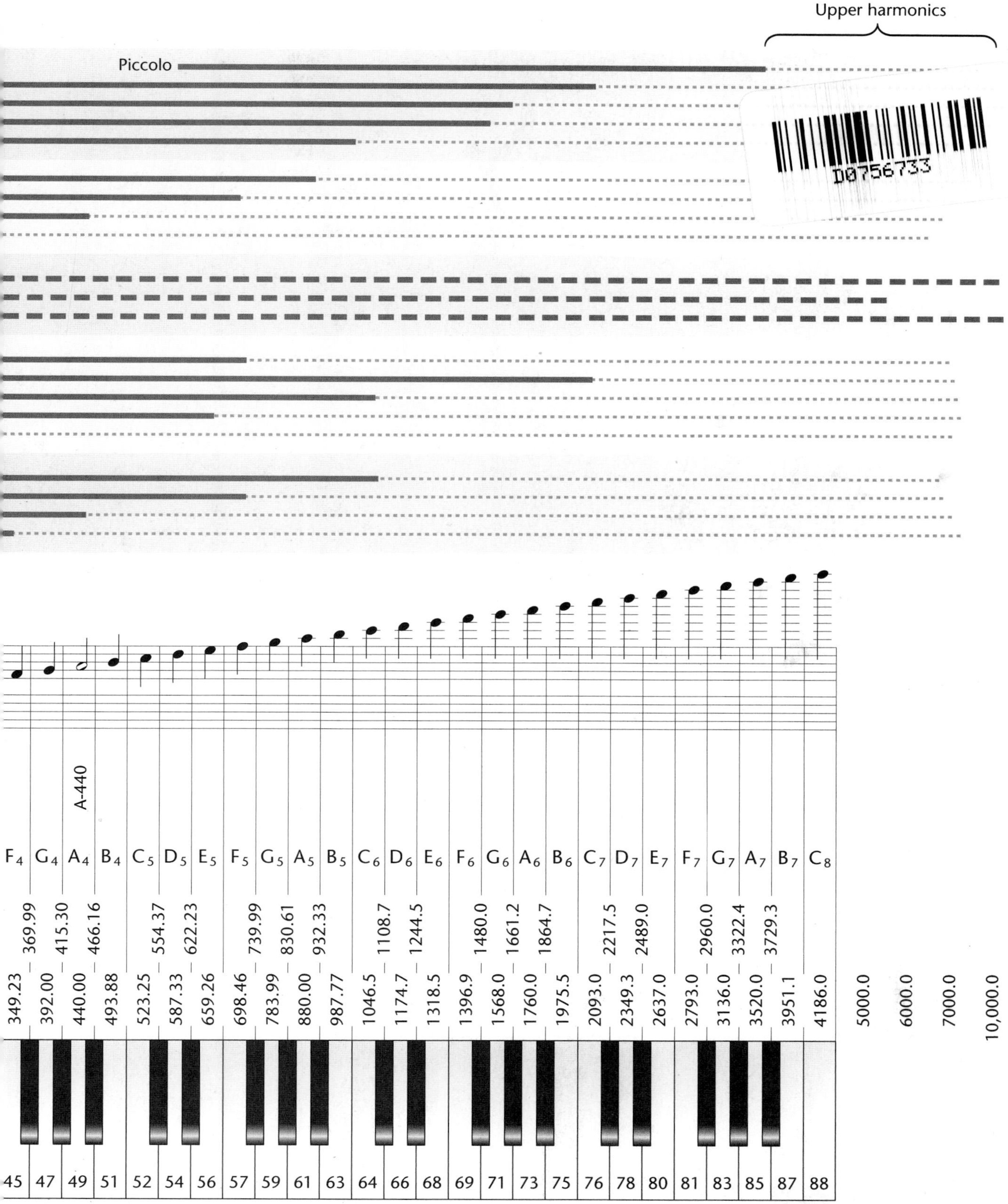
Upper harmonics
Piccolo
A-440
F4 G4 A4 B4 C5 D5 E5 F5 G5 A5 B5 C6 D6 E6 F6 G6 A6 B6 C7 D7 E7 F7 G7 A7 B7 C8
369.99 415.30 466.16 554.37 622.23 739.99 830.61 932.33 1108.7 1244.5 1480.0 1661.2 1864.7 2217.5 2489.0 2960.0 3322.4 3729.3
349.23 392.00 440.00 493.88 523.25 587.33 659.26 698.46 783.99 880.00 987.77 1046.5 1174.7 1318.5 1396.9 1568.0 1760.0 1975.5 2093.0 2349.3 2637.0 2793.0 3136.0 3520.0 3951.1 4186.0
5000.0 6000.0 7000.0 10,000.0
45 47 49 51 52 54 56 57 59 61 63 64 66 68 69 71 73 75 76 78 80 81 83 85 87 88

Audio *in* Media

NINTH EDITION

Stanley R. Alten

Syracuse University

WADSWORTH
CENGAGE Learning™

Australia • Brazil • Japan • Korea • Mexico • Singapore • Spain • United Kingdom • United States

WADSWORTH
CENGAGE Learning™

Audio in Media, Ninth Edition
Stanley R. Alten

Senior Publisher: Lyn Uhl

Publisher: Michael Rosenberg

Development Editor: Laurie K. Dobson

Assistant Editor: Jillian D'Urso

Editorial Assistant: Erin Pass

Media Editor: Jessica Badiner

Marketing Manager: Bryant Chrzan

Marketing Coordinator: Darlene Macanan

Marketing Communications Manager:
 Christine Dobberpuhl

Content Project Manager: Georgia Young

Art Director: Linda Helcher

Print Buyer: Justin Palmeiro

Permissions Editor:
 Margaret Chamberlain-Gaston

Production Service: Ideas to Images

Text Designer: Gary Palmatier

Photo Manager: John Hill

Compositor: Gary Palmatier, Ideas to Images

ISBN-13: 978-0-538-74362-4
ISBN-10: 0-538-74362-X

Wadsworth
20 Channel Center Street
Boston, MA 02210
USA

Cengage Learning is a leading provider of customized learning solutions with office locations around the globe, including Singapore, the United Kingdom, Australia, Mexico, Brazil, and Japan. Locate your local office at **international.cengage.com/region**

Cengage Learning products are represented in Canada by Nelson Education, Ltd.

For your course and learning solutions, visit **www.cengage.com**

Printed in Canada
1 2 3 4 5 6 7   14 13 12 11 10

For Claudette

Brief Contents

Contents

4 Consoles and Control Surfaces   83

13   Field Production: News and Sports   237

14   Sound Design   277

15   Sound Effects   291

16   Music Underscoring   314

17 Music Recording 335

18 Audio for Interactive Media: Game Sound   383

24 Evaluating the Finished Product 497

Advances in audio production continue at an accelerated rate. One purpose of this revision is to stay current in this fast-moving profession. Another is to deal with the interdependent, and blurring, relationship between technique and technology while remembering that technology serves art; it is the means to the end, not the end in itself.

Most of the basic considerations that relate to aural perception, aesthetics, operations, production know-how, and the qualities that go into good sound remain fundamental. It is undeniable that technology has helped make production more accessible, more efficient, and generally less expensive and has facilitated the production of extremely high-quality sound. But a production's ultimate success is due to human creativity, vision, and "ears." As Ham Brosius, pro audio marketing pioneer, once observed, "Respect technology but revere talent." Through its almost three decades as *the* best-selling audio text, *Audio in Media* has tried to balance the relationship between technology and technique and continues to do so in this edition.

A word about the inseparability of computers from audio production: Because there are so many different types of computers and computer software programs in use in an ever-changing landscape, the relationship of computers to audio production is covered only as it applies to producing program materials and not to computer technology, software programs, or operational details. There are many books on the market that handle these areas, to say nothing of the manuals provided with computers and software programs.

As with previous editions, the ninth covers all the major audio and audio-related media: radio, television, film, music recording, interactive media, the Internet, and, new with this edition, mobile media, such as cell phones, iPods, cameras, PDAs, and laptop computers.

Content is designed for the beginner, yet the experienced practitioner will find the material valuable as a reference even after a course of study is completed. The organization facilitates reading chapters in or out of sequence, based on need and level of background, with no disruption in continuity.

This edition has been reorganized, and chapters have been added to better complement subject flow. Overall the chapters are more focused, to make the distribution of content easier to locate and assign. Moreover, chapters are grouped relative to the subject areas of principles, technology, production, and postproduction. All chapters have been updated and refined.

Each chapter is preceded by an outline of its main headings and concluded with a list of its main points. Key terms are identified in **bold italic** and defined in the Glossary. There are more than 100 new and revised illustrations.

The book's companion Web site features chapter summaries, flashcards, crossword puzzles, key terms, main points, a media glossary, information on occupations in audio media, and Web links. For instructors there is an online manual to help guide classroom discussion.

STRUCTURE OF THE BOOK

Part I: Principles

Chapter 1, "Sound and Hearing," introduces the physical behavior of sound and its relationship to our psychophysical perception of sound stimuli. It also includes a section about the importance of healthy hearing and new illustrations related to hearing loss. The chapter has been reorganized to better reflect the subject sequence of its title.

Chapter 2, "Acoustics and Psychoacoustics," develops the material in Chapter 1 as it applies to the objective behavior of received sound, its subjective effect on those who hear it, and how these factors affect studio and control room design and construction.

Part II: Technology

Chapter 3, "Microphones," discusses their principles, characteristics, types, and accessories. The chapter has been reorganized to improve subject flow.

Chapter 4, "Consoles and Control Surfaces," covers signal flow and the design of broadcast and production consoles—analog and digital—and control surfaces. Patching and console automation are also discussed. Because of the many different types, models, and designs of consoles in use and their various purposes, the approach to the material in this edition is generic so that the basic principles are easier to grasp and apply.

Chapter 5, "Recording," covers basic digital theory, digital recorders, digital formats, disk-based recording systems, digital audio on videotape, and film audio formats.

Chapter 6, "Synchronization and Transfers," updates these fundamental aspects of production and postproduction.

Chapter 7, "Signal Processors," discusses their general principles—both stand-alone and plug-ins—and their effects on sound.

Chapter 8, "Loudspeakers and Monitoring," deals with the relationship between loudspeaker selection and control room monitoring, including expanded coverage of stereo and surround-sound monitoring. It also includes a section on headphones.

Part III: Production

Chapter 9, "Sound and the Speaking Voice," is the first of three grouped chapters that focus on the delivery and the signification of nonverbal speech. This chapter concentrates on speech intelligibility and basic considerations in miking and recording speech.

Chapter 10, "Voice-overs and Narration," explains the basic factors in the delivery, production, and functions of these aspects of recorded speech.

Chapter 11, "Dialogue," covers production recording and automated dialogue replacement of recordings made in the studio and on-location. In previous editions, the discussion of dialogue has been grouped with the chapters on sound design. In this edition the chapter was moved because it relates to the speaking voice and because only the director deals with an actor's delivery of dialogue.

Chapter 12, "Studio Production: Radio and Television," covers microphone and production techniques as they apply to studio programs in radio and television.

Chapter 13, "Field Production: News and Sports," concentrates on producing news and sports on-location and includes new material on the growing use of wireless data transmission.

Chapter 14, "Sound Design," introduces the nature and the aesthetics of designing sound, the basic structure of sonic communication, the sound/picture relationship, and strategies for designing sound for traditional and mobile media. It includes a section on the importance of having "ears"—the ability to listen to sound with judgment and discrimination. The chapter also serves as a foundation for the two chapters that follow.

Chapter 15, "Sound Effects," covers prerecorded sound-effect libraries and producing and recording sound effects in the studio and in the field. It includes a new section on vocally produced sound effects and an expanded section on ways to produce sound effects.

Chapter 16, "Music Underscoring," addresses music's informational and emotional enhancement of visual content, with an expanded section of examples.

Chapter 17, "Music Recording," focuses on studio-based recording of live music. It includes the characteristics of musical instruments, ways to mike them, and various approaches to miking ensembles for stereo and surround sound.

Chapter 18, "Audio for Interactive Media: Game Sound," introduces the preproduction, production, and postproduction of audio for games and how they are similar to and different from handling audio for television and film.

Chapter 19, "Internet Production," covers sound quality on the Internet. It includes expanded discussions of online collaborative recording and podcasting and a new section about producing for mobile media.

Part IV: Postproduction

Chapter 20, "Editing," describes the techniques of digital editing. It also addresses organizing the edit tracks; drive and file management; the aesthetic considerations that apply to editing speech, dialogue, music, and sound effects; and the uses of transitions.

Chapter 21, "Mixing: An Overview," is the first of three grouped chapters covering mixing. This chapter introduces the final stage in audio production, when sounds are combined and processed for mastering, final duplication, and distribution. It includes coverage of mixing for the various media and the role of metering in assessment and troubleshooting.

Chapter 22, "Music Mixdown," is devoted to mixing and processing music for stereo and surround sound, with expanded coverage of signal processing.

Chapter 23, "Premixing and Rerecording for Television and Film," includes coverage of the procedures for the premix and rerecording stages; dialnorm; stereo and surround sound; mobile media; and mono-to-stereo and surround sound–to–stereo compatibility.

Chapter 24, "Evaluating the Finished Product," reviews the sonic and aesthetic considerations involved in judging the result of a production.

ACKNOWLEDGMENTS

The success of *Audio in Media* over the years has been due in large part to the interest, advice, and guidance of teachers and practitioners in the field who have been so forthcoming with their expertise. Whatever success the ninth edition enjoys is due in no small measure to their continued guidance and good advice.

To the following reviewers of the ninth edition, I offer my sincere gratitude for their insightful suggestions that helped direct this revision: Jacob Belser, Indiana University; Jack Klotz, Temple University; Barbara Malmet, New York University; William D. Moylan, University of Massachusetts-Lowell; and Jeffrey Stern, University of Miami.

To the following industry and academic professionals for their contributions go my thanks and appreciation: Fred Aldous, senior mixer, Fox Sports; Bruce Bartlett, author and engineer; David Bowles, music producer; Ben Burtt, sound designer; Bob Costas, NBC Sports; Dr. Peter D'Antonio, president, RPG Diffusor Systems; Charles Deenen, audio director, Electronic Arts/Maxis; Dennis Deninger, senior coordinating editor, ESPN; Lee Dichter, rerecording mixer, Sound One; Steve Haas, founder and president, SH Acoustics; Michael Hertlein, dialogue editor; Tomlinson Holman, president of THM Corporation and professor of cinema-television, University of Southern California; House Ear Institute; Dennis Hurd, Earthworks, Inc.; Kent Jolly, audio director, Electronic Arts/Maxis; Nick Marasco, chief engineer, WAER-FM, Syracuse; Sylvia Massy, producer-engineer; Elliot Scheiner, producer-engineer; Mark Schnell, senior audio engineer, Syracuse University; Frank Serafine, composer and sound designer, Serafine Productions; Michael Shane, Wheatstone Corporation; David Shinn, sound-effect and Foley artist; John Terrelle, president and producer, Hothead Productions; Herb Weisbaum, news and consumer reporter, KOMO Radio and TV, Seattle, and MSNBC.com; Dr. Herbert Zettl, professor emeritus, San Francisco State University; and Sue Zizza, sound-effect and Foley artist.

Continued thanks go to Nathan Prestopnik, multimedia developer, for bringing together and drafting the material on game sound and for his help with the material on Internet production in the previous edition that remains current.

To the first-rate folks at Cengage/Wadsworth go my sincere gratitude: Publisher Michael Rosenberg, for his support and guidance; Development Editor Laurie Dobson, who certainly earned that title; Jill Elise Sims for making life so much easier by tracking down the art and the permissions; and Erin Pass, Jillian D'Urso, and Megan Garvey for their added assistance.

As always, heartfelt salutes to project manager and art director Gary Palmatier of Ideas to Images, who brought the design of this edition to life and demonstrated that producing a book can be an art form; to Elizabeth von Radics for her perception, attention to detail, and polished copyediting; and to proofreader Mike Mollett for his keen eye. When it comes to ensuring the quality of *Audio in Media*, they are indispensable.

Special thanks go to my colleague Dr. Douglas Quin, associate professor, Syracuse University, for his contributions to several of the chapters in this edition. They are better because of his knowledge and experience.

Stanley R. Alten

"The engineer has the responsibility to make the audio sound good; the sound designer has the responsibility to make it sound interesting."

Anonymous

"I will always sacrifice a technical value for a production value."

Bruce Swedien, Sound Engineer/Producer

"You can see the picture, but you feel the sound. Sound can take something simple and make it extraordinary, and affect people in ways they don't even realize."

Martin Bruestle, Producer, The Sopranos

"We're invisible, until we are not there."

Mark Ulano, Production Recordist

Murphy's Law of Recording:
"Anything that can sound different, will."

Anonymous

Principles

1

Sound and Hearing

THE IMPORTANCE OF SOUND IN PRODUCTION

In an informal experiment done several years ago to ascertain what effect sound had on television viewers, three tests were conducted. In the first the sound quality of the audio and the picture quality of the video were without flaws. The viewers' general response was, "What a fine, good-looking show." In the second test, the sound quality of the audio was without flaws but the picture quality of the video was tarnished—it went from color to black-and-white and from clear to "snowy," it developed horizontal lines, and it "tore" at the top of the screen. The audience stayed through the viewing but generally had a lukewarm response: "The show was nothing great, just okay." In the third test, the picture quality of the video was without flaws but the sound quality of the audio was tarnished—it cut out from time to time so there was intermittent silence, static was introduced here and there, and volume was sometimes made too loud or too soft. Most of the audience had left by the end of the viewing. Those who stayed said the show was "quite poor."

Viewers may not be as disturbed by small problems in the picture, but problems with the sound often result in calling attention away from the image or from the music on a CD.

Then there are the aesthetics factors, which are covered in the contexts of production and postproduction in this book, such as the vocal emphasis that can change the meaning of a word or phrase from emphatic to pleading to questioning, the sound effect that intensifies an action, or the music underscore that adds drama, romance, or suspense to a scene. In a song the choice and the placement of a microphone and the distribution of the instruments in the aural space can affect the sonority and density of the music.

Disregarding the influence of sound can lead to problems that become disconcerting and distracting, if not disturbing, to audiences. Could that be why they are called "audiences" and not "vidiences"? Attention to sound is too often overlooked to the detriment of a production; it is an effective and relatively low-cost way to improve production values.

THE SOUND WAVE

Sound is produced by vibrations that set into motion longitudinal waves of compression and rarefaction propagated through molecular structures such as gases, liquids, and solids. *Hearing* occurs when these vibrations are received and processed by the ear and sent to the brain by the auditory nerve.

Sound begins when an object vibrates and sets into motion molecules in the air closest to it. These molecules pass on their energy to adjacent molecules, starting a reaction—a *sound wave*—which is much like the waves that result when a stone is dropped into a pool. The transfer of momentum from one displaced molecule to the next propagates the original vibrations longitudinally from the vibrating object to the hearer. What makes this reaction possible is air or, more precisely, a molecular medium with the property of elasticity. *Elasticity* is the phenomenon in which a displaced molecule tends to pull back to its original position after its initial momentum has caused it to displace nearby molecules.

As a vibrating object moves outward, it compresses molecules closer together, increasing pressure. *Compression* continues away from the object as the momentum of the disturbed molecules displaces the adjacent molecules, producing a crest in the sound wave. When a vibrating object moves inward, it pulls the molecules farther apart and thins them, creating a *rarefaction*. This rarefaction also travels away from the object in a manner similar to compression except that it decreases pressure, thereby producing a trough in the sound wave (see Figure 1-1). As the sound wave moves away from the vibrating object, the individual molecules do not advance with the wave; they vibrate at what is termed their *average resting place* until their motion stills or they are set in motion by another vibration. Inherent in each wave motion are the components that make up a sound wave: frequency, amplitude, velocity, wavelength, and phase (see 1-1, 1-2, and 1-9).

FREQUENCY AND PITCH

When a vibration passes through one complete up-and-down motion, from compression through rarefaction, it has completed one cycle. The number of cycles that a vibration completes in one second is expressed as its *frequency*. If a vibration completes 50 *cycles per second (cps)*, its frequency is 50 *hertz (Hz);* if it completes 10,000 cps, its frequency is 10,000 Hz, or 10 *kilohertz (kHz)*. Every vibration has a frequency, and humans with excellent hearing may be capable of hearing frequencies from 20 to 20,000 Hz. The limits of low- and high-frequency hearing for most humans, however, are about 35 to 16,000 Hz. Frequencies just below the *low end* of this range, called *infrasonic*, and those just above the *high end* of this range, called *ultrasonic*, are sensed more than heard, if they are perceived at all.

These limits change with natural aging, particularly in the higher frequencies. Generally, hearing acuity diminishes to about 15,000 Hz by age 40, to 12,000 Hz by age 50, and to 10,000 Hz or lower beyond age 50. With frequent exposure to loud sound, the audible frequency range can be adversely affected prematurely.

Psychologically, and in musical terms, we perceive frequency as *pitch*—the relative tonal highness or lowness of a sound. The more times per second a sound source vibrates, the higher its pitch. Middle C (C4) on a piano vibrates 261.63 times per second, so its fundamental frequency is 261.63 Hz. The A note above middle C has a frequency of 440 Hz, so the pitch is higher. The *fundamental* frequency is also called the *first harmonic* or *primary frequency*. It is the lowest, or basic, pitch of a musical instrument.

The range of audible frequencies, or the *sound frequency spectrum*, is divided into sections, each with a unique and vital quality. The usual divisions in Western music are called octaves. An *octave* is the interval between any two frequencies that have a tonal ratio of 2:1.

The range of human hearing covers about 10 octaves, which is far greater than the comparable range of the human eye; the visible light frequency spectrum covers less than one octave. The ratio of highest to lowest light frequency visible to humans is barely 2:1, whereas the ratio of the human audible frequency spectrum is 1,000:1.

Starting with 20 Hz, the first octave is 20 to 40 Hz; the second, 40 to 80 Hz; the third, 80 to 160 Hz; and

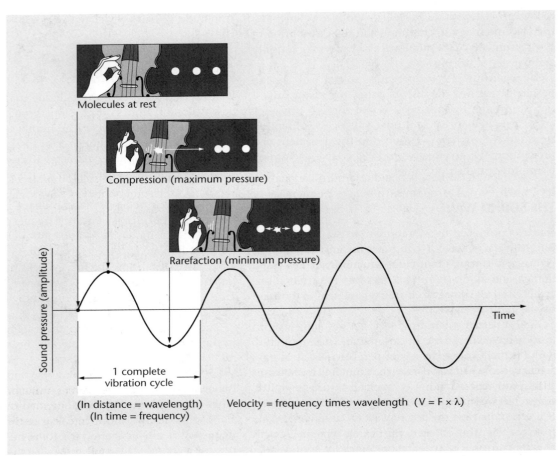

1-1 Components of a sound wave. The vibrating object causes compression in sound waves when it moves outward (causing molecules to bump into one another). The vibrating object causes rarefaction when it moves inward (pulling the molecules away from one another).

so on (see inside back cover). Octaves are grouped into *bass, midrange,* and *treble* and are further subdivided as follows.

■ **Low bass**—first and second octaves (20 to 80 Hz). These are the frequencies associated with power, boom, and fullness. There is little musical content in the lower part of this range. In the upper part of the range are the lowest notes of the piano, organ, tuba, and bass and the fundamental of the bass (kick) drum. (As mentioned previously, a fundamental is the lowest, or basic, pitch of a musical instrument [see "Timbre" later in this chapter].) Sounds in these octaves need not occur often to maintain a sense of fullness. If they occur too often or at too loud a level, the sound can become thick or overly dense. Most loudspeakers are capable of reproducing few, if any,

of the first-octave frequencies. Loudspeakers capable of reproducing second-octave frequencies often do so with varying loudness levels.

■ **Upper bass**—third and fourth octaves (80 to 320 Hz). Most of the lower tones generated by rhythm and other support instruments such as drums, piano, bass, cello, and trombone are in this range. They establish balance in a musical structure. Too many frequencies from this range make it sound boomy; too few make it thin. When properly proportioned, pitches in the second, third, and fourth octaves are very satisfying to the ear because we perceive them as giving sound an anchor, that is, fullness or bottom. Too much fourth-octave emphasis, however, can muddy sound. Frequencies in the upper bass range serve an aural structure in the way the horizontal line serves a visual structure—by providing a foundation. Almost all professional loudspeakers can reproduce the frequencies in this range.

■ **Midrange**—fifth, sixth, and seventh octaves (320 to 2,560 Hz). The midrange gives sound its intensity. It contains the fundamental and the rich lower harmonics and overtones of most sound sources. It is the primary treble octave of musical pitches. The midrange does not necessarily generate pleasant sounds. Although the sixth octave is where the highest fundamental pitches reside, too much emphasis here is heard as a hornlike quality. Too much emphasis of seventh-octave frequencies is heard as a hard, tinny quality. Extended listening to midrange sounds can be annoying and fatiguing.

■ **Upper midrange**—eighth octave (2,560 to 5,120 Hz). We are most sensitive to frequencies in the eighth octave, a rather curious range. The lower part of the eighth octave (2,560 to 3,500 Hz) contains frequencies that, if properly emphasized, improve the intelligibility of speech and lyrics. These frequencies are roughly 3,000 to 3,500 Hz. If these frequencies are unduly emphasized, however, sound becomes abrasive and unpleasant; vocals in particular become harsh and lispy, making some consonants difficult to understand. The upper part of the eighth octave (above 3,500 Hz), on the other hand, contains rich and satisfying pitches that give sound definition, clarity, and realism. Listeners perceive a sound source frequency in this range (and also in the lower part of the ninth octave, up to about 6,000 Hz) as being nearby, and for this reason it is also known as the *presence range*. Increasing loudness at 5,000 Hz, the heart of the presence range, gives the impression that there has been an overall increase in loudness throughout the midrange. Reducing loudness at 5,000 Hz makes a sound seem transparent and farther away.

■ **Treble**—ninth and tenth octaves (5,120 to 20,000 Hz). Although the ninth and tenth octaves generate only 2 percent of the total power output of the sound frequency spectrum, and most human hearing does not extend much beyond 16,000 Hz, they give sound the vital, lifelike qualities of brilliance and sparkle, particularly in the upper-ninth and lower-tenth octaves. Too much emphasis above 6,000 Hz makes sound hissy and brings out electronic noise. Too little emphasis above 6,000 Hz dulls sound.

Understanding the audible frequency spectrum's various sonic qualities is vital to processing spectral balances in audio production. Such processing is called *equalization* and is discussed at length in Chapters 7 and 22.

AMPLITUDE AND LOUDNESS

We have noted that vibrations in objects stimulate molecules to move in pressure waves at certain rates of alternation (compression/rarefaction) and that rate determines frequency. Vibrations not only affect the molecules' rate of up-and-down movement but also determine the number of displaced molecules that are set in motion from equilibrium to a wave's maximum height (crest) and depth (trough). This number depends on the intensity of a vibration; the more intense it is, the more molecules are displaced.

The greater the number of molecules displaced, the greater the height and the depth of the sound wave. The number of molecules in motion, and therefore the size of a sound wave, is called **amplitude** (see 1-2). Our subjective impression of amplitude is a sound's loudness or softness. Amplitude is measured in decibels.

The Decibel

The **decibel (dB)** is a dimensionless unit and, as such, has no specifically defined physical quantity. Rather, as a unit of measurement, it is used to compare the ratio of two quantities usually in relation to acoustic energy, such as sound pressure, and electric energy, such as power and voltage (see Chapter 4). In mathematical terms it is 10 times the logarithm to the base 10 of the ratio between the powers of two signals:

$$dB = 10 \log (P_1 / P_0)$$

P_0 is usually a reference power value with which another power value, P_1, is compared. It is abbreviated *dB* because it stands for one-tenth *(deci)* of a *bel* (from Alexander Graham Bell). The bel was the amount a signal dropped in level over a 1-mile distance of telephone wire. Because the amount of level loss was too large to work with as a single unit of measurement, it was divided into tenths for more-practical application.

Sound-pressure Level

Acoustic sound pressure is measured in terms of **sound-pressure level (dB-SPL)** because there are periodic variations in atmospheric pressure in a sound wave. Humans have the potential to hear an extremely wide range of these periodic variations, from 0 dB-SPL, the **threshold**

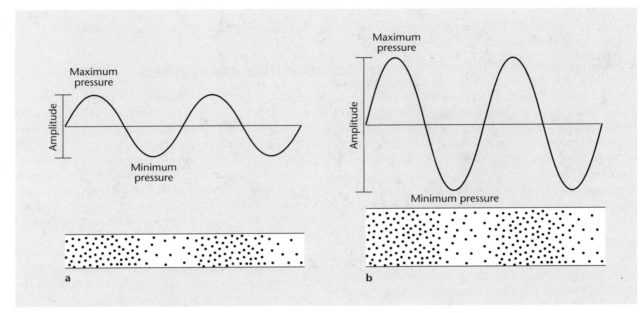

1-2 Amplitude of sound. The number of molecules displaced by a vibration creates the amplitude, or loudness, of a sound. Because the number of molecules in the sound wave in (b) is greater than the number in the sound wave in (a), the amplitude of the sound wave in (b) is greater.

of hearing; to 120 dB-SPL, what acousticians call the ***threshold of feeling;*** to 140 dB-SPL, the ***threshold of pain,*** and beyond. Figure 1-3 shows the relative loudness of various sounds, many that are common in our everyday lives. The range of the difference in decibels between the loudest and the quietest sound a vibrating object makes is called ***dynamic range.*** Because this range is so wide, a logarithmic scale is used to compress loudness measurement into more-manageable figures. (On a linear scale, a unit of 1 adds an increment of 1. On a logarithmic scale, a unit of 1 multiplies by a factor of 10.)

Humans have the capability to hear loudness at a ratio of 1:10,000,000 and greater. A sound-pressure-level change of 1 dB increases amplitude 12 percent; an increase of 6 dB-SPL doubles amplitude; 20 dB increases amplitude 10 times. Sound at 60 dB-SPL is 1,000 times louder than sound at 0 dB-SPL; at 80 dB-SPL it is 10 times louder than at 60 dB-SPL. If the amplitude of two similar sounds is 100 dB-SPL each, their amplitude, when added, would be 103 dB-SPL. Nevertheless, most people do not perceive a sound level as doubled until it has increased anywhere from 3 to 10 dB, depending on their aural acuity.

There are other acoustic measurements of human hearing based on the interactive relationship between frequency and amplitude.

FREQUENCY AND LOUDNESS

Frequency and amplitude are interdependent. Varying a sound's frequency also affects perception of its loudness; varying a sound's amplitude affects perception of its pitch.

Equal Loudness Principle

The response of the human ear is not equally sensitive to all audible frequencies (see 1-4). Depending on loudness, we do not hear low and high frequencies as well as we hear middle frequencies. In fact, the ear is relatively insensitive to low frequencies at low levels. Oddly enough, this is called the ***equal loudness principle*** (rather than the "unequal" loudness principle) (see 1-5). As you can see in Figures 1-4 and 1-5, at low frequencies the ear needs about 70 dB more sound level than it does at 3 kHz to be the same loudness. The ear is at its most sensitive at around 3 kHz. At frequencies of 10 kHz and higher, the ear is somewhat more sensitive than it is at low frequencies but not nearly as sensitive as it is at the midrange frequencies.

In other words, if a guitarist, for example, plucks all six strings equally hard, you do not hear each string at the same loudness level. The high E string (328 Hz) sounds

Apparent Loudness	Ratio to dB	dB-SPL	
		220	12' in front of cannon, below muzzle
		200	
Deafening		180	Rocket engines
		160	Jet engine, close up
		150	Permanent damage to hearing
	10,000,000	140	Threshold of pain Airport runway
	3,162,000	130	Rock band—on-stage; symphony orchestra, triple forte, 30' away
	1,000,000	120	Threshold of feeling; loud vocals in front of ear Thunder
Very loud	316,200	110	Electric guitar amp at maximum volume, 6" away Power tools
	100,000	100	Subway; loud vocals, 6" away Prolonged exposure can cause moderate to severe hearing loss
	31,620	90	Heavy truck traffic; baby crying; trombone, 16" away Brief exposure can cause slight hearing loss
	10,000	80	Acoustic guitar, 1' away
Loud	3,162	70	Busy street
	1,000	60	Average conversation
	316	50	Average office
Moderate	100	40	Subdued conversation
	32	30	Quiet office Recording studio
Faint	10	20	Furnished living room
Very faint	3	10	Insect noises at night, open field
	1	0	Threshold of hearing

1-3 Sound-pressure levels of various sound sources.

1-4 Responses to various frequencies by the human ear. This curve shows that the response is not flat and that we hear midrange frequencies better than low and high frequencies.

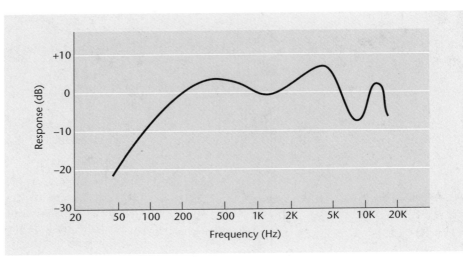

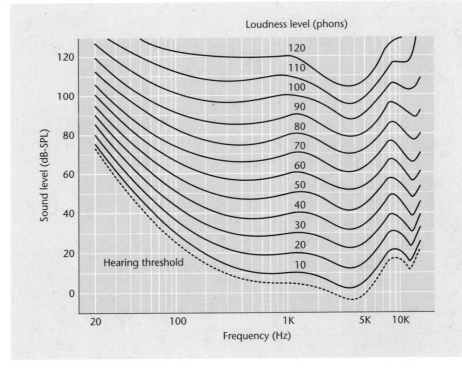

1-5 Equal loudness curves. These curves illustrate the relationships in Figure 1-4 and our relative lack of sensitivity to low and high frequencies as compared with middle frequencies. A 50 Hz sound would have to be 50 dB louder to seem as loud as a 1,000 Hz sound at 0 dB. To put it another way, at an intensity of, for instance, 40 dB, the level of a 100 Hz sound would have to be 10 times the sound-pressure level of a 1,000 Hz sound for the two sounds to be perceived as equal in loudness. Each curve is identified by the sound-pressure level at 1,000 Hz, which is known as the "phon of the curve."

(This graph represents frequencies on a logarithmic scale. The distance from 20 to 200 Hz is the same as from 200 to 2,000 Hz or from 2,000 to 20,000 Hz.) (Based on Robinson-Dadson.)

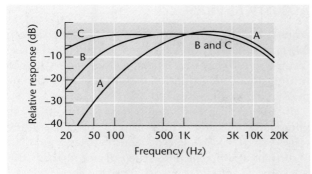

1-6 Frequency responses of the A, B, and C weighting networks.

Weighting Network	dB
A	20–55
B	55–85
C	85–140

louder than the low E string (82 Hz). To make the low string sound as loud, the guitarist would have to pluck it harder. This suggests that the high E string may sound louder because of its higher frequency. But if you sound three tones, say, 50 Hz, 1,000 Hz, and 15,000 Hz, at a fixed loudness level, the 1,000 Hz tone sounds louder than either the 50 Hz or the 15,000 Hz tone.

In a live concert, sound levels are usually louder than they are on a home stereo system. Live music often reaches levels of 100 dB-SPL and higher. At home, levels are as high as 70 to 75 dB-SPL and, alas, too often much higher. Sound at 70 dB-SPL requires more bass and treble boost than does sound at 100 dB-SPL to obtain equal loudness. Therefore the frequency balances you hear at 100 dB-SPL will be different when you hear the same sound at 70 dB-SPL.

In a recording or mixdown session, if the loudness level is high during recording and low during playback, both bass and treble frequencies could be considerably reduced in volume and may be virtually inaudible. The converse is also true: if sound level is low during recording and high during playback, the bass and treble frequencies could be too loud relative to the other frequencies and may even overwhelm them. Because sensitivity of the ear varies with frequency and loudness, meters that measure sound-pressure level are designed to correspond to these variations by incorporating one or more weighting networks.

A *weighting network* is a filter used for weighting a frequency response before measurement. Generally, three weighting networks are used: A, B, and C. The A and B networks bear close resemblances to the response of the human ear at 40 and 70 phons, respectively. (A *phon* is a dimensionless unit of loudness level related to the ear's

subjective impression of signal strength. For a tone of 1,000 Hz, the loudness level in phons equals the sound-pressure level in decibels.) The C network corresponds to the ear's sensitivity at 100 phons and has an almost flat frequency response (see 1-6). Decibel values for the three networks are written as *dBA*, *dBB*, and *dBC*. The level may be quoted in dBm, with the notation "A weighting." The A weighting curve is preferred for measuring lower-level sounds. The B weighting curve is usually used for measuring medium-level sounds. The C weighting, which is essentially flat, is used for very loud sounds (see 1-7).

Masking

Another phenomenon related to the interaction of frequency and loudness is *masking*—the hiding of some sounds by other sounds when each is a different frequency and they are presented together. Generally, loud sounds tend to mask softer ones, and lower-pitched sounds tend to mask higher-pitched ones.

For example, in a noisy environment you have to raise your voice to be heard. If a 100 Hz tone and a 1,000 Hz tone are sounded together at the same level, both tones will be audible but the 1,000 Hz tone will be perceived as louder. Gradually increasing the level of the 100 Hz tone and keeping the amplitude of the 1,000 Hz tone constant will make the 1,000 Hz tone more and more difficult to hear. If an LP (long-playing) record has scratches (high-frequency information), they will probably be masked during loud passages but audible during quiet ones. A symphony orchestra playing full blast may have all its instruments involved at once; flutes and clarinets will probably not be heard over trumpets and trombones, however, because woodwinds are generally higher in frequency and weaker in sound level than are the brasses.

Masking has practical uses in audio. In noise reduction systems, low-level noise can be effectively masked by a high-level signal; and in digital data compression, a desired signal can mask noise from lower resolutions.

VELOCITY

Although frequency and amplitude are the most important physical components of a sound wave, another component—*velocity*, or the speed of a sound wave—should be mentioned. Velocity usually has little impact on pitch or loudness and is relatively constant in a controlled environment. Sound travels 1,130 feet per second at sea level when the temperature is 70° Fahrenheit (F). The denser the molecular structure, the greater the vibrational conductivity. Sound travels 4,800 feet per second in water. In solid materials such as wood and steel, it travels 11,700 and 18,000 feet per second, respectively.

In air, sound velocity changes significantly in very high and very low temperatures, increasing as air warms and decreasing as it cools. For every 1°F change, the speed of sound changes 1.1 feet per second.

WAVELENGTH

Each frequency has a **wavelength**, determined by the distance a sound wave travels to complete one cycle of compression and rarefaction; that is, the physical measurement of the length of one cycle is equal to the velocity of sound divided by the frequency of sound ($\lambda = v/f$) (see 1-1). Therefore frequency and wavelength change inversely with respect to each other. The lower a sound's frequency, the longer its wavelength; the higher a sound's frequency, the shorter its wavelength (see 1-8).

ACOUSTICAL PHASE

Acoustical phase refers to the time relationship between two or more sound waves at a given point in their cycles.[1] Because sound waves are repetitive, they can be divided into regularly occurring intervals. These intervals are measured in degrees (see 1-9).

If two identical waves begin their excursions at the same time, their degree intervals will coincide and the waves will be *in phase*. If two identical waves begin their excursions at different times, their degree intervals will not coincide and the waves will be *out of phase*.

Waves that are in phase reinforce each other, increasing amplitude (see 1-10a). Waves that are out of phase weaken each other, decreasing amplitude. When two sound waves are exactly in phase (0-degree phase difference) and have the same frequency, shape, and peak amplitude, the resulting waveform will be twice the original peak amplitude. Two waves that are exactly out of phase (180-degree phase difference) and have the same frequency, shape, and peak amplitude cancel each other (see 1-10b). These two conditions rarely occur in the studio, however.

It is more likely that sound waves will begin their excursions at different times. If the waves are partially

---

1. *Polarity* is sometimes used synonymously with *phase*; it is not. Polarity refers to values of a signal voltage and is discussed in Chapter 9.

1-8 Selected frequencies and their wavelengths

Frequency (Hz)	Wavelength	Frequency (Hz)	Wavelength
20	56.5 feet	1,000	1.1 feet
31.5	35.8	2,000	6.7 inches
63	17.9	4,000	3.3
125	9.0	6,000	2.2
250	4.5	8,000	1.6
440	2.5	10,000	1.3
500	2.2	12,000	1.1
880	1.2	16,000	0.07

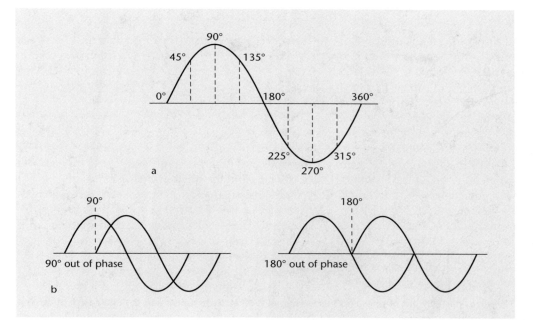

1-9 Sound waves. (a) Phase is measured in degrees, and one cycle can be divided into 360 degrees. It begins at 0 degrees with 0 amplitude, then increases to a positive maximum at 90 degrees, decreases to 0 at 180 degrees, increases to a negative maximum at 270 degrees, and returns to 0 at 360 degrees. (b) Selected phase relationships of sound waves.

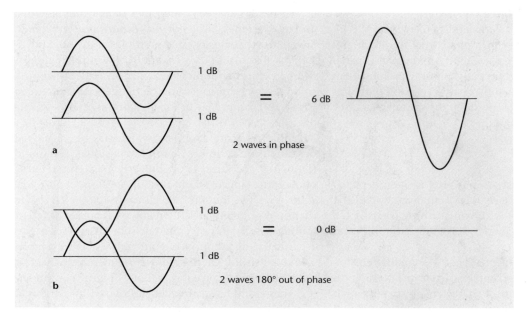

1-10 Sound waves in and out of phase. (a) In phase: Their amplitude is additive. Here the sound waves are exactly in phase—a condition that rarely occurs. It should be noted that decibels do not add linearly. As shown, the additive amplitude here is 6 dB. (b) Out of phase: Their amplitude is subtractive. Sound waves of equal amplitude 180 degrees out of phase cancel each other. This situation also rarely occurs.

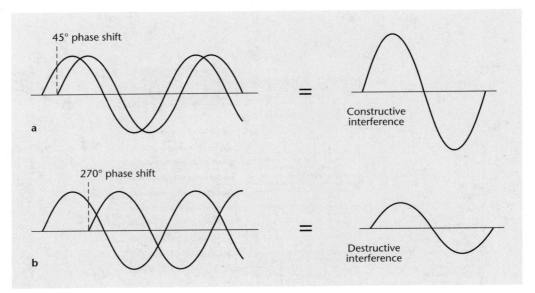

1-11 Waves partially out of phase (a) increase amplitude at some points and (b) decrease it at others.

out of phase, there would be *constructive interference*, increasing amplitude, where compression and rarefaction occur at the same time, and *destructive interference*, decreasing amplitude, where compression and rarefaction occur at different times (see 1-11).

The ability to understand and perceive phase is of considerable importance in, among other things, microphone and loudspeaker placement, mixing, and spatial imaging. If not handled properly, phasing problems can seriously mar sound quality. Phase can also be used as a production tool to create different sonic effects (see Chapter 17, "Music Recording").

TIMBRE

For the purpose of illustration, sound is often depicted as a single, wavy line (see 1-1). Actually, a wave that generates such a sound is known as a *sine wave*. It is a *pure tone*—a single frequency devoid of harmonics and overtones.

Most sound, though, consists of several different frequencies that produce a complex *waveform*—a graphical representation of a sound's characteristic shape, which can be seen, for example, on test equipment and digital editing systems (see 8-21b and 20-1) and in spectrographs (see 1-12). Each sound has a unique tonal mix of fundamental and harmonic frequencies that distinguishes it

from all other sound, even if the sounds have the same pitch, loudness, and duration. This difference between sounds is what defines their *timbre*—their tonal quality, or tonal color.

Harmonics are exact multiples of the fundamental; and its overtones, also known as *inharmonic overtones*, are pitches that are *not* exact multiples of the fundamental. If a piano sounds a middle C, the fundamental is 261.63 Hz; its harmonics are 523.25 Hz, 1,046.5 Hz, and so on; and its overtones are the frequencies in between (see 1-12). Sometimes in usage, harmonics also assume overtones.

Unlike pitch and loudness, which may be considered unidimensional, timbre is multidimensional. The sound frequency spectrum is an objective scale of relative pitches; the table of sound-pressure levels is an objective scale of relative loudness. But there is no objective scale that orders or compares the relative timbres of different sounds. We try to articulate our subjective response to a particular distribution of sonic energy. For example, sound consisting mainly of lower frequencies played by cellos may be perceived as mellow, mournful, or quieting; these same lower frequencies played by a bassoon may be perceived as raspy, honky, or comical. That said, there is evidence to suggest that timbres can be compared objectively because of the two important factors that help determine timbre: harmonics and how the sound

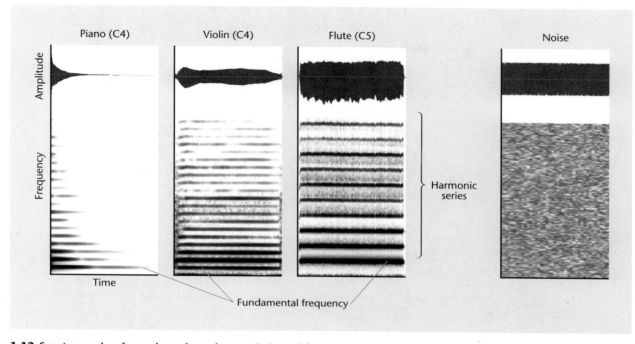

1-12 Spectrographs of sound envelope characteristics and frequency spectra showing differences between musical sounds and noise. Note that the fundamental and the first few harmonics contain more energy and appear darker in the spectrographs and that the amplitude of the harmonic series diminishes at the higher end of the frequency spectrum.

begins—the *attack* (see the following section). Along with intuitive response, objective comparisons of timbre serve as a considerable enhancement to professional ears.[2]

SOUND ENVELOPE

Another factor that influences the timbre of a sound is its shape, or envelope, which refers to changes in loudness over time. A ***sound envelope*** has four stages: attack, initial decay, sustain, and release (ADSR). ***Attack*** is how a sound starts after a sound source has been vibrated. ***Initial decay*** is the point at which the attack begins to lose amplitude. ***Sustain*** is the period during which the sound's relative dynamics are maintained after its initial decay. ***Release*** refers to the time and the manner in which a sound diminishes to inaudibility (see 1-13).

The relative differences in frequency spectra and sound envelopes are shown for a piano, violin, flute, and white-noise sample in Figure 1-12. In the case of the

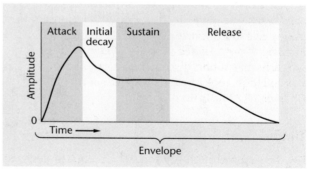

1-13 Sound envelope.

piano and the violin, the fundamental frequency is the same: middle C (261.63 Hz). The flute is played an octave above middle C at C5, or 523.25 Hz. By contrast, noise is unpitched with no fundamental frequency; it comprises all frequencies of the spectrum at the same amplitude.

Two notes with the same frequency and loudness can produce different sounds within different envelopes. A bowed violin string, for example, has a more dynamic

---

2. William Moylan, *Understanding and Crafting the Mix: The Art of Recording,* 2nd ed. (Boston: Focal Press, 2007).

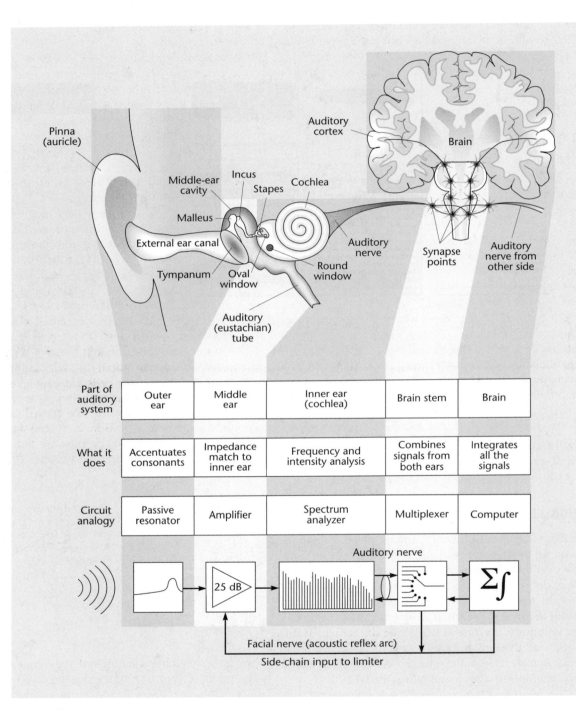

Part of auditory system	Outer ear	Middle ear	Inner ear (cochlea)	Brain stem	Brain
What it does	Accentuates consonants	Impedance match to inner ear	Frequency and intensity analysis	Combines signals from both ears	Integrates all the signals
Circuit analogy	Passive resonator	Amplifier	Spectrum analyzer	Multiplexer	Computer

1-14 Auditory system.

sound overall than does a plucked violin string. If you take a piano recording and edit out the attacks of the notes, the piano will start to sound like an organ. Do the same with a French horn, and it sounds similar to a saxophone. Edit out the attacks of a trumpet, and it creates an oboelike sound.

THE HEALTHY EAR

Having touched on the basic parameters of sound and the characteristics of the sound wave, it is essential to say something about the human ear, hearing, and hearing loss.

The human ear is divided into three parts: the **outer ear**, the **middle ear**, and the **inner ear** (see 1-14). Sound waves first reach and are collected by the *pinna* (or *auricle*), the visible part of the outer ear. The sound waves are then focused through the *ear canal*, or *meatus*, to the *eardrum (tympanum)* at the beginning of the middle ear.

The tympanic membrane is attached to another membrane, called the *oval window*, by three small bones—the *malleus, incus,* and *stapes*—called *ossicles* and shaped like a hammer, an anvil, and a stirrup. The ossicles act as a mechanical lever, changing the small pressure of the sound wave on the eardrum into a much greater pressure. The combined action of the ossicles and the area of the tympanum allow the middle ear to protect the inner ear from pressure changes (loud sounds) that are too great. It takes about one-tenth of a second to react,

however, and therefore provides little protection from sudden loud sounds.

The inner ear contains the *semicircular canals,* which are necessary for balance, and a snail-shaped structure called the *cochlea.* The cochlea is filled with a fluid whose total capacity is a fraction of a drop. It is here that sound becomes electricity in the human head. Running through the center of the cochlea is the *basilar membrane,* resting upon which are sensory hair cells attached to nerve fibers composing the *organ of Corti,* the "seat of hearing." These fibers feed the auditory nerve, where the electrical impulses are passed on to the brain.

It is estimated that there may be as many as 16,000 sensory hair cells at birth. In the upper portion of each cell is a bundle of microscopic hairlike projections called *stereocilia,* or *cilia* for short, which quiver at the approach of sound and begin the process of transforming mechanical vibrations into electrical and chemical signals, which are then sent to the brain. In a symmetrical layout, these sensory hair cells are referred to as "outer" and "inner" sensory hair cells (see 1-15). Approximately 12,000 outer hair cells amplify auditory signals and discriminate frequency. About 140 cilia jut from each cell. The 4,000 inner hair cells are connected to the auditory nerve fibers leading to the brain. About 40 cilia are attached to each inner cell (see 1-16a). Continued exposure to high sound-pressure levels can damage the sensory hair cells, and, because they are not naturally repaired or replaced, hearing loss results. The greater

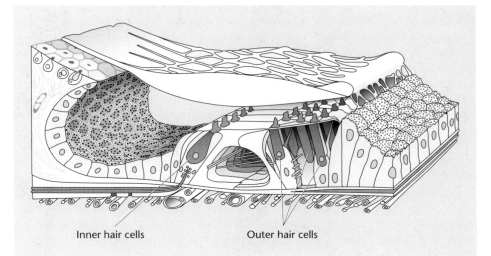

1-15 Artistic representation of the organ of Corti, showing the symmetrical layout of the outer and inner sensory hair cells.

Inner hair cells   Outer hair cells

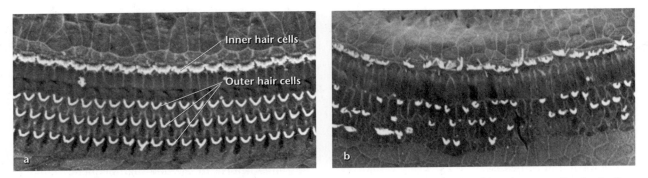

1-16 Scanning electron micrographs of healthy and damaged stereocilia. (a) In the normal cochlea, the stereocilia of a single row of inner hair cells *(top)* and three rows of outer hair cells *(bottom)* are present in an orderly array. (b) In the damaged cochlea, there is disruption of the inner hair cells and loss of the outer hair cells. This damage produced a profound hearing loss after exposure to 90 dBA noise for eight hours six months earlier. Although these micrographs are of the organ of Corti of a lab rat, they serve to demonstrate the severe effects of overexposure to loud sound.

the number of damaged hair cells, the greater the loss of hearing (see 1-16b).

HEARING LOSS

We are a nation of the hard-of-hearing because of the everyday, ever louder noise around us—noise from traffic, airplanes, lawn mowers, sirens, vacuum cleaners, hair dryers, air conditioners, blenders, waste disposals, can openers, snow mobiles, and even children's toys. In modern homes with wood floors, cathedral ceilings, brick or stucco walls, and many windows, sound is reflected and therefore intensified because there is little to absorb it. It is becoming increasingly rare to find a quiet neighborhood.

Parks and campgrounds are inundated with the annoying sounds of generators, boisterous families, and blaring boom boxes. At beaches the lap and wash of gentle surf is drowned out by the roar of jet skis. Cellular phones, MP3 players, and iPods with their ear-mounted headphones or earbuds present an increasing threat to young people, who are showing signs of hearing loss more typical of older adults. At rock concerts, parties, and bars, sound levels are so loud it is necessary to shout to be heard, increasing the din and raising the noise floor even more. In one Manhattan bistro, it is so loud that orders from customers have to be relayed to a person standing on the bar.

More people suffer from hearing loss than from heart disease, cancer, multiple sclerosis, and kidney disease combined. It afflicts one in nine people in the United States and one in five teenagers. Because it is usually not life-threatening, hearing loss is possibly America's most overlooked physical ailment. For the audio professional, however, it can be career-ending.

In industrialized societies some hearing loss is a natural result of aging, but it is not an inevitable consequence. In cultures less technologically advanced than ours, people in their eighties have normal hearing. Short of relocating to such a society, for now the only defense against hearing loss is prevention.

Usually, when hearing loss occurs it does so gradually, typically without warning signs, and it occurs over a lifetime. When there are warning signs, they are usually due to overstimulation from continuous, prolonged exposure to loud sound. You can tell there has been damage when there is ear discomfort after exposure; it is difficult to hear in noisy surroundings; it is difficult to understand a child's speech or an adult's speech at more than a few feet away; music loses its color; quiet sounds are muffled or inaudible; it is necessary to keep raising the volume on the radio or TV; and your response to a question is usually, "What?" The main problem for most people with hearing loss is not the need for an increase in the level of sound but in the *clarity* of sound.

Hearing damage caused by exposure to loud sound varies with the exposure time and the individual. Prolonged exposure to loud sound decreases the ear's sensitivity. Decreased sensitivity creates the false perception that sound is not as loud as it actually is. This usually necessitates an increase in levels to compensate for the hearing loss, thus making a bad situation worse.

After exposure to loud sound for a few hours, you may have experienced the sensation that your ears were stuffed with cotton. This is known as **temporary threshold shift** *(TTS)*—a reversible desensitization in hearing that disappears in anywhere from a few hours to several days; TTS is also called *auditory fatigue.* With TTS the ears have, in effect, shut down to protect themselves against very loud sounds.

Sometimes intermittent hearing loss can occur in the higher frequencies that is unrelated to exposure to loud sound. In such instances elevated levels in cholesterol and triglycerides may be the cause. A blood test can determine if that is the case.

Prolonged exposure to loud sounds can bring on **tinnitus,** a ringing, whistling, or buzzing in the ears, even though no loud sounds are present. Although researchers do not know all the specific mechanisms that cause tinnitus, one condition that creates its onset, without question, is inner-ear nerve damage from overexposure to loud noise levels. (Tinnitus may also be triggered by stress, depression, and anxiety; ear wax and other foreign objects that block the eardrum; trauma to the head or neck; systemic disorders, such as high or low blood pressure, vascular disease, and thyroid dysfunction; and high doses of certain medications, such as sedatives, anti-

depressants, and anti-inflammatory drugs.) Tinnitus is a danger signal that the ears may already have suffered—or soon will—*permanent threshold shift* with continued exposure to loud sound.

Safeguards Against Hearing Loss

As gradual deterioration of the auditory nerve endings occurs with aging, it usually results in a gradual loss of hearing first in the mid-high-frequency range, at around 3,000 to 6,000 Hz, then in the lower-pitched sounds. The ability to hear in the mid-high-frequency range is important to understanding speech because consonants are mostly composed of high frequencies. Hearing loss in the lower-pitched sounds makes it difficult to understand vowels and lower-pitched voices. Prolonged exposure to loud sounds hastens that deterioration. To avoid premature hearing loss, the remedy is simple: do not expose your ears to excessively loud sound levels for extended periods of time (see 1-17 to 1-19).

Hearing impairment is not the only detrimental consequence of loud sound levels. They also produce adverse physiological effects. Sounds transmitted to the brain follow two paths. One path carries sound to the auditory

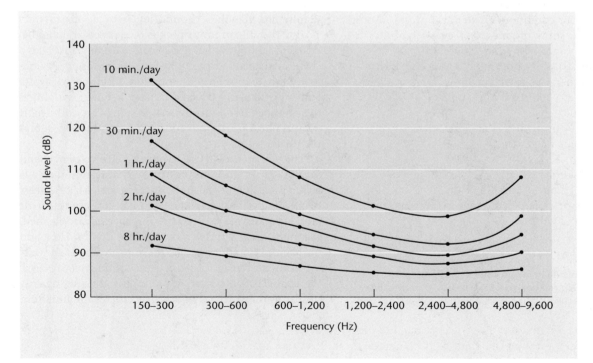

1-17 Damage risk criteria for a single-day exposure to various sound levels.

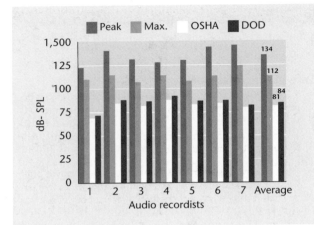

1-18 Peak, average maximum, and calculated average sound-pressure-level exposures by Occupational Safety and Health Administration (OSHA) and Department of Defense (DOD) standards. These results are in relation to the daily exposure to loudness of seven different audio recordists. It is estimated that recordists work an average of eight to 10 hours per day.

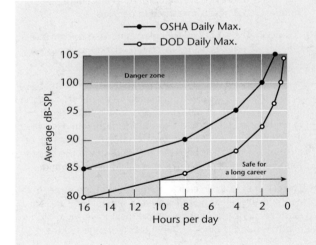

1-19 Allowable daily exposure of sound-pressure levels plotted in relation to OSHA and DOD permissible exposure levels.

center, where it is perceived and interpreted. The other path goes to the brain centers that affect the nervous system. Loud sound taking the latter path can increase heart rate and blood pressure, constrict small blood vessels in the hands and the feet, contract muscles, release stress-related hormones from adrenal glands, disrupt certain stomach and intestinal functions, and create dry mouth, dilated pupils, tension, anxiety, fatigue, and irritability.

When in the presence of loud sound, including amplified music, wear earplugs designed to reduce loudness without seriously degrading frequency response. Some options among available earplugs are custom-fit earmolds, disposable foam plugs, reusable silicon insert plugs, and industrial headsets. The custom-fit earmold is best to use because, as the term suggests, it is made from a custom mold of your ear canal. It is comfortable and does not give you the stopped-up feeling of foam plugs. It provides balanced sound-level reduction and attenuates all frequencies evenly.

Some custom earplugs can be made with interchangeable inserts that attenuate loudness at different decibel levels. The disposable foam plug is intended for onetime use; it provides noise reduction from 12 to 30 dB, mainly in the high frequencies. The reusable silicon insert plug is a rubberized cushion that covers a tiny metal filtering diaphragm; it reduces sound levels by approximately 17 dB. The silicon insert plug is often used at construction sites and firing ranges. The industrial headset has a cushioned headpad and tight-fitting earseals; it provides maximum sound-level attenuation, often up to 30 dB, and is particularly effective at low frequencies. This is the headset commonly used by personnel around airport runways and in the cabs of heavy-construction equipment (see 1-20).

The human ear is a very sophisticated electromechanical device. As with any device, regular maintenance is wise, especially for the audio professional. Make at least two visits per year to a qualified ear, nose, and throat (ENT) specialist to have your ears inspected and cleaned. The human ear secretes wax to protect the eardrum and the cochlea from loud sound-pressure levels. Let the doctor clean out the wax. Do not use a cotton swab. You risk the chance of infection and jamming the wax against the eardrum, which obviously exacerbates the situation.

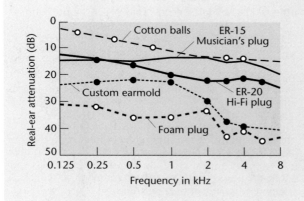

1-20 Attenuation effects of selected hearing-protection devices. Notice that compared with a variety of commonly used hearing protectors, the Musician's and Hi-Fi plugs have relatively even attenuation across the frequency spectrum. (The ER-15 and the ER-20 are products of Etymotic Research,™ which makes a variety of hearing protectors for musicians and hi-fi listeners that attenuate loudness from 9 to 25 dB.)

If you must clean your ears between visits, ask the ENT doctor about the safest way to do it.

Other safeguards include working with listening levels as low as possible, taking regular breaks in a quiet environment during production sessions, and having an audiologist test your hearing at least once a year. Be aware that most standard hearing tests measure octave bands in only the 125 to 8,000 Hz hearing range, essentially the speech range. There are hearing tests with much wider ranges that are more appropriate for the audio professional.

The implications of all this should be obvious, especially if you are working in audio: not only is your hearing in particular and your physiological well-being in general at risk but so is your livelihood.

In this chapter we examined the components of sound waves, how they are heard, without taking into consideration that much of what we hear and choose to listen to is in built-up or enclosed spaces. Behavior of sound waves in such spaces, and our perception of them, is the province of acoustics and psychoacoustics, which is the subject of Chapter 2.

▶ A sound wave is a vibrational disturbance that involves mechanical motion of molecules transmitting energy from one place to another.

▶ A sound wave is caused when an object vibrates and sets into motion the molecules nearest to it; the initial motion starts a chain reaction. This chain reaction creates pressure waves through the air, which are perceived as sound when they reach the ear and the brain.

▶ The pressure wave compresses molecules as it moves outward, increasing pressure, and pulls the molecules farther apart as it moves inward, creating a rarefaction by decreasing pressure.

▶ The components that make up a sound wave are frequency, amplitude, velocity, wavelength, and phase.

▶ Sound acts according to physical principles, but it also has a psychological effect on humans.

▶ The number of times a sound wave vibrates determines its frequency, or pitch. Humans can hear frequencies between roughly 20 Hz (hertz) and 20,000 Hz—a range of 10 octaves. Each octave has a unique sound in the frequency spectrum.

▶ The size of a sound wave determines its amplitude, or loudness. Loudness is measured in decibels.

▶ The decibel (dB) is a dimensionless unit used to compare the ratio of two quantities usually in relation to acoustic energy, such as sound-pressure level (SPL).

▶ Humans can hear from 0 dB-SPL, the threshold of hearing; to 120 dB-SPL, the threshold of feeling; to 140 dB-SPL, the threshold of pain, and beyond. The scale is logarithmic, which means that adding two sounds each with a loudness of 100 dB-SPL would bring it to 103 dB-SPL. The range of difference in decibels between the loudest and the quietest sound a vibrating object makes is called dynamic range.

▶ The ear does not perceive all frequencies at the same loudness even if their amplitudes are the same. This is the equal loudness principle. Humans do not hear lower- and higher-pitched sounds as well as they hear midrange sounds.

▶ Masking—covering a weaker sound with a stronger sound when each is a different frequency and both vibrate simultaneously—is another perceptual response dependent on the relationship between frequency and loudness.

▶ Velocity, the speed of a sound wave, is 1,130 feet per second at sea level at 70°F (Fahrenheit). Sound increases or decreases in velocity by 1.1 feet per second for each 1°F change.

▶ Each frequency has a wavelength, determined by the distance a sound wave travels to complete one cycle of compression and rarefaction. The length of one cycle is equal to the velocity of sound divided by the frequency of sound. The lower a sound's frequency, the longer its wavelength; the higher a sound's frequency, the shorter its wavelength.

▶ Acoustical phase refers to the time relationship between two or more sound waves at a given point in their cycles. If two waves begin their excursions at the same time, their degree intervals will coincide and the waves will be in phase, reinforcing each other and increasing amplitude. If two waves begin their excursions at different times, their degree intervals will not coincide and the waves will be out of phase, weakening each other and decreasing amplitude.

▶ Timbre is the tone quality, or tone color, of a sound.

▶ A sound's envelope refers to its changes in loudness over time. It has four stages: attack, initial decay, sustain, and release (ADSR).

▶ The human ear is divided into three parts: the outer ear, the middle ear, and the inner ear.

▶ In the basilar membrane of the inner ear are bundles of microscopic hairlike projections called cilia attached to each sensory hair cell. They quiver at the approach of sound and begin the process of transforming mechanical vibrations into electrical and chemical signals, which are then sent to the brain.

▶ Temporary threshold shift (TTS), or auditory fatigue, is a reversible desensitization in hearing caused by exposure to loud sound over a few hours.

▶ Prolonged exposure to loud sound can bring on tinnitus, a ringing, whistling, or buzzing in the ears.

▶ Exposure to loud sound for extended periods of time can cause permanent threshold shift—a deterioration of the auditory nerve endings in the inner ear. In the presence of loud sound, use an ear filter (hearing protection device) designed to reduce loudness.

2

Acoustics and Psychoacoustics

When a sound wave is emitted in an enclosed space, it bounces off the surfaces of that space. Each surface affects the travels of the wave, depending on its sound-absorbing properties, size, and shape. Some frequencies are absorbed; others are reflected or diffracted. Some waves travel a short distance, bouncing off surfaces once or twice. Waves that travel longer distances arrive later, weaker, and tonally altered.

The science of a sound wave's behavior—that is, its generation, transmission, reception, and effects—is called *acoustics*. The study that deals with the human perception of acoustics is called *psychoacoustics*. The term *acoustics* is used to describe the physical behavior of sound waves in a room. In that context psychoacoustics is concerned with the relationship of our subjective response to such sound waves.

SPATIAL HEARING

Sound is omnidirectional. Our auditory system can hear acoustic space from all around—360 degrees—in any direction, an ability our visual system does not have. More noteworthy is that in an acoustically complex environment, we are able not only to isolate and recognize a particular sound but also to tell from what direction it is coming. To do this the brain processes differences in both signal *arrival time* and *intensity* at each ear: *interaural time difference (ITD)* and *interaural intensity difference (IID)*, respectively. Interaural intensity difference (IID) is also known as *interaural level difference*.

The ITD and IID occur because the head separates the ears and, depending on which way the head is turned and from what direction the sound is coming, the sound will reach one ear before it reaches the other. The brain compares these differences and tells the listener the sound's location. ITD and IID are frequency-dependent, and it is important to bear in mind the particulars of human hearing and the relative sensitivity we have to different frequencies (see Figure 1-4). Furthermore, as measurements they are most useful in discerning lateral localization, that is, whether a sound is coming from the left or the right. For determining whether a sound is coming from in front, behind, above, or below us, we need to factor in not only the acoustic characteristics of the space but also our physical attributes.

Our ability to localize a sound in space is also affected by our bodies: especially the head, pinnae, and torso. The **head-related transfer function (HRTF)** describes how what we hear is filtered and shaped in establishing its location in three-dimensional space. For example, in addition to serving as passive resonators, pinnae act as filters and tend to reflect frequencies above 4 kHz, whereas sound below 2 kHz is reflected by the torso. The brain's ability to process ITD, IID, and HRTF information makes it possible to hear sound three-dimensionally. This is known as **binaural hearing**, that is, relating to two ears.

Haas and Precedence Effects

When a sound is emitted in a sound-reflectant space, *direct sound* reaches our ears first, before it interacts with any other surface. Indirect sounds, or **reflected sounds**, on the other hand, reach our ears only after bouncing off one or more surfaces. If these small echo delays arrive within a window of 1 to 30 *milliseconds (ms)* of the direct sound, called the **echo threshold**, there are a few perceptual reactions. One, the sound appears to be louder and fuller because of the addition of energies or summing of the direct and indirect sounds; the listener experience is one of a more lively and natural sound. Two, we do not hear the echoes as distinct and separate unless they exceed the intensity of the direct sound by 10 dB or more. They are suppressed, and the direct and reflected sounds are perceived as one coherent event. This is called the **Haas effect**.

The Haas effect gradually disappears and discrete echoes are heard as the time interval between direct and reflected sounds increases from roughly 30 to 50 ms. Furthermore, when hearing a sound and its reflections arriving from different directions at short delay intervals, the listener perceives a **temporal fusion** of both sounds

as coming from the same direction. The first-arriving sound is dominant when it comes to our ability to localize the source, even if the immediate repetitions coming from another location are louder. Fusion and localization dominance are phenomena associated with what is known as the **precedence effect**.

Binaural Versus Stereo Sound

The term *binaural* is often used synonymously with *stereo*, particularly when it comes to sound reproduction. The terms are not synonymous. Binaural sound is three-dimensional; its acoustic space is depth, breadth, and height, whereas stereo is essentially unidimensional sound that creates the illusion of two-dimensional sound—depth and breadth.

Stereo has two static sound sources—the loudspeakers—with nothing but space in between. Although each ear receives the sound at a different time and intensity—the left ear from the left loudspeaker earlier and louder than the right ear and vice versa—the sounds are a composite of the signals from both loudspeakers. Here the brain adds the two signals together, creating the illusion of a fused auditory image in the middle.

Processing of *surround-sound* imaging is somewhat different, but its spatial illusion is still not binaural. Basically, this is why recorded sound cannot quite reproduce the definition, fidelity, and dimension of live sound, even with today's technology. The only way a recording can sound similar to live sound is to record and play it back binaurally (see Chapter 3), although some surround-sound techniques can come close (see Chapters 17, 22, and 23).

DIRECT, EARLY, AND REVERBERANT SOUND

When a sound is emitted in a room, its acoustic "life cycle" can be divided into three phases: direct sound, early reflections, and reverberant sound (see 2-1).

Direct sound reaches the listener first, before it interacts with any other surface. Depending on the distance from the sound source to the listener, the time, T_0, is 20 to 200 ms. Direct waves provide information about a sound's origin, size, and tonal quality.

The same sound reaching the listener a short time later, after it reflects from various surfaces, is **indirect sound**. Indirect sound is divided into **early reflections**, also known as *early sound*, and reverberant sound (see 2-2). Early reflections reaching the ear within 30 ms

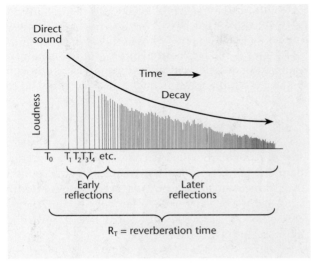

2-1 Anatomy of reverberation in an enclosed space. At time$_0$ (T_0) the direct sound is heard. Between T_0 and T_1 is the initial time delay gap—the time between the arrival of the direct sound and the first reflection. At T_2 and T_3, more early reflections of the direct sound arrive as they reflect from nearby surfaces. These early reflections are sensed rather than distinctly heard. At T_4 repetitions of the direct sound spread through the room, reflecting from several surfaces and arriving at the listener so close together that their repetitions are indistinguishable.

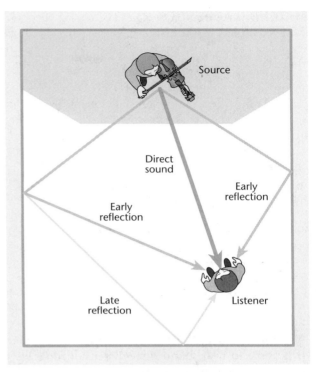

2-2 Acoustic behavior of sound in an enclosed room. The direct-sound field is all the sound reaching the listener (or the microphone) directly from the sound source without having been reflected off of any of the room's surfaces. The early and later reflections of the indirect sound are all the sound reaching the listener (or the microphone) after being reflected off of one or more of the room's surfaces.

of when the direct sound is produced are heard as part of the direct sound. *Reverberant sound,* or **reverberation** (*reverb,* for short), is the result of the early reflections' becoming smaller and smaller and the time between them decreasing until they combine, making the reflections indistinguishable. They arrive outside of the ear's integration time.

Early sound adds loudness and fullness to the initial sound and helps create our subjective impression of a room's size. Reverb creates acoustical spaciousness and fills out the loudness and the body of a sound. It contains much of a sound's total energy. Also, depending on the **reverberation time**, or *decay time* (the time it takes a sound to decrease 60 dB-SPL after its steady-state sound level has stopped), reverb provides information about the absorption and the reflectivity of a room's surfaces as well as about a listener's distance from the sound source. The longer it takes a sound to decay, the larger and more hard-surfaced the room is perceived to be and the farther from the sound source the listener is or senses him- or herself to be.

Reverberation and Echo

Reverberation and *echo* are often used synonymously—but incorrectly so. Reverberation is densely spaced reflections created by random, multiple, blended repetitions of a sound. The time between reflections is imperceptible. If a sound is delayed by 35 ms or more, the listener perceives *echo,* a distinct repeat of the direct sound.

In large rooms discrete echoes are sometimes perceived. In small rooms these repetitions, called **flutter echoes**, are short and come in rapid succession. They usually result from reflections between two parallel surfaces that are highly reflective. Because echoes usually inhibit sonic clarity, studios and concert halls are designed to eliminate them.

MATCHING ACOUSTICS TO PROGRAM MATERIAL

Although the science of acoustics is highly developed, there is no such thing as a sound room with perfect acoustics. The sonic requirements of rock-and-roll and classical music, for example, are different, as they are for a radio studio and a studio used for dialogue rerecording in film and television.

A reverberant studio might be suitable for a symphony orchestra because the reflections add needed richness to the music, as they do in a concert hall. The extremely loud music a rock group generates would swim amid too many sound reflections, becoming virtually unintelligible. At the same time, a studio with relatively few reflections, and therefore suitable for rock-and-roll, would render the sound of a symphony orchestra small and lifeless.

A radio studio is relatively quiet but does have some *room tone,* or atmosphere, so the sound is not too closed down or closetlike. In radio it is important to maintain the intimate sonic rapport between announcer and listener that is essential to the personal nature of the medium. Rerecording dialogue in postproduction for a film or TV drama requires a studio virtually devoid of room tone to prevent acoustics from coloring the dialogue so that room tone appropriate to a scene's setting can be added later.

Rooms with reverberation times of one second or more are considered "live." Rooms with reverberation times of one-half second or less are considered "dry," or "dead" (see 2-3). Live rooms reinforce sound, making it relatively louder and more powerful, especially, although not always, in the lower frequencies. They also tend to

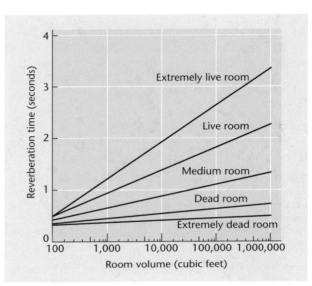

2-3 Room liveness in relation to reverberation time and room size.

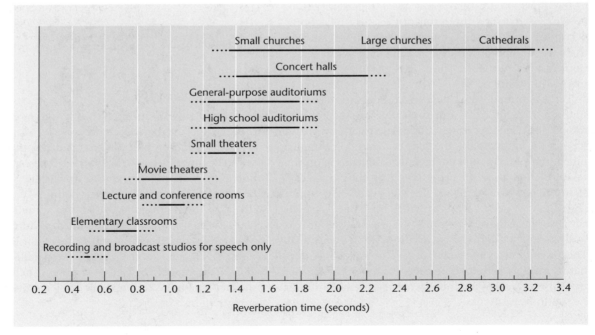

2-4 Typical reverberation times for various performance spaces.

diffuse detail, smoothing inconsistencies in pitch, tonal quality, and performance.

In dry rooms sound is reinforced little or not at all, causing it to be concentrated and lifeless. Inconsistencies in pitch, tonal quality, and other aspects of undesirable performance are readily apparent. In instances where dry rooms are required for recording, signal processing is used to provide appropriate reverberation (see 2-4 and Chapter 7). Liveness can be added by increasing the frequencies between roughly 500 Hz and 2,000 Hz and adding reverberation in the range of one to two seconds. Other aspects to consider in the acoustics of a room or recording, depending on the type of program material, are warmth, intimacy, clarity, and auditory source width.

Warmth is a sonic quality usually associated with the lower frequencies and increased reverberation time—specifically, the frequencies between roughly 125 Hz and 250 Hz—and a high reverb time relative to the midrange frequencies.

Intimacy relates to being part of the performance and connected with the performers. It results from early reflections that follow the direct sound by no more than 15 to 20 ms.

Clarity refers to the ability to hear sonic detail, such as understanding lyrics or the attack of orchestral sections or a solo instrument. Clarity increases as the ratio of direct to reverberant sound decreases. Clarity is extremely high in a dry studio, but the sound would not be enjoyable, so clarity must be judged in relation to the amount of reverb in a sound.

Auditory source width (ASW) refers to how wide a sound source is perceived to be compared with how wide it actually is. This is a result of both the reverberation values in a room or recording and, in a recording, the microphone and panning techniques by which a spatial illusion is created.

Acousticians have calculated optimum reverb times for various types of audio material that have proved suitable for emulation in the production room (see 2-5). That said, preference for the amount of reverberation and reverb time is a matter of individual taste and perception—and perceptions differ, even among the experts. This is one reason why, for example, concert venues of relatively the same dimensions, or acoustic properties, or both, sound different. One hall may be drier and spare sounding, another more reverberant and rich sounding. Then there are concert venues of such dimensions that they require electronic reinforcement through small loudspeakers throughout the hall to ensure optimal distribution of the direct sound and the early and late reflections.

Generally, it is agreed that certain reverb times for speech, pop and rock music, and orchestral music are desirable. For example, for the intimate clarity of speech in radio a drier reverb time value of 0.4 to 0.6 second is

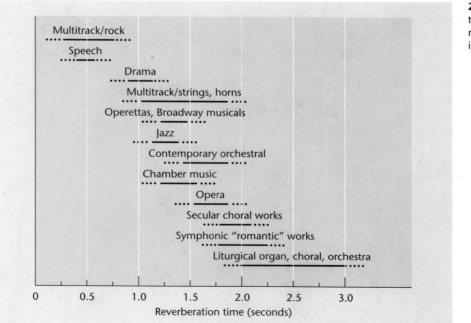

2-5 Optimal reverberation times for various types of music and speech produced indoors.

considered suitable, whereas 0.5 to 0.7 second is acceptable for lecture speech. Too long a reverb time creates a distant, more echoey sound. Too short a reverb time gives speech too dry a quality and is usually uncomfortable for the speaker. Pop and rock require a short reverb time because the music is usually high energy; typically 0.5 to 0.6 second is recommended. Longer reverb times would create too many unwanted sound reflections and wash out too much detail. Orchestral music requires longer reverb times to add fullness and body to the sound; depending on the size of the orchestra, 1.5 to 2 seconds is preferred. Shorter reverb times could adversely affect blending and reduce the music's liveness and vitality.

STUDIO DESIGN

The behavior of sound waves in an acoustic environment and how that behavior affects aural perception leads logically to a consideration of the four factors that influence this behavior: sound isolation, room dimensions, room shape, and room acoustics. These factors are directly related to one overriding concern: noise.

Noise

Noise—unwanted sound—is the number one enemy in audio production. As noted in Chapter 1, noise is everywhere. Outside a room it comes from traffic, airplanes, jackhammers, thunder, rain, and so on. Inside a room it is generated by fluorescent lights, ventilation and heating/cooling systems, computers, and appliances. And these are only the more obvious examples. A few not-so-obvious examples include the "noise" made by the random motion of molecules, by our nervous and circulatory systems, and by our ears. In short, noise is part of our existence and can never be completely eliminated. (Audio equipment also generates *system noise*.) Even though unwanted sound is always present, when producing audio it must be brought to within tolerable

2-6 Noise criteria (NC) curves.

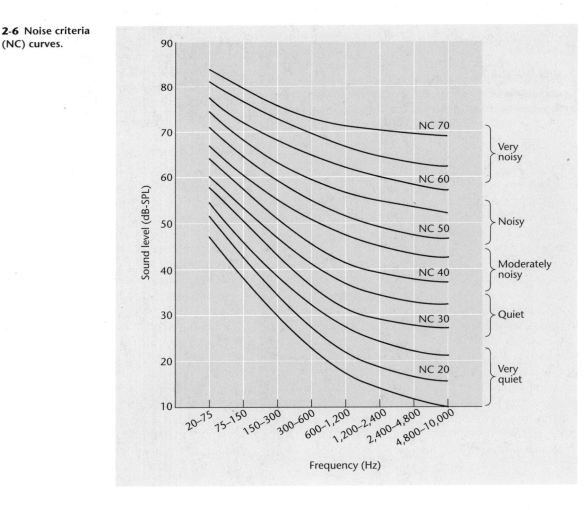

2-7 Recommended NC levels for selected rooms.

Type of Room	Recommended NC Curve	dB
Broadcast and recording studios	NC 15–25	25–35
Concert halls	NC 20	30
Drama theaters	NC 20–25	30–35
Motion picture theaters	NC 30	40
Sports arenas	NC 50	60

levels so that it does not interfere with the desired sound, particularly with digital recording. Among other things, noise can mask sounds, make speech unintelligible, create distraction, cause annoyance, and reduce if not ruin the aesthetic listening experience.

To this end acousticians have developed ***noise criteria (NC)*** that identify, by means of a rating system, background noise levels (see 2-6). From this rating system, NC levels for various types of rooms are derived (see 2-7). This raises the question: once NC levels for a particular room are known, how is noise control accomplished?

Sound Isolation

Sound studios must be isolated to prevent outside noise from leaking into the room and to keep loud sound levels generated inside the room from disturbing neighbors. This is accomplished in two ways. The first is by determining the loudest outside sound level against the minimum acceptable NC level inside the studio. This is usually between NC 15 and NC 25 (approximately 25 to 35 dBA), depending on the type of sound for which the studio is used. It is also done by determining the loudest sound level inside the studio against a maximum acceptable noise floor outside the studio.

For example, assume that the maximum measured noise outside a studio is 90 dB-SPL and the maximum acceptable noise level inside the studio is 30 dB-SPL at, say, 500 Hz. (These values are always frequency-dependent but are usually based on 500 Hz.) This means that the construction of the studio must reduce the loudness of the outside sound level by 60 dB. If the loudest sound inside a studio is 110 dB-SPL and the maximum acceptable noise outside the studio is 45 dB-SPL, the studio's construction must reduce the loudness level by 65 dB.

The amount of sound reduction provided by a partition, such as a wall, floor, or ceiling, is referred to as ***transmission loss (TL)***. Because TL works both ways,

determining partition requirements is equally applicable to sound traveling from inside to outside the studio. Therefore the partitions constructed to isolate the studio in this example would have to reduce the loudness level by at least 65 dB (500 Hz).

Just as it is convenient to define a noise spectrum by a single NC rating, it is useful to measure a partition on the basis of its transmission loss; such a measurement is called ***sound transmission class (STC)***. Sound transmission class varies with the type and the mass of materials in a partition. If a 4-inch concrete block has an STC of 48, it indicates that sound passing through it will be attenuated by 48 dB. An 8-inch concrete block with an STC of 52 attenuates 4 dB more sound than does the 4-inch block. Plastering both sides of the concrete block would add 8 dB more sound attenuation.

Room Dimensions

Sometimes a studio's dimensions accentuate noise by reinforcing certain frequencies, thereby altering, or "coloring," the natural sound. This may also affect the response of a sound's decay (see 2-8). Such coloration affects perception of tonal balance, clarity, and imaging as well. Audio mixed in a control room with these problems will sound markedly different when played in another room. Other factors related to the shape of a studio and the construction materials used therein (discussed in the following two sections) may also affect coloration.

Rooms have particular resonances at which sound will be naturally sustained. These are related to the room's dimensions. ***Resonance*** results when a vibrating body with the same natural frequencies as another body causes it to vibrate sympathetically and increases the amplitude of both at those frequencies if the vibrations are in acoustical phase.

Consider the oft-told story of soldiers on horseback galloping across a wooden bridge. The sound created

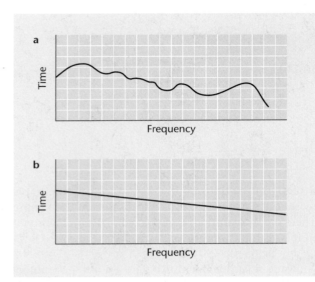

2-8 Reverberation decay responses. (a) Irregular reverb decay, which is undesirable because it creates unwanted sound coloration. (b) Desirable reverb decay, illustrating no resonant coloration. This acoustic condition is always strived for but in practice is rarely attained.

by the hoofbeats on the wood generated the resonant frequency of the bridge, causing it to collapse. In another incident wind excited the resonant frequency of a modern steel-and-concrete bridge, increasing amplitude until it was torn apart.[1] In a television commercial some years ago advertising audiotape, the fidelity of the tape's reproduction was demonstrated by recording a live singer hitting a note that breaks a glass and the tape playback

having the same result. What breaks the glass, of course, is that the note and its loudness hit the resonant frequency of the glass. Most tape recordings could have accomplished the same thing. These are interesting examples, but they are extreme for our purpose.

Resonances occur in a room at frequencies whose wavelengths are the same as or a multiple of one of the room's dimensions. These resonances, called *eigentones,* or, more commonly, *room modes,* are increases in loudness at resonant frequencies that are a function of a room's dimensions. When these dimensions are the same as or multiples of a common value, the resonance amplitude is increased. Such a room's dimensions may be 10 × 20 × 30 feet, or 15 × 30 × 45 feet (see 2-9). This creates unequal representation of the frequencies generated by a sound source. In other words certain frequencies will be reinforced while others will not be. To avoid additive resonances, room dimensions should not be the same, nor be integer multiples of one another. Dimensions of, say, 9 × 10.1 × 12.5 feet or 15 × 27 × 31.5 feet would be satisfactory (see 2-10). It should be noted, however, that although perfect dimensions are the ideal, they are rarely a reality. Most studios will have some resonant frequencies. Figure 2-11 shows a graph of acceptable room ratios.

Resonance is not always bad, however. The tubing in wind and brass instruments, the pipes in an organ, and the human mouth, nose, chest, and throat are resonators. Air columns passing through them excite resonant frequencies, creating sound. Without resonators such as the "box" of a guitar or violin, weak sound sources would generate little sound. Some studios use this principle to construct resonators that help amplify certain frequencies to enhance the type of sound being produced. The following section "Room Acoustics" explains how resonators are also used to absorb sound.

1. Tacoma Narrows Suspension Bridge at Puget Sound, Washington, in 1940.

2-9 Simplified table of reinforced frequencies in a room 10 × 20 × 30 feet. If this table were continued, each frequency that occurs in the height dimension would recur in the other two dimensions.

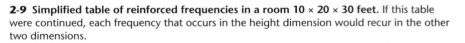

	Height: 10 Feet	Width: 20 Feet	Length: 30 Feet
Fundamental	150 Hz	75 Hz	50 Hz
Second harmonic	300 Hz	150 Hz	100 Hz
Third harmonic	450 Hz	225 Hz	150 Hz
Fourth harmonic	600 Hz	300 Hz	200 Hz
Fifth harmonic	750 Hz	375 Hz	250 Hz
Sixth harmonic	900 Hz	450 Hz	300 Hz
Seventh harmonic	1,050 Hz	525 Hz	350 Hz
Eighth harmonic	1,200 Hz	600 Hz	400 Hz

2-10 Simplified table of frequencies in a studio with dimensions that are not the same as or multiples of a common value. In this example only one frequency, 300 Hz, recurs in another dimension.

	Height: 9 Feet	Width: 10.1 Feet	Length: 12.5 Feet
Fundamental	150 Hz	136 Hz	60 Hz
Second harmonic	300 Hz	272 Hz	85 Hz
Third harmonic	450 Hz	409 Hz	128 Hz
Fourth harmonic	600 Hz	545 Hz	171 Hz
Fifth harmonic	750 Hz	681 Hz	214 Hz
Sixth harmonic	900 Hz	818 Hz	257 Hz
Seventh harmonic	1,050 Hz	954 Hz	300 Hz
Eighth harmonic	1,200 Hz	1,090 Hz	342 Hz

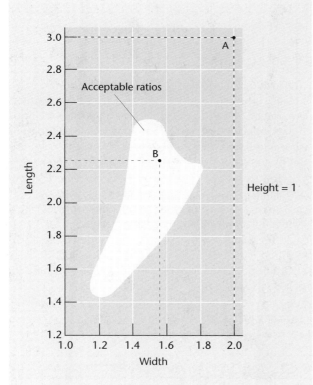

2-11 Acceptable ratios to control room resonances. Using this pictogram, developed by Newman, Bolt, and Baranek in 1957, involves three basic steps: (1) divide all room dimensions by the height (making height equal to 1); (2) plot width and length on the horizontal and vertical scales; and (3) determine acceptability by noting whether the plot is in or out of the "zone."

Room Shape

Acoustics is a science of interacting relationships. Although a studio's walls, floors, and windows may have been properly constructed and their dimensions conform to a set of preferred standards, the room's shape also influences noise reduction and sound dispersion.

Except for bass frequencies, sound behaves like light: *its angle of incidence is equal to its angle of reflectance* (see 2-12). If a studio has reflective parallel walls, sound waves reinforce themselves as they continuously bounce between opposing surfaces (see 2-13). If there are concave surfaces, they serve as collecting points, generating unwanted concentrations of sound (see 2-14a). A studio should be designed to break up the paths of sound waves (see 2-14b and 2-14c).

Typical studio designs have adjacent walls at angles other than 90 degrees and different-shaped wall surfaces, such as spherical, cylindrical, and serrated, to help disperse the sound waves (see 2-15). Even the glass between the studio and the control room is angled toward the floor for sound dispersal (and also to avoid light reflections), but this is not enough to break up the paths of sound waves; they must be controlled once they hit a surface.

Room Acoustics

When sound hits a surface, one reaction—or a combination of five reactions—happens, depending on the surface's material, mass, and design. Sound is absorbed, reflected, partially absorbed and reflected, diffracted, or diffused.

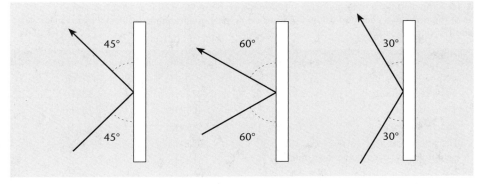

2-12 Angle of incidence and angle of reflectance. In sound, as in light, these angles are equal.

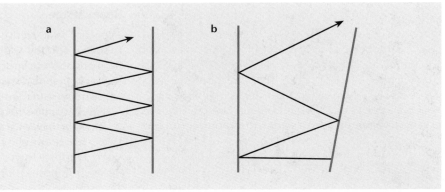

2-13 Parallel walls. (a) Sound waves reflect back along their original paths of travel, thereby generating standing waves that are reinforced, creating echoey sound. (b) Slightly changing the angle of one wall reduces the possibility of the reflections' following repeated paths.

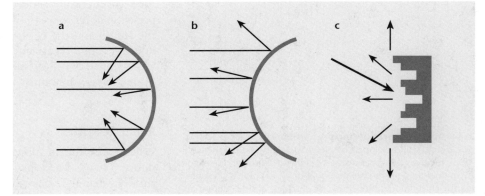

2-14 Shape of a room's surface affecting direction of sound reflections. (a) Concave surfaces concentrate sound waves by converging them. (b) Convex surfaces are more suitable in studios because they disperse sound waves. (c) A quadratic residue diffuser also disperses waves at many different angles.

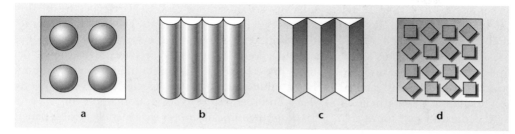

2-15 Studio walls with different surface shapes. (a) Spherical, (b) cylindrical, (c) serrated, and (d) a combination of square and diamond.

Absorption and Reflection

When sound hits a surface and is absorbed, it is soaked up: there is little or no reflection, and the sonic result is lifeless, or dry. When sound hits a surface and is reflected, it bounces off the surface and is perceived as reverberation or echo, depending on its interaction with other live surfaces in the vicinity. Conditions under which sound is completely absorbed or reflected are rare. Most materials absorb and reflect sound to some degree (see 2-16).

The amount of indirect sound energy absorbed is given an acoustical rating called a ***sound absorption coefficient***

(SAC), also known as a *noise reduction coefficient (NRC)*. Theoretically, on a scale from 1.00 to 0.00, material with a sound absorption coefficient of 1.00 completely absorbs sound, whereas material with an SAC of 0.00 is completely sound reflectant. Soft, porous materials absorb more sound than do hard, nonporous materials. Drapes, for example, have a higher absorption coefficient than does glass. Sound absorption ratings for the same material vary with frequency, however. For example: the sound absorption coefficient of a light, porous concrete block at 125 Hz is 0.36, at 500 Hz it is 0.31, and at 4,000 Hz it

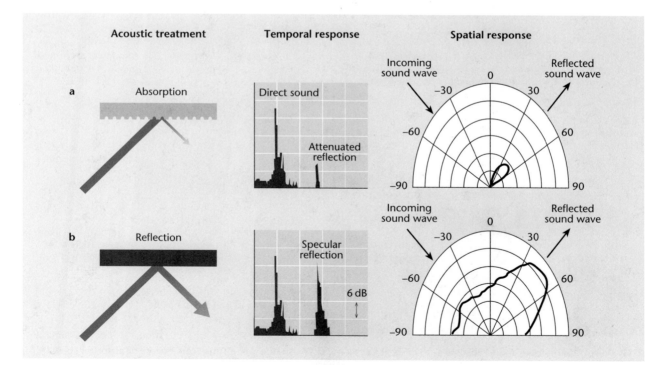

2-16 Absorption and reflection in relation to temporal and spatial response.

is 0.25; heavy plate glass has an SAC of 0.18 at 125 Hz, 0.04 at 500 Hz, and 0.02 at 4,000 Hz; wood parquet's SAC is 0.04 at 125 Hz, 0.07 at 500 Hz, and 0.07 at 4,000 Hz.[2]

Three types of acoustic absorbers are porous absorbers, diaphragmatic absorbers, and Helmholtz absorbers.

Porous absorbers come in an ever increasing variety of materials, shapes, and sizes, including polyurethane and melamine foams (see 2-17), sintered glass, transparent fiber-free panels and films, absorptive building materials such as wood and plaster, and metal bass management plate absorbers. Porous absorbers are most effective with high frequencies. Because the wavelengths of high fre-

quencies are short, they tend to get trapped in the tiny air spaces of the porous materials. The thicker and denser the absorbent, the greater the sound absorption—but only to a point. If the material is overly dense, it will act more like a hard wall and reject high-frequency sound. In the middle and lower frequencies, however, an overly dense absorber improves absorption.

Diaphragmatic absorbers are generally flexible panels of wood or pressed wood mounted over an air space. When a sound wave hits the panel, it resonates at a frequency (or frequencies) determined by the stiffness of the panel and the size of the air space. Other sound waves of the same frequency (or frequencies) approaching the panel, therefore, are dampened. Diaphragmatic absorbers are used mainly to absorb low frequencies; for this reason they are also called *bass traps* (see 2-18). This principle can also be applied to absorbing high frequencies.

---

2. A list of sound absorption coefficients for many types of materials can be found at the Web sites of acoustic providers; for an example see *www.acousticalsurfaces.com/acoustic_IOI/101_13.htm.*

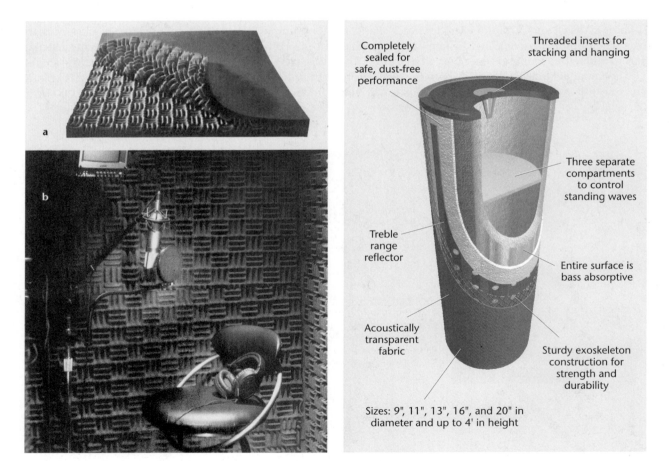

2-17 Polyurethane-foam sound absorber. (a) In sheet form, ready to install. (b) Applied to a voice-over room to control unwanted acoustic reflections.

2-18 Anatomy of a Tube Trap™ acoustic absorber (bass trap).

Because it is difficult to completely dissipate standing waves, especially in small rooms and even with optimal acoustics, bass traps are usually designed to introduce significant absorption for frequencies between 30 Hz and 100 Hz.

A **Helmholtz absorber,** also called a *Helmholtz resonator,* is a tuned absorber designed to remove sound at specific frequencies or within specific frequency ranges, usually the lower-middle frequencies. It functions, in principle, not unlike the action created when blowing into the mouth of a soda bottle. The tone created at the frequency of the bottle's resonance is related to the air mass in the bottle. By filling the bottle with water, the air mass is reduced, so the pitch of the tone is higher.

Diffraction

When sound reaches a surface, in addition to being partially absorbed and reflected, it *diffracts*—spreads around the surface. The amount of **diffraction** depends on the relationship between wavelength and the distances involved. You will recall that each frequency has a wavelength; bass waves are longer, and treble waves are shorter. Hence the diffraction of bass waves is more difficult to control acoustically than the diffraction of treble waves.

Diffusion

The overriding challenge for the acoustician is controlling the physical behavior of sound waves in a studio. The goal is the even distribution of sound energy in a room so that its intensity throughout the room is approximately uniform (see 2-19). This is called **diffusion**.

No matter how weak or strong the sound and regardless of its wavelength, the diffused energy is reduced in amplitude and spread out in time, falling off more or less exponentially. Figures 2-20 and 2-21 are diffusers that meet specific needs. Figure 2-22 displays an example of a combined acoustic treatment.

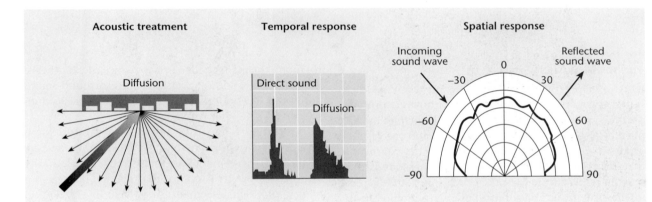

2-19 Diffusion in relation to temporal and spatial response.

2-20 Abffusor.™ Provides reflection control by simultaneously using absorption and diffusion down to 100 Hz for all angles of incidence.

2-21 Omniffusor.™ Sound diffuser that scatters sound into a hemisphere; useful when omnidirectional coverage and high sound attenuation are desired.

2-22 Acoustic treatment system showing a room with absorbers, diffusers, and bass traps.

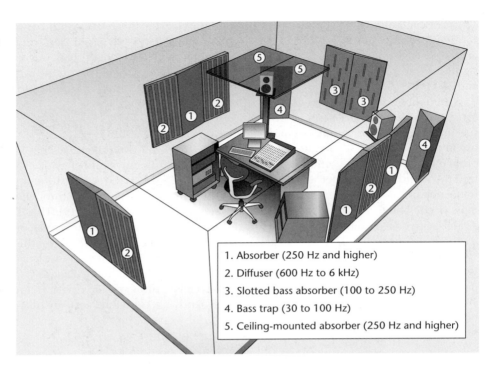

1. Absorber (250 Hz and higher)
2. Diffuser (600 Hz to 6 kHz)
3. Slotted bass absorber (100 to 250 Hz)
4. Bass trap (30 to 100 Hz)
5. Ceiling-mounted absorber (250 Hz and higher)

Variable Acoustics

Basic principles of acoustics apply to any room in which sound is generated. As noted earlier, however, a room's purpose greatly influences how those principles are applied. If a studio is used for rock music and speech, the acoustics must absorb more sound than they diffuse so that there is minimal interference from other sounds and/ or from reverberation. On the other hand, studios used for classical music and some types of jazz should diffuse more sound than they absorb to maintain balanced, blended, open sound imaging.

Theoretically, this means that a studio designed to fulfill one sonic purpose is inappropriate for another. In fact, to be more functional, some studios are designed with variable acoustics. They have adjustable panels, louvers, or partitions and portable baffles, or *gobos,* to alter diffusion, absorption, and reverb time (see 2-23 to 2-25).

CONTROL ROOM DESIGN

Purpose also affects design differences between studios and control rooms. Studios are designed for sound that is appropriate for microphone pickup, whereas control rooms are designed for listening to loudspeakers. Therefore, to accurately assess the reproduced sound in a control room, the main challenge is to reduce the number of unwanted reflections at the stereo and surround-sound monitoring locations so that they are relatively reflection-free zones.

In facilities designed by professional control room architects and acousticians, monitoring environments are less problematic than they are in the burgeoning number of project or personal studios that may be housed in a living room, den, basement, or garage. In either case, however, unless the monitoring room is acoustically suitable for its sonic purpose, it seriously inhibits the ability to accurately evaluate the sound quality of audio material. (Control room monitoring is discussed in Chapter 8, "Loudspeakers and Monitoring.")

ERGONOMICS

Sound control is obviously the most important factor in studio and control room design, but human needs should not be ignored. Production is stressful enough without personnel having to endure poor lighting, hard-to-reach equipment, uncomfortable chairs, and so on. Designing an engineering system with the human element in mind is called ***ergonomics***. This section discusses a few of the more important ergonomic considerations in higher-end

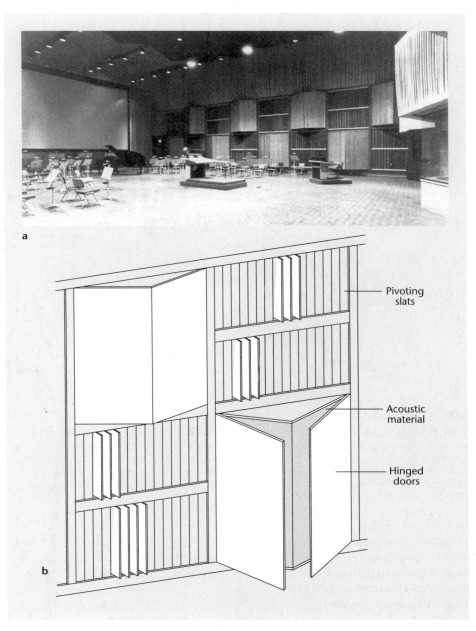

2-23 Acoustic treatment along walls. (a) Scoring stage with alternating doors and slats that can be opened or closed to vary acoustics. (b) Detail of doors and slats shown in (a).

Pivoting slats

Acoustic material

Hinged doors

a

b

audio facilities. Any advice that can be accommodated in the personal studio, however, will ameliorate working conditions there as well.

■ **Lighting** Studio and control room atmosphere are important in a production session, and lighting—adjustable lighting in particular—goes a long way in enhancing the environment. One audio operator may like a lot of light in the control room, whereas another may prefer it dim.

Talent, particularly musicians, may like low-key lighting, assorted colored lights, or flashing lights, depending on the emotional bolstering they may need.

■ **Size** Ample room for personnel and equipment should prevent a cramped, claustrophobic feeling.

■ **Position of equipment** Equipment and remote controls should be situated within arm's reach; equipment

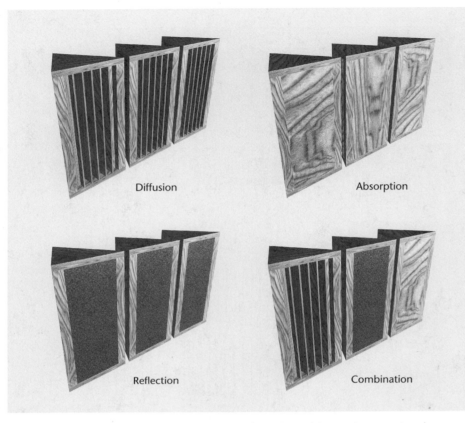

Diffusion

Absorption

Reflection

Combination

2-24 Trifussor.® Variable equilateral triangle prism acoustic modules can be rotated to expose absorptive, reflective, and diffusive sides in any combination, thereby refining reverb times. For example, in recording an orchestra, the modules adjacent to strings and woodwinds could be turned to their reflective side to enhance these weaker-sounding instruments, and panels nearer brass and tympani could be turned to their absorptive side to help control these strong-sounding instruments.

that cannot be so positioned should be easily accessible. The operator should be situated to have optimal hearing and line-of-sight. If there is a dedicated section for a producer, a director, and observers, raise the area so that the views of console operations, video monitors, and studio activities are unobstructed.

■ **Furniture** Furniture should be functional, rather than just decorative, and reflect as little sound as possible. Chairs should be comfortable and move around easily on wheels without squeaking. A chair should be adjustable, have a five-point base so that it does not tip, and be flexible when sliding or leaning. Most people prefer armrests and even flexible headrests. A chair should give

back support, particularly in the lower back, and not cut off blood circulation in the legs. Cushions should be firm and shaped to support the body. If different contoured chairs are needed to accommodate the regular control room personnel, they're worth the investment.

■ **Floor covering** Rugs should be static-free and permit anything on wheels to move about easily.

■ **Color coding** The amount of hardware in a control room can pose a challenge for personnel who need to quickly reach for the right piece of equipment. But trying to locate a particular control, among the hundreds on the console, the computer screen, signal processors, and so on, can be even more of a challenge. Color coding

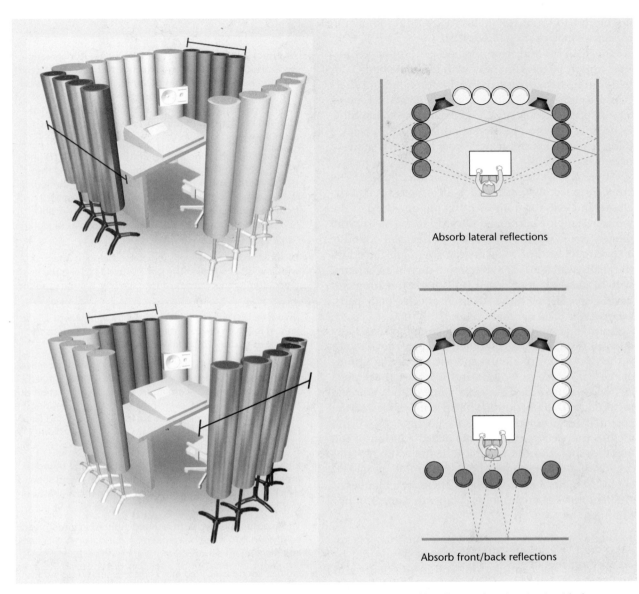

Absorb lateral reflections

Absorb front/back reflections

2-25 Acoustic treatment for rooms with less-than-desirable acoustics. One way of handling such a situation is with the Attack Wall,™ a portable array of reflective/absorptive acoustic traps that can be positioned in various ways around the console and the recordist.

can help. Depending on the equipment and the controls, using different-colored ties, paints, or labels can make it easy to identify a function, patch cord, sample library, or channel grouping. For hard-disk production, computer software is available to color-customize various functions for easier identification and to be more restful on the eyes.

■ **Digital audio workstation** With the proliferation of digital recording and editing systems, many hours a day are spent at *digital audio workstations (DAWs)*. The repetitive nature of computer operations over extended periods of time can lead to chronic pain in the fingers, hands, arms, shoulders, and back, ranging from mild discomfort to serious disability, a condition known as *repetitive strain,* or *stress, injury (RSI).*

The main RSI risk factors include: performing a repetitive motion in the same way with the same body part; performing a repetitive activity with force; putting direct pressure on nerves, tendons, bones, or joints by keeping a body part rested against a hard surface; maintaining, or holding an object in, a fixed position; and keeping a joint in a forced position away from its normal centered or neutral position.

There are ways to prevent or reduce RSI. At the DAW, keep feet flat on the floor, arms horizontal at the elbow, and eyes lined up with the top one-third of the monitor. Employ cushioned tabletop surfaces. To avoid mouse-related strain, switch among a trackball, a mouse, a touchpad, and/or a keyboard. There are mice and trackballs available that allow you to plug in an external switch, such as a foot pedal. Do simple stretching and flexing exercises with the adversely affected body parts. Take regular breaks and just relax.[3]

Another factor to consider with computers (and any other noise-generating equipment in the control room) is the noise from the fan(s) and the sputtering sounds of the hard drive as it reads and writes. If the sounds are loud enough, they can mask some of the audio being produced, to say nothing of the annoyance and the potential distraction they cause. If a microphone is being used in the vicinity, there is the added concern of the noise leaking into the recording. If the computer and other noise-generating equipment cannot be moved out of the control room or studio, there are a number of different types of enclosures available to dampen if not eliminate the noise.

■ **Access** Studios and control rooms are busy places. Production and performance personnel should not be disturbed by the comings and goings of clients and other observers. Access into and out of production rooms should be easy, allowing activities to continue without distraction or interruption.

When the ergonomics in a production venue are lacking, it puts undue mental and physical strain on personnel, reducing concentration and perceptual acuity and thereby increasing the risk of a subpar product. Production is demanding enough: make it as efficient and easy on yourself as possible.

---

3. From Philip DeLancie, "Engineering Without Pain," *Mix,* February 1999, p. 80.

MAIN POINTS

▶ Acoustics is the science of sound, including its generation, transmission, reception, and effects. Psychoacoustics deals with the human perception of sound. The term *acoustics* is also used to describe the physical behavior of sound waves in a room. In that context psychoacoustics is concerned with the relationship of our subjective response to such sound waves.

▶ By processing the time and intensity differences (ITD and IID, respectively) of a sound reaching the ears, and the head-related transfer function (HRTF) that filter the sound, the brain can isolate and recognize the sound and tell from what direction it is coming. This makes it possible to hear sound three-dimensionally and is known as binaural hearing.

▶ Direct sound reaches the listener first, before it interacts with any other surface. The same sound reaching the listener after it reflects from various surfaces is indirect sound.

▶ To be audible a sound reflection arriving up to 30 ms (milliseconds) after the direct sound must be about 10 dB louder, in which case the direct and reflected sounds are perceived as one. This is known as the Haas effect.

▶ When hearing two sounds arriving from different directions within the Haas fusion zone, we perceive this temporal fusion of both sounds as coming from the same direction as the first-arriving sound, even if the immediate repetitions coming from another location are louder. Fusion and localization dominance phenomena are associated with what is known as the precedence effect.

▶ Binaural and stereo sound are different. Binaural sound is three-dimensional, and stereo has two static sound sources, which create the illusion of a fused, multidimensional auditory image.

▶ The acoustic "life cycle" of a sound emitted in a room can be divided into three phases: direct sound, early reflections, and reverberant sound.

▶ Indirect sound is divided into early reflections (early sound) and reverberant sound (reverb).

▶ Early reflections reach the listener within about 30 ms of when the direct sound is produced and are heard as part of the direct sound.

▶ Reverberant sound is the result of the early reflections' becoming smaller and smaller and the time between them decreasing until they combine, making the reflections indistinguishable.

▶ Reverb is densely spaced reflections created by random, multiple, blended reflections of a sound.

▶ Reverberation time, or decay time, is the time it takes a sound to decrease 60 dB-SPL after its steady-state sound level has stopped.

▶ If sound is delayed by 35 ms or more, the listener perceives echo, a distinct repeat of the direct sound.

▶ Direct sound provides information about a sound's origin, size, and tonal quality. Early reflections add loudness and fullness to the initial sound and help create our subjective impression of room size.

▶ Reverberation adds spaciousness to sound, fills out its loudness and body, and contains most of its tonal energy.

▶ Because no one sound room is acoustically suitable for all types of sound, it is important to match studio acoustics to sonic material.

▶ Rooms with reverberation times of one second or more are considered "live." Rooms with reverb times of one-half second or less are considered "dry," or "dead."

▶ Four factors influence how sound behaves in an acoustic environment: sound isolation, room dimensions, room shape, and room acoustics.

▶ Noise is any unwanted sound (except distortion) in the audio system, the studio, or the environment.

▶ The noise criteria (NC) system rates the level of background noise.

▶ Sound isolation in a room is measured in two ways: by determining the loudest outside sound level against the minimum acceptable NC level inside the room, and by determining the loudest sound level inside the studio against a maximum acceptable noise floor outside the room.

▶ Transmission loss (TL) is the amount of sound reduction provided by a partition, such as a wall, floor, or ceiling. This value is given a measurement called sound transmission class (STC).

▶ The dimensions of a sound room—height, width, and length—should not equal or be exact multiples of one another. Room dimensions create additive resonances, reinforcing certain frequencies and not others and thereby coloring the sound.

▶ Resonance, another important factor in studio design, results when a vibrating body with the same natural frequencies as another body causes that body to vibrate sympathetically, thereby increasing the amplitude of both at those frequencies if the variables are in acoustical phase.

▶ The shape of a studio is significant for good noise reduction and sound dispersion.

▶ When sound hits a surface, one or a combination of five reactions occurs: it is absorbed, reflected, partially absorbed and reflected, diffracted, or diffused.

▶ The amount of indirect sound energy absorbed is given an acoustical rating called a sound absorption coefficient (SAC), also known as a noise reduction coefficient (NRC).

▶ Three classifications of acoustic absorbers are porous absorbers, diaphragmatic absorbers, and Helmholtz absorbers or resonators.

▶ When sound reaches a surface, in addition to being partially absorbed and reflected, it diffracts—or spreads around the surface.

▶ Diffusion is the even distribution of sound energy in a room so that its intensity throughout the room is approximately uniform.

▶ To be more acoustically functional, many studios are designed with adjustable acoustics—movable panels, louvers, walls, and gobos (portable baffles) to alter diffusion, absorption, and reverb time.

▶ Studios are designed for sound that is appropriate for microphone pickup. Control rooms are designed for listening through loudspeakers.

▶ To accurately assess the reproduced sound in a control room, the main challenge is to reduce the number of unwanted reflections at the monitoring location(s) so that it is a relatively reflection-free zone.

▶ Ergonomics addresses the design of an engineering system with human comfort and convenience in mind.

Technology

3

Microphones

The analogy can be made that microphones are to audio production what colors are to painting. The more colors and hues available to a painter, the greater the possibilities for coloration on a visual canvas. In recording sound the more models of microphones there are, the greater variety of tones on the sonic palette and, hence, the greater the possibilities for coloration in designing an aural canvas. To make the point using a lexical analogy: "Every mic is part of [the] sonic vocabulary. Every mic describes an event differently."[1] The 2009 Grammy Awards telecast, for example, employed more than 600 microphones.[2]

When choosing a **microphone,** or *mic,* there are three basic features to consider: operating principles, directional characteristic(s), and sound response. Appearance may be a fourth feature to consider if the mic is on-camera. Cost and durability may be two other considerations.

OPERATING PRINCIPLES

Like the loudspeaker, the microphone is a transducer, but it works in the opposite direction: instead of changing electric energy into acoustic energy, it changes acoustic energy into electric energy. The electric energy flows through a circuit as voltage.

1. Joel Hamilton, "I Miked the Unsane," *EQ,* September 2005, p. 6.

2. Steve Harvey, "Grammys Shine in 5.1," *TV Technology,* March 4, 2009.

Impedance

In measuring an electric circuit, a foremost concern is *impedance*—that property of a circuit, or an element, that restricts the flow of *alternating current (AC)*. Impedance is measured in **ohms** (Ω), a unit of resistance to current flow. The lower the impedance in a circuit, the better. Microphones used in professional audio are low imped-ance. Low-impedance microphones (and equipment) have three advantages over high-impedance mics: they generate less noise; they are much less susceptible to hum and electrical interference, such as static from motors and fluorescent lights; and they can be connected to long cables without increasing noise. Professional mics usually range in impedance from 150 to 600 ohms.

Transducing Elements

The device that does the transducing in a microphone is mounted in the mic head and is called the *element*. Each type of mic gets its name from the element it uses. The elements in professional microphones operate on one of two physical principles: magnetic induction and variable capacitance.

Magnetic Induction

Magnetic induction uses a fixed magnet and a movable dia-phragm to which a small, lightweight, finely wrapped coil is attached. The coil is suspended between the poles of the fixed magnet and attached to the diaphragm. When the coil moves through the magnetic field in response to the sound waves hitting the diaphragm, it produces volt-age proportional to the sound-pressure level (SPL). Such mics are called **moving-coil microphones** (see Figure 3-1).

Another type of mic employing magnetic induction is the **ribbon microphone** (see 3-2). Instead of a moving coil, it uses a metal ribbon attached to a fixed magnet. As the ribbon vibrates from the pressure of the sound waves, voltage is generated. Generally, in the earlier generations of ribbon mics the ribbon is situated vertically; in many modern ribbon mics, it is positioned horizontally. The longitudinal positioning and the more advanced ribbon design have helped make it possible to house modern ribbon mics in smaller, lighter-weight casings than the older models (see 3-3).

There are also **active ribbon microphones** that use an **amplifier** system, which requires phantom power (see 3-4). **Phantom power** is a method of remotely pow-ering an amplifier or impedance converter by sending voltage along the audio cable (see the following section, "Variable Capacitance"). Among the advantages of the

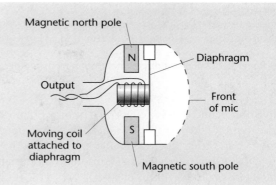

3-1 The element of a moving-coil microphone.

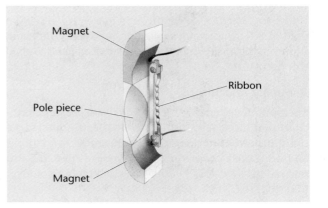

3-2 The element of a ribbon microphone.

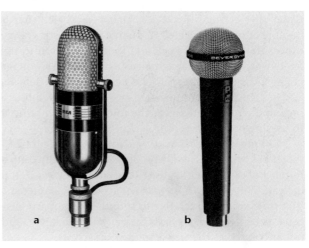

3-3 Ribbon microphones. (a) Older model with vertical ribbon. Newer versions of this type of ribbon mic are still being manufactured. (b) Newer model with small, longitudinal ribbon.

3-4 Royer R-122 active bidirectional ribbon microphone.

active ribbon microphone over conventional ribbons are higher output and sensitivity, wider and flatter frequency response, and the ability to handle higher sound levels before distortion (see "General Transducer Performance Characteristics" later in this chapter).

Mics that use the magnetic induction principle are classified as **dynamic microphones**. This includes the moving-coil and ribbon transducers. In practice, however, the moving-coil mic is referred to as a *dynamic* mic and the ribbon as a *ribbon* mic; the term *moving coil* is seldom used in referring to a *dynamic* mic. To avoid confusion, however, the term *moving coil,* instead of *dynamic,* is used throughout this book.

Variable Capacitance

Microphones operating on the *variable capacitance* principle transduce energy using voltage (electrostatic) variations, instead of magnetic (electromagnetic) variations, and are called **capacitor microphones**. They are also referred to as *condenser microphones,* which is a holdover from the past.

The element consists of two parallel plates separated by a small space (see 3-5). The front plate is a thin, metalized plastic diaphragm—the only moving part in the mic head—and the back plate is fixed. Together these plates or electrodes form a *capacitor*—a device that is capable of holding an electric charge. As acoustic energy moves the diaphragm back and forth in relation to the fixed back plate, the capacitance change causes a voltage change, varying the signal. The signal output is delicate and has a very high impedance, however, and requires a preamplifier (mounted near the mic capsule) to bring it to useable proportions.

Most preamps in capacitor microphones use a transistor circuit, which generally produces a clean sound. But a number of capacitor mics use a tube circuit in the preamp instead. This is due to the particular sonic characteristic that **tube microphones** give to sound, which many perceive as being more present, livelier, more detailed, and not as colored as the transistorized capacitors.

Because the capacitor requires polarizing voltage and the preamplifier requires power voltage to operate,

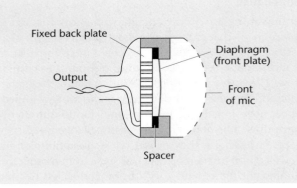

3-5 Cross-section of the element of a capacitor microphone.

capacitor microphones must have a separate power source either from batteries contained inside the mic or from an external, or phantom, power supply. External power eliminates the need for batteries and may be supplied from the console, studio microphone input circuits, or portable units.

Some capacitor microphones have an electret diaphragm. An *electret* is a material (high-polymer plastic film) that can hold a charge permanently, eliminating the need for external polarizing voltage. Because a small battery is all that is required to power the preamp, *electret microphones* can be made more compact, which facilitated the design of lavaliers and mini-mics.

Laser-based Microphone

In the ever-constant quest to eliminate distortion from microphones, a laser-based mic has been developed. At this writing it is still in the experimental stage but deserves attention because it could revolutionize microphone design. The technology is described as a ***particulate flow detection microphone:*** "A stream of air infused with particles passes through a chamber within the outer casting near the top, where the particles are perturbed by sound waves entering from the back. A laser beam passes through the stream, which modulates its intensity, and a photosensor converts that modulated light into an electrical signal analogous to the original sound wave" (see 3-6).[3] The process eliminates all nonlinearities in the conversion from acoustic to electric energy, hence making the sound distortion-free.

---

3. Scott Wilkinson, "Light Mic," *Electronic Musician,* March 2007, p. 28.

From *Electronic Musician*, March 2007, p. 28.

3-6 Laser-based microphone called particulate flow detection microphone.

Dual-element Microphones

Some microphone models combine transducing elements for particular applications. One such design combines capacitor and moving-coil elements in phase to take advantage of each element's different sonic characteristics (see 3-7). Other mic designs may use two capacitor or moving-coil elements to ensure more-uniform response or to minimize proximity effect or both (proximity effect is discussed later in this chapter), or to use the separate diaphragms to provide different responses.

GENERAL TRANSDUCER PERFORMANCE CHARACTERISTICS

Each type of microphone is unique. It is not a matter of one microphone being better than another but that one mic may be more suitable for a particular application. Moving-coil microphones are rugged, generate low self-noise, tend to be less susceptible to humidity and wide temperature variations, and handle high sound-pressure levels without distortion. They are usually less expensive than the other professional types and come in a wide variety of makes and models.

The element of a moving-coil mic has more mass than that of a ribbon or capacitor mic and therefore has greater inertia in responding to sound vibrations. This results in a slower response to *transients*—sounds that begin with a quick attack, such as a drum hit or breaking glass, and then quickly decay. (Capacitor microphones have the lowest mass of the three types of professional mics, which makes them best suited to handle transient sounds. The ribbon mic has relatively low mass; its transient response is between that of the moving-coil mic and the capacitor mic.) The inertia of the moving-coil element has another effect on pickup: with increased mic-to-source distance, high-frequency response is reduced. Generally (there are a number of exceptions), the frequency response of moving-coil mics is transparent; they tend not to color sound.

Ribbon microphones are not widely used today except in music recording and for the speaking voice. They are more expensive than many moving-coil mics and have to be handled with care, particularly when it comes to loud sound levels.

Older ribbon mics have mediocre high-frequency response, which can be turned into an advantage because it gives sound a warm, mellow quality. This attribute complements digital recording, which can produce an edged, hard sound quality. Modern ribbon mics have a more extended high-frequency response. As pointed out earlier, compared with most ribbon mics the active ribbon microphone has a higher output and sensitivity, a wider and flatter frequency response, and the ability to handle higher sound levels before distortion. Generally, ribbon mics have low self-noise, but they also have the lowest output level of the three major types. This means a poorer signal-to-noise ratio if the mic is too far from the sound source or if the cable run is too long.

Capacitor microphones are high-performance instruments. They have a wide, smooth frequency response and reproduce clear, airy, detailed sound. They are the choice among professional-quality mics when it is necessary to record sounds rich in harmonics and overtones. Capacitor mics have high sensitivity, which makes them the preferred choice for distant miking; high-end response is not hampered by extended mic-to-source distances. They also have the highest output level, which gives them a wide signal-to-noise ratio. These advantages come at a cost, however; capacitors are generally the most expensive type of microphone, although excellent capacitor models are available at lower prices.

DIRECTIONAL CHARACTERISTICS

A fundamental rule of good microphone technique is that a sound source should be *on-mic*—at an optimal distance

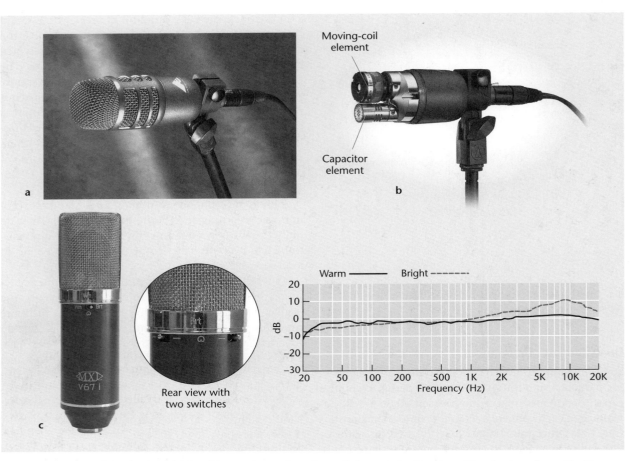

3-7 Dual-element microphones. (a) Mic with capacitor and moving-coil elements in phase for miking the bass drum. The idea behind the dual element is to preserve the full open sound of the drum and to capture the punch and the attack of the beater (see Chapter 17). (b) The arrangement of the two elements in (a). (c) Capacitor mic with two selectable diaphragms and their response curves. The front-side diaphragm produces a warm, lush sound; the rear-side diaphragm produces a brighter, airier sound.

from the microphone and directly in its pickup pattern. *Pickup pattern,* formally known as **polar response pattern**, refers to the direction(s) from which a mic hears sound.

Microphones work in a three-dimensional soundfield; sounds arrive at a mic from all directions. Depending on the design, however, a microphone is sensitive only to sound from all around—**omnidirectional**; its front and rear—**bidirectional**; or its front—**unidirectional** (see 3-8). Omnidirectional mics are also called *nondirectional;* and unidirectional mics are also called *directional.* **Cardioid** is yet another commonly used name for a unidirectional microphone because its pickup pattern is heart-shaped (see 3-8c and 3-12c). Five unidirectional patterns are in common use: *subcardioid* (also called *wide-angle cardioid*),

cardioid, supercardioid, hypercardioid, and *ultracardioid* (see 3-9).

A microphone's pickup pattern and its transducer classification are unrelated. Moving-coil mics are available in all pickup patterns except bidirectional. Ribbon mics are bidirectional, hypercardioid, or *multidirectional*—providing more than one pickup pattern. Capacitor mics come in all available pickup patterns, including multidirectional. Figures 3-8 and 3-9 show basic microphone directionalities. The precise pattern varies from mic to mic. To get a better idea of a microphone's pickup pattern, study its polar response diagram (see the following section).

A microphone's unidirectionality is facilitated by ports at the side and/or rear of the mic that cancel sound com-

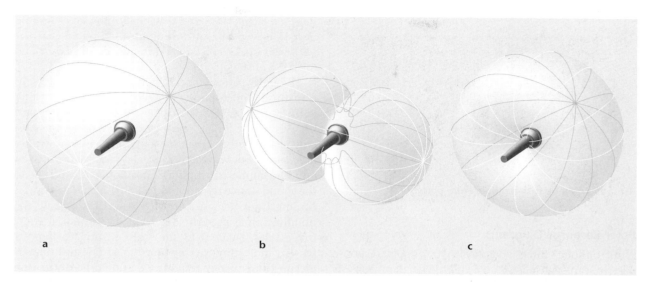

3-8 Pickup patterns. (a) Omnidirectional, (b) bidirectional, and (c) unidirectional, or cardioid.

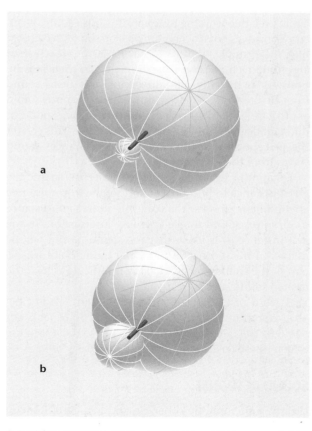

3-9 Pickup patterns. (a) Supercardioid and (b) hypercardioid.

ing from unwanted directions. For this reason you should not cover the ports with a hand or with tape. Directional mics are referred to as ***single-entry-port microphones***, or *single-D*™—having ports in the capsule; or as ***multiple-entry-port microphones***, also called *variable-D*™—having ports in the capsule and along the handle. In a single-entry directional mic, the rear-entrance port handles all frequencies (see 3-10). A multiple-entry directional mic has several ports, each tuned to a different band of frequencies (see 3-11). The ports closer to the diaphragm process the higher frequencies; the ports farther from the diaphragm process the lower frequencies. Ports also influence a mic's proximity effect, which is discussed later in this chapter.

Port

3-10 Microphone with single entry port. *Note:* This figure and Figure 3-11 indicate the positions of the ports on these mics. The actual ports are concealed by the mic grille.

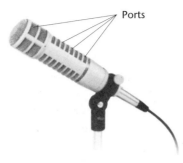

Ports

3-11 Microphone with multiple entry ports.

Polar Response Diagrams

A microphone's directional sensitivity, or polar response pattern, can be displayed on a graph. The graph consists of concentric circles, usually divided into segments of 30 degrees. Reading inward, each circle represents a decrease in sound level of 5 dB. The graph depicts response sensitivity in relation to the angle of sound incidence.

The omnidirectional polar pattern shows that sound is picked up almost uniformly from all directions (see 3-12a). The bidirectional polar pattern is most sensitive to sound coming from the front and the rear and least sensitive to sounds entering the sides (see 3-12b).

The cardioid polar pattern illustrates sensitivity to sounds arriving from the front and front-sides. It shows a reduced sensitivity of about 6 dB at the sides and least sensitivity, 15 to 25 dB, in the rear (see 3-12c). The subcardioid has a wider front and front-side and therefore a less directional pickup pattern than does the cardioid.

The supercardioid is more directional at the front than the cardioid. At the sides it is about 9 dB less sensitive and least sensitive at 125 degrees away from the front (see 3-12d). The hypercardioid polar pattern illustrates its highly directional frontal pickup, a 12 dB reduced sensitivity at the sides, and its areas of least sensitivity 110 degrees away from the front (see 3-12e).

Here's a brief comparison of the cardioid, supercardioid, hypercardioid, and ultracardioid pickup patterns: The cardioid mic has a wide-angle pickup of sound in front of the mic and maximum sound rejection at its rear. The supercardioid mic has a somewhat narrower on-axis response and less sensitivity at the rear-sides than the cardioid mic. It has maximum difference between its front- and rear-hemisphere pickups. The hypercardioid mic has a far narrower on-axis pickup and has its maximum rejection at the sides compared with the supercardioid mic.

Its rear rejection is poorer than that of the supercardioid mic, however. The ultracardioid microphone has the narrowest on-axis pickup and the widest off-axis sound rejection of the directional mics (see 3-12f).

The polar pattern diagrams shown here are ideals. In actual use a microphone's directional sensitivity varies with frequency. Because treble waves are shorter and bass waves are longer, *the higher the frequency, the more directional a mic becomes; the lower the frequency, the less directional a mic becomes, regardless of pickup pattern.* Even omnidirectional microphones positioned at an angle to the sound source tend not to pick up higher frequencies coming from the sides and the rear, thus making the nondirectional pattern somewhat directional at these frequencies. Figure 3-13 shows an example of a polar pattern indicating the relationship of on- and off-axis pickup to frequency response. It should be noted that a microphone's polar pattern is not an indication of its *reach*—a mic's relative effectiveness in rejecting reverberation (see 3-14).

Although *reach* is the term commonly used to describe a mic's relative working distance, it is misleading. A microphone does not reach out to pick up sound. A cardioid mic, for example, appears to have a farther reach than an omnidirectional mic. The difference in their pickup, however, is that the omnidirectional mic hears sound from all directions, whereas the cardioid mic hears sound approaching mainly from the front, rejecting sound in different degrees from the sides and the rear. This creates the perception that the cardioid mic enhances sound waves from the front.

For another example, use an omnidirectional mic at a given distance to pick up a sound source in a noise-free environment; now use the same mic at the same distance to pick up a sound source at a busy intersection. In the first instance, it is likely that the sound pickup will be usable. In the second instance, the traffic noise will be part of the sound pickup, making it difficult to hear the desired sound source clearly, if at all.

A word of caution about polar patterns: Don't believe everything you read. Looking good on paper is not enough. The microphone has to be put to the test in use to determine its actual response, particularly off-axis.

SOUND RESPONSE

Clearly, a microphone's operating principle (transducer) and directional characteristics affect the way it sounds. There are other sonic features to consider as well, which

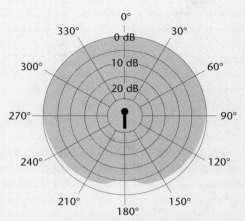

a. Omnidirectional polar pattern

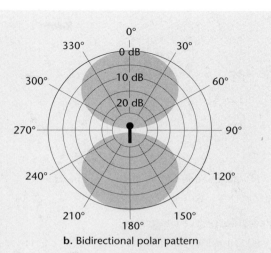

b. Bidirectional polar pattern

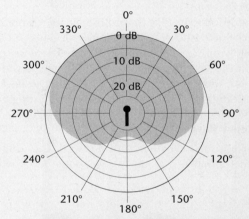

c. Unidirectional, or cardioid, polar pattern

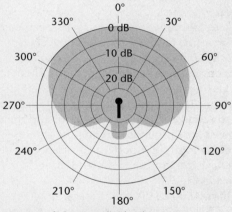

d. Supercardioid polar pattern

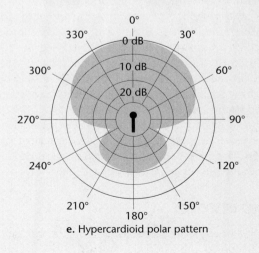

e. Hypercardioid polar pattern

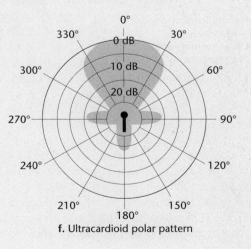

f. Ultracardioid polar pattern

3-12 Principal microphone polar patterns.

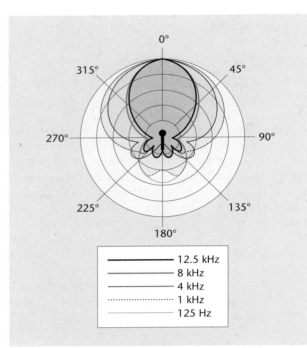

3-13 Polar pattern indicating differences in directionality at certain frequencies. Notice that the lower the frequency, the less directional the pickup.

are detailed on the mic's specification sheet. The specifications are either generalized, giving the response details of a particular line of models for potential buyers, or they are specific to, and included with, the actual mic when it is purchased.

Microphone specifications are useful because they can shortcut the selection process. With the hundreds of professional mics available, it is difficult to try more than a few of them at any one time. If you are looking for a mic with a particular polar pattern, frequency response, overload limit, and so on, reading a spec sheet can eliminate those mics that do not meet your needs. A word of caution, however: even when a spec sheet suggests that you may have found the "right" mic, regardless of how detailed the specifications are, there is only one ultimate test before selection—*listening and doing what your ears tell you.*

In addition to its type (transducer element) and directional characteristic(s), a microphone's spec sheet includes the following sonic features: frequency response, overload limit, maximum sound-pressure level, sensitivity, self-noise, and signal-to-noise ratio. Proximity effect and humbucking are also considerations when selecting a mic.

Frequency Response

A microphone's *frequency response* is the range of frequencies that it reproduces at an equal level, within

3-14 Differences in relative working distances among omnidirectional, cardioid, supercardioid, and hypercardioid microphones and their relative effectiveness in rejecting reverberation.

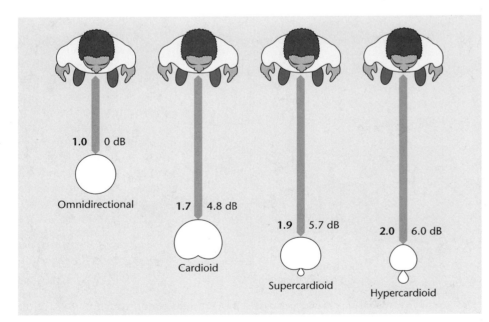

a margin of ±3 dB; that is, at a given level a frequency will not be more or less than 3 dB off. A mic's frequency response indicates how faithfully it transduces acoustic energy into electric signals and with what coloration, if any.

A mic's *frequency response curve* is displayed as a graph with the vertical line indicating amplitude (dB) and the horizontal line indicating frequency (Hz) (see 3-15). It shows the tonal balance of the microphone pickup at a designated distance from a sound source, usually 2 or 3 feet.

When the curve is reasonably straight, or *flat*, response has little coloration—all frequencies are re-produced at relatively the same level. But flat is not necessarily desirable. In looking at a response curve, it is important to know for what purpose the microphone was developed and what your sonic requirements are. In Figure 3-15, for example, the bass begins rolling off at 150 Hz, there is a boost in the high frequencies between 4,000 Hz and 10,000 Hz, and the high end rolls off beyond 10,000 Hz. Obviously, this particular mic would be unsuitable for instruments such as the bass drum, organ, and cello because it is not very sensitive to the lower frequencies from these instruments. It is also unsuitable for high-frequency sound sources, such as cymbals, the piccolo, and the female singing voice, because it is not that sensitive to their higher frequencies or harmonics. The mic was not designed for these purposes, however; it was designed for the speaking voice, and for this purpose it is excellent. Reproduction of frequencies through the critical upper bass and midrange is flat, the slight boost in the upper midrange adds presence, and the roll-offs

in the bass and the treble are beyond the ranges of most speaking voices.

Overload Limit

All microphones will distort if sound levels are too high—a condition known as *overload*—but some mics handle it better than others. Moving-coil and capacitor microphones are not as vulnerable to distortion caused by excessive loudness as are ribbon mics. Moving-coil mics can take high levels of loudness without internal damage. Using a ribbon mic when there may be overload risks damaging the element, particularly with older models.

In the capacitor system, although loud sound-pressure levels may not create distortion at the diaphragm, the output signal may be great enough to overload the electronics in the mic. To prevent this many capaci-tors contain a built-in pad. Switching the pad into the mic system eliminates overload distortion of the mic's preamp, thereby reducing the output signal so many decibels (see 3-28a).

Maximum Sound-pressure Level

Maximum sound-pressure level is the level at which a microphone's signal begins to distort. If a microphone has a maximum sound-pressure level of 120 dB-SPL, it means that the mic will audibly distort when the level of a sound source reaches 120 dB-SPL. A maximum sound-pressure level of 120 dB is good, 135 dB is very good, and 150 dB is excellent.

In a microphone distortion is measured as *total har-monic distortion (THD)*, a specification that compares the output signal with the input signal and measures the level differences in harmonic frequencies between the two. THD is measured as a percentage; the lower percentage, the better.

In microphones a commonly used level of total har-monic distortion is 0.5 percent (1 percent is also used). Therefore if the THD is listed as "< 0.5% up to 140 dB-SPL," it means that the mic has less than 0.5 percent THD up to 140 dB-SPL.

Sensitivity

Sensitivity measures the voltage that a microphone produces (in *dBV,* a unit of measurement for expressing the relationship of decibels to voltage, with decibels referenced to 1 V) at a certain sound-pressure level. It indicates how loud a microphone is. Capacitor mics

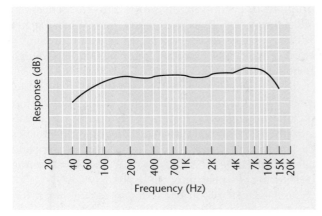

3-15 Frequency response curve of the Electro-Voice 635A mic.

are the loudest; ribbon mics are the quietest. Sensitivity does not affect a mic's sound quality, but it can affect the overall sound quality of a recording. A microphone with high sensitivity has a high voltage output and will not require as much gain as a mic with low sensitivity. Ribbon and small moving-coil mics have low sensitivity (–85 dBV), larger moving-coil mics have medium sensitivity (–75 dBV), and capacitor mics have high sensitivity (–65 dBV).

Self-noise

Self-noise, also known as *equivalent noise level,* indicates the sound-pressure level that will create the same voltage as the inherent electrical noise, or hiss, that a microphone (or any electronic device) produces. Self-noise is measured in dB-SPL, A-weighted. A fair self-noise rating is around 40 dB-SPL(A), a good rating is around 30 dB-SPL(A), and an excellent rating is 20 dB-SPL(A) or less.

Signal-to-noise Ratio

Signal-to-noise ratio (S/N) is the ratio of a signal power to the noise power corrupting the signal and is measured in decibels. In relation to microphones, S/N is the difference between sound-pressure level and self-noise. For example, if the microphone's maximum sound-pressure level is 94 dB and the self-noise is 30 dB-SPL, the signal-to-noise ratio is 64 dB. The higher the S/N, the less obtrusive is the noise. An S/N of 64 dB is fair, 74 dB is good, and 84 dB and higher is excellent.

Proximity Effect

When any microphone is placed close to a sound source, bass frequencies increase in level relative to midrange and treble frequencies. This response is known as ***proximity effect*** or *bass tip-up* (see 3-16).

Proximity effect is most pronounced in pressure-gradient (ribbon) microphones—mics in which both sides of the diaphragm are exposed to incident sound. Response is generated by the pressure differential, or gradient, between the sound that reaches the front of the diaphragm relative to the sound that reaches the rear. As mic-to-source distance decreases, acoustic pressure on the diaphragm increases. Because pressure is greater at lower frequencies and the path between the front and the rear of the diaphragm is short, bass response rises.

Response of directional microphones is, in part, pressure-gradient and therefore also susceptible to proximity effect but not to the extent of ribbon mics. Om-

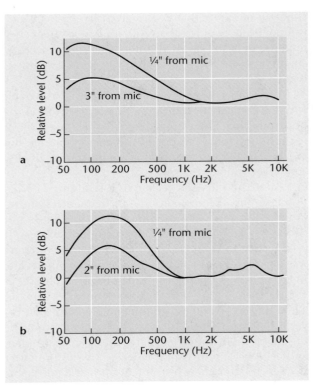

3-16 Proximity effect. (a) A typical cardioid moving-coil mic and (b) a cardioid capacitor mic.

nidirectional microphones are not subject to proximity effect unless the mic is close enough to the sound source to be almost touching it.

Proximity effect can be a blessing or a curse, depending on the situation. For example, in close-miking a bass drum, cello, or thin-sounding voice, proximity effect can add power or solidity to the sound source. When a singer with a deep bass voice works close to the mic, proximity effect can increase boominess, masking middle and high frequencies.

To neutralize unwanted proximity effect (rumble, or 60-cycle hum), most microphones susceptible to it include ***bass roll-off***, a feature of a limited in-mic equalizer (see 3-28a). When turned on, the roll-off attenuates bass frequencies several decibels from a certain point and below, depending on the microphone, thereby canceling or reducing any proximity effect (see 3-17).

Because bass roll-off has so many advantages, it has become a common feature even on mics that have little or no proximity effect. In some models bass roll-off has been extended to include several different frequency set-

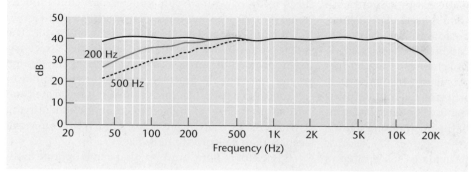

3-17 Bass roll-off curves.

tings at which attenuation can occur, or different levels of attenuation at the same roll-off frequency (see 3-18).

Another way to reduce proximity effect is to use a multiple-entry-port directional microphone because these mics have some distance between the rear-entry low-frequency ports and the sound source. At close mic-to-source distances, however, most multiple-entry-port microphones have some proximity effect.

To avoid proximity effect at close working distances down to a few inches, directional mics have been de-

signed that are frequency independent. One such mic uses two transducers—one to process high frequencies, the other to process low ones. This *two-way system* design also produces a more linear response at the sides of the microphone.

Hum

Hum is an ever-present concern in audio in general and in microphone pickup in particular. In a microphone it

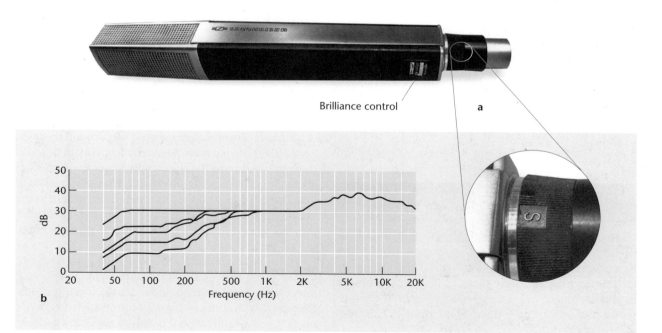

3-18 (a) Five-position roll-off control and (b) its effect on bass response. S = speech, M (not shown) = music. This particular microphone also has a brilliance control. The response curve (b) shows the curve when the high-frequency boost is switched into the pickup.

is typically produced by stray alternating current (AC) magnetic fields at 50 or 60 Hz and is particularly a problem in dynamic mics. One way to minimize hum is to use balanced mic cables and connectors (see "Cables" and "Connectors" later in this chapter). Twisted-pair mic cables with good shield coverage are recommended; the braided shield is particularly effective. When using a microphone splitter or a direct box, be sure it is transformer-isolated (for coverage of the microphone splitter, see Chapter 13; for direct box see Chapter 17). Because dynamic microphones are particularly susceptible to hum, use one with a humbuck coil.

Humbucking

Humbucking is not so much a response characteristic as it is a feature built into many moving-coil microphones. It is designed to cancel the effect of induced hum by introducing a 50/60 Hz component equal in level and opposite in polarity to the offending hum. Because the original and the introduced hums are opposite in polarity, they cancel each other. Humbucking is effected with a **humbuck coil** that is built into the microphone system and requires no special operation to activate it. The effectiveness of the hum reduction varies with the microphone.

MICROPHONE MODELER

A *microphone modeler* is not an actual microphone but a microphone simulator that can be added to a hard-disk recording system as a plug-in (see 3-19). It is designed to emulate the sounds of most professional-grade microphones.

Say you have a track recorded with a Sennheiser MD421 and you want to make it sound as though it had

3-19 Microphone modeler.

been recorded with a Neumann U-87. The mic modeler removes from the audio the characteristics of the original microphone and applies those of the target mic. The microphone modeler can be used either after a track has been recorded or during recording to shape the desired sound. Although the process is not completely accurate in reproducing a particular mic's sound, it does create good virtual similarities of a given microphone's identifying characteristics, thereby providing a much larger mic collection than a recordist might have.

It is useful to note, however, that a microphone modeler cannot make a $30 dynamic mic sound like a $3,000 tube-type capacitor; and because many factors affect a recording, such as a studio's acoustics, the microphone preamplifier, and mic-to-source distance, it cannot make poorly recorded material sound good.

SPECIAL-PURPOSE MICROPHONES

Certain mics have been designed to meet particular production needs because of their size, pickup characteristics, sound, appearance, or a combination of these features. A number of different types of mics can be considered special-purpose: lavalier (mini-mic), shotgun, parabolic, headset and earset, contact, boundary, noise-canceling, multidirectional, stereophonic, middle-side, infinitely variable pattern, binaural and surround-sound, High Definition,™ digital, and USB.

Lavalier Microphones (Mini-mics)

The first TV microphone created primarily for looks was the small and unobtrusive **lavalier microphone** (see 3-20), although by today's standards it was not so small and unobtrusive. The microphone was hung around the neck, hence the name (*lavaliere* is French for "pendant"). Today these mics are indeed quite small and are also known as *miniature microphones,* or **mini-mics**. They are attached to a tie, to the front of a dress in the sternum area or at the neckline, or to a lapel. When they have to be concealed, they are placed in the seam or under clothing, behind the ear, or in the hair.

Mini-mics designed for use under the chin have two things in common: most are omnidirectional, although directional minis are used under certain conditions (see Chapter 13), and many have a built-in high-frequency boost. The omnidirectional pickup is necessary because, with the mic mounted away from the front of the mouth, a speaker does not talk directly into it but *across* it. A directional response would not pick up much room

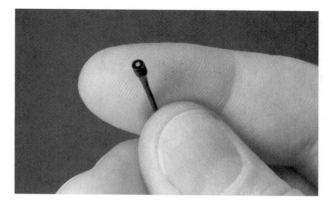

3-20 Lavalier miniature microphone. This model measures ¹/₁₀ inch in diameter. It features three protective caps that both keep moisture out and alter the mic's color and frequency response to match desired applications. Frequency responses using the three protective caps are flat, +0 dB; bright, +4 dB; and very bright, +8 dB.

presence and would sound too dead. In addition, as a speaker talks, high frequencies, which are directional, travel straight ahead. The chin cuts off many of the less directional high frequencies with longer wavelengths that otherwise would reach the mic. The built-in high-frequency boost compensates for this loss. If you hold in front of your mouth a mini-mic that was designed for use under the chin, its response will be overly bright and hissy. Their sensitivity to breathing and popping sounds also makes mini-mics unsuitable for use in front of the mouth; they have no pop filter, although windscreens come with many models (see "Windscreens and Pop Filters" later in this chapter).

The mini-mics in common use are electret capacitors. Generally they fall into two groups: the *proximity-prone mini-mic*, which adds presence to close speech while reducing background sound, and the *transparent mini-mic*, which picks up more ambience, thereby blending more naturally with the overall sound.

Shotgun Microphones

Television created the need for a good-looking on-camera microphone, but the need for an off-camera mic first became apparent in sound motion pictures. The problem was to record performers' voices without the microphone's being visible. Directors had many ingenious ways to hide a mic on the set; they used flowerpots, vases, lamps, clothing, and virtually anything else that could conceal a mic. These attempts only made more obvious the need for a mic capable of picking up sound from a distance.

The solution was the *shotgun microphone*. The basic principle of all shotgun mics is that they attenuate sound from all directions except a narrow angle at the front. This creates the perception that they have greater reach. Compared with an omnidirectional microphone, mic-to-source pickup can be 1.7 times greater with a cardioid, 1.9 times greater with a supercardioid, and 2 times greater with a hypercardioid and not affect on-mic presence (see 3-14). Some shotguns are better than others, so be careful when choosing one, especially for use in mediocre acoustic environments. The main consideration should be how well it discriminates sound, front-to-back, in a given situation.

The comparison can be made between a shotgun mic and a telephoto lens on a camera. A telephoto lens compresses front-to-back space. Shot with such a lens, an auditorium, for example, would appear smaller, with the rows of seats closer together than they really are. A shotgun mic does the same thing with acoustic space: it brings the background and the foreground sounds closer together. The extent of this spatial compression depends on the mic's pickup pattern. Of the three types of shotgun pickups—super-, hyper-, and ultracardioid—the supercardioid compresses front-to-rear sound the least and the ultracardioid compresses it the most.

Shotgun mics can sacrifice quality for a more focused pickup. One reason why is because shotguns are usually used for speech, and the frequency ranges of the male and female speaking voices are not very wide. Another reason is that the shotgun becomes less directional at lower frequencies, as do all directional mics, due to its inability to deal well with wavelengths that are longer than the length of its tube, called the *interference tube*. Interference tubes come in various lengths from 6 inches to 3 feet and longer. The longer the interference tube, the more highly directional the microphone. If the tube of a shotgun mic is 3 feet long, it will maintain directionality for frequencies of 300 Hz and higher—that is, wavelengths of approximately 3 feet or less. For 300 Hz and lower, the mic becomes less and less directional, canceling fewer and fewer of the lower frequencies. Many shotgun mics do have bass roll-off, however.

Stereo Shotgun Microphone   The shotgun mic is also available in a stereo design. Models vary in characteristics. One design is compact and lightweight, measuring a little more than 9 inches long and weighing about 5 ounces.

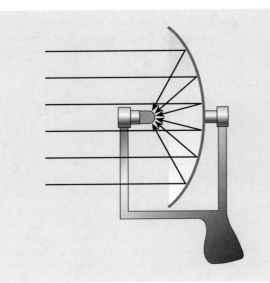

3-21 Stereo shotgun microphone. This model provides three switchable modes: normal, mono, and wide. In the normal mode, pickup is quite focused and stereo localization is accurate. In the mono mode, extremely sharp directivity is maintained for the aimed frontal sound source(s). The wide mode is designed for stereo recording of sound effects and any other source that requires a wide pickup. Pickup in the wide mode is 140 degrees.

3-22 Parabolic microphone system. The system uses a concave dish that concentrates the incoming sound waves, based on the principle that a sound wave's angle of incidence is equal to its angle of reflectance (see Chapter 2). The attached microphone can be wired or wireless. With wireless mics the transmitter is usually attached to the parabolic reflector (see "Wireless Microphone System" later in this chapter).

It has independent cardioid and bidirectional capacitor elements and three switchable stereo modes: left/right stereo-wide; left/right stereo-narrow; and middle-side. Figure 3-21 shows another stereo shotgun design.

Parabolic Microphone System

Another microphone that is used for long-distance pickup, mainly outdoors at sporting events, film and video shoots, in gathering naturalistic recordings of sounds in the wild, and for surveillance, is the *parabolic microphone system*. It consists of either an omni- or a unidirectional mic facing inward and attached to a parabolic reflector. Fine-tuning the pickup is done by moving the device that holds the mic forward and backward. Some parabolic systems enable electronic magnifying by several decibels of faint or distant sounds. Parabolic systems are also available with a built-in recorder.

More than canceling unwanted sound, the parabolic dish, which is concave, concentrates the sound waves from the sound source and directs them to the microphone (see 3-22). As with the shotgun mic, the parabolic mic is most effective within the middle- and high-frequency ranges; its sound quality is not suitable for critical recording.

Headset and Earset Microphones

Sports broadcasting led to the development of the *headset microphone*—a mic mounted to headphones. The microphone is usually a moving-coil type with a built-in pop filter because of its ability to handle loud sound-pressure levels that sports announcers project. It may be omnidirectional for added event ambience or cardioid to keep background sound to a minimum. Hypercardioid models are designed for high rejection of unwanted sounds.

The headphones can carry two separate signals: the program feed through one headphone and the director's feed through the other. The headset system frees the announcer's hands and frontal working space. Another benefit is that the announcer's distance from the mic does not change once the headset is in place. Small and lightweight headset mics are also available. They are particularly popular with singers doing TV or live concerts and for dance-oriented performances (see 3-23).

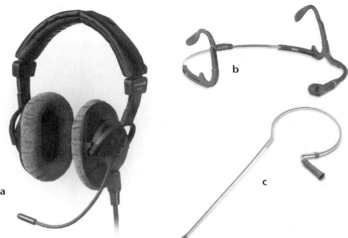

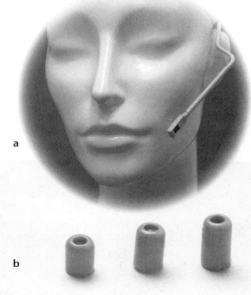

3-23 Headset microphone systems.
(a) Headset microphone system with omnidirectional mic. (b) Small headset microphone system with cardioid mic for vocalists, singing instrumentalists, and radio talk-show hosts. (c) Headset mic with a flexible, telescoping band that fits snugly around the back of the head and is easily concealed under the hair. It has a telescoping boom that can be bent for a custom fit. Headset microphone systems can be wired or wireless.

The ***earset microphone*** has no headband. It consists only of an earpiece cable connected to a microphone, usually omni- or unidirectional. If keeping a mic unobtrusive is important, the earset microphone is far less apparent on-camera than are headset models (see 3-24).

Contact Microphones

Not to quibble about semantics, but some lavaliers, particularly the miniature models, can be classified as ***contact microphones*** and vice versa. Essentially, the difference between the two is that a contact mic, also called an *acoustic pickup mic,* has been specially designed to attach to a vibrating surface (see 3-25a). Instead of picking up airborne sound waves as conventional mics do, it picks up vibrations through solid materials. Exact positioning of a contact mic is important if the sound is to be free of standing-wave resonance from the vibrating surface, especially if it is a musical instrument.

Contact mics come in various impedances, so it is important to select low-impedance models for professional recording. They also come in different designs. One electret capacitor version is enclosed in a strip and

3-24 Earset microphone. (a) This model comes with protective caps (b) to keep perspiration, makeup, and other foreign materials out of the microphone. The caps also provide different high-frequency responses to control the amount of presence or crispness in the sound. Earset mics can be wired or wireless.

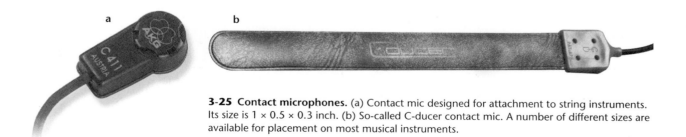

3-25 Contact microphones. (a) Contact mic designed for attachment to string instruments. Its size is 1 × 0.5 × 0.3 inch. (b) So-called C-ducer contact mic. A number of different sizes are available for placement on most musical instruments.

is flexible enough to adhere to almost any surface, flat or curved (see 3-25b).

Boundary Microphones

When a conventional microphone is placed on or near a surface, such as a wall, floor, or ceiling, sound waves reach the mic from two directions—directly from the sound source and reflected from the nearby surface. The reflected sound takes longer to reach the microphone than the direct sound because it travels a longer path. This time difference causes phase cancellations at various frequencies, creating a *comb-filter effect,* which gives sound an unnatural, hollow coloration (see 3-26). The *boundary microphone* positions a mini–capacitor mic capsule very close to, but at an optimal distance from, a sound-reflecting plate—the boundary. At this optimal distance, direct and reflected sound travel the same distance and reach the mic at about the same time, thereby eliminating phase cancellations. Any comb filtering occurs out of the range of human hearing.

Boundary microphones may be mounted on rectangular or circular plates. If the mic is positioned centrally on a symmetrical plate, acoustical phasing from the edges of the plate may interfere with pickup and cause irregularities in response. Therefore some mics are positioned off-center.

Boundary microphones have an electret transducer. Their pickup pattern is half omnidirectional or hemispheric, half cardioid, half supercardioid, or stereophonic. Their response is open and, in suitable acoustics, spacious (see 3-27).

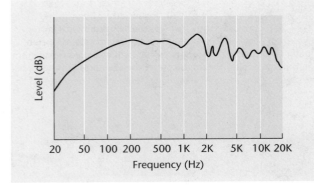

3-26 Comb-filter effect. Delayed reflected sound combined with direct sound can create this effect.

Noise-canceling Microphones

As stated earlier a shotgun mic is designed to pick up at a distance and in so doing focuses sound by reducing unwanted background noise, so long as it is correctly aimed and does not pull in unwanted ambience from behind the primary sound source. The *noise-canceling microphone* is also intended to reject unwanted ambient sound, but it is designed for use close to the mouth. Because of its particular electronics, the noise-canceling mic must be used close to the sound source. If it is held even a short distance away, the performer's sound may be clipped, and the pickup may be *off-mic* entirely.

Noise Suppression

It is also possible to reduce unwanted background noise using conventional microphones. The sound-pressure level from a sound source in a free field doubles by 6 dB each time the distance is halved (see the discussion of the inverse square law in Chapter 13). Therefore in noisy surroundings moving a mic closer to the desired sound source increases the on-mic level as the background noise remains constant. This type of noise suppression is more effective with directional microphones than with non-directional mics because they better concentrate on-axis pickup. With directional mics subject to the proximity effect, it is important to neutralize the effect or the sound will be too bassy.

Multidirectional Microphones

Microphones with a single directional response have one fixed diaphragm (or ribbon). By using more than one diaphragm and a switch to select or proportion between them, or by including more than one microphone capsule in a single housing, a mic can be made *multidirectional,* or *polydirectional,* providing two or more ways to pick up sound from various directions (see 3-28).

System Microphones

One multidirectional mic of sorts is the *system microphone,* which uses interchangeable heads or capsules, each with a particular pickup pattern, that can be mounted onto a common base (see 3-29). Because these systems are capacitors, the power supply and the preamplifier are in the base, and the mic capsule simply screws into the base. Any number of directional capsules—omnidirectional and bidirectional, cardioid, supercardioid, and hypercardioid—can be interchanged on a single base.

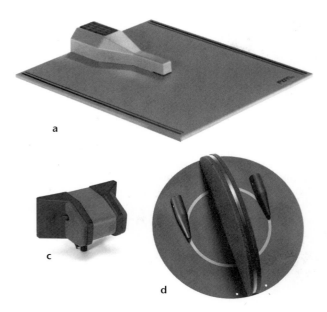

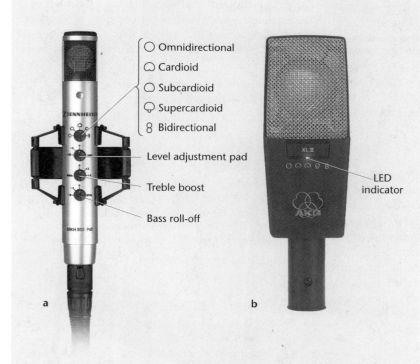

3-27 Boundary microphones with various pickup patterns.
(a) Hemispheric. (b) Hypercardioid. (c) SASS™ (Stereo Ambient Sampling System) stereo boundary mic, which uses two boundary mics, with a foam barrier between them. It is manufactured by Crown Audio, which calls its boundary mics PZMs (pressure zone microphones). (d) This stereo boundary mic features dual omnidirectional mics separated by a modified Jecklin disc baffle (see 17-6). Each mic is omnidirectional at low frequencies and unidirectional at high frequencies.

○ Omnidirectional
◠ Cardioid
○ Subcardioid
♀ Supercardioid
8 Bidirectional

Level adjustment pad

Treble boost

Bass roll-off

LED indicator

3-28 Multidirectional microphones with five pickup patterns: omni-directional, subcardioid, cardioid, supercardioid, and bidirectional.
(a) This microphone also has a three-position level adjustment pad (0, –6 dB, and –12 dB; second control from the top), a three-position treble boost at 10 kHz (0, +3 dB, and +6 dB; third control from top), and a bass roll-off at 50 Hz (–3 dB and –6 dB; bottom control). See "Overload Limit" and "Proximity Effect" earlier in this chapter. (b) Multidirectional microphone with two-color (green and red) LEDs (light-emitting diodes). Green shows the function selected; red indicates overload—the output signal is distorted. As the microphone is moved off-axis, illumination of the LED dims.

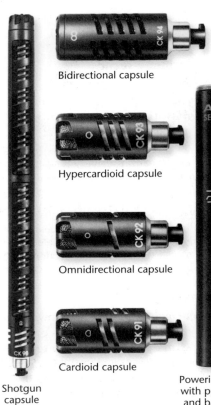

Bidirectional capsule

Hypercardioid capsule

Omnidirectional capsule

Cardioid capsule

Shotgun capsule

Powering module with preamplifier and bass roll-off

3-29 System microphone.

3-30 A stereo pair of matched ribbon mics mounted one above the other in a single casing. The two ribbons' pickup patterns are 90 degrees off-axis from each other.

3-31 Stereo microphone with one rotating capsule. The upper capsule in this model can rotate 270 degrees horizontally; the lower capsule is stationary. Two 3-way switches control the polar response, high-pass filtering, and –10 dB pad for each capsule.

3-32 Stereo microphone with two rotating capsules. The angle between the microphone's axes can be adjusted continuously in the range from 0 to 180 degrees.

Some system mic models may only include two or three directional capsules.

Stereophonic Microphones

Stereophonic microphones are actually microphone capsules with electronically separate systems housed in a single casing or separate casings. The stereo mic has two distinct elements which, in some models, can be remotely controlled. Generally, stereo mics are configured in one of three ways: the lower and upper elements are stationary (see 3-30); one element is stationary and the other element rotates 180 to 360 degrees to facilitate several different stereo pickup patterns, depending on the pickup design (see 3-31); or both elements rotate (see 3-32). Stereo mics also come in shotgun designs.

Middle-side Microphones

Most **middle-side (M-S) microphones** consist of two mic capsules housed in a single casing. One capsule is designated as the midposition microphone aimed at the sound source to pick up mostly direct sound; it is usually cardioid. The other capsule is designated as the side-position mic. It is usually bidirectional, with each lobe oriented 90 degrees laterally to the sides of the sound source to pick up mostly ambient sound. The outputs of the cardioid and bidirectional capsules are combined into a sum-and-difference matrix through a controller that may be external or internal (see 3-33 and 3-34).

Infinitely Variable Pattern Microphones

Instead of having selectable pickup patterns, the *infinitely variable pattern microphone* allows fine adjust-

3-33 Combined middle-side and stereo microphone. In the stereo mode, this microphone uses its internal matrix to mix the middle and side signals. In the *L* (low) position, the stereo image spread is small. In the *M* (medium) position, it is wider. The *H* (high) position provides the widest stereo spread. In the M-S output mode, the internal stereo matrix is bypassed. The pickup from the front-facing mic capsule is cardioid, and from the side-facing capsule it is bidirectional.

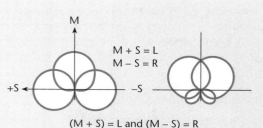

$$M + S = L$$
$$M - S = R$$

$(M + S) = L$ and $(M - S) = R$
In summed mono [L + R], the S component disappears
$(M + S) + (M - S) = 2M$

3-34 M-S pickup pattern and capsule configuration.

ments to any position from omnidirectional through bi- and unidirectional patterns (see 3-35).

Binaural and Surround-sound Microphone Systems

Binaural microphony picks up sound in three, instead of two, dimensions. The addition of vertical, or height, information to the sonic depth and breadth reproduced by conventional stereo and M-S mics makes sound quite spacious and localization very realistic. Surround sound adds greater front-to-rear depth and side-to-side breadth (assuming side placement of the loudspeakers) than stereo but not quite the vertical imaging or sonic envelopment of binaural sound.

A number of binaural and surround-sound microphones are available. The following section includes a few of the better-known models.

Binaural Microphone Head

The **binaural microphone head** (also known as *artificial head* or *dummy head* [Kunstkopf] *stereo*) consists of an artificial head with a pair of pinnae ear replicas and a matched pair of omnidirectional capacitor microphones or mic capsules placed in the ear canals (see 3-36). Some binaural microphone systems go so far as to construct the head and the upper torso based on statistical averaging and variations in real humans. Some even feature felt hair

3-35 Infinitely variable tube microphone. In addition to its variable pickup patterns, this capacitor mic has a variable high-pass filter (bass roll-off) and a variable pad.

— Pickup patterns

— Bass roll-off

— Pad

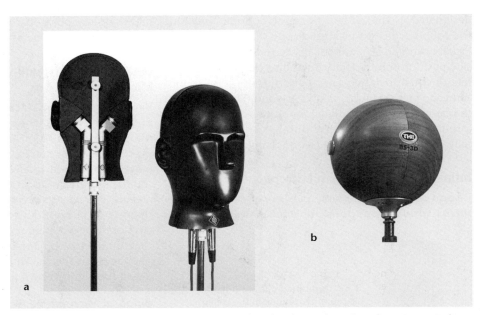

3-36 Binaural microphone heads. (a) Two omnidirectional capacitor microphones mounted in "ear" cavities reproduce binaural sound. At the bottom of the unit is a switch for different power supply modes and balanced and unbalanced output signals. Inside the head are additional switches for 10 dB attenuation and the high-pass filter. To hear the full binaural effect, it is necessary to listen with headphones. Recordings made with this and some other binaural microphone models that are played back through loudspeakers reproduce aural imaging similar to conventional stereo but with a much deeper sound stage. (b) The Binaural Sphere uses matched omnidirectional microphones on either side of a sphere. The sphere is a compact hardwood ball with gold-plated grilles on either side, which house the two mic capsules.

and shoulder padding to simulate the characteristics of hair and clothing.

There are three essential differences between how a stereo microphone hears sound and how humans hear it.

1. With stereo there is no solid object, like the head, between the microphones. When sound comes from the left, particularly the midrange and high frequencies, it reaches the left ear sooner and with greater intensity than it does the right ear. The sound reaching the right ear is delayed, creating a *sound shadow.* The converse is also true: sound coming from the right is louder in the right ear and casts a sound shadow in the left ear. The listener's shoulders and torso also reflect sound.

2. With the low frequencies, this shadow is largely neutralized because the longer wavelengths diffract around the head. Therefore we depend on their time of arrival—relative phases—for perceptual clues (see also "Spatial Hearing" in Chapter 2).

3. The human ear itself also modifies sound. The folds in the outer ear (pinnae) resonate and reflect sounds into the ear canal, causing phase cancellations at certain frequencies.

Combined, these *head-related transfer functions (HRTF)* are the theoretical bases for binaural head construction and recording (see Chapter 2). Binaural sound is an extraordinary listening experience. It has not been commercially viable, however, because it is possible to get its full effect only through stereo headphones; loudspeakers will not do nearly so well.

SoundField Microphone System

The **SoundField microphone system** is a method of recording an entire soundfield as defined by absolute sound pressure and three pressure gradients of the front/rear, left/right, and up/down directions. The microphone contains four mic subcardioid capsules mounted in a tetrahedron arrangement (see 3-37). The outputs of these

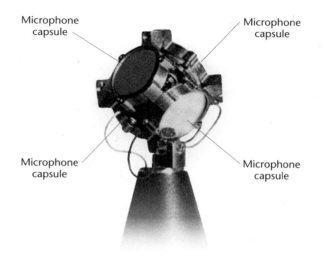

3-37 Four rotating capsules of the SoundField microphone system.

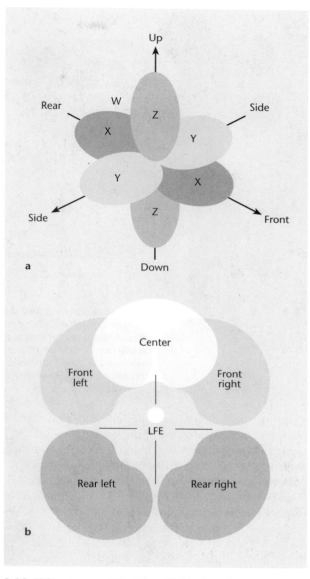

3-38 Pickup arrays of the SoundField microphone system. (a) Basic pickup arrays and (b) 5.1 surround-sound pickup array—five cardioid microphones (center, left and right front, and left and right surround) plus an omnidirectional low-frequency enhancement (LFE) channel.

capsules are fed into a matrix controller to reproduce a number of different pickups.

Three of the signals—the X, Y, and Z channels—describe the space around the microphone in the X (front/rear), Y (left/right) and Z (up/down) dimensions and are equivalent to recordings made with three figure-of-eight microphones at right angles to one another. The fourth channel, known as W, is equivalent to a recording made with an omnidirectional microphone and provides a reference for the three other channels (see 3-38).

The four outputs, known as the *A-format,* feed the high left-front-right-rear and the low right-front-left-rear information into the matrix network. After the signals are mixed, they are converted into the so-called *B-format,* from which they can be manipulated to produce a variety of pickups. The resulting three-dimensional sound is quite spacious, and localization is realistic although it does not provide quite the enveloping sonic experience of binaural sound. But SoundField recordings do not require headphones for listening; they do, however, require four loudspeakers—two in front of the listener and two to the rear. SoundField has given this fully immersing sound experience the name *ambisonic.*

There are different SoundField controller configurations designed for particular applications, such as broadcast, music recording, sporting events, and surround sound. The surround-sound system can be either hardware- or software-controlled (see 3-39).

Holophone Microphone System

The original **Holophone™ *microphone system*** consists of seven miniature omnidirectional capacitor microphone elements housed in a 7.5 × 5.7–inch fiberglass epoxy ellipsoid that is shaped like a giant teardrop. The elliptical

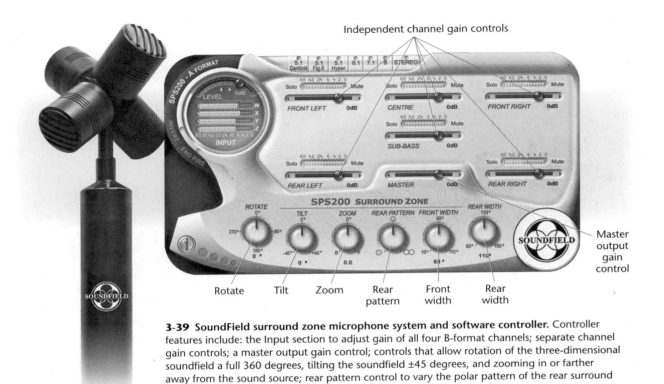

Independent channel gain controls

Master output gain control

Rotate Tilt Zoom Rear pattern Front width Rear width

3-39 SoundField surround zone microphone system and software controller. Controller features include: the Input section to adjust gain of all four B-format channels; separate channel gain controls; a master output gain control; controls that allow rotation of the three-dimensional soundfield a full 360 degrees, tilting the soundfield ±45 degrees, and zooming in or farther away from the sound source; rear pattern control to vary the polar pattern of the rear surround channels; and front and rear width to vary the front and rear stage width.

shape of the Holophone is designed to emulate the characteristics of the human head. Sound waves diffract around the mic as they do around the head, producing realistic, spacious sonic imaging. Five microphone connections are for front-left-right-left surround and right-surround pickup, with the front (or center) element at the tip of the teardrop. Another mic is positioned on top for height. The seventh microphone is dedicated to low-frequency pickup. This configuration is consistent with the 5.1 surround-sound protocol which, in reproduction, calls for frontal loudspeakers left, center, and right, plus a loudspeaker for low-frequency enhancement and two loudspeakers left-rear and right-rear (see Chapters 8, 17, 22, and 23). The Holophone comes with a control module that allows for manipulating the seven signals.

Another Holophone microphone includes a system that adds an eighth mic to enable 7.1 surround sound (see 3-40). It houses mic capsules for left, center, right, left-rear surround, center-rear surround, right-rear surround, top, and low-frequency pickup. There is also a camera-mountable 5.1 Holophone system for field recording (see 3-41).

Atmos 5.1 Surround Microphone System

The *Atmos 5.1 surround microphone system* consists of a control console and an adjustable surround microphone (see 3-42). The console is the command center for the mic's various surround configurations, controlling output assignment and panning. It also includes features found on conventional consoles, such as microphone amplifiers, pads, phase reversal, phantom power, filters, and sends (see Chapter 4).

The microphone unit consists of five matched cardioid capsules mounted on a spiderlike stand. The capsules can be manually rotated 90 degrees and the pickup patterns remotely controlled. The left, center, and right capsules are positioned in a triangle, with each microphone 6.9 inches from the center. These mics can be positioned in a straight line if desired. The two rear mic capsules are about 24 inches to the back with a 60-degree offset.

Schoeps Surround Microphone System

The *Schoeps surround microphone system* (the KFM 360) combines the features of its stereo model, which uses

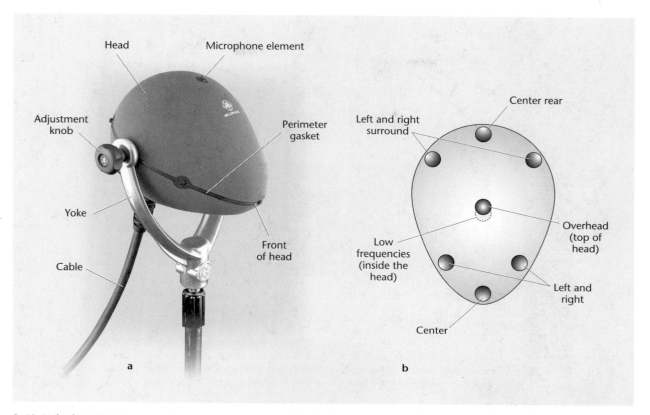

3-40 **Holophone™ 7.1 surround-sound microphone system.** (a) Holophone microphone head. (b) Positions of the eight microphone capsules.

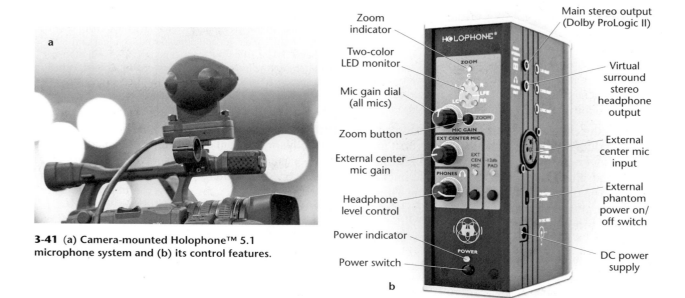

3-41 (a) Camera-mounted Holophone™ 5.1 microphone system and (b) its control features.

3-42 Atmos 5.1 surround-sound microphone and control console.

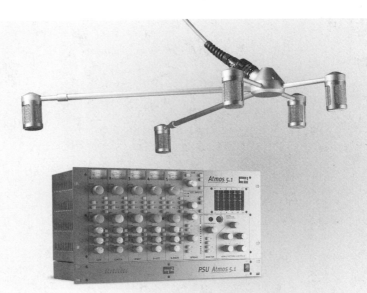

3-43 Schoeps surround microphone system. (a) Omni- and bidirectional microphones mounted on a sphere. (b) Digital processor. This unit derives four channels (L, R, LS, and RS) from the microphone signals. A center-channel signal is obtained from the two front signals. An additional output channel carries only the frequencies below 70 Hz. The front stereo image width is adjustable, and the directional patterns of the front-facing and rear-facing pairs of "virtual microphones" can be chosen independent of one another.

two omnidirectional capacitor capsules flush-mounted on either side of a sphere, with two bidirectional microphones—one on each side of the sphere, facing front and rear. The positive phase of the bidirectional mics faces forward. The diameter of the sphere is about 7 inches. This system also includes a digital processor used to derive the six 5.1 surround-sound signals (see 3-43).

High-definition Microphones

The term *High Definition Microphone*™ is a trademark of Earthworks, Inc., and refers to its line of very high-quality mics and their proprietary technology. But so-called

high-definition microphones, regardless of manufacturer, generally include similar sonic characteristics.

The guidelines for the Earthworks line provide an idea of what those characteristics are:

■ *Better impulse response.* This is the ability of a microphone to accurately respond to transients (see 3-44). Impulse response is a measure of a mic's overall sonic accuracy and fidelity.

■ *Shorter diaphragm settling time.* This increases a mic's ability to pick up low-level sounds by ceasing to vibrate sooner than conventional diaphragms. If a

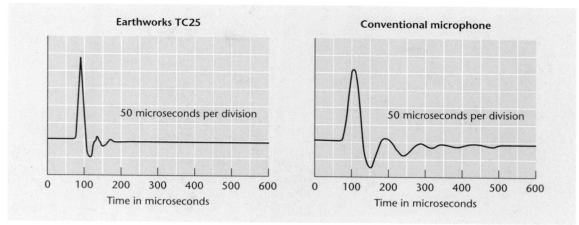

3-44 Impulse response graphs.

diaphragm is still vibrating from a previous sound, it tends to mask or color the sounds that follow.

■ *Extended frequency response.* This is essential in a high-definition microphone. Studies have shown that sounds beyond 20 kHz influence our perception of overall sound quality.

■ *Minimal signal path.* Fewer electronic features, such as switchable patterns, pads, and filters, provide a purer and less altered signal.

■ *Low distortion at high sound-pressure levels* up to and beyond 140 dB-SPL.

■ *Improved polar pattern.* This feature stabilizes the polar response over a microphone's operating frequency range to reduce deteriorating frequency response over the pickup pattern and the phasing at its edges (see 3-45).

Digital Microphones

Given digital technology's relatively rapid ascendancy to dominance in sound production, by comparison it has taken a while to develop a basic component of the audio chain: the digital microphone. Among the problems have been developing an acceptable analog-to-digital converter in the mic and meeting industry standards for creating, controlling, and transmitting digital signals.

When conventional mics are used in digital recording, the analog signal is converted to a digital signal at some point in the sound chain—but after it leaves the microphone. With the *digital microphone* system, the analog signal is converted to digital at the mic capsule, which means that the signal going through the sound chain is digital immediately after it is transduced from acoustic energy into electric energy.

USB Microphones

The *USB microphone* was developed for those who want to record directly into a computer without an audio interface, such as a console, control surface, or mixer. (*USB* stands for *Universal Serial Bus,* a protocol used worldwide for data transfer between peripheral devices and computers.) The USB mic has become popular in podcasting (see Chapter 19) and for other prosumer-friendly applications in which production requirements are not as involved as they are in more-professional-quality audio productions. Generally, first-generation USB mics had mediocre sound quality. That has changed, however, with the array of high-quality models now available.

Like all microphones classified as digital, USB mics have a built-in analog-to-digital (A/D) converter. They are available in both moving-coil and capacitor models. With capacitor USB mics, it is important to make sure that, because they use phantom power (which can generate noise) and because USB power can be noisy in the first place, the mic has compensating power conditioning and noise filtering to ensure sound quality that can run from decent to excellent. Another possible source of noise is the quality, or lack thereof, of the A/D converter.

Frequency response among USB mics varies from as narrow as 40 Hz to 14 kHz to as wide as 20 Hz to 20 kHz.

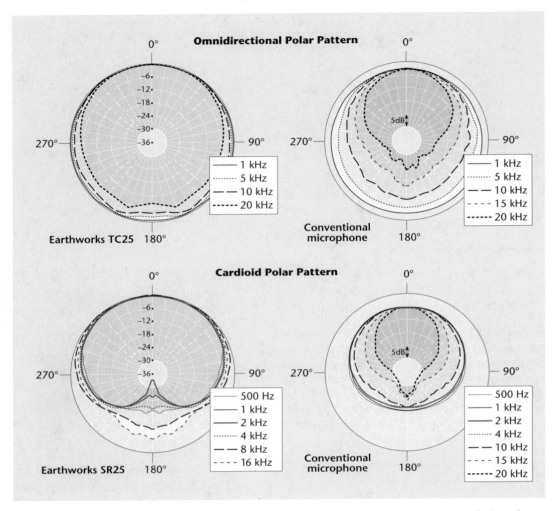

3-45 Polar pattern comparisons between a High Definition Microphone™ and a conventional microphone.

Bit depth is generally 16-bit or 18-bit, with sampling rates that range from 8 to 48 kHz (see Chapter 5). Features such as a pad, an internal shock mount, bass roll-off, and variable pickup patterns vary with the mic. It is wise to keep in mind that regardless of how good the USB microphone may be, if there are problems with sound quality, the cause may be the programs being used or the applications to which the USB mic is connected. One such problem may be *latency*—the period of time it takes data to get from one designated point to another (see Chapter 6).

USB Microphone Converter

The development of the **USB microphone converter** (or *USB microphone adapter*) makes it possible to connect

any dynamic or capacitor XLR mic to a computer via USB (see "Connectors" later in this chapter). Depending on the model, a converter may include a microphone preamp, phantom power, headphone monitoring, and level controls for mic balancing and playback (see 3-46).

High-definition Microphone for Laptop Computers

The mediocre to poor sound quality in laptop computers has long been a bane of users. Upgraded loudspeakers have not helped that much because of the poor quality of available microphones. This problem has been alleviated with the development of a high-definition digital microphone for laptops and other broadband devices.

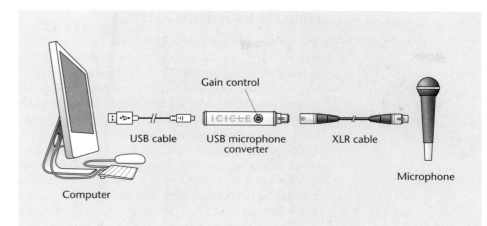

3-46 USB microphone converter flow chart. This particular converter from Blue Microphones is called Icicle. Shure also manufactures a USB adapter catalogued X2U.

According to the specifications of the manufacturer (Akustica, Inc.), the microphone has wideband frequency response and complies with the audio performance requirement for wideband transmission in applications such as **Voice over Internet Protocol (VoIP)**, delivering high-definition voice quality (see Chapters 13 and 19). It is surface-mountable and provides an *L/R* user-select function that allows a single device to be configured as either a left or a right microphone (see 3-47).

Other Special-purpose Microphones

Three other types of special-purpose microphones warrant mention: the recording microphone, the ice zone mic, and the underwater mic.

Many recorders have built-in microphones. Now there is a microphone with a built-in recorder. The model shown in Figure 3-48 combines an omnidirectional capacitor mic with a digital recorder that uses flash memory. (Flash memory can be electrically erased and reprogrammed without the need for power to maintain the information stored on the chip.) This easily portable all-in-one system greatly facilitates audio production in the field (see Chapter 13). For a discussion of flash recorders, see Chapter 5.

The *ice zone mic* is designed for implantation in an ice rink to pick up the skating sounds. The *underwater mic,* or *hydrophone,* is designed for recording sound underwater (see 3-49). Incidentally, if the need arises to record sound underwater in the absence of the specially designed underwater mic, wrapping a small conventional mic in a thin, airtight plastic cover will work. Of course, the connector cannot be submerged.

3-47 High-definition digital microphone for laptop computers and other broadband devices.
Courtesy of Akustica

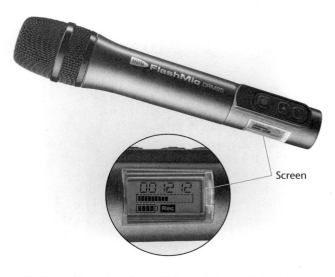

Screen

3-48 Recording microphone. This model is the FlashMic recorder/microphone.

3-49 Underwater microphone. This waterproof mic is designed to handle high sound-pressure levels. It is omnidirectional and uses a piezoelectric element. Piezoelectric elements are usually either crystal or ceramic. The cable is high-quality, vulcanized to the body of the mic, and fitted with a standard XLR connector (see "Connectors" later in the chapter).

WIRELESS MICROPHONE SYSTEM

The **wireless microphone system**, also called a *cordless mic*, an *FM mic*, a *radio mic*, and a *transmitter mic*, consists of three main components (four, if you count the mic): transmitter, antenna, and receiver (see 3-50). Additional system components may include cables and distribution systems. A standard mic is used with the system in one of four ways: lavalier, handheld, headset, and boom.

The lavalier system typically uses a mini-mic connected to a battery-powered bodypack transmitter, which may be wired or wireless. The handheld wireless mic operates with the transmitter and the microphone in a single housing (see 3-51). The headset and earset mics use the bodypack transmitter. The boom microphone's transmitter is usually a plug-on (see 3-52; see also 11-6). The plug-on is a wireless transmitter with an XLR connector (discussed later in this chapter) that plugs into the end of the mic.

The microphone's signal is sent to the transmitter, which converts it to a radio signal and relays the signal to a receiver anywhere from several feet to many yards away, depending on the system's power. The receiver converts the radio signal back to an audio signal. The transmitter usually includes a flexible wire antenna and controls for on/off power, frequency selection, microphone loudness, and microphone mute. Status lights indicate when the mic is on or off, the battery is low, and the signal is overloading.

The transmitter may include other features such as integrated time code transmission (see Chapter 6), audio recording with time code to a flash memory card, and interruptible foldback (see Chapter 13).

3-50 Wireless microphone system.
(a) Pocket transmitter. (b) Receiver.

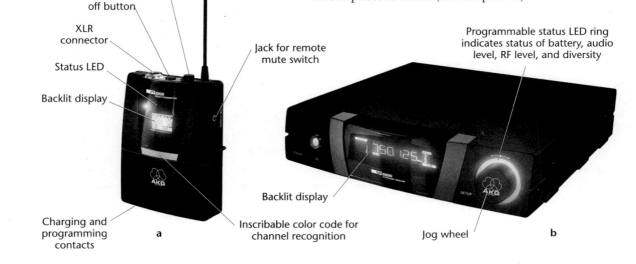

Mute switch

Lockable on/off button

XLR connector

Status LED

Backlit display

Jack for remote mute switch

Charging and programming contacts

a

Inscribable color code for channel recognition

Backlit display

Programmable status LED ring indicates status of battery, audio level, RF level, and diversity

Jog wheel

b

Interchangeable mic element

Status LED

Backlit display

Bottom controls include: jog switch for setting all function parameters, charging and programming contacts, lockable on/off button, and mute switch

3-51 **Wireless handheld transmitter.**

3-52 **Plug-on wireless microphone transmitter.**

The receiver usually includes the antenna(s) and controls for frequency selection (the frequency must match that of the transmitter); the signal level; the squelch-mute threshold control so the receiver picks up the desired signal and mutes when the signal is turned off; and indicator status lights to indicate the level of the incoming signal, the level of the audio being sent from the receiver down the signal chain, mute, and diversity operation (see "Diversity reception" later in this discussion).

Before using a wireless microphone system, there are a few operational and performance criteria to consider: frequency assignment and usage, diversity reception, audio circuitry, sound quality, transmission range, antenna, and power supply.

■ **Frequency assignment and usage** Wireless microphone systems transmit on frequencies in the *very high frequency (VHF)* and *ultra high frequency (UHF)* bands. The VHF ranges are: low band—49 to 108 *megahertz (MHz);* and high band—174 to 216 MHz. The UHF ranges are: low band—470 to 698 MHz; and high band—900 to 952 MHz. The 700 MHz band, which was also used for wireless microphone transmissions, was reassigned in 2009 by the Federal Communications Commission (FCC) for new commercial services and public safety use. Most wireless mic manufacturers anticipated the reallocation and no longer produce wireless systems that transmit in the 700 MHz band.

The differences between VHF and UHF wireless mic systems relate to bandwidth, flexibility, power, multipath reception, and cost. Because the VHF bandwidth is far narrower than UHF, there is much less room for available frequencies (see 3-53). This limits both its use in large metropolitan areas, where the spectrum is crowded with VHF TV and FM radio stations, and its flexibility in operating a number of wireless systems simultaneously. Therefore using low-band VHF wireless systems is not recommended because the band is prone to interference from many users. Also, transmitter power is limited, and the required antenna size limits portability.

▶ *Multipath* Wireless systems in the higher frequencies, and therefore transmitting shorter wavelengths,

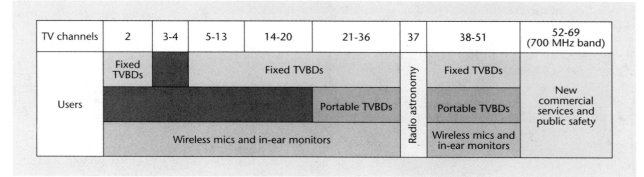

TV channels	2	3-4	5-13	14-20	21-36	37	38-51	52-69 (700 MHz band)
Users		Fixed TVBDs	Fixed TVBDs			Radio astronomy	Fixed TVBDs	New commercial services and public safety
					Portable TVBDs		Portable TVBDs	
		Wireless mics and in-ear monitors					Wireless mics and in-ear monitors	

3-53 **New FCC frequency allocations after the digital television (DTV) transition.** (*TVBD* is short for *personal and portable TV band devices,* previously referred to as white space devices [WSDs]).

are vulnerable to instances of **multipath** reception, a physical phenomenon in which more than one *radio frequency (RF)* signal from the same source arrives at the receiver's front end, creating phase mismatching (see 3-54).

▶ *Fixed- and variable-frequency systems* Wireless microphones operate on either a fixed- or a variable-frequency system. **Fixed-frequency wireless microphone systems,** which are less expensive than variable systems, are useful in situations where the mic does not change locations or there are relatively few FM and TV stations in the area or both. These factors make it relatively easy to find an available operating frequency and the wireless system to match it. In large cities, or if the mic is used in different locations, the **variable-frequency wireless microphone system** is necessary. Also known as *frequency-agile systems,* some of these use a technology that automatically selects the best channels at any given time for seamless microphone performance.

■ **Diversity reception** A wireless microphone system transmits radio waves from a transmitter, through the air, to a receiver. Because the waves are transmitted line-of-sight, there is the danger that the radio waves will encounter obstructions en route to the receiver. Another potential hindrance to signal reception could result from the transmitter's being out of range. The problem with multipath reception may be a third difficulty. Any of these problems creates a dropout or null in the transmission. **Dropout** is a momentary loss of the signal at the receiver. The technique used to deal with dropout is known as **diversity reception**.

There are three types of diversity reception. *Space diversity* places antennas far enough apart so that at least one receives an unobstructed signal (see 3-55). *Phase-switching diversity* shifts phase in the receiver so that one antenna's signal phase-shifts to reinforce the other rather than cancel it. *Audio-switching diversity* uses two receivers and switches to the one getting the stronger signal. It is the fastest and quietest of the three types of diversity reception.

When a wireless system is used in a controlled environment where dropout is not a problem, a **nondiversity receiver** can be used. Nondiversity systems have a single antenna mounted on the receiver. They are generally less expensive than diversity systems.

To check if a wireless system is operating correctly, walk the signal path from the transmitter to the receiver, speaking into the microphone as you go. If you hear dropout, buzzing, or any other sonic anomaly, note the location(s). First check the system to make sure it is in proper working order. If it is, change microphone placement or receiver location if you can and retest the signal transmission.

■ **Audio circuitry** The nature of radio transmission inhibits the quality of the audio signal. To counteract this the audio signal is processed in two ways, through equalization and companding.

Equalization, in this instance, involves a pre-emphasis and a de-emphasis of the signal to minimize the level of hiss (high-frequency noise) that is unavoidably added

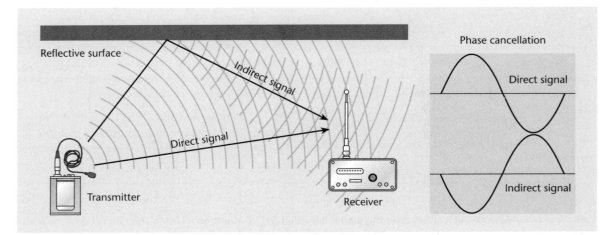

3-54 Multipath dropout.

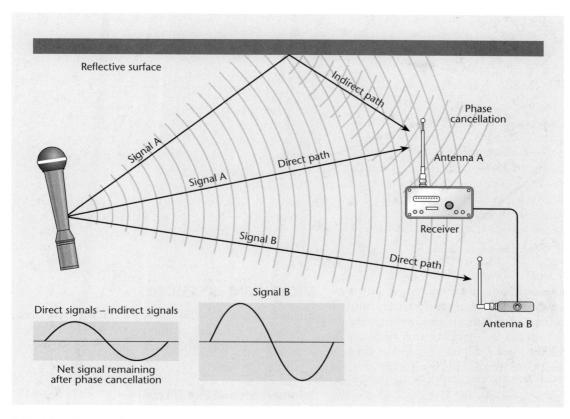

3-55 Diversity reception.

during transmission. **Pre-emphasis** boosts the high frequencies in transmission; **de-emphasis** reduces the high-frequency noise at the receiver. The equal but opposite process reduces noise by up to 10 dB.

Companding, a contraction of the words *compressing* and *expanding*, compensates for the limited dynamic range of radio transmission. The input signal varies over a range of 80 dB and is compressed at the transmitter to a range of 40 dB, a factor of 2 to 1. At the receiver the signal is expanded by 40 dB to its original dynamic range, a factor of 1 to 2. Even though companding sometimes creates noise, coloration, and the audible pumping sound caused by compander mistracking, particularly in less expensive systems, a wireless mic is always far better off with companding than without it (see 3-56).

Another process important to signal reception at the receiver is called **squelch**. The function of this circuit is to silence or mute the receiver's audio output when there is no radio signal. Otherwise the "open" receiver could pick up background radio noise or another signal.

■ **Sound quality** Wireless microphone systems vary widely in quality. Clearly, in professional audio only a system with wide frequency response and dynamic range should be used. Frequency response should be well beyond the frequency range of the sound being recorded. Good wireless systems are now capable of dynamic ranges up to 115 dB. A system with poorer dynamic range needs more compression at the transmitter and more expansion at the receiver, creating an annoying squeezed sound that results from companding loud levels.

■ **Transmission range** The transmission range of wireless microphone systems varies from as short as 100 feet to as long as 2,500 feet. The range of a given system is provided in its specifications. Transmission range should be based on need. Obviously, a shorter range would suffice in a studio or theater, whereas a longer range would be necessary in a stadium or in a long shot for a film.

■ **Antenna** The antenna should be fully extended and several feet away from any obstruction, including the

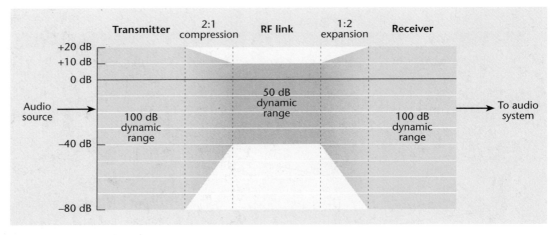

3-56 Compander action.

floor. With transmitters avoid taping "whip" antennas (and bodypacks) to the skin, as perspiration inhibits signal transmission. Both the transmitter and the receiver antennas should be oriented either vertically or horizontally. If they are not, it hinders reception. Because performers usually stand, the most common antenna position is vertical. Some antennas are more effective than others. To improve system performance, a dipole antenna could increase signal pickup by 3 dB or more.

■ **Power supply** Wireless mic systems use a variety of battery types, such as AA, 9 V, and VDC (voltage DC). Battery lifetime varies from a few hours to up to 10 hours. Alkaline batteries are good, but lithium batteries last longer. To reduce power supply problems, batteries should be replaced before they have a chance to run down. It is simply not worth holding up a production session to save a few cents, trying to squeeze maximum life out of a battery.

Analog Versus Digital Wireless Microphone Systems

Wireless microphones systems are available in analog and digital formats. By digitizing the signal, the audio gets converted to digital right away at the transmitter. It is then sent to the receiver, where the data are received, checked for errors, corrected (if necessary), and converted back to analog. This process has several advantages over analog; among them are a more robust signal; considerable reduction, if not elimination, of interference and overall noise in RF in the radio path; and reduction of the need for squelch.

MICROPHONE ACCESSORIES

Microphones come with various accessories. The most common are windscreens and pop filters, shock mounts, cables, connectors, and stands and special-purpose mounts.

Windscreens and Pop Filters

Windscreens and *pop filters* are designed to deal with distortion that results from blowing sounds caused by breathing and wind, the sudden attack of transients, the hiss of sibilant consonants like *s* and *ch,* and the popping plosives of consonants like *p* and *b.* (In practice the terms *windscreen* and *pop filter* are used interchangeably, but for clarity of discussion here they are given slightly different applications.)

Windscreens are mounted externally and reduce the distortion from blowing and popping but rarely eliminate it from particularly strong sounds (see 3-57). A pop filter is built-in and is most effective against blowing sounds and popping (see 3-58). It allows very close microphone placement to a sound source with little fear of this type of distortion.

Windscreens also slightly affect response, somewhat reducing the crispness of high frequencies (see 3-59). Many directional microphones with pop filters are designed with a high-frequency boost to compensate for reduced treble response.

Pop filters, also known as *blast filters,* are mainly found in moving-coil, newer ribbon, and some capacitor microphones, particularly directional models because they are more susceptible than omnidirectional mics to breath

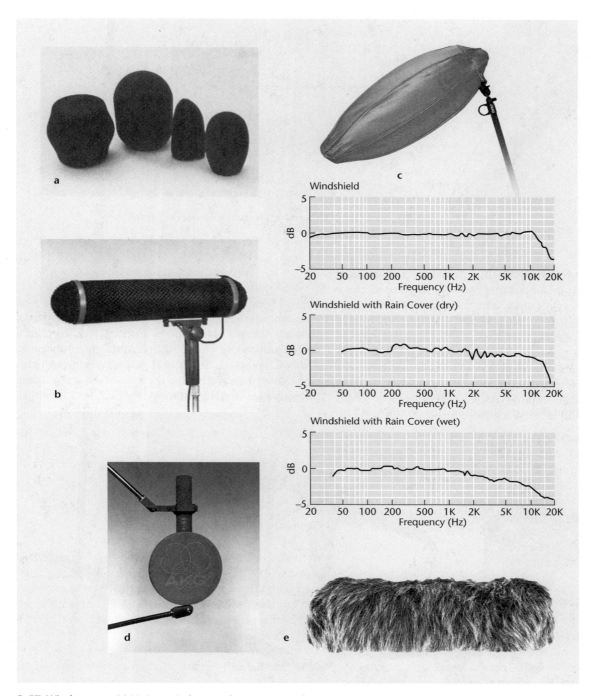

Windshield

Windshield with Rain Cover (dry)

Windshield with Rain Cover (wet)

3-57 Windscreens. (a) Various windscreens for conventional microphones. (b) So-called zeppelin windscreen enclosure for shotgun microphone. (c) Lightweight collapsible windshield consisting of a light metal frame covered with a fine-mesh foam material. The windshield comes with a rain cover. The response curves illustrate the differences in response characteristics without the rain cover, with the rain cover dry, and with the rain cover wet. It should be noted that all windscreens affect frequency response in some way. (d) Stocking (fabric) windscreen designed for use between the sound source and the microphone. This particular model has two layers of mesh material attached to a lightweight wooden ring. (e) Windscreen cover, or windjammer, to cover zeppelin-type windscreens.

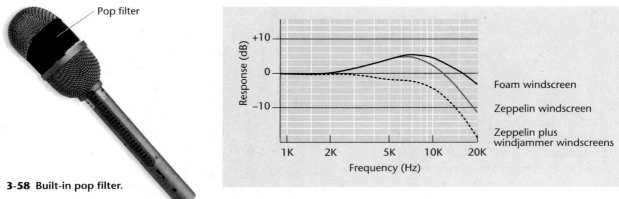

3-58 Built-in pop filter.

3-59 The effect of various windscreens on frequency response.

and popping noise due to their partial pressure-gradient response. (They are also more likely to be used closer to a sound source than are other microphone types.) An omnidirectional mic is about 15 dB less sensitive to wind noise and popping than is a unidirectional mic of similar size.

Another way to minimize distortion from sibilance, transients, blowing sounds, and popping is through microphone placement. (These techniques are discussed throughout the chapters that deal with production.)

Shock Mounts

Because solid objects are excellent sound conductors, the danger always exists that unwanted vibrations will travel through the mic stand to the microphone. To reduce noises induced by vibrations, place the microphone in a ***shock mount***—a device that suspends and mechanically isolates the mic from the stand (see 3-60). Some microphones are designed with a shock absorber built-in.

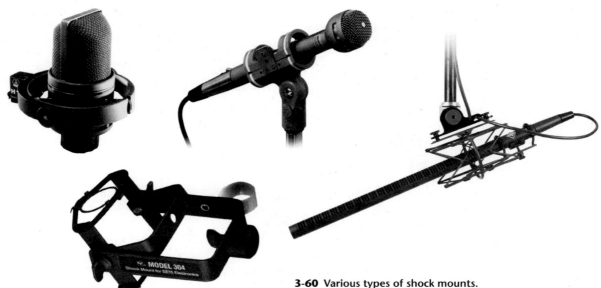

3-60 Various types of shock mounts. See also 3-28a.

Cables

A microphone cable is either a ***balanced line***—consisting of two conductors and a shield—or an ***unbalanced line***—consisting of one conductor with the shield serving as the second conductor. A quad mic cable uses a four-conductor design for added noise control. As with all professional equipment, the balanced line is preferred because it is less susceptible to electrical noise.

When winding mic cable, do not coil it around your arm, and be careful not to make the angle of the wrap too severe or it can damage the internal wires. It is also a good idea to secure the cable with a clasp specially made for this purpose to prevent it from getting tangled (see 3-61).

Connectors

Most professional mics and mic cables use a three-pin plug that terminates the two conductors and the shield of the balanced line. These plugs are generally called ***XLR connectors*** (*X* is the ground or shield, *L* is the lead wire, and *R* is the return wire). Usually, the female plug on the microphone cable connects to the mic, and the three-prong male plug connects to the console (see 3-62). It is always important to make sure that the three pins in

3-61 Microphone cable. To keep cable intact and avoid damage to internal wires and connections, coil and secure cable when not in use.

all microphones being used in a session are connected in exactly the same way. If pin 1 is ground, pin 2 is positive, and pin 3 is negative, all mics must be wired in the same configuration; otherwise the mismatched microphones will be electrically out of polarity and reduce or null the audio level.

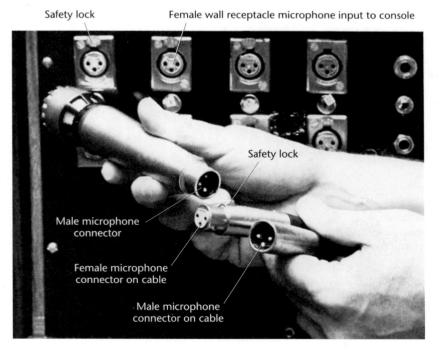

Safety lock

Female wall receptacle microphone input to console

Safety lock

Male microphone connector

Female microphone connector on cable

Male microphone connector on cable

3-62 Microphone connectors. The female cable connector plugs into the male microphone connector; the male cable connector plugs into the female wall receptacle, which is connected to the microphone input on the console.

Microphone Mounts

Just as there are many types of microphones to meet a variety of needs, numerous microphone mounts are available for just about every possible application. Commonly used microphone mounts are shown in Figures 3-63 to 3-72.

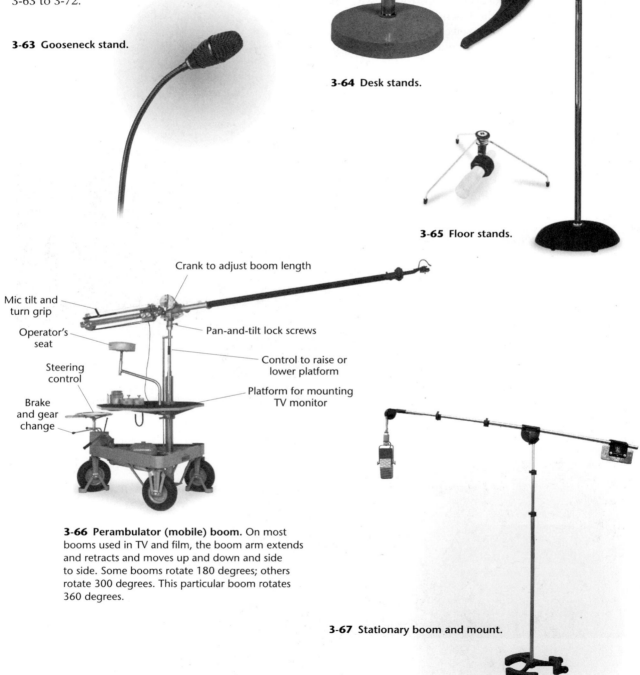

3-63 Gooseneck stand.

3-64 Desk stands.

3-65 Floor stands.

Crank to adjust boom length

Mic tilt and turn grip

Operator's seat

Pan-and-tilt lock screws

Steering control

Control to raise or lower platform

Brake and gear change

Platform for mounting TV monitor

3-66 Perambulator (mobile) boom. On most booms used in TV and film, the boom arm extends and retracts and moves up and down and side to side. Some booms rotate 180 degrees; others rotate 300 degrees. This particular boom rotates 360 degrees.

3-67 Stationary boom and mount.

3-68 Handheld "fishpole" boom.

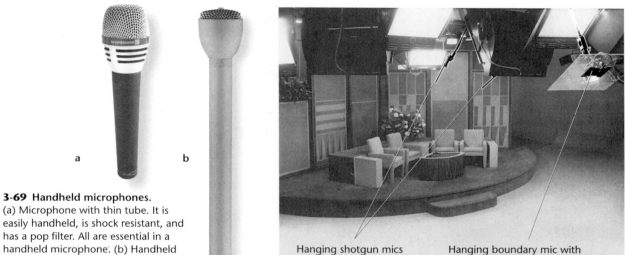

a   b

3-69 Handheld microphones.
(a) Microphone with thin tube. It is easily handheld, is shock resistant, and has a pop filter. All are essential in a handheld microphone. (b) Handheld mic with a long handle for added control in broadcast applications and to provide room for a microphone flag.

Hanging shotgun mics
for hosts and guests

Hanging boundary mic with
reflector for audience pickup

3-70 Hanging microphones.

3-71 Hidden microphone.

Lavalier mic taped
to rearview mirror

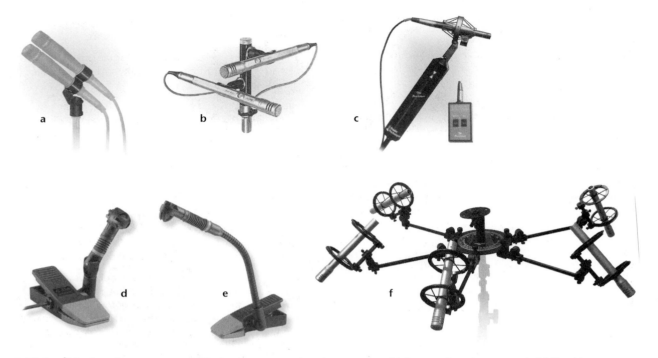

3-72 Special microphone mounts. (a) Redundant mono microphone mount. (b) Stereo microphone mount. (c) Remote panner boom mount and control module. (d) Hypercardioid microphone and mount for attachment to drums. (e) Hypercardioid microphone and mount for attachment to brass and woodwind instruments. (f) Mount for surround-sound miking.

MICROPHONE CARE

Poor care of audio equipment adversely affects sound quality—this cannot be stressed enough. Moisture from high humidity or breath can greatly shorten a microphone's life. When moisture is a problem, a windscreen will help protect the microphone element. Avoid blowing into a mic to check if it is on. There is not only the problem of moisture but the force can drive particles through the grille and onto the diaphragm.

Ribbon mics are especially sensitive to the force of air pressure from blowing into the grille. Capacitor mics are also sensitive to air turbulence, not only from blowing but from fans and blowers. In fact, a breath blast can perforate a capacitor mic's diaphragm. Be sure to turn off phantom power when a capacitor mic is not in use. The electric charge attracts dust to the mic's diaphragm.

While the phantom power is on, do not plug or unplug the mic cable; the abrupt power change could damage the mic's preamp.

Dirt, jarring, cigarette smoke, oil from hands, and pop filters clogged with saliva and/or lipstick also reduce microphone efficiency. Microphones should be cleaned and serviced regularly and kept in carrying cases when not in use.[4] Microphones left on stands between sessions should be covered with a cloth or plastic bag but not so tightly as to create a condensation problem. The working environment should be temperature- and humidity-controlled, kept clean, and vacuumed regularly.

---

4. See "Cleaning Microphones" at *www.shure.com/ProAudio/Products/us_pro_ea_cleaning.*

MAIN POINTS

▶ Microphones are transducers that convert acoustic energy into electric energy. The device that does the transducing is called the element.

▶ The elements in professional microphones operate on one of two physical principles: magnetic induction and variable capacitance.

▶ Professional microphones (and equipment) are low impedance.

▶ The two types of professional mics that use magnetic induction are the moving-coil mics and the ribbon mics. The type of professional microphone using variable capacitance is the capacitor mic.

▶ Capacitor microphones require a power supply to operate.

▶ Although it is still in the experimental stage, the laser-based particulate flow detection microphone could revolutionize microphone design by, among other things, eliminating distortion from mics.

▶ Some microphone models are dual-element, combining the moving-coil and capacitor designs or incorporating two capacitor or two moving-coil elements.

▶ Each type of microphone is unique. One type is not so much better than another as it is more suitable for a particular application.

▶ Microphones pick up sound from essentially three directions: all around—omnidirectional; front and rear—bidirectional; and front only—unidirectional.

▶ The unidirectional, or cardioid, design has even narrower pickup patterns. They are supercardioid, hypercardioid, and ultracardioid.

▶ A microphone's directional sensitivity can be displayed graphically in a polar response diagram.

▶ A microphone's unidirectionality is facilitated by ports at the side and/or rear of the mic that cancel sound coming from unwanted directions.

▶ Directional sensitivity in a unidirectional microphone varies with frequency: the higher the frequency, the more directional the pickup; the lower the frequency, the less directional the pickup.

▶ A microphone's frequency response is the range of frequencies that it produces at an equal level, within a margin of ±3 dB. Its frequency response curve can be displayed as a graph.

▶ All microphones will distort if sound levels are too high—a condition known as overload.

▶ Maximum sound-pressure level (SPL) is the level at which a microphone's output signal begins to distort.

▶ To help protect against loudness distortion, many capacitor mics are equipped with a pad to reduce overloading the mic's electronics.

▶ Sensitivity measures the voltage that a microphone produces (dBV) at a certain sound-pressure level. It indicates how loud a microphone is.

▶ Self-noise, also known as equivalent noise level, indicates the sound-pressure level that will create the same voltage as the inherent electrical noise, or hiss, a microphone (or any electronic device) produces.

▶ Signal-to-noise ratio (S/N) is the ratio of a signal power to the noise power corrupting the signal and is measured in decibels. In relation to microphones, S/N is the difference between sound-pressure level and self-noise.

▶ Bidirectional and most directional microphones are susceptible to proximity effect, or bass tip-up—an increase in the level of bass frequencies relative to midrange and treble frequencies—when they are placed close to a sound source. To neutralize proximity effect, most of these microphones are equipped with bass roll-off.

▶ Hum is an ever-present concern in microphone pickup. In a mic it is typically produced by stray AC (alternating current) magnetic fields at 50 or 60 Hz and is particularly a problem in dynamic mics. There are several ways to minimize hum.

▶ One method used to reduce hum is the humbuck coil that is built into some dynamic microphones.

▶ A microphone modeler is not an actual microphone but a microphone simulator that can be added to a hard-disk recording system as a plug-in. It is designed to emulate the sounds of most professional-grade microphones.

▶ Microphones have been developed for special purposes: the lavalier and mini-mics to be unobtrusive; the shotgun and parabolic mics for long-distance pickup; the headset and earset mics to keep background sound to a minimum by maintaining a close mic-to-source distance; the contact mic for use on a vibrating surface; the boundary mic for use on a boundary (a hard, reflective surface) so that all sound pickup at the microphone is in phase; the noise-canceling mic for use close to the mouth with excellent rejection of ambient sound; multidirectional and system microphones, which have more than one pickup pattern; stereophonic, middle-side (M-S), and infinitely variable pattern microphones; the binaural mic for three-dimensional sound imaging; the surround-sound mics for surround-sound pickup; the high-definition mic for extremely high-quality reproduction; the digital mic, which converts the analog signal to digital when the acoustic energy is transduced to electric energy; the USB mic to record directly to a computer without an audio interface; the recording microphone—a mic with a built-in recorder; the ice zone mic to pick up ice-skating sounds; the underwater mic, or hydrophone, to record underwater sounds; and the wireless mic for greater mobility and flexibility in plotting sound pickup regardless of camera-to-source distance.

▶ When using a wireless microphone system, consider the following operational and performance criteria: frequency assignment and usage, diversity reception, audio circuitry, sound quality, transmission range, antenna, and power supply.

▶ Windscreens and pop filters are used to reduce distortion caused by wind and transients. An external shock mount, or a built-in shock absorber, is used to prevent unwanted vibrations from reaching the microphone element.

▶ Standard accessories used for professional microphones include the following: twin conductor cables called balanced lines, XLR connectors, and various types of stands and clips for microphone mounting.

▶ Proper care is very important to the functioning and the sound quality of a microphone.

4

Consoles and Control Surfaces

A *console* (also known as a ***board***, *mixer*, or, in Europe, *mixing desk*) takes input signals and amplifies, balances, processes, combines, and routes them to broadcast or recording.[1] Many consoles also store operational data. Mixers do essentially the same thing, but the console is larger in most models, is more complex, performs several processing functions, and is designed essentially for use in the studio. In the majority of modern console systems, many if not most functions are computer-assisted. The ***mixer*** is smaller and, compared with studio-size consoles, performs limited processing operations, which may or may not be computer-assisted.

Although mixers can be used anywhere, their size and compactness make them highly portable, so they are typically used away from the studio, in the field. Some are equipped with a built-in recorder (see 13-19). Mixers are covered in Chapter 13, "Field Production: News and Sports."[2]

---

1. The different types and models of consoles and control surfaces available today are considerable. Their purposes and particular designs differ. To cover the subject with specificity would be unwieldy. Moreover, the details that apply to one console or control surface may not apply to another. They do have certain functions in common, however. Therefore to deal with the topic manageably, the approach in this chapter is generic; the intent is to cover in general the operational features of the main types of consoles and control surfaces.

2. Not to get bogged down in terminology, but the term *mixer* is often used synonymously with *console*. Some mixers include additional features that are found on consoles, and some small- and medium-format consoles have limited features that could classify them as large mixers.

Consoles today are available in various configurations; they use different technologies and are designed for specific production purposes. There is no one system that can be used as a generalized example of all the systems out there. They can be grouped into broad categories, however. A console may be analog or digital; appropriate for on-air broadcast, production, or postproduction; and software-based and used as a virtual console with a digital audio workstation.

ANALOG AND DIGITAL CONSOLES

In an *analog console,* audio signals flow in and out of physical modules through inboard wires and circuits. To add flexibility to the signal flow, an inboard patch bay consisting of jacks wired to the console's components facilitates the routing and the rerouting of signals within the console and to and from studio outboard equipment. Patch cords plug into the jacks to direct signal flow (see "Patching" later in this chapter).

In a *digital console,* incoming analog audio signals are converted to digital information at the inputs, and interfaces handle the routing and the signal processing. If the audio entering the console is already digitized, of course no conversion is necessary. Routing and rerouting of signals are also handled by patching, but operations are managed through the console's interfaces, which are inboard. There are no jacks or patch cords needed to effect connections.

Modern analog and digital consoles are capable of data storage, and the operation of many analog models is computer-assisted. Digital consoles almost always incorporate at least some computer-assisted functions.

A *virtual console* is a simulated console displayed on a computer screen that is part of the software of a digital recording program. Its functions are similar to those of a conventional console and are controlled by a mouse or control surface (see "Control Surfaces" later in this chapter).

ON-AIR BROADCAST CONSOLES

A console used for on-air broadcasts (including *podcasts—* see Chapter 19) is designed to handle audio sources that are immediately distributed to the audience. Whatever is not live has been already produced and packaged and requires only playback. Therefore an on-air broadcast console needs more controlling elements to manage rapid transitions. In a radio disc jockey program, those transitions are between disc jockey, music, and spot an-

nouncements; in an interview or panel program, they are among host, guest(s), call-ins from listeners, and spot announcements. In radio and television news, there are the studio-based anchor(s), field reporters, and recorded segments to deal with. Mix-minus (covered in Chapter 13) is essential for creating custom mixes for reporters waiting to come on the air from the field. *Snapshot memory* of console parameters enables event storage and recall of a program's baseline settings at the beginning of the program's next broadcast, so operators do not have to take the time to reset those parameters manually.

The on-air broadcast console and consoles in general have at least three basic control sections: input, output, and monitor. The **input section** takes an incoming signal from a microphone, CD player, recorder, or phone-in caller. Each input channel is configured for either low-level sound sources, such as microphones, or high-level sound sources, such as recorders and CD players. The loudness level of each channel is regulated by a **fader** (usually sliding, as opposed to rotary). A delegation switch on each channel can either turn off the signal flow or route it to one of three destinations: *program,* which sends it to the console's output; to the *monitor* section so that it can be heard; or to a second monitor system, called *audition* or *cue.* The audition or cue system makes it possible to listen to program material while preparing it for broadcast, without its being heard on the air.

At the **output section**, there is a **master fader** to handle the combined signals feeding to it from the input channels. This is the last stop at the console before the output signal is further routed and transmitted.

For stereo, faders usually carry a tandem left/right stereo signal. Some on-air consoles may use stereo pairs, with the left fader carrying the left signal and the right fader carrying the right signal.

Input and output signals are heard as sound through monitor loudspeakers. As they pass through the console, however, they are in the form of voltage. Therefore meters are necessary to measure the voltages in the input and output sections. By using the fader, these voltages can be kept within acceptable limits. (Meters are discussed later in this chapter.)

On-air consoles include a variety of other features, such as equalization, compression, and limiting, depending on the complexity of the broadcast and the need for signal processing and programmed functions. A console designed for broadcast may also be able to do double duty and handle off-air production needs as well, as explained in the following section. Figure 4-1 displays the signal flow of a basic generic broadcast console.

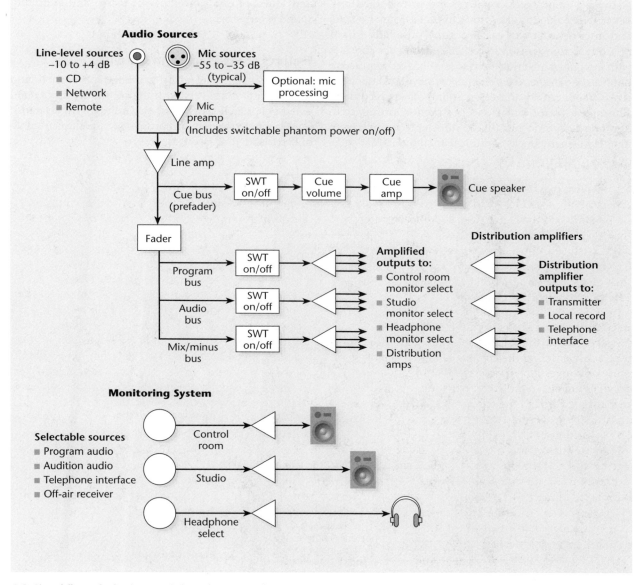

4-1 Signal flow of a basic generic broadcast console.

PRODUCTION CONSOLES

Production consoles are necessary for producing and post-producing music, film, and video sound tracks, sports, and such live-to-recording programs as parades and variety, talk, and awards shows. They must be capable of handling many sound sources simultaneously and employing the diversity of tasks involved in dynamics processing—equalization, compression, noise gating, reverberation, and delay—necessary for "sweetening" and mixing.

Automation is a necessity. It allows operational data from production sessions to be stored on and retrieved from disk. In film and television, automated panning facilitates the matching of movement to picture. A production console for music recording often requires a number of *submixers* to **premix** groups of similar voicings, such as strings, backup vocals, and the components of a drum set.

Network TV news is essentially a one- or two-mic show, yet with recorded music intros, reports from the field, and interviews, it can easily occupy the many inputs of a production console. Specialized, compact consoles with integrated machine interface systems are required to handle the unique requirements of automated dialogue replacement (ADR) and Foley sound-effects recording. Consoles used for music and postproduction mixes in film and television must have sufficient capabilities to handle the many tracks of musical instruments, dialogue, and sound effects as well as the stereo and surround-sound processing.

Features of the Production Console

The number of features on a production console and how they interface vary with the console's purpose and whether it is analog or digital. Regardless of these factors, however, most production consoles incorporate a number of basic functions (see 4-2).

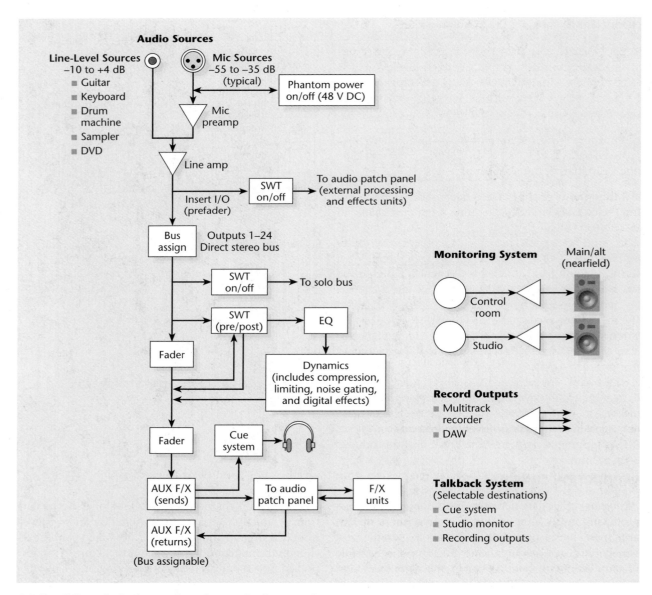

4-2 Signal flow of a basic generic analog production console.

In the following list, sequence of functions, signal flow, section designations, groupings, and terminology will differ depending on the console architecture and manufacturer. But most of the features are found on the majority of production consoles.

■ **Input/output (I/O) channel** During recording, the *input/output,* or *I/O, channel strip* processes and delegates incoming signals and sends them on for recording (see 4-3). During mixing the I/O section processes signals from the recorder and routes them to the master section, where they are combined into mono, stereo, or surround channels and routed for the master recording.

■ **Input selector control** You will recall that two types of signal sources feed to input modules: low-level, such as microphones, and high-level, such as recorders and CD players. The *input selector control* delegates which type of signal source enters the input section.

■ **Phantom power** *Phantom power,* when activated, provides voltage (48 V DC, or direct current) for capacitor mics, eliminating the need for batteries.

■ **Microphone preamplifier** A microphone signal entering the console is weak. It requires a *mic preamplifier* to increase its voltage to a usable level.

A word about mic preamps in consoles: Whether the audio is analog or digital, each component in the signal flow must be as noise-free as possible. Given the low-noise, high-sensitivity, and high-SPL specifications of many of today's microphones, it is important that the mic preamp be capable of handling a mic's output without strain. If the console's preamp is inadequate to meet this requirement, it is necessary to use an outboard mic preamp (see 4-4).

Inboard or outboard, a good-quality mic preamp must deliver high gain, low circuit noise (hiss), high *common-mode rejection ratio (CMRR)*—the ratio between signal gain and interference rejection—freedom from *radio frequency (RF)* interference, and freedom from ground-induced buzz or hum.

Console preamps may be located many feet from a microphone. The more circuitry a signal navigates, the greater the chance for increased noise. By placing a mic preamp in close proximity to a microphone and amplifying mic signals to the required levels before they travel very far, noise can be dramatically reduced. A mic preamp should be stable at very low and/or very high gain settings. The CMRR values should be at least 80 to 90 dB at crucial frequencies, such as 50 to 60 Hz and

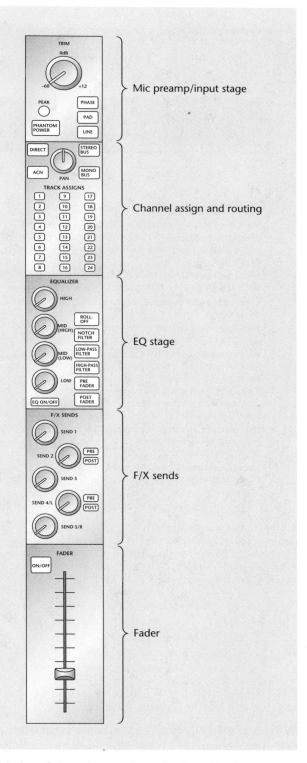

4-3 Generic input/output channel strip and its features.

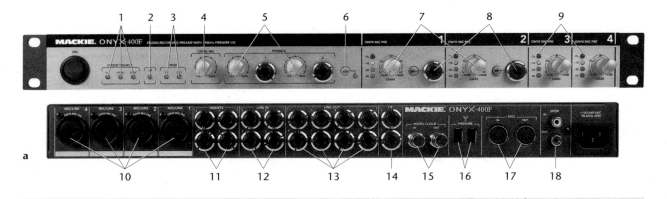

1. **Clock source indicators** LEDs indicate current clock source—internal, word clock input, or S/PDIF input

2. **FireWire indicator** Green LED illuminates when the Onyx 400F establishes a valid FireWire connection with a Mac or PC

3. **MIDI I/O activity** These 2 LEDs flash whenever MIDI data appear at the MIDI In and MIDI Out connections

4. **Control room volume** Volume control for studio reference monitors

5. **Headphone control** Front-mounted twin ¼" headphone jacks and individual volume controls

6. **Phantom power** Switch activates +48 V DC at all four microphone inputs for powering condenser mics; includes LED indicator

7. **Channel gain** Sensitivity controls for channels 1 and 2 (mic/line/instrument inputs) and channels 3 and 4 (mic/line input levels)

8. **Instrument inputs** Convenient, front-mounted ¼" instrument input with impedance switch for direct-recording guitars and basses

9. **Level indicators** Four-segment LED meters for channels 1 through 4 indicate post-gain, post-insert signal intensity

10. **Mic/line inputs** Combo connectors for microphones, keyboards, drum machines, and other peripherals

11. **Inserts** TRS send/return connections for inserting outboard processors after the Onyx mic preamps and before the Onyx 400F's A/D converters

12. **Line inputs** Balanced/unbalanced ¼" TRS inputs for line-level devices like keyboards and drum machines

13. **Line outputs** Balanced/unbalanced ¼" analog connections fed directly by your DAW or by an internal DSP matrix mixer

14. **Control room outputs** Balanced/unbalanced ¼" TRS connections for studio reference monitors

15. **Word clock I/O** Dual BNC connections for synchronizing multiple digital devices

16. **FireWire connections** For connecting to a Mac or PC; second connector provided for daisy-chaining additional devices like external hard drives

17. **MIDI I/O** Standard 5-pin DIN connectors for keyboards, controllers, control surfaces, and other MIDI-enabled devices

18. **S/PDIF I/O** RCA connectors for digital I/O at up to 192 kHz sampling rate

4-4 Microphone preamplifiers. (a) Four-microphone preamplifier and its features. (b) This is a stereo mic preamp with phantom power, switchable to a middle-side (M-S) matrix. It includes two low-cut filters (20 Hz and 150 Hz) and can be AC- or battery-powered. TRS = tip, ring, sleeve.

above 10 kHz—not just at 1 kHz, the only frequency at which many mic preamps are measured.

■ **Trim or gain** The *trim* is a gain control that changes the input sensitivities to accommodate the nominal input levels of various input sources. Trim boosts the

lower-level sources to usable proportions and prevents overload distortion in higher-level sources.

■ **Pad** A *pad* reduces the power of a signal. On a console it is placed ahead of the mic input transformer to prevent overload distortion of the transformer and the mic preamplifier. It is used when the trim, by itself, cannot prevent overload in the mic signal. The pad should not be used otherwise because it reduces signal-to-noise ratio.

■ **Overload indicator** The *overload indicator,* also called a *peak indicator,* tells you when the input signal is approaching or has reached overload and is clipping. It is usually a *light-emitting diode (LED).* In some consoles the LED flashes green when the input signal is peaking in the safe range and flashes red either to indicate clipping or to warn of impending clipping.

■ **Polarity (phase) reversal** *Polarity reversal* is a control that inverts the polarity of an input signal 180 degrees. Sometimes called *phase reversal,* it is used to reverse the polarity of miswired equipment, usually microphones, whose signal is out of phase with the signal from a piece of similar equipment correctly wired. Sometimes intentional polarity reversal is helpful in canceling leakage from adjacent microphones or in creating *electroacoustic* special effects by mixing together out-of-phase signals from mics picking up the same sound source.

■ **Channel assignment and routing** This is a group of switches on each channel used to direct the signal from that channel to one or more outputs; or several input signals can be combined and sent to one output. For example, assume that three different microphone signals are routed separately to channels 1, 3, and 11 and the recordist wishes to direct them all to channel 18. By pressing assignment switch 18 on channels 1, 3, and 11, the recordist feeds the signals to channel 18's active combining network and then on to recorder track 18.

An *active combining network (ACN)* is an amplifier at which the outputs of two or more signal paths are mixed together to feed a single track of a recorder. To save space the assignment switches are sometimes paired, either alternately—1 and 3, 2 and 4, and so on—or adjacently—1 and 2, 3 and 4, et cetera. In relation to stereo, odd numbers are left channels and even numbers are right channels.

■ **Direct switch** The *direct switch* connects the channel signal to the channel output, directing the signal to its own track on the recorder, bypassing the channel ACN and thus reducing noise. For example, using the direct switch routes the signal on, say, channel 1 to recorder track 1, the signal on channel 2 to recorder track 2, and so on.

■ **Pan pot** A *pan pot* (short for *panoramic potentiometer*) is a control that can shift the proportion of sound to

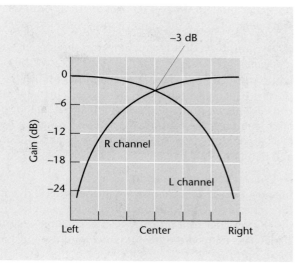

4-5 Effect of a typical pan pot.

any point from left to right between two output buses and, hence, between the two loudspeakers necessary for reproducing a stereo image (see 4-5). Panning is also necessary in surround sound to delegate signals left-to-right, front-to-rear (or to rear-side), and rear side-to-side. To hear a signal louder in one bus than in the other, the pan pot varies the relative levels being fed to the output buses. This facilitates the positioning of a sound source at a particular place in the stereo or surround field between or among the loudspeakers.

■ **Equalizer and filter** An *equalizer* is an electronic device that alters a signal's frequency response by boosting or attenuating the level of selected portions of the audio spectrum. A *filter* alters frequency response by attenuating frequencies above, below, or at a preset point. Most production consoles have separate equalizer controls for selected frequencies grouped in the bass, midrange, and treble ranges. Filters are usually high-pass and low-pass. Upscale consoles have additional equalizer ranges, such as low and high bass and low and high treble, as well as more filter effects. (Equalizers and filters are discussed in Chapter 7.)

The *equalization (EQ)* module may also have prefader and postfader controls. That is, any equalization or filtering can be assigned before or after the channel fader. Before, or *prefader,* means that the level control at the EQ module is the only one affecting the loudness of the channel's equalization. After, or *postfader,* means that the main channel fader also affects the EQ level. In the postfader mode, the level control at the EQ module is still operational but the main channel fader overrides it.

■ **Dynamics section** Production consoles may include a *dynamics section* in each I/O module or, as is the case with most digital models, in a separate, centralized section to which each channel has access. This adds to a console's signal-processing power and often includes, at least, compression, limiting, and noise gating. Multieffects processing may also include delay, reverb, phasing, and flanging (see Chapter 7).

■ **Channel/monitor control** Some production consoles include a *channel/monitor control* in the EQ and dynamics sections that switches the equalizer, dynamics, and usually selected *send* functions either into the channel signal path for recording or into the monitor signal path for monitoring.

■ **Cue and effects sends (pre- or postfader)** *Cue send* is a monitor function that routes a signal from an input channel to the headphone, or foldback, system. *Foldback* is a monitor system that feeds signals from the console to the headphones. The cue send level control adjusts the loudness of the headphone signal before it is sent to the master cue sends in the monitor module.

At the input channel, the cue send can be assigned before or after the channel fader. Before, or *prefader cue*, means that the level control at cue send is the only one affecting the loudness of the channel's cue send. After, or *postfader cue*, means that the main channel fader also affects the cue send level. In the postfader mode, the level control at cue send is still operational, but the main channel fader overrides it.

Pre- and postfader controls add flexibility in providing performers with a suitable headphone mix. In music recording, for example, if the musicians were satisfied with their headphone mix and did not want to hear channel fader adjustments being made during recording, cue send would be switched to the prefader mode. On the other hand, if the musicians did want to hear changes in level at the channel fader, cue send would be switched to the postfader mode.

The *effects* (*F/X* or *EFX*) send, feeds the input signal to an external (outboard) signal processor, such as a reverberation unit, compressor, or harmonizer (see Chapter 7). The effects send module is also called *auxiliary (aux) send, reverb send,* and *echo send.*

Effects send can feed a signal to any external signal processor so long as it is wired to the console's patch bay (see "Patching" later in this chapter). Such a connection is not needed with dynamics processing that is inboard as it is with most modern analog and digital consoles. After the "dry" send signal reaches the outboard signal processor, it returns "wet" to the effects return in the master section for mixing with the main output. The wet signal may also feed to a monitor return system.

The send function also has pre- and postfader controls whereby any signal can be sent before or after the channel fader.

■ **Solo and prefader listen** Feeding different sounds through several channels at once can create an inconvenience if it becomes necessary to hear one of them to check something. Instead of shutting off or turning down all the channels but the one you wish to hear, activating the *solo* control, located in each input module, automatically cuts off all other channels feeding the monitor system; this has no effect on the output system. More than one solo can be pushed to audition several channels at once and still cut off the unwanted channels.

The solo function is usually prefader. On some consoles, therefore, it is called *prefader listen (PFL)*. In consoles with both solo and prefader listen functions, PFL is prefader and solo is postfader.

■ **Mute (channel on/off)** The *mute* function, also called *channel on/off,* turns off the signals from the I/O channel. During mixdown when no sound is feeding through an input channel for the moment, it shuts down the channel or mutes it. This prevents unwanted channel noise from reaching the outputs.

■ **Channel and monitor faders** The *channel and monitor faders* control the channel level of the signal being recorded and its monitor level, respectively. During recording, channel levels to the recorder are set for optimal signal-to-noise ratio. Level balances are made during mixdown. To enable the recordist to get a sense of what the balanced levels will sound like, the monitor faders are adjusted to taste, with no effect on the signal being recorded.

Meters

It is a paradox in sound production that the way to determine levels in consoles and mixers is visually—by watching a meter that measures the electric energy passing through an input or output. Audio heard through a monitor system is acoustic, but it passes through the console as voltage, which cannot be heard and therefore must be referenced in another way.

That said, a word about determining levels with your eyes: it can done only to a point. Meters can reflect problems that may not be perceived; or, if they are perceived, a meter may identify the problem when you may not be able to. As such, meters can be considered analogous to test equipment. In recording—and in mixing in particular—however, it is the ear that should determine audio quality and sonic relationships. After all, it is the sound that matters (see Chapter 21).

Sound in Electrical Form

For sound (acoustic) energy to be processed through electrical equipment, it must be *transduced,* or converted, into electric energy. Electric energy is measured in decibels in relation to power—dBm—and voltage—dBu or dBv, dBV, and dBFS. It is difficult to fully discuss these

4-6 Power and voltage measurements in dB.

dBFS (decibel full-scale) is the highest level in digital sound that can be recorded before distortion. On a digital meter, it is 0 dB. For example, –10 dB would be 10 dB below full-scale.

dBm is the original electrical measurement of power. It is referenced to 1 *milliwatt (mW)* as dissipated across a 600-ohm (Ω) load. 600 ohms is the standard circuit resistance of a telephone line. (A *resistor* is a device that opposes the flow of current.) Any voltage that results in 1 mW is 0 dBm, which is the same as 0.775 *volt (V)* across a 600-ohm impedance. +30 dBm is 1 *watt (W)*; +50 dBm is 100 W.

dBu, or *dBv,* is a unit of measurement for expressing the relationship of decibels to voltage—0.775 V to be exact.* The *u* stands for *unterminated.* The figure comes from 0 dBm, which equals 0.775 V. *dBu* is a more flexible reference than *dBm* because it permits use of the decibel scale to obtain a relative level without regard to a standard impedance, that is, 600 ohms. It is a measurement most useful in professional audio.

dBV is also a measure of voltage but with decibels referenced to 1 V. This measurement is used where the dBm—600 ohm/1 mW—value is impractical, as it is with the measurement of microphone sensitivity where the zero reference is 1 V. +10 dBV is equal to 20 V. Otherwise, dBV is not often used in professional audio.

*Originally, the reference symbol *dBu* was designated *dBv,* but because *dBv* was often confused with *dBV* it was changed to *dBu.* Both are still used—*dBu* mainly in the United States, and *dBv* mainly in Europe.

measurements here because they involve mathematical formulas and technical terminology that are beyond the scope of this book (see 4-6).

In measuring an electric circuit, a foremost concern is *impedance*—that property of a circuit, or an element, that restricts the flow of *alternating current (AC).* Impedance is measured in *ohms* (Ω), a unit of resistance to current flow. The lower the impedance in a circuit, the better.

VU Meter

The volume-unit meter has been a mainstay for decades and is still found on equipment in use today. But on most new consoles and recording equipment, it is rarely incorporated. The preferred meters today are peak indicators (see "Peak Meters" later in this section).

The *volume-unit (VU) meter* is a voltage meter originally designed to indicate level as it relates to the human ear's perception of loudness. It reflects a signal's perceived volume, but it is not fast enough to track rapid transients. With a complex waveform, the VU meter reads its average loudness level and less than the waveform's peak voltage. Hence there is headroom built into a console using VU meters so that a signal peaking above 0 level will not distort. (The VU meter uses a linear scale wherein 100 percent of modulation is equal to 0 VU on the volume-unit scale.) *Headroom* is the amount of level equipment can take, above working level, before overload distortion occurs. For these reasons and given the fact that with digital sound there is no headroom—a level over 100 percent of modulation will distort—the VU meter cannot provide the more exacting measures required for signal processing and recording that peak indicators can.

Two calibrated scales are on the face of the VU meter: a percentage of modulation scale and a volume-unit scale (see 4-7). A needle, the volume indicator, moves back

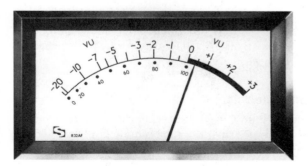

4-7 Volume-unit (VU) meter.

and forth across the scales, pointing out the levels. The needle responds to the electric energy passing through the VU meter. If the energy level is excessively high, the volume indicator will **pin**—hit against the meter's extreme right-hand side. Pinning can damage the VU meter's mechanism, rendering the volume indicator's reading unreliable.

Percentage of modulation is the percentage of an applied signal in relation to the maximum signal a sound system can handle. It is a linear scale wherein 100 percent of modulation is equal to 0 VU on the volume-unit scale. Therefore 30 percent of modulation is equal to slightly less than –10 VU, 80 percent of modulation is equal to –2 VU, and so on.

Any sound below 20 percent of modulation is too quiet, or ***in the mud***; and levels above 100 percent of modulation are too loud, or ***in the red***. (The scale to the right of 100 percent is red.) As a guideline the loudness should "kick" between about –5 and +1, although the dynamics of sound make such evenness difficult to accomplish, if not aesthetically undesirable. Usually, the best that can be done is to ***ride the gain***—adjust the faders from time to time so that, on average, the level stays out of the mud and the red. Fader movements can also be automated (see "Console Automation" later in this chapter).

When manually operating the faders, ride the gain with a light, fluid hand and do not jerk the faders up and down or make adjustments at the slightest fall or rise in loudness. Changes in level should be smooth and imperceptible because abrupt changes are disconcerting to the listener, unless an abrupt change is called for in, say, a transition from one shot to another.

When the VU meter is in the red, it is a warning to be cautious of loudness distortion. All modern consoles with VU meters are designed with headroom so that a signal peaking a few decibels above 0 VU will not distort.

Because a VU meter is designed to reflect a signal's perceived loudness, it does a poor job of indicating transient peaks, which is a main reason why peak meters are preferred.

Peak Meters

Whereas the VU meter is mechanical, most peak meters are electronic. Their rise time is quite fast because there is no mechanical inertia to overcome. A ***peak meter*** is able to track peak program levels, thereby making it a more accurate indicator of the signal levels passing

through the console and a safer measure when dealing with digital audio.

Peak meters read out in *bargraphs*, using LED or plasma displays.

LED Meters *LED*s are small light sources (*LED* stands for light-emitting diode). The meters are arranged horizontally or vertically. Usually, green LEDs indicate safe levels and red ones register in the overload region. On professional equipment the LEDs are about 2 dB apart, so resolution is fair (see 4-8).

Plasma Displays *Plasma displays* are columns of light that display safe levels in one color, usually green, and

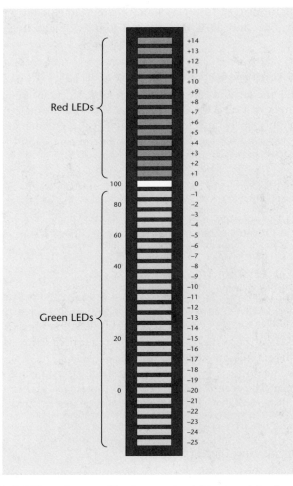

4-8 LED peak meter. Numbers on the right are peak levels; numbers on the left are their equivalent to VU meter levels.

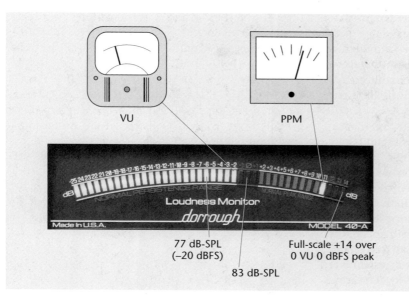

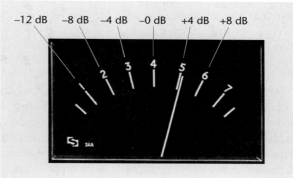

4-9 Loudness meter. This meter is roughly analogous to a VU meter and a peak program meter combined. It establishes a relationship between the root mean square (RMS) and the peak content of a signal. When riding the gain for balanced loudness, peaks should be driven to the brink of the top set of three LEDs (red), while the RMS should be driven to the brink of the center set of three LEDs (red). This is defined as relative loudness, in 1 dB steps. When the signal peaks in the red, the levels should be reduced slightly.

VU

PPM

77 dB-SPL
(−20 dBFS)

83 dB-SPL

Full-scale +14 over
0 VU 0 dBFS peak

overload levels in red. They are more complex than LED meters and have excellent resolution, with an accuracy of 1 dB. One version of a plasma display meter is roughly analogous to a VU meter and peak program meter (see 4-10) combined, thereby establishing a relationship between average and peak levels (see 4-9).

Meter Controls

In modern consoles meters also have the capability of measuring more than just output signal levels. Controls on the meter panel can be assigned to read bus, cue send, cue return, and monitor mix levels.

Peak Program Meter

Another type of peak indicator is the ***peak program meter (ppm)*** (see 4-10). With the ppm, as signal levels increase there is a warning of impending overload distortion. The level indicator makes this easier to notice because its rise time is rapid and its fallback is slow.

The ppm's scale is linear and in decibels, not volume units. The scale's divisions are 4 dB intervals, except at the extremes of the range; and zero-level is 4, in the middle of the scale.

Optimizing Digital Levels

One goal in processing audio through the signal chain is to make sure that the levels at each stage are optimal. Given the several stages in the sound chain, from micro-

4-10 Peak program meter with equivalent dB values. Dual-movement ppms with two indicators are for two-channel stereo applications.

phone to console to recording to mixing to mastering, this is easier said than done. With a console alone, there are a number of reference and overload scales for analog and digital signal levels. They involve a great deal of math that is beyond the scope of this book.

In general, however, there are approaches to optimizing level control in consoles using the available metering. Because just about all production today is handled in the digital domain and there is no headroom with digital signal processing, it makes sense to set the loudest levels below 0 level to avoid ***clipping***—distortion. How far below depends on the dynamics of the audio material.

Bear in mind that setting levels too low could create signal-to-noise problems with quiet passages.

Meters in digital audio consoles are calibrated in **decibel full-scale (dBFS)**, a unit of measurement for the amplitude of digital audio signals. Zero dBFS occurs when all the binary bits that make up the digital signal are on, that is, are read as 1's (as opposed to 0's, when the digital signal is off). It is the highest digital level that can be encoded, so anything above 0 dBFS will clip. Therefore setting the digital level at, say, –20 dBFS provides a headroom of 20 dB before overload distortion occurs.

Still another measuring system has been developed and proposed by mastering engineer Bob Katz. Called the **K-system**, it integrates measures of metering and monitoring to standardize reference loudness.[3] Apparently, many recordists do not find peak meters all that reliable and are using VU meters once again. The K-system is an attempt to establish a reliable, standard 0-level measurement that means the same thing to everyone.

Master Section

The **master section** contains the master controls for the master buses, the master fader, the master effects sends and returns, level and mute controls, meters, and other functions (see 4-11).

■ **Master buses** After a signal leaves an input/output module, it travels to its assigned *bus(es)*. In many consoles these signals may be grouped for premixing at submaster buses before being finally combined at the master bus(es). There may be any number of submaster buses, but usually there are only a few master buses because final output signals are mixed down to a few channels, such as two-channel stereo and six- (or more) channel surround sound.

■ **Master fader** The *master fader* controls the signal level from the master bus to the recorder. Most master faders are configured as a single fader carrying a tandem left/right stereo signal; some are configured as a stereo output pair with the left fader carrying the left signal and the right fader carrying the right signal. A console may have two, four, eight, or more such faders or sets of faders to handle stereo and surround sound. Sometimes there is a mono master fader as well.

■ **Master effects sends (aux send, reverb send, and echo send)** The *effects sends* from the I/O channels are

3. See Bob Katz, *Mastering Audio,* 2nd ed. (Boston: Focal Press, 2007), p. 176.

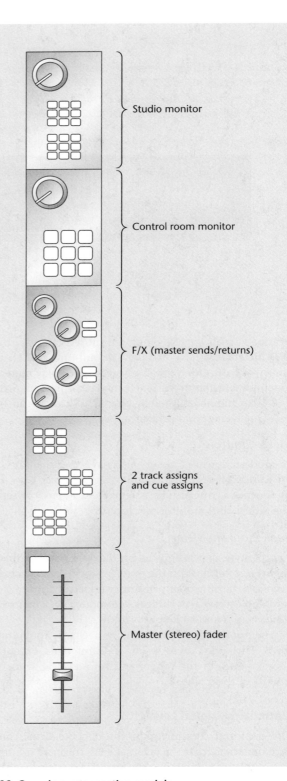

4-11 Generic master section module.

Studio monitor

Control room monitor

F/X (master sends/returns)

2 track assigns and cue assigns

Master (stereo) fader

first routed to the master effects sends before being output to an outboard signal processor.

■ **Master effects returns (aux return, reverb return, and echo return)** Signals routed to an outboard signal processor from the master sends are returned at the master returns and mixed with the main program signal.

■ **Level, mute, PFL, solo, and pan pot** Each master aux send and aux return usually has a level control and a mute switch. The master returns also usually have PFL, solo, and pan controls.

■ **Meters** Most modern production consoles provide peak metering for each master fader; a mono meter to indicate the level of a summed stereo signal; a phase meter to show the phase relationship between the left and right stereo signals or among the surround signals; metering to monitor surround-sound levels; and metering to display master send and/or return levels. Some consoles also have meters for the control room monitor outputs.

Monitor Section

Monitor functions, such as setting monitor level and panning for each channel, may be performed by the I/O module. The *monitor section,* among other things, allows monitoring of the line or recorder input, selects various inputs to the control room and studio monitors, and controls their levels.

■ **Recorder select switches** These switches select a recorder for direct feed to the monitor system, bypassing the I/O controls. There may also be *aux in* switches for direct feeds to the monitor system from other sound sources such as a CD player or a recorder.

■ **Send switches** These route signals from the sends to the input of the control room or studio monitors or both.

■ **Mix switches** These select the mix input (i.e., stereo or surround sound) for the monitor system.

■ **Speaker select switches** These select the control room or studio loudspeakers for monitoring. There is a level control for each set of loudspeakers. Monitor sections also have a *dim* switch for the control room monitors. Instead of having to turn the monitor level down and up during control room conversation, the dim function reduces monitor level by several decibels or more at the touch of a button.

A monitor section may also have a pan pot, mutes for the left and right channel signals to the control room, and a phase coherence switch. The *phase coherence* switch inverts the left-channel signal before it combines with the right-channel signal. If the stereo signals are in phase, sound quality should suffer, and, in particular, the sonic images in the center (between the two loudspeakers) should be severely attenuated. If the phase coherence check improves the mono signal, there is a problem with the stereo signal's mono compatibility.

Additional Features

Additional features found on most consoles include talkback, slate, and oscillator.

■ **Talkback** The *talkback* permits the recordist in the control room to speak to the studio performers or music conductor or both via a console microphone. The talkback may be directed through the studio monitor, headphones, or a slate system.

■ **Slate/talkback** Many multichannel consoles also have a *slate* feature that automatically feeds to a recording anything said through the talkback. It is a convenient way to transcribe information about the name of the recording, the artist, the take number, and so on.

■ *Oscillator* An *oscillator* is a signal generator that produces pure tones or sine waves (sound waves with no harmonics or overtones) at selected frequencies. On a console it is used both to calibrate the console with the recorder so that their levels are the same and to put reference tone levels on recordings.

CHANNEL STRIPS

In general, a *channel strip* refers to one channel (usually input) of a console. In the past the sound quality of some console channel strips have been so highly regarded that they were ordered separately from the console manufacturer and rigged to a power supply and input/output connections for stand-alone use. A microphone could be plugged directly into the channel strip and the signal sent directly to a recorder, thereby producing a purer and far less complex signal path while eliminating the need to deal with a larger console.

Today stand-alone and plug-in channel strips are so popular that they have become a separate product category. They may include some or most of the functions usually found in most conventional and virtual console channel strips, such as a microphone preamp, equalization, compression, limiting, de-essing, and noise-gating (see 4-12 and 4-13).

4-12 Stand-alone channel strip. This rack-mountable model is designed to reproduce the sound from vintage Neve console models. It includes a mic preamp, a three-band equalizer, high- and low-frequency shelving, high-pass filters, and phantom power. The *silk* control is designed to reduce negative feedback and adjust the frequency spectrum to provide a more musical sound.

4-13 Channel strip plug-in. This software from Metric Halo includes input gain and trim, polarity reversal, a six-band parametric equalizer, high- and low-frequency shelving, expander/gate, compressor, delay, and time alignment; it also displays detailed visual feedback about the effects of the processing applied.

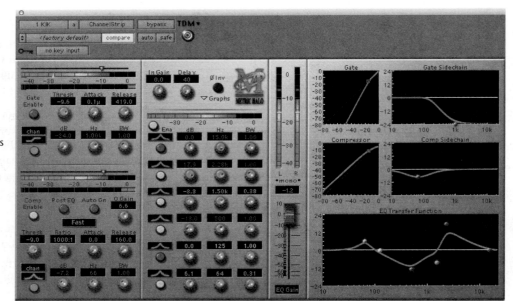

PATCHING

Audio facilities require flexibility in sending signals to various components within the console and to and from outboard equipment in the control room.[4] In studios where active components are not wired directly to one another but to the console or outboard gear or both, one or more patch bays are required. A ***patch bay*** is a central terminal that facilitates the routing of sound through pathways not provided in the normal console design. Each hole in the patch bay (or *patch panel*), called a ***jack***, becomes the connecting point to the input or output of each electronic component in the sound studio (see 4-14). *Patching* is the interconnecting of these inputs and outputs using a ***patch cord*** (see 4-15 and 4-16). In this context a patch bay is more like an old-fashioned telephone switchboard.

In digital consoles there is no separate patch bay. Patching is handled internally without the need for special wiring or patch cords (see "Digital Consoles" later in this chapter). Control surfaces can handle signal routing using network routers (see "Control Surfaces" later in this chapter).

In a well-equipped and active analog facility, the patch bay could become a confusing jungle of patch cords. In all studios, regardless of size and activity, a signal travels some paths more often than others. For example, it is more likely that a signal in a console will travel from

---

4. Although patching operations are handled internally in many of the consoles produced today, there are a sufficient number of facilities with equipment that requires patching to warrant coverage here.

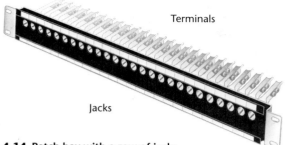

4-14 Patch bay with a row of jacks.

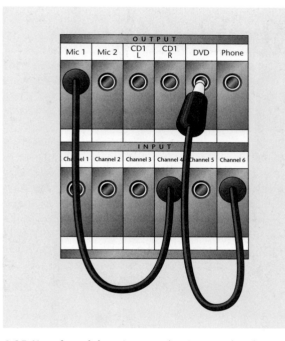

4-15 Use of patch bay. Any sound source wired to the patch panel can be connected to any other one with a patch cord plugged into the appropriate jack.

mic (or line) input to pan pot to equalizer to assignment control to fader, rather than directly from mic (or line) input to output bus. It is also more likely that a signal will travel from mic to console to recorder rather than directly from a mic to a recorder.

As a way of both reducing the clutter of patch cords at the patch bay and simplifying production, terminals wired to certain equipment can also be wired, or *normaled,* to one another. A *normal* connection is one that permits a signal to flow freely among components without any patching. To route a signal through components that have terminals not normaled or wired to one another,

patch cords are put in the appropriate jacks to *break normal*—that is, to interrupt the normal signal flow—thus rerouting the signal. In some patch bays, normaling can be done manually, without the need for rewiring.

The ability to reroute a signal is also advantageous when equipment fails. Suppose a microphone is plugged into studio mic input 1, which connects directly to console channel 1, and channel 1 becomes defective. With all inputs and outputs connected at the patch bay, the defective console channel 1 can be bypassed by patching the output from studio mic input 1 to any other working console channel.

Here are some other features of patch bays.

■ **Input/output** Patch bays are usually wired so that a row of input jacks is directly below a row of output jacks. By reading a patch bay downward, it is possible to get a good idea of the console's (or studio's) signal flow.

■ **Full-normal and half-normal** Input jacks are wired so that a patch cord always interrupts the normal connection. These connections are called *full-normal.* Output jacks may be wired as either full-normal or *half-normal*—connections that continue rather than interrupt signal flow. Hence a half-normal connection becomes a junction rather than a switch.

■ **Multiple** Most patch bays include jacks called *multiples,* or *mults,* that are wired to one another instead of to any electronic component. Multiples provide the flexibility to feed the same signal to several different sources at once.

■ **Tie line** When the only patch bay in a control room is located in the console, the other control room equipment, such as CD and DVD players and signal processors, must be wired to it to maintain flexibility in signal routing. *Tie lines* in the patch bay facilitate the interconnecting of outboard devices in the control room. When a control room has two patch bays, one in the console and one for the other control room equipment, tie lines can interconnect them. The tie line is also used to interconnect separate studios, control rooms, or any devices in different locations.

General Guidelines for Patching

■ Do not patch mic-level signals into line-level jacks and vice versa. The signal will be barely audible in the first instance and will distort in the latter one.

■ Do not patch input to input or output to output.

■ Unless jacks are half-normaled, do not patch the output of a component back into its input, or feedback will occur.

■ When patching microphones make sure that the fader controls are turned down. Otherwise, the loud popping sound that occurs when patch cords are inserted into jacks with the faders turned up could damage the microphone or loudspeaker element.

Plugs

The patch-cord plugs most commonly used in professional facilities are the *¼-inch phone plug* and the *bantam phone plug*. The bantam (also called *mini* and *tiny telephone*) plug, and the smaller patch panel with which it is used, has all but replaced the larger ¼-inch phone plug and its patch panel (see 4-16).

These plugs are either *unbalanced*—tip and sleeve—or *balanced*—tip, ring, and sleeve (see 4-17). An unbalanced audio cable has two conductors: a center wire and a braided shield surrounding it. A balanced audio cable has three conductors: two center wires and a braided shield. The balanced line is preferred for professional use because it is not so susceptible to electrical interference and can be used in long cable runs without undue loss in signal-to-noise ratio.

Computer Patching

Instead of hardware-based patch panels, many modern consoles in general and most digital consoles in particular handle patching using computer programming. Routing signals via patching does not require a physical patch bay or cords. At the touch of a few keys, routing information is entered into a programmer, which tells the electronic patch panel to connect the selected signal source to the desired console channel. All patching commands can be stored for future use. Computer patching is convenient, flexible, and tidy. It is worth emphasizing, however, the importance of keeping track of all the patching assignments. Otherwise it could lead to confusion in managing the signal flows.

CONSOLE AUTOMATION

Given today's complex production consoles and the myriad procedures involved in mixing many tracks to a few, console automation has become indispensable. It

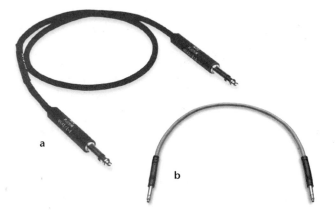

4-16 Patch cords with (a) ¼-inch phone plugs and (b) bantam (mini or tiny telephone) phone plugs.

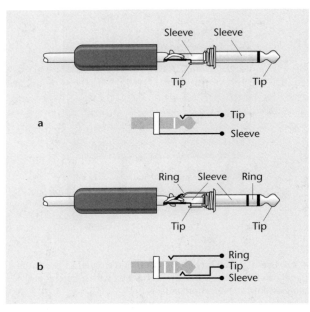

4-17 (a) Mono unbalanced phone plug and (b) stereo balanced phone plug.

greatly facilitates operations by automatically keeping track of the various mixer settings and by storing the information for recall at any time.

Types of Automation Systems

There are four types of automation systems in consoles: voltage-controlled automation, moving-fader automation, software-controlled automation, and MIDI-based automation.

Voltage-controlled Automation

In voltage-controlled automation, fader levels (and other functions) are regulated by two types of amplifiers. The **voltage-controlled amplifier (VCA)** is used to decrease level, unlike conventional amplifiers that become unstable if operated with loss. It is regulated by external DC voltage. In a typical VCA-equipped console, faders vary the DC control voltage that changes the VCA's gain in relation to the fader movement. This control voltage is digitized and stored for later retrieval. In addition to fader levels, it is possible to automate channel and group mutes, solo functions, and inboard signal processors, such as the equalizer. The **digitally controlled amplifier (DCA)** is an amp whose gain is remotely controlled by a digital control signal.

Moving-fader Automation

Moving-fader, also called *flying-fader, automation* drives a small servo-motor that is attached to the fader instead of using DC voltage to control a VCA. As the control voltages are regenerated, it activates the motor, which moves the fader automatically; no hand-operated assistance is necessary. It is possible to control automatically one fader or groups of faders at the same time.

Software-controlled Automation

Software-controlled automation uses specially designed computer programs for console automation. It is usually employed in disk-based recording systems.

Adjustments are made through *virtual faders* displayed on a video monitor. A virtual control is simulated on a computer monitor and adjusted at the computer keyboard, with a mouse, or by using a touchscreen. More-complex programs, in addition to automated level control, also allow automated control of all inboard signal processing, such as equalization, panning, compression, and effects.

MIDI-based Automation

MIDI, short for **Musical Instrument Digital Interface,** is a communications protocol. The *digital* refers to a set of instructions in the form of digital (binary) data, like a computer program, that must be interpreted by an electronic sound-generating or sound-modifying device, such as a synthesizer, that can respond to the instructions. *Interface* refers to the hardware connection that permits the control signals generated by one device to be transmitted to another. A specified system of digital commands and hardware interface allows musical instruments and other devices to communicate with one another.

In the same way that MIDI can automate musical instruments, it can also be used to automate console operations, such as fader levels, send and return levels, EQ, and pans. MIDI-automated consoles may physically resemble consoles with conventional automation or may be "black boxes" with input and output jacks. These boxes may use either a virtual console computer graphic interface or dedicated controllers with slides and knobs that control the box through MIDI commands.

MIDI console automation has limitations in handling the large amounts of data that other types of automation do not have. But because many conventional console automation systems are so complex, some recordists turn to MIDI-based automation systems as a simpler alternative.

Snapshot and Continuous Automation   Two methods are used to handle data changes in console automation: snapshot control and continuous control. With *snapshot control* the automation system takes an instant reading of the console settings for recall from storage. The reading reflects the state of the console at a particular moment. With *continuous,* or *dynamic, control,* the motion of the mixer controls is recorded. Gradual changes of parameters, from small adjustments in level to larger changes such as fades, are stored as they are made over time.

Operating Modes

Console automation systems have at least three basic operating modes: write, read, and update. All functions may be used independently on any or all channels.

■ **Write mode** The *write mode* is used to create an automated mix. In the write mode, the automation system monitors and stores data from the faders. Only current fader movements are stored in the write mode.

■ **Read mode** The *read mode* plays back or recalls the stored automation data. In the read mode, which is also called *safe mode,* the console's faders are inoperative. They take their control voltage information only from the stored data on the disk to reproduce the "recorded" fader movements in real time.

■ **Update mode** The *update mode* allows the operator to read the stored information at any time and make changes simply by moving the appropriate fader. A new data track is generated from the original data track with the changes that have been made.

Advantages of Console Automation

Mixing various sounds once they are recorded can be exacting and tedious. It requires dozens, maybe hundreds, of replays and myriad adjustments to get the right equalization, reverberation, blend, spatial balance, timing of inserts, and so on. Comparing one mix with another is difficult unless settings are written down (which is time-consuming) so that controls can be returned to previous positions if necessary. It is not uncommon to discard a mix because someone forgot to adjust one control or decided after a few days to change a few settings without noting the original positions. Then the controls have to be set up all over again. Mixing one song can take many hours or even days; a production can take months.

Console automation greatly facilitates the recordkeeping and the accuracy of mixing; it makes the engineer's arms "longer." Many productions are so involved that they would be nearly impossible without automation.

Disadvantages of Console Automation

As necessary as automation is in so much of audio production, it also has some disadvantages. It tends to be confusing, even to experienced operators. Some systems are so complex that it is easy to lose track of the many operations necessary to perform a mix, which defeats the purpose of automation. Some systems may not play back exactly what the operator wrote. If the mix is complex, a difference of a few decibels overall may not be perceptible. That would not be the case, however, in more-subtle mixes.

Automation systems, like all computer systems, are vulnerable to crashing. Getting the system operational again, even assuming that you had the forethought to make a backup copy of the mix before completion, often involves a frustrating loss of production time and continuity, to say nothing of the financial cost.

An aesthetic concern with automation is "sameness." Unless an automated mix is done with skill, its dynamics can sound the same from beginning to end.

The disadvantages of console automation notwithstanding, most audio production today would be difficult without it.

DIGITAL CONSOLES

Aside from their differences in technologies, the main innovation in digital consoles compared with analog consoles is the divorcing of circuitry from panel controls. The control surface still comprises the familiar controls—faders, equalizer, input selectors, sends, returns, and so on—but there is no physical connection between the controls on the console surface and the audio circuit elements, nor are specific controls necessarily dedicated to particular channels.

With an analog console, the controls in one input/output channel strip must be duplicated for each channel strip in the console. With digital consoles many of these functions pass through a central processor, eliminating the need for duplication and making it possible to increase the number of operations in a smaller surface area. Operational commands are recorded in the system's memory for recall at any time and are assignable.

For example, instead of having an EQ module in each channel strip, the console is designed into a central control panel to which all channels have access. Select, say, channel 1 and pass its signal through the equalizer in the central control panel; make the desired EQ adjustments, which are recorded in the console's memory; then move on to, say, channel 2 and pass its signal through the equalizer; make the desired EQ adjustments, which are recorded in the console's memory; and so on. With most digital consoles today, the same can be done with other dynamic effects that are part of the central control panel, such as compression, limiting, noise gating, and delay, as well as effects sends, monitor levels, and panning. (A pan control may also be included in each channel strip.)

The **assignable console** design has several advantages over conventional production consoles. In addition to making many more operations possible in a more compact chassis, signals can be handled more quickly and easily because functions are grouped and, with fewer controls, there are fewer operations to perform; patching can be accomplished at the touch of a few keys, inboard, without the need for a patch bay and patch cords (see 4-18).

Digital consoles are available in three basic configurations. One configuration is actually an analog console that is digitally controlled. The signal path is distributed and processed in analog form, but the console's control parameters are maintained digitally.

The second configuration is the all-digital console, which uses two approaches. The analog input signal

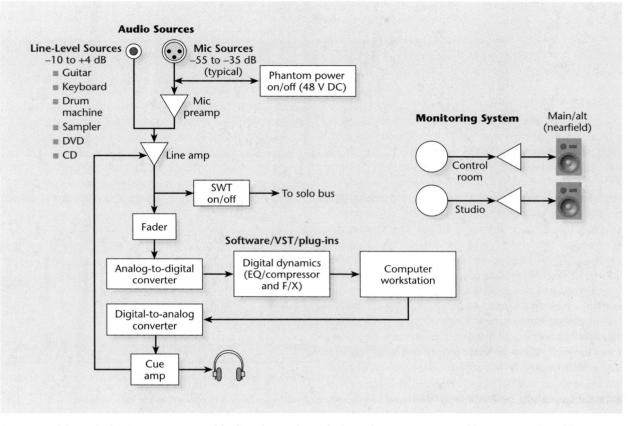

4-18 Signal flow of a basic generic assignable digital console. Each channel strip is separate and houses a number of functions typical of a channel strip on most consoles. In an assignable console, however, functions such as EQ, compression, noise gating, and delay are located in a central processing unit and can be individually custom-assigned to each channel strip and retained in the console's memory.

is first encoded into a digital signal, or it is directly accepted as digital information. In either case, the data are distributed and processed digitally. The output might be decoded back into analog or may remain in digital form, depending on its destination.

A third type of digital mixer is actually a virtual console. As the term suggests, a *virtual console* is not a console per se but an integrated system that combines a hard-disk computer and specialized software to record and process audio directly to disk. Instead of feeding a sound source to a conventional console, it is fed directly to the computer. The controls are displayed on the computer monitor and look like those of a typical analog console—faders, EQ, panning, sends, returns, and so on (see 4-19). Operations and functions are manipulated using some type of **human interface device (HID)**, such as a mouse,

keyboard, joystick, or touchscreen, although these tools are not always suited to the hands-on control associated with various aspects of audio production. Mixing with a mouse and a keyboard can be cumbersome and awkward at best. An increasingly diverse range of HIDs, called *control surfaces* or *work surfaces,* provide more-tactile means of control across a spectrum of digital audio systems, devices, and software applications.

CONTROL SURFACES

In much the same way that digital tablet and pen technology liberated graphic artists from the limitations of creating with a keyboard and a mouse, an audio **control surface** provides a tactual means of controlling the various elements of sound production. Also called a *work*

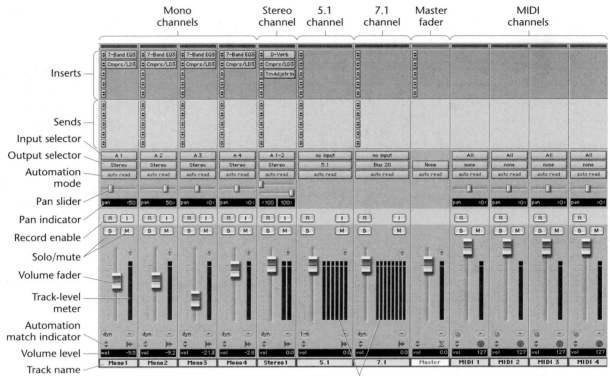

4-19 Virtual console, shown in what is referred to in recording/editing software programs as the mix window.

surface, the design, features, and appearance of such a control surface vary according to its function: from a dedicated virtual instrument or *digital signal processing (DSP)* plug-in controller to universal and hybrid work surfaces (see 4-20 to 4-22). Generally, there are no actual audio signals present inside a simple control surface, only control circuitry that sends digital instructions to the device doing the actual audio signal processing.

Depending on the *digital audio workstation* environment and the technology employed, control surfaces may function or be configured in different ways. The most popular means of connecting a control surface to a host computer or other peripheral device is via the MIDI standard (see "MIDI-based Automation" earlier in this chapter; see also Chapter 6). Other equipment may support a number of connections: a proprietary interface; a Universal Serial Bus (USB) port; a FireWire cable, which generally provides more-rapid data and media transfer and access speeds than USB; or an Ethernet connection.

Universal and hybrid control surfaces often integrate analog and digital audio signals and paths with DSP control capability across a complement of compatible

4-20 Control surface designed to facilitate editing of DSP and virtual instrument plug-ins with a variety of different software. This controller may be used as a stand-alone solution or in tandem with other control surface components for analog-style control over tracks and plug-ins.

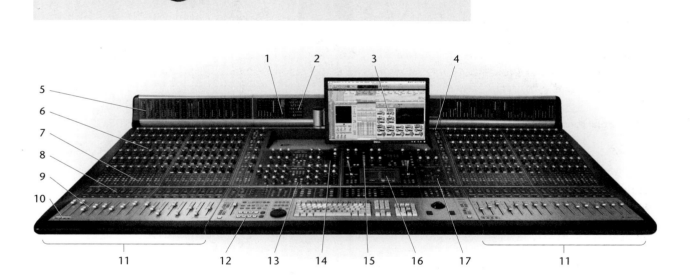

4-21 Universal control surface. This model provides transport, automation, and DSP functions without the need for a mouse or keyboard. Used primarily for mixing, it resembles an analog mixing console. Controls include *record, play, stop, fast-forward, rewind,* and other frequently used editing functions. A job/shuttle wheel facilitates positioning and scrub-editing.

1. **Talkback microphone**
2. **Time scale displays and location indicators**
3. **Virtual console display**
4. **Channel strip master section** affects how channel strips behave globally. Dedicated buttons control such assignments as I/O and automation. Also available to the left of the main unit.
5. **LED meter bridge display**
6. **Rotary encoder section**
7. **Channel strip mode controls**
8. **Channel strip function controls**
9. **Channel faders**
10. **Modifier keys**
11. **Fader module** contains individual channel strips that control processing and routing functions.
12. **Transport section** controls recorder transport functions, such as *play, stop, record, fast-forward,* and *fast-rewind.*
13. **EQ section**
14. **Dynamics section** includes controls for limiter/compressor and expander/noise gate plug-ins.
15. **Monitor section**
16. **Visual pan indicator**
17. **Zoom/navigation section**

4-22 Integrated D-Control™ work surface for Digidesign® ICON systems, showing key features.

programs. Control surfaces can be used in most types of audio production: in performance, from dedicated control over MIDI devices including virtual instruments, synthesizers, samplers, and sequencing software applications; and in recording, mixing, DSP, and automation.

Another use for a control surface is via router connectivity, thereby enabling access to a broadcast station's or production facility's entire network of audio sources and assets. A dedicated control surface such as the one shown in Figure 4-23 works with a network router.

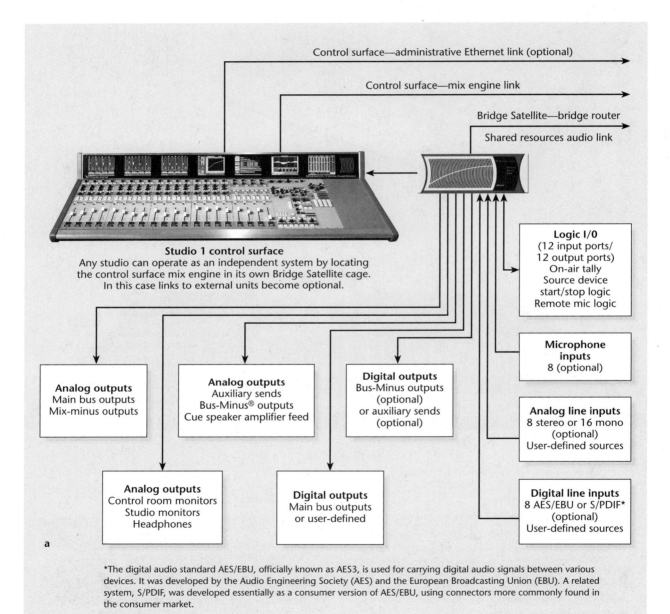

Control surface—administrative Ethernet link (optional)

Control surface—mix engine link

Bridge Satellite—bridge router

Shared resources audio link

Studio 1 control surface
Any studio can operate as an independent system by locating the control surface mix engine in its own Bridge Satellite cage. In this case links to external units become optional.

Logic I/0
(12 input ports/
12 output ports)
On-air tally
Source device
start/stop logic
Remote mic logic

Microphone inputs
8 (optional)

Analog outputs
Main bus outputs
Mix-minus outputs

Analog outputs
Auxiliary sends
Bus-Minus® outputs
Cue speaker amplifier feed

Digital outputs
Bus-Minus outputs
(optional)
or auxiliary sends
(optional)

Analog line inputs
8 stereo or 16 mono
(optional)
User-defined sources

Analog outputs
Control room monitors
Studio monitors
Headphones

Digital outputs
Main bus outputs
or user-defined

Digital line inputs
8 AES/EBU or S/PDIF*
(optional)
User-defined sources

a

*The digital audio standard AES/EBU, officially known as AES3, is used for carrying digital audio signals between various devices. It was developed by the Audio Engineering Society (AES) and the European Broadcasting Union (EBU). A related system, S/PDIF, was developed essentially as a consumer version of AES/EBU, using connectors more commonly found in the consumer market.

4-23 (a) Dedicated control surface and its input and output connections. With this model it is possible to select any combination of input signals in the entire Bridge system and create a multitude of mixes. The system can handle any live broadcast segment or complex, layered production programming. Because of the inboard routing control, all mixes can be directed to any destination in a facility.

Input channel   Master section   Dynamics section

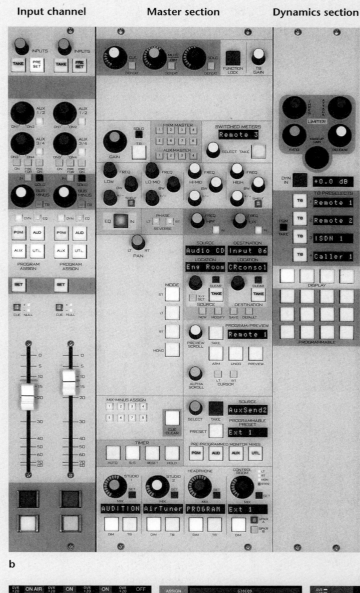

- Programmable EQ and dynamics
- 4 stereo output buses
- 4 stereo auxiliary sends
- 8 mix-minus outputs
- Bus-Minus® output with individual talkback and solo on every input channel
- Full-scale digital peak and VU metering
- Extensive talkback and communication circuits
- 2 studio, control room, and headphone circuits
- Function lockout feature
- Programmable source access
- Independent operation (no personal computer required)
- Intuitive graphic interface setup software
- Logic follow source
- On-air safety locks
- Event storage and recall
- 12 user-programmable switches, 4 programmable talkback switches
- Automation-friendly protocol
- Event scheduling software available
- Automatic failsafe digital signal-processing (DSP) card option
- Automatic failsafe central processing unit (CPU) card option
- Switched meters with systemwide access

b

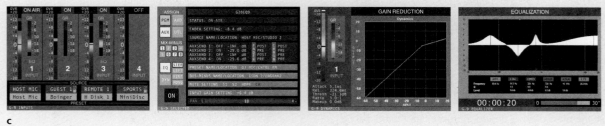

c

4-23 *(continued)* (b) Detail of an input channel, master section, and dynamics section with a list of features. (c) LCD screens for input, channel status, dynamics, and equalization.

Digital consoles and control surfaces have several advantages over their all-analog counterparts, especially as more and more facets of audio production move into the digital domain. They are virtually distortion- and noise-free; every control move—manual or preprogrammed—is stored and retrieved digitally with a greater degree of accuracy. For example, manipulating a knob or—in the parlance of the control surface—a *rotary encoder* sends a set of precise, digital instructions to a device. This is far more efficient than manually modulating voltage control through a potentiometer, with all its associated system noise, artifacts, and margin of user error from one move to the next. Control parameters may be combined or matrixed in such a way that one control instruction can direct several preprogrammed functions to occur simultaneously. Physical inboard and outboard patch bays are unnecessary, although limited in control surfaces compared with the routing flexibility in digital consoles; a compact chassis preserves valuable control room space; and, given the variety and the efficiency of operational potential and capacities, compared with their analog cousins, whether the console or control surface is modest or upscale, there are enough models available to suit any budget and production requirement.

MAIN POINTS

▶ Consoles and mixers take input signals and amplify, balance, process, combine, and route them to broadcast, recording, or other destinations in a facility.

▶ The differences between a mixer and a console are that a mixer is small, highly portable, and performs limited processing functions, whereas a console is larger and performs numerous processing functions. In most modern consoles, these functions are computer-assisted.

▶ The term *mixer* is often used synonymously with *console*. Some mixers include additional features that are found on consoles, and some small- and medium-format consoles have limited features that could classify them as large mixers.

▶ Consoles today are available in various configurations, use different technologies, and are designed for particular production purposes. A console may be analog or digital; appropriate for on-air broadcast, production, or postproduction; software-based and used as a virtual console with a hard-disk recorder; or it may be a control surface.

▶ Regardless of their design, purpose, and complexity, consoles have at least the three basic control sections: input, output, and monitor. Many consoles have an additional master control section.

▶ The input section takes incoming signals and routes them to the output section.

▶ The output section routes signals to broadcast, recording, or a router.

▶ The monitor section enables signals to be heard.

▶ On-air broadcast consoles, particularly for radio, do not have to be as elaborate as production consoles because most of the audio they handle has been produced already. But modern consoles for radio have sophisticated features, such as digital signal processing (DSP), computer-assisted operations, and routing flexibility.

▶ The features of production consoles generally include the input/output (I/O) section consisting of an I/O channel strip; input selector control; phantom power; microphone preamplifier input module; microphone preamplifier; trim or gain; pad; overload, or peak, indicator; polarity (phase) reversal; channel assignment and routing; direct switch; pan pot; equalizer and filter; dynamics section; channel/monitor control; cue and effects (F/X or EFX) sends (pre- or postfader); solo and prefader listen (PFL); mute (channel on/off); channel and monitor faders; and meters.

▶ For acoustic sound to be processed through electrical equipment, it must be transduced, or converted, into electric energy. Electric energy is measured in decibels in relation to power—dBm—and voltage—dBu or dBv, dBV, and dBFS.

▶ In measuring an electric circuit, a foremost concern is impedance—that property of a circuit, or an element, that restricts the flow of alternating current (AC). Impedance is measured in ohms (Ω), a unit of resistance to current flow. The lower the impedance in a circuit, the better.

▶ The volume-unit (VU) meter is a voltage meter that measures the amount of electric energy flowing through the console. The meter has two scales: percentage of modulation and volume units. Percentage of modulation is the percentage of an applied signal in relation to the maximum signal a sound system can handle.

▶ Peak meters, which today are preferred over the VU meter, track peak program levels, thereby making them a more accurate indicator of signal levels passing through a console.

▶ Peak meters read out in bargraphs using light-emitting diodes (LEDs) or plasma displays.

▶ With the peak program meter (ppm), as signal levels increase there is a warning of impending overload distortion. The level indicator makes this easier to notice because its rise time is rapid and its fallback is slow.

▶ One goal in processing audio through the signal chain is to make sure that the levels at each stage are optimal. Given the several stages in the sound chain, from microphone to console to recording to mixing to mastering, this is easier said than done.

▶ Meters in digital audio consoles are calibrated in decibel full-scale (dBFS), a unit of measurement for the amplitude of digital audio signals. Zero dBFS occurs when all the binary bits that make up the digital signal are on.

▶ The master section includes master buses, the master fader, the master effects sends and returns, level and mute controls, meters, and other functions.

▶ The monitor section includes recorder select, send, mix, and speaker select switches. It may also have a pan pot, mutes, and a phase coherence switch.

▶ Other common features of production consoles include talkback, slate/talkback, an oscillator, and, in analog consoles, a patch bay.

▶ A channel strip refers to one channel (usually input) of a console. It can be ordered separately from the console manufacturer and rigged to a power supply and I/O connections for stand-alone use.

▶ A patch bay is a central routing terminal that facilitates the routing of sound through pathways not provided in the normal console design. The patch bay makes multiple signal paths possible. Patch cords plugged into jacks connect the routing circuits.

▶ The signal paths that are used most often are wired together at the terminals of the patch bay. This normals these routes and makes it unnecessary to use patch cords to connect them. It is possible to break normal and create other signal paths by patching.

▶ Plugs at the end of patch cords are either unbalanced, comprising a tip and a sleeve, or balanced, comprising a tip, ring, and sleeve.

▶ Instead of hardware-based patch panels, many modern consoles in general and all digital consoles in particular handle patching using computer programming.

▶ Console automation makes it possible to automate fader functions, decoding positional information as adjustments in level are made. The data are stored in and retrieved from computer memory.

▶ There are four types of console automation systems in use: voltage-controlled automation, moving-fader automation, software-controlled automation, and MIDI-based automation.

▶ Console automation systems have at least three basic operating modes: write, read, and update.

▶ Digital consoles use the assignable concept in three configurations: in an analog console that is digitally controlled, in an all-digital console, and in a virtual console which is not a console per se but an integrated system that combines a hard-disk computer and specialized software to record and process audio directly to disk.

▶ With digital consoles, instead of individual controls for channel-to-track routing on each channel strip, these functions have been centralized into single sets so they can be assigned to any channel. Once assigned, the commands are stored in the console's computer, so different functions can be assigned to other channels. There is no physical connection between the controls on the console surface and the audio circuit elements.

▶ A control surface, or work surface, provides external control of a virtual audio environment. There are two main types of control surfaces: general-purpose controllers that can work with a wide range of gear and dedicated controllers that work with specific software.

5

Recording

Until the advent of experimental digital audio recording in the 1960s and commercial digital recordings in the early 1970s, the format used was analog. In **analog recording** the waveform of the signal being processed resembles the waveform of the original sound—they are analogous. The frequency and the amplitude of an electrical signal changes continuously in direct relationship to the original acoustic sound waves; it is always "on." If these continuous changes were examined, they would reveal an infinite number of variations, each instant different from any adjacent instant. During processing, noise—electrical, electronic, or tape—may be added to the signal. Hence the processed signal is analogous to the original sound plus any additional noise (see Figure 5-1).

Although some audio production is still done in analog, mostly in music recording, and the format still has passionate supporters, analog is being used less and less. Producers who continue to record in analog cite its warmer, more elegant sound; its sonic proportion that they feel is more complementary to music; its more forgiving production format—technical problems are not as apparent as they are with digital; and its less intensive production process.

These advantages notwithstanding, the reality is that the analog format in audio production is obsolescent. Professional audiotape recorders are no longer being manufactured except on special order; they are not shown at trade shows; at this writing only one company in the United States manufactures audiotape; and the majority of analog audiotape recorders in professional studios have been relegated to the storage room. Analog videotape recorders (VTRs) have been supplanted by digital VTRs

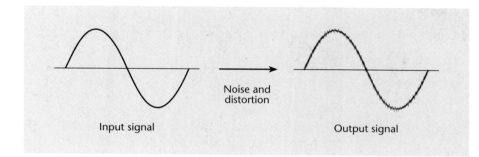

5-1 Analog recording process.

Input signal

Noise and distortion

Output signal

because of digital video recording's superior sound and picture. Now even digital videotape recorders are on the way out, being replaced by disc recorders.

When compared with analog, the advantages of digital audio are overwhelming. The digital format is virtually noise-free, sound quality is crystal clear, many copies of the original recording can be made without loss in sound quality, data storage and production flexibility are substantially increased, more can be accomplished in less time and with less equipment, equipment is not as costly given the technology's processing power, and today's signal processors can furnish most of the sonic attributes of analog sound if desired. (Despite these advantages, digital audio is not without its sonic impurities. Data compression, discussed later in this chapter and in Chapters 19 and 23, for example, can have detrimental effects on digital sound quality.)

The decision to concentrate on digital recording in this chapter is not an indictment of the analog format but a reflection of the audio industry's transition from analog to digital sound. For those who are still recording in analog, a full discussion of analog audiotape recording can be found at *www.cengage.com/rtf/alten/audioinmedia9e.*

DIGITAL AUDIO

Instead of an analogous relationship between the acoustic sound and the electronically processed signal, recording audio in the digital format uses a numerical representation of the audio signal's actual frequency and amplitude. In analog, *frequency* is the time component and *amplitude* is the level component. In digital, *sampling* is the time component and *quantization* is the level component.

Sampling

Sampling takes periodic samples (voltages) of the original analog signal at fixed intervals and converts them to

digital data. The rate at which the fixed intervals sample the original signal each second is called the *sampling frequency,* or *sampling rate.* For example, a sampling frequency of 48 kHz means that samples are taken 48,000 times per second, or each sample period is ¹⁄₄₈,₀₀₀ second. Because sampling and the component of time are directly related, a system's sampling rate determines its upper frequency limits. Theoretically, the higher the sampling rate, the greater a system's frequency range.

It was determined several years ago that if the highest frequency in a signal were to be digitally encoded successfully, it would have to be sampled at a rate at least twice its frequency.[1] In other words, if high-frequency response in digital recording is to reach 20 kHz, the sampling frequency must be at least 40 kHz. Too low a sampling rate would cause loss of too much information (see 5-2).

Think of a movie camera that takes 24 still pictures per second. A sampling rate of ¹⁄₂₄ second seems adequate to record most visual activities. Although the camera shutter closes after each ¹⁄₂₄ second and nothing is recorded, not enough information is lost to impair perception of the event. A person running, for example, does not run far enough in the split second the shutter is closed to alter the naturalness of the movement. If the sampling rates were slowed to 1 frame per second, the running movement would be quick and abrupt; if it were slowed to 1 frame per minute, the running would be difficult to follow.

A number of sampling rates are used in digital audio. The most common are 32 kHz, 44.056 kHz, 44.1 kHz, 48 kHz, and 96 kHz. For the Internet, sampling rates below 32 kHz are often used (see Chapter 19). To store more audio data on computer disks, usually submultiples

---

1. This concept was developed by a Bell Laboratories researcher, Harry Nyquist. To honor his discovery, the sampling frequency was named the Nyquist frequency.

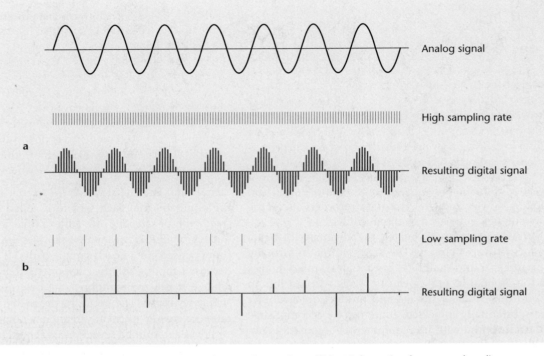

5-2 Sampling. (a) A signal sampled frequently enough contains sufficient information for proper decoding.
(b) Too low a sampling rate loses too much information for proper decoding.

of 44.1 kHz are used, such as 22.05 and 11.025. Multiples of 44.1 kHz (88.2 kHz and 176.4 kHz) and 48 kHz (96 kHz and 192 kHz) are used for greater increases in frequency response.

The international sampling rate—32 kHz—is used for broadcast digital audio. Because the maximum bandwidth in broadcast transmission is 15 kHz, the 32 kHz sampling rate is sufficient. For laser disc, compact disc, and digital tape recording, 44.056 kHz, 44.1 kHz, and 48 kHz, respectively, are used. Generally, standards for the *digital versatile disc (DVD)* are 48 kHz and 96 kHz. DVDs comprise several formats, however, some of which use higher sampling rates, as does the **Super Audio Compact Disc (SACD)** (see 5-3; see also "Digital Versatile Disc" later in this chapter).

Depending on the comparative sampling frequencies, there may or may not be a significant difference in frequency response. For example, 44.1 kHz and 48 kHz sound almost alike, as do 88.2 kHz and 96 kHz. But the difference between 48 kHz and 96 kHz is dramatic. Among other things, 44.1 kHz and 48 kHz do not have the transparent response of the higher sampling rates. *Transparent sound* has a wide and flat frequency response,

5-3 Selected sampling frequencies and their applications.

kHz	Applications
16	Used in some telephone applications and data reduction
18.9	CD-ROM/XA (extended architecture) and CD-interactive (CD-I) standard for low- to moderate-quality audio
32	Used in some broadcast systems and the R-DAT (digital audiocassette recorder) long-play mode
37.9	CD-ROM/XA and CD-I intermediate-quality audio using ADPCM (adaptive differential pulse-code modulation)
44.1	Widely used in many formats, including the CD
48	Used in several formats, including R-DAT and digital video recorders
88.2, 96, 176.4, and 192	Double and quadruple sampling rates standardized as options in the DVD-Audio format and used in some high-end equipment
2.8224	Used in the Super Audio Compact Disc (SACD) format

a sharp time response, clarity, detail, and very low noise and distortion.

Oversampling

The Nyquist theorem states that to be successfully digitally encoded, the highest frequency in a signal has to be sampled at a rate at least twice its highest frequency. The very best that most humans hear is around 20 kHz. That means a sampling frequency of 40 kHz should be adequate. So why is there a need for *oversampling* at frequencies far higher than 40 kHz?

The reason is that sampling at higher rates not only creates a wider frequency response but also spreads the noise of the analog-to-digital conversion process over a wide frequency range. The noise that is in the ultrasonic range is beyond human hearing. When the signal is converted from digital back to analog, the conversion process has to deal only with the noise in the audible frequency range.

Quantization

While sampling rate affects high frequency response, the number of bits taken per sample affects dynamic range, noise, and distortion. As samples of the waveform are taken, these voltages are converted into discrete quantities and assigned values, a process known as **quantization**. The assigned value is in the form of *bits,* from *bi*nary dig*its.* Most of us learned math using the decimal, or base 10, system, which consists of 10 numerals—0 through 9. The binary, or base 2, system uses two numbers—0 and 1. In converting the analog signal to digital, when the voltage is off, the assigned value is 0; when the voltage is on, the assigned value is 1.

A quantity expressed as a binary number is called a *digital word:* 10 is a two-bit word, 101 is a three-bit word, 10101 is a five-bit word, et cetera. Each *n*-bit binary word produces $2n$ discrete levels. Therefore a one-bit word produces two discrete levels—0,1; a two-bit word produces four discrete levels—00, 01, 10, and 11; a three-bit word produces eight discrete levels—000, 001, 010, 011, 100, 101, 110, and 111; and so on. So the more quantizing levels there are, the longer the digital word or **word length** must be. (Word length is also referred to as *bit depth* and *resolution.*)

The longer the digital word, the better the dynamic range. For example, the number of discrete voltage steps possible in an 8-bit word is 256; in a 16-bit word, it is 65,536; in a 20-bit word, it is 1,048,576; and in a 24-bit

word, it is 16,777,216. The greater the number of these quantizing levels, the more accurate the representation of the analog signal and the wider the dynamic range (see 5-4 and 5-5).[2]

This raises a question: how can a representation of the original signal be better than the original signal itself? Assume that the original analog signal is an ounce of water with an infinite number of values (molecules). The amount and the "character" of the water changes with the number of molecules; it has one "value" with 500 molecules, another with 501, still another with 2,975, and so forth. But all together the values are infinite. Moreover, changes in the original quantity of water are inevitable: some of it may evaporate, some may be lost if poured, and some may be contaminated or absorbed by dust or dirt.

But what if the water molecules are sampled and then converted to a stronger, more durable form? In so doing a representation of the water would be obtained in a facsimile from which nothing would be lost. But sufficient samples would have to be obtained to ensure that the character of the original water is maintained.

For example, suppose that the molecule samples were converted to ball bearings and a quantity of 1 million ball bearings was a sufficient sample. In this form the original water is not vulnerable to evaporation or contamination from dust or dirt. Even if a ball bearing is lost, they are all the same; therefore, losing one ball bearing does not affect the content or quality of the others.

Audio Data Rate

A higher sampling rate does not necessarily ensure better frequency response if the word length is short and vice versa. Uncompressed digital audio is expressed by two measurements, word length (or bit depth) and sampling frequency, such as 16-bit/44.1 kHz. The two numbers are used to compute the data rate of uncompressed audio.

Bit depth defines the digital word length used to represent a given sample and is equivalent to dynamic range. Larger bit depths theoretically yield greater dynamic range. The *sampling frequency* determines the audio

---

2. In quantizing the analog signal into discrete binary numbers (voltages), noise, known as *quantizing noise,* is generated. The signal-to-noise ratio (S/N) in an analog-to-digital conversion system is 6 dB for each bit. A 16-bit system is sufficient to deal with quantizing noise. This gives digital sound an S/N of 96 dB (6 dB × 16-bit system), which is pretty good by analog standards; but by digital standards, 20-bit systems are better at 120 dB, and 24-bit systems are dramatically better at 144 dB.

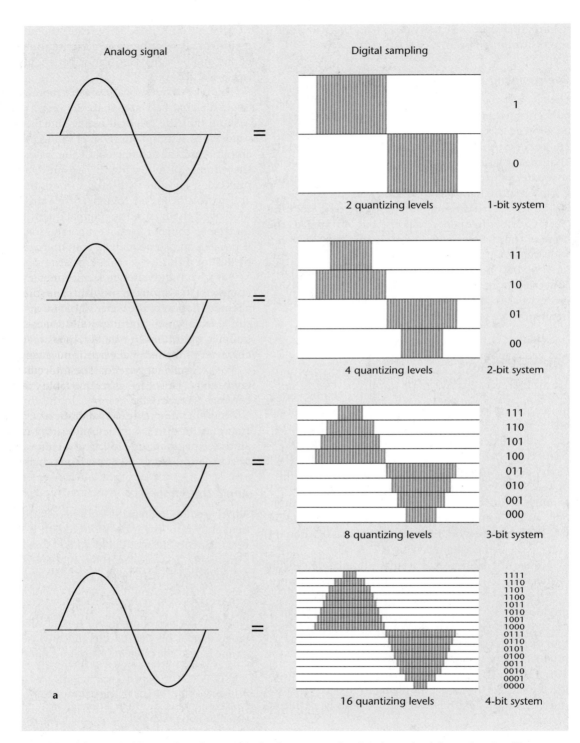

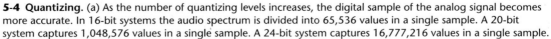

5-4 Quantizing. (a) As the number of quantizing levels increases, the digital sample of the analog signal becomes more accurate. In 16-bit systems the audio spectrum is divided into 65,536 values in a single sample. A 20-bit system captures 1,048,576 values in a single sample. A 24-bit system captures 16,777,216 values in a single sample.

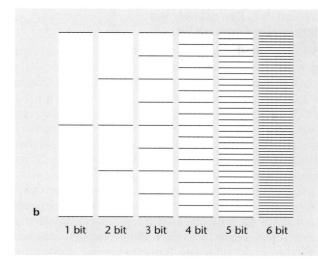

5-4 Quantizing. *(continued)* (b) The addition of a single bit doubles the data that a digital device can capture.

5-5 Quantizing resolutions and applications.

Bit Depth	Dynamic Range	Application
8	44 dB	Older PCs and multimedia applications yielding low-quality audio.
16	92 dB	Many professional recorders and multimedia PCs. The standard for CD and R-DAT. Widely used in consumer-grade media.
20	116 dB	High-quality professional audio and mastering.
24	140 dB	Very high-quality recording, including DVD-Audio.

bandwidth. Higher sampling frequencies theoretically yield wider audio bandwidth.

The relationship between sampling frequency and quantization is called the **audio data rate.** The formula for determining the audio data rate is *bit depth times sampling frequency.* For example, the data rate of 16-bit/44.1 kHz stereo audio would be computed as follows: $(16 \times 44{,}100 \div 1{,}024 \div 8) \times 2 = 172$ kilobytes per second (KB/s). Division by 1,024 converts from bits to kilobits. Division by 8 converts from kilobits to kilobytes. Multiplying by 2 gives the data rate for stereo audio.

TECHNOLOGIES AND FORMATS

A number of audio formats are on the market and, regardless of their popularity or lack thereof, they are all vulnerable to the coming of more-advanced technologies. This is not new in the world of research and development of course, but the rapidity with which formats are being developed and replaced raises concerns among producers, studio owners, and marketers alike that this morning's new technology could be obsolescent by afternoon and obsolete by evening. Not only does this create a potential cost-effectiveness problem but it becomes unwieldy to keep so many technologies operational for clients who may prefer one format over another.

Not long ago the era of digital recording began with the *open-reel stationary head recorder,* similar in appearance and operation to its analog cousin. These machines were

supplanted by the *rotary-head cassette digital audiotape recorder (R-DAT).* The rotary head, rather than stationary head, imprints a wider bandwidth on the tape, which makes it possible to encode digital-quality audio on a small format tape. The rotary-head design also led to the development of the *modular digital multitrack recorder (MDM),* which used videotape, and a *rotary-head open reel digital audiotape recorder.* These formats have given way to audio recording with removable-media and fixed disk–based systems.

The *digital cartridge disk record/playback system* and its analog predecessor had been mainstays for decades in on-air broadcast production. The digital cart system has been supplanted by computer-based systems that program *playlists* of music, spot announcements, bumpers, and other types of program materials and play them back using touchscreen technology for instant access.

For those using R-DATs, MDMs, the open-reel digital audiotape recorder and other tape-based recorders, and the digital cart system, see *www.cengage.com/rft/alten/ audioinmedia9e* for coverage of these recorder/players.

The digital versatile disc was heralded as the successor to the *compact disc (CD).* The DVD is far superior in data storage to the CD, yet a few of its formats, such as DVD-ROM and DVD-RAM, are not making inroads. The CD is still very much with us as a personal recording medium, but sales of music CDs are dramatically lower. This, of course, is due in large part to music downloading on the Internet. With its extraordinary sound quality, the Super Audio Compact Disc was acclaimed as *the* format for audiophiles. It has not been as successful as hoped because it is expensive and the number of recordings in the format are not extensive. It may not be around much longer. Now the high-density optical disc is being touted as the format of the future to replace all other disc formats. Who knows what format will be developed to replace the high-density optical disc if, indeed, it succeeds in supplanting the DVD. In the discussion that follows, be aware that the many formats available today may not be around tomorrow.

TAPELESS RECORDING SYSTEMS

Tapeless digital recording systems have supplanted tape-based units as the audio production tools of choice. They have many advantages over tape-based recording: all data are digital; recording, playback, editing, and signal processing are possible in a self-contained unit; information retrieval is nonlinear and virtually instantaneous; encoded data can be nondestructive; synchronization options are extensive; and storage capacity is considerably greater. Not to be overlooked are the significantly increased creative and technical possibilities these systems afford and the fact that they are widely available and cost-effective.

Removable-media and fixed disk–based systems can be divided into two groups: record/playback and distribution. *Record/playback systems* are used in production and postproduction. *Distribution systems* are what the final product is transferred to for release to the marketplace. Examples of distribution systems are the CD and the DVD, which can also be used for recording and playback during production. Because this book deals with the audio production process, only record/playback systems are addressed in this chapter.

REMOVABLE-MEDIA RECORDING SYSTEMS

Removable-media recording systems either in relatively widespread use professionally, or seeking to become so, include the compact disc, digital versatile disc, high-density optical disc, and memory card. The *mini disc™ (MD™)* is another removable recording medium. It was originally intended for the consumer market and became an inexpensive alternative to higher-priced disk-based systems, particularly in radio, broadcast journalism, and project studios. Due to the advent of more-robust removable-media systems with greater recording and editing flexibility and data storage capacity, however, mini disc recording is now seldom used. (See *www.cengage.com/rft/alten/audioinmedia9e* for coverage of the mini disc recording system.)

Recordable, Rewritable, and Interactive Compact Discs

The *recordable compact disc (CD-R)* has unlimited playback, but it can be recorded on only once. The CD-R conforms to the standards document known as *Orange Book*. According to this standard, data encoded on a CD-R does not have to be recorded all at once but can be added to whenever the user wishes, making it more convenient to produce sequential audio material. But CD-Rs conforming to the Orange Book standard will not play on any CD player.

To be playable on a standard CD player, the CD-R must conform to the *Red Book* standard, which requires that a table of contents (TOC) file be encoded onto the disc.[3] A TOC file includes information related to subcode and copy prohibition data, index numbering, and timing information. The TOC, which is written onto the disc after audio assembly, tells the CD player where each cut starts and ends. Once it is encoded, any audio added to the disc will not be playable on standard CD players due to the write-once limitation of CD-R. It is therefore important to know the "color book" standards with which a CD recorder is compatible. Details of these standards are beyond the scope of this book but are available on the Internet.

Compact-disc recorders are available in different recording speeds: for example, single- (1×), double- (2×), quad- (4×)—up to 16× speed. Single-speed machines record in real time; that is, at the CD's playback speed, 2× machines record at twice the playback speed, reducing by half the time it takes to create a CD, and so on. For the higher recording speeds, the computer and the hard drive must be fast enough.

Playing times vary with the CD format. CDs for *consumer format* use a 63-minute blank disc. Disc length for

---

3. In addition to the Orange and Red Book standards, there are Yellow, Green, White, Blue, and Scarlet Book standards. The *Yellow Book* format describes the basic specifications for computer-based CD-ROM (compact disc–read-only memory). The *Green Book* format describes the basic specifications for CD-I (compact disc–interactive) and CD-ROM XA (the *XA* is short for extended *a*rchitecture). It is aimed at multimedia applications that combine audio, graphic images, animation, and full-motion video. The *White Book* describes basic specifications for full-motion, compressed videodiscs. The *Blue Book* provides specifications for the HDCD (high-definition compact disc) format, such as Digital Versatile Disc–Audio (DVD-A). The *Scarlet Book* includes the protocol for the SACD.

the *professional format* is 63 minutes (550 megabyte [MB]), 74 minutes (650 MB), or 80 minutes (700 MB).

The **rewritable CD (CD-RW)** is a considerable improvement over the CD-R because it can be recorded on, erased, and used many times again for other recordings. If the driver program supports it, erase can even be random.

Like the CD recorders, CD-RW drives operate at different speeds to shorten recording time.

After the Orange Book, any user with a CD recorder drive can create a CD from a computer. CD-RW drives can write both CD-R and CD-RW discs and can read any type of CD.

CDVU+ (pronounced "CD view plus") is a compact disc with interactive content. It was created by the Walt Disney Company to reverse the decline in music CD sales. In addition to the music, it includes multimedia material such as band photos, interviews, and articles relevant to the band or the music or both.

Digital Versatile Disc

When the DVD first appeared on the scene in 1996, it was known as the "digital videodisc." With its potential for expandability and the relatively quick realization of that potential, it was redubbed **digital versatile disc (DVD)**. And versatile it is. It has all but replaced the CD-ROM as a common storage medium and has begun to supplant other disc formats, including the CD. One indication of its versatility is the alphabet soup of DVD formats. It may therefore provide a clearer perspective of the medium to include a few of DVD's distribution formats before discussing the production formats.

The DVD is the same diameter and thickness as the compact disc, but it can encode a much greater amount of data. The storage capacity of the current CD is 650 MB, or about 74 minutes of stereo audio. The storage capacity of the DVD can be on a number of levels, each one far exceeding that of the CD. For example, the single-side, single-layer DVD has a capacity of 4.7 billion bytes, equivalent to the capacity of seven CD-ROMs; the double-side, dual-layer DVD with 17 billion bytes is equivalent to the capacity of 26 CD-ROMs.

The CD has a fixed bit depth of 16 bits and a sampling rate of 44.1 kHz. DVD formats can accommodate various bit depths and sampling rates. The CD is a two-channel format and can encode 5.1 (six channels) surround-sound but only with data reduction (see "DVD-Audio").

Currently, the DVD formats are DVD-Video (DVD-V), DVD-Audio (DVD-A), DVD-Recordable (DVD-R) author-ing and general, DVD-Rewritable (DVD-RW), and another rewritable format, DVD+RW. (Two other formats, DVD-ROM and DVD-RAM, have not made their anticipated inroads in the marketplace and therefore are not covered here.) Of these formats, of interest for our purposes are DVD-Audio and the recordable and rewritable formats (see 5-6).

DVD-Audio

DVD-Audio (DVD-A) is a distribution medium with extremely high-quality audio. To get a better idea of DVD-A, we can compare it with *DVD-Video (DVD-V)*, the first DVD format marketed. DVD-V is a high-quality motion picture/sound delivery system. The audio portion can have up to eight audio tracks. They can be one to eight channels of linear digital audio; one to six channels of Dolby Digital 5.1 surround sound; or one to eight channels (5.1 or 7.1 surround) of MPEG-2 audio.[4] There are provisions for *Digital Theater System (DTS)* and *Sony Dynamic Digital Sound (SDDS)* as well.

Sampling rates can be 44.1, 48, or 96 kHz, with a bit depth of 16, 20, or 24 bits. Although these digital specifications yield high-quality audio, the transfer bit rate for audio is limited to 6.144 *megabits per second (Mbps)*. This means that there is room for only two audio channels at a sampling rate of 96 kHz and a bit depth of 24 bits (abbreviated 96/24). The best multichannel audio would be 48/20.

The DVD-A can hold 9.6 Mbps. This provides six channels of 96/24 audio. To accomplish the increased storage room, *Meridian Lossless Packing (MLP)* data compression is used. It gives a compression ratio of about 1.85 to 1. (**Lossless compression** means that no data is discarded during the compression process; during **lossy compression** data that is not critical is discarded.)

DVD-A is also flexible. It is possible to choose the number of channels—one to six; the bit depth—16, 20, or 24; and the sampling frequency—44.1, 48, 88.2, 96, 176.4, or 192 kHz (see 5-7).

Another advantage of DVD-A is that it is *extensible*, meaning it is relatively open-ended and can utilize any

---

4. MPEG-2 is a compression protocol. This and other compression schemes are explained in Chapter 19. In general, data compression represents an information source using the fewest number of bits. Audio compression reduces the size of audio files using algorithms referred to as codecs. *Codec* is a contraction of the words *coder-dec*oder or *compression-dec*ompression algorithm.

5-6 Popular DVD formats, features, and disc capabilities.

DVD Formats	Features	Disc Capacity/Notes
DVD-Video (DVD-V)	High-quality picture and audio Movie titles, live video, education video	Single-sided 4.7 gigabyte (GB)/8.5 GB Double-sided 9.4 GB/17 GB
DVD-Audio (DVD-A)	High-quality audio Music titles	Playback-only medium Distribution
DVD-Recordable (DVD-R) Authoring	DVD authoring (content check)	Single-sided 4.7 GB Write-once, read many
DVD-Recordable (DVD-R) General	Streaming onetime write archiving	Single-sided 4.7 GB Copy protection included on disc
DVD-Rewritable (DVD-RW)	AV-oriented Consumer recorder—sequential	Single-sided 4.7 GB Rerecordable disc No defect management Maximum 1,000 times—sequential read, write
DVD-Rewritable (DVD+RW)	Sequential, random recording CLV, CAV recording	Single-sided 4.7 GB Double-sided 9.4 GB Defect management handled by drive Rewrite 32 KB data block Maximum 1,000 rerecordable cycles

From Mark Waldrep, "The A to Z's of DVD," *Videography*, August 2001, p. 64.

5-7 DVD-Audio playback times.

Audio Contents Combination	Channel Combination	Playback Time per Disc Side			
		4.7-inch Disc		3.1-inch Disc	
		Single-layer	Dual-layer	Single-layer	Dual-layer
2-channel only	48K/24-bit/2 channel	258 minutes	469 minutes	80 minutes	146 minutes
2-channel only	192K/24-bit/2 channel	64 minutes	117 minutes	20 minutes	36 minutes
2-channel only	96K/24-bit/2 channel	125 minutes	227 minutes	39 minutes	70 minutes
Multichannel only	96K/24-bit/6 channel	86 minutes	156 minutes	27 minutes	48 minutes
2-channel and multichannel	96K/24-bit/2 channel + 96K/24-bit/3 channel and 48K/24-bit/2 channel	76 minutes each	135 minutes each	23 minutes each	41 minutes each

From Philip DeLancie, "Music Meets Multimedia," *Mix*, December 2000, p. 40.

future audio coding technology. DVD-A's recording time is 74 minutes, but it can hold up to seven hours of audio on two channels with lesser sound quality. DVD-A can also encode text, graphics, and still pictures. It should be noted that DVD-A discs are not compatible with CD players, and some DVD-A discs will not play in some current DVD players because DVD-A was specified well after DVD-V.

Recordable DVDs

The recordable DVD (DVD-R) is the high-density equivalent of the CD-R. It is a write-once format that can store 3.95 *gigabytes (GB)* on a single-sided disc and 7.9 GB on a double-sided disc. It takes about 50 minutes to record a single-sided DVD-R. It provides both DVD flexibility and program quality.

Two formats are used to record DVDs. They are designated DVD+R and DVD-R. Both formats record, but they write their data in different ways, so they are incompatible; a DVD+R recording will not play on a DVD-R machine and vice versa. This problem has been overcome with DVD recorders that handle both formats and are designated DVD±R.

There are two categories of DVD-R: general and authoring. The general format was developed for business and consumer applications, such as data archiving and onetime recording. Authoring was designed to meet the needs of professional content developers and software producers. Both general and authoring media can be read by all DVD drives, but technical differences make it impossible to write to DVD-R authoring media using the general DVD-R media system.

DVD Authoring   Although the complexities of DVD authoring and its required software are beyond the scope of this book, it may be useful to say a few things about this important aspect of DVD production. *DVD authoring* is that phase of DVD production when the user decides what goes onto the DVD, then applies the appropriate software to implement the process and burns the DVD.

Implementation involves three basic stages: transcoding, authoring, and burning. In *transcoding* (also called *encoding*), media files are converted from their original format to MPEG-2, the lossy compression format required for DVD. What goes onto the DVD is handled with authoring software. Content includes the principal video/audio program materials and other information, such as the number of chapter, or index, points the disc will have to enable random selection of sections on the disc; subtitles; and text. After configuring the structure of the DVD and previewing the content, the user burns the data to the DVD itself, usually using one of the rewritable formats as opposed to the recordable DVD format.

Although no two authoring projects are alike, the process usually requires a considerable amount of computer disk space and is quite time-consuming. Transcoding, authoring, and burning can take as much as five times the length of the actual playing time of the DVD.[5]

Rewritable DVDs

There are three basic types of rewritable DVD: DVD-RW, DVD+RW, and MVI.

---

5. From Dennis Miller with Chris Armbrust, "The Inside Track," *Electronic Musician,* May 2003, p. 42.

DVD-RW   DVD-RW is the rewritable version of DVD-R. Two differences between DVD-RW and CD-RW are the way they are written and their storage capacity. DVD-RW employs *phase-change technology,* which means that the phase of the laser light's wavefront is being modulated to write to the medium. In the erase mode, the material (a photopolymer medium) is transferred back into its original crystalline state, allowing data to be written to the disc again and again. The other way to write to DVD is the *organic-dye process,* a nonreversible method. In essence, rewritable discs using this process are write-once media. DVD-RW has a capacity of 4.7 GB and is compatible with DVD-R and DVD-ROM players. A primary application for DVD-RW is authoring media for content development of DVD-ROM and DVD-V.

DVD+RW   DVD+RW is an erasable format using phase-change technology that has been developed to compete with DVD-RAM. Data capacity for a single-sided disc is 4.7 GB; for a double-sided disc it is 9.4 GB. DVD+RW drives can write CD-Rs and CD-RWs and read CDs, DVD-ROMs, DVD-Rs, and DVD-RWs.

MVI   *MVI (Music Video Interactive)* is a DVD-based format being marketed by Warner Music Group. It encodes three zones of content audio (full music album), video (interviews, behind-the-scenes footage), and interactive (applications that allow modification and manipulation of the disc's content). MVI is available in multiple formats including MP3 for copying to portable players and a high-definition version. The video is compatible with DVD-Video players, but incompatible with CD players.

High-density Optical Disc Formats

High-density optical disc technology is another entrant into the competition to meet the demands of high-definition (HD) media. The most familiar format at this writing is the Blu-ray Disc. Another high-density optical disc format, HD DVD, was developed to compete with the Blu-ray Disc but lost out and is no longer marketed.

Blu-ray Disc

The *Blu-ray Disc (BD)* format was developed to enable recording, playback, and rewriting of *high-definition television (HDTV).* It produces not only superior picture quality but superior audio quality as well. The name derives from the blue-violet laser used to read and write data.

Single-sided, single-layer 4.7-inch discs have a recording capacity of 25 GB; dual-layer discs can hold 50 GB.

5-8 Differences between Blu-ray Disc and DVD.

Parameters	BD	BD	DVD	DVD
Recording capacity	25 GB	50 GB	4.7 GB	9.4 GB
Number of layers	Single-layer	Dual-layer	Single-layer	Dual-layer
Data transfer rate	36 Mbps	36 Mbps	11.08 Mbps	11.08 Mbps
Compression protocol	MPEG-2* MPEG-4* AVC* VC-1*	MPEG-2 MPEG-4 AVC VC-1	MPEG-2	MPEG-2

*MPEG-2 is the compression standard for broadcast-quality video and audio. MPEG-4 also supports high-quality video and audio and 3D content. *Advanced Video Coding (AVC)* is part of the MPEG-4 protocols. It is the compression standard for high-definition video and audio and achieves very high data compression. *VC-1* is a specification standardized by the Society of Motion Picture and Television Engineers (SMPTE) and implemented by Microsoft as Windows Media Video 9. It relates specifically to the decoding of compressed content.

Double-sided 4.7-inch discs, single-layer and dual-layer, have a capacity of 50 GB and 100 GB, respectively. The recording capacity of single-sided 3.1-inch discs is 7.8 MB for single-layer and 15.6 GB for dual-layer. The double-sided, single-layer 3.1-inch disc holds 15.6 MB of data; the dual-layer disc holds 31.2 GB. These recording capacities are far greater than those of DVDs (see 5-8).

The 25 GB disc can record more than two hours of HDTV and about 13 hours of *standard television (STV).* About nine hours of HDTV can be stored on a 50 GB disc and about 23 hours of STV. Write times vary with drive speed and disc format (see 5-9).

Blu-ray supports most audio compression schemes. They include, as mandatory, lossless pulse code modulation (PCM), Meridian Lossless Packing (MLP), and TRUE HD two-channel; as optional, it supports DTS HD. The mandatory lossy compression protocols are Dolby Digital, Dolby Digital Plus (developed especially for HDTV and Blu-ray), DTS, and MPEG audio.

Other Blu-ray formats now available or in development are the Mini Blu-ray Disc that can store about 7.5 GB of data; BD-ROM, a read-only format developed for prerecorded content; the BD5 and BD9 discs with lower storage capacities, 4,482 MB and 8,152 MB, respectively; the Blu-ray recordable (BD-R) and rewritable (BD-RW) discs for PC data storage; BD-RE, a rewritable format for HDTV recording; and the Blu-ray Live (BD Live) disc, which addresses Internet recording and interactivity.

Given Blu-ray's overall superiority to DVDs in data storage and quality, it has been slow in gaining acceptance. Four reasons why are because the players and discs are more expensive than those for the DVD; users do not perceive the qualitative differences as being sufficiently superior to DVD to justify the higher cost; the DVD is well

5-9 Drive speed, data rate, and write times (in minutes) for Blu-ray Discs.

Drive Speed	Data Rate Mbps	Data Rate MB/s	Single-layer	Dual-layer
1×	36	4.5	90	180
2×	72	9	45	90
4×	144	18	23	45
6×	216	27	15	30
8×	288	36	12	23
12×	432	54	8	15

established and heavily invested; and, for the consumer, the number of titles in the format is limited.

Other Optical Disc Formats

As if there were not enough formats out there, here are a few more that are either already available or in development.

Digital Multilayer Disc (DMD) This disc is the successor to the fluorescent multilayer disc. Currently, it can store 22 to 32 GB of data, with the potential for 100 GB of storage space.

Ultra Density Optical Disc (UDO) This disc, in two versions, can store up to 60 GB and 120 GB, respectively.

Holographic Versatile Disc (HVD) This format uses two lasers in a single beam and can hold up to 3.9 *terabytes (TB)* of information. (One TB is equal to 1 trillion bytes, or 1,000 gigabytes; 1 gigabyte is equal to 1 billion bytes.)

Protein-coated Disc (PCD) This disc uses a theoretical optical disc technology and is still in development. Potentially, it would greatly increase the storage capacity of the holographic versatile disc. The process involves coating a normal DVD with a light-sensitive protein, which would give the disc up to a 50 TB capacity.

EVD and FVD Still two other disc formats are the enhanced versatile disc (EVD) and the forward versatile disc (FVD). The EVD was developed in China to compete with DVD-Video and reproduce HDTV-quality image and sound. The FVD was developed in Taiwan and is a less expensive alternative for high-definition content. Depending on its number of layers, it can encode from 5.4 to 15 GB of data.

Memory Recorders

A *memory recorder* is a portable digital recorder that has no moving parts and therefore requires no maintenance. The storage medium is a *memory card*, a nonvolatile memory that can be electrically recorded onto, erased,

and reprogrammed. *Nonvolatile* means that the card does not need power to maintain the stored information.

Memory cards have taken portability in digital recording to a new level. They are quite small, easily fitting into the palm of a hand. They hold a substantial quantity of data for their size and have fast read access times. They are a robust recording medium, as are the recorders, which makes the technology highly suitable for production on-location.

Examples of memory cards include flash cards such as CompactFlash, flash memory sticks (a family of formats so named because the original cards were about the size and the thickness of a stick of chewing gum), Secure Digital (SD) memory cards, and SmartMedia. The PC-MCIA card (named for the Personal Computer Memory Card International Association) is yet another recording medium used in memory recorders. Depending on the recorder, the flash card may be removable or fixed.

Several models of memory recorders are available. Depending on the design, the storage medium, recording configurations, recording times, bit depths, and sampling frequencies vary. Three examples of memory recorders and their features are displayed in the accompanying three figures (see 5-10 to 5-12).

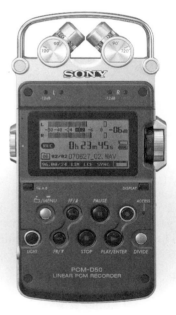

5-10 Sony PCM-D50. Among this model's features are a 4 GB flash memory, PCM stereo and WAV recording format, 96/24 sampling rate and bit depth, USB port, and two built-in electret capacitor microphones with two stereo coverage positions—X-Y and wide-angle (see Chapter 17). The recorder weighs 13 ounces.

5-11 Nagra ARES-MII. This model, shown with a stereo microphone (two cardioid elements), also comes with an omnidirectional (monaural) clip-on mic and has an external microphone connection. Its flash memory, which is nonremovable, can encode up to 2 GB of data using either the PCM or MPEG compression recording methods. Recording capacity is 2 hours 52 minutes in stereo, 69 hours 26 minutes in mono, and up to 144 hours using compression. Other features include voice-activated recording; internal loudspeaker; internal, graphic, non-destructive editor (the original material remains unchanged); 8 to 48 kHz sampling rates; 64 to 384 KB/s bit rates; low-pass filter; USB port; and more than 10 hours of operation on two AA batteries. It is easily handheld and weighs approximately 7 ounces.

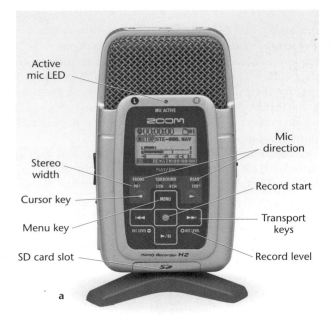

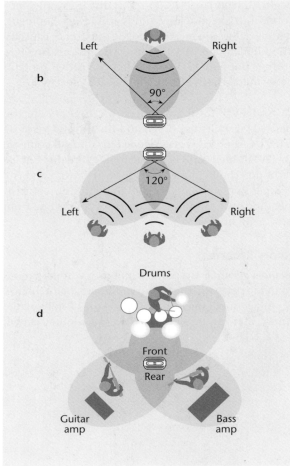

5-12 Zoom H2. (a) This model includes four cardioid microphone capsules, which allow (b) front 90-degree, (c) rear 120-degree, and (d) 360-degree pickup. The 360-degree pickup facilitates conversion of a recording to 5.1 surround sound. It comes with a 512 MB Secure Digital card but can accommodate up to a 16 GB card, allowing for as much as 24 hours of recording time using the 16-bit/44.1 kHz WAV format. The data formats include WAV (44.1 kHz, 48 kHz, and 96 kHz at 16- or 24-bit), MP3 to 320 Kbps, and variable bit rate (bit rate is not constant). Other features include a metronome, a guitar/bass tuner, a low-pass filter, voice-activated recording, and a USB interface. It weighs 4 ounces.

Hard-disk Recorders

Digital recorders also use fixed and removable hard disks. Compared with memory recorders, they usually provide better sound quality and greater recording flexibility (see 5-13, 5-14, and 5-15). They are available in portable and rack-mountable models.

Storage Capacity

The amount of data that memory and hard-disk recorders can encode is impressive given their size. But all technology has its limitations. When using these recorders, especially in the field, it is essential to know their storage capacities in advance so that you do not get caught shorthanded (see 5-16).

DIGITAL AUDIO WORKSTATIONS

Like many digital audio recorders, a *digital audio workstation (DAW)* records, edits, and plays back. But unlike digital audio recorders, DAWs have considerably greater processing power because of the software programs they use. Generally, there are two types of DAW systems: computer-based and integrated.

Computer-based Digital Audio Workstation

A computer-based DAW is a stand-alone unit with all processing handled by the computer. A software program facilitates recording and editing (see Chapter 20). Most programs also provide some degree of digital signal processing (DSP), or additional DSP may be available as

5-13 Nagra VI. This model is the successor to the Nagra-D and DII multitrack digital recorders. It has six channels, four microphone and two line; a 120 GB internal hard disk and a removable flash card; approximately 20 minutes of six-track 48 kHz 24-bit recording per gigabyte of available disk/card space; sampling rates of 44.1 kHz, 48 kHz, 88.2 kHz, and 96 kHz; 16- and 24-bit Broadcast Wave File (BWF) and is iXML compatible for metadata; channel mixing of the four mic inputs to channels 5 and 6; and noise suppression. The recorder weighs 8.3 pounds with the rechargeable lithium-ion battery pack.

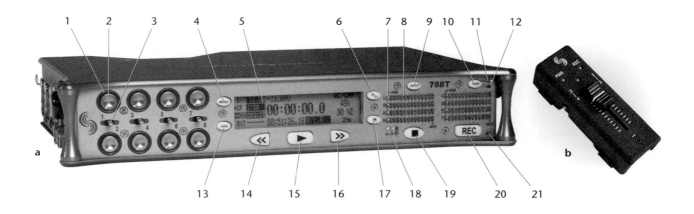

1. **Input activity ring LEDs** (indicates input activity for each input)

2. **Input gain control** (controls analog and digital input gain)

3. **Input selector/solo switch** (pushed left selects odd-numbered inputs; pushed right selects even-numbered inputs)

4. **Menu key**

5. **LCD display**

6. **Tone key** (activates tone oscillator)

7. **Track arm LEDs** (indicates that the respective track is armed to record)

8. **Level meter LEDs** (indicates level in dBFS)

9. **Input key** (accesses track setup menu)

10. **Power key**

11. **Power/charge LED**

12. **Headphone output peak LED** (indicates overload of headphone amp)

13. **HDD key** (enters the take list and the drive directory)

14. **Rewind key**

15. **Play key**

16. **Fast-forward key**

17. **LCD backlight key**

18. **Media activity key LEDs** (indicates storage media activity)

19. **Stop/pause key**

20. **Record key**

21. **Record LED**

5-14 Sound Devices 788T and its control features. (a) This model is about the size of a small paperback book and weighs about 3.6 pounds without the battery. It includes eight mic/line inputs, a selectable sampling rate up to 98 kHz with selectable sampling rate converters on each digital input, peak/VU meters, a word clock, time code, and internal hard drive and a flash slot, FireWire and USB connections, and a separate USB keyboard input for control. (b) Remote fader controller includes two 2-position toggle switches; programmable to control *record, start/stop,* and other functions; and LEDs to indicate record and power status. It can be mounted to a boom pole.

5-15 Deva 16. This model is a 16-track hard-disk recorder for film and television production. It uses a built-in hard disk, DVD-RAM, or flash media. Resolution is 16 or 24 bit with sampling rates from 44.1 to 192 kHz. Among its features are a built-in slate microphone (see Chapter 4); time code reader and generator; all working frame rates; EQ, high-pass, and notch filters; delay, compressor, and expander; FireWire port; and color touchscreen. The unit weighs 7.4 pounds.

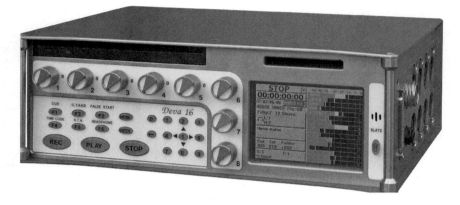

5-16 Required storage capacity for a one-hour recording.

Number of Tracks	Bit Depth	Sampling Rate	Storage Needed
2	16	44.1 kHz	606 MB
2	24	44.1 kHz	909 MB
2	24	96 kHz	1.9 GB
8	16	44.1 kHz	2.4 GB
8	24	44.1 kHz	3.6 GB
8	24	96 kHz	7.7 GB
16	16	44.1 kHz	4.8 GB
16	24	44.1 kHz	7.1 GB
16	24	96 kHz	15.4 GB
24	16	44.1 kHz	7.1 GB
24	24	44.1 kHz	10.7 GB
24	24	96 kHz	23.3 GB

an add-on so long as the computer has sufficient storage capacity.

For recording, typical computer-based DAWs support either two-track or multitrack production and include a virtual mixer and record transport controls (*play, record, rewind,* and so on). The relationships of channels to inputs, outputs, and tracks are not directly linked. Once the computer-based audio data is recorded and stored, it can be assigned to any output(s) and moved in time.

For example, a DAW may have four inputs, eight outputs, 16 channels, and 256 virtual tracks. This means that up to four inputs can be used to record up to four channels at one time; up to eight channels at one time can be used for internal mixing or routing; up to 16 channels (real tracks) are simultaneously available during playback; and up to 256 separate *soundfiles*[6] can be maintained and assigned to a virtual track.

Virtual tracks provide all the functionality of an actual track but cannot be played back simultaneously. For example, in a 16-channel system with 256 virtual tracks, only 16 tracks can play back at once. Think of 16 stacks of index cards totaling 256 cards. Assume that each stack is a channel. A card can be moved from anywhere in a stack to the top of the same stack or to the top of another stack. There are 256 cards, but only 16 of them can be on top at the same time. In other words, any virtual track can be assigned to any channel and slipped along that channel or across channels.

It is difficult to discuss recording operations generically because terms, configurations, and visual displays differ from system to system. Layout and control functions, however, are similar to those in recording consoles (see Chapter 4). Depending on the DAW, a system may have more or fewer signal-processing capabilities in its recording software.

Sound Card

A computer must have a **sound card** to input, manipulate, and output audio. It either comes with the computer or must be purchased separately and installed. In either case, it is important to make sure that the card is compatible with the computer's platform—PC, Macintosh, or other proprietary system. Also, because the sound card interfaces with other audio equipment, it is necessary to know your input/output requirements, such as the types of balanced or unbalanced connectors and the number

---

6. Audio that is encoded onto the disk takes the form of a *soundfile*. The soundfile contains information about the sound such as amplitude and duration. When the soundfile is opened, most systems display that information.

of recording channels the card has to handle. Signal-to-noise ratio is another consideration. A sound card capable of –70 dB and below is necessary for producing professional-quality audio.

Integrated Digital Audio Workstation

An *integrated DAW* not only consists of the computer and its related software but may also include a console; a control surface—either universal or one specially designed for use with a particular software program; a *server* for integration with and networking to a collection of devices, such as other audio, video, and MIDI sources within or among facilities in the same or different locations; and a *storage area network* for transfer and storage of data between computer systems and other storage elements, such as disk controllers and servers. A DAW's systemwide communication with other external devices, and communication between devices in general, is facilitated through the distribution of digital interfaces. Those in common use are *AES/EBU, S/PDIF, SCSI, iSCSI, MADI,* and *FireWire* (see 5-17).

Although a server and a storage area network greatly facilitate operations in broadcast and production facilities, their programming and management are the provinces of computer and other technical personnel. Therefore the following two sections address their functions only briefly.

Server

A *server* is a computer dedicated to providing one or more services over a computer network, typically through a request-response routine. These services are furnished by specialized server applications, which are computer programs designed to handle multiple concurrent requests.[7]

In relation to a broadcast or audio production facility, a server's large-capacity disk arrays record, store, and play back hours of entire programs, program segments, news clips, music recordings, and CD and DVD sound effects and music libraries—in other words just about any recordable program material. A server can run a number of programs simultaneously. For example, a director can access a sound bite for an on-air newscast while a producer in another studio accesses an interview for a documentary still in production and an editor in still another studio accesses music and sound-effect cues for a commercial.

---

7. *Source:* Wikipedia.

5-17 Digital interfaces.

AES/EBU is a professional digital audio connection interface standard specified jointly by the Audio Engineering Society (AES) and the European Broadcast Union (EBU). Its standard calls for two audio channels to be encoded in a serial data stream and transmitted through a balanced line using XLR connectors.

S/PDIF (Sony/Philips Digital Interface) is the consumer version of the AES/EBU standard. It calls for an unbalanced line using phono connectors. S/PDIF is implemented on consumer audio equipment such as CD players.

SCSI (Small Computer Systems Interface) is the standard for hardware and software command language. Pronounced "scuzzy," it allows two-way communication between, primarily, hard-disk and CD-ROM drives to exchange digital data at fast speeds. SCSI can also be used with other components, such as scanners.

iSCSI (Internet SCSI) is a standard based on the Internet Protocol (IP) for linking data storage devices over a network and transferring data by carrying SCSI commands over IP networks.

MADI (Multichannel Audio Digital Interface) is the standard used when interfacing multichannel digital audio. It allows up to 56 channels of digital audio to be sent down one coaxial cable.

FireWire is a low-cost networking scheme that is a more formidable cable interface than SCSI. Powering is flexible, modes are asynchronous/isosynchronous within the same network, and compatibility is backward and forward with continuous transmission in either direction. Because it can interface with just about anything electronic, with fewer problems of compatibility than with other interfaces, in the appropriate applications FireWire has become the interface of choice.

Storage Area Network

A *storage area network (SAN)* can be likened to the common flow of data in a personal computer that is shared by different kinds of storage devices, such as a hard disk, a CD or DVD player, or both. It is designed to serve a large network of users and handle sizeable data transfers among different interconnected data storage devices. The computer storage devices are attached to servers and remotely controlled.

DIGITAL AUDIO NETWORKING

Through telephone lines a recording can be produced in real time between studios across town or across the country with little or no loss of audio quality and at a

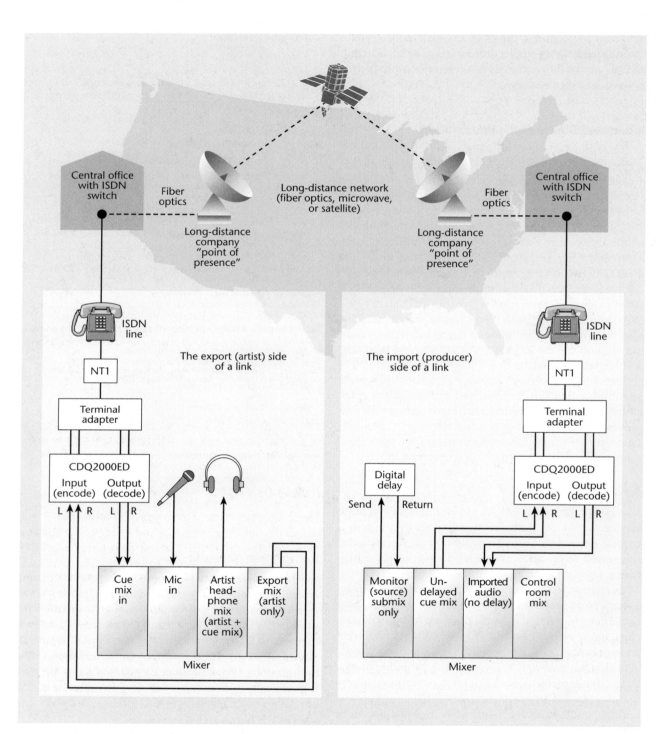

5-18 Long-distance recording. In this illustration NT1 is a network terminator that protects the network from electrical malfunctions. CDQ2000ED code enables you to send a cue mix to an artist in another location, delay the mix sent to your monitors, not delay the received artist's solo signal, mix the two, give direction, and make production judgments in real time.

relatively low cost. Computer technology has also facilitated long-distance audio production via the Internet. This aspect of digital audio networking—online collaborative recording—is discussed in Chapter 19.

Integrated Services Digital Network (ISDN) is a public telephone service that allows inexpensive use of a flexible, wide-area, all-digital network (see 5-18 and 5-19). With ISDN it is possible to have a vocalist in New York, wearing headphones for the foldback feed, singing into a microphone whose signal is routed to a studio in Los Angeles. In L.A. the singer's audio is fed through a console, along with the accompaniment from, say, the San Francisco studio, and recorded. When necessary, the singer in New York, the accompanying musicians in San Francisco, and the recordist in L.A. can communicate with one another through a talkback system. Commercials are being done with the announcer in a studio in one city and the recordist adding the effects in another city. And unlike much of today's advanced technology, ISDN is a relatively uncomplicated service to use.

Until now ISDN recording while locked to picture has been difficult because, of course, standard ISDN lines do not carry images; therefore, while recording audio remotely, the talent is unable to see the picture. A technique has been developed that overcomes this problem, however.[8]

DIGITAL AUDIO ON DIGITAL VIDEOTAPE

Digital recording of video, like audio, has moved toward disk; but unlike audiotape, digital videotape is still employed. There are several systems in use. The major differences among them have more to do with the way they process video than with their audio processing. There are also differences in compatibility among systems, tape width, and recording time.

Sound in *digital videotape recorders (DVTRs)* is digital quality. The differences in audio among the various systems come down to bit rate and number of audio channels.

Due to the number of DVTR systems available and the fact that their principal advantages and disadvantages have more to do with video than audio, a discussion of these systems is better left to the television production

---

8. For the particulars of this technique, which are beyond the scope of this book, see Ron DiCesare, "Audio Know-how," *Post Magazine,* March 2008, p. 28.

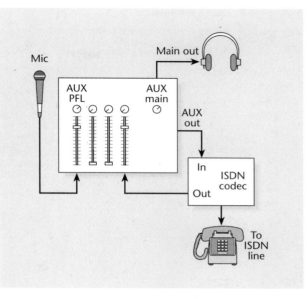

5-19 Simplified setup for long-distance recording. A codec is a device that encodes a signal at one end of a transmission and decodes it at the other end.

From Jeffrey P. Fisher and Harlan Hogan, *The Voice Actor's Guide to Home Recording* (Boston: Thomson Course Technology, 2005), p. 73.

books. Figure 5-20, however, gives a brief summation of the similarities and the differences among the audio formats of today's more common digital videotapes.

AUDIO ON FILM

There are three basic types of film—silent, sound, and magnetic—and they come in two gauges: 35 *millimeter (mm)* and 16 mm, which is rarely used today (see 5-21). ***Silent film*** carries no sound information; it consists of the picture area and two columns of sprocket holes, one on each edge of the film. It is used during shooting when picture and sound are recorded separately—picture with a camera, and sound with an audio recorder (see "Synchronizing Sound and Picture in Film" in Chapter 6). ***Sound film*** carries both picture and optical sound. The optical process is used for release prints and is done photographically in a laboratory. In 16 mm optical film, the optical audio track replaces the sprocket holes on one edge of the film.

Magnetic film is similar to audiotape in that it contains all sound and no picture, and it has similar magnetic characteristics, but it is the same size as regular film stock

5-20 Digital videotape formats.

Type	Number of Digital Audio Channels	Maximum Tape Time	Sound Channel Coding
DV (digital video), also known as MiniDV	2	60/80 minutes	16-bit at 48 kHz
	4		12-bit at 32 kHz
DVCAM	4	Mini-cassette: 40 minutes	16-bit at 48 kHz
		Standard cassette: 184 minutes	12-bit at 48 kHz
DVCPRO (D-7)	2	Small and medium cassettes: 66 minutes	16-bit at 48 kHz
		Large cassette: 126 minutes	
DVCPRO50	4	92 minutes	16-bit at 48 kHz
DVCPRO HD (high-definition) (D-12)	8	46 minutes	16-bit at 48 kHz
Digital8	2	60 minutes	16-bit at 48 kHz
Digital-S (D-9)	4	124 minutes	16-bit at 48 kHz
HDCAM (D-11)	4	124 minutes	20-bit at 48 kHz

and contains sprocket holes. Magnetic film is available either full coat or stripe coat, and it records analog sound.

With ***full coat*** the oxide coating covers most or all of the film width (see 5-22). The 16 mm variety is usually full width for single-track monaural audio; 35 mm full coat has 3, 4, or 6 magnetic stripes, with clear base between, for 3-, 4-, or 6-channel recording.

In 35 mm ***stripe coat***, there are two stripes of oxide: a wide stripe for recording single-track mono and a narrow balance stripe to ensure that the film wind on reels is smooth. In 16 mm the oxide stripe coat is either down the edge of the film (*edge track*) or down the center of the film (*center track*).

Sound quality—dynamic range, signal-to-noise ratio, and frequency response—in 16 mm magnetic film is mediocre. In fact, 16 mm gave way first to analog videotape because of its better picture and sound quality and lower cost, which then gave way to digital videotape because of its even better picture and sound quality. Now digital videotape is giving way to disk recording, which provides still better picture and sound quality than digital videotape. With such enhancements as Dolby processing, digital audio, and surround sound, plus considerably improved theater loudspeaker systems, 35 mm audio quality is quite excellent (see 5-23).

5-21 16 mm film stock formats.

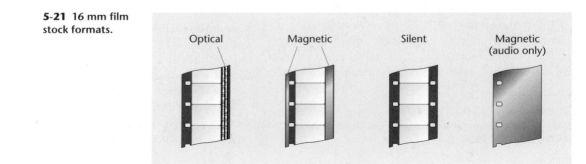

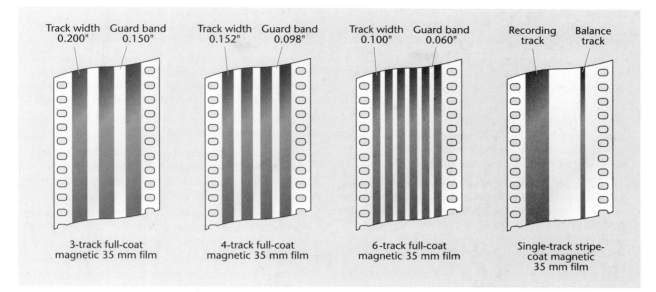

Track width 0.200" Guard band 0.150"

Track width 0.152" Guard band 0.098"

Track width 0.100" Guard band 0.060"

Recording track Balance track

3-track full-coat magnetic 35 mm film

4-track full-coat magnetic 35 mm film

6-track full-coat magnetic 35 mm film

Single-track stripe-coat magnetic 35 mm film

5-22 Types of 35 mm magnetic film.

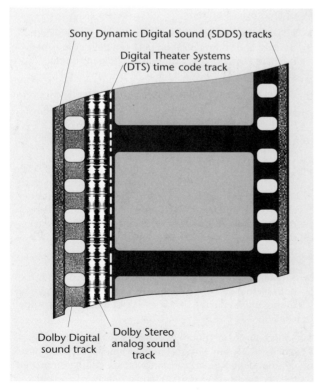

Sony Dynamic Digital Sound (SDDS) tracks

Digital Theater Systems (DTS) time code track

Dolby Digital sound track

Dolby Stereo analog sound track

5-23 Position of digital sound tracks on a 35 mm film release print.

▶ In analog recording, signals are oriented on the tape in patterns analogous to the waveform of the original signal. The signal is continuous—it is always "on."

▶ Digital audio uses a numerical representation of the sound signal's actual frequency and amplitude. In analog, frequency is the time component, and amplitude is the level component. In digital, sampling is the time component, and quantization is the level component.

▶ Sampling takes periodic samples (voltages) of the original analog signal at fixed intervals and converts them to digital data. The rate at which the fixed intervals sample the original signal each second is called the sampling frequency, or sampling rate.

▶ A number of sampling rates are used in digital audio. The most common are 32 kHz, 44.056 kHz, 44.1 kHz, 48 kHz, and 96 kHz.

▶ As samples of the waveform are taken, these voltages are converted into discrete quantities and assigned values. This process is known as quantization.

▶ Bit depth defines the digital word length used to represent a given sample and is equivalent to dynamic range. Word length is also referred to as resolution.

▶ The relationship between sampling frequency and quantization is called the audio data rate.

▶ Tapeless digital recording systems use either removable media or fixed hard disks; some use both. These systems fall into two categories: record/playback and distribution.

▶ Removable-media recording systems in relatively widespread use professionally include the compact disc (CD), digital versatile disc (DVD), and memory card.

▶ The recordable compact disc (CD-R) is a write-once medium with unlimited playback. The rewritable CD (CD-RW) is like recording tape in that it can be recorded on, erased, and used again for other recordings. The CDVU+ ("CD view plus") is a compact disc with interactive content.

▶ The digital versatile disc is the same diameter and thickness as the compact disc but it can hold a much greater amount of data. DVDs come in a variety of formats: DVD-Video (DVD-V), DVD-Audio (DVD-A), DVD-ROM, DVD-Recordable (DVD-R) authoring and general, DVD-RAM, and two rewritable formats—DVD-RW and DVD+RW.

▶ DVD-Audio differs from DVD-Video in that there is much more storage room for audio data. DVD-A can provide a greater number of extremely high-quality audio channels.

▶ Recordable and rewritable DVDs are high-density versions of the CD-R and the CD-RW. Two formats are used to record DVDs. They are designated DVD+R and DVD-R and are incompatible with one another. There are two categories of DVD-R: general and authoring. The general format was developed for business and consumer applications, such as data archiving and onetime recording. Authoring was designed to meet the needs of professional content developers and software producers. MVI (Music Video Interactive) is a DVD-based interactive format being marketed by Warner Music Group.

▶ High-density optical disc formats are designed to meet the demands of high-definition (HD) media. The most popular format at this writing is the Blu-ray Disc (BD). Other high-density optical formats include the Digital multilayer disc (DMD), ultra density optical disc (UDO), holographic versatile disc (HVD) protein-coated disc (PCD), enhanced versatile disc (EVD), and forward versatile disc (FVD).

▶ A memory recorder is a portable digital recorder that has no moving parts and therefore requires no maintenance. Its storage medium is a memory card, a nonvolatile memory that can be electrically recorded onto, erased, and reprogrammed. The card does not need power to maintain the stored information.

▶ Examples of memory cards include flash cards such as CompactFlash, flash memory sticks, Secure Digital (SD) memory cards, and SmartMedia. The PCMCIA card is yet another recording medium used in memory recorders.

▶ Digital recorders also use fixed and removable hard disks. Compared with memory recorders, they usually provide better sound quality and greater recording flexibility.

▶ A digital audio workstation (DAW) records, edits, and plays back. DAWs have considerable processing power because of the software programs they use. Generally, there are two types of DAW systems: computer-based and integrated.

▶ A computer-based DAW is a stand-alone unit with all processing handled by the computer.

▶ A computer must have a sound card to input, manipulate, and output audio. A sound card with a signal-to-noise ratio (S/N) of –70 dB and below usually ensures that it can produce professional-quality audio.

▶ An integrated DAW not only consists of the computer and its related software but may also include a console, a control surface, a server, and a storage area network.

▶ A server is a computer dedicated to providing one or more services over a computer network, typically through a request-response routine.

▶ A storage area network (SAN) can be likened to the common flow of data in a personal computer that is shared by different kinds of storage devices such as a hard disk, a CD or DVD player, or both.

▶ A DAW's systemwide communication with other external devices, and communication between devices in general, is facilitated through the distribution of digital interfaces such as AES/EBU, S/PDIF, SCSI, iSCSI, MADI, and FireWire.

▶ Digital audio networking using the Integrated Services Digital Network (ISDN) makes it possible to produce a recording in real time between studios across town or across the country with little or no loss in audio quality and at relatively low cost.

▶ Digital videotape recorders (DVTRs) come in a variety of formats, which differ more in the way they process video than with their audio processing. The differences in audio among the various systems come down to bit rate and number of audio channels. All sound in DVTRs is digital quality.

▶ There are three types of film: silent, sound, and magnetic.

▶ Silent film carries no sound information. Sound film carries both picture and optical sound. Magnetic film contains all sound and no picture. It comes in either full coat or stripe coat.

▶ Sound quality in 16 mm (millimeter) magnetic film is mediocre. In 35 mm with such enhancements as Dolby processing, digital audio, and surround sound, plus improved theater loudspeaker systems, audio quality is excellent.

6

Synchronization and Transfers

Little in production and postproduction can be accomplished without *synchronization*—the ability to lock two or more signals or devices that have microprocessor intelligence so that they operate at precisely the same rate. That includes almost any combination of audio, video, and film equipment, from a simple audio-to-audio or audio-to-video recorder interface—analog or digital, tape or disk—to a complete studio system that interfaces a digital audio workstation (DAW), console, synthesizer, sequencer,[1] effects processor, and other equipment throughout a facility.

Accurate synchronization requires a system to code and coordinate the recording media and the controlling mechanisms to ensure that signals remain in sync.

TIME CODES

Of the various time codes available, two are mainly used today: SMPTE time code, which is the most employed, and MIDI time code.

SMPTE Time Code

SMPTE time code (pronounced "sempty") was originally developed to make videotape editing more efficient; its identifying code numbers are broken down into hours, minutes, seconds, and frames. The code number

---

1. A *sequencer* is a device that can record performance data for synthesizers and other electronic instruments and, during playback, pass on that data to the instruments so that they play what has been recorded.

129

01:22:48:15 is read as 1 hour, 22 minutes, 48 seconds, and 15 frames. Videotape has 30 *frames per second (fps),* or 29.97, to be exact. Each 1/30 second of each video frame is tagged with a unique identifying number called a **time code address**. The advantages of time coding became immediately apparent and were soon applied to coding audiotape.

Even though tape is rarely used now, and DAWs have internal databases to keep multiple audio (and video) tracks in sync, time coding is used as a reference. It is a convenient and precise way of identifying segments to the split second; and, more importantly, time codes are necessary to standardize references and/or sync tracks when they are transferred to external devices. SMPTE is named for the Society of Motion Picture and Television Engineers.

MIDI Time Code

MIDI time code (MTC) was developed as a way to translate SMPTE time code into MIDI messages. An absolute timing reference, SMPTE time code remains constant throughout a program. In MIDI recording, timing references are relative and vary with both tempo and tempo changes. Because most studios use SMPTE time code addresses (as opposed to beats in a musical bar) as references, trying to convert between the two timing systems to cue or trigger an event would be tedious and time-consuming.

MIDI time code allows MIDI-based devices to operate on the SMPTE timing reference independent of tempo. In MIDI devices that do not recognize MTC, integrating an MTC sequencer is necessary. Converting SMPTE to MTC is straightforward: SMPTE comes in and MTC goes out.

Using MTC with a computer requires a MIDI interface to convert a MIDI signal into computer data and vice versa. It may be a circuit card, a sound card with MIDI connectors, or a control surface. Many computer recording/editing software programs have MIDI capability, so synchronizing a project to MTC or SMPTE time code is just a matter of accessing the program's appropriate synchronization page.

Time Formats with Computer-based Recorder/Editors

Computer-based recorder/editors incorporate at least SMPTE time code for reference; many systems also include other time formats for internal use, such as real time, music time, and film time. These format names differ among programs, but their functions are essentially comparable.

Real time displays the time scale in actual minutes and seconds. Many systems are able to refine real time to tenths, hundredths, and thousandths of a second.

Music time is in bars and beats and usually requires tempo data on which to base it. It can be adjusted to preserve relative timing to a variety of values, such as quarter-note, quarter-triplet, eighth-note, eighth-triplet, and so on.

Film time displays the time scale in feet and frames.

MIDI time code is included in hard-disk recorder/editor systems with MIDI capability. MTC is accurate to a quarter of a frame.

As noted earlier, the need for time coding in digital recorder/editors is sometimes questioned because of their internal databases that keep tracks in sync wherever they are moved and placed in the computer. So long as the entire audio production is done on a computer, coding does not matter. If the audio is exported to other devices, however, coding becomes essential for synchronization.

SYNCHRONIZING DIGITAL EQUIPMENT

Synchronizing digital equipment requires keeping the digital data synchronized in the digital domain. For example, a computer processes data at a much faster rate than the real-time devices that may be connected to it. Time code alone cannot keep the digital interconnectivity of data compatible. Every digital audio system has a signal generated inside the device that controls sampling frequency. This signal is commonly known as a word clock. The **word clock**, sometimes also referred to as a *sample clock* or *digital clock,* is an extremely stable synchronization signal that is used to control the rate at which digital audio data are converted or transmitted. It is responsible for the timing associated with moving audio data from one digital device to another. If the word clocks of different audio devices are not in sync, resulting problems in the data transfer can seriously degrade the audio signal.

The word-clock generator is usually built-in to a **converter**. Analog-to-digital converters (abbreviated *ADC, A/D,* or *A to D*) change continuous analog signals into discrete digital numbers. Digital-to-analog converters (abbreviated *DAC, D/A,* or *D to A*) reverse the operation. The ADC and the DCA are contained in the same device.

Jitter

A word-clock signal cues every audio device in the system to record, play back, or transfer each sample at the same time. It is important to note that with digital audio the determining sync factor is the sampling frequency, not the time code rate. In analog recording, the determining sync factor is the time code rate. A degradation in the word-clock signals among the digital devices being interfaced can create *jitter*—a variation in time from sample to sample that causes changes in the shape of the audio waveform. Jitter creates such adverse sonic effects as reduced detail, harsher sound, and ghost imaging. The best way to avoid jitter in syncing digital devices is to use a dedicated low-jitter master clock generator (see Figure 6-1).

It is important to underscore that in digital studios there can be only one master clock to control the clocks of the other digital devices. Uncompressed digital audio plays at a fixed rate. Although two or more devices in the signal chain can be set to run at the same sampling frequency, it is unlikely that the word clocks in each of these devices will run at the same time, which creates discontinuities in the audio streams.

Other ways to avoid jitter are to use balanced, well-shielded digital cables of the correct impedance; use short cables (longer cables are more subject to interference and data delays);[2] keep digital and analog cables separate; and use the most accurate clock source as the master time reference if a master clock generator is not employed.

Driver Support and Latency

An audio *driver* is a program that allows the transfer of audio signals to and from an audio interface. Examples of audio driver formats are *ASIO,* the Audio Stream Input Output protocol, which allows multiple channels of simultaneous input and output; *DAE* (short for *digital audio extraction*), a multichannel driver that runs with a compatible host such as Pro Tools, Logic, and Digital Performer; *Direct I/O,* which works with Digidesign interfaces as a multichannel driver only; *MAS* (Digital Performer's MOTU Audio System), which offers resolutions up to 24-bit and 96 kHz and multiple simultaneous input and output channels; *SoundManager,* which records and plays mono and stereo files up to 16-bit and 44.1 kHz; *Wave,* which can be used with a variety of audio interfaces; and *WDM* (Windows Driver Model), a multichannel driver.

---

2. Standard tested limits of cable runs to maintain accuracy and reduce risk of delay are Ethernet/10Base-T or 100Base-T—328 feet; USB 1.0 (low-speed)—9 feet 10 inches; USB 2.0 (high-speed)—16 feet 5 inches; and FireWire—14 feet 9 inches.

6-1 Syncing multiple digital devices to a master clock generator.

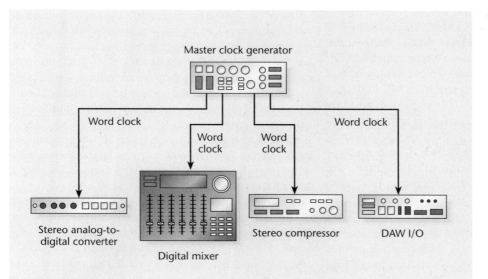

Master clock generator

Word clock

Word clock

Word clock

Word clock

Stereo analog-to-digital converter

Digital mixer

Stereo compressor

DAW I/O

Aside from its functionality in meeting needs, a driver with low latency (less than about 5 ms) is critical. **Latency** is the period of time it takes for data to get from one designated point to another. In audio, latency is the signal delay through the driver and the interface to the output. Some of the drivers noted above have low latency; others have a moderate amount.

Latency does not in and of itself affect sound quality. The problem is with synchronization. It is roughly analogous to recording with and without *selective synchronization,* or *Sel Sync,* in analog multitrack tape recording. In feeding a live signal for recording from, say, a vocal, while an already-recorded signal from an accompanying piano is playing back, both the record head and the playback head of the recorder are activated. This causes a delay in the signals created by the distance between the two heads; the signal being recorded is out of sync with the signal playing back. Sel Sync puts the appropriate tracks of the record head into the playback mode, thereby synchronizing the live input signal with the recorded playback signal. Little or no latency in a digital system "selectively synchronizes" the input and playback signals.

There is a way to avoid the problem of latency altogether, with audio interfaces that include the ability to mix incoming signals with already-recorded audio coming from the computer and then send the signal back out in sync.

FRAME RATES

Five frame rate standards are used within SMPTE time code: 23.976, 24, 25, 29.97, and 30 frames per second. *Frame rate* refers to the number of film or video frames displayed in 1 second of real time.

23.976 fps   This is the frame rate used in high-definition (HD) video where the HD camera is substituting for film. The format is called ***24p***. The *24* refers to the standard frames-per-second rate used for film applications in the United States. The *p* stands for *progressive,* which refers to the scanning method used in producing a video picture. The audio recorder used with 24p, and with most audio production recording, runs at 30 fps. The discrepancy in the two different frame rates is resolved when picture and sound are transferred for postproduction editing.

Some newer digital audio and video recorder/editors allow for 23.976 and 24p time code display and synchronization. Hence there is no need for a conversion to 30 fps unless material is output to a television standard.

24 fps   This is the frame rate used for pure film applications in the United States. Once a film is shot and transferred to a DAW for postproduction, 24 fps is not used.

25 fps   This is the frame rate used in Europe for film and video shot for television.

29.97 fps and 30 fps   To consider these two frame rates, it is first necessary to understand the implications of drop frame and non–drop frame.

Drop Frame and Non–Drop Frame

In the days before color television, the frame rate of U.S. black-and-white TV was 30 fps. With color TV the rate was reduced to 29.97 fps to allow easier color syncing of new programs and reproduction of black-and-white programs. Today American television and videotape recorders run at 29.97 fps.

The problem with 30 fps time code running at 29.97 fps is that it comes up 108 frames short every hour. To correct this problem, a time code format called drop frame was developed. *Drop frame* skips the first two frame counts in each minute, except for each tenth minute (00, 10, 20, etc.), to force the time code to match the clock time.

Solving one problem, however, created another. A frame rate of 29.97 fps for, say, a 1-minute commercial will show as exactly 1 minute on a clock but will read 00:00:59:28 on a time code display. One hour of real time will read out as 00:59:56:12. In editing, not working with whole numbers can be bothersome, to say nothing of trying to get an exact program time in broadcasting. To resolve this problem, the 30 fps and 29.97 fps frame rates can be adjusted between drop frame and non–drop frame.

Drop frame is necessary when precise timing is critical and when synchronizing audio to video. But in most other production—audio and video—*non–drop frame* is used because it is easier to work with. It is worth remembering that recordings used in any given production must employ one mode or the other; the two modes are not interchangeable.

For the uses of the 29.97 fps and 30 fps codes in their drop frame and non–drop frame modes, see 6-2. Given the array of frame rates in use and whether they are drop frame or non–drop frame, it is not uncommon during complex productions either to lose track of what was used and when or to misunderstand the requirements of a particular stage in the production chain. Some frame rates and counts are incompatible, such as 29.97 fps drop frame and non–drop frame. Others may be compatible

From Tomlinson Holman, *Sound for Film and Television*, 2nd ed. (Boston: Focal Press, 2002), p. 144.

6-2 29.97 and 30 fps frame rates, counts, and their primary uses.

Frame Rate (fps)	Frame Count	Primary Uses
29.97	Non–drop frame	Postproduction editorial, original video production, and delivery masters for some nonbroadcast uses such as DVD-V
29.97	Drop frame	Delivery masters for broadcast and original video production on episodic television
30	Non–drop frame	Shooting film for music video or commercials for television at 24 fps or 30 fps
30	Drop frame	Used with 24 fps film origination of episodic or long-form television when the delivery master requirement is 29.97 drop frame

in certain ways, such as 30 fps drop frame that can be converted to 29.97 fps drop frame in the process of transferring film and audio to a DAW. If possible, avoid mix-ups by using the frame rate and the frame count needed for the final delivery master throughout production and postproduction.

Some digital recorder/editors differentiate between the drop frame and non–drop frame time code displays. Non–drop frame uses colons between the numbers—00:00:00:00, whereas drop frame uses semicolons—00;00;00;00. An easy way to remember which is which is that dropping off the lower dot indicates the drop frame format.

SYNCHRONIZING SOUND AND PICTURE IN FILM

The problem with recording sound and picture synchronously in film production is that audio recorders do not have sprocket holes like film does; moreover, they run at different speeds. The solution to the problem is the technique known as ***double-system recording:*** sound and picture are recorded separately and in sync; the camera records the picture, and the audio recorder handles the sound. ***Single-system recording*** records both sound and picture on the same medium, which today is either videotape or, more likely, disk. It is particularly convenient and efficient in TV news, where time is of the essence (see Chapter 13). But if extensive postproduction is necessary and sound quality is important, double-system recording is used.

Time Code Synchronization

The method of synchronizing sound and picture in double-system recording today is with time code. Al-

though picture and sound are shot together, they are not in true sync because of the differences in recording rate between film and audio. To sync them properly, the editor has to know the precise point at which the picture and the sound recording began. For this purpose a ***clapslate*** is used (see 6-3). The clapslate (also called *slate, clapboard,* or *sticks*) is filmed just before each take, after the camera and the recorder have begun rolling.

The clapslate serves three purposes: One, it displays a running time code. Two, depending on the model, it can display the names of the production, director, and cameraperson; the number of the scene and the take; the number of the sound take; the date; and whether the shot is interior or exterior. Three, on top of the slate is a

6-3 Time code clapslate.

clapstick, which is lifted and then snapped closed to produce a loud sound. At the moment the clapstick closes, the time code showing at that instant freezes; that is the start point or sync mark that tells the editor at exactly what frame to begin synchronizing sound with picture. Once sound has been recorded, it is usually transferred to a DAW for postproduction editing.

A note of caution: When time code is recorded during production, it is continuous. When the material is transferred for editing, any discontinuity in time code can be confusing. Therefore a continuous time code should be recorded for editing. This, however, could create two sets of time code numbers, one for the production and one for the edited material. Good recordkeeping is essential to avoid mix-ups.

TRANSFERS

Copying sound (or picture) from one audio (film or video) device to another is commonly called a *transfer.* The term *dub,* in popular use for decades and still in the audio lexicon, means essentially the same thing.

Analog-to-analog Audio Transfers

Analog-to-analog transfers are rarely done these days unless it is to preserve the sonic authenticity of a recording for archival purposes. In dubbing an analog recording from a vinyl record to analog tape, each transfer of material loses a *generation,* worsening the signal-to-noise ratio (S/N) (see 6-4). Using only top-notch equipment and noise reduction software that can act on such sounds as clicks, scratches, hum, rumble, hiss, and surface noise can

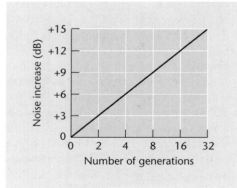

6-4 The effect that transferring an analog-to-analog recording has on sound quality.

minimize loss of audio quality. The loss in S/N is more acute when transferring from a vinyl record to analog tape than from analog tape to analog tape because the sound on a vinyl record is already several generations down due to the multigenerational steps in the mastering process.

In transferring material to open-reel analog tape, it is best to begin recording the sound a few seconds after the tape has started spinning to prevent the sound from *wowing in*—gradually reaching full speed. Even the finest analog open-reel audiotape recorders take at least one second to reach full speed. If the tape recorder has automated cueing, startup time is more precise and dependable.

Analog-to-digital Audio Transfers

Two primary considerations in transferring analog audio to digital audio are maintaining levels and not reducing dynamic range. Remember that if a signal goes "into the red" in analog recording, there is usually some headroom before distortion occurs. Once a signal is "in the red" with digital sound, it is already distorted. Therefore in doing an analog-to-digital transfer, the first step is to do equipment *calibration*—adjust all levels to a standard so that their measurements are similar. For example, a reading of, say, 0 VU on the console should produce an equivalent reading of 0 VU or –20 dBFS digital signal level on the recorder(s).

In setting levels to avoid distortion and maintain dynamic range, one fairly obvious approach is to set the level of the digital recorder at 0 VU during the loudest passages in the analog recording. This helps ensure that all levels will be 0 VU or below. In quiet passages, however, the level may be too low. For the sake of audibility, it may be necessary to use gentle signal processing to slightly raise the lower-level signal. Of course any technique has to take into account the program material. Transferring classical music requires a different aesthetic than transferring rock; dealing with dialogue may not require as many sonic adjustments as dealing with the dynamics of sound effects but may require the use of *dialnorm* (short for *dialogue normalization*—see Chapter 23).

Unless it is necessary, most signal processing is avoided in the transfer, or kept to a minimum, so as not to alter the original sound. This usually does not include transfers that are done to correct obvious audio deficiencies, such as using equalization and compression to enhance the clarity of the original analog recording, especially if it is down a generation or more. Nor does it include taking advantage of the powerful noise reduction capabilities of digital signal processing, which "clean" the sound without altering it.

Digital-to-digital Audio Transfers

Making a digital-to-digital transfer can be a straightforward process or—given the differences in quality among recording systems, the platforms they use, and susceptibility to digital errors—it can require some care. In any transfer of a digital signal from one digital device to another, the sampling frequency must be the same. If the sampling rate of the original recording is 48 kHz, for example, the mixer through which the signal is sent for transferring must also be set at 48 kHz.

In practice, though, when importing digital sources to a DAW, it is possible that the sampling rates of the various sources may be different. For example, the sampling rate of a CD is 44.1 kHz; digital videotape is usually 48 kHz; Internet and multimedia audio might be 32 or 22.050 kHz. By taking a few precautions, the havoc of sampling errors can be avoided. Try to use as few sampling-rate conversions as possible. Determine what the final sampling rate is to be and set the DAW to this rate. If the final sampling rate is 44.1 or 48 kHz, most DAWs can convert between these rates internally.

The number of bits (word length) being transferred is not as important as the matching of sampling rates so long as the master (source) and the slave (destination) devices are using the same digital formats, such as AES/EBU, S/PDIF, FireWire, and so on. That said, keeping the word length as long as possible during transfer helps reduce distortion: 24-bit is better than 16 bit. Moreover, feeding a 16-bit signal to a 24-bit device is more desirable than feeding a 24-bit signal to a 16-bit device. In the former instance, the 24-bit device will usually add zeros to fill out the digital word. In the latter instance, the last 8 bits are cut off, thereby introducing some distortion.

Other procedures worth noting in making digital transfers are as follows:

■ Digital audio data cables and word-clock lines need to be the same length. Cable length affects timing, which affects the phase relationship of the word clock to the digital audio data.

■ Make sure that all signals—time code, digital audio, and word clock—are flowing from the source recording to the destination recording. Check signal flow and make sure that there are no pops or clicks.

■ Avoid using wild time code during formatting. *Wild time code* occurs when the time code generator used for the original recording was not locked to the device that made the recording.

■ With tape make sure that there is plenty of preroll and keep the transfer start point consistent.

■ Use high-quality digital audio cables.

■ Transferring a WAV, AIFF (Audio Interchange File Format), or Sound Designer II file, for example, rather than a digital audio signal ensures a virtually perfect copy because it is an exact duplicate of the original file.

■ With FireWire, which has become the interface of choice, audio transfers over a computer connection are virtually trouble-free. This standardized high-speed connection can be used not only with audio, including multichannel, but also with devices such as computers, hard drives, CD burners, digital video, and scanners. With FireWire it now possible to connect up to 63 devices. When a new bus bridge (in development at this writing) becomes available, it will be possible to connect more than 60,000 devices together on a common bus. There are two standards of FireWire: 400 and 800. FireWire 400 has a maximum speed of 400 Mbps per second; 800 has a maximum speed of 800 Mbps per second. Three types of connectors are associated with FireWire: the 4-pin found on devices such as video recorders and Windows PCs; the 6-pin for Apple computers; and the 9-pin for FireWire 800. Maximum cable length is about 15 feet.

When a disk recorder is involved in a transfer either from within the computer from one hard-drive location to another or from one computer to another, the copy is exactly like the original. Digital tape-to-tape transfers or transfers to or from CD-Rs, CD-RWs, DVD-Rs, and the rewritable DVDs may or may not be exactly like the original due to digital errors and problems with error correction that may occur during the transfer process.

Transfers into a disk recorder usually involve either a file transfer or a streaming audio transfer. A *file transfer* is nonlinear and digital to digital. A *streaming transfer* is linear and may involve either analog or digital sources.

File transfers are done at higher-than-normal audio speeds. That cuts down the wait time compared with streaming audio transfers, which are in real time. Streaming audio transfers are also susceptible to digital bit errors; and if the error coding breaks down, interpolated data may be substituted into the missing portions, creating noticeable audio problems after several generations (see 6-5 and 6-6).

Transferring Audio Files for Accompanying Video

There are precautions to take when transferring audio files for accompanying video, particularly when they come from systems dedicated to image editing.

■ Avoid changing software during the project.

■ Use file naming that is precise, logical, easily understood, and not duplicated elsewhere.

■ Make sure that any file name extensions that are used, such as .wav, .aiff, and the like, are carried through the transfer.

■ Properly format the export media and start from an empty file structure.

■ Make sure that the recorded tracks are laid out logically, especially if different people are involved in editing and mixing the transferred material.

■ Verify that the start times match the sequence times.

■ Audio should be in hard sync before transfer because it is difficult to see sync on low-resolution video.[3]

Altering Audio in Transferring for Special Effects

Once a sound has been recorded, during transfer any number of things can be done to alter its sonic characteristics for use as a special effect. Because these are particularly useful techniques in dealing with sound effects, this aspect of transferring is discussed in Chapter 15.

---

3. Suggestions based on Tomlinson Holman, *Sound for Digital Video* (Boston: Focal Press, 2005), p. 156.

6-5 Audio file formats.

Formats	Applications and Characteristics
AIFF (Audio Interchange File Format)	Created for use on Macintosh computers, but most professional PC programs can read and write AIFF files. Supports bit resolutions in multiples of eight, but most AIFF files are 16- to 24-bit.
BWF (Broadcast Wave Format)	PC and Mac compatible. An enhanced WAV file that supports metadata. Files may be linear or lossy coded using MPEG-1 or MPEG-2. Adopted by the AES/EBU as a standard interchange.
SDII (Sound Designer II)	Developed by Digidesign for use on Mac computers. Supports sampling frequencies up to 48 kHz by Digidesign and up to 96 kHz through MOTU (Mark of the Unicorn).
WAV (Waveform)	Developed by Microsoft and accepted by most DAWs. Supports a variety of sampling rates and bit resolutions and a number of audio channels.

6-6 Project exchange formats.

Formats	Applications and Characteristics
AAF (Advanced Authoring Format)	File interchange format designed for video postproduction and authoring. Transfers audio and video files. AAF is expected to replace OMF. Unlike MXF, AAF is designed to be used with works-in-progress.
AES31 (Audio Engineering Society)	Supported by most DAWs but not Digidesign. Audio-only interchange.
OMF 1 and 2 (Open Media Format)	Produced by Digidesign but interchanges with most DAWs. Transfers audio and picture files.
MXF (Material Exchange Format)	Based on the AAF data model. Transfers audio and video files in a streamable format. MXF is used to transfer completed projects on a networked DAW.

MAIN POINTS

▶ Synchronization provides the ability to lock two or more signals or devices so that they operate at precisely the same rate.

▶ Accurate synchronization requires a system to code the recording media and the controlling mechanisms to ensure that signals remain in sync.

▶ Of the various time codes available, two are mainly used today: SMPTE time code, which is the most employed, and MIDI time code.

▶ SMPTE time code's identifying code numbers are broken down into hours, minutes, seconds, and frames. Each encoded value is called a time code address.

▶ MIDI time code (MTC) translates SMPTE time code into MIDI messages.

▶ Computer-based recording/editing systems include one or more of the following time formats: real time, music time, film time, and MIDI time code.

▶ To avoid the problem of latency altogether, use audio interfaces that include the ability to mix incoming signals with already-recorded audio coming from the computer, then send the signal back out in sync.

▶ Every digital audio system has a signal, known as a word clock (also called a sample clock or digital clock), generated inside the device that controls sampling frequency. It is an extremely stable synchronization signal that is used to control the rate at which digital audio data is converted or transmitted. With digital audio, sampling rate is the determining sync factor.

▶ The word-clock generator is usually built-in to a converter, which changes the analog signal into digital numbers and vice versa.

▶ A degradation in the word-clock signals among the digital devices being interfaced can create jitter—a variation in time from sample to sample that causes changes in the shape of the audio waveform.

▶ An audio driver is a program that allows the transfer of audio signals to and from an audio interface.

▶ It is critical to select a driver with low latency (less than about 5 ms). Latency is the period of time it takes for data to get from one designated point to another. In audio, latency is the signal delay through the driver and the interface to the output.

▶ Frame rate refers to the number of film or video frames displayed in 1 second of real time.

▶ Five frame rate standards are used within SMPTE time code: 23.976, 24, 25, 29.97, and 30 frames per second (fps).

▶ Frame rates for television are in either drop frame or non–drop frame format. Drop frame time code is time-accurate because it makes up for the error that results from the difference between the 29.97 fps and the 30 fps rate of video. Non–drop frame is the original video time code calculated at 30 fps. The two modes are not interchangeable.

▶ In double-system recording, sound and picture are recorded separately and in sync; the camera records the picture, and an audio recorder handles the sound.

▶ In single-system recording, both sound and picture are recorded on the same medium.

▶ In double-system recording, time code is used for synchronization.

▶ In double-system recording, a clapslate makes both a visible and an audible sync mark on the film and the audio recording, respectively. This helps identify and synchronize scenes during their transfer from the audio recording to a DAW and in editing.

▶ Copying sound (or picture) from one audio (film or video) device to another is called a transfer or a dub.

▶ Common audio transfers are analog to analog, analog to digital, and digital to digital.

▶ In transferring audio files for accompanying video, there are precautions to take to ensure accurate transfer particularly when they come from image-editing systems.

▶ In transferring audio, the sound can be altered for special effects.

7

Signal Processors

ignal processors are devices used to alter some characteristic of a sound. Generally, they can be grouped into four categories: spectrum processors, time processors, amplitude processors, and noise processors. A *spectrum processor,* such as the equalizer, affects the spectral balances in a signal. A *time processor,* such as a reverberation or delay device, affects the time interval between a signal and its repetition(s). An *amplitude processor* (or *dynamic processor*), such as the compressor-limiter, affects a signal's dynamic range. A *noise processor* does not alter a signal so much as it makes the signal clearer by reducing various types of noise.

Some signal processors can belong to more than one category. For example, the equalizer also alters a signal's amplitude and therefore can be classified as an amplitude processor as well. The flanger, which affects the time of a signal, also affects its frequency response. A de-esser alters amplitude and frequency. Compression and expansion also affect the time of an event. In other words, many effects are variations of the same principle.

A signal processor may be dedicated to a single function—that is, an equalizer just equalizes, a reverberation unit only produces reverb, and so on—or it may be a multieffects unit. The processing engine in a multieffects unit can be configured in a variety of ways. For example, one model may limit, compress, and pitch-shift, and another model may provide reverb as well as equalize, limit, compress, and noise-gate.

Signal processors may be inboard, incorporated into production consoles (see Chapter 4); outboard standalone units; or plug-ins—additions to whatever signal processing that is already integral to a hard-disk recording/editing system. In the interest of organization, the signal processors covered in this chapter are arranged by category in relation to their primary discrete function and are then discussed relative to multieffects processors. Examples in each category include outboard units, plug-ins, or both.

PLUG-INS

A *plug-in* is an add-on software tool that gives a hard-disk recording/editing system signal-processing alternatives beyond what the original system provides. Plug-ins include not only the familiar processing tools—equalization, compression and expansion, reverb, delay, pitch shifting, and so on—but also an array of capabilities that place at the recordist's fingertips virtually limitless potential for creating entirely new effects at comparatively little cost.

Plug-in programs are available separately or in bundles. *Bundles* include a number of different signal-processing programs, usually dedicated to a particular purpose. For example, there are bundles that include various noise reduction programs; sound sculpting with software to control time, pitch, instrument sound, rhythmic contour, and dimension; surround sound with such functions as 360-degree sound rotation, width, and distance panning; diagnostics for various types of sonic and technical analyses; and typical signal processing, such as reverb, delay, equalization, de-essing, compression/limiting, and stereo imaging.

STAND-ALONE SIGNAL PROCESSORS VERSUS PLUG-INS

No signal processor—stand-alone or plug-in—is a panacea. There are, however, considerations that influence the choice between a stand-alone unit and a plug-in.

Generally, given their comparative processing power, plug-ins are less expensive because they can incorporate as many or more functions than stand-alone units. Also, software programs are less costly to produce and market than mechanical-electronic units, and there is a greater user demand for them.

Ergonomically, stand-alone units are easier to employ because they can be adjusted while handling other equipment operations. It is also easier to operate actual controls than it is to navigate a mouse through various software functions. And computer monitors can display only so much information, which makes dealing with several plug-ins for a given session difficult.

Differences in the sound quality are a matter of design; but because there is an ever-growing number of companies producing plug-in software, one must be cautious about the audio quality of the programs they provide. Moreover, the pressure to reduce demand on the central processing unit (CPU) often results in plug-ins with reduced sound quality. Plug-ins also vary in their "tonalities." Some are musical, and some are not. Professional-grade stand-alone units are generally of high quality and produce excellent sound.

All that said, however, because of their convenience, comparatively lower cost, processing power, availability of bundles, and the ever-increasing momentum toward completely computerized production facilities, plug-ins are the way of the future in signal processing.

SPECTRUM PROCESSORS

Spectrum processors include equalizers, filters, and psychoacoustic processors.

Equalizers

The best-known and most common signal processor is the *equalizer*—an electronic device that alters frequency response by increasing or decreasing the level of a signal at a specific portion of the spectrum. This alteration can be done in two ways: by *boost* or *cut* (also known as *peak* or *dip*) or by *shelving*.

Boost and cut, respectively, increase and decrease the level of a band of frequencies around a *center frequency*—the frequency at which maximum boost or cut occurs. This type of *equalization (EQ)* is often referred to as *bell curve* or *haystack* due to the shape of the response curve (see Figure 7-1).

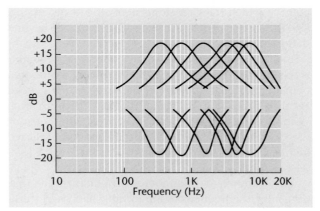

7-1 Bell curve or haystack showing 18 dB boost or cut at 350 Hz, 700 Hz, 1,600 Hz, 3,200 Hz, 4,800 Hz, and 7,200 Hz.

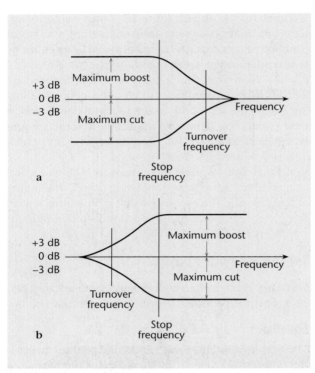

7-2 (a) Low-frequency shelving equalization and (b) high-frequency shelving equalization. The turnover frequency shown is where the gain is 3 dB above (or below) the shelving level—in other words, the frequency where the equalizer begins to flatten out. The stop frequency is the point at which the gain stops increasing or decreasing.

Shelving also increases or decreases amplitude but by a fixed amount, gradually flattening out, or shelving, at the maximum selected level when the chosen (called *turnover* or *cutoff*) frequency is reached. The *stop frequency* is the point at which the gain stops increasing or decreasing. Level then remains constant at all frequencies beyond that point (see 7-2).

In other words, with boost/cut EQ, when a frequency is selected for boost or cut by a certain amplitude, that frequency is the one most affected. Adjacent frequencies are also affected but by gradually lesser changes in level. With shelving EQ, all frequencies above (high-frequency shelving) or below (low-frequency shelving) the selected frequency are equally increased or decreased by the level selected.

The number of frequencies on equalizers varies. Generally, the frequencies are in full-, half-, and third-octave intervals. If the lowest frequency on a full-octave equalizer is, say, 50 Hz, the other frequencies ascend in

octaves: 100 Hz, 200 Hz, 400 Hz, 800 Hz, and so on, usually to 12,800 Hz. A half-octave equalizer ascends in half octaves. If the lowest frequency is 50 Hz, the intervals are at or near 75 Hz, 100 Hz, 150 Hz, 200 Hz, 300 Hz, 400 Hz, 600 Hz, and so on. A third-octave equalizer would have intervals at or near 50 Hz, 60 Hz, 80 Hz, 100 Hz, 120 Hz, 160 Hz, 200 Hz, 240 Hz, 320 Hz, 400 Hz, 480 Hz, 640 Hz, and so on.

Obviously, the more settings, the better the sound control—but at some cost. The more settings there are on an equalizer (or any device, for that matter), the more difficult it is to use correctly because problems such as added noise and phasing may be introduced, to say nothing of having to keep track of more control settings.

Two types of equalizers are in general use: fixed-frequency and parametric.

Fixed-frequency Equalizer

The *fixed-frequency equalizer* is so called because it operates at fixed frequencies usually selected from two (high and low), three (high, middle, and low), or four (high, upper-middle, lower-middle, and low) ranges of the frequency spectrum (see 4-3). Typically, the high and low fixed-frequency equalizers on consoles are shelving equalizers. The midrange equalizers are center-frequency boost/cut equalizers. Each group of frequencies is located at a separate control, but only one center frequency at a time per control may be selected. At or near each frequency selector is a level control that boosts or cuts the selected center and band frequencies. On consoles where these controls are concentric to save space, the outer ring chooses the frequency, and the inner ring increases or decreases level.

A fixed-frequency equalizer has a preset **bandwidth**— a range of frequencies on either side of the center frequency selected for equalizing that is also affected. The degrees of amplitude to which these frequencies are modified form the **bandwidth curve**. If you boost, say, 350 Hz a total of 18 dB, the bandwidth of frequencies also affected may go to as low as 80 Hz on one end and up to 2,000 Hz on the other. The peak of the curve is 350 Hz—the frequency that is boosted the full 18 dB (see 7-1). The adjacent frequencies are also boosted but to a lesser extent, depending on the bandwidth. Because each fixed-frequency equalizer can have a different fixed bandwidth and bandwidth curve, it is a good idea to study the manufacturer's specifications before you use one. A measure of the bandwidth of frequencies an equalizer affects is known as the **Q**.

Graphic Equalizer

The *graphic equalizer* is a type of fixed-frequency equalizer. It consists of sliding, instead of rotating, controls that boost or attenuate selected frequencies. It is called "graphic" because the positioning of these controls gives a graphic representation of the frequency curve set. (The display does not include the bandwidth of each frequency, however.) Because each frequency on a graphic equalizer has a separate sliding control, it is possible to use as many as you wish simultaneously (see 7-3).

Parametric Equalizer

The main difference between a *parametric equalizer* (see 7-4) and a fixed-frequency equalizer is that the parametric has continuously variable frequencies and bandwidths, making it possible to change a bandwidth curve by making it wider or narrower, thereby altering the affected frequencies and their levels. This provides greater flexibility and more precision in controlling equalization.

In other words, in parametric EQ it is possible to vary the Q from anywhere between high-Q settings, which produce narrow bands of frequencies, to low-Q settings, which affect wider bands of frequencies (see 7-5).

Paragraphic Equalizer

A *paragraphic equalizer* combines the sliding controls of a graphic equalizer with the flexibility of parametric equalization (see 7-6).

Filters

A *filter* is a device that attenuates certain bands of frequencies. It is a component of an equalizer. There are differences between attenuating with an equalizer and with a filter, however. First, with an equalizer attenuation affects only the selected frequency and the frequencies on either side of it, whereas with a filter all frequencies above or below the selected frequency are affected. Second, an equalizer allows you to vary the amount of drop

7-3 Graphic equalizer. This model is dual-channel, with 31 EQ bands at one-third octave intervals from 20 Hz to 20 kHz. Equalization gain is switchable between ±6 dB and ±12 dB. It also includes a high-pass filter.

7-4 Parametric equalizer. This model includes four EQ bands, each with six switch-selectable frequencies and 14 dB of fully sweepable level increase or attenuation. The low-middle and high-middle are the parametric bands and can switch between narrow and wide bandwidths. The low- and high-frequency bands can switch between boost/cut and shelving EQ. Also included is a switchable high-pass filter at 30 Hz to reduce rumble.

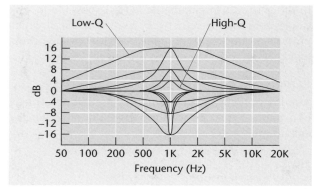

7-5 Selectable bandwidths of a parametric equalizer showing the effects of low-Q and high-Q settings.

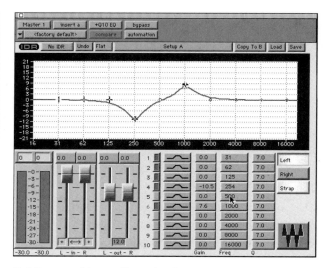

7-6 Paragraphic equalizer plug-in.

in loudness; with a filter the drop is usually preset and relatively steep.

Among the most common filters are high-pass, low-pass, band-pass, and notch.

High- and Low-pass Filters

A *high-pass (low-cut) filter* attenuates all frequencies below a preset point; a *low-pass (high-cut)* **filter** attenuates all frequencies above a preset point (see 7-7).

Suppose in a recording that there is a bothersome rumble between 35 Hz and 50 Hz. By setting a high-pass filter at 50 Hz, all frequencies below that point are cut and the band of frequencies above it continues to pass—hence the name *high-pass (low-cut) filter.*

The low-pass (high-cut) filter works on the same principle but affects the higher frequencies. If there is hiss in a recording, you can get rid of it by setting a low-pass filter at, say, 10,000 Hz. This cuts the frequencies above that point and allows the band of frequencies below 10,000 Hz to pass through. But keep in mind that all sound above 10 kHz—the program material, if there is any, along with the hiss—will be filtered.

Band-pass Filter

A *band-pass filter* is a device that sets high- and low-frequency cutoff points and permits the band of frequencies in between to pass (see 7-8). Band-pass filters are used more for corrective rather than creative purposes.

Notch Filter

A *notch filter* is also used mainly for corrective purposes. It can cut out an extremely narrow band, allowing the

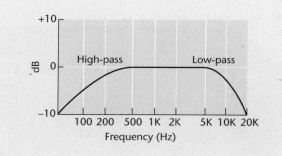

7-7 High-pass (low-cut) and low-pass (high-cut) filter curves.

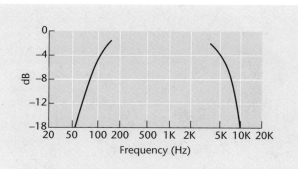

7-8 Band-pass filtering. The frequencies below 120 Hz and above 5,000 Hz are sharply attenuated, thereby allowing the frequencies in the band between to pass.

frequencies on either side of the notch to pass. For example, a constant problem in audio is AC (alternating current) hum, which has a frequency of 60 Hz. A notch filter can remove it without appreciably affecting the adjacent frequencies.

Psychoacoustic Processors

A *psychoacoustic processor* is designed to add clarity, definition, overall presence, and life, or "sizzle," to program material. Some units add tone-generated odd and even harmonics[1] to the audio; others are fixed or program-adaptive high-frequency equalizers. A psychoacoustic processor might also achieve its effect by adding comb filtering and by introducing narrow-band phase shifts between stereo channels. One well-known psychoacoustic processor is the Aphex Aural Exciter.™

TIME PROCESSORS

Time processors are devices that affect the time relationships of signals. These effects include reverberation and delay.

Reverberation

Reverberation, you will recall, is created by random, multiple, blended repetitions of a sound or signal. As these repetitions decrease in intensity, they increase in number. Reverberant sound increases average signal level and adds depth, spatial dimension, and additional excitement to the listening experience.

A reverb effect has two main elements: the initial reflections and the decay of those reflections (see Chapter 2). Therefore reverb results when the first reflections hit surfaces and continue to bounce around until they decay. In creating reverb electronically, using the parlance of audio, a signal is sent to the reverb processor

---

1. Each harmonic or set of harmonics adds a characteristic tonal color to sound, although they have less effect on changes in timbre as they rise in pitch above the fundamental. In general, even-number harmonics—second, fourth, and sixth—create an open, warm, filled-out sound. The first two even harmonics are one and two octaves above the fundamental, so the tones blend. Odd-number harmonics—third and fifth—produce a closed, harsh, stopped-down sound. The first two odd harmonics are an octave plus a fifth and two octaves plus a major third above the fundamental, which bring their own tonality to the music.

as *dry sound*—without reverb—and is returned as *wet sound*—with reverb.

The types of reverberation in current use are digital, convolution, plate, and acoustic chamber. Reverb plug-in software may be considered a fifth type. There is also *spring reverberation,* which is rarely employed today because of its mediocre sound quality. It is sometimes used, however, in guitar amplifiers because of its low cost and small size and when the musician is going for the particular sound quality spring reverbs produce.

Digital Reverberation

Digital reverberation is the most common type today. Most digital reverb devices are capable of producing a variety of different acoustic environments. Generally, when fed into the circuitry and digitized, the signal is delayed for several milliseconds. The delayed signal is then recycled to produce the reverb effect. The process is repeated many times per second, with amplitude reduced to achieve decay.

Specifically, in digital reverb there are numerous delay times that create discrete echoes, followed by multiple repetitions of these initial delays to create the ambience, which continues with decreasing clarity and amplitude. High-quality digital reverb units are capable of an extremely wide range of effects, produce high-quality sound, and take up relatively little room.

Digital reverb systems can simulate a variety of acoustical and mechanical reverberant sounds, such as small and large concert halls, bright- and dark-sounding halls, small and large rooms, and small and large reverb plates (see "Plate Reverberation" on the next page). With each effect it is also possible to control individually the attack; decay; diffusion (density); high-, middle-, and low-frequency decay times; and other sonic colorings.

One important feature of most digital reverb units is *predelay*—the amount of time between the onset of the direct sound and the appearance of the first reflections. Predelay is essential for creating a believable room ambience because early reflections arrive before reverberation. It also helps create the perception of a room's size: shorter predelay times give the sense of a smaller room and vice versa.

There are two other common reverb effects. *Reverse reverb* builds up before it decays. With *gated reverb* the reverb is cut off just after the sound is established so there is no reverb tail.

Most digital reverb systems are programmed and programmable. They come with preprogrammed effects but

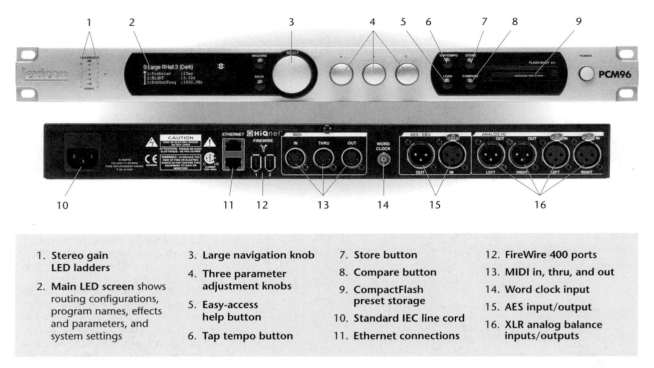

1. **Stereo gain LED ladders**	3. **Large navigation knob**	7. **Store button**	12. **FireWire 400 ports**
2. **Main LED screen** shows routing configurations, program names, effects and parameters, and system settings	4. **Three parameter adjustment knobs**	8. **Compare button**	13. **MIDI in, thru, and out**
	5. **Easy-access help button**	9. **CompactFlash preset storage**	14. **Word clock input**
	6. **Tap tempo button**	10. **Standard IEC line cord**	15. **AES input/output**
		11. **Ethernet connections**	16. **XLR analog balance inputs/outputs**

7-9 Digital reverberation processor, front and rear views. This model includes monaural and stereo reverbs for 28 effects, including chamber, hall, plate, room, chorus/flange, and delay. There are digital audio workstation automation and FireWire streaming through a plug-in format, CompactFlash preset storage, and sampling rates of 44.1 kHz, 48 kHz, 88.2 kHz, and 96 kHz.

also permit new ones to be programmed in and stored for reuse (see 7-9).

Convolution Reverb

Convolution reverb is a sample-based process that multiplies the spectrums of two audio files. One file represents the acoustic signature of an acoustic space. It is called the *impulse response (IR)*. The other file is the source, or *carrier*. It takes on the characteristics of the acoustic space when it is multiplied by the IR. Hence it has the quality of having been recorded in that space. By facilitating the interaction of any two arbitrary audio files, convolution reverb provides a virtually infinite range of unusual sonic possibilities.

Among the more common uses of convolution reverb is providing the actual likeness of real acoustic spaces interacting with any sound source you wish—such spaces as Boston's Symphony Hall, Nashville's Ryman Auditorium, a particular recording stage, a living room, a kitchen, or a jail cell (see 7-10). The process can create effects, such as exotic echoes and delays, a single clave or marimba hit, and different tempos and timbres.

Plate Reverberation

The *reverberation plate* is a mechanical-electronic device consisting of a thin steel plate suspended under tension in an enclosed frame (see 7-11). It is large and heavy and requires isolation in a separate room. A moving-coil driver, acting like a small speaker, vibrates the plate, transducing the electrical signals from the console into mechanical energy. A contact microphone (two for stereo) picks up the plate's vibrations, transduces them back into electric energy, and returns them to the console. The multiple reflections from the vibrating plate create the reverb effect.

The reverberation plate is capable of producing a complex output, but it is difficult to change its characteristics. Generally, plates have long reverb times (more than two seconds) at high frequencies that produce a crisp, bright decay. They are susceptible to overload, however. With louder levels low frequencies tend to increase disproportionately in reverb time compared with the other frequencies, thus muddying sound. Rolling off the unwanted lower frequencies helps, but too much roll-off reduces a sound's warmth.

b

7-10 Reverberation plug-ins. (a) This sampling reverberation plug-in offers one-, two-, and four-channel sampled acoustic environments ranging from real halls, to cathedrals, to bathrooms, to closets. It also provides the means for users to create their own acoustic samples. (b) This convolution reverb plug-in, among other things, facilitates the shortening and the lengthening of reverb times while maintaining the coherence of an acoustic space; making an acoustic space sound clearer or denser; manipulating the reverb's stereo spaciousness; setting the reverb tail; separately adjusting a sample's low, middle, and high frequencies; and controlling the length of the actual real-time convolution.

7-11 Reverberation plate.

Acoustic Chamber Reverberation

The *acoustic reverberation chamber* is a natural and realistic type of simulated reverb because it works on acoustic sound in an acoustic environment. It is a room with sound-reflective surfaces and nonparallel walls to avoid *flutter echoes*—multiple echoes at a rapid, even rate—and *standing waves*—apparently stationary waveforms created by multiple reflections between opposite, usually parallel, surfaces. It usually contains two directional microphones

(for stereo), placed off room center, and a loudspeaker, usually near a corner angled or back-to-back to the mic(s) to minimize the amount of direct sound the mic(s) pick up. The dry sound feeds from the console through the loudspeaker, reflects around the chamber, is picked up by the mic(s), and is fed back wet into the console for further processing and routing.

Reverb times differ from chamber to chamber. Generally, however, reverb time should be about 3.5 seconds at 500 Hz and about 1.25 seconds at 10,000 Hz. Reverb times can be varied by using movable acoustic baffles.

Although an acoustic chamber creates very realistic reverberation, a top-of-the-line chamber is expensive to build. It should be at least 2,000 cubic feet in size (too small a room is poor for bass response), it requires good soundproofing, and it must be isolated. Even with a chamber, studios use other reverb devices to provide additional sonic alternatives.

It is possible to convert a basement, spare room, hallway, staircase, or even such spaces as a shower stall, tiled bathroom, metal heating duct, or galvanized garbage can into a passable acoustic chamber for a relatively low cost. The keys to making such spaces effective are sound-proofing from outside sonic interferences; choosing a professional-quality microphone(s) and loudspeaker; ensuring that the loudspeaker size is suitable to the size of the space; and placing microphone(s) and loudspeaker optimally in the space and relative to one another.

Choosing a Reverberation System

In choosing a reverb system, personal taste notwithstanding, the system should sound natural. Make comparisons by auditioning different reverb units. Take a familiar sound and run it through the system's presets. Here are some sonic details to listen for: the high end should be bright and lifelike, and the low end should not thicken or muddy the sound; good diffusion is essential (*diffusion* refers to the density of the sound—increasing diffusion produces a heavier sound; decreasing diffusion produces a thinner, lighter sound); repeats should be numerous and random, and decay response should be smooth; and there should be an absence of flutter, twang, "boing," and tinniness.

A good test for checking for muddy sound is to listen to a singer; if the reverb system makes the lyrics more difficult to understand, it is not clear or transparent enough. To check for density and randomness of the early reflections, try a transient sound such as a sharp drumbeat or a handclap; poorer reverb systems will produce a sound like an acoustic flutter. To check for randomness of the later reflections, listen to a strong male voice completely wet—with no dry feed from the reverb send on the console; if the lyrics are clear, the combined wet and dry signals will probably be muddy.

It also helps to listen to familiar recordings and pay attention to how reverb is used overall on specific instruments or groups of instruments and on the vocal. Try to discern what the reverb is doing, such as blending the voicings, adding spaciousness, creating a special effect, or articulating the sound of a particular room or concert hall.

Reverberation and Ambience

In considering a reverberation system, it is helpful to keep in mind that reverberation and ambience, often thought of as synonymous, are different. Reverb is the remainder of sound that exists in a room after the source of the sound is stopped.[2] *Ambience* refers to the acousti-

cal qualities of a listening space, including reverberation, echoes, background noise, and so on.[3] In general, reverb adds spaciousness to sound; ambience adds solidity and body.

Delay

Delay is the time interval between a sound or signal and its repetition. By manipulating delay times, it is possible to create a number of echo effects (see "Uses of Delay" below). This is done most commonly with an electronic digital delay.

Digital Delay

Digital delay is generated by routing audio through an electronic buffer. The information is held for a specific period of time, which is set by the user, before it is sent to the output. A single-repeat delay processes the sound only once; multiple delays process the signal over and over. The amount and the number of delay times vary with the unit (see 7-12).

Two delay parameters that are important to understand are delay time and feedback.

Delay time regulates how long a given sound is held and therefore the amount of time between delays. *Feedback,* also known as *regeneration,* controls how much of that delayed signal is returned to the input. Raising the amount of feedback increases the number of repeats and the length of decay. Turning it down completely generates only one repeat.

The better digital delays have excellent signal-to-noise ratio, low distortion, good high-frequency response with longer delay times, and an extensive array of effects. They are also excellent for prereverb delay. Lower-grade units are not as clean-sounding, and high-frequency response is noisier with longer delay times.

Uses of Delay

Delay has a number of creative applications. Among the common effects are doubling, chorus, slap back echo, and prereverb delay.

■ **Doubling** One popular use of delay is to fatten sound. The effect, which gives an instrument or voice a fuller, stronger sound, is called **doubling**. It is created by setting

---

2. Glenn D. White and Gary J. Louie, *The Audio Dictionary,* 3rd ed. (Seattle: University of Washington Press, 2005), p. 331.

3. Ibid, p. 16.

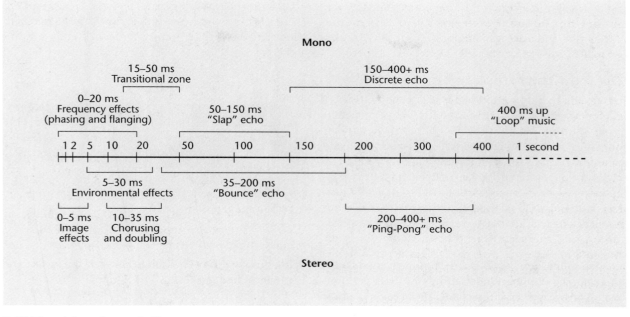

7-12 Time delay values and effects.

the delay to about 15 to 35 ms. These short delays are like early sound reflections and lend a sense of openness or ambience to dead-sounding instruments or voices.

Doubling can also be done live by recording one track and then overdubbing the same part on a separate track in synchronization with the first. Because it is not possible to repeat a performance exactly, variations in pitch, timing, and room sounds add fullness or openness to sound. By continuing this process, it is possible to create a chorus effect.

■ **Chorus** The *chorus effect* is achieved by recirculating the doubling effect. The delay time is about the same as in doubling—15 to 35 ms—but is repeated. This effect can make a single voice sound like many and add spaciousness to a sound. Two voices singing in a relatively dead studio can be made to sound like a choir singing in a hall by chorusing the original sound.

■ **Slap back echo** A *slap back echo* is a delayed sound that is perceived as a distinct echo, much like the discrete Ping-Pong sound emitted by sonar devices when a contact is made. Slap back delay times are generally short, about 50 to 150 ms.

■ **Prereverb delay** As mentioned in the discussion of digital reverb, there is a definite time lag between the arrival of direct waves from a sound source and the arrival of reflected sound in acoustic conditions. In some reverb systems, there is no delay between the dry and wet signals. By using a delay unit to delay the input signal before it gets to the reverb unit, it is possible to improve the quality of reverberation, making it sound more natural.

Flanging

Flanging is produced electronically. The signal is combined with its time-delayed replica. Delay time is relatively short, from 0 to 20 ms. Ordinarily, the ear cannot perceive time differences between direct and delayed sounds that are this short. But due to phase cancellations when the direct and delayed signals are combined, the result is a *comb-filter effect*—a series of peaks and dips in the frequency response. This creates a filtered tone quality that sounds hollow, swishy, and outer space–like (see 7-13).

In addition to the various delay times, flangers typically provide feedback rate and depth controls. *Feedback*

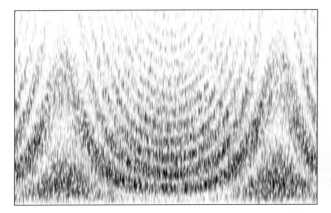

7-13 Spectrogram of the flanging effect.
Source: Wikipedia

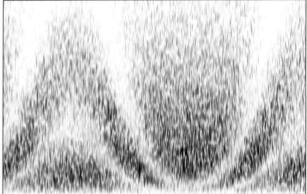

7-14 Spectrogram of the phasing effect.
Source: Wikipedia

rate determines how quickly a delay time is modulated; for example, a feedback rate setting of 0.1 Hz performs one cycle sweep every 10 seconds. *Depth controls* adjust the spread between minimum and maximum delay times; depth is expressed as a ratio.

Many flangers provide controls to delay feedback in phase or out of phase. In-phase flanging is "positive," meaning that the direct and delayed signals have the same polarity. Positive flanging accents even harmonics, producing a metallic sound. Out-of-phase flanging is "negative," meaning that the two signals are opposite in polarity, accenting odd harmonics. Negative flanging can create strong, sucking effects like a sound being turned inside out.

Phasing

Phasing and flanging are similar in the way they are created. In fact, it is sometimes difficult to differentiate between the two. Instead of using a time-delay circuit, however, phasers use a phase shifter. Delays are very short, between 0 ms and 10 ms. The peaks and the dips are more irregular and farther apart than in flanging, which results in something like a wavering vibrato that pulsates or undulates (see 7-14). Phasers provide a less pronounced pitched effect than flangers do because their delay times are slightly shorter, and the phasing effect has less depth than with flanging.

Phasers use two parameters that control modulation of the filters: rate (or speed) and depth (or intensity). *Rate* determines the sweep speed between the minimum and the maximum values of the frequency range. *Depth* defines the width of that range between the lowest and the highest frequencies.

Morphing

Morphing is the continuous, seamless transformation of one effect (aural or visual) into another. For example, in Michael Jackson's video *Black and White*, a Chinese woman is transformed into an African-American man, who is transformed into an Irishman, who is transformed into a Hispanic woman, and so on. In *Terminator II* the silver terminator could melt, slither through cracks, and transform into various objects; and in *Matrix* characters change shape and form as though they were made of plastic. These effects are more than sophisticated dissolves (the sonic counterpart of a dissolve is the *crossfade*). Morphing is a complete restructuring of two completely different and independent effects. Because most audio-morphing effects are delay-based, audio-morphing devices can be classified as time processors (see 7-15).

A few examples of audio morphing are: turning human speech or vocal lines into lines impossible to be spoken or sung by a human; turning sounds that exist into sounds that do not exist; spinning vowel-like sounds, varying their rate and depth, and then freezing them until they fade away; flanging cascades of sound across stereo space, adding echo, and varying the envelope control of rates; adding echoing rhythms to a multivoice chorus which become more dense as they repeat, with the effect growing stronger as the notes fade away; and taking a musical instrument and adding pitch sweeps that dive into a pool of swirling echoes that bounce from side to side or end by being sucked up.

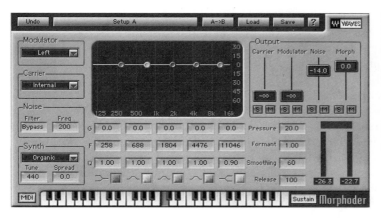

7-15 Morphing. This plug-in, called the Morphoder, is a processor of the vocoder type (see "Voice Processors" later in this chapter). It allows two audio signals to be combined using one source as a modulator input and a synthesizer as the carrier. The effect is that the synthesizer will "talk" and actually say the words spoken by the voice; or a drum track can be the modulator, resulting in a rhythmic keyboard track in sync with the drum track.

AMPLITUDE PROCESSORS

Amplitude, or *dynamic, processors* are devices that affect dynamic range. These effects include such functions as compression, limiting, de-essing, expanding, noise gating, and pitch shifting.

Compressor

The term *compressor* is customarily linked with the term *limiter.* They do basically the same signal processing but to different degrees. The *compressor* is a processor whose output level increases at a slower rate as its input level increases (see 7-16). It is used to restrict dynamic range because of the peak signal limitations of an electronic system, for artistic goals, due to the surrounding acoustical requirements, or any combination of these factors.

Compressors usually have four basic controls—for compression ratio, compression threshold, attack time, and release time—each of which can affect the others. Some compressors also include a makeup gain control.

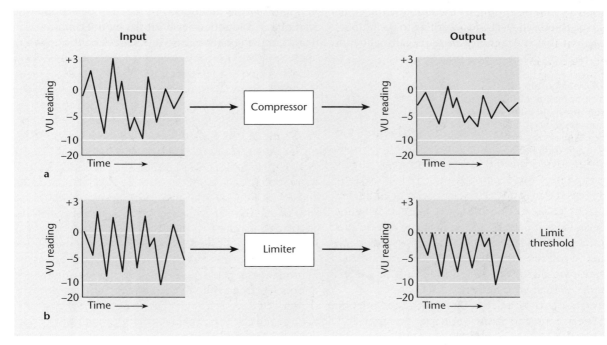

7-16 Effect of (a) compression and (b) limiting.

Compressor plug-ins may have additional features that act on a signal's dynamics.

The **compression ratio** establishes the proportion of change between the input and the output levels. The ratios are usually variable, and, depending on the compressor, there are several selectable points between 1.1:1 and 20:1. Some recent compressor designs change ratios instantaneously, depending on the program's dynamic content and the range of control settings. If you set the compression ratio for, say, 2:1, it means that for every 2 dB increase of the input signal, the output will increase by 1 dB; at 5:1, a 5 dB increase of the input signal increases the output by 1 dB. In other words it "reins in" excessive program dynamics. This is how sound with a dynamic range greater than the equipment can handle is brought to usable proportions before distortion occurs.

The **compression threshold** is the level at which compression ratio takes effect. It is an adjustable setting and is usually selected based on a subjective judgment of where compression should begin. It is difficult to predetermine what settings will work best for a given sound at a certain level; it is a matter of listening and experimenting. The compressor has no effect on the signal below the threshold-level setting. For an illustration of the relationship between compression ratio and threshold, see 7-17.

Once the threshold is reached, compression begins, reducing the gain according to the amount the signal exceeds the threshold level and according to the ratio set. The moment that the compressor starts gain reduction

is called the **knee**. **Hard knee compression** is abrupt; **soft knee compression** is smoother and less apparent.

Attack time is the length of time it takes the compressor to start compressing after the threshold has been reached. In a good compressor, attack times range from 500 *microseconds (μ)* to 100 ms. Depending on the setting, an attack time can enhance or detract from a sound. If the attack time is long, it can help bring out percussive attacks; but if it is too long, it can miss or overshoot the beginning of the compressed sound. If the attack time is too short, it reduces punch by attenuating the attacks, sometimes producing popping or clicking sounds. When it is controlled, a short attack time can heighten transients and add a crisp accent to sound. Generally, attack time should be set so that signals exceed the threshold level long enough to cause an increase in the average level. Otherwise gain reduction will decrease overall level. Again, your ear is the best judge of the appropriate attack time setting.

Release time, or *recovery time*, is the time it takes a compressed signal to return to normal *(unity gain)* after the input signal has fallen below the threshold. Typical release times vary from 20 ms to several seconds. It is perhaps the most critical variable in compression because it controls the moment-to-moment changes in the level and therefore the overall loudness. One purpose of the release-time function is to make imperceptible the variations in loudness level caused by the compression. For example, longer release times are usually applied to

7-17 The relationship of various compression ratios to a fixed threshold point. The graph also displays the difference between the effects of limiting and compression.

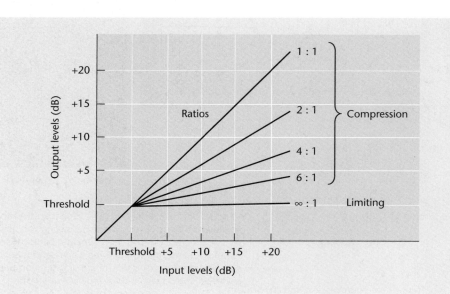

music that is slower and more legato (that is, smoother and more tightly connected); shorter release times are usually applied to music that is fast.

Generally, release times should be set long enough that if signal levels repeatedly rise above the threshold, they cause gain reduction only once. If the release time is too long, a loud section of the audio could cause gain reduction that continues through a soft section.

These suggestions are not to imply rules—they are only guidelines. In fact, various release times produce different effects. Some enhance sound, others degrade it, as the following list of potential effects suggests.

■ A fast release time combined with a low compression ratio makes a signal seem louder than it actually is.

■ Too short a release time with too high a ratio causes the compressor to pump or breathe. You actually hear it working when a signal rapidly returns to normal after it has been compressed and quickly released.

■ A longer release time smoothes a fluctuating signal.

■ A longer release time combined with a short attack time gives the signal some of the characteristics of a sound going backward. This effect is particularly noticeable with transients.

■ A release time longer than about half a second for bass instruments prevents harmonic distortion.

■ Too long a release time creates a muddy sound and can cause the gain reduction triggered by a loud signal to continue through a soft one that follows.

Makeup gain allows adjustment of the output level to the desired optimum. It is used, for example, when loud parts of a signal are so reduced that the overall result sounds too quiet.

Broadband and Split-band Compressors

Compressors fall into two categories: broadband and split-band. A *broadband compressor* acts on the dynamic range of the input signal across the entire frequency spectrum. The *split-band compressor* affects an input signal independently by splitting the audio into multiple bands, as needed, and then recombining the outputs of the bands into a single mono or stereo broadband signal. Good split-band compressors provide separate threshold, ratio control, attack and release times, and makeup gain for each compression band (see 7-18).

The split-band compressor allows for finer control of dynamic range. For example, a bass can be compressed in the low end without adversely affecting the higher

a Broadband compressor

Left channel
Center channel
Right channel
Left surround
Right surround
Low-frequency enhancement

b Split-band compressor

7-18 Compressor plug-ins. (a) A broadband compressor that can be used to control the dynamic range in recording and mixing 5.1 surround sound. (b) A split-band compressor that provides three separate bands of compression with graphic, adjustable crossover points among the three. Each band has its own settings, facilitating control over the entire spectrum of the signal being compressed, and a solo control that isolates an individual band for separate monitoring. This model has 64-bit processing and metering with numerical peak and RMS (root mean square) value displays.

end. Conversely, speech can be de-essed without losing fullness in the lower end.

Limiter

The *limiter* is a compressor whose output level stays at or below a preset point regardless of the input level. It has a compression ratio between 10:1 and infinity; it puts a ceiling on the loudness of a sound at a preset level (see 7-16). Regardless of how loud the input signal is, the output will not go above this ceiling. This makes the limiter useful in situations where high sound levels are frequent or where a performer or console operator cannot prevent loud sounds from distorting.

The limiter has a preset compression ratio but a variable threshold; the threshold sets the point at which limiting begins. Attack and release times, if not preset, should be relatively short, especially the attack time. A short attack time is usually essential to a clean-sounding limit.

Unlike compression, which can have little effect on the frequency response, limiting can reduce high-frequency response. Also, if limiting is severe, the signal-to-noise ratio drops dramatically. What makes a good limiter? One that is used infrequently but effectively, that is, except in broadcasting, where limiting the signal before transmission is essential to controlling peak levels and hence overload distortion.

De-esser

The *de-esser* is basically a fast-acting compressor that acts on high frequencies by attenuating them. It gets rid of the annoying hissy consonant sounds such as *s, z, ch,* and *sh* in speech and vocals. A de-esser may be a stand-alone unit or, more common, built into compressors and voice processors.

Uses of Compressors and Limiters

Compressors and limiters have many applications, some of which are listed here.

■ Compression minimizes the wide changes in loudness levels caused when a performer fails to maintain a consistent mic-to-source distance.

■ Compression smoothes the variations in attack and loudness of instruments with wide ranges or wide sound-pressure levels, such as the guitar, bass, trumpet, French horn, and drums. It can also smooth percussive sound effects such as jangling keys, breaking glass, and crashes.

■ Compression can improve the intelligibility of speech in an analog tape recording that has been rerecorded, or dubbed, several times.

■ Compressing speech or singing brings it forward and helps it jump out of the overall mix.

■ Compression reduces apparent noise if the compression ratios are low. Higher ratios add more noise.

■ Limiting prevents high sound levels, either constant or momentary, from saturating the recording.

■ The combination of compression and limiting can add more power or apparent loudness to sound.

■ The combination of compression and limiting is often used by AM radio stations to prevent distortion from loud music and to bring out the bass sounds. This adds more power to the sound, making the station more obvious to someone sweeping the dial.

■ Compression in commercials is used to raise average output level and thus sonically capture audience attention.

Expander

An *expander,* like a compressor, affects dynamic range (see 7-19a). But whereas a compressor reduces it, an expander increases it. Like a compressor, an expander has variable ratios and is triggered when sound reaches a set threshold level. The ratios on an expander, however, are the inverse of those on a compressor but are usually gentler: 1:2, 1.5:2, and so on. At 1:2 each 1 dB of input expands to 2 dB of output; at 1:3 each 1 dB of input expands to 3 dB of output. Because an expander is triggered when a signal falls below a set threshold, it is commonly used as a noise gate.

Noise Gate

Like the compressor, the expander/*noise gate* has the same dynamic determinants but they act inversely to those of the compressor. In addition to ratio settings, there is threshold: When the input signal level drops below the threshold, the gate closes and mutes the output. When the input signal level exceeds the threshold, the gate opens. Attack time determines how long it takes for the gate to go from full-off to full-on once the input level exceeds the threshold. Attack times are usually quite short—1 ms or even less. Longer attacks tend to chop off fast transients on percussive sounds. Release time

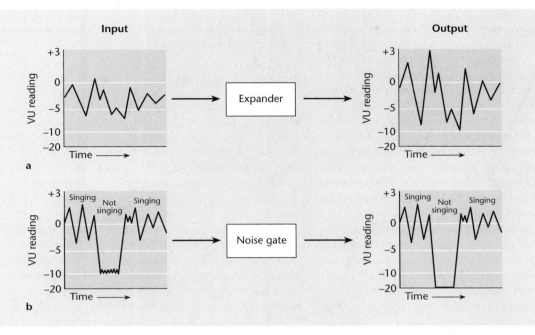

7-19 **Effect of (a) expansion and (b) noise gating.** Without noise gating, ambient noise is masked during singing and audible when singing is not present. Noise gating eliminates the ambient noise when there is no singing.

sets the time required for the gate to go from full-on to full-off once the signal level falls below the threshold. Another control is the *key input,* sometimes called a *side chain input,* which allows a different signal to be fed in to govern the gating action, such as using a bass drum as the key signal to turn another sound on and off in time with the bass drum's rhythm.

The noise gate is used primarily as a fix-it tool to reduce or eliminate unwanted low-level noise from amplifiers, ambience, rumble, noisy tracks, and leakage. It also has creative uses, however, to produce dynamic special effects. As an example of a practical application, assume that you have two microphones—one for a singer and one for an accompanying piano. When the singer and the pianist are performing, the sound level will probably be loud enough to mask unwanted low-level noises. But if the pianist is playing quietly and the vocalist is not singing, or vice versa, the open, unused microphone may pick up these noises (see 7-19b).

An obvious solution to this problem is to turn down the fader when a microphone is not being used, cutting it off acoustically and electronically; but this could become hectic for a console operator if there are several sound sources to coordinate. Another solution is to set the expander's threshold level at a point just above the quietest sound level that the vocalist (or piano) emits. When the vocalist stops singing, the loudness of the sound entering the mic falls below the threshold point of the expander, which shuts down, or gates, the mic. When a signal is above the threshold, there is no gating action and therefore no removal of noise.

The key to successful noise gating is in the coordination of the threshold and the ratio settings. Because there is often little difference between the low level of a sound's decay and the low level of noise, in gating noise you have to be wary that you do not cut off program material as well. Always be careful when you use a noise gate; unless it is set precisely, it can adversely affect response.

As mentioned, noise gates are also used to create effects. Shortening decay time of the drums can produce a very tight drum sound. Taking a 60 Hz tone and feeding it so that it is keyed or triggered by an electric bass can produce not only a simulated bass drum sound but also one that is synchronized with the bass guitar.

Pitch Shifter

A *pitch shifter* is a device that uses both compression and expansion to change the pitch of a signal. It is used to correct minor off-pitch problems, create special effects, or change the length of a program without changing its pitch. The latter function is called *time compression/expansion.* For example, if a singer delivers a note slightly flat or sharp, it is possible to raise or lower the pitch so that it is in tune. A pitch shifter also allows an input signal to be harmonized by mixing it with the harmonized signal at selected pitch ratios.

A pitch shifter works by compressing and expanding audio data. When the audio is compressed, it runs faster and raises pitch; it also shortens the audio segment. When the audio is expanded, it lowers pitch and lengthens the audio data. During processing, therefore, the pitch shifter is also rapidly cutting and pasting segments of data at varying intervals.

The basic parameter for pitch shifting is transposition. *Transposing* is changing the original pitch of a sound into another pitch; in music it is changing into another key. Transposition sets the harmony-line interval, typically within a range of ±1 or 2 octaves. A pitch shifter may also include a delay line with feedback and predelay controls.

Depending on the model or software, a pitch shifter may also be capable of **speed-up pitch-shifting**, which changes the timbre and the pitch of natural sounds. Speed-up pitch-shifting is sometimes referred to as the "chipmunk effect."

As a time compressor, a pitch shifter can shorten recorded audio material with no editing, no deletion of content, and no alteration in pitch (see 7-20).

NOISE PROCESSORS

Noise processors reduce or eliminate noise from an audio signal. With the advent of **digital signal processing (DSP)** plug-ins, these processors have become powerful tools in getting rid of virtually any unwanted noise. In fact, because noise reduction with digital processing is so effective, getting rid of recorded and system noise has become far less of a problem than it once was. It has also been a boon to audio restoration.

Software programs are dedicated to getting rid of different types of noise such as clicks, crackles, pops, hum, buzz, rumble, computer-generated noise, unwanted background ambience, and recovery of lost signals due, for example, to *clipping.* They are available in bundles with separate programs for particular types of noise reduction.

Digital noise reduction is able to remove constant, steady noises. In a vocal track with high-level background noise from lights, ventilating fans, and studio acoustics, almost all the noise can be removed without affecting voice quality.

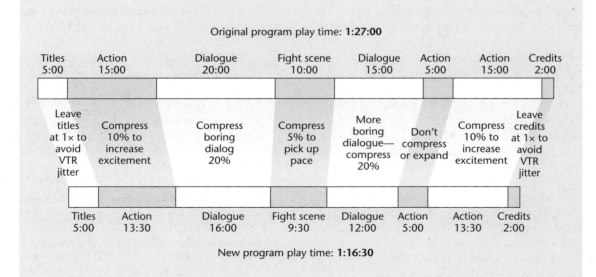

7-20 Time compression of an event sequence.

In digital noise reduction, there are parameters to control and balance. It is important to consider the amount of noise being removed from the signal, the amount of signal being removed from the program material, and the amount of new sonic colorations being added to the signal. Failure to coordinate these factors can sonically detract from the program material if not exacerbate the original noise problem.

Here are a few points to consider when using noise reduction[4]:

◼ Always preview before processing and have a backup copy.

◼ To maintain perspective, continue to compare the processed sound with the unprocessed sound.

◼ Do not rely only on automatic settings. They may not precisely produce the desired effect or may introduce unwanted artifacts or both.

◼ Use the "noise only" monitoring feature to check the part of the audio being removed by the software.

◼ In heavy noise situations, a multiband expander or an EQ boost in the frequency range of the target audio helps make the audio clearer.

----

4. Based on Mike Levine, "Noises Off," *Electronic Musician*, August 2008, p. 50.

◼ In rhythmic material be careful that the noise reduction processing does not adversely affect the rhythmic patterns or the transient response.

MULTIEFFECTS SIGNAL PROCESSORS

A *multieffects signal processor* combines several of the functions of individual signal processing in a single unit. The variety and the parameters of these functions vary with the model; but because most multieffects processors are digital, they are powerful audio-processing tools albeit, in some cases, dauntingly complicated. Figure 7-21 shows two examples of stand-alone multieffects processors. There are also plug-in bundles that provide just about every signal-processing function. Most multieffects processors have a wide frequency response, at least 16-bit resolution, and dozens of programmable presets.

Voice Processors

One type of popular multieffects processor used for voice work is the *voice processor* (also referred to as a *vocoder*). Because of its particular application in shaping the sound of the all-important spoken and singing voice, it warrants some attention here.

A voice processor can enhance, modify, pitch-correct, harmonize, and change completely the sound of a voice, even to the extent of gender. Functions vary with the model, but in general a system may include some,

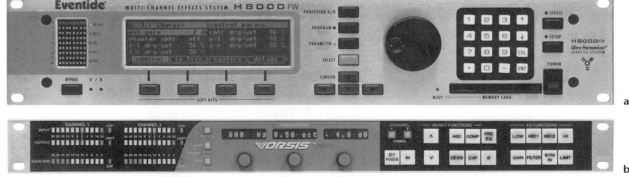

Courtesy of Eventide

7-21 Multieffects processors. (a) This device is a 24-bit eight-channel processor with 1,800 programs that include pitch shifting; tempo and compression modes; ambience; plate, acoustic chamber, and inverse reverb; tremolo; chorus; flanging; detune; 174-second delay; and echo. The processor offers eight discreet channels of processing, 5.1 surround effects, and stereo effects. (b) This device includes parametric EQ; high-pass, low-pass, and notch filters; a multiband compressor; a de-esser; an expander; and a limiter. It also comes with software to control one or more of these processors via a standard Ethernet local area connection.

many, or most of the following: preamp, EQ, harmonizer, compression, noise gate, reverb, delay, and chorus. Voice-modeling menus create different textures and may include any number of effects for inflections; spectral changes in frequency balance; *vibratos* (variations in the frequency of a sound generally at a rate of 2 and 15 times per second; *glottals* (breathiness, rasp, and growl); warp (changes in *formants*—a frequency band in a voice or musical instrument that contains more energy and loudness than the neighboring area); harmony processing that provides multivoice harmonies; and pitch shifting in *semitones,* or in *cents*—¹⁄₁₀₀ semitone. Voice processors are available in rack-mounted models and as plug-ins.

OTHER TYPES OF PLUG-INS

In addition to plug-ins that perform the relatively familiar signal-processing functions, specialized plug-ins add almost infinite flexibility to sound shaping. Among the hundreds available are programs for mastering—the final stage in preparing audio material for duplication; stereo and surround-sound calibration, panning, and mixing; musical synthesis with patches included; virtual instrumentation of just about any musical sound source, such as keyboards, fretted instruments, horns, drums, and full orchestras; metering, metronome, and instrument tuning; time alignment of vocals, dialogue, and musical instruments; simulation of various types of guitar amplifiers; software sampling with multiformat sound libraries; and emulation—making digital audio sound like analog.

FORMAT COMPATIBILITY OF PLUG-INS

Plug-ins come in a number of different formats. Before purchasing one make sure that it is compatible with your software production system. For example, the most popular formats for Windows are Steinberg's Virtual Studio Technology (VST) and Direct X, which is a group of application program interfaces. Because formats come and go, as do software programs, listing here which plug-in formats are compatible with which production systems would be unwieldy and become quickly outdated. A check of vendors' Web sites can provide their available plug-ins and the systems with which they are compatible.

MAIN POINTS

▶ Signal processors are used to alter some characteristic of a sound. They can be grouped into four categories: spectrum; time; amplitude, or dynamic; and noise.

▶ A plug-in is an add-on software tool that gives a hard-disk recording/editing system signal-processing alternatives beyond what the original system provides.

▶ Plug-ins incorporated in hard-disk recording/editing systems add to digital signal processing (DSP) not only the familiar processing tools—equalization (EQ), compression and expansion, reverb, delay, pitch shifting, and so on—but also an array of capabilities that place at the recordist's fingertips virtually limitless potential for creating entirely new effects at comparatively little cost.

▶ Plug-in programs are available separately or in bundles. Bundles include a number of different DSP programs.

▶ The equalizer and the filter are examples of spectrum processors because they alter the spectral balance of a signal. The equalizer increases or decreases the level of a signal at a selected frequency by boost or cut (also known as peak and dip) or by shelving. The filter attenuates certain frequencies above, below, between, or at a preset point(s).

▶ Two types of equalizers in common use are the fixed-frequency and the parametric.

▶ The most common filters are high-pass (low-cut), low-pass (high-cut), band-pass, and notch.

▶ Psychoacoustic processors add clarity, definition, and overall presence to sound.

▶ Time processors affect the time relationships of signals. Reverberation and delay are two such effects.

▶ The four types of reverberation systems used for the most part today are digital, convolution, plate, and acoustic chamber; reverb plug-in software may be considered a fifth type.

▶ Digital reverb reproduces electronically the sound of different acoustic environments.

▶ Convolution reverb is a sample-based process that multiplies the spectrums of two audio files. One file represents the acoustic signature of an acoustic space. It is called the impulse response (IR). The other file, or source, takes on the characteristics of the acoustic space when it is multiplied by the IR. Hence it has the quality of having been recorded in that space.

▶ The reverberation plate is a mechanical-electronic device consisting of a thin steel plate suspended under tension in an enclosed frame, a moving-coil driver, and a contact microphone(s).

▶ The acoustic reverberation chamber is a natural and realistic type of simulated reverb because it works on acoustic sound in an acoustic environment with sound-reflective surfaces.

▶ An important feature of most digital reverb units is predelay—the amount of time between the onset of the direct sound and the appearance of the first reflections.

▶ Delay is the time interval between a sound or signal and its repetition.

▶ Delay effects, such as doubling, chorus, slap back echo, and prereverb delay, are usually produced electronically with a digital delay device.

▶ Flanging and phasing split a signal and slightly delay one part to create controlled phase cancellations that generate a pulsating sound. Flanging uses a time delay; phasing uses a phase shifter.

▶ Morphing is the continuous, seamless transformation of one effect (aural or visual) into another.

▶ Amplitude, or dynamic, processors affect a sound's dynamic range. These effects include compression, limiting, de-essing, expanding, noise gating, and pitch shifting.

▶ With compression, as the input level increases, the output level also increases but at a slower rate, reducing dynamic range. With limiting, the output level stays at or below a preset point regardless of its input level. With expansion, as the input level increases, the output level also increases but at a greater rate, increasing dynamic range.

▶ A broadband compressor acts on the dynamic range of the input signal across the entire frequency spectrum. The split-band compressor affects an input signal independently by splitting the audio into multiple bands, as needed, and then recombining the outputs of the bands into a single mono or stereo broadband signal.

▶ A de-esser is basically a fast-acting compressor that acts on high-frequency sibilance by attenuating it.

▶ An expander, like a compressor, affects dynamic range. But whereas a compressor reduces it, an expander increases it.

▶ A noise gate is used primarily to reduce or eliminate unwanted low-level noise, such as ambience and leakage. It is also used creatively to produce dynamic special effects.

▶ A pitch shifter uses both compression and expansion to change the pitch of a signal or the running time of a program.

▶ Noise processors are designed to reduce or eliminate such noises as clicks, crackles, hum, and rumble from an audio signal.

▶ Multieffects signal processors combine several of the functions of individual signal processors in a single unit.

▶ A voice processor, also referred to as a vocoder, can enhance, modify, pitch-correct, harmonize, and change completely the sound of a voice, even to the extent of gender.

▶ There are highly specialized plug-ins that add almost infinite flexibility to sound shaping.

▶ When selecting a plug-in, it is important to know whether it is compatible with a given hard-disk production system.

8

Loudspeakers and Monitoring

The *sound chain* begins with the microphone, whose signal is sent to a console or mixer for routing and then processed, recorded, and heard through a loudspeaker. Although the loudspeaker is last in this signal flow, no matter how good the other components in the audio system are *the quality of every sound evaluated is based on what you hear from a loudspeaker interacting with the room acoustics*. More than with any other component, knowing a loudspeaker's sonic characteristics in relation to the acoustic environment is fundamental to the accurate monitoring and appraisal of audio material.

The solution seems straightforward enough: select the best loudspeaker for the given room. But which is best? Is it the most expensive? The largest? The loudest? The one with the widest, flattest frequency response? The one suitable for symphonic music, jazz, country, or hard rock?

Although a loudspeaker is critical to every audio operation, choosing the one most suited to your needs is not so straightforward. The loudspeaker is capable of reproducing a wide variety and range of sounds, more than any musical instrument or other component in the sound chain. Therefore choosing the "right" loudspeaker involves several decisions; each influences later ones, and many are mainly subjective.

In deciding which loudspeaker is "best," consider several factors: frequency response, linearity, amplifier power, distortion, dynamic range, sensitivity, polar response, arrival time, and polarity. Placement also affects the sound. These factors are discussed later in this chapter. Perhaps the two fundamental criteria for loudspeakers most audio professionals agree on are that they are able to handle with equal impartiality the frequencies between, at least, 30 to 16,000 Hz and loudness levels of 120 dB-SPL.

TYPES OF LOUDSPEAKERS

The loudspeaker is a *transducer*—it converts one form of energy into another: electric energy into acoustic energy. (Another example of a transducer is the microphone, which works in the opposite direction, converting acoustic energy into electric energy (see Chapter 3, "Microphones"). Also like microphones, loudspeakers are available with three different types of elements: the moving-coil, ribbon, and capacitor designs. But unlike microphone usage, the *moving-coil loudspeaker* is, by far, the most common.

The moving-coil principle can be easily applied to a wide variety of loudspeakers, from inexpensive transistor radio speakers to the highest-quality studio monitors, and for relatively low cost compared with other loudspeaker designs (see "Transducing Elements" in Chapter 3). Moving-coil speakers are also sturdier and can handle louder sound-pressure levels. When the ribbon principle is employed, it is usually only in the high-frequency, or tweeter, components of the loudspeaker. One advantage of the *ribbon loudspeaker* is its smooth high-frequency response.

The *electrostatic loudspeaker* is rarely used. Also called a *capacitor loudspeaker,* it is expensive and cannot produce the loud sound levels required in so much of today's audio production. That said, the sound quality of the best electrostatic loudspeaker models is rarely equaled by the other types of speakers.

LOUDSPEAKER POWERING SYSTEMS

Loudspeakers are powered either externally or internally. Externally powered speakers are called *passive loudspeakers;* internally powered speakers are called *active loudspeakers.* With a passive loudspeaker, an external amplifier feeds power to the speaker elements. With an active loudspeaker, power amplifiers are built-in, and each speaker element has its own amplifier.

Theoretically, a loudspeaker should be able to reproduce all frequencies linearly—that is, having an output that varies proportionately with the input. In reality, however, this does not occur. A loudspeaker that is large enough to generate low-frequency sound waves most likely will not be able to efficiently reproduce the high

frequencies. Conversely, a speaker capable of reproducing the shorter wavelengths may be incapable of reproducing the longer waves.

To illustrate the problem, consider that many radio and television receivers contain a single speaker; even many stereo radios and recorders contain only one loudspeaker in each of the two loudspeaker enclosures. Because a single speaker has difficulty coping with the entire range of audible frequencies, a compromise is made: the long and the short wavelengths are sacrificed for the medium wavelengths that a single, midsized loudspeaker can reproduce more efficiently. Therefore, regardless of a recording's sound quality, a receiver with just one loudspeaker cannot reproduce it with full-frequency response.

Crossover Network and Drivers

To widen the loudspeaker's frequency response and make reproduction of the bass and the treble more efficient, the *crossover network* was created. Also, individual speaker elements, called *drivers,* were developed to handle the different physical requirements necessary to emit the long, powerful bass frequencies and the short, more directional treble frequencies.

The crossover network divides the frequency spectrum between the low and the high frequencies. The actual point, or frequency, where the bass and the treble divide is called the *crossover frequency*. A driver large enough to handle the low frequencies is dedicated to the bass, and a driver small enough to handle the high frequencies is dedicated to the treble. Informally, these drivers, or loudspeakers, are called the *woofer* and the *tweeter*. Low- and high-frequency drivers are contained in a single cabinet. The size of the drivers is related to the power output of the loudspeaker system.

If a loudspeaker system divides the frequency spectrum once, it is called a *two-way system loudspeaker*. The crossover frequency in a two-way system is in the neighborhood of 1,500 to 2,000 Hz. Lows from the crossover feed the woofer power amplifier, which is directly connected to the woofer; highs from the crossover feed the tweeter power amp, which is directly connected to the tweeter. A loudspeaker may have more than one driver for each frequency range.

A loudspeaker system that uses two crossover networks is called a *three-way system loudspeaker,* and one that has three crossover networks is called a *four-way system loudspeaker*. Three-way systems divide the frequency spectrum at roughly 400 to 500 Hz and 3,500 to 5,000 Hz.

Four-way systems divide it at anywhere between 400 to 500 Hz, 1,500 to 2,000 Hz, and 4,500 to 6,000 Hz.

Passive and Active Crossover Networks

Two types of crossover networks are used in loudspeakers: passive and active. In a *passive crossover network,* the power amplifier is external to the speakers and therefore precedes the crossover (see Figure 8-1). This design can create certain problems: output level at the crossover frequency is usually down by a few decibels; intermodulation distortion is more likely to occur, particularly at loud levels; and harmonic distortion may be heard in the high frequencies.

In an *active crossover network,* the crossover precedes the power amps and operates at low power levels. In a two-way system loudspeaker, one amp receives the low-frequency signals and drives the woofer; the other amp receives the high-frequency signals and drives the tweeter. This is known as a *biamplification,* or *biamped,* system (see 8-2).

An active crossover network has several advantages over a passive one. It is usually less expensive; it reduces distortion; and, if distortion occurs in either the woofer or the tweeter, it will not be transferred to the other component. Power use is more efficient because a lower-power amp can drive the tweeter, which requires less power than

8-1 Passive two-way crossover system. (a) Layout. (b) Frequency response curves assuming crossover frequencies of 1,500 Hz.

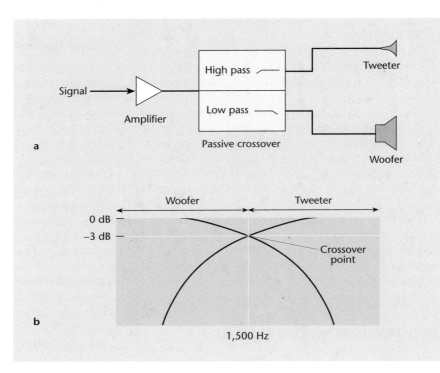

8-2 Biamped monitor system with an active crossover.

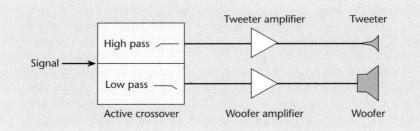

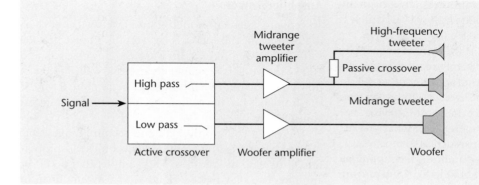

8-3 Biamped monitor system with both active and passive crossovers.

the woofer. Transient response is better, especially in the lower frequencies.

A disadvantage of active loudspeakers is that if an amplifier fails, the entire speaker has to be serviced. It is not possible to substitute another amp, which can be done with a passive loudspeaker.

Active three-way system loudspeakers can be *triamped,* meaning that each speaker is driven by its own amp. Some active three-way systems may be biamped, in which case a passive crossover is added before the tweeter to create the three-way design (see 8-3).

SELECTING A MONITOR LOUDSPEAKER

Loudspeakers are sometimes compared to musical instruments in that they produce sound. But it is more accurate to say that they reproduce sound. And unlike any musical instrument, a loudspeaker has the capability of generating a far wider frequency response and a greater dynamic range.

Loudspeakers are not like purely electronic components such as consoles, which can be objectively tested and rationally evaluated. No two loudspeakers sound quite the same. Comparing the same make and model of loudspeakers in one room tells you only what they sound like in that acoustic environment; in another room they may sound altogether different. Furthermore, a loudspeaker that satisfies your taste might be unappealing to someone else.

A loudspeaker's specifications can be used only as a reference. No matter how good a speaker looks on paper, keep in mind that the measurements are based on tests made in an *anechoic chamber*—a room with no reflections of any kind.

Another problem in loudspeaker evaluation is that in comparison tests, which are done by switching back and forth between two monitors or switching among more than two monitors, auditory memory is quite short—only a few seconds at best. By the time one is listening to a second set of monitors, or monitor number 3, recalling what the comparisons in the first set were or what monitor 1 sounded like is unreliable. This is why it is essential to employ objective testing when evaluating a loudspeaker (see "Calibrating a Loudspeaker System" later in this chapter).

Even as methods for evaluating loudspeakers improve, it is still difficult to suggest guidelines that will satisfy the general population of audio professionals, though they will agree that monitors used for professional purposes should meet certain performance requirements.

Frequency Response

Evaluating *frequency response* in a loudspeaker involves two considerations: how wide it is and how flat, or linear, it is. Frequency response ideally should be as wide as possible, from at least 40 to 20,000 Hz. But the relationship between the sound produced in the studio and the sound reproduced through the listener's receiver/loudspeaker becomes a factor when selecting a monitor loudspeaker.

For example, TV audio can carry the entire range of audible frequencies. You may have noticed during a televised music program, however, that you see certain high- and low-pitched instruments being played but you hear them only faintly or not at all. Overhead cymbals are one example. Generally, their frequency range is between 300 Hz and 12,000 Hz (including overtones), but they usually begin to gain good definition between 4,500 Hz and 8,000 Hz, which is well within the frequency of television transmission. The highest response of many home TV receivers is about 6,000 Hz, however, which is below a good part of the cymbals' range.

Assume that you wish to boost the cymbal frequencies that the home TV receiver can barely reproduce. Unless you listen to the sound over a monitor comparable in output level and response to the average TV speaker, you cannot get a sense of what effect the boost is having. But that monitor will not give you a sense of what viewers with upgraded TV sound systems, such as stereo and surround sound, are hearing. (The audio in *high-definition television [HDTV]* has great potential to level the playing field between the sonic fidelity of the transmission and that of the reception, but it depends on the audio quality of the commercial TV tuner and the willingness of the consumer to purchase an HDTV set.)

Due to the differences between the potential sound response of a medium and its actual response after processing, transmission, and reception, most professional studios use at least two types of studio monitors: one to provide both wide response and sufficient power to reproduce a broad range of sound levels, and the other with response and power that reflect what the average listener hears. Many studios use three sets of monitors to check sound: mediocre-quality loudspeakers with mostly midrange response and limited power output, such as those in portable and car radios, portable and desktop TVs, computer-grade speakers, and small playback devices; average-quality loudspeakers with added high and low response, such as moderately priced component systems; and high-quality loudspeakers with a very wide response and high output capability.

Linearity

The second consideration in evaluating frequency response in a loudspeaker is how linear it is. **Linearity** means that frequencies being fed to a loudspeaker at a particular loudness are reproduced at the same loudness. If they are not, it is very difficult to predetermine what listeners will hear. If the level of a 100 Hz sound is 80 dB going in and 55 dB coming out, some—if not most—of the information may be lost. If the level of an 8,000 Hz sound is 80 dB going in and 100 dB coming out, the information loss may be overbearing.

Loudspeaker specifications include a value that indicates how much a monitor deviates from a flat frequency response by either increasing or decreasing the level. This variance should be no greater than ±3 dB.

Amplifier Power

To generate adequately loud sound levels without causing distortion, the loudspeaker amplifier must provide sufficient power. At least 30 *watts (W)* for tweeters and 100 W for woofers are generally necessary. Regardless of how good the rest of a loudspeaker's components are, if the amp does not have enough power, efficiency suffers considerably.

There is a commonly held and seemingly plausible notion that increasing amplifier power means a proportional increase in loudness; for example, that a 100 W amplifier can play twice as loud as a 50 W amplifier. In fact, if a 100 W amp and a 50 W amp are playing at top volume, the 100 W amp will sound only slightly louder. What the added wattage gives is clearer and less distorted reproduction in loud sonic peaks.

Distortion

Discussion of amplifier power naturally leads to consideration of *distortion*—appearance of a signal in the reproduced sound that was not in the original sound (see 8-4). Any component in the sound chain can gener-

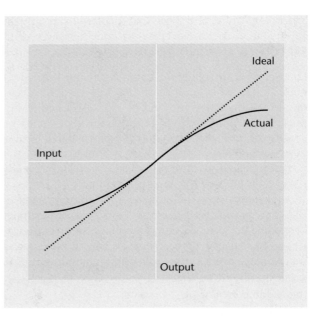

8-4 Generalized graphic example of distortion. Ideally, a reproduced sound would change in direct proportion to the input. Realistically, the relationship between input and output is rarely linear, resulting in distortion, however slight or significant it may be.

From Brian Smithers, "Sonic Mayhem," *Electronic Musician*, August 2007, p. 66.

ate distortion. Because distortion is heard at the reproduction (loudspeaker) phase of the sound chain, regardless of where in the system it was generated, and because loudspeakers are the most distortion-prone component in most audio systems, it is appropriate to discuss briefly the various forms of distortion: intermodulation, harmonic, transient, and loudness.

Intermodulation Distortion

The loudspeaker is perhaps most vulnerable to **intermodulation distortion (IM)**, which results when two or more frequencies occur at the same time and interact to create combination tones and dissonances that are unrelated to the original sounds. Audio systems can be most vulnerable to intermodulation distortion when frequencies are far apart, as when a piccolo and a baritone saxophone are playing at the same time. Intermodulation distortion usually occurs in the high frequencies because they are weaker and more delicate than the low frequencies.

Wideness and flatness of frequency response are affected when IM is present. In addition to its obvious effect on perception, even subtle distortion can cause listening fatigue.

Unfortunately, not all specification sheets include percentage of IM, and those that do often list it only for selected frequencies. Nevertheless, knowing the percentage of IM for all frequencies is important to loudspeaker selection. A rating of 0.5 percent IM or less is considered good for a loudspeaker.

Harmonic Distortion

Harmonic distortion occurs when the audio system introduces harmonics into a recording that were not present originally. Harmonic and IM distortion usually happen when the input and the output of a sound system are **nonlinear**—that is, when they do not change in direct proportion to each other. A loudspeaker's inability to handle amplitude is a common cause of harmonic distortion. This added harmonic content is expressed as a percentage of the total signal or as a component's *total harmonic distortion (THD)*.

Transient Distortion

Transient distortion relates to the inability of an audio component to respond quickly to a rapidly changing signal, such as that produced by percussive sounds. Sometimes transient distortion produces a ringing sound.

Loudness Distortion

Loudness distortion, also called *overload distortion*, occurs when a signal is recorded or played back at a level of loudness that is greater than the sound system can handle. The clipping that results from loudness distortion creates a fuzzy, gritty sound.

Dynamic Range

Overly loud signals give a false impression of program quality and balance; nevertheless, a loudspeaker should be capable of reproducing loud sound levels without distorting, blowing fuses, or damaging its components. An output capability of 120 dB-SPL can handle almost all studio work. Even if studio work does not often call for very loud levels, the monitor should be capable of reproducing them because it is sometimes necessary to listen at a loud level to hear subtlety and quiet detail. For soft passages at least 40 dB-SPL is necessary for most professional recording/mixing situations.

It is worth noting that although monitors in professional facilities have a dynamic range of up to 80 dB (40 to 120 dB-SPL), the dynamic range in consumer loudspeakers is considerably less. Even the better ones may be only 55 dB (50 to 105 dB-SPL).

Sensitivity

Sensitivity is the on-axis sound-pressure level a loudspeaker produces at a given distance when driven at a certain power (about 3.3 feet with 1 W of power). A monitor's sensitivity rating gives you an idea of the system's overall efficiency. Typical ratings range from 84 to more than 100 dB.

In real terms, however, a sensitivity rating of, say, 90 dB indicates that the loudspeaker could provide 100 dB from a 10 W input and 110 dB from a 100 W input, depending on the type of driver. It is the combination of sensitivity rating and power rating that tells you whether a monitor loudspeaker will be loud enough to suit your production needs. Generally, a sensitivity rating of 93 dB or louder is required for professional applications.

Polar Response

Polar response indicates how a loudspeaker focuses sound at the monitoring position(s). Because it is important to hear only the sound coming from the studio or the recording, without interacting reflections from the control

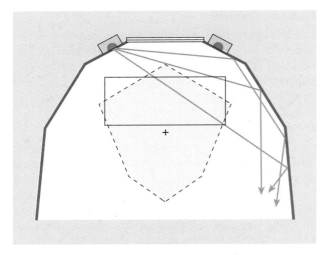

8-5 The shaded area in this control room design is a reflection-free zone.

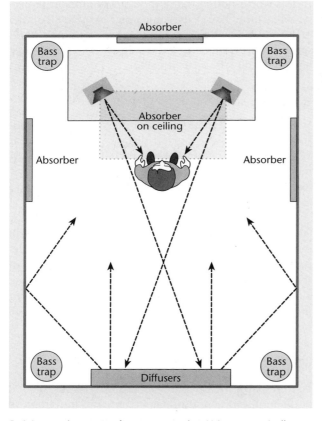

8-6 Improving control room acoustics. Using strategically placed absorbers, diffusers, and bass traps can help control unwanted room reflections.

room walls (vertical surfaces) and the ceiling or floor (horizontal surfaces), dispersion must be controlled at the monitoring locations so that it is a relatively reflection-free zone (see 8-5).

This is easier said than done, particularly with bass waves, which are difficult to direct because of their long wavelengths. With bass waves the room's size, shape, and furnishings have more to do with a speaker's sound than does the speaker's inherent design. Therefore bass traps and other low-frequency absorbers are included in control room design to handle those bass waves not focused at the listening position (see 8-6 and 8-7; see also 2-25).

Frequencies from the tweeter(s), on the other hand, are shorter, more directional, and easier to focus. The problem with high frequencies is that as the wavelength shortens, the pattern can narrow and may be off-axis to the listening position. Therefore the *coverage angle*, defined as the off-axis angle or point at which loudspeaker level is down 6 dB compared with the on-axis output level, may not be wide enough to include the entire listening area.

To help in selecting a loudspeaker with adequate polar response, specifications usually list a monitor's horizontal and vertical coverage angles. These angles should be high enough and wide enough to cover the listening position and still allow the operator or listener some lateral movement without seriously affecting sonic balance (see 8-8).

Figures 8-5, 8-6, and 8-8 display examples of reflection-free zones and coverage angles using conventional two-loudspeaker setups for stereo monitoring. Surround sound presents altogether different acoustic challenges because monitors are located to the front and the rear and/or the sides of the listening position. Theoretically, therefore, for surround monitoring there should be an even distribution of absorbers and diffusers so that the rear-side loudspeakers function in an acoustic environment that is similar to the frontal speaker array. The problem is that this approach renders mixing rooms designed for stereo unsuitable for surround sound because stereo and surround require different acoustic environments (see "Monitoring Surround Sound" later in this chapter).

Arrival Time

Even if coverage angles are optimal, unless all reproduced sounds reach the listening position(s) at relatively the same time they were produced, aural perception will be impaired. When you consider the differences in size and power requirements among drivers and the wavelengths they emit, you can see that this is easier said than done.

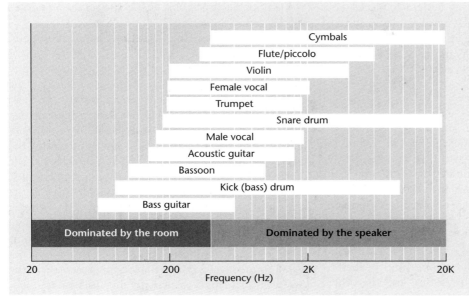

8-7 Room and loudspeaker influences on the response of selected musical instruments. At frequencies lower than 300 Hz, the room is the dominant factor. Above 300 Hz the inherent loudspeaker characteristics dominate response.

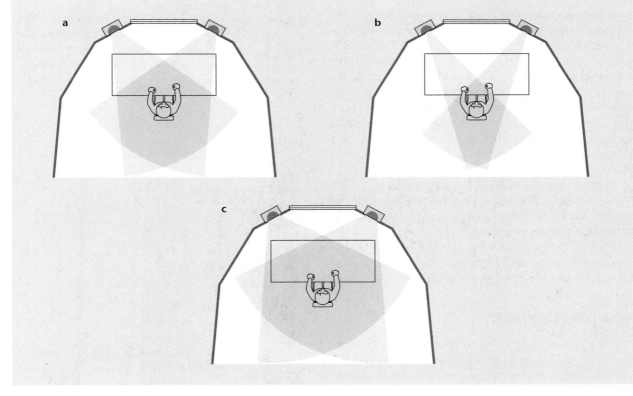

8-8 Coverage angles of monitor loudspeakers. (a) Desirable coverage angle. Alternative coverage angles include (b) loudspeakers with narrow radiation, which produce a sharp aural image and less envelopment, and (c) loudspeakers that radiate more broadly, which increase envelopment but reduce imaging.

In two-, three-, and four-way system loudspeakers, the physical separation of each speaker in the system causes the sounds to reach the listener's ears at different times. *Arrival times* that differ by more than 1 ms are not acceptable in professional applications.

Polarity

Sometimes, although dispersal and arrival time are adequate, sound reaching a listener may not be as loud as it should be, or the elements within it may be poorly placed. For example, a rock band may be generating loud levels in the studio, but the sounds in the control room are, in relative terms, not so loud; or an actor is supposed to be situated slightly left in the aural frame but is heard from the right loudspeaker.

These problems may be the result of the loudspeakers' polarity being out of phase: one loudspeaker is pushing sound outward (compression), and the other is pulling sound inward (rarefaction) (see 8-9). *Polarity* problems can occur between woofer and tweeter in the same loudspeaker enclosure or between two separate loudspeakers. In the latter case, it is usually because the connections from loudspeaker to amplifier are improperly wired; that is, the two leads from one loudspeaker may be connected to the amplifier positive-to-negative and negative-to-positive, whereas the other loudspeaker may be connected positive-to-positive and negative-to-negative. If you think that sound is out of phase, check the sound-level meters. If they show a similar level and the audio still sounds skewed, the speakers are out of phase; if they show different levels, the phase problem is probably elsewhere.

Another way to test for polarity problems is to use a *9-volt (V)* battery. Attach the battery's positive lead to the loudspeaker's positive lead and the battery's negative lead to the loudspeaker's negative lead. Touching the battery's positive lead should push the speaker outward. If the speaker moves inward, it is out of polarity. All speakers in a cabinet should move in the same direction.

MONITOR PLACEMENT

Where you place monitor loudspeakers also affects sound quality, dispersal, and arrival time. Loudspeakers are often designed for a particular room location and are generally positioned in one of four places: well toward the middle of a room, against or flush with a wall, at the intersection of two walls, or in a corner at the ceiling or on the floor. Each position affects the sound's loudness and dispersion differently.

A loudspeaker hanging in the middle of a room radiates sound into what is called a *free-sphere* (or *free-field* or *full space*), where, theoretically, the sound level at any point within a given distance is the same because the loudspeaker can radiate sound with no limiting obstacles or surface (see 8-10). If a loudspeaker is placed against a wall, the wall concentrates the radiations into a *half sphere* (or *half space*), thereby theoretically increasing the sound level by 3 dB. With loudspeakers mounted at the intersection of two walls, the dispersion is concentrated still more into a *one-quarter sphere,* thus increasing the sound level another 3 dB. Loudspeakers placed in corners at the ceiling or on the floor radiate in a *one-eighth sphere,* generating the most-concentrated sound levels in a four-walled room. A significant part of each increase in the overall sound level is due to the loudness increase in the bass (see 8-11). This is particularly the case with frequencies at 300 Hz and below. It is difficult to keep them free of excessive peaks and boominess, thereby inhibiting a coherent, tight bass sound.

For informal listening one of these monitor positions is not necessarily better than another; placement may depend on a room's layout, furniture position, personal taste, and so on. As noted, in professional situations it is preferable to flush-mount loudspeakers in a wall or

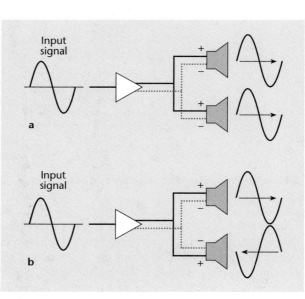

8-9 Loudspeaker polarity. (a) Cone motions in phase. (b) Cone motions out of phase.

From David Miles Huber, *Modern Recording Techniques*, 5th ed. (Focal Press), p. 419. © 2001 Focal Press. Reprinted with permission of Elsevier, Ltd.

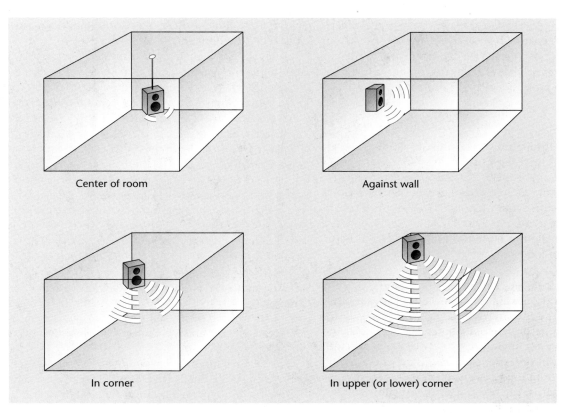

8-10 Four typical loudspeaker locations in a room and the effects of placement on overall loudness levels.

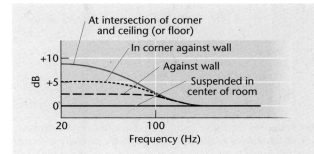

8-11 Effects of loudspeaker placement on bass response.

soffit (see 8-16). The most important thing in monitor placement is to avoid any appreciable space between the loudspeaker and the wall and any protrusion of the loudspeaker's cabinet edges. Otherwise the wall or cabinet edges, or both, will act as secondary radiators, degrading frequency response. By flush-mounting loudspeakers, low-frequency response becomes more efficient, back-wall reflections and cancellation are eliminated, and cabinet-edge diffraction is reduced.

Monitoring Stereo

Stereo creates the illusion of two-dimensional sound by imaging depth—front-to-back—and width—side-to-side—in aural space. It requires two discrete loudspeakers each of which, in reality, is producing monaural sound but creating a phantom image between them (see 8-12). In placing these loudspeakers, it is critical that they be positioned to reproduce an accurate and balanced stereo image. The monitoring system should be set up symmetrically within the room. The distance between the speakers should be the same as the distance from each speaker to your ears, forming an equilateral triangle with your head. Also, the center of the equilateral triangle should be equidistant from the room's side walls (see 8-13).

The locations of the front-to-back and side-to-side sound sources are where they should be. If the original material has the vocal in the center (in relation to the two

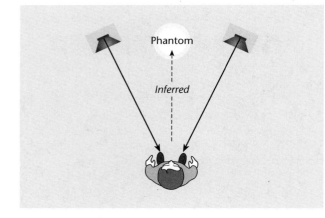

8-12 Why we perceive a phantom image.

From Dave Moulton, "Median Plane, Sweet Spot, and Phantom Everything," *TV Technology,* November 2007, p. 34.

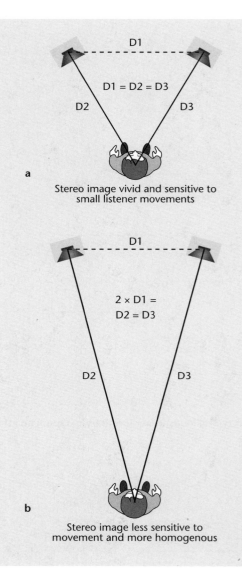

loudspeakers), the first violins on the left, the bass drum and the bass at the rear-center, the snare drum slightly left or right, and so on, these should be in the same spatial positions when the material is played through the monitor system. If the listener is off the median plane, it skews the stereo imaging (see 8-14). The designated stereo listening position is known as the **sweet spot**.

A recent development in loudspeaker design eliminates the sweet spot by using a single loudspeaker enclosure to reproduce two-channel stereo, thereby doing away with the cancellation or reinforcement of certain frequencies that results when distances from the listener to the speakers are not equal. As noted, anyone sitting even slightly off from the sweet spot hears a different sound (see 8-14).

The design includes a central speaker driver aimed forward and two drivers facing sideways—each oriented at 90 degrees to the central driver. The forward-facing driver reproduces the main signal, which is the sum of the left and right channels (L + R). The side drivers reproduce the difference signal (L – R) with one driver being 180 degrees out of phase with the other (see 8-15).[1]

Far-field Monitoring

Most professional audio-mixing rooms use at least two sets (or groups) of frontal loudspeakers. One set is for *far-field monitoring*, consisting of large loudspeaker systems that can deliver very wide frequency response

8-13 To help create an optimal travel path for sound from the loudspeakers to the listening position, carefully measure the loudspeaker separation and the distance between the loudspeakers and the listening position. (a) The distance between the acoustic center (between the loudspeakers) and the listening position is equal. In this arrangement head movement is restricted somewhat and the stereo image will be emphasized or spread out, heightening the sense of where elements in the recording are located. Shortening D2 and D3 will produce a large shift in the stereo image. (b) The distance between the acoustic center and the listening position is about twice as long. With this configuration the movement of the head is less restricted and the stereo image is reduced in width, although it is more homogeneous. The more D2 and D3 are lengthened, the more monaural the stereo image becomes (except for hard-left and hard-right panning).

---

1. From Scott Wilkinson, "Sweet Space," *Electronic Musician,* August 2008, p. 30.

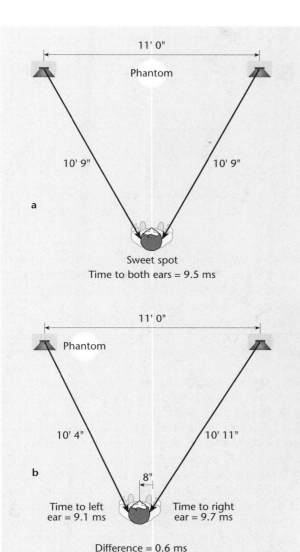

8-14 Phantom imaging on and off the median plane.

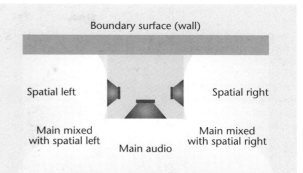

8-15 **Reproducing two-channel stereo from a single loudspeaker enclosure.** This concept was designed by the company airSound.

8-16 Positions of far-field and near-field monitors.

at moderate to quite loud levels with relative accuracy. Due to their size and loudness capabilities, these loudspeakers are built into the mixing-room wall above, and at a distance of several feet from, the listening position (see 8-16). Far-field loudspeakers are designed to provide the highest-quality sound reproduction.

Near-field Monitoring

Even in the best monitor–control room acoustic environments, the distance between wall-mounted loudspeakers and the listening position is often wide enough to generate sonic discontinuities from unwanted control room reflections. To reduce these unwanted reflections, another set of monitors is placed on or near the console's meter bridge (see 8-16).

Near-field monitoring reduces the audibility of control room acoustics by placing loudspeakers close to the listening position. Moreover, near-field monitoring improves source localization because most of the sound reaching the listening position is direct; the early reflections that hinder good source localization are reduced to the point where they are of little consequence. At least that is the theory; in practice, problems with near-field monitoring remain (see 8-17).

Among the requirements for near-field monitors are: loudspeakers that are small enough to put on or near

8-17 Near-field monitoring. (a) If a meter bridge is too low, early reflections will bounce off the console, degrading the overall monitor sound reaching the operator's ears. (b) One way to minimize this problem is to place the near-field monitors a few inches in back of the console.

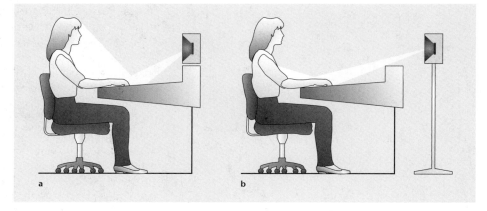

the console's meter bridge without the sound blowing you away; a uniform frequency response from about 70 to 16,000 Hz, especially smooth response through the midrange; a sensitivity range from 87 to 92 dB; sufficient amplifier power; and good vertical dispersion for more-stable stereo imaging.

It is worth remembering that many near-field monitors have a built-in *high-pass filter* to protect the bass unit from overload. The filter is generally set around 50 Hz. Being unaware that the loudspeaker is removing this part of the spectrum can lead to low-frequency balancing problems.

Monitoring Surround Sound

Surround sound differs from stereo by expanding the dimension of depth, thereby placing the listener more in the center of the aural image than in front of it. Accomplishing this requires additional audio channels routed to additional loudspeakers.

The most common surround-sound format (for the time being) uses six discrete audio channels: five full-range and one limited to low frequencies (typically below 125 Hz), called the *subwoofer*. Hence the format is known as *5.1*. The loudspeakers that correspond to these channels are placed front-left and front-right, like a stereo pair; a center-channel speaker is placed between the stereo pair; and another stereo pair—the surround speakers—are positioned to the left and right sides, or left-rear and right-rear, of the listener. (Unlike stereo, there is no phantom image in surround's frontal loudspeaker arrangement. The center-channel speaker creates a discrete image.) The subwoofer can be placed almost anywhere in the room because low frequencies

are relatively omnidirectional, but it is usually situated in the front, between the center and the left or right speaker (see 8-18). Sometimes it is positioned in a corner to reinforce low frequencies.

A problem in positioning the center-channel speaker is the presence of a video monitor if it is situated on the same plane as the loudspeakers. Mounting the center speaker above or below the monitor is not the best location. If it is unavoidable, however, keep the tweeters close to the same plane as the left and right speakers, which may require turning the center speaker upside down. If the image is being projected, it becomes possible to mount the center speaker behind a micro-perforation screen, as they do in movie theaters.

If the center-channel speaker is on the same plane as the left and right loudspeakers, it is closer to the monitoring position and therefore its sound travels a shorter path than the sound coming from the outside speakers. This tends to create a center-channel sonic image that is louder than and, hence, forward of the sounds coming from the speakers on either side. There are four ways to compensate for this aural imbalance:

1. Use a somewhat smaller center speaker, taking care to ensure that its frequency response is similar to that of the left and right speakers.

2. Position the center speaker at an optimal distance behind the outside speakers so that their left-center-right arrangement forms a slight semicircle.

3. Reduce the loudness of the center channel to a level that appropriately balances the information coming from left, center, and right.

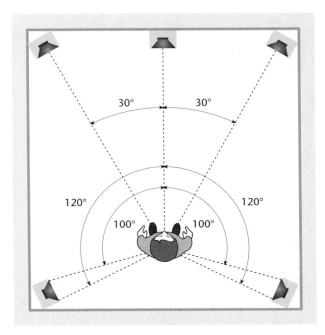

8-18 **International Telecommunications Union guideline for arranging loudspeakers in a surround-sound setup.** In a 5.1 system, the front-left and front-right speakers form a 60-degree angle with the listener at the apex; the center-channel speaker is directly in front of the listener. The surround speakers are usually placed at an angle between 100 and 120 degrees from the front-center line.

4. Slightly delay the center-channel audio so that it is in the correct position acoustically.

You could also use some combination of these four approaches. The important thing is to take the steps necessary to ensure that the sound coming from the center channel is not disproportionate to the sound coming from the left and right channels.

As for the subwoofer, there is widespread opinion about placement and, in some cases, whether there should be more than one. The main problems are controlling acoustically the powerful low-frequency sound waves, particularly in small rooms, and dealing with the subwoofer's loudness level so that it does not overwhelm the mix.

Perhaps the most common placement for the subwoofer is between the left and center or the center and right-front loudspeakers, usually at floor level. Advocates of this positioning cite that such placement makes aural imaging easier. Detractors claim that low bass tends to mask too much of the sound coming from the other front speakers. Another approach is to place the subwoofer in a front corner for the smoothest, most extended low-frequency response. Some subwoofers are especially designed for corner placement. The potential problem here is that typically any loudspeaker placed in a corner produces a bass boost (see 8-11). Placing the subwoofer to the middle and side of the mixing room is yet another approach, the rationale being that the sound is, theoretically at least, distributed evenly between the front and surround speakers. But this approach can imbalance aural perception because the left or right ear, depending on which side of the listening position the subwoofer is located, is receiving the stronger sound.

It has been suggested that, because the subwoofer is monaural, two will create more-natural spatial imaging and improve the spaciousness of the low-frequency information. The specific approach (advanced by David Griesinger of Lexicon) recommends that the two subwoofers be placed to either side of the listening position but be driven 90 degrees out of phase to help control additive low-bass response. There is also the notion that a subwoofer should be used only in a mixing room that can handle it acoustically. Otherwise, just go with the 5 in the 5.1 arrangement.

When dealing with location of the subwoofer(s), some kind of signal processing may be necessary to obtain a satisfactory sound. Equalization may be necessary to create as flat an overall frequency response as possible. Time delay may be used to enable some correction of the time relationship between the subwoofer and the other loudspeakers.

A primary consideration with surround-sound setups is making sure the room is large enough, not only to accommodate the additional equipment and loudspeaker placement specifications but also to handle the relatively high loudness that is sometimes necessary when monitoring surround sound. There is also the factor of surround-sound systems that go beyond the 5.1 configuration, such as 6.1 and 7.1, up to 10.2 (see 8-19).

In fact, trends suggest that *7.1* is increasing in popularity and may supplant 5.1. In addition to the 5.1 configuration, the two added channels in 7.1 are fed to left- and right-side speakers (see 8-20) to improve sound localization, especially of ambience. Also see Chapters 22 and 23 for discussions of mixing surround sound for music mixdowns and for television and film.

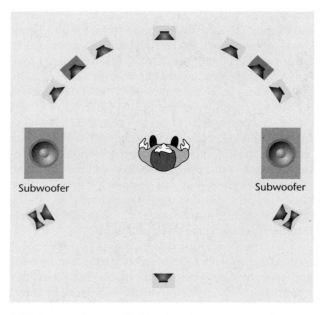

8-19 Surround-sound 10.2 loudspeaker arrangement.

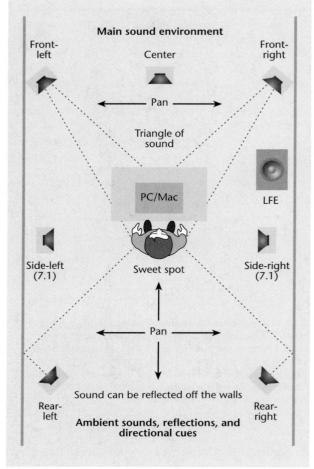

From Chris Middleton, *Creating Digital Music and Sound* (Boston: Focal Press, 2006), p. 160.

8-20 7.1 surround-sound monitoring.

CALIBRATING A LOUDSPEAKER SYSTEM

As important as "educated ears" (see Chapter 14) and personal taste are to monitor selection and evaluation, it is critical to obtain an objective measure of the correlation between monitor sound and room sound using a calibration system. *Calibration* helps ensure that a system's measurements meet a specified or desired standard. A critical component in a calibration system is the *spectrum analyzer*—a device that, among other things, displays the frequency response of an electrical waveform in relation to the amplitude present at all frequencies. It may do this over an assigned period of time or, if it is a *real-time analyzer (RTA)*, on an instantaneous basis (see 8-21). It is also possible to calibrate using a sound-pressure-level meter. But SPL meters provide only approximate levels, and RTAs are preferred.

When problems with frequency response show up, particularly serious ones, avoid the temptation to offset them with equalization. For example, if control room acoustics boost loudspeaker sound by, say, 6 dB at 250 Hz, try not to equalize the monitors by, in this case, attenuating their response 6 dB at 250 Hz. Aside from adding noise by running the signal through another electronic device, an equalizer can change the phase relationships of the audio that passes through it.

To deal with discontinuities in the monitor–control room interface, look to the source of the problem and correct it there. It may be necessary to change or modify the monitor, monitor position, power amplifier, or sound-diffusing materials or correct an impedance mismatch between sections of the monitor system. Whatever it takes, "natural" provides a truer sonic reference than "artificial," especially if the recording has to be evaluated or further processed in a different control room.

Still, taking the "natural" approach may not be practical logistically, ergonomically, or financially. There are several alignment systems available that are an improvement over using conventional equalizers to correct problems with the monitor–control room interface.

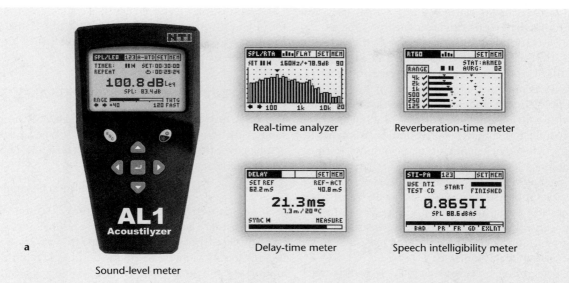

Sound-level meter

Real-time analyzer

Reverberation-time meter

Delay-time meter

Speech intelligibility meter

a

Time-code clock

Digital level meters

Left/right balance meter

Left-channel oscilloscope

Left-channel spectragram

Left-channel spectragraph

Left-channel power history meter

Lissajous phase scope

Phase Torch™ band limited phase meter

Right-channel oscilloscope

Right-channel spectragram

Right-channel spectragraph

Right-channel envelope display

b

Left-channel envelope display

Right-channel power history meter

8-21 Two audio analysis systems. (a) Palm-sized portable acoustical analyzer and its various features. (b) This stand-alone or software plug-in system includes Lissajous phase scopes, audio frequency oscilloscopes, power balance meters, level meters with physical unit calibration, audio spectrum analyzers, spectragram spectral history meters, correlation meters, correlation history meters, Phase Torch frequency-sensitive meters to compare phase differences between two channels, envelope history meters, band power history meters, and peak and RMS (room mean square) power history meters.

One such system is called *MultEQ,* which uses test tones through the sound system and measures the room's acoustics at various listening positions. It then creates a tuned inverse filter that counteracts the room-based distortions. The technology is not limited to bands of frequencies as are most equalizers but has hundreds of control points using *finite impulse response filters.* Compared with conventional equalizers, this allows for the more accurate and complete correction of anomalies in the time and frequencies domains of the monitor–control room interface.

Another alternative is to install monitors with built-in digital signal processing bundled with analysis software that measures deviations from linear response in the monitor–control room interface. Once measured, corrective equalization helps flatten overall response. Some of these systems are automated.

It is worth noting, however, that many recordists agree that no corrective monitor–control room alignment system can do as good a job as a well-trained professional.

Calibrating the 5.1 Surround System

Engineers take various approaches to calibrating loudspeakers in a surround system, depending on which calibration system they use. Generally, however, for 5.1, setting a reference level for the five main loudspeakers is done first. At the outset of calibration, it is important to have the proper subwoofer positioned where the real-time analyzer shows it to have the smoothest response. Reference levels vary with the program material. When the reference level of the speakers is added for film, it is usually 85 dB-SPL; for television it is 79 dB-SPL, and for music it is 79 to 82 dB-SPL.

Graphic display technologies help evaluate surround-sound monitoring (see 8-22). Calibration is usually handled by engineers, and detailing the procedure is beyond the scope of this book.[2]

EVALUATING THE MONITOR LOUDSPEAKER

The final test of any monitor loudspeaker is how it sounds. Although the basis for much of the evaluation is subjective, there are guidelines for determining loudspeaker performance.

■ Begin with rested ears. Fatigue alters aural perception.

■ Sit at the designated stereo listening position—the optimal distance away from and between the loudspeakers. This sweet spot should allow some front-to-back and side-to-side movement without altering perception of loudness, frequency response, and spatial perspective. It is important to know the boundaries of the listening position(s) so that all sound can be monitored on-axis within this area (see 8-8 and 8-13).

■ If repositioning near-field monitors is necessary, changes of even a few inches closer or farther away or from side to side can make a considerable difference in how the sound is perceived.

■ There is no one best listening position with surround sound. Moving around provides different perspectives

2. To provide an idea of the process and the measurements involved, see "Calibrating the 5.1 System" by Bobby Owsinski at *www.surroundassociates.com/spkrcal.html.* Also see Jeffrey P. Fisher, *Instant Surround Sound* (San Francisco: CMP Books, 2005), pp. 49–51.

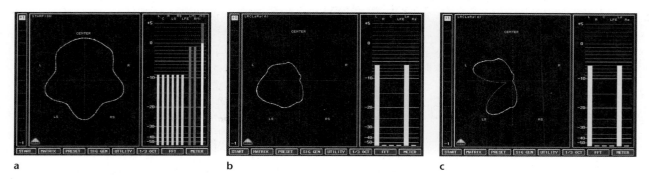

8-22 Visual displays of surround-sound monitoring. (a) Same signal in all channels. (b) Left and left-surround signals in phase. (c) Left and left-surround signals out of phase.

without significantly changing clarity, dimension, and spatial coherence (see 8-18).

■ When evaluating monitors in general and near-field monitors in particular, the tendency is to be drawn to the bass response. The focus should be on overall clarity.

■ Use material with which you are intimately familiar for the evaluation, preferably on a high-quality digital disc. Otherwise, if some aspect of the sound is unsatisfactory, you won't know whether the problem is with the original material or the loudspeaker.

For example, with speech the male voice is a good test to reveal if a loudspeaker is boomy; the female voice helps determine if there is too much high-end reflection from nearby surfaces. With music consider how the following sonic details would change tonally from speaker to speaker: an overall sound with considerable presence and clarity, the depth and the dynamic range of symphonic music, the separation in the spatial imaging of instruments, a singer whose sound sits in the lower midrange, the sounds of fingers on guitar strings and frets or fingernails plucking the strings, the kiss of the hammers on piano strings, the wisp of brushes on a snare drum, the deep bass response of an organ, the punch of the kick drum, and the upper reaches of a flute's harmonics. Such tests, and there are many others, facilitate the judging of such things as a loudspeaker's bass, midrange, and treble response; dynamic response; imaging; clarity; and presence.

■ Keep in mind that as bass response becomes more prominent, midrange clarity suffers due to masking.

■ Listen at a comfortable loudness level; 85 dB-SPL is often recommended.

■ Listen for sounds you may not have heard before, such as hiss, hum, or buzz. Good monitors may reveal what inferior monitors cover up; or the sounds could indicate that the monitors you are listening to have problems. In either case, you have learned something.

■ In listening for spatial balance, make sure that the various sounds are positioned in the same places relative to the original material. As an additional test for stereo, put the monitor system into mono and check to make sure that the sound appears to be coming from between the two loudspeakers. Move toward the left and right boundaries of the sweet spot. If the sound moves with you before you get near the boundaries, reposition the monitors, then recheck their dispersion in both stereo and mono until you can move within the boundaries of the listening position without the sound following you or skewing the placement of the sound sources. If monitor repositioning is necessary to correct problems with side-to-side sound placement, make sure that it does not adversely affect front-to-back sound dispersion to the listening position.

■ In evaluating monitor loudspeakers for surround sound, consider the following: Is the imaging of the sound sources cohesive, or is it disjointed? Does the sound emanate from the appropriate loudspeaker location, or does it seem detached from it? In moving around the listening environment, how much of the positional information, or sonic illusion, remains intact? How robust does that illusion remain in another listening environment? If there are motion changes—sound moving left-to-right, right side–to–right front, and so on—are they smooth? Does any element call unwanted attention to itself?

■ In evaluating treble response, listen to the cymbal, triangle, flute, piccolo, and other high-frequency instruments. Are they too bright, crisp, shrill, harsh, or dull? Do you hear their upper harmonics?

■ In testing bass response, include such instruments as the tuba and the bass, as well as the low end of the organ, piano, bassoon, and cello. Sound should not be thin, boomy, muddy, or grainy. For example, notes of the bass guitar should be uniform in loudness; the piano should not sound metallic.

■ Assess the transient response, which is also important in a loudspeaker. For this drums, bells, and triangle provide excellent tests, assuming they are properly recorded. Good transient response reproduces a crisp attack with no distortion, breakup, or smearing.

■ If you are evaluating a number of different loudspeakers, compare only a few at a time and take notes. Trying to remember, for example, how different speakers color the presence range, their differences in low-end warmth, or their degree of darkness or brightness is unreliable. Our ability to retain precise auditory information is limited, particularly over time and when comparison testing.

Other important elements to evaluate, such as intermodulation, harmonic, transient, and loudness distortion, were discussed earlier in this chapter.

Monitoring in an Unfamiliar Control Room

When doing a session in a facility you have not worked in before, it is essential to become thoroughly familiar with the interaction between its monitor sound and its room sound. A relatively quick and reliable way to get an objective idea of that interaction is to do a real-time analysis. It is also crucial to put the real-time analysis into perspective with reference recordings and your ears.

Reference recordings on CD, CD-ROM, or DVD can be commercial recordings with which you are entirely familiar or discs specially designed to help assess a listening environment or both. Knowing how a recording sounds in a control room whose monitors and acoustics you are intimately familiar with is a good test in determining the sonic characteristics of, and among, the monitors and the acoustics in a new environment. For example, if you know that a recording has a clear high-end response in your own control room but the high end sounds thinner in another control room, it could indicate, among other things, that the other studio's monitors have inadequate treble response, the presence of harmonic distortion, a phase problem, the room's mediocre sound diffusion, or any combination of these factors.

Digital discs specially produced for referencing are also available. They are variously designed to test monitor and/or room response to a particular instrument, such as a drum set; individual or groups of instruments, such as the voice and clarinet, or strings, brass, and woodwinds; various sizes and types of ensembles, such as orchestras, jazz bands, and rock groups; room acoustics; spatial positioning; and spectral balances (see Bibliography).

HEADPHONES

Headphones (also referred to as "cans") are a too-often-overlooked but important part of monitoring, especially in field production. The following considerations are basic when using headphones for professional purposes:

■ Although frequency response in headphones is not flat, listen for as wide and uncolored a response as possible.

■ You must be thoroughly familiar with their sonic characteristics.

■ They should be *circumaural* (around-the ear), as air-tight as possible against the head for acoustical isolation, and comfortable.

■ The fit should stay snug even when you are moving.

8-23 **5.1 Headphone monitoring system.** This particular system is called Headzone. It includes stereo headphones and a digital processor that accepts 5.1 signal sources. The processor uses modeling software to reproduce a surround-sound image. It also provides the ability to turn your head while the virtual sound sources stay in the correct spatial positions as they do in control room monitoring through separate loudspeakers. The processor takes various types of connectors, such as a three-pin socket for static ultrasonic receivers, six phono (RCA) sockets for unbalanced 5.1 analog inputs, and a standard six-pin FireWire socket for linking to a computer. The processor can be remotely controlled.

■ And, although it may seem obvious, stereo headphones should be used for stereo monitoring, and headphones capable of multichannel reproduction should be used for monitoring surround sound (see 8-23).

Headphones are usually indispensable in field recording because monitor loudspeakers are often unavailable or impractical. In studio control rooms, however, there are pros and cons to using headphones.

The advantages to using headphones are: sound quality will be consistent in different studios; it is easier to hear subtle changes in the recording and the mix; there is no aural smearing due to room reflections; and because so many people listen to portable players through headphones or *earbuds,* you have a reasonably reliable reference to their sonic requirements.

The disadvantages to using headphones are: the sound quality will not be the same as with the monitor loudspeakers; the aural image forms a straight line between your ears and is unnaturally wide; in panning signals for stereo, the distance between monitor loudspeakers is greater than the distance between your ears—left and right sounds are directly beside you; there is no interaction between the program material and the acoustics, so the tendency may be to mix in more artificial reverberation than necessary; and, in location recording, if open-air, or *supra-aural,* headphones are used, bass response will not be as efficient as with circumaural headphones, and outside noise might interfere with listening.

Headphones and Hearing Loss

As pointed out in Chapter 1, high sound levels from everyday sources such as loudspeakers, loud venues, hair dryers, and lawn mowers are detrimental to hearing. Potentially, that is even more the case with headphones because they are mounted directly over the ear or, with earbuds, placed inside the ear. Outdoors the problem is exacerbated by the tendency to boost the level so that the program material can be heard above the noise floor. Listening over an extended period of time can also result in cranking up the level to compensate for listening fatigue.

It has been found that listening to headphones at a loud level after only about an hour and a quarter can cause hearing loss. One recommendation is called the *60 percent/60-minute rule:* limit listening through headphones to no more than one hour per day at levels below 60 percent of maximum volume. You can increase daily listening time by turning down the level even farther.

One development in headphone technology to help reduce the potential of hearing loss is the active ***noise-canceling headphone.*** Designs differ, but generally the noise-canceling headphone detects ambient noise before it reaches the ears and nullifies it by synthesizing the sound waves. Most noise-canceling headphones act on the more powerful low to midrange frequencies; the less powerful higher frequencies are not affected. Models may be equipped with a switch to turn the noise-canceling function on or off and may be battery-operated.

Passive noise-canceling can be employed with conventional circumaural headphones. The better the quality of headphones and the tighter the fit, the more effective the reduction of ambient noise.

In-ear Monitors

The ***in-ear monitor (IEM)*** was developed for use by musicians in live concerts to replace stage monitors. They allow the performers to hear a mix of the on-stage microphones or instruments, or both, and provide a high level of noise reduction for ear protection. Due to the convenience of adjusting the sound levels and the mix of audio sources to personal taste, ***in-the-ear monitoring*** has become increasingly popular with performers in broadcasting and recording. The problem with IEMs is that a performer who prefers loud sound levels or has hearing loss may increase the loudness of the IEM to a harmful level, thereby negating its noise reduction advantage.

One company, Sensaphonics, has developed a sound-level analyzer, *dB Check,* to measure the sound-pressure levels reaching the ear canal so that users can determine not only their actual monitoring level but also how long they can safely listen at that volume. dB Check works only with earphones that are company products, however. The expectation is that this or a similar technology will be made available by other manufacturers so that the monitoring levels of not only IEMs but also other types of earphones can be measured.

MAIN POINTS

▶ The sound chain begins with the microphone, whose signal is sent to a console or mixer for routing and then processed, recorded, and heard through a loudspeaker.

▶ Loudspeakers are transducers that convert electric energy into sound energy.

▶ Loudspeakers are available in the moving-coil, ribbon, and electrostatic, or capacitor, designs. The moving-coil loudspeaker is by far the most common.

▶ Loudspeakers that are powered externally are called passive loudspeakers. Those that are powered internally are called active loudspeakers.

▶ A single, midsized speaker cannot reproduce high and low frequencies very well; it is essentially a midrange instrument.

▶ For improved response, loudspeakers have drivers large enough to handle the bass frequencies and drivers small enough to handle the treble frequencies. These drivers are called, informally, woofers and tweeters, respectively.

▶ A crossover network separates the bass and the treble frequencies at the crossover point, or crossover frequency, and directs them to their particular drivers.

▶ Two-way system loudspeakers have one crossover network, three-way system loudspeakers have two crossovers, and four-way system loudspeakers have three crossovers.

▶ In a passive crossover network, the power amplifier is external to the speakers and precedes the crossover. In an active crossover network, the crossover precedes the power amps.

▶ Each medium that records or transmits sound, such as a CD or TV, and each loudspeaker that reproduces sound, such as a studio monitor or home receiver, has certain spectral and amplitude capabilities. For optimal results audio should be produced with an idea of how the system through which it will be reproduced works.

▶ In evaluating a monitor loudspeaker, frequency response, linearity, amplifier power, distortion, dynamic range, sensitivity, polar response, arrival time, and polarity should also be considered.

▶ Frequency response ideally should be as wide as possible, from at least 40 to 20,000 Hz.

▶ Linearity means that frequencies being fed to a loudspeaker at a particular loudness are reproduced at the same loudness.

▶ Amplifier power must be sufficient to drive the loudspeaker system, or distortion (among other things) will result.

▶ Distortion is the appearance of a signal in the reproduced sound that was not in the original sound.

▶ Various forms of distortion include intermodulation, harmonic, transient, and loudness.

▶ Intermodulation distortion (IM) results when two or more frequencies occur at the same time and interact to create combination tones and dissonances that are unrelated to the original sounds.

▶ Harmonic distortion occurs when the audio system introduces harmonics into a recording that were not present originally.

▶ Transient distortion relates to the inability of an audio component to respond quickly to a rapidly changing signal, such as that produced by percussive sounds.

▶ Loudness distortion, or overload distortion, results when a signal is recorded or played back at an amplitude greater than the sound system can handle.

▶ To meet most any sonic demand, the main studio monitors should have an output-level capability of 120 dB-SPL and a dynamic range of up to 80 dB.

▶ Sensitivity is the on-axis sound-pressure level a loudspeaker produces at a given distance when driven at a certain power. A monitor's sensitivity rating provides a good overall indication of its efficiency.

▶ Polar response indicates how a loudspeaker focuses sound at the monitoring position(s).

▶ The coverage angle is the off-axis angle or point at which loudspeaker level is down 6 dB compared with the on-axis output level.

▶ A sound's arrival time at the monitoring position(s) should be no more than 1 ms; otherwise, aural perception is impaired.

▶ Polarity problems can occur between woofer and tweeter in the same loudspeaker enclosure or between two separate loudspeakers.

▶ Where a loudspeaker is positioned affects sound dispersion and loudness. A loudspeaker in the middle of a room generates the least-concentrated sound; a loudspeaker at the intersection of a ceiling or floor generates the most.

▶ For professional purposes it is preferable to flush-mount loudspeakers in a wall or soffit to make low-frequency response more efficient and to reduce or eliminate back-wall reflections, cancellation, and cabinet-edge diffraction.

▶ Stereo sound is two-dimensional; it has depth and breadth. In placing loudspeakers for monitoring stereo, it is critical that they be positioned symmetrically within a room to reproduce an accurate and balanced front-to-back and side-to-side sonic image.

▶ Loudspeakers used for far-field monitoring are usually large and can deliver very wide frequency response at moderate to quite loud levels with relative accuracy. They are built into the mixing-room wall above, and at a distance of several feet from, the listening position.

▶ Near-field monitoring enables the sound engineer to reduce the audibility of control room acoustics, particularly the early reflections, by placing loudspeakers close to the monitoring position.

▶ Surround sound differs from stereo by expanding the depth dimension, thereby placing the listener more in the center of the aural image than in front of it. Therefore, using the 5.1 surround-sound format, monitors are positioned front-left, center, and front-right, and the surround loudspeakers are placed left and right behind, or to the rear sides of, the console operator. A subwoofer can be positioned in front of, between the center and the left or right speaker, in a front corner, or to the side of the listening position. Sometimes in the 5.1 surround setup, two subwoofers may be positioned to either side of the listening position.

▶ 7.1 surround sound, which is growing in popularity, feeds the two added channels to left- and right-side speakers. The additional speakers improve sound localization.

▶ As important as personal taste is in monitor selection and evaluation, calibration of a monitor system is critical to the objective measurement of the correlation between monitor sound and room sound.

▶ In adjusting and evaluating monitor sound, objective and subjective measures are called for.

▶ Devices such as a spectrum analyzer measure the relationship of monitor sound to room sound. Although part of testing a monitor loudspeaker involves subjectivity, there are guidelines for determining performance.

▶ When evaluating the sound of a monitor loudspeaker, it is helpful to, among other things, use material with which you are intimately familiar and to test various loudspeaker responses with different types of speech and music.

▶ Headphones are an important part of monitoring, particularly on-location. The following considerations are basic when using headphones for professional purposes: the frequency response should be wide, flat, and uncolored; you must be thoroughly familiar with their sonic characteristics; they should be circumaural (around-the ear), as airtight as possible against the head for acoustical isolation, and comfortable; the fit should stay snug even when you are moving; and, although it may seem obvious, stereo headphones should be used for stereo monitoring, and headphones capable of multichannel reproduction should be used for monitoring surround sound.

▶ Headphones can be detrimental to hearing because they are mounted directly over the ears or, with earbuds, placed inside the ears. Outdoors the problem is exacerbated by the tendency to boost the level so that the program material can be heard above the noise floor.

▶ To help reduce the potential of hearing loss, the active noise-canceling headphone detects ambient noise before it reaches the ears and nullifies it by synthesizing the sound waves.

▶ Passive noise-canceling can be employed using high-quality conventional circumaural headphones that fit snugly over the ears.

▶ The in-ear monitor (IEM) allows a performer to hear a mix of on-stage microphones or instruments, or both, and provides a high level of noise reduction for ear protection. Since their development, IEMs are used for other monitoring purposes. One company has developed a sound-level analyzer for the specific purpose of measuring in-the-ear monitoring levels to guard against excessive loudness.

Production

9

Sound and the Speaking Voice

The production chain generally begins with the performer—announcer, disc jockey, newscaster, narrator, actor, interviewer/interviewee, and so on. How that speech is handled depends on four factors: the type of program or production—disc jockey, news, commercial, documentary, audiobook, drama, and so on; whether it is produced on radio or, as in the case of film and television, using the single- or multicamera technique; whether it is done in the studio or in the field; and whether it is live, live-to-recording,[1] or produced for later release. Before covering the techniques specific to those applications, it is worthwhile to provide an overview of sound and the speaking voice.

FREQUENCY RANGE

The frequency range of the human speaking voice, compared with that of some musical instruments, is not wide (see the diagram on the inside front cover). Fundamental voicing frequencies produced by the adult male are from roughly 80 to 240 Hz; for the adult female, they are from roughly 140 to 500 Hz. Harmonics and overtones carry these ranges somewhat higher (ranges for the singing voice are significantly wider—see Chapter 17).

---

1. Not to quibble about semantics, but the term *live-to-recording* seems more appropriate these days than the more familiar and commonly used term *live-to-tape*. Although videotape in particular is still used to record program material, digital storage systems consisting of disk arrays are becoming the recording and distribution media of choice (see Chapter 5).

Despite these relatively narrow ranges, its harmonic richness makes the human voice a highly complex instrument. Frequency content varies with the amount of vocal effort used. Changes in loudness and intensity change pitch. Loud speech boosts the midrange frequencies and reduces the bass frequencies, thus raising overall pitch. Quiet speech reduces the midrange frequencies, lowering overall pitch.

In relation to the recording/playback process, if speech (and audio in general) is played back at a level louder than originally recorded, as is possible in radio and film, the lower-end frequencies will be disproportionately louder. If speech (and audio in general) is played back at a quieter level than originally recorded, as is possible in radio and TV, the lower-end frequencies will be disproportionately quieter.

Regardless of the dynamic range in voicing sounds, speech must be intelligible while maintaining natural voice quality. Moreover, in audio production speech must also be relatively noise-free. Although background noise does not affect speech intelligibility when the noise level is 25 dB below the speech level, such a *signal-to-noise ratio (S/N)* is still professionally unacceptable. Even when the S/N is adequate, other factors, such as distance between speaker and listener, the listener's hearing acuity, and other sounds can adversely affect speech intelligibility. These factors as they relate to aural perception in general are discussed elsewhere in this book. Two other influences on speech intelligibility—sound level and distribution of spectral content—are covered in the following sections.

SOUND LEVEL

Speech intelligibility is at a maximum when levels are about 70 to 90 dB-SPL. At higher levels intelligibility declines slightly. It also declines below 70 dB-SPL and falls off rapidly under about 40 dB-SPL. Distance between speaker and listener also affects intelligibility: as distance increases, intelligibility decreases (see the discussion of the inverse square law in Chapter 13).

DISTRIBUTION OF SPECTRAL CONTENT

Each octave in the audible frequency spectrum contributes a particular sonic attribute to a sound's overall quality (see Chapter 1 and the diagram on the inside back cover). In speech certain frequencies are more critical to intelligibility than others. For example, an absence of frequencies above 600 Hz adversely affects the intelligibility

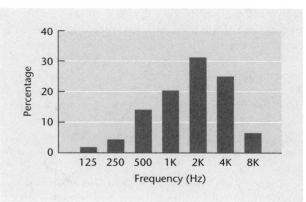

9-1 Percentage of contribution to speech intelligibility in one-octave bands.

of consonants; an absence of frequencies below 600 Hz adversely affects the intelligibility of vowels.

Various procedures have been developed to evaluate and predict speech intelligibility. One such procedure is based on the relative contribution to intelligibility by various frequencies across one-third-octave and full-octave ranges (see Figure 9-1).

INFLUENCES OF NONVERBAL SPEECH ON MEANING

Delivering words from a page, whether they are in a commercial, documentary, or drama, involves more than just reading them aloud. Words carry meaning, of course. It is often not what is said, however, but *how* it is said that conveys the meaning's overall intent.

Examples of how nonverbal speech influences meaning include emphasis, inflection, speech patterns, pace, mood, and accent.

Emphasis

Emphasis—stressing a syllable or a word—is important to all speech—voice-overs, narration, and dialogue. It often conveys the meaning of what is being said. When a clerk says, "Have a nice day," is the good wish believable? Is it delivered mechanically or with sincerity? The sound (emphasis) tells you. On paper the words "How are you?" suggest concern for someone's welfare. But often the words are used as another way of saying "Hello" or making a perfunctory recognition with no expression of concern. Emphasis is what tells you so. Moreover, it is possible to emphasize the *how,* the *are,* or the *you* and communicate three different meanings. The words remain the same; the aural emphasis alters the message.

Take the line "He'd kill us if he got the chance." If it were delivered with the emphasis on us—"He'd kill *us* if he got the chance"—the meaning conveyed would be defensive, that is, unless we kill him first. If the emphasis were on *kill*—"He'd *kill* us if he got the chance"—it suggests that the "us" did something to him first or that the "us" did something that would provoke him if he found it out.

The question "What are you doing here?" can take on entirely different meanings depending on which word is stressed. Emphasizing *what* indicates surprise. Stressing *are* could suggest exasperation. Accenting *you* is asking why someone else is not there or why "you" are there at all. Placing the emphasis on *doing* wants to know what "you" are up to by being here. Putting the stress on *here* questions why "you" are not elsewhere.

Inflection

Inflection—altering the pitch or tone of the voice—can also influence verbal meaning. By raising the pitch of the voice at the end of a sentence, a declarative statement becomes a question. Put stress on it, and it becomes an exclamation. Take the sentence "My country, right or wrong." As a declarative statement, it is a fact. As a question, it introduces skepticism or satiric bite, perhaps even anguish. As an exclamation it becomes an aggressive statement or one of pride.

"So help me God" is usually said at the end of an oath, as a declarative statement with almost equal emphasis on *help me God.* But if a pleading inflection were added to the words *help me,* it would underscore the weight of responsibility now borne by the new office holder.

Speech Patterns

Speech patterns are important to natural-sounding speech and believable characterization. Although these patterns may be inherent in the script, a writer must be equally aware of how words should sound. If the speaker is supposed to be highly educated, the vocabulary, sentence structure, and speech rhythms should reflect erudition. If the speaker is being formal, vocabulary and sentence structure should be precise, and speech rhythms should sound even and businesslike. Informality would sound looser, more relaxed, and more personal. A performer role-playing someone from the nineteenth-century

should speak with a vocabulary and syntax that evokes that period to modern ears. That is, unless the character has a modern outlook and temperament, which would make the sound of contemporary vocabulary and sentence structure appropriate.

Pace

The *pace* of spoken words can convey nonverbal information about the passion, urgency, or boredom of a situation.

For example, in a drama:

She: Go away.

He: No.

She: Please.

He: Can't.

She: You must.

He: Uh-uh.

Certainly, there is not much verbal content here apart from the obvious. But by pacing the dialogue in different ways, meaning can be not only defined but also changed. Think of the scene played deliberately, with each line and the intervening pauses measured, as opposed to a rapid-fire delivery and no pauses between lines. The deliberately paced sound design can convey more stress or, perhaps, more inner anguish than the faster-paced version. On the other hand, the faster pace can suggest nervousness and urgency.

Mood

Sound affects the *mood* or feeling of words and sentences. Aside from meaning, the sound of *dine* is more refined than the sound of *eat.* If the idea is to convey an edge to the action, *eat* is the better choice. *Lounge* has a softer, more gradual sound than *bar.* *Bestial* conveys more of a sense of the word's meaning than *barbaric* because of its harder sounds and shorter, more staccato attacks at the beginning of its two syllables. Choosing a better-sounding word, notwithstanding, its textual meaning cannot be ignored.

In the lines "lurid, rapid, garish, grouped" by poet Robert Lowell and "Strong gongs growing as the guns boom far" by G. K. Chesterton, the sounds in the words not only contribute to the overall meaning but are contained in the other words to further enhance the mood of the line.

In this passage about a sledgehammer from the poem "A Shiver" by Seamus Heaney, the interaction of similar sounds adds melodic and rhythmic qualities to the force of the poem's mood:

> The way you had to heft and then half-rest
> Its gathered force like a long-nursed rage
> About to be let fly: does it do you good
> To have known it in your bones, directable,
> Withholdable at will,
> A first blow that could make air of a wall,
> A last one so unanswerably landed
> The staked earth quailed and shivered in the handle?[2]

Consider the following translations of the same line from Dante's *Purgatorio:*

> I go among these with my face down.

> Among these shades I go in sadness.

The first sounds graceless and heavy-handed. The sound of the second is more emotional, rhythmic, and vivid.

Accent

An *accent* can tell you if a speaker is cultured or crude, an American from rural Minnesota or someone from China, England, or India. It can also color material. A story set in Russia depicting events that led to the 1917 Bolshevik Revolution with an all-British cast may have superb acting and dialogue, but the refined, rounded, mellifluous British sound may not be so effective as the more guttural Slavic sound and may not give the necessary edge to people and events. Shakespeare played by actors with deep southern drawls would sound unnatural. Films rerecorded from one language to another rarely sound believable.

BASIC CONSIDERATIONS IN MIKING SPEECH

Of the more important and generally subjective influences on sound shaping are a studio's acoustics and microphone selection and placement. Acoustics in relation to various program materials is discussed in Chapter 2. The following section considers how acoustics generally relate to the speech studio. Microphones directly affect the quality of recorded and transmitted sound. But because no two audio people achieve their results in exactly the same way, there can be no hard-and-fast rules about

---

2. Seamus Heaney, *District and Circle: Poems* (New York: Farrar, Straus, and Giroux, 2006), p. 5.

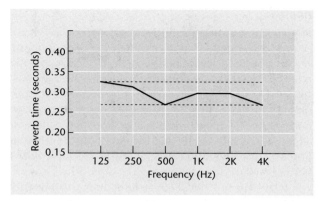

9-2 Measured reverberation time of a speech studio with good acoustics.

From Blazo Guzina, "How to Optimize Speech for Air," *Radio World,* March 1, 2004, p. 39. © Blazo Guzina. Courtesy of IMUS Publishing.

selecting and positioning microphones. The purpose of discussing mic technique in this and subsequent chapters is to suggest possible approaches, using as examples the types of situations you are most likely to encounter.

Acoustics in the Speech Studio

The acoustics in a studio used for speech should be relatively reverberant-free so as not to unduly color the sound, particularly in radio (see Chapter 12). A reverberation time of about 0.3 second (±0.05 second) is generally recommended. Studios requiring deader acoustics may have a lower limit of 0.25 second; studios requiring a somewhat livelier acoustic environment may have an upper limit of 0.35 second. As noted in Chapter 2, reverb time should be flat and decay time even (see 9-2; see also 2-8b).

Sometimes a slight boost in the low frequencies and a gradual roll-off in the high frequencies are desirable to add a bit of depth and solidity to the voice while reducing harshness in the consonants. Keep in mind that room acoustics notwithstanding, microphone choice and mic-to-source distance also affect sound quality.

Phase and Polarity

Before moving on it is necessary to say a word about phase and polarity. In acoustics **phase** is the time relationship between two or more sound waves at a given point in their cycles (see Chapter 1). In electricity **polarity** is the relative position of two signal leads—the high (+) and the low (–)—in the same circuit.

Phase

Phase is an important acoustic consideration in microphone placement. If sound sources are not properly placed in relation to mics, sound waves can reach the mics at different times and be out of phase. For example, sound waves from a source (performer or musical instrument) that is slightly off-center between two spaced microphones will reach one mic a short time before or after they reach the other mic, causing some cancellation of sound. Perceiving sounds that are considerably out of phase is relatively easy: when you should hear sound, you hear little or none. Perceiving sounds that are only a little out of phase is not so easy.

By changing relative time relationships between given points in the cycles of two waves, a *phase shift* occurs. Phase shift is referred to as *delay* when it is equal in time at all frequencies. Delay produces a variety of out-of-phase effects that are useful to the recordist (see Chapter 7). To detect unwanted phase shift, listen for the following: unequal levels in frequency response, particularly in the bass and the midrange; slightly unstable, wishy-washy sound; or a sound source that is slightly out of position in relation to where it should be in the aural frame.

One way to avoid phase problems with microphones is to follow the *three-to-one rule:* place no two microphones closer together than three times the distance between one of them and its sound source. If one mic is 2 inches from a sound source, for example, the nearest other mic should be no closer to the first mic than 6 inches; if one mic is 3 feet from a sound source, the nearest other mic should be no closer than 9 feet to the first; and so on (see 9-3).

If a sound source emits loud levels, it might be necessary to increase the ratio between microphones to 4:1 or even 5:1. Quiet levels may facilitate mic placement closer than that prescribed by a ratio of 3:1.

Phasing problems can also be caused by reflections from surfaces close to a microphone bouncing back into the mic's pickup. This condition is discussed in Chapters 12 and 17.

Polarity

Signals in a microphone circuit that are electrically out of polarity, depending on degree, considerably reduce sound quality or cancel the sound altogether. A common cause of mics' being out of polarity is incorrect wiring of the microphone plugs. Male and female XLR connectors used for most mics have three pins: a ground, a positive pin

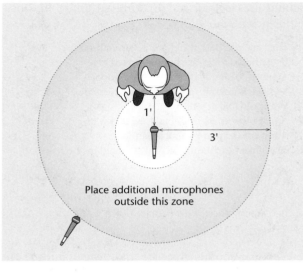

9-3 Three-to-one rule. Most phasing problems generated by improper microphone placement can be avoided by placing no two mics closer together than three times the distance between one of them and its sound source.

for high output, and a negative pin for low output. (XLR five-pin connectors are used for stereo microphones.) Mic cables house three coded wires. All mics in the same facility must have the same-number pin connected to the same-color wire. If they do not and are used simultaneously, they will be electrically out of polarity.

To check the polarity of two mics, first make sure that both are delegated to the same output channel. Adjust the level for a normal reading as someone speaks into a mic. Turn down the fader and repeat the procedure with another mic. Then open both mics to the normal settings. If the meter reading decreases when the levels of both mics are turned up, there is a polarity problem. The obvious way to correct this condition is to rewire the equipment, assuming the problem is not in the mic itself. If there is no time for that, most multichannel consoles and hard-disk recording systems have a polarity reversal control that reverses polarity by 180 degrees (see Chapter 4).

Microphones for the Speaking Voice

When miking any instrument, the microphone of choice should be the one that best complements its sound. That includes the most sonically complex instrument of all: the human voice.

Sound Quality

Sometimes in choosing the "right" microphone, circumstances make the decision for you. For example, if a transparent sound is desirable, a good moving-coil mic may be the best selection; if mellowness is the primary consideration, a ribbon mic may be most suitable; if detail is important, the capacitor mic may be the likely pick. Remember that each type of microphone has particular attributes (see "General Transducer Performance Characteristics" in Chapter 3).

Keep in mind, however, that the "general transducer performance characteristics" are just that: *general*. There are exceptions to many of the characteristics noted. For example, many moving-coil microphones have transparent sound. Some moving-coil mics have midrange coloration, which makes them highly suitable for the speaking voice because they add some richness to the sound. Capacitor mics for the most part add enrichment and detail. This also makes them suitable for the speaking voice, but they can produce a more sculpted sound than desired. With voices that are already rich in harmonics, a capacitor mic may make the speaker sound edgier or more assertive. There are capacitors, however, that have a flatter response curve, thus making the sound more transparent and less sculpted or edgy yet still preserving the detail (see also "Recording Voice-overs" in Chapter 10).

The evaluation of a mic for speech includes at least four criteria: *clarity*—detail, accuracy, and lack of saturation; *presence*—open yet stands out; *richness*—little or no coloration but full, deep, and warm; and *versatility*—flexibility across different speech applications (important because many of the better microphones are expensive). Other features may also be desirable, such as a built-in pop filter and a shock mount, pad and roll-off controls, variable pickup patterns, and reduced off-axis response.

Directional Pattern

Another common decision in microphone selection is the directional pattern. Usually, the choice is between an omnidirectional and a unidirectional mic. Again circumstances sometimes make the decision for you. In a noisy environment, a unidirectional mic discriminates against unwanted sound better than does an omnidirectional one; to achieve a more open sound, the omnidirectional mic is the better choice. If there is an option of choosing either pickup pattern, each has certain advantages and disadvantages, depending on the demands of a given situation (see 9-4 and 9-5).

9-4 The omnidirectional microphone.

Advantages	Disadvantages
Does not have to be held directly in front of the mouth to provide adequate pickup	Does not discriminate against unwanted sound
Does not reflect slight changes in the mic-to-source distance	Is difficult to use in noisy environments
Gives a sense of the environment	Presents greater danger of feedback in reverberant locations
Is less susceptible to wind, popping, and handling noises	
Is not subject to the proximity effect	
Is natural sounding in rooms with good acoustics	

9-5 The unidirectional microphone.

Advantages	Disadvantages
Discriminates against unwanted sound	Must be angled correctly to the mouth, or the performer will be off-mic
Gives little or no sense of the environment (which could also be a disadvantage)	May be subject to the proximity effect
Significantly reduces the danger of feedback in reverberant locations	Is susceptible to wind and popping, unless there is a pop filter
	Is more susceptible to handling noises
	Requires care not to cover the ports, if handheld
	Is less natural sounding in rooms with good acoustics

Bidirectional microphones are rarely used because the audio from two people speaking into the same mic is processed through a single channel and cannot be manipulated without difficulty. Moreover, getting the right level and ambience balances could be time-consuming. At times a bidirectional pattern is used for a single speaker (or singer) to add some ambient pickup through the open rear lobe of the mic instead of employing an omnidirectional mic, which may add more ambience than desired.

Based on the differences detailed in Figures 9-4 and 9-5, the omnidirectional pickup pattern seems to be the more useful of the two. In fact, unidirectional mics are more widely used, which does not necessarily suggest that they are better. As with the choice of mic transducer type, so it is with deciding on a directional pattern. A microphone's suitability depends on the sonic requirements, not on favoritism.

Mic-to-source Distance

Speech is usually *close-miked;* that is, the distance between the talent and the microphone is about three to six inches, depending on the force of the delivery and the material being performed. Close-miking in the studio produces an intimate sound with little acoustic coloration from ambience. On-location it reduces the chance of unwanted sound from interfering with or distracting attention from the spoken content, particularly with a directional microphone.

The closer a mic is to a sound source, the warmer, more detailed, denser, more oppressive (if too close) the sound, and the closer the listener perceives the speaker to be. The farther a mic is from the sound source, the less warm, less detailed, thinner (if there is little reverberation) the sound, and the more distant the listener perceives the speaker to be.

In most situations involving speech, the performer must be picked up at close range to ensure that the words are heard clearly and are immediately intelligible. In the studio this is to avoid any interference from ambience, noise, or other unwanted sounds; on-location it is to reduce as much as possible these sonic interferences.

MAIN POINTS

▶ The production chain (in nonmusic production) generally begins with the talking performer and therefore involves considerations that relate to producing speech.

▶ How speech is produced depends on the type of program or production; the medium—radio, TV, film—and, in TV and film, whether the production technique is single- or multicamera; whether it is done in the studio or in the field; and whether it is live, live-to-recording, or produced for later release.

▶ The frequency range of the human voice is not wide compared with that of other instruments. The adult male's fundamental voicing frequencies are from roughly 80 to 240 Hz; for the adult female, they are from roughly 140 to 500 Hz. Harmonics and overtones carry these ranges somewhat higher (ranges for the singing voice are significantly wider).

▶ Speech intelligibility is at a maximum when levels are about 70 to 90 dB-SPL. Certain frequencies, particularly in the midrange, are also more critical to speech intelligibility than others. For example, an absence of frequencies above 600 Hz adversely affects the intelligibility of consonants; an absence of frequencies below 600 Hz adversely affects the intelligibility of vowels.

▶ Influences of nonverbal speech on meaning include emphasis, inflection, speech patterns, pace, mood, and accent.

▶ Acoustics in a speech studio should be relatively reverberant-free so as not to unduly color sound.

▶ Acoustical phase refers to the time relationship between two or more sound waves at a given point in their cycles. Polarity is the relative position of two signal leads—the high (+) and the low (–)—in the same circuit. When these waves or polarities are in phase—roughly coincident in time—their amplitudes are additive. When these waves or polarities are out of phase—not coincident in time—their amplitudes are reduced.

▶ By changing relative time relationships between given points in the cycles of two sound waves, a phase shift occurs. Phase shift is referred to as delay when it is equal in time at all frequencies.

▶ Evaluation of a microphone for speech includes at least four criteria: clarity, presence, richness, and versatility.

▶ Factors that influence a microphone's effect on the sound of the speaking (and singing) voice are its sound quality, directional pattern, and mic-to-source distance.

▶ The closer a mic is to a sound source, the warmer, more detailed, denser, more oppressive (if too close) the sound, and the closer the listener perceives the speaker to be.

▶ The farther a mic is from the sound source, the less warm, less detailed, thinner (if there is little reverberation) the sound, and the more distant the listener perceives the speaker to be.

10

Voice-overs and Narration

Performing speech generally involves either the voice-over or dialogue (covered in Chapter 11). *Voice-over (VO)* is the term used when a performer records copy to which other materials, such as sound effects, music, dialogue, and visuals, are added, usually at a later time. There are two types of voice-over material: *short form,* such as spot announcements, and *long form,* such as documentaries and audiobooks.

A solo performer delivering copy into a microphone may seem straightforward to produce. It is more involved than that, however. Speech sounds are harmonically and dynamically complex. Producing vocal sound involves the lungs, chest, diaphragm, larynx, hard and soft palates, nasal cavities, teeth, tongue, and lips. There is also the dynamic interaction of all these elements through time. Moreover, it is not only the words but the way in which they are performed that influence meaning as well (see Chapter 9). And there is the added pressure of having no place to hide: no accompanying voices, musical instruments, or reverberant acoustics to distract from or mask a mediocre performance. In sum: delivering copy meaningfully requires good voice acting.

VOICE ACTING

Voice acting differs from screen (and stage) acting because, in addition to the words, the only other way to convey meaning is vocally—through the sound of the words. A voice actor infuses sonic flair into copy, making words believable and memorable.

Voice acting is a profession, and most of what is involved in developing and training talent, auditioning, preparing demo reels, and handling the wide variety of copy that is part of the advertising and programming worlds is beyond the scope of this book. What can be addressed here to some extent are some of the considerations a voice actor deals with when coming to grips with how copy should sound.

Voice Quality

There is no such thing as the perfect voice. A voice actor may have a deep, rich voice suitable for the serious sell of life insurance or a documentary about the gravity of war but unsuitable for a lighthearted commercial about a vacation in Cancun. Different voice-overs call for different voice qualities and styles of delivery. Some voice actors are capable of changing their voice quality to suit the message. The more variety of vocal qualities a voice actor can deliver, the better the chances of getting work.

Message

Another aspect of voice acting is knowing the character of the script and how to deliver the appropriate sound. Sound in this case refers not only to voice quality but to inflection, emphasis, rhythm, phrasing, and attitude.

In advertising, for example, the product is often sold indirectly. What is actually being sold is an appeal, such as family security, social acceptance, health, guilt, fear, companionship, sexual attraction, curiosity, loyalty, and so on. Infusing a reading with the appropriate message is critical to the believability of the sell.

For example, take a product we will call LoCal. Instead of going through an entire commercial, using one line should make the point. Let's say the line is: "LoCal—no calories, just lots of good taste."

To get the right reading, a voice actor should determine what the appeal is. Why do people use diet products? They are concerned about gaining weight. Therefore the sell is "Don't worry—you can use this product without the anxiety of putting on pounds." Think about the sound when you say, "Don't worry." Then use that inflection in delivering the line so that in addition to the information that LoCal has no calories, just lots of good taste, the sound says, "Don't worry."

Audience

Another factor in voice acting is knowing the audience to whom the copy is appealing. Clearly, one speaks to, say, a teenage audience in a different style, pace, and mood than to an audience of retirees, the product notwithstanding. But do not speak to the target audience at large: have an individual in mind. Picture your one-person audience and address him or her. One of the legends of radio, Arthur Godfrey, once advised that when you speak to thousands, you reach no one. When you speak to one person, you reach thousands.

Radio Commercial Example The following radio commercial is for the Opulent 3QX, an expensive, full-sized luxury sedan. The target audience is affluent, suburban, college-educated, and in their late thirties to early sixties. The Modest MV is a midpriced, family-type minivan. The target audience is in the socioeconomic middle class, urban-suburban, with at least a high school education, and in their midtwenties to late thirties.

ANNOUNCER:

Today is a big day at your [Opulent/Modest] dealer. The exciting new [year] [Opulent 3QX/Modest MV] is on display. And as a way of saying "Come on down," your [Opulent/Modest] dealer will include five oil changes, including checkups, free when you purchase a new [Opulent 3QX/Modest MV] before October first. Even if you decide not to buy, there's a free gift for you just for coming down and saying hello. That's at your [Opulent 3QX/Modest MV] dealer now.

The commercial is straightforward, indeed routine. Sound can not only bring it to life but change its impact to suit the two different audiences, even though the copy is the same.

The spot calls for an announcer—a voice actor. But what type of voice actor? It is not enough for the talent to have a "good" voice. Voice quality and delivery must be compatible with the content of the message. If the message is "having a good time," the voice actor should sound that way, delivering the copy with a smile in the voice and buoyancy in the intonation. If the message is lighthearted or comedic, the sound of the delivery should be playful, whimsical, or offbeat. A serious message is better served with a composed, perhaps cultured delivery from a performer who sounds that way.

Voice actors for the Opulent and Modest commercials must consider the products themselves. The Opulent is an expensive luxury automobile usually affordable to upper-middle- and upper-class professionals with a college education and social position. The Modest, on the other hand, is generally a lower-middle- to middle-class automobile affordable to a broad group of people including blue- and white-collar workers, some with a high school education and some college educated, some with and some without social position. These two groups of consumers call for two different approaches.

The performer delivering the commercial for the Opulent may have a cultured sound: rounded-sounding vowels, deliberate pacing, stable rhythm, and somewhat aloof yet friendly. Among the important words to be emphasized are *new, gift,* and, of course, the product's name.

The sound for the Modest commercial would be brisker and more animated. The performer might sound younger than the one for the Opulent and more like the person next door—warm, familiar, and friendly. Pacing might be quicker and rhythms syncopated. The important words to emphasize are, at least, *big, exciting, free, come on down,* and the product's name.

No doubt there are other, equally valid approaches to the commercial. The point is that the same words take on different meanings and address different audiences just by changing the sound, pacing, and emphasis of the delivery.

Word Values

Another aspect of voice acting in delivering key words and phrases is by appropriately sounding them. The following word combinations should obviously take different sonic emphases: *soft/hard, love/hate, happy/sad, good/bad, lively/dull, quiet/loud,* and so on. The phrase "and the assault continued" as the good guys beat the bad guys may take a straightforward, prideful delivery compared with the same phrase delivered questioningly or wonderingly in describing a brutality.

Character

Delivering copy may require doing a character voice, such as a doctor, a corporate executive, a mother, or Brad the Bunny. Understanding the character is important to a convincing, believable reading. There are two questions to consider: *Why is your character speaking—what is the reason, the motivation?* and *Who is your character—what are the basic traits?* In either case, the character is not you. It is important to understand that you must "come out of yourself" and *be* that character.

Doing a character may require a change in voice coloration, that is, altering the size and the tonality of the vocal sound. Using different parts of the body creates changes in the voice. For example: from the top of the head (tiny); through the nose (nasal); from the top of the cheeks (bright); from the front of the mouth (crisp); from under the tongue (sloppy); from the throat (raspy); from the back of the throat (breathy); from the chest (boomy); from the diaphragm (strong); and from the stomach (bassy).[1]

Although this brief discussion of voice acting has mainly used commercials for examples, the principles apply to all types of audio materials—documentary, audiobooks, animation, and dialogue.

Prerecorded Voice Collections

Not all producers or broadcasters can afford hiring voice-over talent, or they may have the budget but not the requisite availability of performers. Prerecorded voice collections are available featuring a wide variety of words, phrases, sayings, and vocal sounds that can be used in voice-over production either in lieu of a bone fide voice actor or to supplement a performance (see Figure 10-1).

Automating Voice-overs

Voice-overs are done not only for onetime performances such as spot announcements, documentaries, and audiobooks but also for productions that require large amounts of copy that have to be duplicated, such as videogames, speaking dictionaries, and telephone voice-responses. For example, hundreds of voice-overs may be required for a video game, or thousands of recordings of pronunciations may be needed for an online dictionary. And all must be done without error. To meet such demands, automation is a necessity.

Software programs are available to handle these needs. One such program, voXover, allows you to write or import a script and automate it. The script can be displayed to the performer on the system's teleprompter. Each recording is automatically named and annotated as called for in the script, and takes can be sorted, rearranged, renamed, and exported.

RECORDING VOICE-OVERS

In recording voice-overs the essentials are neutral acoustics; selecting a microphone that is most complementary to the performer's voice; taking care to avoid plosives, sibilance, and breathiness; setting the optimum mic-to-source distance and avoiding fluctuations in on-mic presence; keeping levels uniform and handling any signal

---

1. From James R. Alburger, *The Art of Voice Acting,* 2nd ed. (Boston: Focal Press, 2002), p. 147.

Vocalizations

55 Cheering—individual
56 Booing—individual
57 Whistling
58 Singing—warm-ups
59 Singing—adults
60 Singing, nursery rhymes—kids
61 Nursery rhymes—adult
62 Yodeling
63 Auctioneer (mono)
64 Auctioneer (stereo)
65 Drunk
66 Whisper
67 Whisper with effects
68 Aliens
69 Animals—misc. (humans imitating)

70 Animals—dogs (humans imitating)
71 Animals—cats (humans imitating)
72 Animals—wolves (humans imitating)
73 Instruments—drums (humans imitating)
74 Instruments (humans imitating)
75 Sermon—priest
76 Argument—couple
77 Sex—couple

Words and Phrases

39 Hello/greetings
40 Hello/greetings—foreign
41 Good-bye
42 Good-bye—foreign
43 Etiquette 1 of 2
44 Etiquette 2 of 2

45 Etiquette—foreign
46 Occasion/event
47 Occasion/event—foreign
48 Congratulations, cheers
49 Endearment
50 Endearment—foreign
51 Calls to attention
52 Calls of caution
53 Calls to action
54 Courtroom
55 Church and prayer
56 Calls, distress
57 Police
58 Restaurant bar
59 Taxi
60 Waiter
61 Response: "yes," "no," "maybe"

10-1 Selected examples of vocal production elements from one prerecorded library.

processing with care; recording to facilitate editing in postproduction; and making the performer comfortable.

Acoustics   Recording speech begins with good acoustics. Mediocre acoustics can make speech sound boxy, oppressive, ringy, or hollow. Suitable acoustics are more important to speech than to singing: the spectral density and the energy the singing voice generates can somewhat overcome mediocre acoustics. Also, in multitrack recording other tracks can mask less-than-acceptable acoustics on a vocal track to say nothing of the "distraction" of a good lyric or performance.

In recording speech for voice-overs, suitable acoustics are dry. There should be few, if any, reflections. The less the ambient coloration, the less the "contamination" to the speech track and the easier it is to mix the voice with other elements. That said, the acoustics should not be oppressively dry or the voice-over will sound lifeless.

Microphone Selection   Recording the voice-over may not seem particularly demanding, especially given the multifarious nature of today's production environment. But producing a solo performer and a microphone is a considerable challenge: there is no place to hide.

Generally, the high-quality capacitor is the microphone of choice for voice-overs because of its ability to reproduce vocal complexities and handle transient sounds. Keep in mind, however, that selecting a particular mic should be based on the one that best complements the actor's voice quality. Many voice actors know which mic suits them best. Use it. Otherwise, as noted in Chapters 3 and 9, there are plenty of mics to suit a particular sonic need: mics that sound crisp and bright, warm but not overly bright, transparent, or silky in the treble range; mics with bass roll-off to reduce low-end density, presence-boost control to enhance midrange definition, proximity effect to add a fuller or warmer low-end, or high sensitivity/high output for added gain.

Directional pickup patterns are preferred because they reduce ambience and produce a more intimate sound. Sometimes shotgun mics are used for added punch. If a slightly open sound is called for, a bidirectional mic can add some ambient pickup through the open rear lobe. An omnidirectional mic may pick up too much ambience.

Plosives, Sibilance, and Breathiness   Avoiding plosives, sibilance, breathiness, and tongue and lip smacks is handled in two ways. The first method is to place the mic capsule on line with, or slightly above, the performer's upper lip so that the pickup is not directly in the slipstream yet still on-mic (see 17-60). The second means is by using a windscreen; the fabric windscreen is preferred over the conventional windscreen because of its better high-frequency response (see 3-57d). If a fabric windscreen is not available, a microphone with a built-in pop filter works well (see 3-58).

Mic-to-source Distance Mic-to-source distance depends on the strength, resonance, and intensity of the performer's delivery, but it should be close enough to retain intimacy without sounding too close or oppressive—3 to 4 inches is a good distance to start with.

Be careful to avoid fluctuations in mic-to-source distance that result from a voice actor's using body movement to help give expression or emotion to the performance. This can result in changes in ambience or levels or both.

Recording Levels and Signal Processing Recording is usually done flat so that there's no sonic "baggage" to deal with in the mix or if the recording has to be continued on another day or in a different studio. Any signal processing done during recording is typically quite minimal, such as using a high-pass filter to remove low end that creates unwanted density and eats up headroom, or a low-pass filter to remove high end that is beyond the upper harmonics of the desired sound. For the most part, though, signal processing is handled in the mixing stage.

For example, a dull-sounding voice may get a slight boost in equalization between 3,000 Hz and 4,000 Hz. Presence may be added at 5,000 Hz. At frequencies between 3,000 Hz and 5,000 Hz, however, care must be taken to avoid bringing out hiss or sibilance. If there is a problem with sibilance that mic selection and placement cannot address, a de-esser may eliminate the problem. Boosting the low midrange from 150 to 250 Hz and the treble range from 8,000 to 10,000 Hz provides added punch. Some compressing of speech is almost always done if the voice-over is to be mixed with other sonic elements. This is especially so with spot announcements to make them stand out from the other broadcast program material. Compression with a fast attack and a slow release and a compression ratio of about 4:1 adds impact to the voice. Gentle compression can smooth levels for a more natural sound.

In producing a voice-over, if ambience is important to the overall delivery, it may be necessary to record it separately, after the performer finishes recording, by letting the recorder *overroll*—that is, keep running for a while. This makes it possible to maintain a consistent background sound in the mix, if it is required, by editing in the recorded ambience during the pauses in the voice-over and, in so doing, avoiding ambience "drop outs" on the voice-over track. Such changes may be subtle, but they are perceptible as differences in the openness and closeness of the aural space.

It is also essential to maintain consistency in voice quality, energy, and interpretation from take to take. This is especially challenging during a long session and when sessions run over two or more days. Not doing so makes it difficult to match recorded segments during postproduction editing. To reduce the possibility of having to deal with this problem, if you have any say in casting voice-over talent, avoid hiring someone for long-form work who is used to doing spot announcements.

Editing One time-consuming factor often overlooked in recording speech is the editing: how long it takes to repair plosives, breath gasps, sibilance, and mouth noises that get through, even with a windscreen; fluffs of words or phrases that require retakes; and the segments that must be deleted after letting a reading continue through poorly delivered passages to help the performer establish a rapport with the mood and the pulse of the copy. When possible, it is usually better to try for a trouble-free retake right away than to try and grapple with time-consuming editing later on. "Fixing it in post" should not be viewed as a stopgap for a sloppy production.

Performer Comfort Making the performer comfortable is of the utmost importance. Dealing with an unhappy performer creates added stress, but even the most professional of actors cannot do their best work in discomfort or under unnecessary strain.

Be professional, of course, but also try to be casual, informal, friendly, supportive, and, perhaps most important, diplomatic. Many performers are sensitive and emotionally vulnerable. A joke and laughter always help ease the natural tensions of a recording session and put the performer more at ease.

Most performers prefer doing a voice-over while standing. It allows for better breathing and vocal control because the diaphragm is free to move, and it helps the body language, which often makes for a better performance. Long-form readers may prefer sitting, mainly due to the endurance factor.

For standing performers, scripts are usually placed on music stands, padded and angled to avoid reflections back into the mic. Seated performers generally use desktop copy stands, also padded and angled. In both cases the stands are high enough that the performer does not have to look down at the script, thereby going off-mic. If a performer is seated, make sure the chair is comfortable.

Keep water and healthful energy foods on hand. Water at room temperature is better for the voice than hot or cold liquid. Adding a few drops of lemon juice to the water can keep mouth noises to a minimum, and chewing gum between takes keeps the mouth moist. Coffee and tea with caffeine and dairy products dry out the voice.[2] If phlegm begins to cause throat-clearing, which either holds up the recording session or has to be edited out, it is better if the talent swallows. Throat-clearing tends to bring up more phlegm.

Voicing-over Background Music or Sound Effects

Once a voice-over or narration is recorded, typically it is then mixed with other elements in a production. In recording spot announcements such as commercials and promos in radio, because they are usually short, an announcer often voices-over music, effects, or both at one sitting. A typical spot may call for music to be attention-getting at the open, then faded under during the announcement, returned to the opening level when the spoken part of the announcement concludes, and then either faded out or played to its conclusion. This format is called a *donut*—fading the music after it is established to create a hole for the announcement and then reestablishing the music at its former full level.

The problem with fading music, or any sound, is that the high and low frequencies and the overall ambience are faded as well, thus dulling the music. Using equalization it is possible to cut a hole (instead of fading a hole) in the music by attenuating the midrange frequencies that clash with or mask the announcer. This creates sonic room for the announcer while maintaining the music's presence, the low- and high-end response, and the ambience.

The procedure involves selecting the band of frequencies in the music that conflict with the announcer's intelligibility when they are at the same level, and attenuating the conflicting frequencies the necessary amount. When

the announcer speaks, the music equalization (EQ) is switched in; when the announcer is not speaking, it is switched out.

Another technique used to balance levels between an announcer and music, or between an announcer and other sounds such as crowd noise or traffic, is to feed each sound through a limiter and set one limiter to trigger the response of the other. In the case of a voice-over music announcement, the limiter controlling the music would be set to reduce the music level to a preset point when it is triggered by the limiter controlling the announcer's sound. As soon as the announcer speaks, the limiters' actions automatically reduce the music level. When the announcer stops speaking, the announcer's limiter triggers the music's limiter to restore the music to its preset louder level.

This can also be done with a limiter and a compressor. This practice has been used for years, but you have to be careful when setting the limit levels. If they are not precise, you will hear the limiters' annoying pumping action as they increase and decrease the levels.

To facilitate balances between the announcer and the music bed, there are music libraries specifically for use with spot announcements. These include cuts with reduced dynamic range, thereby giving a producer a choice of supporting music with either full or limited dynamic range.

When the voice of an announcer or a narrator is mixed with background music or sound effects, the copy is the most important element. This is why the performer's voice is in the foreground. If the music or effects become as loud as or louder than the performer, it forces the audience to struggle to focus attention on one of the competing elements, thereby inhibiting communication. This does not mean that the music and the effects must remain in the background. During a pause in the copy, the background can be increased in level or, if it is kept under the announcer, it can be varied to help accent the message, thereby providing sonic variety to heighten interest and pace.

In audio production it is worthwhile to remember that *sonic variety attracts the ear*. In fact, whether it is audio or video, the human perceptual system likes change. Shifts in focus, directed by the production, hold audience attention, particularly these days when changes from cut to cut are so rapid-fire. This is not to suggest that confused, cluttered, frenetic production is advised. Obscuring the message with production pyrotechnics makes for poor communication.

---

2. From Perry Anne Norton, "Recording the Spoken Word," *Electronic Musician*, February 2007, p. 33.

Using Compression

Using compression enhances the spoken word by giving it clarity and power. It also helps keep speech from being overwhelmed by sound effects or music and brings it forward in the mix. With analog sound, compression facilitates recording at a hotter level, thereby reducing distortion and noise, particularly at low levels. Compressing in the digital domain improves bit processing. In an overall mix, compression adds more cohesion and balance. Compression also has limitations: Too much of it dulls sound and makes it lifeless. It can also accentuate sibilance. Heavy compression may produce the annoying pumping sound of the compressor's action and also increase, rather than decrease, noise.

Like for most aspects of audio production, there are no prescribed rules for employing compression, but a few guidelines provide a starting point for experimentation.[3] It is also worth noting that it may take time to perceive the effects of compression because they can be subtle.

■ In close-miking speech, try a compression ratio of 2:1 or 3:1 and adjust the threshold until there is a 3 or 4 dB gain reduction. Use a fast attack time and a slow release time. With this and all of the following guidelines, use the makeup gain to restore any lost level.

■ Using a music bed, start with a 2:1 ratio and a fast attack time. Adjust the threshold until there is a 4 to 6 dB gain reduction.

■ With sound effects—which may not need compression and can be considerably changed with it—experiment with a ratio range of 3:1 to 6:1. Set gain reduction at 6 dB. Use a fast attack time and a medium release time.

■ Dealing with room tone and ambience usually requires only light compression: a ratio of 1.5:1 or 2:1, a 2 to 4 dB gain reduction, a fast attack time, and a medium release time.

■ Compressing the overall mix is better processed using a low ratio, a 3 to 6 dB gain reduction, a medium to medium-fast attack time, and a medium release time.

Backtiming and Deadpotting

Using prerecorded music to underscore or end a spot announcement, narrative, dialogue, or program theme

---

3. From Loren Alldrin, "The Joys of Compression," *Radio World*, July 21, 1999, p. 55.

song may involve backtiming and deadpotting to ensure that it ends at the appropriate time. Prerecorded material has a fixed total time. Suppose in a commercial that the section of music used to end a spot is 18 seconds long but only the last 11 seconds of it are needed. To get the music to end when the commercial ends, assuming a 30-second spot, the music has to start 12 seconds into the commercial. Subtracting the time of an individual element from the total time of a program or program segment is known as **backtiming**.

Deadpotting, also known as *deadrolling*, refers to starting a recording with the fader turned down all the way. To get the music to end when the spot ends, begin playing the music 12 seconds after the spot begins; just do not raise the fader. The music recording will deadpot—play with no sound feeding through—until you are ready for it. At that point, fade it in; because it started at the right time, it will also end on time. And ending music is usually a more effective close than fading it out. Of course, computers and automation can handle operations automatically once the data have been entered.

NARRATION

Narration is usually descriptive; that is, a narrator describes events from outside the action, not as a participant but as an observer. Three types of narration are direct, indirect, and contrapuntal.

Direct narration describes what is being seen or heard. If we see or hear an automobile coming to a stop, a car door opening and closing, footsteps on concrete and then on stairs, and a wooden door opening and closing, and are told as much, the narration is direct. If, on the other hand, the narrator tells us that the person emerging from the car and going into the building is an ambassador on an urgent mission and is meeting with his counterparts from other countries who are waiting in the building, it is **indirect narration**: what you are being told is not evident in what is being shown. Indirect narration adds more information to the picture. **Contrapuntal narration**, as the term suggests, counterpoints narration and action to make a composite statement not explicitly carried, or suggested, in either element. For example, the action may contain people happily but wastefully consuming a more-than-ample meal, while the narration comments on the number of starving people in the world. The conflict between the two pieces of information makes a separate, third, comment—a *tertium quid*.

These examples may suggest that indirect and contrapuntal narration are better than direct narration because they supplement and broaden information and therefore provide more content. Indirect and contrapuntal narration are preferable if the action is somewhat obvious. But direct narration is useful when the picture or the sounds may not convey the necessary meaning. It is also helpful in educational or instructional programs, when information requires reinforcement to be remembered and understood.

MAIN POINTS

▶ Performing speech generally involves either the voice-over (VO)—recording copy to which other sonic material is added—or dialogue. Voice-over material includes short-form material, such as spot announcements, and long-form material, such as documentaries and audiobooks.

▶ Speech sounds are harmonically and dynamically complex.

▶ Voice acting involves taking the words off the page and conveying meaning, making them believable and memorable.

▶ Among the considerations of a voice actor in bringing the appropriate delivery to copy are voice quality, message, audience, word values, and character.

▶ Prerecorded voice collections provide a variety of words, phrases, sayings, and vocal sounds to use in the absence of, or to supplement, a voice actor.

▶ When hundreds of voice-overs may be required for such projects as video games and online dictionaries, automation is necessary and software programs are available to handle these needs.

▶ Recording speech begins with good acoustics. Mediocre acoustics can make speech sound boxy, oppressive, ringy, or hollow.

▶ Producing a solo performer and a microphone is a considerable challenge: there is no place to hide.

▶ Among the things to avoid in recording speech are plosives, sibilance, breathiness, and tongue and lip smacks.

▶ Mic-to-source distance depends on the strength, resonance, and intensity of the performer's delivery, but it should be close enough to retain intimacy without sounding too close or oppressive.

▶ In terms of recording levels, recording is usually done flat so that there's no sonic "baggage" to deal with in the mix or if the recording has to be continued on another day or in a different studio. Any signal processing done during recording is typically quite minimal.

▶ In producing a voice-over, if ambience is important to the overall delivery, it may be necessary to record it separately, after the performer finishes recording, by letting the recorder overroll.

▶ One time-consuming factor often overlooked in recording speech is the editing. If mistakes are made, rather than leave them for the editor, try for trouble-free retake.

▶ Making the performer comfortable is of the utmost importance.

▶ Doing a voice-over when elements such as background music and sound effects are to be added later requires care to ensure that, when mixed, these elements do not interfere with the intelligibility of the copy.

▶ In mixing audio for a spot announcement, fading the music after it is established to create a hole for the announcement and then reestablishing the music at its former full level is called a donut.

▶ Using compression, in moderation, enhances the spoken word by giving it clarity and power.

▶ Backtiming is a method of subtracting the time of a program segment from the total time of a program so that the segment and the program end simultaneously.

▶ Deadpotting, also called deadrolling, is starting a recording with the fader turned down all the way.

▶ Three types of narration are direct, indirect, and contrapuntal.

11

Dialogue

In audio the principal challenge during the production of drama is recording dialogue. Sound effects are usually handled in postproduction; music always is. Recording dialogue on the set is known as *production recording*. Regardless of the venue—studio or on-location—or the medium—radio, television, or film—*recording dialogue that is clear, intelligible, and as noise-free as possible is the production recordist's goal*. Even when dialogue is to be ultimately recorded or rerecorded in postproduction, it is important to preserve an actor's performance on the set, if for no other reasons than for timing and interpretation (see also "Automated Dialogue Replacement" later in this chapter).

A production recording also preserves the sonic record of takes. Many things happen in life that are difficult to remember, much less re-create—the precise rhythmic nuance of dialogue, the unplanned cough or sputter that furnished a perfect dramatic highlight, the train that happened to go by at exactly the right moment. The live situation is more real and more delicate than the re-created one.

To this point Sir Roger Moore (James Bond, Agent 007, 1973–1985) has said, "In evaluating the success of the dailies [rushes] I don't look at my performance to decide if I had succeeded in the scene. It's the sound of [my] voice and delivery that tells me that."[1]

Even though the sound crew involved in recording dialogue on the set is responsible to the director, and

---

1. From an interview on *Night Talk,* BIT Channel, November 12, 2008.

is too often considered secondary, or even less, to the picture-making process, as production recordist Mark Ulano observed, "We're invisible, until we're not there."[2]

RECORDING DIALOGUE IN MULTI- AND SINGLE-CAMERA PRODUCTION

Capturing dialogue on the set in a multicamera or single-camera production usually means employing a boom, body-mounted wireless, or plant microphone or a combination of the three. The type of mic generally preferred is the capacitor—mini-mic and shotgun.

Using the Boom

The important decisions in using a boom are logistical and aesthetic. They involve plotting the best mic positions and angles for each scene in a production to ensure optimal aural balance, keeping the boom out of the lighting pattern so that its shadow does not fall across the set, making sure that the boom does not get in the way of the performers, making sure that the boom can move freely, trying to keep cameras and boom out of the audience's line-of-sight as much as possible, and positioning the boom at mic-to-source distances that are relative to the fields of view of the shots to help maintain acoustic perspective between sound and picture.

It is worth noting that because of the logistical and operational concerns associated with using the boom, many directors use the wireless body mic instead, regardless of whatever sonic advantages the boom may have in a given situation (see "Using Wireless Body Microphones" later in this section). Their thinking is that easier is better and more economical; any aesthetic shortcomings can be offset in postproduction. Reality notwithstanding, always try to take the best aesthetic approach.

Blocking

In dramatic productions miking decisions are made during the preproduction planning stages when you work out the **blocking**—the movements of performers, cameras, and sound boom(s). Blocking begins with a *floor plan*—a diagram, drawn to scale, showing where scenery, cameras, mics, and performers will be positioned.

If there is limited physical movement by the performers and the set is small, one boom microphone can usually handle the action, provided the performers are not

more than 6 to 9 feet from the mic when they speak. If physical movement is active, the set is large, or both, two booms and sometimes wireless body mics are used. In multicamera staged productions, two booms are standard. When using two booms, one is usually positioned to cover the front and the front-left of a set (looking into the set); the other covers the rear and the rear-right.

Perambulator Boom

In studios it is also necessary to think about the boom mount when blocking. The *perambulator boom,* for instance, is large, bulky, and difficult to move quickly over extended distances, especially when cameras, cables, and set furniture are in the way (see 3-66). It is easier to leave the boom mount in place and swing, extend, or retract the boom arm to cover the action. If the boom has to be moved, use boom movers because it is time-consuming and inconvenient to have the operator come down from the boom seat each time the boom has to be repositioned.

An evident but vital concern is making sure the boom mic does not get into the picture. If it is positioned out-of-shot in a close-up, it would obviously show up in a longer shot if not repositioned. The boom should also be out of an audience's line-of-sight as much as possible. Although TV studios have TV monitors for the audience, it is to the program's advantage to make the audience feel like part of the event, especially with comedy.

If the boom stays just above (or below) the frame line, the acoustic mic-to-source distance should be proportional to the size of the shot, matching the aural and visual space, which is one of the boom's main aesthetic advantages.

Here are a few guidelines to using the boom:

■ Position the boom above and angled in front of the performer's mouth. Remember: sound comes from the mouth, not from the top of the head.

■ Establish mic-to-source operating distance by having the performer raise an arm at a 45-degree angle toward the tip of the mic and extend a finger; the finger should just touch the mic. Appropriate working distances can be planned from there. For example, if the mic-to-source distance in a close-up is 3 feet, in a medium shot it could be about 6 feet, and in a long shot up to 9 feet.

■ Directional shotgun microphones compress distance between background and foreground. Aim the mic directly at the performer(s) so as not to increase background sound.

---

2. Heather Johnson, "Tips from the Pros: Location Production Audio," *ProAudio Review,* August 2008, p. 22.

◼ Hypercardioid shotgun mics have considerable rear sensitivity, so avoid pointing the back end toward a source of unwanted noise, such as ventilators, parabolic lights, and so on.

◼ Capacitor shotguns are high-output, high-sensitivity instruments and therefore can be used at somewhat longer mic-to-source distances than moving-coil mics without degrading sound quality. Also, high-frequency response in moving-coil mics falls off with increased mic-to-source distance.

◼ To facilitate learning the shot changes in a multicamera production, provide each boom operator with *cue sheets* and, if possible, place a TV monitor on the boom (assuming a perambulator boom) or near it. Also provide headphones that feed the program sound to one ear and the director's cues to the other ear. Boom movers should also have access to cue sheets. Rehearse each shot so that the exact mic-to-source distances are established.

◼ Rehearse all boom operations. Even the slightest movements such as bending down or turning the head while talking can require complicated boom maneuvers. For example, as a head turns while talking, the boom has to be panned and the mic rotated at the same time.

◼ If a performer has a tendency to do "head whips" while interacting with other guests or because dialogue interaction calls for it, play the mic in front, keeping movement to a minimum so the speech sound and ambience are consistent.

◼ Have preparatory discussions with the sound recordist or mixer.

◼ Learn about lighting. A boom operator has to know what side of a set to work from so that the boom does not throw a shadow. Outside it is necessary to be opposite the sun side so that the boom shadow falls away from the performer.

◼ Anticipate the performer's movements so that the boom leads, rather than follows, the talent.

◼ Position the boom's base toward the front of the set, not to the side. From the side it is difficult to judge the microphone's height in relation to the cameras because cameras are usually placed in an arc around the front of the set.

◼ Indoors or outdoors it is wise to use a windscreen, especially with a capacitor shotgun because it is particularly susceptible to wind noise. A windscreen permits rapid,

abrupt boom movements without distortion from the increased force of air created by such movements.

Due to the size of perambulator booms, they may be unwieldy in small sets or difficult to maneuver when relatively frequent repositioning is called for, especially if there is no boom mover. An alternative is the fishpole boom.

Fishpole Boom

The *fishpole boom* is used in-studio when larger booms cannot negotiate small spaces, but mostly it is the microphone mount of choice in field production. It is more mobile, easier to manage, takes up less space, and requires fewer crew than wheeled booms. A fishpole is handheld and therefore can be moved around a set with relative ease (see Figure 11-1).

Fishpole booms come in various lengths, and most have a telescoping tube that can be extended or retracted (see 11-2). Shorter fishpoles can extend from 16 inches to more than 6 feet and weigh as little as 11 ounces; medium-sized fishpoles can extend from 23 inches to 8 feet and weigh about 14 ounces; longer fishpoles can extend from just under 3 feet to more than 16 feet and weigh a little more than a pound.

The fishpole boom does present a few problems. It can get heavy if it has to be carried about the set or held for any length of time, particularly if the mic is weighty. It can be difficult to control precisely, particularly in wider shots when it has to be held high. Furthermore, handling noises can be heard if the fishpole operator is not careful.

The following are some preparatory and operational tips for using the fishpole boom, particularly in field production (see 11-3 to 11-5):

◼ It is politic to remember that in field production the boom operator is the sound department's eyes and ears on the set.

◼ Operating a fishpole boom is intense and exhausting work. Be well rested and physically conditioned. Build endurance by holding a fishpole for progressively longer periods of time. If one is not available, practice with a bucket or weights at the end of a broom handle.

◼ Wear clothing that is comfortable and relatively loose fitting. Dark clothes help avoid reflections. Because fishpole miking often involves being on your feet for extended periods of time plus a lot of walking and running, forward and backward, sneakers with thick soles are comfortable and quiet.

11-1 Using a fishpole with a directional microphone pointed at the performer's mouth from (a) above and (b) below. The mic's position depends on the focal length and the angle of the shot. Better sound is usually obtained by positioning the mic above the performer because sound rises and the bounce from the floor or ground can brighten the pickup.

Mushroom pole base
Attach accessories to bottom coupling
Low-handling-noise finish
Two sets of slots accommodate most types of mic cables
Captive collet
Collar with directional dimples
Telescoping sections

11-2 Fishpole boom and its features.

■ Know the script. If one is not available or if last-minute copy changes have been made, learn the body gestures of the performers just before they speak to help anticipate boom movements.

■ Always use a windscreen, especially with directional capacitor mics, which are particularly sensitive to even minute air movement. Barrier, mesh-style windscreens are quite effective (see 3-57b), especially with a collapsible mesh windshield (see 3-57c) or windjammer (see 3-57e).

■ Always use a shock mount. High-quality microphones, particularly capacitors with high sensitivity, are apt to pick up sound conductance through the metal tube. It

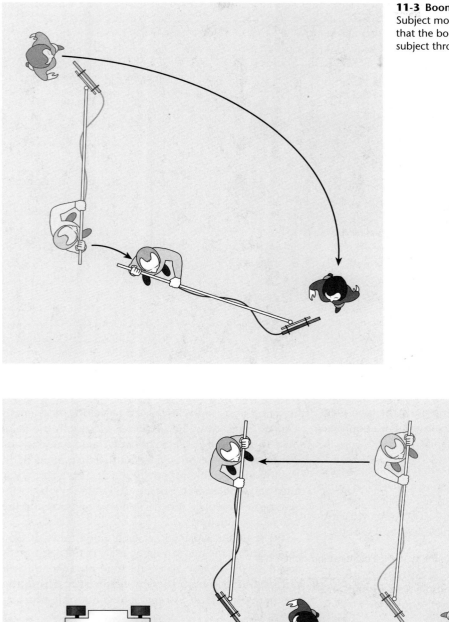

11-3 Boom leading subject. Subject movement requires that the boom lead the subject through the space.

11-4 Moving the boom for broad movements. For broad movements, such as characters moving in front of a dollying camera, the boom operator must walk backward or sideways when leading.

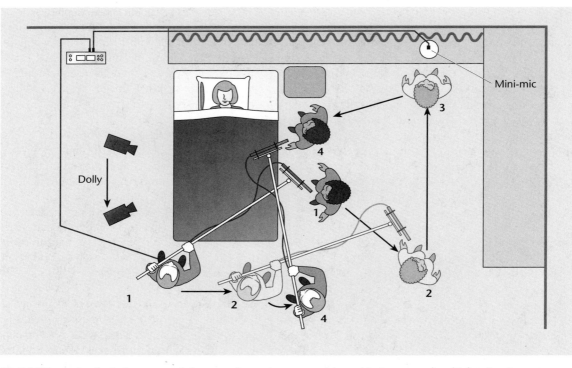

11-5 Miking complicated movement. In cases of complex movement, a subject may need multiple mic setups.

is a good idea to tape foam rubber around the tube a few inches above the handgrip and below the microphone mount to inhibit sound conductance.

■ Use high-quality headphones when operating a fishpole boom. Except for the recordist, who may be at some distance, there is no other way to tell what sounds are being picked up or how they are balanced, particularly in relation to the foreground and background sounds.

■ Be sure that there is enough cable and cleared space on the floor if the fishpole mic must move with the performer(s). To avoid the cable problem altogether, and if it is feasible, boom-mount a wireless mic (see 11-6).

■ Remove all jewelry before recording and wear gloves to help dampen handling noise.

■ If the fishpole has to be held for any length of time, secure a flag holder around the waist and sit the pole end in its pocket. Some longer fishpoles come with a handle grip on the pole to help support it against the body.

The advantage of the boom-mounted microphone on-location, as in the studio, is that by varying its distance to the sound source you can make it reflect the focal length of shots. This advantage applies especially in the field, where there is more likely to be background sound whose relationship to the principal sound source often helps establish the overall sonic environment. This technique is called ***perspective miking*** because it establishes the audio viewpoint. Moreover, it helps convey the mood and the style of a production.

If a scene takes place in a seedy hotel room, for example, aiming the mic at a slight angle to the performer's mouth so that it also picks up more room sound will "cheapen" the sound, thereby better articulating the visual atmosphere. If a scene is to convey an anticipa-

11-6 Wireless boom mic with mounted transmitter.

tory ambience, widening mic-to-source distance even in a tight shot creates an open sound that encompasses background sounds such as a clock ticking, a board creaking, a drink being poured, an owl hooting, a siren screaming, and so on. (Of course, both of these examples require the director's OK.)

Fishpole booms also permit positional changes to compensate for problems with perspective. In handling a strong voice against a weak one, the mic can be placed closer to the weak voice but aimed at the strong voice, evening out the overall level. In addition to perspective and flexibility, overhead miking in general tends to provide a crisp, natural sound compared with body mics, which are often sterile in texture.

Perspective

The challenge in operating any boom is to maintain aural perspective while simultaneously keeping the boom mic out of the picture and keeping the performers in the mic's pickup pattern. To create a realistic setting, sound and picture must work together; the aural and visual perspectives should match.

It is logical to assume that if you see two performers talking in the same plane, you should hear them at relatively the same loudness; if you see one performer close up engaged in dialogue with another actor farther away, the performer who is closer should sound louder. *Do not confuse perspective with loudness.* Loudness aside, it is hearing more or less of the surroundings relative to the positions of the performers that helps create perspective.

Two performers talking in the same plane would have the same relative loudness but the background sounds and/or ambience would be minimized. With two performers in different planes, one, say, in a *close up (CU)* and one in a *medium shot (MS),* the sound of the performer in the MS would include more background sounds and/or ambience compared with the performer in the CU.

Performers in the Same Plane The easiest way to pick up performers talking in the same plane and to maintain their aural relationship is to position the microphone equidistant between them and close enough so that they are on-mic (see 11-7). If one performer walks a short distance away, blocking will have determined either how far the boom can follow, keeping the performer on-mic yet remaining close enough to get back in time to cover the other performer, or whether a second boom should be used (see 11-8 and 11-9).

Performers in Different Planes During a scene it is typical for shots to change from, say, a medium shot of a group with performer A talking, to a close-up of performer A, to a close-up of performer B responding, to another medium shot of the group, to a close-up of performer C talking, and so on. To keep visual and aural perspective consistent, the sound in the medium shots should not be quite as loud as the sound in the close-ups and should include more of the background sounds and ambience.

In a medium shot compared with a close-up, for example, the boom has to be higher and therefore farther

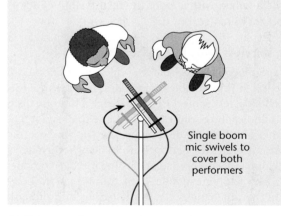

11-7 Two performers on the same plane. The easiest way to boom-mic them is to place the microphone equidistant between them and swivel it back and forth.

Single boom mic swivels to cover both performers

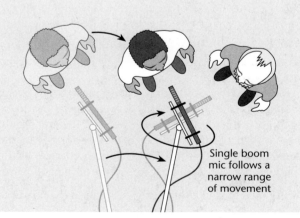

11-8 Two performers on the same plane but with some movement. One boom mic can be used when there is some movement of performers on the same plane and the distances between them remain minimal.

Single boom mic follows a narrow range of movement

11-9 Two performers on the same plane but with significant movement. Two boom mics may be needed when blocking calls for more-dynamic movement, as it often does.

from the actors. In a long shot compared with a medium shot, the mic has to be higher and farther still. The aural difference in the mic-to-source distance, reflected by the acoustic change in the loudness level and the proportion of direct to indirect waves, should match the visual difference in the audience-to-source distance.

Regardless of the visual perspective, however, the audience must hear the performers clearly. Someone close up should sound more present than someone farther away—but only to a certain extent. A performer in a close-up shot should not sound on top of the audience, and the audience should not have to strain to hear a performer in a long shot. The mic also has to be close enough to a performer that it does not pick up too much ambience or background sounds. You have to cheat a bit with mic placement to reduce the unwanted reflections so that the difference in loudness levels is obvious but not disconcerting.

Suppose a scene calls for two performers to talk several feet apart. First, the distance between them has to be within the microphone's range. Second, the mic should be between them but closer to the performer in the foreground (see 11-10). Third, if further changes in the loudness level are necessary, the range of the boom arm should be increased to get the mic closer or the performers' positions should be changed. If the performers are too far apart to cover with one boom, use two (see 11-11).

Remember, within the same scene and locale, differences in loudness levels and background sounds or am-

bience should be apparent but not marked. Don't worry about the slight discrepancies between the visual and aural perspectives. If the audio sounds realistic enough, the psychological effect of the picture's perspective should make up for the difference between the two.

Adjusting Microphone Levels at the Mixer   Using the fader to change the aural perspective does not work. Increasing loudness will bring sound closer, and decreasing it will move sound farther away. But unless loudness changes are minor, using the fader to make level adjustments that are obvious not only affects loudness but changes ambient and background sound relationships as well. Remember: with a fader the relationship of actors on a set may change, but the space itself does not.

Using Wireless Body Microphones

Most audio people agree that if a wired microphone can do the job, it is preferable to a wireless mic because it is more reliable, less subject to interference and noise from motors and cabling, and not vulnerable to dropout. On the other hand, many directors prefer the wireless mic because it liberates the performer from being tethered to a cord. This has been a particular blessing in staged productions where actors are mobile. The advantages of the body mic are that dialogue is clear, intelligible, and present, with minimal background sound. The disadvantages are that sonic perspective, regardless of a shot's focal length, is the same and the sound tends to be sterile.

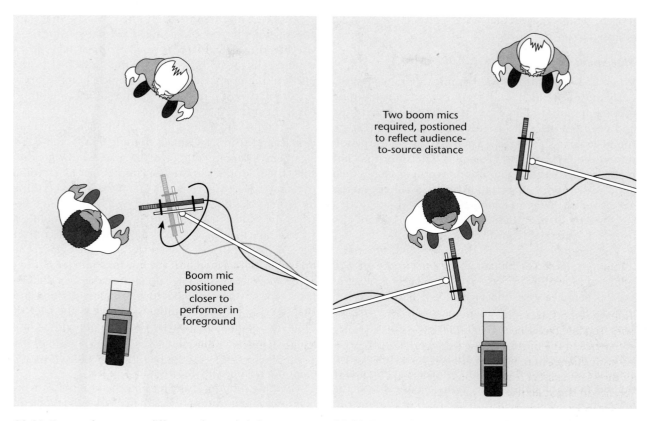

11-10 Two performers on different planes and close enough to be covered by one boom. The microphone should be placed between the performers, but mic-to-source distance should reflect audience-to-source distance. In other words, the person who looks closer should be louder.

11-11 Two performers on different planes and too far apart to be covered by one boom. Two booms should be used. To some extent mic-to-source distance should complement camera-to-source distance.

It is possible to compensate for these drawbacks to some extent. There are two basic types of mini-mics used for body miking: proximity-prone and transparent. ***Proximity-prone mini-mics*** tend to add presence to close dialogue and reject background sound. ***Transparent mini-mics*** have a more open and natural sound and pick up more ambience. The advantage of transparent mini-mics is that sound can be blended more naturally with boom and plant mics; their disadvantage is that they pass more ambience.

Body mics are usually omnidirectional; directional mini-mics have not proved practical. They have to be pointed precisely in the direction of the sound, which, in body-miking actors or in using plant mics, is often not effective. Also remember that sound-canceling ports are

what make a mic directional. Clothes or mounting tape could block some of the ports and thereby degrade pickup.

When using a wireless body mic, consider all of the following: aural perspective, microphone placement, number of mics in use, and sound levels.

Perspective

The main sonic difference between a body-mounted wireless mic and a boom mic is in creating aural perspective. Remember, with a boom mic-to-source distance is adjusted with the shot, thereby automatically matching aural/visual perspective (at least in theory). When a wireless mic is attached to the body, mic-to-source distance is close and never varies, regardless of the shot's focal length, which means that aural perspective must be adjusted in postproduction.

Placement

When body-mounting a wireless mic for drama, it obviously must be hidden, so the type of fabric and clothing become important factors in deciding what mic to use and where to place it. For this reason, before miking a sound designer should make a point to consult the person responsible for wardrobe. Remember that cotton does not make as much rustling sound as do synthetic fabrics such as polyester, rayon, nylon, and Dacron. Synthetic fabrics are also more likely to conduct static electricity, which creates interference, than are wool, suede, cotton, and leather. Leather does, however, make noise.

The design of performers' clothing is also important. A microphone can be hidden inside a tie, in the seam of a shirt or blouse, in a pocket, in the collar of a jacket or sweater, behind a scarf, under a bodice, and so on. Certain mics are less susceptible than others to interference from such noises as rustling, jostling, and static electricity; you have to test to determine which is best. Obviously, a mic with a windscreen and shock absorbency is better than a mic without one or both, but a windscreen also makes the mic more difficult to hide. Tying a loose knot in the microphone cable underneath the head of the mic can sometimes, but not always, reduce or eliminate clothing noise. If the proximity of the mic to the mouth creates problems with sibilance, popping, and nose blast, invert the mic (so long as it is omnidirectional).

Clothing style also affects where a mic can be hidden—costumes from different periods and cultures pose different challenges. Hiding a mic on a performer playing an eighteenth-century Austrian prince clothed from neck to ankle in tight-fitting raiment presents one type of problem; hiding a mic on a woman in a low-cut, strapless dress presents another. Here, again, the person handling wardrobe can help. Maybe a pocket for the microphone can be sewn underneath the prince's vest; the bodice of the dress can be tubed and the mic placed inside. It is, of course, easier to hide a microphone in loose-fitting clothes than in tight-fitting ones. Loose-fitting garments also reduce the chance of picking up rustling sounds.

If possible, it is best to have the microphone in the open. Try to mount it in the shadow area of a coat lapel, sew it to the material, or stick it through material to look like a button, tie clasp, or brooch. Use mini-mics that are available in black, which is easier to conceal than gray or shiny metal.

An externally mounted mini-mic can be made inconspicuous by camouflaging it to match wardrobe. Use marking pens to color small strips of tape, foam windscreens, or both, which are then attached to the mic and the clasp, thereby subduing their appearance. An alternative is to use small patches of felt or cloth to cover the mic.

Two types of clothing noise often encountered are contact and acoustic. Contact clothing noise is caused by a garment's flapping into or rubbing across the mic capsule. The solution is to carefully immobilize all clothing that may cause this problem by taping down everything on either side of the mic. Try sandwiching the mic between two sticky triangles of tape (formed by folding a strip of tape like a flag, sticky side out). Because contact noise can also be caused when clothing rubs against the mic cable, form a loop near the mic for strain relief, then apply a few lengths of tape along the cable. Try double-faced tape or sticky triangles to immobilize clothing and keep it from rubbing. Another adhesive is the type of caulk used as a weather seal for windows. It bonds to fabric and dampens induced noises from the fabric and the cable. Avoid using too much damping material, however; extra material usually means added noise.

Clothing rubbing against itself generates noise; treating the clothing with static guard may solve the problem. A spray mist of water can soften starched fabrics. Because synthetic fabrics are much noisier than natural fibers, they should be avoided whenever possible.

Never allow the mic line and the antenna to cross when rigging a wireless body mic. It is also important to keep the antenna rigid and not looped over itself; a good way to anchor the antenna is to affix a rubber band to the tip and then safety-pin the rubber band to the clothing. If the antenna has to run in a direction other than straight up and down or to the side, invert the transmitter pack and let the mic cable, rather than the antenna, loop. Check the performer to make sure that the mic and the cable are secure—tape tends to loosen from moisture, and costumes tend to shift from movement—but be careful not to do this too often; many actors are uncomfortable wearing wireless mics, do not like to be bothered with adjustments, or both. Waterproof sealants and sweat-resistant mics can minimize the moisture problems of loosening tape and degraded transmission.

All of this is well and good, but what can you do when the costume, such as a man's bathing suit or chain mail on a knight, makes it difficult to use a body mic? In the case of the bathing suit, cooperation may be needed from the hairdresser: with skill, a wireless microphone can be hidden in the hair; sound does rise and the body does resonate. For female voices mic placement toward the front hairline is better for their high-frequency response. For the male voice, placing the mic behind the ear or over the ear, attached to a specially made ear clip, is better for low-end pickup. For wigs and hairpieces, there are toupee clips to which a mic can be attached. Avoid placing the mic under the gauze of a wig, however, because of head sweat and reduced high-frequency response. The chain mail, on the other hand, may be too noisy for any successful body miking, in which case either take a more conventional miking approach or rerecord the dialogue in postproduction.

Still another reason for working with wardrobe is to arrange with the costumer when to mount the body mic on the performer. The best time is usually when the performer is dressing at the start of the production day, even if the mic will not be needed right away. By mounting the mic before production begins, the performer has more time to get used to it, and shooting does not have to be interrupted to place the mic when it is needed. Moreover, a performer has a great deal to think about, and disrupting concentration to body-mount a mic is not a good idea.

Using Two or More Wireless Microphones

The use of two or more wireless microphone systems in the same immediate area requires that they be on different and, preferably, widely separated frequencies to avoid interference. But the wireless systems and mics should be of similar make and model to ensure sonic consistency. If this is not possible and only different systems and mics are available, each performer should be given the same make and model to use throughout production so at least the individual's sound is uniform.

An ever-present problem with body mics is noise, not only from fabric but also from props in a pocket that may jingle or rustle, such as coins, keys, or paper. For example, suppose two (or more) actors using wireless mics are exchanging dialogue at relatively close proximity. Actor A is nervously jangling coins, and the sound is interfering with the pickup of his dialogue. Assuming the pocket containing the coins is closer to the body mic than it is to the mouth, actor A's dialogue probably is also being picked up by actor B's mic but with the sound of the coins not as loud. In postproduction the recording from actor B's microphone can be used in place of the recording from actor A's mic. This enables continued use of the

wireless systems, which may be desirable for logistical or other reasons. This technique also helps solve problems of unwanted or unintelligible overlapping dialogue.

Controlling Levels

A frequent problem in recording dialogue is trying to maintain suitable levels when performers are speaking at different and varying loudnesses. If sound is too loud, level is "in the red"; if sound is too quiet, level is "in the mud." Controlling levels both to avoid distortion, particularly with digital sound, and to keep sound above the noise floor yet still preserve the relative dynamics of the performers is handled in different ways, depending on the miking.

Suppose that in a scene a distraught man is alternately sobbing and shouting at a woman, who is responding in a quiet, controlled voice, trying to calm him. In such a scene, the level changes would be wide and acute and difficult to ride. Putting a limiter on the sound is not always preferred nor recommended because it can reduce sound quality. Nor may it be possible through blocking to place the mics to compensate for the widely fluctuating levels. And it is imprudent to depend completely on postproduction to fix problems that occur in sound recording during production; by then the sound may be beyond repair because either it is distorted or the signal-to-noise ratio is unacceptable. To handle the widely varying sound levels, either boom or body mics may be employed.

When using the boom, recordists in a situation like this may set the level on the loudest sound emitted, in this case the man's shouts. If the shouts are set at, say, –27 dBFS (–7 VU), it ensures that there is sufficient headroom before *clipping*. This makes riding levels less critical in situations where the dynamic range is wide and changes quickly, and it keeps both dialogue and ambience in perspective. Exactly what meter level to set depends on the level at which the man's voice peaks. Or, as was suggested earlier in this chapter, the mic can be placed closer to the weaker voice but aimed at the strong voice, evening out the overall level.

In terms of perspective, by setting a maximum loudness level the woman's level will be quite a bit lower than the man's because she has a less powerful voice and is speaking quietly. But increasing her loudness level during the quiet interchanges will also increase her ambience disproportionately to the man's. This creates different background noise levels between the two performers as well as different spatial relationships. If quieter levels are at or below the noise floor, slight adjustments in microphone selection or placement, performer placement, or voice projection can be made, or compression can be used. (Another alternative to using the boom is to shoot and mike the scene entirely from the woman's perspective.)

With the body mic, handling the scene is somewhat easier. Because each performer is individually miked, it is possible to set and control levels separately. If in the scene the woman also has to shout at the man, perhaps to admonish him to stop feeling sorry for himself, another option is to put two wireless mics on each performer. Levels for one pair of mics would be set for the louder dialogue, and levels for the other pair set for the quieter dialogue. The production mixer then has four faders to manage, but overall sound quality will probably be better, and the editor has more to work with in postproduction.

Here are some other tips to keep in mind when considering or using wireless body mics:

■ When complex movement is called for, do not automatically choose a wireless body mic before considering whether good boom work can meet the challenge. Remember that a boom-mounted microphone produces a more realistic sound.

■ Because wireless mics are subject to interference from noise, avoid using them in heavy-traffic areas, such as downtown streets, parking lots, highways, airports, or in areas where there are frequent *radio frequency (RF)* transmissions.

■ Place the receiver properly—in line-of-sight with the transmitter and as close to the set as possible.

■ Check transmission frequencies to make sure that no one else in the area is using your band(s).

■ Do a sound check by walking around the same area(s) the performers will be using.

■ Adjust the gain control on the transmitter for each performer.

■ Always power down; that is, do not turn off the transmitter without turning off the receiver. Otherwise the receiver will keep looking for a signal and could lock into unpleasant VHF white noise. (**White noise** is a wideband noise that contains equal energy at each frequency, as opposed to **pink noise,** which is wideband noise that maintains constant energy per octave. Both types of noise are generally used for testing electronic audio equipment.)

■ Bring backup wireless systems and plenty of fresh batteries, preferably longer-lasting lithium batteries.

Plant Microphones

Plant microphones, also called *fixed mics,* are positioned around a set to cover action that cannot be easily picked up with a boom or a body mic or to provide fill sound. A plant mic can be either a conventional size or, preferably, a capacitor mini-mic. Plant mics can be hidden practically anywhere—in flowers, on a desktop nameplate, in a doorway, on the edge of a windowsill, on an automobile visor, or in a plant, which is where the term originated.

Because a plant mic is almost always used along with the main boom or body mic, beware of phasing from overlapping sound. Also, if possible, try to match the perspective sound quality of the main and plant mics; that will probably be easier to do with a boom mic than with a body mic.

Multiple Miking with Different Microphone Mounts

As pointed out earlier, miking dialogue for staged productions might involve using a combination of approaches, incorporating boom, body, and plant mics.

For example, in a single-camera production a master shot and then various perspectives of the shot are recorded in separate takes. A *master shot* is a single shot of an entire scene from a far-enough distance to cover all the action. Suppose the scene is a party in a large living room, where host and hostess are mingling with guests and exchanging pleasantries. The master shot would be a wide shot of the room, taking in all the action. Other takes might consist of a group shot with host, hostess, and a few guests and three-, two-, and one-shots of the host and hostess in a selected exchange with one person in the group.

To take advantage of all the sonic possibilities, the sound of each take should be recorded. By audio-recording as many takes as possible, the various sonic qualities and perspectives provide the editor with more options in cutting sound and picture. For example, the master shot could be miked from overhead, using boundary mics with hemispheric, or stereo, pickup to capture the overall hubbub. Directional overhead mics could be added for more-selective but still open pickup of particular interactions among host and hostess and certain guests or groups of guests. The middle-side (M-S) mic is yet another alternative. The directional capsule can be used to pick up selective sounds, and its side capsules can be used to pick up the more-open sounds. The advantage of the M-S mic is that middle and side imaging can be handled separately in the mix, so using the M-S mic during production recording does not necessarily commit the mixer to its entire pickup in postproduction. The same is not true with conventional stereo miking.

Wireless mics attached to host and hostess would record their dialogue for close-ups to be shot later. In the group shot, a boom mic with an omnidirectional or wide-angle pattern could be used for the overall pickup to provide a more open sonic perspective than is possible with the directional overhead mics. For the tighter three-, two-, and one-shots, body-mounted wireless mics provide the sonic complement to these closer cutaways. Also, with a multitrack recorder there is no reason not to continue using the overhead mics for each take to provide additional recordings of the ambient party sounds.

The point is that in a single-camera production, shooting each scene several times to record as many different visual perspectives as possible is part and parcel of the technique. Each shot often requires time to reposition the camera, trim the lighting, adjust the performers' clothes, and touch up hair and makeup. If such pains are taken for the picture, similar time and attention should be given to the sound so that the recorded audio also has as many different perspectives as possible. Although enlightened directors do this, even today too many directors still give sound short shrift to the detriment of the finished product (see "How Directors Can Help the Audio Crew" later in this chapter).

By the standards of most multicamera productions for television, the length of each continuous shot recorded in a single-camera production is often relatively short. Long takes are uncommon, because when performer and camera movement change appreciably, it is often also necessary to reposition performers, crew, and equipment. But long takes over relatively far-flung distances are done from time to time.

A key to such takes, in addition to having mics strategically mounted and located, is the placement of recorders. Clearly, more than one recorder is necessary to handle a long take over some distance. The placement of recorders is dictated by the length of mic cable runs, the transmission range of a wireless mic system, or both, and if necessary where the recorders and their operators can be hidden.

RECORDING DIALOGUE IN THE FIELD

In production always be prepared. Time is money, to say nothing of the physical and psychological angst caused by unnecessary delays. This applies even more so to field production, where away from the security and the controlled environment of the studio, if something can go wrong, it will. And it applies to dialogue as well as to other materials produced in the field, such as news and sports, which are covered in Chapter 13.

Preproduction Planning

Before actual production gets under way, decisions are made about the production site, the equipment, and any specific needs. Some of these decisions may be out of the sound person's control. But even as a consultant, the sound person can facilitate the preparation and the production of audio by anticipating problems and needs and by being ready to provide knowledgeable advice when asked. The importance of proper preparation for on-location production cannot be overemphasized. Consider the loss of time and money, to say nothing of the inconvenience to all the people involved, if you hold up production or have to accommodate a less-than-desirable situation because the sound crew is short a person or someone brought the wrong microphone, forgot the batteries for the recorder, neglected to pack the tool kit, planned to mount a heavy camera crane on soft soil, chose a shooting site several days in advance of production without realizing that a building nearby was slated for demolition on the day of recording, scouted the shooting site at noon although the script called for the scene to take place at dusk, or selected a site filled with ragweed without checking whether any of the key people were allergic to pollen. Planning to shoot on-location is a careful, meticulous procedure involving more than just decisions about production and in the end worth whatever time it takes.

Selecting a Location

In selecting a shooting site, sound designers prefer one with suitable acoustics indoors and no distracting sounds outdoors, although these qualities are rarely found away from the controlled environment of the studio. The first thing to understand about a production site is that directors are interested in what it *looks* like, not what it sounds like. The second thing is to be prepared to deal with unwanted sound. If possible, try to reduce the difficulties by suggesting to the director those sites with the fewest sound problems. But keep in mind that where you shoot is determined by the demands of the picture, not of the sound.

Because the main challenge in doing a production on-location is to record the principal sound source with little or no sonic leakage from either the acoustics or the other sound sources, it is of considerable help to the sound crew if the location site is evaluated with noise control in mind and judged on what is possible to achieve in neutralizing unwanted sound.

Dealing with Unwanted Sound

Unwanted sound is generated by many sources. Some are obvious; others are not so obvious: the low-frequency rumble from traffic that becomes a midrange hiss on a wet day, blowing sound from wind, clatter from a nearby office, excessive reverb from rooms that are too live, buzz from fluorescent lights, jet roar from planes that fly over the production site, noise from construction, church bells that ring on the hour, a far-off foghorn, barking dogs, chirping birds, clanking pipes, creaking floorboards, refrigerators, computers, machinery, and so on.

Being aware of the problems is not enough—you have to know what, if anything, to do about them. For example, you can usually roll off low-frequency rumble from traffic, but the midrange hiss from wet tires on a wet surface is difficult to equalize out or even reduce with a noise processor plug-in. Gentle wind presents little problem for a mic equipped with a pop filter and a windscreen. With capacitor mics these filters will not completely offset the effect of noise from strong winds, although the mesh-style zeppelin windscreen and windjammer are quite effective, especially when used together. If a room is reverberant, you can make it less so by placing a lot of sound-absorbent material out-of-shot and using tight, highly directional miking; but these techniques may not work in large, extremely reverberant spaces. If the director insists on a site where sound problems cannot be neutralized, plan to rerecord the audio in the studio during postproduction.

If possible, schedule shooting during times when sites are least noisy. In locations where there are popular nightspots, shopping areas, and other types of clamor, plan to shoot after hours unless you want these sounds to be part of the soundscape.

Two other considerations in choosing a production site with audio in mind are the available space and the power supply. Make sure the fishpole operator has enough room to move with the action and maneuver the boom. If the production site does not have enough power outlets or wattage, or if the circuits are noisy, plan to bring the main and backup power supplies.

Prerecorded Material

Any prerecorded announcements, sound effects, or music used during production must be included in preproduction planning. Also plan for the equipment to be used to play and reproduce them: disc player, recorder, loudspeaker(s), and so on.

Other Equipment and Materials

Anticipating the need for less-obvious but nevertheless important equipment and materials is also part of preproduction planning. Many production recordists rent equipment packages, which vary depending on production needs. For example, a basic package for sound-effect gathering or documentary may include a recorder with a built-in microphone or a separate shotgun mic, windscreen and shock mount, mic cable, fishpole, and headphones. A package for a theatrical-style production may include, in addition to the equipment in a basic package, a production mixer; a sound cart; a laptop computer with recording/editing software; additional microphones, including mini- and stereo mics and cables; and a carrying bag. When renting an equipment package, test it before you arrive on-location to make sure all the equipment is in working order.

The following are among other necessary items to have handy, where appropriate (also see Chapter 13).

- AC [alternating current] power checker
- Adjustable wrench
- Backup microphones and mic accessories, such as cables, connectors, windscreens, and shock mounts
- Batteries for every piece of equipment using them
- C-clamp, pony clips, and various clips for body-mounted mics
- Clip leads
- Colored marking pens to camouflage body-mounted mics
- Cotton swabs
- Disk drives
- Drill and drill bits

- Flashlight or lantern light
- Fuses
- Headphone amp
- Knee bench
- Log sheets or a laptop computer to record time, location, and content of production information
- Lubes and glues
- Memory cards
- Mic stands
- Measuring tape
- Multimeter
- Nut drivers
- Oscillator
- Oscilloscope
- Pens and paper
- Pocketknife
- Rope
- Scripts and rundown sheets
- Soldering pencil
- Sound blanket
- Sound-pressure-level meter
- Stopwatch
- Tape—duct, masking, and waterproof (sweatproof)
- Tool kit with ruler, needle-nose and regular pliers, wire cutters, Phillips-head and conventional screwdrivers, hammer, awl, file, and saw
- Umbrellas
- Vise grip
- Walkie-talkies

Blocking and Rehearsing

Despite the considerable flexibility that technology provides in producing staged material, scenes are still shot one at a time, out of sequence, and in segments. Each shot is blocked and lighted, and camera movements are rehearsed. Just as the visual elements must be painstakingly planned and practiced, so should the audio. For each shot mic positions are blocked, movements are rehearsed, and sound balances are determined.

The responsibilities of the sound crew are in some ways perhaps greater than those of the people responsible for producing the picture. The sound crew is often left on its own, not because the director does not care (although this is sometimes the case) but because audio is usually the one major production component of film and TV that a director is likely to know least about. As a result, blocking and rehearsing become all the more important for the audio crew. The director may proceed with shooting when the pictorial elements are in place and assume that, or not bother to check if, sound is ready. It had better be! As pointed out earlier, too many directors who would understand a delay if a light had to be repositioned would have little patience if a similar delay were due to, say, a microphone that had to be changed.

Production Dialogue Recording

Most of the same considerations that apply to recording dialogue in the studio also apply to field recording, including the challenge of getting the sound right with little leeway for experimentation, refinement, or, should something go wrong, repair. Perhaps one difference between studio and field production recording is the additional pressure that comes from being away from the controlled environment of the studio, particularly when a director has an aesthetic distaste for rerecording dialogue in postproduction and indicates a strong desire to use the original sound in the final mix. Being flexible and imaginative in solving problems is essential to good production recording.

Suppose a director wants to shoot a scene with constrained action in a very large stone-and-marble room using a boom, but because of authenticity does not want to rerecord the dialogue in postproduction. The reverberation is so dense, however, that the actors cannot pick up cues from one another. Clearly, the walls and the ceiling cannot be acoustically treated—the room is far too large. What the production recordist did in this actual situation was devise a canopy secured to four extendable legs and position it over the action. In addition, a rolling, absorbent, 20-foot-high baffle was used to reduce the length of the room and therefore the reverberant space. It should be noted that this type of solution would not have worked had the scene required a lot of movement.

In a scene, particularly a long one, with a lot of movement in a contained but live space, employing as many different microphone setups as possible may, in the long run, be the expedient approach; that is, so long as the number of mics can be controlled given the mixer and the recorder being used. For example, a boom mic may be able to capture only some of the action; the squeaks from an actor's costume may be picked up by the body mic; and in part of the scene, the actors may be blocked too close to the reflective surfaces for a usable pickup by a plant mic. By using all three microphone mounts and recording all the dialogue from them on separate tracks, an editor has the choice of the best-sounding dialogue tracks. Of course, it is then up to the editor or the mixer, or both, to process the overall pickups so that the perspectives and the ambience are seamless. But if it works, the director has a live production recording and does not have to resort to automated dialogue replacement (discussed later in this chapter).

Suppose that a director wants an actor to sing while revving a racecar engine on a racetrack. Clearly, the engine sound will drown out the singing. But with a noise-canceling mic positioned correctly on the actor, the singing should be front-and-center and the lyrics intelligible.

With a conventional mic, it is possible to use noise suppression (see 11-12). If the sound-pressure level of a sound source is high enough, it is possible to close-mike the source and reduce leakage. Remember: sound-pressure level from a point source in a free field doubles by 6 dB

11-12 Dialogue noise suppressor. This unit provides automated (to time code) dialogue noise suppression. Its features include on-board scenes, a recall system, moving faders, sample rates up to 96 kHz, Pro Tools integration, and near-zero latency.

each time the distance is halved (see the discussion of the inverse square law in Chapter 13). Therefore in noisy surroundings, moving a mic closer to the desired sound source increases the on-mic level as the background noise remains constant.

These are the success stories. There are conditions under which no amount of ingenuity can make it possible to record much usable dialogue on the set, regardless of a director's intent, such as when the shooting schedule is so tight that construction on one part of the set has to continue while action is shot on another part of the set, or when on the day of shooting an unanticipated paving crew is digging up a nearby street with a jackhammer and it is not possible to reschedule the shoot. In such cases most if not all of the dialogue has to be rerecorded in postproduction (see "Automated Dialogue Replacement" later in this chapter).

That said, actors generally prefer the natural environment and interactions on the set to the sterility of the automated dialogue replacement (ADR) studio. As good as postproduction can be, most believe that it cannot quite capture the dozens of tiny sounds that correspond to physical movements, such as a sniff, soft exhales of anxiety, the caress of a touch, and the rustle of a newspaper page against the edge of the table. Although ADR gives directors complete control and often saves time and money, most actors agree that it is no substitute for the real thing, assuming that it is possible to record a usable "real thing" on the set.

Signal Processing and Production Recording

Signal processing is rarely used during production recording except for, perhaps, bass roll-off and a slight midrange boost to help punch dialogue. Anything else, such as compression, heavy equalization, and so on, is usually done in postproduction. Productions shot with a single camera are done out of sequence and with different takes of most scenes; prematurely processing sound on the set could cause myriad matching problems, particularly with stereo and surround sound. Spatial imaging should be left to postproduction. To attempt it during production recording makes little sense because there is no way to know how a scene will ultimately be edited.

The only "processing" usually done in production recording is riding the mic level and balancing the loudness extremes of each sound source. It is important to perform these operations with smooth and imperceptible changes using a top-quality mixer or recorder whose controls are easy to see and access. Slight gain adjustments using faders on equipment of mediocre quality are often too apparent in the recording, especially with digital audio.

Recording

Regardless of the microphone used during production, audio pickup is only half the sound equation. Recording is the other half. And the more tracks there are available, the better the chances of both producing usable audio from the set and providing the sound editor with more choices in postproduction.

Today this is less of a problem than ever before. With single-system recording, digital video cameras have at least four high-quality audio tracks available. For double-system recording, roadworthy digital recorders furnish at least four digital audio tracks (see 5-14 and 5-15).

The advantages of multitrack recording on the set are obvious: it facilitates various miking arrangements and therefore allows better control of dialogue, background, and even sound-effect recording. For example, take a simple outdoor scene in which a couple is walking in the countryside and focal lengths vary from wide shots to close-ups. One approach could be to use two body mics for the couple and a separate microphone—omnidirectional or boundary—to pick up background sound. Recording the three tracks separately not only allows control of each sonic element during production and postproduction but also reduces the need for the extra step of dialogue rerecording, potentially at least.

In dramatic productions, because scenes are often shot a few times from different perspectives, the preceding example may be shot as a master scene of the couple, then as close-ups from first the man's and then the woman's perspective. This allows an editor to cut from shots of the couple to individual shots of their interaction.

As for miking, because the master scene would be shot wider than the one-shot close-ups, clip-on boundary microphones could be used as the body mics. The audio would be more open and include more background sound than would that of the typical mini-mic, better reflecting the wider focal lengths of the shot. During the one-shots the boundary mic could be changed to a mini-mic to sonically articulate the closer focal lengths and reduce background sound. A separate mic to record background sound could still be employed for added flexibility in mixing. The microphone's pickup pattern may be omnidirectional, directional, or hemispheric, depending on the quality of the background sound required. Indeed all three pickups may be recorded on separate tracks to further increase flexibility in the mix, but be careful of

additive ambience—a cumulative build of ambience as the separate tracks are combined.

Having the luxury of recording one source per track also presents its own set of challenges: it takes more time to plan and set up, and simultaneously monitoring several inputs in multitrack recording is difficult. An approach some recordists take is to adjust and sample all input levels before a shot, establish the headroom level, and then watch the meters during recording, laying down the tracks at optimum loudness. Another approach is to use muting. Even in multitrack production recording, it is unlikely that several tracks will be recorded at the same time. Once a principal track has been recorded, it can be muted during the recording of another track. The danger in this, however, is that if a muted track is being used for cueing purposes, the recordist could miss the cue. A way to avoid this problem is to simply lower the levels of the previously recorded track so that they are audible but not competing with the level of the track being recorded. Even so, this solution still takes bifurcated concentration and nimble fingers.

Regardless of the venue, it is always wise to record plenty of ambience of the performance area. This is of great help in solving problems of matching during postproduction editing.

It is worth noting here that a production recordist is also responsible for making sure that the mixer, recorder, and distribution system are adequate to the task. They must be able to handle the number of mics on the set, the cable runs from wired mics (which must be long enough to reach from the set to the production recordist's location or the distribution system, or from the set to the mixer/recorder), the receivers used with wireless mics, and some signal processing (see Chapter 13).

Reality Programs

All of the above is well and good for most conventionally produced programs. The so-called reality shows are another story and present a unique challenge. As more than one production recordist has suggested, the problems of a feature film pale in comparison to the problems of dealing with sound environments in less-than-hospitable locations and the unpredictable actions of the participants.

In reality programs dialogue from the participants is usually handled with wireless body mics, plant mics, and the fixed mics on the digital camcorders (see 13-8). But plenty of postproduction signal processing is inevitable to clean up dialogue that is full of different types of noise, such as varying background sounds, unintelligible words, overlapping lines, and clicks, pops, and mic knocks. As talented and proficient as the productions' recordists are, without postproduction most if not all of the production audio from reality shows would be unusable.

Sound crew who work on reality programs agree that the battle to make dialogue intelligible and match it shot to shot is constant. Every shot presents a problem. "The actor might have a camera and mic in his eyeglasses and have to fight to keep his head steady. There's traffic noise, people are whispering to each other…[and] segments are shot on different days at different locations."[3]

Another contributing factor to the problem of getting intelligible dialogue is the placement of hidden mics, which can be anywhere—in a dashboard, tree, potted plant, or beaded necklace. The recordist has to hope that participants will deliver their lines reasonably on-mic and that weather and background sound will not be inhibiting factors in recording the dialogue. There are few opportunities for retakes. Dialogue that would easily qualify for rerecording in film has to be made usable in reality TV.[4] When this is not possible, some productions have to resort to subtitles.

Recording dialogue for reality programs is indeed challenging but not unavailing. Certainly, postproduction processing is absolutely necessary to clean up the audio tracks. It is also vital to use time code during recording as a guide to match sounds from the various mics. There is a forgiving element as well. Due to the documentary feel of most reality programs, the audience is comfortable with their cinéma vérité production values. There is not the same expectation of polish as there would be with a theatrical television drama.

Production Sound-effect Recording

Although most sound effects in a staged production are handled in post, some directors prefer to use as many sounds recorded on the set as possible. They feel that because those sounds were recorded in their actual ambient environment and perspective in relation to the sound of the dialogue, they are more realistic than sounds that are postproduced. See Chapter 15 for a comprehensive discussion of sound-effect production.

---

3. Christine Bunish, "Audio for Reality TV," *Post Magazine,* January 2004, p. 28.

4. From Dan Daley, "Get Real," *Film and Video,* January 2004, p. 35.

Noise Reduction

Because noise is an ever-present annoyance, and because of the clarity of digital sound, the value of noise reduction cannot be stressed enough, especially in relation to dialogue and field recording. Even though digital noise-processing plug-ins are powerful tools in eliminating noise from a recording during postproduction, it saves considerable time and expense in the long run if noise reduction is attended to throughout the production process. In addition to noise processing, which is implemented after the fact, there are a number of ways to deal with noise before (and during) the fact.

Use only the highest-quality microphones and recording equipment. With directional mics make sure they have excellent off-axis rejection. Remember that many capacitor mics have high output, so it is ordinarily unnecessary to increase their levels appreciably during quiet interchanges, thereby avoiding a boost in background noise. The output of moving-coil mics may be too low to pick up quiet levels without noise. Moreover, capacitor mics do not have to be brought as close to a sound source, so you avoid the problems of popping and sibilance.

A noise suppressor helps (see 11-12), as does equalization. By rolling off the low frequencies, noise from ventilation systems and room rumble are reduced. (Some directors have the air-conditioning turned off during shooting.) Cutting the high frequencies reduces hiss. With dialogue it is possible to use a relatively narrow frequency range because the speaking voice has little low- and high-frequency content.

Putting gentle compression on a voice raises the quieter levels above the noise floor. Using a noise gate can also reduce ambient noise level, but take care that its action is not perceptible. A de-esser reduces sibilance, but be careful of too much signal processing during recording because once it is part of a recording it is very difficult to remove, and the more electronic devices in the signal chain, the worse the signal-to-noise ratio. That said, use whatever miking technique or signal processing is necessary to reduce rumble, AC hum, buzz, and hiss—they are unacceptable in a recording. Better to deal with these problems during production recording than to try to fix them in post. Keep in mind, however, that any signal processing during recording should be conservative and knowledgeably applied; otherwise it will cause more problems than it solves.

A primary source of acoustic noise is the sets. Art directors can eliminate many potential noise problems by following a few principles of acoustic design, such as constructing sets whose walls are not parallel, using absorptive materials (including sound-absorbing paint), and building flooring that does not squeak—unless the director wants this effect.

Directors can also reduce ambient noise by not blocking action near a flat surface or, worse, a corner. Regardless of the quality of the mic and the effectiveness of the sound-absorbing materials, it is difficult to avoid signal degradation when sound bounces from walls and corners into a mic at close range. Too much sound absorption is not good, either. Heavy carpeting on a set, for example, could make sound lifeless.

In field-recording venues, no matter how carefully chosen with sound in mind, there may be background noise problems from wind, traffic, ventilation, and so on. Although the point has been made before, it bears repeating: background noise, once it becomes part of a recording, is difficult to remove without altering the sound quality of the program material, noise processing plug-ins notwithstanding.

HOW DIRECTORS CAN HELP THE AUDIO CREW

During a shoot the activities of most folks on the set are readily apparent. Everyone knows what the director, assistant director, cameraperson, costumer, electrician, and so on, do. Film and video are dominated by visual considerations. It takes more people to produce picture than it does to produce sound. Except for handling the microphones, the recorder, and any audio playback equipment needed for cues, what the few people on the sound crew do is a mystery to most of the other production personnel. Whereas the visual aspects of filming or video recording can be seen by everyone, only the sound mixer and the microphone handler can hear what is being recorded. Moreover, a director will usually understand if there is a request to delay shooting because a shadow needs to be eliminated; asking for a delay to eliminate a hum, however, may not be met with quite the same response.

If the director enlightens the entire image-producing team on how to avoid or minimize audio problems, it goes a long way toward audio efficiency and economy, not only in production but in postproduction as well.

Preproduction, discussed earlier in this chapter, is a good place to start. On the set the *cameraperson* can use a sound-absorbing blimp to mask camera noise. The *lighting*

director can mount lights high enough to allow sufficient headroom for the boom operator and prevent noise from the lights from being picked up by the microphones. *Special-effect techs* should keep noise-making devices, such as a rain machine or a fan to blow curtains or foliage, away from the reach of mics or baffled to muffle their sound. As noted earlier *wardrobe* can avoid noisy fabrics, consider the impact of jewelry, and design clothing for easier placement of body mics. *Props* can reduce noise, for example, by putting a pad under a tablecloth to muffle dish and utensil sounds, by using fake ice cubes in drinking glasses to reduce clinking sounds, and by spraying shopping bags with water mist to prevent paper crackle. *Grips* can reduce dolly squeaks, put talcum powder around the rubber wheels, secure fixtures that rattle, and oil noisy hinges. The *assistant director* or designated overseer should arrange with local officials to have traffic cleared and make sure that no noise-generating public works project is scheduled near the performance area at the time of shooting.

The audio crew can help itself in a number of ways already pointed out in this chapter, including recording all takes—whether usable or not—to make editing easier and to always have a sync reference with which to work.

Production personnel should be equipped with walkie-talkies or cell phones (if feasible) so that they can coordinate their activities, particularly if the set is far-flung.[5] Communication among the audio personnel is vital, before and during a location shoot. Of considerable help too is making sure the budget and the director allow for running test recordings before shooting begins.

PRODUCTION RECORDING AND THE SOUND EDITOR

Production recordists can be of considerable help in giving sound editors flexibility by how they record dialogue on the set. This is no small consideration given the pressures, expense, and usually limited time of postproduction. In other words multitrack recording is often better than split-track recording (using the two tracks of a stereo recorder separately as monaural tracks [see Chapter 13]). If a scene or show uses one or two mics, there is no problem recording split-track. But when a shot uses several mics, a multitrack recorder provides more possibilities

5. Based on John Coffey, "To: Directors, From: Your Sound Department," *Mix*, February 2001, p. 141.

for track assignments and for recording dialogue with minimal sonic encumbrance from other pickups.

AUTOMATED DIALOGUE REPLACEMENT

Automated dialogue replacement (ADR), also known as *automatic dialogue replacement,* is handled in postproduction. During ADR dialogue is recorded or rerecorded, depending on the outcome of the production recording, the director's aesthetic preference, or both. Generally, there are two schools of thought about this process.

Some directors believe that an original performance is preferable to a re-created one and that the background sounds that are part of the dramatic action are a natural part of the sonic environment just as shadow is a natural part of light. They therefore prefer to use the dialogue and other sounds recorded during production, assuming that pickup is tight enough that the intelligibility of the dialogue and the sonic balances are acceptable. Other directors prefer dialogue recorded with a minimum of background sound. They want to control the ambience and other elements separately in postproduction, where they can also hone an actor's performance. Regardless of preference, however, there are times when ADR is the only way to capture dialogue, as it usually is, for example, in far-flung battle and chase scenes, scenes involving considerable actor movement, and scenes that require several microphones.

In general ADR in theatrical film and video is not done as much as it once was. In the past if, say, hundreds of lines per script were rerecorded, today it may be roughly a quarter that many or less. A few reasons for the change are the considerable improvement in wireless microphones; using wireless mics along with boom and plant mics to better cover sound on the set and provide the dialogue editor with more flexibility; and mixers and digital recorders that can reliably handle, synchronize, and data- and signal-process several mic feeds separately or simultaneously without sacrificing sound quality.

Purpose and Process

Automated dialogue replacement is done in a *dialogue recording studio,* a relatively dry room (reverberation time is at most 0.4 second for average-sized studios, but it is usually around 0.2 second) with a screen and microphone(s) (see 11-13). The control room is separate from the studio. As the picture is displayed on the screen, the performer, wearing headphones, stands before a mic and synchronizes the dialogue to his or her mouth and lip movements on the screen. Dry rooms are necessary so that the background sound added later can be laid in with as little prerecorded ambience as possible. Too

11-13 Dialogue recording studio.

dry a studio, however, absorbs the vitality of an actor's performance and could create a claustrophobic feeling.

Not only is ambience kept to a minimum in ADR but audio enhancements are also exiguous to give the sound editor and the rerecording mixer the most possible latitude. Compression or a microphone pad may be applied to keep a signal from overmodulating. Sometimes spare equalization is employed to smooth intercut dialogue and transitions.

The *automated* in automated dialogue replacement refers to the computer-controlled aspect of the procedure. The equipment is programmed to start, shuttle between cue points, and stop automatically. The computer also puts the recorder in *record* or *playback* and selects the desired playback track(s) in a multitrack recording. Cue points are designated in time code or in feet and frames.

Dialogue rerecording is also referred to as *looping* because the process once involved putting the dialogue sequences into short film loops so they could be repeated again and again without interruption. Each short section was rehearsed until the actor's dialogue was in sync with the picture and then recorded. The procedure is still the same, only today it is automated and the picture medium may be videotape or, more likely, a digital video display.

In ADR there are a few points and procedures worth remembering:

- Screen and analyze the scenes to be recorded and break them down line by line.

- Study the actor's tone, pitch, and emotion in the production recording.

- Note such things as dialogue that is to be shouted, whispered, and so on.

- Get to know what the performer's normal speaking voice sounds like because voice quality is quite different between a first take early in the day and a take 12 hours later.

- Another reason to get to know what the performer sounds like normally is to gauge scenes calling for projected or quiet delivery—you'll have an idea of what adjustments to make in microphone placement and levels.

The ADR studio is a sterile setting for a performance. The acoustics are dry, there is no set to help create a mood or establish a sense of environment, and there is rarely interaction among actors—they usually record their lines while working alone.

When it comes to ADR, the distinction is made between performers and trained actors. Performers often have a problem becoming the character in the absence of people on the set and a camera to play to. A trained actor, on the other hand, has an easier time adjusting to the sterile environment of the dialogue recording studio.

But even with trained actors, it is important to make them comfortable and be sensitive to any mood swings that may create inconsistencies in their performance. If an actor is having trouble nailing a line, be patient and supportive. Of course it is up to the director to deal with the actor. But the audio personnel handling the ADR can also be helpful by making suggestions, assuming the director welcomes such help.

For all talent, but particularly for the performers in ADR, listen carefully to delivery in relation to believability and how a performance will sound after background audio is added. For example, if a scene calls for an actor to talk loudly over the noise of, say, a racecar, the dialogue's force and accentuation must be convincing. Also, the dialogue may sound sufficiently loud in the quietness of the studio, but once the racecar sound is added the delivery may not be forceful enough.

Adding the sound of a scene's background environment to the actor's headphone mix sometimes helps enliven the performance. It may not be possible to use the precise background called for in the picture, but adding some presence helps counteract the sterility of the ADR studio.

Recordkeeping is an often-overlooked but very important part of ADR (and of the production process in general). Keeping accurate records of track assignments and making notes about each take is not only necessary to avoid confusion but of immeasurable help to the editors and mixers, who will be working with the dialogue tracks in postproduction. A director may choose the reading of a particular line even though the beginning of a word may not be as crisp as it should be. By noting that in the record, an editor can try to find the same sound, delivered more crisply, elsewhere in the recording and edit it in, or the mixer may be able to use equalization to add the desired amount of crispness—all with the director's approval, of course.

The five elements generally considered to be most important in ADR are pitch, tone, rhythm, emotion, and sync. The goals are to maintain consistency and to make the dialogue sound like an original production recording.

Microphone Selection and Technique

Keeping in mind that there are as many opinions about how to deal with mics and miking technique as there are ADR supervisors, it is generally agreed that the microphone used on the set does not have to be the same in ADR. Because the purpose of ADR is to record the clearest, cleanest dialogue (in a good, synced performance), only the finest mics are chosen. The particular mic will vary according to the situation. For example, recording an intimate, warm sound may call for a large-diaphragm capacitor. If the tone is not sufficiently robust, a second mic may be positioned between the mouth and the sternum to add a chestier sound. Extremely tight dialogue may require a shotgun to close down the dry acoustics even more. Screams may necessitate a moving-coil mic to avoid overload distortion and undue coloration.

Ordinarily, ADR involves straight-on recording. Such elements as perspective and signal processing are added later, though movement may be attended to through mic positioning or by having the actor move. These techniques are used more to move the voice around a bit for level to achieve some of the naturalness of the production recording. For example, if on the set an actor walks into a scene and then comes toward the camera, in ADR the actor can start a bit off-mic and then walk to the mic. Or if there is a change in mic angle but the perspective, in-studio, sounds too close, moving the actor or the mic a bit father away may provide the needed adjustment. If the ambience in back-to-back shot changes does not match and can be made seamless in ADR, it gives the dialogue editor one less problem to deal with.

Loop Groups

In scenes calling for background voices, called walla, loop groups are used. *Walla* consists of spoken words to create ambient crowd sound usually without anything discernible being said. A *loop group* comprises everyone from professional actors who do walla for a living, or some part thereof, to anyone who happens to be around and is hired by the postproduction or ADR supervisor.

The function of a loop group is to provide whatever type of background sound the script calls for—from moans and kisses to all types of crowd audio for restaurant scenes, mobs, sporting events, office hubbub, and so on. Using a loop group is far less expensive than paying principal actors to essentially make sounds.

During actual shooting, a loop group will mouth the words, instead of actually saying them, so their background does not interfere with the actors' production recording. The loop group adds the words in ADR. Usually, whatever is being said is kept at a low level just to convey a sense of location and atmosphere.

When certain words are designed to come through, these *callouts* are edited into holes where there is no dialogue or into shots with little visual or aural action. For example, in a fight scene when the favorite has his opponent against the ropes, the callout may be "Knock him out!" Or if the champ is on the canvas, the callout may be "Get up, you bum!" In a restaurant scene, in addition to the background conversational walla, you may hear callouts such as, "Would you care for another cup of coffee?" or "Thank you, come again."

A common loop group assignment is to cover nonspecific sounds for an actor, such as breaths, groans, and grunts. Again, it is much cheaper than having an A-list performer do them.

In situations where budget or availability of talent precludes using a loop group, there are the prerecorded voice collections to fall back on (see Chapter 10).

Automated Dialogue Replacement in the Field

Developments in computer hardware and software technology have made it possible to do automated dialogue replacement in the field by combining such resources as a laptop computer using specially designed dialogue-recording software. This is particularly useful in productions that are shot mostly on-location and in locales that are not close to a studio (see 11-14).

The ability to handle ADR in the field saves considerable time in postproduction. It is also advantageous to the actors, who can redo their lines relatively soon after a take. This helps ensure a fresher performance instead of having to wait until all shooting is completed before doing the dialogue replacement in-studio.

Dialogue Rerecording: Pros and Cons

Dialogue rerecording frees picture from sound and gives the director more control. When there is a choice between using the original dialogue or rerecording it, directors and sound designers disagree about the benefits of looping. The question becomes: are the added sonic control and assurance of first-rate audio quality and refined performance worth the loss of spontaneity and the unexpected?

On the one hand, regardless of the subject and the style of the material, art is illusion, so there is no reason not to use whatever means necessary to produce the most polished, well-crafted product possible. Every sonic detail must be produced with the same care and precision as

11-14 Two screen examples from an ADR software program. (a) Spotting screen showing dialogue prompt, in and out cue times, and performance notes. (b) Cue list.

every visual detail. Anything less than excellent sound (and picture) quality reduces the effect of the illusion.

Dialogue replacement also provides a director with more flexibility in shaping the sound of the dialogue. For example, for a character, say, in jail speaking within hard-surfaced areas of metal and concrete, the sound should be hard-edged and icy. When the character is then released out in the world, in the more natural, open environment, he should have a warmer, less contained sound. Producing these sonic differences and maintaining their consistencies in the two different environments is more easily handled in the controlled acoustics of an ADR studio and with whatever signal processing is added afterward.

On the other hand, quality of performance is more important than quality of sound; "natural" is more realistic and hence more effective. Because actors as a rule do not like to re-create their performances in a rerecording studio, dialogue looping is rarely as good as the original performance recording. Even though lines sound different as a shooting day progresses, because the actor's voice changes, the difference between a production line and a looped line is always much greater than the difference between two production lines.

MAIN POINTS

▶ Recording dialogue on the set is known as production recording.

▶ The principal challenge during production is recording dialogue that is clear, intelligible, and as noise-free as possible.

▶ Recording dialogue on the set of a multi- or single-camera production usually means employing a boom, body-mounted wireless, or plant microphone or a combination of the three. The microphones of choice are usually the capacitor mini-mic and the shotgun mic.

▶ Miking decisions are made in preproduction planning during blocking, when the movements of performers and cameras are worked out.

▶ The main sonic difference between boom and body-mounted microphones is aural perspective. The boom better reproduces the mic-to-source distances that are relative to the shots' fields of view. This helps maintain acoustic perspective between sound and picture. On the other hand, the body-mounted mic always picks up dialogue that is clear and present with a minimum of background sound, but sonic perspective remains the same regardless of a shot's focal length.

▶ The challenge in operating a boom is to maintain aural perspective while simultaneously keeping the performers in the mic's pickup pattern and, of course, the mic out of the frame.

▶ Do not confuse perspective with loudness.

▶ Care must be taken when using a body mic to ensure that it is inconspicuous and that it does not pick up the sound of clothes rustling. Cotton does not make as much rustling sound as do synthetic fabrics.

▶ Plant, or fixed, microphones are positioned around a set to cover action that cannot be easily picked up with a boom or body mic.

▶ Preproduction planning is essential in any production but especially so when working in the field, away from the security and the resources of the studio. Preproduction planning involves selecting a location, determining how to deal with unwanted sound, preparing prerecorded material, and anticipating all primary and backup equipment needs.

▶ Make sure that all equipment to be used in the field is thoroughly tested beforehand.

▶ Even though a director may redo dialogue in postproduction, the production recordist must still try to record the clearest, most intelligible noise-free dialogue as possible.

▶ Dealing with unwanted sound on the set is an ever-present challenge to the audio crew. But being aware of problems is not enough—you have to know what, if anything, to do about them.

▶ Reality programs present their own challenges in dialogue recording in comparison with theatrical feature films. Among other things, recordists have to deal with sound environments in less-than-hospitable locations and the unpredictable actions of the participants.

▶ Be wary of employing signal processing during production recording. It affects the dialogue audio throughout postproduction.

▶ The value of noise reduction throughout the production process cannot be overemphasized, especially in relation to dialogue and field recording.

▶ If the director enlightens the entire picture-producing team on how to avoid or minimize audio problems, it goes a long way toward audio efficiency and economy, not only in production but in postproduction as well.

▶ Production recordists can be of considerable help in giving sound editors flexibility by how they record dialogue on the set.

▶ In automated dialogue replacement (ADR), dialogue is recorded or rerecorded in postproduction so there is complete control over the acoustic environment. Any background sound, ambience, or sound effects are added to the dialogue track(s) in post.

▶ ADR, also known as looping, is done in a dialogue recording studio, a relatively dry room with a screen and a microphone.

▶ ADR frees picture from sound and gives the director more flexibility and control. On the other hand, it requires the actor to re-create a performance, which is not as natural or authentic as the real thing.

▶ The five elements generally considered to be most important in ADR are pitch, tone, rhythm, emotion, and sync.

▶ In scenes calling for background voices, called walla, loop groups are used.

12

Studio Production: Radio and Television

In radio, performers are for the most part stationary. Whether they are seated or standing, microphone positioning during a broadcast changes relatively little. When performers do change, it is usually to adjust for a small shift in their position. Under these apparently straightforward circumstances, however, there are a number of miking techniques to consider.

MIKING THE SINGLE SPEAKER IN RADIO

Positioning a microphone in front of a seated or standing performer—disc jockey, newscaster, talk-show host, guest—is the most common placement. The mic usually is mounted on a flexible swivel stand suspended in front of the performer (see Figure 12-1); sometimes it is on a table stand (see 12-2).

In selecting and positioning the mic, it is important to keep excessive sound that is reflected from room surfaces, furniture, and equipment from reaching the mic. This can result in comb filtering, creating a hollow sound quality.

To minimize the sound reflections reaching the microphone, a performer should work at a relatively close mic-to-source distance and use a directional mic. How directional depends on how much front-to-rear sound rejection is needed. Usually, however, cardioid is the pickup pattern of choice. It gives the performer some flexibility in side-to-side movement without going off-mic and produces the intimate sound essential to creating radio's lip-to-ear rapport with the listener. Keep in mind that with more-directional mics, side-to-side movement becomes more restricted.

12-1 Microphone mounted on a flexible swivel stand.

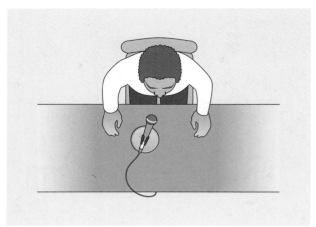

12-2 Performer speaking into a microphone mounted on a desk stand.

Because radio studios are acoustically quiet, there is little need for highly directional mics unless more than a few performers are using microphones in close proximity. One problem with using too directional a mic is the usually drier and more closed sound it produces.

It is difficult to suggest an optimal mic-to-source working distance because voice projection and timbre vary from person to person, but here are a few guidelines:

■ Always stay within the mic's pickup pattern.

■ Maintain voice level between 60 and 100 percent of modulation; some stations like it between 80 and 100 percent. With digital sound, level cannot exceed 0 dBFS or the audio will distort. Hence maximum level should ride below 0 dBFS to allow for headroom.

■ Working too close to a mic may create oppressive and unnatural sound that is devoid of ambience.

■ Working too close to a mic emphasizes tongue movement, lip smacking, and teeth clicks. It could also create proximity effect.

■ Working too far from a mic diffuses the sound quality, creating spatial distance between the performer and the listener.

Sometimes a mic is positioned to the side of or under a performer's mouth, with the performer speaking across the mic face (see 12-3). Usually, this is done to reduce the popping and sibilance that often occur when a performer talks directly into a mic.

Speaking across a directional microphone can reduce these unwanted sounds. Unless the mouth-to-mic angle is within the microphone's pickup pattern, however, talking across the mic degrades the response. To eliminate popping and reduce sibilance without overly degrading the response, use a windscreen, use a mic with a built-in pop filter, or point the mic at about a 45-degree angle above, below, or to the side of the performer's mouth, depending on the mic's pickup pattern (see 12-4).

In positioning a mic, make sure that its head is not parallel to or facing the tabletop. Remember that the angle of a sound's incidence is equal to its angle of reflectance in midrange and treble frequencies (see 2-12). Therefore sound waves bouncing from the table will reflect back into the mic's pickup pattern, creating the comb-filter effect. When any hard surface is close to a mic, such as a table, console, computer monitor, or window, the mic should be angled so that the sound waves do not reflect directly back into it (see 12-5 and 12-6).

When changing the mic's angle presents a problem, if possible cover the hard surface with a soft material to absorb most of the unwanted reflections. This reduces popping and sibilance. It is also a good idea to mount the mic in a shock absorber if it does not have one built-in. This reduces or eliminates jarring and handling noises.

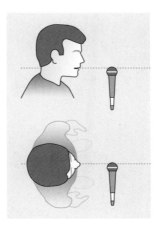

12-3 Directional microphone positioned so that the performer speaks across the mic face. This placement reduces popping and sibilance, but the directional pattern should be wide-angle cardioid, cardioid, or supercardioid so that frequency response is not adversely affected.

12-4 Speaking at a 45-degree angle into a directional mic.

Space and Perspective: Monaural, Stereo, and Surround Sound

AM and FM radio are broadcast in stereo, and a growing number of stations are transmitting surround sound, yet talent is still miked monaurally. In monaural sound, aural space is one-dimensional—that is, perceived in terms of depth—so perspective is near-to-far. Reverberation notwithstanding, *the closer a mic is placed to a sound source, the closer to the audience the sound source is perceived to be; the farther a mic is placed from a sound source, the farther from the audience the sound source is perceived to be.* If the mic is omnidirectional, both the closer and more distant sounds are perceived as more open than if the mic is directional; a directional microphone reproduces a closer, tighter sound.

In stereo sound, aural space is two-dimensional—that is, perceived in terms of depth and breadth—so perspectives are frontally near-to-far and side-to-side. Moreover, stereo space includes more ambience than does monaural space. Stereo miking involves using either two microphones or a stereo mic (see "Stereophonic Microphones" in Chapter 3, "Stereo Microphone Technique" later in this chapter, and "Other Types of Stereo Microphone Arrays" in Chapter 17).

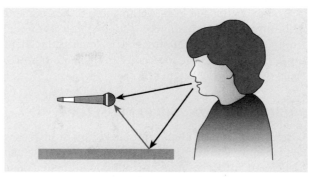

12-5 Incorrect placement of microphone. Indirect sound waves reflecting back into a mic cause phase cancellations that degrade the response. To avoid this a microphone should not be placed parallel to or more than a few inches from a reflective surface.

12-6 Correct placement of microphone. Placing a microphone at an angle to a reflective surface prevents indirect sound from bouncing back into the mic.

Stereo radio transmission and reception have little effect on single-speaker miking; talent is still miked with one microphone. If the performer is not sonically "stage-center," localization is disconcerting to the listener. Stereo sound in stereo radio is in the music and often in the spot announcements but not in the spatial positioning of the talent. Even when two or more persons are miked, their positions in the aural frame are usually stage-center. If there is any stereo spacing at all, it is quite conservative.

Surround sound is also two-dimensional—near-to-far and side-to-side. But with surround sound, its near-field is in front of the listener, its far-field is behind the listener, and the side fields are literally to the listener's sides. (Depending on the mix and the loudspeaker array, surround sound can create the sonic illusion of height.)

Even with the added spatial imaging that is possible with surround sound, unless it is for dynamic positional requirements in spot announcements and drama, talent is still positioned front and center in the aural frame to avoid disconcerting listener focus.

RADIO INTERVIEW AND PANEL SETUPS

When there is more than one speaker, as in interview and panel programs, it is customary today to mike each participant with a separate microphone for better sonic control. Directional mics, usually cardioid or supercardioid, are preferred. If the participants are sitting opposite one another, the cardioid is sufficient because it is least sensitive at 180 degrees off-axis. If the participants are sitting side-by-side, facing the host, the supercardioid could be a better choice; its on-axis response allows sufficient side-to-side head movement, and it is less sensitive at the sides than is the cardioid. The hypercardioid mic would also work in the latter situation, but there are the potential problems of restricted head movement due to its quite narrow on-axis pickup and of reduced sound quality because of its poorer rejection at 180 degrees. In any case, microphones are commonly fixed to flexible mic mounts to free frontal working space and to make minor positioning adjustments easier (see 12-7).

When multiple microphones are used, they must have the same directional pattern. Mics with different polar patterns, say, a cardioid mic used with a supercardioid mic, will have perceptible sonic differences. With the cardioid and supercardioid mics, for example, the cardioid will produce a more open sound than the supercardioid; or, to put it another way, the supercardioid will sound tighter than the cardioid.

In choosing a microphone for a guest, consider that the person may be unfamiliar with mic technique, be nervous, or speak more softly or loudly than usual. Choosing an end-fed, instead of a side-fed, mic makes it easier for the guest to focus the direction toward which to speak. Also, an end-fed mic is usually smaller than a side-fed mic and therefore less intimidating. (For an example of a side-fed mic, see Figure 3-60 top left; for an end-fed mic, see top right.)

The lavalier mic is another option. The speaker cannot be off-mic and tends to forget it is there. The potential problem here is that most lavaliers are omnidirectional, and even in suitable acoustics the sound may be too open and airy. Directional lavaliers, on the other hand, may create a sound that is too dry.

12-7 Radio talk/interview studio.

In miking a radio program with two or more participants, the host and the guests are in the studio and an operator is in the control room, or the host operates the control panel in the studio at the table where the guests are sitting. The studio control panel can usually also handle telephone feeds for listener call-in. Some radio stations even put a simple control console at the guest stations. In both situations host and guests have their own directional microphones or, as is often the case with telephone call-in programs, headset mics.

A headset mic facilitates the feeding and the balancing of all program information to each participant, reduces problems of mic placement, allows host and guests more freedom of head movement, and clears desk space for scripts and note taking. Because it is radio, appearance is of no concern unless the radio program is televised (simulcast), which is done with some programs on a regular basis. Then some attention to appearance does become a factor. Whether televised or not, the participants must be comfortably and sensibly arranged for optimal interaction (see 12-8).

Using a microphone processor may also be wise. Most studio mics are capable of producing the necessary dynamic range for voice, but other equipment may not be, particularly if there are multiple audio sources. A mic

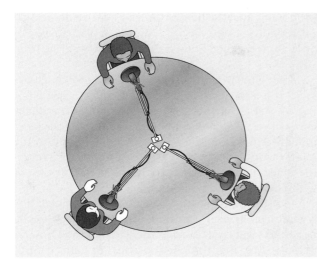

12-8 Example of an arrangement for a radio panel program. Because in radio there is less concern about appearance on the set, mics can be selected and arranged primarily for sound quality, without inconveniencing the panelists of course. This illustration is based on an actual arrangement using high-quality Neumann U-87 multidirectional microphones, set on the cardioid pickup pattern, and fabric windscreens.

processor can provide compression and some general gain reduction as needed. Many mic processors also offer equalization (EQ). Care must be taken with processing, however, so that the audio sounds natural (see 12-9).

Another way to keep the audio from all mics in check is to use an *automatic microphone mixer.* By linking the host and guest microphone processors, the host can maintain control, particularly if things get out of hand, because the automatic mic mixer can be set so that the host's signal will duck the guests' audio slightly. But using an automatic mic mixer can be chancy. If it is less than high quality or is not properly adjusted, its action can be audible, thus reducing audio quality and creating a distraction (for a thorough discussion of the automatic mic mixer, see Chapter 13).

RADIO DRAMATIZATIONS

Dramatizations produced in radio today are played out mostly in commercials and other types of spot announcements. Except for some drama done on public radio and in some colleges, the days of bona fide radio drama have long since passed. What has carried over, however, are many of the microphone and production techniques that were used.

Dramatizations on radio entail creating sound to compel the listener to "see" mental images—to create a "theater of the mind." The stimuli that trigger the imagination are words, sound effects, and music as well as the methods used to produce these elements. Generating illusions of perspective and movement begin with techniques of miking.

Single-microphone Technique

Using one microphone in radio dramatization involves positioning performers at the mic and having them play to it as if it were the ear of the audience. This requires selecting an appropriate mic and properly mounting it. Creating a sense of perspective and, if necessary, movement makes the "visual" illusion effective. The technique was used in radio drama throughout its heyday, before technology made it easier to use the multimicrophone approach. With a number of mics, performers can be miked separately to allow greater sound control during recording. This has made the multimicrophone approach the technique of choice. Nevertheless it may be useful to discuss how one microphone can be used effectively in radio dramatizations.

Microphone Selection and Mounting

The best microphone to use for the single-mic technique is a multidirectional capacitor. Capacitors give the human voice a rich, realistic timbre. Ribbon mics are good for voice, but some ribbons, particularly older models, lack the high-frequency response that gives sound its

12-9 Microphone processor. The features of this model include control of all audio parameters; a low-noise mic preamp; phantom power; parametric EQ and high and low shelving; a de-esser, compressor, expander, and limiter; 44.1 kHz, 48 kHz, and 96 kHz sampling rates; a 24-bit audio-to-digital/digital-to-audio converter; a voice phase scrambler; and TCP/IP Ethernet remote control.

lifelike quality, assuming the medium reproduces those frequencies and a performer's harmonics reach into the high-frequency range.

As for moving-coil mics, several models have excellent voice response, but almost all are either omnidirectional or unidirectional. If the number of performers changes within a dramatization or during a take, it is easier to set up one multidirectional microphone than to change mics every time the situation requires.

The preferred microphone mount for radio dramatizations is the boom. It gives easy access to the mic, there is no floor stand to get in the way, and, with shock mounting, there is less chance of sound conductance from movement across the studio floor.

Another advantage of the boom is that performers deliver their lines standing, which is better for breathing. It also allows some freedom of movement for performers who like to swing an arm to help their delivery—or both arms if one hand is not holding the script.

Creating Perspective

To create perspective acoustically, performers are positioned at appropriate distances relative to the mic and to one another, as the dramatic action dictates. If an actor is close to the mic, the audience perceives the sound as near, the space as small, or both, particularly with a directional microphone. If a performer is farther from the mic, the sense of distance increases and the space seems larger. If a man and a woman are on-mic, playing opposite each other in a scene that calls for them to be equally enthusiastic, position the man farther from the mic than the woman is to compensate for the (usually) more powerful male voice. If they are equidistant from the mic, the man will sound closer than the woman does (see 12-10). The audience's perspective will be from the performer in the closer position. This assumes a relatively quiet, acoustically controlled studio. In a more open ambience, moving an actor too far from the mic to compensate for a stronger voice would also increase the level of his room tone, thereby placing him in an aural frame that is different from that of the more soft-spoken actor.

Maintaining perspective does not always mean keeping voice levels balanced. If a scene requires one character to call to another from a distance, perspective is created by placing on-mic the actor who is supposed to be closer and off-mic the one who is supposed to be farther away.

Creating Movement

If movement is involved, such as someone leaving or entering a room, there are three ways to create the effect: by moving from the live to the dead side of a directional microphone or vice versa, by turning in place toward or away from the mic, or by walking toward or away from the mic.

Moving the fader up or down—also known as a *board fade*—will also create the effect of coming or going but not so well as having the performers do it. The difference between the two techniques is that using the fader influences not only the actor's voice level but also the room's acoustics. When a person enters or leaves a room, the space does not change; only the person's position within it changes.

Once the proper aural balances are determined, it is a good idea to mark the studio floor with tape so the performers will know exactly where to stand and how far to move. Marking the floor also assists in traffic control around a mic when several performers are in a scene and have to yield and take the on-mic position.

Multimicrophone Technique

With multitrack recording, producing a dramatization can take advantage of all the flexibility that it affords. Performers can be miked separately to allow greater sound control during recording. Then the various tracks can be processed, edited, and mixed in postproduction. Although added sound control is an advantage of this technique, there are also disadvantages: it may be more difficult to obtain natural spatial relationships and perspective between performers, the appropriate acoustic environments have to be added in postproduction, and it requires the additional time and expense of a postproduction session. Today it is rare not to take some time to process a recording in postproduction, however.

For the sound shaping of individual performances, particularly when using effects, and for the added flexibility in production, including stereo and surround sound, the multimicrophone approach is the technique of choice.

Stereo Microphone Technique

When stereo placement of the performers is called for, and the multimicrophone technique is employed during recording, spatial placement in the stereo frame is done in postproduction through panning. If the "single" microphone approach is used, the performers must be stereo-miked during recording; otherwise it is difficult to position them in stereo space in postproduction.

A number of the production techniques applicable to monaural radio dramatizations also apply to stereo, but

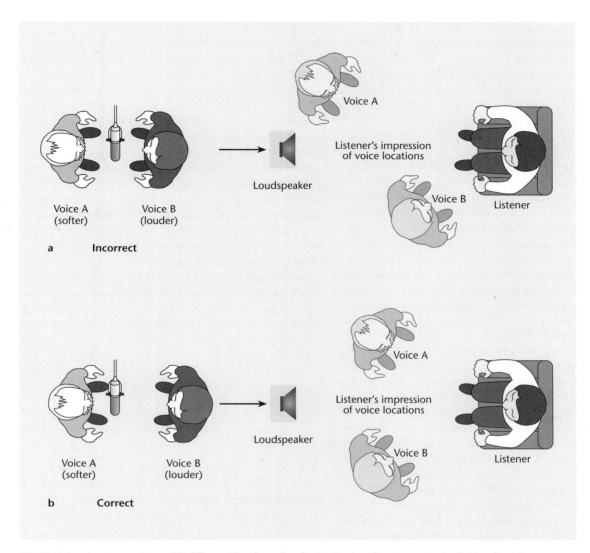

12-10 Balancing two voices with different loudness levels. Positioning the stronger voice farther from the microphone keeps the voices in proper aural perspective relative to the listener. But do not position the stronger voice too far from the mic or it could take on an ambient quality noticeably different from that of the softer voice.

stereo does bring its own set of challenges, not the least of which is *mono compatibility*. Although stereo has been around for many years, and AM and FM radio transmit in stereo, enough of the audience still listens in mono, particularly to AM radio, for it to be a factor in recording and mixing. This means that material recorded in stereo should be capable of also being reproduced in mono.

Stereo requires two discrete signals: A (left) and B (right). To reproduce these signals in mono, they are summed: A + B. *Discrete stereo* is also referred to as *sum-and-difference stereo* because one channel is summed

(A + B) and the other channel is subtracted (A − B). If the stereo signals are in phase when they are added, level can increase 3 to 6 dB; if the signals are out of phase in stereo, they cancel in mono. It is therefore critical during recording to make sure that problems with stereo-to-mono compatibility are anticipated.

Stereo miking uses two microphones (or microphone capsules) to feed each discrete signal to a separate channel. Sound reaches the mics with intensity and time differences. The difference in arrival time between the signals reaching the two mics creates phase problems later when combining the signals to mono. The narrower the angle or space between the mics, the less the difference in arrival time between the signals reaching them.

There are a number of ways to mike for stereo. One technique—coincident miking—ensures stereo-to-mono compatibility; another—near-coincident miking—can be mono-compatible if the angle or space between the mics is not too wide. Coincident and near-coincident arrays are also called *X-Y miking*.

Coincident miking positions two microphones, usually directional, in virtually the same space with their diaphragms located vertically on the same axis (see Chapter 17). This arrangement minimizes the arrival time difference between the signals reaching each mic. Stereo imaging is sharp, and sound localization is accurate.

Near-coincident miking positions two microphones, usually directional, horizontally on the same plane, angled a few inches apart. They may be spaced or crossed (see Chapter 17). The wider angle or space between the mics adds more depth and warmth to the sound, but stereo imaging is not as sharp as it is with the coincident array. As a guideline in radio dramatizations, keep the angle or space between the mics to 90 degrees or less. At more than 90 degrees, not only could mono compatibility be a problem but the stereo image would be more diffuse.

In stereo miking, the lateral imaging of the stereo field is also important. If the angle between the mics is too narrow, sound will be concentrated toward the center (between two loudspeakers). If the angle between the mics is too wide, sound will be concentrated to the left and the right, with little sound coming from the center, a condition referred to as "hole in the middle." The angle between the mics is contingent on the width of the sound source: the wider the source, the wider the angle; the narrower the source, the narrower the angle. (If a sound source is too wide for the coincident and near-coincident arrays, as may be the case with orchestral ensembles in concert halls, spaced mics are employed—see Chapter 17.)

In stereo radio dramatizations, performers are usually not widely spaced at a single microphone. The center of the stereo space is where the main action is likely to take place. Too much "Ping-Ponging" of sound left and right can create dislocation of the sound sources, confusing the listener. If action is played left or right of center, it is usually not too wide afield.

Assuming that there are no acute acoustic problems, the inclusive angle between the mics should be between 60 and 90 degrees. At the least that is a good starting point; further positioning depends on the number of people in the scene and the size of the aural "set."

Using the multimicrophone approach, on-mic spacing is not a factor. Stereo imaging is handled in postproduction.

Perspective

When positioning performers take care to ensure that they are in the same positions and perspectives as the associated voices. If a script calls for conversation among performers in various parts of a room, they cannot be grouped around the mics—some closer, some farther—in stereo as they would be in mono. To maintain the stereo perspective, each actor should be in about the same position, relative to the others, as he or she would be if the situation were real (see 12-11).

More studio space is required for stereo radio dramatizations than for mono because the dead sides of the microphones cannot be used for approaches to and retreats from the mics. To produce the illusion of someone walking from left to right, a performer cannot simply walk in a straight line across the stereo pickup pattern. If that happened, the sound at the center would be disproportionately louder than the sound at the left and the right, and the changes in level would be too abrupt. To create a more realistic effect, a performer has to pass the mics in a semicircle. Also, studio acoustics should be dry because they are much more apparent with stereo than they are with mono.

Surround-sound Technique

As noted in Chapter 8, surround sound adds greater front-to-rear depth and side/rear breadth to aural imaging. A main difference—and advantage—in using surround sound rather than stereo in dramatic radio productions is being able to position performers much as they would be on a stage and recording them from those perspectives. This can be done during recording by using surround-sound microphony (see Chapter 3) or by using conventional multitrack-recording techniques and handling the surround-sound placements through panning in postproduction. See Chapters 17, 22, and 23 for more-detailed coverage of surround-sound techniques.

Handling sound effects in surround can also add to the spatial imaging. Make sure, however, between the positioning of the actors and the sound effects in surround that the overall perspectives do not confuse the listening audience.

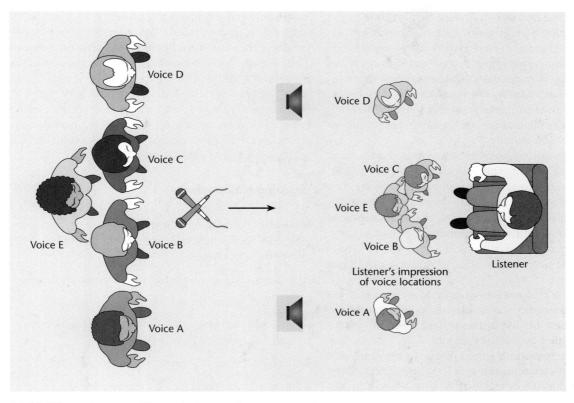

12-11 Effects of stereo-miking technique on listener perception.

MIKING SPEECH FOR MULTICAMERA TELEVISION

Television productions aired live or live-to-recording generally use the multicamera approach. By employing two or more cameras and feeding the signals to a switching console, a shot from one camera can be broadcast (or recorded) while other cameras prepare the next shots—in essence, "editing as you go." Sound is similarly handled during live or live-to-recording production. Postproduction time is limited due to an imminent or relatively imminent broadcast deadline. Programs such as parades and news, sports, and interview, panel, talk, awards, and game shows are carried live or live-to-recording and use the multicamera production technique.

Productions that do not have an imminent release deadline, such as theatrical TV dramas, films made for television, magazine programs, and commercials, frequently use the single-camera production approach. Scenes are shot one at a time—first from a general perspective and then from various individual perspectives.

These different views are edited during postproduction into a meaningful sequence of events to build the structure and set the pace. In postproduction, dialogue and sound effects are recorded (or rerecorded if necessary), and music is added.

This categorizing is not to imply fixed production conventions; it is simply a generalization. For example, many game shows and episodes of soap operas are shot well in advance of their broadcast dates yet use the multicamera approach. Often commercials shot in studios, as opposed to on-location, also use the multicamera technique.

NEWS AND INTERVIEW PROGRAMS

In news and interview programs, the participants are usually seated at a desk or on an open set to lend a behind-the-scenes vitality to the image. The mic almost universally used in these situations is the omnidirectional capacitor wireless mini-mic. It is unobtrusive and easy to mount; its sound quality with speech is excellent; the omnidirectional pickup pattern ensures that ambience is natural and that a performer will stay on-mic regardless of head movement; and being wireless eliminates the hassle of running, plugging in, and hiding cords if the director wants to make the miking even more unobtrusive and easier to handle. Even though they may be less unobtrusive, the reason newscasters (and panelists) often wear two mini-mics is simply for backup in case the on-air capacitor mic system fails.

If the mini-mic is wired, be careful that the mic cord does not pick up rubbing sounds when a performer, such as a weathercaster, moves within a small set. The performer should use a belt clip, leave enough play in the mic cord so that it drags across the floor as little as possible, and avoid sudden, wrenching motions. If the mic cord is put underneath a pant leg or dress to keep it out of sight, it is a good idea to tape it to the leg to reduce rustling sounds.

If background sound is troublesome, which is unlikely in a broadcast studio, the directional mini-mic may be a suitable alternative. But it does restrict head movement and can produce too closed a sound.

Generally, for optimal sound pickup the recommended placement for a mini-mic is in the area of the wearer's sternum—hooked to a tie, shirt, or dress—6 to 8 inches below the chin. Frequently, the mic is attached to the lapel, but beware of getting it too close to the mouth or the sound may be too dry.

In interview programs the host sometimes sits behind a mic mounted on a desk stand. Usually, the mic is not live. It is being used as a set piece to create a closer psychological rapport between the host and the television audience, to fill the open table space in front of the host, or both. Otherwise, with a few exceptions, desk mics are seldom used.

If you do use a live desk mic, select one that is good-looking so it does not call attention to itself; position it so that it does not block the performer's face or interfere with the performer's frontal working space; use one with a built-in shock mount to isolate the mic from desk noises; and make sure the mic-to-source angle is on-axis.

PANEL AND TALK PROGRAMS

Television panel and talk programs employ a few basic set arrangements. When the host or moderator is seated, guests sit in a line either diagonal to and facing the host; or, if an audience is participating in the show, the guests sit in a horizontal line facing the audience, and the host moves between them and the audience. Sometimes the set design is in the shape of an inverted U. The moderator sits at the top center of the U, with the interviewers usually to the moderator's right and the guest(s) to the moderator's left, across from the interviewers. Panel participants might also sit in a semicircle, with the moderator opposite them at the center of the arc. To create a more visual dynamic, the set arrangement may be trapezoidal, with the moderator at the narrower end and the guests along either of the diagonal sides.

Choosing a Microphone

Mini-mic In most circumstances, for host and guest alike, the mini-mic's multiple advantages make it the microphone of choice:

- It is unobtrusive and tends to disappear on-camera.

- It is easy to mount.

- It is easily adaptable to use with a wireless system, which is how it is mostly employed.

- It keeps the mic-to-source distance constant.

- It reduces the need for frequent loudness adjustments once the levels have been set.

- It requires no special lighting or additional audio operator, as does a boom mic.

- It enables participants to be placed comfortably on a set without concern for maintaining levels and mic-to-source distances.

- It eliminates concern about participants' handling the mic, as could happen with desk mics.

The mini-mic's main disadvantage is that it's a single-purpose microphone. It rarely sounds good used away from the body.

Hand Mic In some situations in panel and talk programs, microphone mounts, other than the body-positioned mini-mic, are preferred. For a host moving about a set among guests or going into the audience for questions, the handheld mic is the popular choice.

In situations where the studio is very large and the audience is seated amphitheater-style, except for overall coverage mics of the audience sound, handheld mics are the only choice for host, guests, and audience participants.

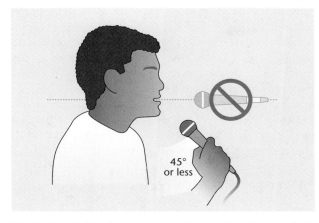

12-12 Handheld microphone positioning. Ideally, a handheld mic should be positioned 6 to 12 inches from the user's mouth at an angle of 45 degrees or less. Positioning the mic at an angle of about 90 degrees may result in popping sounds when consonants like *p* and *t* are pronounced.

The handheld microphone has these advantages:

■ It allows the host to control the audience questioning.

■ It allows the host to control mic-to-source distances.

■ Like the desk mic, it helps the host generate a closer psychological rapport with the television audience.

The handheld mic should have a built-in pop filter to minimize sibilance and popping and an internal shock mount to eliminate handling noise. Optimal position is 6 to 12 inches from the mouth, pointing upward at about a 45-degree angle (see 12-12).

A disadvantage of the handheld mic is that it ties up one of the host's hands. This is not a problem with the boom mic, which for some situations is the mic of choice.

Boom Mic   When guests are coming and going during the course of a show, for example, the boom mic is often used once they are seated. It is less awkward than having a guest put on and take off a mini-mic on-camera or having a guest hold a mic. Usually, no more than a few guests are seated on the set at any one time, which allows one boom to cover the group adequately. In this type of situation, the host generally uses a live desk mic for several reasons: to set the host apart from the guests; to enhance, psychologically, the rapport with the television audience; and to avoid the lighting and logistical problems that result from having two booms on a set in close proximity.

Whenever one boom covers two or more people in conversation, the boom operator has to make sure that none of the program's content is inaudible or off-mic. A good boom operator must therefore quickly learn the speech rhythms and inflections of the people talking, listen to their conversations, anticipate the nonverbal vocal cues that signal a change in speaker, and, when the change occurs, move the mic from one speaker to another quickly and silently.

If performers are seated, there is little need to do anything but rotate the mic itself. If performers are mobile, moving the boom arm and extending and retracting it are also important aspects of good boom operation (see Chapter 11).

Controlling Multiple Sound Sources

Individually miking several program participants can be a challenge for the console operator trying to control various levels simultaneously, especially when other sound sources such as the announcer, bumper (intro and outro) music, and recorded spot announcements are also part of the operator's responsibilities. It is best to use as few mics as possible in a given situation to reduce system noise, phasing, and coordination problems. But with the multichannel console and sophisticated signal processing, many recordists prefer separate control of each sound source to more-conservative miking techniques. To help reduce the problems associated with controlling multiple, simultaneous microphone voice feeds, the console operator has a number of options.

One option is to put a moderate limit or some compression on each mic once levels are set. With the mini-mic and handhelds, the proximity of the mic to the speaker's mouth is close enough to be a potential problem with loud sound surges and consequent overloading. Limiting keeps such surges under control, helping maintain more-uniform levels. Also, because mic-to-source distance with a mini-mic is close, there is little problem with voice levels being too quiet; such may not be the case with the boom. With the boom mic, compression helps keep quieter voices above the noise floor and louder voices from overloading, although there is some risk with this technique. If compression values are not properly set, the compressor's effects on the signals could result in an audible pumping sound.

When omnidirectional mini-mics are used closer than the recommended 3:1 ratio, phasing problems can create the hollow "tin can" sound that results from comb filtering. Compression is definitely needed to reduce the dynamic range of each mic. If that is not sufficient, it might be necessary to put adjacent microphones out of phase with each other. When adjacent mics are out of phase, a null is created between them, which keeps the same sound from reaching an adjacent mic at slightly different times by canceling the delayed sound. This technique works only if the participants are not mobile and do not lean into the null. Omnidirectional mini-mics can also be a problem in less-than-acceptable studio acoustics. Many TV studios are designed primarily with picture in mind, at the expense of sound; and in TV studio sets, walls are often concave and hard, which focuses and reflects sound.

A way to avoid the problems created by omnidirectional mini-mics is to use directional mini-mics. They interact less and can be left at or near operating levels without having to keep riding gain. Directional mics also help with **upcuts**, where a participant's first few utterances are barely heard until the audio operator responds. But keep in mind that directional mini-mics, and directional mics in general, produce a drier, more closed sound than do omnis, a characteristic that some directors tend not to like for speech. They also require that participants control head movements to stay on-mic.

Using a noise gate is yet another way to handle these phasing problems, although it can be a solution that is more trouble than it is worth. Setting precise thresholds takes time, and the gating effect may be audible as microphones are opened and closed.

Still another alternative to controlling multiple sound sources is to use an automatic microphone mixer, discussed in Chapter 13.

Miking the Audience

When a talk show (or almost any entertainment program) takes place before an audience, the crowd response becomes integral to the program's presentation. Applause, laughter, and other reactions contribute to the show's spontaneity and excitement. The presence of an audience creates two challenges for the sound designer: the people at home must be able to hear the audience, and the audience must be able to hear the participants, wherever they are in the studio.

For the home viewer, the studio audience should sound relatively close and uniform so that the viewer feels part of the action. No single voice or cadence or group of similar-sounding voices (that is, high-pitched cackle, halting laugh, children, elderly women, and so

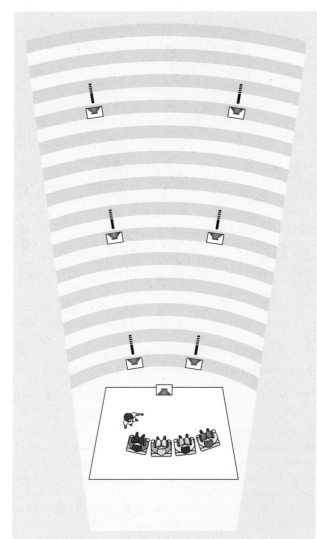

12-13 Talk-show studio with audience area. Shotgun microphones are placed above the audience in quadrants for uniform and controlled directional pickup. Above and behind the mics are small directional loudspeakers situated to avoid feedback and to cover specific audience areas. A small loudspeaker above the stage feeds the audience sound to the guests during questioning. Depending on the studio size and layout, this loudspeaker may be phased so that it covers a narrow stage area or to avoid interference with the studio loudspeakers or both.

forth) should predominate, unless that is the intention. (Some game shows, for example, whose viewers consist mainly of a particular demographic group like to have that group sonically evident in its audience reaction.)

One way to achieve these ends is to mount directional shotgun microphones several feet above the audience and distribute them in equal quadrants throughout the audience area for uniform pickup (see 12-13; see also 3-70). The type of shotgun—cardioid, supercardioid, or hypercardioid—depends on how broad or focused you want the pickup to be. Keep in mind that with shotguns good off-axis frequency response is vital; poor off-axis response results in unwanted coloration that can be quite pronounced in inferior mics.

Sometimes, depending on the studio acoustics and the size of the audience, omnidirectional mics or boundary mics with hemispheric pickup patterns are also used to help blend the overall audience sound. Figures 12-14 and 12-15 illustrate a few other approaches.

To free the operator's hands for other audio control operations, audience microphones are sometimes controlled by a foot pedal under the console. The pedal is used to open and close the mics.

For the audience to hear the program participants, loudspeakers must be mounted in the audience area of the studio. This places microphones and loudspeakers close together, creating the potential for *feedback*—that high-pitched squeal from a signal feeding from a mic to a loudspeaker, around and around. To avoid feedback the loudspeakers are situated so that their sound is off-axis to the microphones' pickup pattern (see 12-13).

If the loudspeaker is too loud, however, feedback will occur anyway. To minimize this risk, smaller, more directional loudspeakers are used, and their levels are kept moderate. If the danger of feedback persists, yet smaller loudspeakers may be employed or their sound may be compressed, or both.

A small loudspeaker above the stage feeds audience sound to the guests during questioning. Depending on the studio size and layout, this loudspeaker may be phased so that it covers a narrow stage area or to avoid interference with the studio loudspeakers or both.

Generally, the larger the audience and therefore the venue, the fewer audience mics are needed because of the fuller sound of the audience reaction reinforced by the longer reverb time. The converse is also generally true: the smaller the audience and the venue, the more mics are needed to help fill the thinner audience sound and the shorter reverb time.

"Producing" Audience Response

Audiences usually react in two ways: by laughing and by applauding. (There are programs in which some verbal responses from the audience are part of the "action.") Raising the levels of these sounds when they occur adds to their uplift and to the program's overall fun and excitement. This is known as *milking the audience*. But such

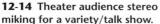

12-14 Theater audience stereo miking for a variety/talk show.

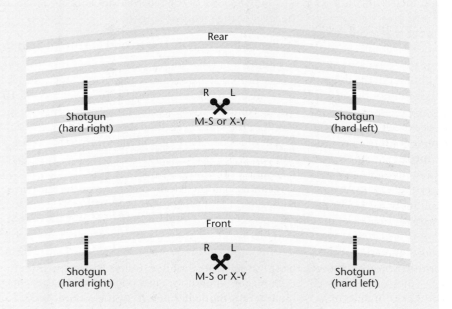

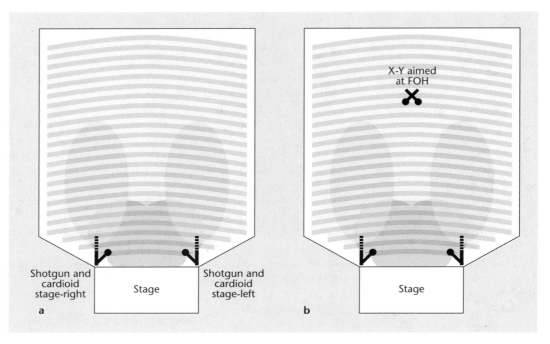

12-15 Two other examples of audience miking. (a) Pairs of cardioid and shotgun microphones are placed stage-left and stage-right. The cardioids are aimed at the nearest segment of the audience. The shotguns are aimed farther back in the hall. (b) This mic arrangement supplements the mics in (a) with another pair of cardioid mics arranged in an X-Y pattern aimed toward the front of the hall (FOH).

level adjustments have to be accomplished gracefully; they cannot be abrupt. Skillfully done, increasing the level of laughter can add to its infectiousness, thus reinforcing the impact of a funny line or joke; in the case of applause, it can heighten its intensity, perhaps even its enthusiasm.

The audience sound may be controlled by a limiter. When the audience mics reach the limit level, the limiter kicks in to increase apparent loudness but not the actual peak level.

Audiences do not always react as expected, however. When a funny line or a climactic moment is not greeted with the anticipated intensity of laughter or applause, recorded applause and laugh tracks are sometimes used to reinforce, or "sweeten," audience reactions. Disks with different types and degrees of audience reactions are run continuously but are played with the faders off, a technique known as **deadpotting** or *deadrolling* (see Chapter 10.) Or they can be played on an effects-replay device that can store effects and perform looping functions as well (see 12-16).

Laughter and applause sometimes occur relatively close together. When this happens, because applause is louder than laughter, the general guideline is to decrease the loudness level of the recorded applause and increase the level of the recorded laughter.

Audience Reaction in Stereo and Surround Sound

In mixing audience sound with the sound of the program's principal participants for stereo and surround, there are no hard-and-fast rules. To avoid having the sounds compete with one another, common sense dictates that the audience sound should not be at the same level as or louder than the sound of the program participants or, worse, that the audience reaction drowns out the sound of the participants.

A common approach in stereo is to center the participants' sound and fill the left-to-right stereo space with audience sound, keeping the audience level lower in the center to avoid interfering with the participants' audio. Another approach is to place audience sound left and right of participants' center-positioned audio.

In surround, audience mics can be fed to the rear or side-rear surround channels to provide a spacious effect to the overall program audio.

12-16 Effects replay device. This model can hold up to 1,000 music and sound-effect cuts and retrieve them instantly. Built-in editing enables head and tail trims as well as fade-ins and fade-outs. Recording formats are 16- and 24-bit, and it supports WAV files.

MAIN POINTS

▶ In radio, in particular, when positioning a microphone in front of a seated or standing performer it is important to keep excessive sound that is reflected from surfaces, furniture, and equipment from reaching the mic to preserve the medium's sonic intimacy.

▶ To reduce unwanted sounds such as popping and sibilance, use a mic with a windscreen or pop filter or speak within the pickup pattern across the mic, or both.

▶ The closer a mic is placed to a sound source, the closer to the audience the sound source is perceived to be; the farther a mic is placed from a sound source, the farther from the audience the sound source is perceived to be.

▶ In disc jockey, interview, and panel programs, the participants should sound as though they are coming from the front and center of the aural space. With more than one participant, using individual microphones, the loudness levels for the participants must be similar if the sound is to be perceived as coming from the front and center of the aural space.

▶ Dramatizations on radio involve creating a "theater of the mind," using sound to impel the listener to "see" the action.

▶ To create perspective using one microphone in radio dramatization, performers are positioned at appropriate distances relative to the mic and to one another, as the dramatic action dictates.

▶ Using the multimicrophone technique in radio dramatization, perspective is created in the postproduction mix.

▶ For stereo radio dramatizations, coincident or near-coincident microphone arrays (also called X-Y miking) are usually employed. Coincident miking positions two microphones, usually directional (or a stereo mic), in virtually the same space with their diaphragms located vertically on the same axis. Near-coincident miking positions two mics, usually directional, horizontally on the same plane, angled a few inches apart.

▶ A main difference and advantage of surround-sound miking of radio dramatizations is being able to position performers much as they would be on a stage and recording them from those perspectives or recording them conventionally and creating those perspectives in postproduction.

▶ In radio, microphones can be placed anywhere without regard for appearance so long as the participants are comfortable and the mics do not get in their way. If the radio program is also televised, some care for appearance should be taken. In television, if a mic is not in the picture, it must be positioned close enough to the performer so that the sound is on-mic.

▶ Generally, for optimal sound pickup the recommended placement for a mini-mic is in the area of the performer's sternum, about 6 to 8 inches below the chin.

▶ In television a desk mic is often used as a prop. If the desk mic is live, make sure it does not block the performer's face, interfere with the performer's frontal working space, or pick up desk noises.

▶ The handheld mic allows the host to control audience questioning and mic-to-source distance and, like the desk mic, helps generate a closer psychological rapport with the audience.

▶ The boom microphone, like the mini-mic hidden under clothing, is used when mics must be out of the picture. Often one boom mic covers more than one performer. To provide adequate sound pickup, and to move the boom at the right time to the right place, the boom operator must anticipate when one performer is about to stop talking and another is about to start.

▶ Different techniques are used in controlling levels, leakage, and feedback of mic feeds from multiple sound sources: following the three-to-one rule, moderate limiting or compression, noise gating, or using an automatic microphone mixer.

▶ If an audience is present, it must be miked to achieve an overall sound blend and to prevent one voice or group of voices from dominating.

▶ Increasing audience laughter or applause, or both, by using recorded laughter or applause tracks adds to a program's spontaneity and excitement. But these effects should not be so loud as to compete with the sound of the program participants.

▶ For stereo, audience sound is usually panned left-to-right with a lower level in the center. Or it is placed left and right of center, where the participants' audio is placed. For surround sound, feeding audience mics to the rear channels provides a spacious effect to the overall program audio.

13

Field Production: News and Sports

Production is a challenge no matter where it takes place. But in the field, away from a controlled studio environment, it presents its own particular problems, especially given the immediate and relatively immediate demands of live and live-to-recording broadcasting. Yet field production is almost as commonplace as studio production. Producers go on-location—or on a *remote*, as broadcasters often refer to field production—to cover news and sports, to do a disc jockey program promoting a sponsor, to heighten realism in a drama, to add authenticity to a setting, or to provide surroundings that are difficult or impossible to reproduce in a studio.

Field production for radio and television can be grouped into two basic categories: electronic news gathering (ENG) and electronic field production (EFP). ENG uses highly portable equipment to cover news for live or imminent broadcast. EFP involves more-complex productions, such as parades, sporting events, and awards programs.

ELECTRONIC NEWS GATHERING

Electronic news gathering (ENG) refers to radio or TV news gathered or broadcast in the field. ENG covers broadcast news as it is happening. Specifically, it now pertains to news in the field that is transmitted terrestrially. This is to differentiate it from *satellite news gathering (SNG)* and *digital satellite news gathering (DSNG)*. These differences in field reporting are in the modes of transmission and delivery, rather than in the way news is covered and collected.

Radio ENG

Radio ENG (often abbreviated *RENG*) is relatively uncom-plicated to produce and can be broadcast on the spot with comparative logistical ease. It usually involves a reporter with portable recording and, if necessary, transmitting equipment. At its most basic, all that the radio reporter needs to record a story are a microphone and a recorder. To send the story to the radio station's newsroom, add a transmitting device. Even when somewhat more elaborate production is called for, a microphone mixer or portable console, an edit-capable recorder or laptop computer with recording/editing software and Internet access, or a mobile unit can usually handle it.

Microphone

Because RENG usually involves one reporter delivering a story or doing an interview, the handheld, omnidirec-tional, moving-coil microphone with a pop filter and an internal shock mount is generally the mic of choice. Capacitor mics are not as rugged, they are susceptible to wind distortion, and they require a power supply. A handheld mic requires no mounting and takes no time to set up. Field reporting is often done outdoors, and a pop filter is better at reducing unwanted wind sound than is a windscreen; nevertheless, if the situation requires, it does not hurt to use a pop filter and a windscreen just to be safe. If wind or traffic rumble is severe, a high-pass filter can be plugged into the mic line to diminish bassy noise (see Figure 13-1). Omnidirectional moving-coil mics do not have a bass roll-off control, but conditions should justify using the high-pass filter because it may also attenuate desired low frequencies. If a microphone mixer is used, some have filters built-in (see "Microphone Mixer" later in this section).

13-1 High-pass filter. This device can be plugged into a microphone line to reduce unwanted low frequencies below 100 Hz by 12 dB per octave. It helps eliminate electrical and mechanical noise in an audio system, such as 60 Hz electrical hum from AC power lines and low-frequency rumble caused by wind noise or an air-conditioning system. A similar-looking low-pass filter is also available to reduce unwanted high-frequency sounds.

When hum and electrical noise, such as from motors and fluorescent lights, are the problems, a quad mic cable (a four-conductor design available from a number of manufacturers) can greatly reduce these sonic nuisances. There is also the powerful tool of digital noise reduction that can be used to deal with these noises after recording. With news, of course, dependence on any postproduction always assumes time permitting.

An omnidirectional mic maintains a sense of environ-ment. The body blocks sounds coming from behind the reporter, reducing the overall level of background noise. Mic-to-source distance can be adjusted simply by mov-ing the microphone closer to or farther from the mouth to compensate for noisy environments. If a locale is too noisy, try a directional microphone, but be aware that directional mics are more prone to wind noise than are omni mics. Also their on-axis response is drier and more concentrated than that of omnis, so working too close to the mic can create a denser, more closed sound.

Recorder

Digital sound quality has not been essential to news, although it has not been detrimental either; but with the advent of high-definition broadcasting, it is no longer a luxury but a necessity. In addition to sound quality, there are the storage and editing capabilities of digital recorders; their robustness; and their speed and preci-sion in cueing (see "Memory Recorders" and "Hard-disk Recorders" in Chapter 5).

Knowing the best way to take advantage of a recorder's editing capabilities can speed assembling reports almost as soon as they are recorded. For stories that have imme-diacy or do not require additional production, or both, reporters may edit and mix a story in the field. Some news directors, however, prefer that no editing or mixing be done in the field, choosing to have the raw voice tracks, sound bites, and natural sounds sent directly to the sta-tion for processing there, particularly if more-elaborate production is necessary.

Setting levels to avoid distortion before any recording is done is always important, particularly in the field and especially with news. There isn't the security of studio surroundings, and news events are usually not repeatable. Remember that there is no headroom in digital recording; once a digital signal goes "into the red," it is useless. In digital systems that use 16-bit sampling, the level should be set at –12 dBFS or below. In 18-bit systems or higher, setting the level at –18 dBFS is recommended.

Microphone Mixer

When one microphone is used for field reporting, it is a simple matter to plug it directly into the recorder. If two mics are needed, a recorder with two mic inputs suffices (assuming in both cases that the recorder uses balanced connectors). When there are more mics than recorder inputs, or if the recorder takes an unbalanced mini- or phono plug (see 13-13), it calls for a *microphone mixer,* of which there are two types: passive and active.

A ***passive microphone mixer*** combines individual inputs into one output without amplifying the signal. When there are only two on-mic sound sources, such as a reporter and an interviewee, as is often the case in news, a passive mic mixer with two inputs and one output is easy and convenient to use.

An ***active microphone mixer*** allows amplification control of each audio source and usually includes other processing features as well (see 13-2). The format can be mono or stereo, and operation can be manual or automatic. Signal flow is straightforward: mics are plugged into the mixer's input channels, where their signals are preamplified and their loudness levels are controlled by faders, usually rotary pots. The signals are then routed to the output channel, where they are combined, and a master fader controls their overall loudness level before they are sent on to broadcast or recording. In the field, monitoring is usually done through headphones.

In addition to the features shown in Figure 13-2, more-elaborate portable mixers may have additional inputs to accommodate recorders and CD players, and interfaces for direct transmission to the station using a phone line, ISDN, Internet Protocol, and laptop computer (see the following section).

Transmission

In the world of news, where stories must be filed fast and first, field reporters often do not have the luxury of bringing their stories back to the newsroom, nor do they have to, given today's technology. They can easily transmit them to the station from the field for direct broadcast or recording. Various transmitting systems are used, the most common of which are the mobile telephone (land line), cellular telephone, remote transmitter, wireless fidelity (WiFi), and Internet Protocol.

The *mobile telephone* is a radio unit connected to telephone equipment that sends the signal to phone wires for transmission to the station. With mobile phones it is possible to call anyone, anywhere. Sound quality is mediocre but can be improved with a telephone line interface (see 13-3). Mobile telephones are vulnerable to *radio frequency (RF)* and electrical interference from high-voltage lines, transformers, and motors. This is another reason why the interface is used; the better ones have a balanced line to protect against interference.

The ubiquitous *cellular telephone* is similar to a mobile telephone, but instead of sending signals over wires

13-3 Telephone audio interface. This handheld device is used to send audio in and out of wired phone lines, cell phones, and PBX (private branch exchange) multichannel phone systems. Among its features are an XLR input with a mic/line switch, an XLR phone mix output that switches to an intercom link, and the capability of working with ISDN phone lines. It weighs 1.5 pounds.

13-2 Microphone mixer. This mic mixer is compact, rugged, and lightweight (2.25 pounds) and can be strapped over the shoulder. Among its features are four mic/line inputs, master gain control, slate mic, phantom power, high-pass filter, pan control, compressor/limiter, main headphone output jack and headphone jack for a boom operator, LED VU meters with brightness switch for viewing in direct sunlight, and battery operation up to 14 hours.

it sends them over radio waves through a computer-controlled network of ground stations. Because areas in a locale are divided into cells, the cell phone can serve as an inexpensive mobile unit as calls are automatically transferred from one ground station to another. Among the advantages of cell phones are improved sound quality and greater flexibility in feeding material to the station (see 13-4 and 13-5).

Devices are available that can route audio from any telephone into a computer sound card. Once recorded the audio can be played back into the phone line and sent to the broadcast facility (see 13-6).

The *remote transmitter,* more commonly called a *remote pickup,* or *RPU,* allows a reporter freedom of movement. (It is also referred to as a *Marti* after a leading RPU manufacturer, although RPUs are made by several companies.)

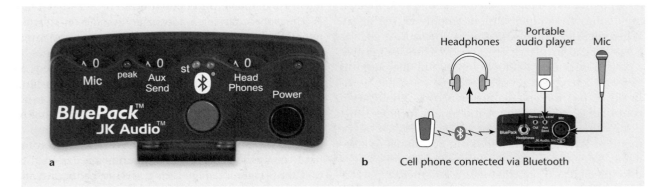

13-4 Cell phone connector, front and back views. (a) This device pairs to a cell phone like a Bluetooth wireless headset. It houses a microphone and headphone preamp; a stereo line input jack, allowing a recording to be mixed into a broadcast; a stereo line output jack, providing the mic signal in the left channel and Bluetooth audio in the right channel; and thumbwheel controllers for mic and headphone levels. The unit weighs 10 ounces. (b) Rear view shows the mic and the headphone connected and the Bluetooth connection to the cell phone. The aux(iliary) send can be used for prerecorded sound clips. The studio is then dialed up for transmission. Bluetooth is a wireless protocol for exchanging data over short distances from fixed and mobile devices.

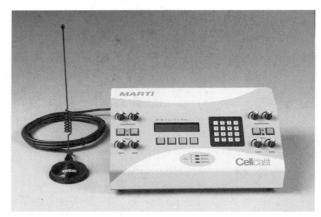

13-5 Remote transmitter. This unit is designed for use with a cell phone or a standard phone line. It includes a four-channel mixer; separate level controls for each of four mics and headset channels; inputs switchable to program or cue; a 20-position speed-dial memory, up to 39 digits per number; and a VU meter. It weighs 5.1 pounds.

13-6 Telephone handset audio tap. This device connects between the handset and the base of a telephone. Attached cables connect to the in- and out-jacks of the computer sound card. It can continuously route both sides of a conversation to the mic input of the sound card. This particular model will not work with a telephone with a keypad in the handset. Other similar devices will, however.

It may be used for direct broadcast from the remote unit, or it can be removed from a news mobile unit and operated on AC current. It also has better sound quality than the other types of mobile transmission; in some units frequency response extends from 20 to 15,000 Hz. Remote transmitters have inputs for at least one microphone and one line source, such as a recorder. Many also include a basic mixer.

The disadvantages of some RPUs include their vulnerability to RF and electrical interference; their inability to entirely cover large metropolitan areas, which means they must be supplemented with a cell phone; their size and weight compared with smaller and lighter transmitting devices; and, oddly enough, their sound quality, which makes it seem as though reports were done in the studio. (Some news directors feel that location-quality sound in field reports adds authenticity and the sense of "being there.") Fully portable RPUs are also available (see 13-4).

Wireless fidelity is wireless broadband Internet access. It enables a reporter to e-mail audio files back to a base station. With specific software at both ends, audio files can be transmitted directly without cumbersome equipment, using a pocket-sized recorder/editor, a WiFi connection, and a transmission device. Wireless fidelity is usable up to about 300 feet from the WiFi transceiver station.

Internet Protocol (IP) is the method used to send data from one computer to another over the Internet. Increasingly, IP is being brought into broadcast stations' electronic news-gathering capability and, as such, is referred to as ***IP ENG***. ENG field reporters and mobile units outfitted with IP can transmit news stories via such paths as cellular, WiFi, and WiMAX[1] connections. IP has supplemented or reduced dependence on conventional microwave and satellite mobile units to the extent that the major networks are employing it more and more.

Integral to many portable devices used for remote transmission back to the broadcasting facility is the ***codec*** (a contraction of en*cod*er/*dec*oder), which encodes a signal at one end of a transmission and decodes it at another end. This can take place over a *POTS (plain old telephone system)* line or an ISDN-compatible line or using a computer interface. Devices with codec capability

usually offer more than one mic/line input/output, a telephone jack, and a keypad for dialing. In addition to signal transmission, it enables communication with personnel at the other end.

Mobile Unit

Although some radio stations have need of a ***mobile unit*** to cover news in the field—anything from a car to a van (which may do double duty for on-location disc jockey and other types of promotional broadcasts)—most stations these days can adequately handle on-location reporting with the highly portable recording and transmitting equipment discussed earlier in this section.

When a mobile unit is employed, it is usually due to news coverage that requires more equipment, production flexibility, and greater transmission capability (i.e., satellite) than portable gear (which can be handled by one or two people) can accommodate.

In addition to meeting a reporter's typical recording and transmission needs, mobile units are designed to facilitate the producing, editing, mixing, packaging, and broadcasting of stories. Larger mobile units are literally small studios on wheels, some with an extendable mast that can be raised to a height of several feet for microwave transmission.

Headphones

Headphones are an important but often-overlooked piece of equipment in field production (see Chapter 8). Regardless of the medium—radio, TV, film, or music recording—the purpose of the production, or its scale, headphones are as important on-location as loudspeakers are in the studio. Unless there is another way to monitor audio, headphones are the only reference you have to sound quality and balance. Use the best headphones available, study their frequency response, and get to know their sonic characteristics. First-rate headphones are expensive but worth it. They have a wide, flat response; they are sensitive; they have superb channel separation (for stereo and multichannel sound); and their cushioned earpieces keep outside sound from leaking through. All these characteristics are essential in producing audio on-location, when loudspeakers are unavailable.

It is also to your advantage to have a headphone amplifier (see 13-7), which enables you to monitor a mix at a convenient level without affecting the original signal sources. This is particularly useful when the loudness of background sound makes it difficult to hear program

---

1. *WiMAX* is short for *Worldwide Interoperability for Microwave Access.* It provides wireless data transmission over the Internet with access just about anywhere. WiMAX has become a wireless alternative to cable and DSL. (*DSL* stands for *digital subscriber loop* or, more recently, *digital subscriber line.* It provides data transmission over a local telephone network.)

13-7 Headphone amplifier. This model can accommodate four headphones, with a loudness control for each one. The master loudness control allows matching to the audio source so that the individual volume controls operate at convenient levels. There is high headroom to avoid clipping at loud levels. (The manufacturer warns, however, that ear protection is the user's responsibility.) The unit weighs 1 pound.

audio. By plugging headphones into a headphone amplifier and plugging the amp into the mic mixer headphone output, you can not only drive the headphone gain to the desired loudness level but can also control the levels of other headphone feeds. A headphone amp works well not only in the field but in studio recording when more than one performer requires foldback.

Guidelines for Submissions from the Field

Many broadcast networks and stations have guidelines for the submission of news reports from the field or from affiliates. These guidelines vary with the news organization. For example, a station may accept reports via ISDN lines, the Internet and its various protocols, File Transfer Protocol (FTP) uploads via FTP software, FTP uploads via Web browsers, or direct-dial (modem) serial or Point-to-point Protocol (PPP) connections. Therefore a field reporter (or engineer) should be versed in the various audio transmission protocols.

Audio may be preferred in a WAV (uncompressed) file to ensure high-quality sound. If the news director accepts compressed material, compression should be done after the uncompressed recording has been produced, not before.

Television ENG

The obvious differences between radio and television ENG are the addition of the camera and the equipment necessary to transmit picture as well as sound, plus the added production considerations that go along with video. That said, using the single-system recording technique greatly simplifies field coverage of TV news, where time is of the essence.

In *single-system recording,* both sound and picture are recorded on the same medium; in the case of ENG, the medium is usually disk; videotape is being used less and less. The recording device is a *camcorder*—a portable TV camera with a video recorder that also records audio feeds.

Camcorder

The *camcorder* is a combination camera and recorder that is portable, lightweight, battery-powered, and operated handheld or shoulder-borne (see 13-8). Most camcorders used today are digital and take a disk; some use mini-DV (Digital Video) or SP videocassette tape. The recorder is either built into the camera unit or dockable to it. With the advent of the digital field recorder, the era of ENG has become the era of *digital news gathering (DNG).*

Most camcorders come with a mounted shotgun microphone and inputs for handheld mics. Other types of microphones are also used, such as the Holophone (see 3-41a) and the stereo mic (see 13-8). Most camcorders are also equipped to handle wireless mic systems.

Camcorders vary in the number of audio channels they furnish. Some provide two channels, usually 16-bit with a sampling rate of 48 kHz, four channels at 12-bit and 32 kHz, or both. Some are also capable of cut-and-paste in-camera editing. Recording times vary with the recording format; hard disk and flash recorders have greater recording capacities than do videotape.

Microphone

As in RENG the handheld, omnidirectional, moving-coil microphone with a pop filter and a built-in shock mount is still the mic of choice for TV ENG because the omni pickup pattern provides a sense of sonic environment and the reporter can control mic-to-source distance. If the environment is too noisy, a directional mic may be more suitable. The mic may be wired or, as is more likely today, wireless. The reporter carries the transmitter, and the receiver is usually mounted on the camera.

Handheld microphones in TV usually carry a *mic flag*—the small box mounted on the mic showing the station

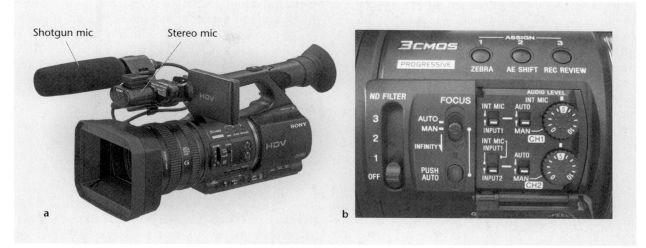

13-8 Camcorder. (a) This model records onto CompactFlash, hard-disk drive, or digital videotape (HDV, DVCAM, and DV). It includes both a mounted shotgun microphone and a built-in stereo mic. (b) Among the audio features are two XLR inputs; an intuitive switching system—channel 1 can be fed by the internal mic or whatever is plugged into XLR 1, while channel 2 can be fed by the internal mic, XLR 1, or XLR 2; the two XLRs can be switched from *mic* to *mic-to-line;* level controls for each input; phantom power; and an audio status check displayed on the camera's liquid crystal display (LCD).

logo. Make sure it does not cover the microphone's grille area, or it can adversely affect directional response and sound quality.

The convenience of wireless mics is undeniable. That notwithstanding, most audio people advise against using them when a wired mic will do the job. Wireless systems are not as reliable as wired mics; there are problems with interference, dropout, and noise from the camera, motors, cabling, and so on. This advice is particularly noteworthy when field-recording dramatic material (see Chapter 11).

When using a wireless mic, be sure to check for RF interference beforehand. This is easy to do using a handheld scanner set to the wireless mic's frequencies. If wireless reception is a problem, putting the beltpack receiver on the front of the reporter instead of on the side or back (out of sight, of course) should improve signal pickup.

When camera-to-source distance is wide, placing the receiver closer to the reporter, if possible, minimizes dropout and multipath reflections. In rainy and snowy conditions, mounting the beltpack just above the ankle and placing the receiver as close to the ground as possible can minimize poor reception because of absorption.

Although audiences are accustomed to seeing a microphone in the picture, particularly in news, care still must be taken to keep the mic from being too obtrusive. In typical stand-up reports and on-the-scene interviews, this

is usually not a problem. But if an interview is lengthy, it may be preferable to take the time to body-mount two mini-mics. It could be annoying to the audience (and the person being interviewed) to see one handheld mic moved back and forth between reporter and interviewee for several minutes. On the other hand, if there is nothing to occupy the reporter's hands, using body mics may be more of a distraction. Moreover, unless the camera operator directs the viewer where to look with the video, the viewer may find it distracting without a handheld mic in the picture to help focus attention. Given these potentials for viewer annoyance, savvy photographers and reporters "produce" an interview by varying shots to avoid distraction and sameness.

As pointed out earlier, camcorders also come with an attached or built-in microphone. Usually, the mic is a capacitor shotgun that in some models is stereo. The attached mic has a number of advantages: it allows one person to operate audio and video simultaneously; the mic of choice is super- or hypercardioid to pick up sound several feet away; when used in addition to the reporter's mic, it provides another sound pickup; and, when it is the only mic used, it frees the reporter's hands.

The fixed camera mic also has a number of disadvantages: the mic may pick up sound from a zoom lens motor or a hum from the monitor; if it is highly directional, which it usually is, it has to be pointed straight at the sound source to reduce unwanted sound; and it cannot adequately handle shots that change from one focal length to another. Unless the camera moves, it is difficult to adjust the sound for a change from, say, a medium shot to a close-up or a long shot.

A final disadvantage of the camera mic is due to the *inverse square law*—the acoustic situation in which the sound level changes in inverse proportion to the square of the distance from the sound source. Outdoors, when mic-to-source distance is doubled, the sound-pressure level drops approximately 6 dB, thus reducing loudness to one-fourth. Conversely, cutting the mic-to-source distance in half increases loudness approximately 6 dB (see 13-9). The precise effect of this law depends on the openness of the area and the directionality of the microphone.

Camcorder Audio Inputs, Outputs, and Controls

Professional camcorders have a number of features that may vary with the model and be known by somewhat different terms. Generally, they include at least two balanced microphone inputs to record two separate audio channels. There are also line-level inputs to receive audio from another video recorder, audio recorder, or other line-level sound sources. An *audio input selector* tells the recorder whether the signal is coming from the camera or from a microphone or line source.

Camcorders may have an input feature called an *automatic gain control (AGC)*. Avoid using it. AGC automatically boosts sound level when loudness falls below

a preset (built-in) level. During recording, when there is no foreground sound for the mic to pick up, the AGC brings up the background sound as it seeks volume. If a reporter makes slight pauses when delivering a story, it may be possible to hear the increases in background sound level as the AGC automatically increases volume. AGC should not be confused with a built-in limiter, which can be useful.

The outputs on a camcorder are for feeding sound to another recorder—audio or video—and for monitoring through headphones. Some camcorders have an RF output that mixes audio and video together and makes it possible to see and hear the recording on a conventional TV set. On recorders with two audio channels, an *audio monitor control* selects which one is heard in the headphones; in the *mix* position, both channels are heard together. Camcorders also have an intercom jack.

In addition to the usual recorder controls—*play, record, stop,* and so on—an *audio dub* function allows the recording of new audio onto a prerecorded disk or tape without erasing the video. Record-level controls adjust the loudness of the input, output, and monitor audio. Camcorders also have a meter to monitor audio levels.

Despite the convenience and the handiness of the audio-level controls on camcorders, be aware that they may not be as finely tuned as similar controls on an audio recorder and microphone mixer. The primary function of camcorders, after all, is recording picture. If there is a problem with the camcorder's mic or audio controls, try feeding the sound through a mic mixer (see 13-2),

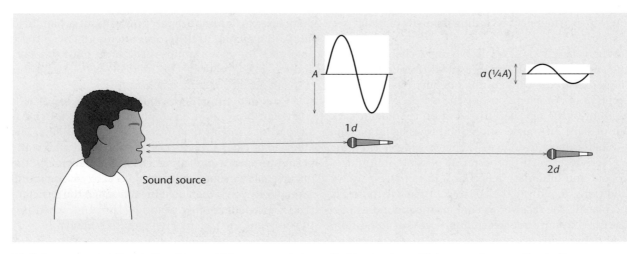

13-9 Inverse square law. As the distance *(d)* from a sound source doubles, loudness *(A)* decreases in proportion to the square of that distance.

13-10 Camcorder XLR adapter. This device is designed to feed XLR audio to any camcorder and can be mounted under the camera or to a belt. It is switchable between mic and line inputs. Two inputs can be mixed to both channels or, for stereo, one input can feed both channels. There are also two ⅛-inch mono jack connectors. Frequency response is 20 Hz to 20 kHz. The unit weighs 13.5 ounces.

a separate audio recorder, or an adapter (see 13-10). When using a mic mixer with a camcorder, make sure in advance that it will improve sound quality; sometimes it does the opposite. Always monitor the sound through high-quality headphones.

Transmission and Mobile Units

Similar to the way radio field reporting is handled, a TV field reporter can record a story, transfer it to a laptop computer, edit it, and send the files via the Internet to the newsroom server. If more-elaborate production is required, the unedited files can be sent to the station for the necessary additional processing. When field coverage of a story is involved and requires more equipment and transmission capability than a videographer and reporter can handle, a mobile unit may be employed. ENG mobile units, even at their most basic, obviously require more technical support than do RENG vehicles, not only because of the video component but also because of the transmission requirements. ENG vans require more space and therefore may provide additional audio support that includes a more complex mixer, signal processors, recorders, and shelf-type loudspeakers. It is worth noting that what often influences the equipment brought into the field is not production need but how many people are on the production crew.

ENG Production

The main purpose of ENG is to facilitate fast access to the news scene, quick setup time, uncomplicated pro-duction, immediate distribution if necessary, and simple postproduction when time permits and production circumstances require. In news the immediacy is more important than the aesthetics, but this is not to say that news producers ignore production values. They simply do the best they can under the circumstances.

Preproduction

Preproduction planning in ENG is obviously difficult because news can occur anywhere at any time. The best you can do is always be prepared. In audio, preparation means making sure that the following items are available and ready:

- AC adapters and extension cords
- Alligator clips and leads
- Backup phantom power for capacitor mics
- Backup recorder
- Battery charger
- Clamp-on mic stands for a podium
- Codec (if it is not integral to the transmission/communications system being used)
- Distribution amplifier for multiple feeds (see 13-11)
- Duct and masking tape
- Extra and fresh battery supplies for recorders, mic mixers, wireless microphone systems, and capacitor mics (if no phantom power is available)—lithium batteries provide extended operating time
- Extra mic cables, belt clips for body mics, and windscreens
- High-pass filters to insert into the mic line to cut low-frequency noise
- High-quality headphones and headphone amplifier
- Line-to-mic adapters to match impedance from auditorium amplifiers
- Log sheet or laptop computer for recordkeeping: time, location, and content of recorded information; problems with audio quality; and suggestions that anticipate editing
- Microphone splitter (see 13-21)
- Nondirectional and directional handheld mics and lavalier mini-mics

■ Pads (40 dB) if line-to-mic adapters are insufficient to reduce level

■ Phone tap (see 13-12)

■ Plastic waterproof coverings to protect equipment against excessive moisture and rain

■ Plenty of the recording medium being used (i.e., disks, flash cards, and so on)

■ Portable microphone mixer

■ Surge protector

■ Tool kit

■ USB A-to-B adapter cord

■ XLR, phone, phono, and mini plugs and adapters (see 13-13)

In addition to ensuring that all the items needed are available:

■ Prep the gear to make sure it is working properly.

■ Plug in all connecting equipment to ensure that it is compatible and, if necessary, interchangeable.

■ Try to avoid using equipment that is vulnerable to inclement weather, rough handling, or crashing. If that is not feasible, use the most robust and dependable gear available and thoroughly check out the backup equipment.

Production

Field production often presents the problem of background sound's interfering with the intelligibility of the on-mic/on-camera reporters. In news, however, sense of locale is important to reports from the field, particularly in radio. In fact, as noted earlier, some news producers do not want the sound quality of *actualities*—reports from the field—upgraded to studio quality precisely to preserve location presence.

Miking the Stand-up News Report The omnidirectional, moving-coil, handheld microphone is used most often in stand-up news reports from the field. It picks up enough background sound to provide a sense of environment in normal conditions without overwhelming the reporter's sound. It is possible to control the balance of background-to-reporter sound by moving the mic closer to or farther from the speaker (see 13-14). The closer the mic-to-source distance, the greater the reduction in background sound. Remember the inverse square law (see 13-9).

Another advantage of the omni mic is that it can be held comfortably below the mouth in a relatively unobtrusive position on-camera. For interviews the mic can be situated between reporter and interviewee without necessarily having to move it back and forth for questions and answers (see 13-15).

In noisy environments an omnidirectional microphone may not discriminate enough against unwanted sound even at a close mic-to-source distance. In such a situation, a directional mic may be suitable. The sound balance between reporter and background can still be maintained by moving the mic closer to or farther from the reporter's mouth. But remember that directional mics must be held at an appropriate angle to be on-axis to the mouth (see 13-16). Moreover, during interviews the mic must be moved back and forth between interviewer and

Output volume pots control the level at the corresponding rear-panel output XLR

Individual clip LEDs on all 8 outputs and on each of the 2 inputs indicate signal overload

Combine switch converts the DA-2 from a 2 × 4 configuration to a 1 × 7 distribution amp

Signal-present LEDs on each of the input channels indicate that the signal is being applied to the input

Channel 1/2 select switch determines which channel's input signal is fed to the headphone circuit for monitoring

Headphone circuit monitors the signals coming into the DA-2 inputs

13-11 **Distribution amplifier for multiple microphone feeds and its features.**

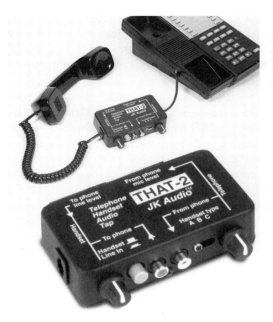

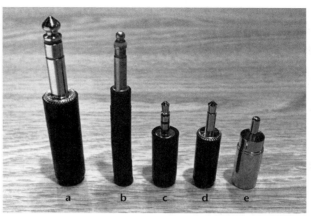

13-13 Common connectors for audio. Left to right: (a) ¼-inch balanced (tip/ring/sleeve) stereo phone plug. (b) Bantam balanced stereo phone plug—phone plugs are used for microphone- or line-level audio signals and as a headphone connector; phone plugs are also unbalanced (tip/sleeve). (c) Mini stereo plug. (d) Mini mono plug—mini plugs are used for mic inputs, headphones, iPods, and other consumer gear; they are unbalanced. (e) RCA or phono plug—RCA/phono plugs are used for line-level inputs and outputs and are unbalanced; they are used as connectors on many compact mixers and consumer equipment and usually come in left (white) and right (red) pairs. (See 3-62 for XLR connectors, not shown here.)

13-12 Phone tap. This device is used as an interface for recording audio from a standard telephone line.

13-14 Reducing background sound. (a) Holding an omni-directional microphone at chest level usually creates an optimal mic-to-source distance. (b) If background noise is high, its level can be reduced by decreasing the mic-to-source distance.

13-15 Using an omnidirectional microphone for on-location interviews. It can be positioned between the principals, usually with little need for repositioning, at least in quiet surroundings.

interviewee if the sound is to be on-mic. In television the microphone should not obstruct the mouth.

To provide a stereo feel to the stand-up report, use a middle-side (M-S) microphone. Recall that the M-S mic combines a cardioid and a bidirectional pickup in a single casing (see 3-33). By speaking into the front of the mic, the reporter's audio is monaural and on-mic; the bidirectional sides pick up the ambience, providing expanded sonic imaging to the on-scene story. This technique assumes that the environmental sound is not loud enough to overwhelm the reporter's narrative and that time permits setting up the M-S mic. If after recording circumstances do not facilitate reproducing the stereo M-S image, the middle, or mono, signal can be separated from the side pickup with no loss in sound and no problem with mono compatibility.

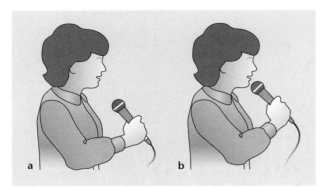

13-16 Miking when on-location background noise is too loud. Use a directional microphone either (a) several inches from the mouth or (b) close to it, depending on the performer's voice projection. Because the mic is directional, it must be held at the proper angle if the performer is to be on-mic. With cardioids and supercardioids, the angle does not have to be as severe as it would with a hypercardioid mic because of their wider on-axis response compared with the quite narrow on-axis response of the hypercardioid mic.

Split-track Recording In an interview there is another way to control the audio balances between reporter and background sounds or to enhance stereo imaging. *Split-track recording* employs a recorder with at least two separate audio tracks, such as a stereo recorder and camcorder. Using two microphones it is possible to feed the output of each to a separate channel. It is like doing a mini-multitrack recording, rather than stereo, to better control the audio quality and the mix of two sound sources. If the recorder has more than two mic inputs, it is indeed possible to do a mini-multitrack recording.

In a stand-up report, for example, the speaker can hold the microphone close to the mouth to minimize background sound. The other mic is used to record just background sound. When the elements are recorded separately, the two can be balanced properly in the mix under controlled conditions.

In an interview the two principals can be miked separately, or one mic can be used between them with the second mic used to pick up background sound. In either case, the two mic feeds facilitate more control over the sound balance. If one voice is dominating the other in an interview, using two mics makes it possible to employ a polarity reverse cable on the dominant voice to partially cancel it.

Split-track recording may not be possible or necessary on an everyday basis, or with recorders that have either a built-in stereo mic or two mics in relatively fixed positions. In each case, being able to control the proportional mic-to-source distances and levels of talent and background sounds is difficult. When it is feasible, however, the improvement that split-track recording provides in audio quality and control is worth the time if you have it. Not only is this technique useful in ENG but it can also be applied in any type of field recording.

Recording Background Whether you record using the split-track method or put all the audio on one track, make sure you record enough background sound (indoor or outdoor) by doing an *overroll*—running the recorder in *record* for a while either before or after recording. Background sound is useful in postproduction editing to bridge transitions and cover awkward edits (see Chapter 20).

If tying up a camcorder to record an overroll is an inconvenience, bring a backup audio recorder and a microphone to record additional background sound separately.

Transmission and Mix-minus

When the distance between the reporter and the station is thousands of miles or if the signal is being sent via satellite, there will be a slight delay between the time the reporter's words are spoken and the time they reach the station. The reporter's words are fed back through an *interruptible foldback (IFB) system.* The system is used to connect the director, producer, and other control room personnel with the performer(s), through an earpiece, to convey directions before and during a broadcast. The earpiece is small enough to be inserted into the ear canal and carries program sound, the performer's voice included. When the director or anyone else connected to the system has an instruction for the performer, the program feed to the performer's earpiece is interrupted for the instruction.

When the reporter's words are fed back through the IFB earpiece, the reporter and the crew will hear the reporter's words after they have been spoken. This is analogous to the disorientation a public-address announcer hears in a stadium when the spoken words are heard a split second after they are delivered. To avoid disorientation the station sends the incoming report back to the field *mix-minus;* that is, all the audio is returned minus the reporter's words.

Mix-minus can be used in any situation in which sound is being returned via a foldback or IFB system. Some consoles and mixers include a mix-minus module, which is particularly useful for call-in programs. It facilitates a variety of mix-minus feeds to studio guests and listeners calling in. It also comes in handy in double remotes, where one personality is broadcasting from, say, an auto show and another performer is taking audience questions in another area of the show while the overall program host is at the station's studio handling phone-in comments from listeners. Mix-minus makes it possible for the talent at the two remote locations to hear one another and the main studio in real time and without echo. Another example is in a music recording when the conductor wishes to hear only the orchestra in the headphones, minus the vocalist, or vice versa.

ELECTRONIC FIELD PRODUCTION

Electronic field production (EFP) refers to video production done on-location, involving program materials that take some time to produce. The major differences between ENG and EFP are scale, time, and purpose; in principle they are the same. They both make it possible to produce program material in the field. But whereas ENG is designed to cover news events quickly, EFP is used to produce, more deliberately, such material as entertainment programs, drama, sports, documentaries, and commercials. Therefore EFP generally takes more time in planning, production, and postproduction and usually results in a technically and aesthetically superior product.

Small-scale EFP

EFP can be divided into small-scale and large-scale productions. The main difference between them is in the complexity of the production and, therefore, the amount of equipment and personnel required. Commercials, documentaries, disc jockey programs, and local sports can be produced with a minimum of hardware and people, whereas a nationally telecast football game, a parade, or the Grammy Awards show cannot.

Radio

Electronic field production in radio is usually limited to personality programs such as disc jockey and talk shows, as well as sports. Sometimes it may involve a live concert.

The absence of the visual component in radio drastically cuts down on production needs, compared with TV and film, and on the time needed for preproduction. In sports, for example, a few microphones, a mixer or portable mixing console, and a POTS codec are suf-

ficient. A disc jockey program can be mounted with a self-contained remote unit consisting of a microphone, CD and DVDs players, and a mixer.

Vans are also used in radio remotes. They may be ENG units equipped with CD players and recorders, or EFP units with removable side panels so the personalities can be seen.

Transmission

Remote radio broadcasts carried by a local station use wired telephone services if they must be transmitted across distances too far for RPU transmission, or if they would be difficult to carry by microwave because of the hundreds of relay stations needed to get the signal from one area to another. Using a satellite to beam signals for long-range transmission also solves this problem, although the solution is not cheap. Generally, satellites are used for global and continental transmission by networks and syndicated programmers.

There are several wired telephone services, analog and digital. They range from an inexpensive and relatively poor-quality dial-up voice line for radio remotes; to more-expensive, higher-quality voice lines; to digital transmission with high quality and greater data capacity. The number of services and their technical parameters are the domain of the engineer and are beyond the purview of this book.

There is one useful bit of information to pass on about telephone lines for remote broadcasting: When a line is installed, one terminus will be at the broadcast station. The other terminus—called the *telco drop*—will be at the remote site. Make sure you know where the phone company has left that terminal block; otherwise valuable and frantic time could be spent searching for it.

Television

Small-scale EFP for television is closer to ENG; large-scale EFP is more like a major studio production. Because ENG is covered earlier in this chapter, we'll move on to large-scale EFP.

Large-scale EFP

Large-scale electronic field production involves recording or broadcasting an event, such as a baseball game, a parade, or an awards program, on the spot. As major productions these events require the same technical support on-location that large-scale productions require in the studio. A huge trailer (sometimes more than one)—

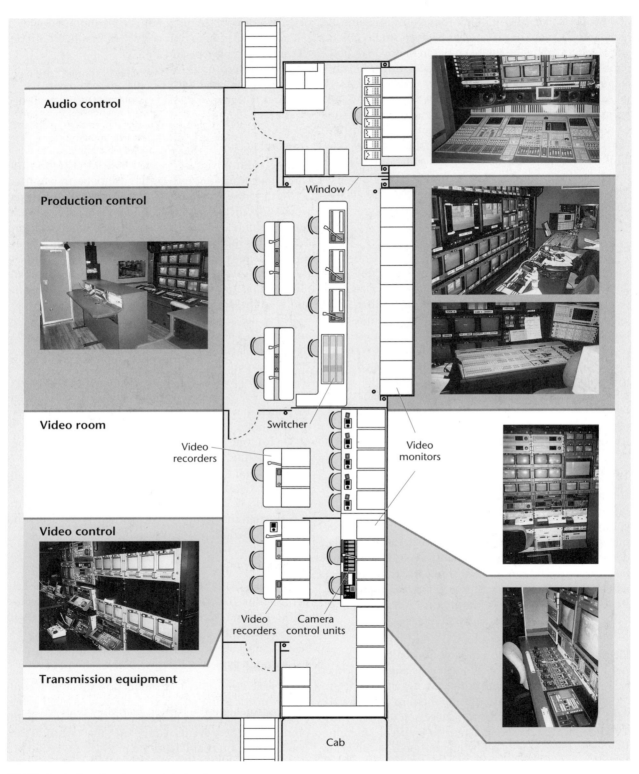

13-17 Control centers in a remote truck.

13-18 Interior of an audio mobile unit. Among the types of equipment provided in this mobile unit are 48-channel automated console, hard-disk recorder/editors, time code reader/generator, more than 100 microphones, most types of signal processors, main and near-field monitors, audio and video communications systems, cables, and powering equipment.

literally a studio-type technical facility on wheels—and the dozens of engineering and production personnel to go with it provide that support (see 13-17). The trailer contains all the equipment necessary to process and route signals from the many cameras and microphones that cover the event outside the truck and from the video and studio sources, such as instant replay, slow motion, and sound gear, inside the truck.

Audio-only mobile units run in size from a large van to a 10- or 12-wheel truck. Generally, they contain the types of equipment found in recording-studio control rooms: multichannel console; digital audio workstation with signal-processing plug-ins; additional recorders; outboard, rack-mounted signal processors; plus cables, generators, and other types of powering equipment (see 13-18). Audio mobile units are used for on-location concert production and for awards programs and TV and film shoots to support the video EFP or film unit.

MULTICAMERA EFP

Events produced in the field are either covered or staged. A covered event occurs regardless of media, and production conforms to the event (at least in theory). Sports, parades, and concerts are examples of covered events. Staged events, such as drama, variety, and awards shows, are produced especially for the media and are more

tightly controlled. The production approach to an event depends on the type of event it is.

Covered events usually require the multicamera TV approach. Several cameras feed a switcher, several microphones feed a mixer, and all signals feed to recording or broadcast or both. Shots are selected as the event progresses, and there is little or no postproduction. Staged events can be produced using the multicamera TV or single-camera film approach. The event is constructed in postproduction.

The following sections cover multicamera EFP of speeches, news conferences, and sporting events.

Remote Survey

Except for news (as opposed to news features, mini-documentaries, and the like), field production takes careful planning. The more complex the production, the more detailed the planning must be. To address the logistics of, among other things, what equipment will be needed and where it will be positioned, a remote survey is essential. A *remote survey* consists of an inspection of a production location by key production and engineering personnel and the written plan they draft based on that inspection. The plan helps coordinate the ordering and the setting up of equipment and the communication hookup among the key production people during shooting or broadcast. A remote survey, also called a *site survey,* can take whatever form suits the particular need.

In surveying a field location, diagrams and photographs of the various shooting areas at the production site are often required and are always helpful. Camera and mic positions, cable and power runs, signal feeds, and other equipment locations can be easily determined at a glance. Clearing access to the site and acquiring police permits and written permissions from property owners are also necessary.

Production meetings are essential, particularly after the remote survey has been completed. If something is to go wrong, and it usually does, it is more likely to occur in the field than in the studio. In *production meetings* key personnel coordinate their responsibilities, explain their needs, discuss audio and video, and resolve problems. The remote *production schedule,* including setup and rehearsal times, is also planned. Scheduling production meetings seems like common sense, but you would be surprised at how many field productions proceed without them. As you might expect, these particular productions are apt to be more nerve-racking, to run over schedule, to cost more, and to be aesthetically inferior. Paradoxically, in this business of communications, communication is sometimes the one element that is overlooked.

In doing a remote survey for audio-related needs, depending on the type of production, the following are factors to consider:

■ **Power supply and other electrical needs** Determine whether the venue has sufficient power and electrical support; if not, plan to bring the necessary power and electrical equipment.

■ **Test the electric circuits** If using the available electrical outlets, plug in a microphone and a recorder to check for noise and signal interference from other transmissions in the area.

■ **Acoustics** If the venue is indoors, make sure that the sound is not too reverberant for optimal microphone pickup of the speakers; if it is, bring sound absorbers to place out-of-shot to help control unwanted reflections.

■ **Noise** Do the site survey at the time of day planned for the broadcast or recording to check for noise from traffic, an adjacent or upstairs room, or a nearby factory or airport. Find out from the appropriate city official if any road work or building demolition is planned for the production day(s).

■ **Public-address system** If the venue has its own public-address (PA) system, determine whether its sound quality is good enough to use. If it is, get permission to do so; if it's not, get permission to bring and set up the necessary communications equipment.

■ **Microphones and recorders** Determine what wired and wireless mics, recorders, cabling, and cable runs to bring. With wireless mics check the placement of the transmitter and the receiver to ensure that the signal is unobstructed and that there is no interference from motors and other noise-generating equipment.

■ **Action radius** For the purposes of blocking, determining the length of cable runs, and calculating the distances involved between the transmitters and the receivers of wireless mic systems, check the size of the area over which the action will occur.

■ **Headphones, loudspeakers, and intercom systems** Determine the type(s) and the number of headphones needed. If loudspeakers are used, decide on their placement and the control of their sound throw to avoid interference with microphone pickup. Determine what field intercom systems are necessary (see "Field Intercom Systems" below).

Portable Mixing Systems

As noted earlier in this chapter, there are many portable audio recorders available with various albeit limited recording, mixing, and editing capabilities. In productions that involve picture (other than news), such as video commercials and film, particular demands may require more functions than typical ENG mixers can handle. In such cases there are multichannel portable mixers and small consoles with signal processing and mixing capabilities that also facilitate coordination with and synchronization to picture. Some models include an inboard recorder (see 13-19).

Field Intercom Systems

Intercommunication among personnel is always vital during production. This is particularly so in the field, where crew and facilities are more widely dispersed than in the studio.

Among the intercom systems employed in the field are IFB, program sound receiver, paging, intercom, cellular telephone, and walkie-talkie. (The IFB system is covered earlier in this chapter.)

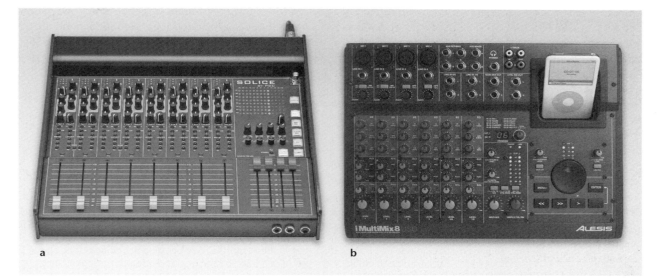

13-19 Portable mixers for EFP. (a) This model includes the following features: eight input channels with phantom power and parametric EQ; eight mix buses; input channels 1 and 2 and channels 3 and 4 that can be ganged for stereo recording; sunlight-readable LED peak program metering; slate microphone; remote roll; communication to boom operators; speaker output that follows mixer headphone selection for playback; and iPod input jack. The unit weighs 14 pounds. (b) Tabletop mixer with iPod recorder measuring 13.38 × 3 × 9.75 inches and weighing 5 pounds, 13 ounces. This model includes four input channel strips with eight channels—four mono and two stereo; two of the input channels can be switched to high impedance for recording electric guitar and bass; stereo output to the iPod; phantom power; three-band equalizer per channel; 100 preset programs containing reverbs (hall, room, plate, chamber), chorus, flange, delay, and pitch shift; limiter; and 16-bit/44.1 kHz and 48 kHz recording.

The *program sound receiver,* which looks like a pager, lets you hear the sound portion of the telecast to monitor the director's cues.

Paging systems are wireless and similar to the small, belt-clipped receivers used by people who have to be contacted when they are not near a telephone.

Field *intercom systems* are wireless and similar to those used in the studio. They enable two-way communication between the remote truck and the production crew.

The *cellular telephone* can be used to feed a performer program sound and IFB information, particularly when the performer is beyond a station's transmitting range.

The *walkie-talkie* is a handheld, two-way communications device with adequate reach if the field site is not too widespread. It can also be interfaced with other intercom devices.

Production of Speeches and News Conferences

Recording someone speaking from a podium at an event such as a press conference, a dinner, an awards ceremony, and the like is an everyday assignment in broadcasting.

In preparing for such an event, it is important to know whether you will be taking the sound from your own microphone(s), from the house PA system, or from a common output feed other than the PA system, called a *multiple* or *press bridge.*

Setting Up Your Own Microphones

The directional microphone is usually the best one to use for a speaker at a podium. Its on-axis response focuses the sound from the speaker, and its off-axis cancellation reduces unwanted room and audience noises (see 13-20).

Cardioid microphones are most frequently used at a podium due to their wider on-axis response and because the audience faces the back of the mic, where a cardioid is least sensitive. Supercardioids may be better, however; though they are slightly more directional at the front than are cardioids, it is not enough to seriously inhibit side-to-side head movement, and their area of least sensitivity begins at the sides, about 125 degrees off-axis.

The advantages of setting up and using your own microphones are that you have control of the sound quality and exclusive use of the content. Nevertheless, there are

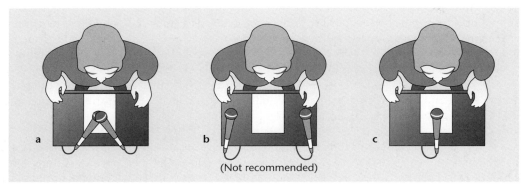

13-20 Common techniques for miking a podium speaker with directional microphones. (a) This mic placement provides a wide, smooth response and allows comfortable side-to-side head movement but is often unnecessary. (b) This array is not recommended because it requires the speaker to remain between the mics to ensure smooth response. (c) In many situations a single cardioid or supercardioid mic is sufficient, that is unless more than one mic is needed to feed multiple sources. Two parallel microphones, one above the other (see 3-72a) or three triangularly arrayed mics are often used in podium setups for redundancy.

situations in which you have little or no say in these matters and have to take your sound from a common source.

Public-address Pickups

Talks delivered in many types of rooms and halls require a public-address system so that the audience can hear the speaker. The miking for the PA system is at the podium. On occasion adding your mics to those already at the podium could create clutter that may be visually distracting and also obscure the speaker from some of the audience. In such instances you may have to take the audio feed from the PA system.

This entails patching into an output jack in the PA amplifier or PA control panel and feeding the signal to your mixer. It should not interfere with the loudspeaker sound because the PA feed from the podium mics is usually split into at least two separate routing systems. Because many PA loudspeaker systems are not noted for their sound quality, this arrangement gives you some control over the audio. If the house technicians control the sound feed, which is often the case, it is necessary to coordinate your needs with them in advance.

Splitting Microphones

An alternative to a PA pickup is splitting the microphone feed. This is manageable if your station or company is the only one, or one of only a few, covering an event. Otherwise, mic and cable clutter could result.

Microphone splitting is usually accomplished with a transformer-isolated microphone splitter (see 13-21). It

13-21 Microphone splitter. This model provides one direct and two transformer-isolated outputs. Each output has a ground lift switch.

splits the mic signal to the PA system (or other source) and your mic mixer, isolating the two feeds and thereby reducing the possibility of hum.

Multiple Pickups

Several stations or networks often cover the same event. If they all set up microphones at the podium, not only would the clutter be unsightly but a good sound pickup might depend on how lucky the producer was in getting a mic close enough to the speaker. This often happens at news conferences, sometimes because the speaker believes that a clutter of mics makes the event appear important. To the audio person, however, this is not ideal or preferred. If the facilities exist, it is better to take the sound from a multiple.

A **multiple** (not to be confused with the mult that interconnects jacks on a patch bay [see Chapter 4]) is a distribution amplifier—an amp with several individual line- and mic-level outputs. It can take many physical forms, but generally it is a device with output connectors to which news crews connect their equipment. Each station then obtains a separate, good-quality sound feed without struggle by patching into one of the amplifier's output connectors. Such a feed is usually agreed upon in advance by those involved and is set up either cooperatively by them or by the sound people who operate the in-house audio system. This type of multiple is also known as a **press bridge**, *press mult box,* or *presidential patch* (see 13-22). Microphones used for questions from the audience are connected to the multiple as well. Thus all networks and stations get the same high-quality feed from the few mics used.

A challenge periodically encountered on remotes (and in studio broadcasts) is the need to mike several speakers at a conference, symposium, press parley, entertainment program, and the like. The obvious way to produce such a program is to use a multichannel mixer and manually control the mic levels of each participant. But, depending on the number of participants, this could become unwieldy, especially if the operator has to handle other sound sources such as announcer, recorder, or CD players, or a combination of these elements. And, with a number of mics being open at the same time, other problems could occur, such as comb filtering, ambient noise and/or reverberation buildup, and, if a PA system is operating, feedback. The device that is often employed to overcome these problems is the automatic microphone mixer.

Automatic Microphone Mixer

The **automatic microphone mixer** controls a group of live microphones in real time, turning up a mic when someone is talking and turning down the mics of the participants who are not talking. While the automatic mic mixer may incorporate such functions as limiting, compressing, AGC, and noise gating, the term *automatic mixing,* per se, means controlling multiple mics so that the system goes where it is needed.

In the early days of the technology, automatic mic mixers had a number of problems: the gating action that opened and closed the mics was perceptible; in noisy venues the noise level at the mic was sometimes higher than the voice level; it was difficult for some automatic mixers to discriminate between background noise and low-level speech reaching an adjacent mic; and additive background levels when several mics were open at the same time caused feedback, excessive room ambience, or both.[2]

Today's systems have largely overcome these problems. The gating action is relatively seamless, and noise-adaptive threshold settings activate a mic for speech while maintaining the natural studio/room ambience (see 13-23 and 13-24). An automatic mic mixer may be able to do only so much, however. Figure 13-25 lists several tips for addressing the most common problems associated with having multiple open microphones.

Precautions to Take

Speeches and press conferences are real-world events. As such they are often unpredictable, sometimes hectic, and usually involve using different types of equipment. It is therefore wise to take a few sensible precautions to minimize unpleasant surprises:

■ Ensure that equipment (such as microphones and recorders) and accessories (such as recording media, cables, and connectors) are functioning properly and that all batteries are fresh.

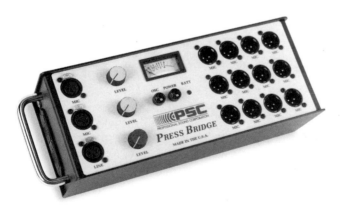

13-22 Press bridge. This multiple has three inputs—two mic level and one line level, each with independent level controls—and 12 outputs, providing transformer-isolated, mic-level audio feeds. A VU meter and an internal tone oscillator are provided to set levels. The unit can be powered for 12 hours from two 9 V batteries.

2. Dan Dugan; see *www.dandugan.com.*

13-23 Four snapshots of an automatic micro-phone mixer's action on speech in a three-mic setup. (a) The first frame shows no one speaking; the sound levels at all mics are low. The system fades all channels to a medium gain that sums to the equivalent of one mic at full gain. (b) The second frame shows one person speaking. The system automatically fades the gain to full, while the other two inputs are turned down. (c) The third frame shows a different person speaking. The system automatically fades the gain to full, while the other two inputs are turned down. (d) The fourth frame shows two people speaking simultaneously. The system automatically shares the gain between them, while the other input is turned down.

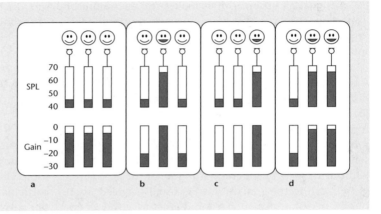

Example from the Dugan Speech System™; see *www.dandugan.com.*

13-24 Application of an automatic microphone mixer. A simplified version of the Dugan Speech and Music Systems™ used for *Late Night with David Letterman.* The mixers are inserted into the console. For the specific needs of the program, the sound designer, Dan Gerhard, used the music system to mix the voices on-stage as the threshold for the audience mics. This makes the voices duck the audience mics, suppressing reverberation from the PA in the mix, but they pop right back up between the words to catch audience nuances.

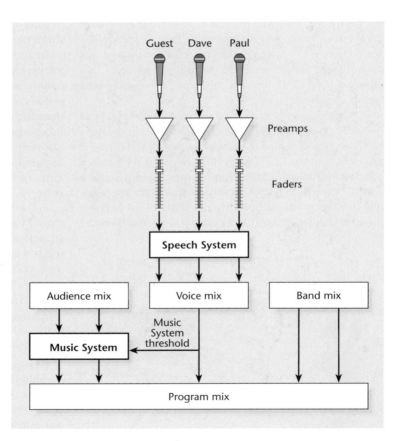

■ Make sure that all recording media have sufficient memory and that cables and wires are not broken or frayed.

■ Double-check that components are correctly wired.

■ Do a test recording to ensure that there is no hum or buzz in the circuit(s).

■ Check that audio levels between the output of the mult and the input of the recorder match and, with digital media, that there is enough headroom to avoid distortion.

■ Be confident that you are thoroughly familiar with the equipment; some gear is fairly straightforward; other

13-25 Suggested solutions for multiple-open-microphone problems.

Problem	Indicators	Tips
Comb filtering	Thin, hollow sound	Reduce number of mics Observe three-to-one rule
Excessive ambient noise reverberation	Distant, washed-out sound Loss of clarity and intelligibility	Reduce number of mics Reduce mic-to-source distances
Feedback	Feedback before the system is loud enough for the audience to hear it	Reduce number of mics Reduce mic-to-source distances Increase mic-to-loudspeaker distances

equipment is quite formidable with vast arrays of features and menus.

■ If you know the speech or press conference assignment in advance, arrive early enough to set up and test the gear to ensure that it is working, thereby helping avoid last-minute chaos. Getting there early may also get you in a more favorable position proximate to the action.

PRODUCTION OF SPORTS PROGRAMS

Sound in sports broadcasting is essential to the excitement of the event. It provides three basic elements—the sound of the announcers, the sound of the crowd, and the sound of the game action—which are handled somewhat differently for television than they are for radio.

Television Sports Audio

In TV sports the presence of the visual element, paradoxically, puts more of a demand on the audio than the absence of picture does in radio (see "Radio Sports Audio" later in this chapter).

The Announcers

In sports broadcasting the announcers have to be heard clearly, whether they project their voices over the constant din of a large, vocal crowd or speak quietly during a golf game or tennis match. In TV no microphone is better suited to meet both of these demands than the headset mic (see 3-23). The mic's design allows it to be positioned close to the announcer's mouth for optimal pickup of normal and quieter-than-normal speech while permitting the announcer to sit or stand. Its moving-coil element and built-in pop filter can withstand loud speech levels without overloading the mic, although

limiting or compressing may be necessary with some systems. The unidirectional pickup pattern reduces sound leakages from outside sources, and the omnidirectional pattern adds more background color. Microphones on more-recent headset systems have some degree of noise canceling to better control crowd sound that can compete with, or worse, overwhelm, the announcers' sound. Each earpiece can carry separate information—the director's cues on one and the program audio on the other—and the space in front of the announcer can be kept clear for papers, TV monitors, and other paraphernalia.

It is also critical that the announcers hear themselves in the headphone mix and have a means of communicating with the director through the IFB. To this end headphone and talkback controls are often placed within an announcer's reach as is a "cough button" to kill the announcer's mic when the throat must be cleared.

The Crowd

Crowd sound is vital to the excitement of most sporting events. The cheers, boos, and general hubbub punctuate the action, adding vitality and making the audience at home feel a part of the action.

Depending on the venue, crowd sound is picked up by dedicated crowd microphones, the mics that are used to pick up the action sounds, or a combination of both. Dedicated crowd mics are generally employed in outdoor stadiums because sound is more diffuse in an open space than it is indoors. The microphones—usually shotguns either separate or in X-Y pairs, a stereo mic, a middle-side mic, or some combination of these arrays—are positioned facing the crowd. They are mounted either low in the stands, aimed toward the crowd; high in the stands at press box level, aimed straight ahead; suspended with the mic's back off-axis to the P.A.; on the field; or a combination of the four.

Philosophies differ about the number of mics to use for adequate crowd sound pickup. Generally, overmiking can destroy clarity. This makes a location survey mandatory because each stadium and arena has its own acoustics and seating patterns. For example, some outdoor stadiums are more live than others; the proximity of the crowd to the field may be closer in one stadium than in another; an indoor arena may have a concave roof relatively close to, or farther away from, the playing surface—all of which have a direct effect on the density and the loudness of crowd sound.

One notable example of the need for location surveys and testing is a professional football game broadcast by NBC many years ago, without the announcers. It was an experiment to determine how well crowd and action sounds could sustain the game's excitement. (The experiment was also in response to the still valid criticism that sports announcers, particularly color commentators, talk too much.) The game was at season's end and meaningless, but the experiment failed because it was a sonically dull broadcast: it turns out that the stadium was built on sand, which absorbed much of the action and crowd sounds.

In addition to the typical needs considered in a location survey, such as type of microphones, mic assignments, length of cable required, and so on, there are a number of steps to take in making decisions related to crowd pickup:

■ Identify points where sound is more intense or live or both. Sound-collecting points, usually at the concavities of stadiums and arenas, are good places to begin.

■ Remember that sound is louder and more concentrated in enclosed venues than in open ones. In domed stadiums sound collects at and bounces from the concave roof to the crown of the playing surface. If microphones near the playing surface are not properly positioned, their sound quality will be degraded.

■ Avoid dead spots where crowd sound will be hollow, thin, and unexciting.

■ If attendance is likely to be less than capacity, ascertain which seats are usually filled and place the crowd mics in those areas.

■ Be aware that home-team fans are likely to far outnumber those of a visiting team. To help maintain excitement no matter which team generates it, position a mic in front of or near the section where the visiting fans are

seated, particularly if the game is important or involves a heated rivalry.

The Action

The sound of the action itself adds impact to a sporting event: the whoosh of the ball crossing the plate, the whomp of its hitting the catcher's mitt, and the crack of the bat on the ball in baseball; the signal calling of the quarterback and the crunch of hitting linemen in football; the skating sounds and the slamming of bodies against the boards in hockey; the bouncing ball, squeaking sneakers, and swish of the ball through the net in basketball; and so on. In fact, many sports producers consider the action sounds as important as—or more important than—the crowd sound.

To capture these sounds, separate microphones, other than the crowd mics, are used. The mics are mounted close to the area of play and pointed toward the action. Action sounds can also be enhanced in sports where the playing surface is a source of sound and mics can be embedded in it, such as with hockey and skateboarding. In skateboarding, for example, as many as 80 pickups, 40 on either side, are screwed into the vert (skating surface) to provide a continuous sonic movement of the skateboard.

A synthesis of the various approaches to mic placement for picking up action and crowd sounds used by the major networks in various sports is illustrated in Figures 13-26 to 13-36. Keep in mind that these illustrations are just that—examples. They do not represent the approach of any particular broadcast or cable network, nor are they to be construed as preferred techniques.

The Players

To add even more of a dynamic to sports sound coverage, the development of extremely small wireless transmitters facilitates miking the participants without interfering with their play. One such wireless system, the PlayerMic® is $35/100$ inch in thickness, 1.5 inches wide, and 4 inches long. It weighs 1 ounce and 1.8 ounces combined—transmitter and mini-mic. The body pack is rubberized and waterproof. The system can be manually operated or remotely controlled.

Because most sporting events are carried on a several seconds' delay, players' sounds, comments, and outbursts can be monitored for their enhancement to the game action and broadcast suitability. This also helps in integrating their sounds at an appropriate level in the overall game mix so that they are intelligible without standing out.

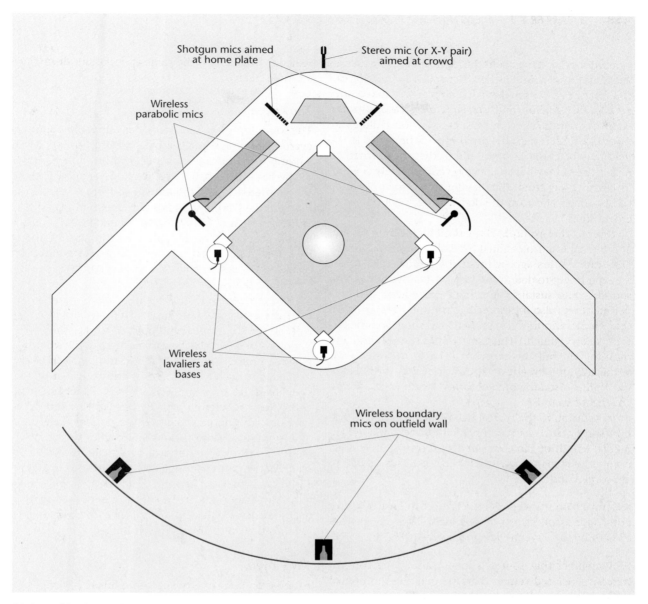

Shotgun mics aimed
at home plate

Stereo mic (or X-Y pair)
aimed at crowd

Wireless
parabolic mics

Wireless
lavaliers at
bases

Wireless boundary
mics on outfield wall

13-26 Miking baseball. Although most baseball sound is broadcast in mono-compatible stereo, only the crowd sound is miked for and reproduced in stereo. The main crowd mic, either a stereo mic or an X-Y pair of shotguns, is usually situated behind home plate, facing the crowd. For additional crowd sound reinforcement and to help pick up the sound of an outfielder crashing against the wall, wireless boundary mics are mounted on the outfield wall in left, center, and right fields. These mics are panned to enhance the stereo imaging of the crowd sound. Shotgun mics aimed at the plate pick up action sounds of the ball whooshing across the plate, the umpire's call, and the crack of the bat. The left shotgun mic (looking in toward home plate) is used when a right-handed batter is at the plate; the right shotgun is used when a left-handed batter is up. Only one shotgun at a time is live. For the whooshing sound of the ball crossing the plate, the level of the working shotgun mic is boosted for that split second of time. Other action sounds from the field are picked up by omnidirectional parabolic mics at the camera locations at first and third bases and wireless lavaliers at first, second, and third bases. Omnidirectional mics are employed because they reproduce a wider image than do unidirectional mics. Because all sound sources except the crowd are mono, too narrow an image of the action sounds would be disconcerting when switching back and forth between them and crowd reaction sounds.

In surround-sound miking for baseball, crowd sound is usually the only element produced in surround. Pickup for the surround mix comes from dedicated crowd microphones. Depending on the stadium, these mics are usually mounted at various field-level positions or hung from underdeck supports or both, facing toward the crowd. The mics are shotguns or parabolic mics or a combination of both. Precise positioning depends on the best sound-collecting points in the stadium. (See "Surround Sound" later in this chapter.)

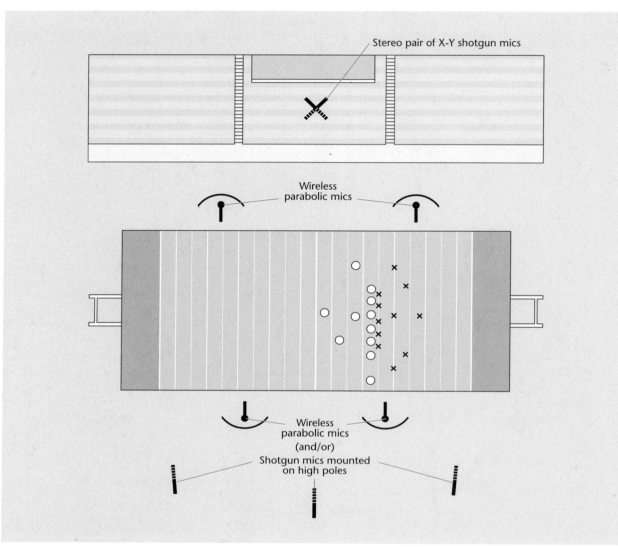

13-27 Miking football. Crowd sound is picked up through a stereo pair of shotgun mics, or a middle-side mic, placed in the stands usually at press box level and pointed straight across the stadium. Crowd sound is also picked up by shotgun mics mounted on the sideline cameras (not shown) and/or shotguns mounted on high poles, depending on how well or poorly the crowd sound carries. The crowd mics are mixed for stereo. Wireless parabolic mics pick up the sounds of field action such as the quarterback signals and the colliding linemen. Four parabolic mics are usually employed, two on either side of the field, each assigned to cover from the 50-yard line to the end zone. Sometimes the umpire positioned behind the defensive line is miked for additional pickup of the game action. Before the game it is important to ensure that the wireless mics transmit unobstructed sound, with no dropout, over their entire coverage area. Also at field level is a wireless handheld mic for the on-field color/interview announcer.

To add more game color, a microphone may be mounted on each goal post on the off chance that the football hits it on a field goal or point-after attempt; a supercardioid is mounted on the cable cam—a remotely controlled camera that moves on a cable above the field for added fill; and a very small wireless transmitter is mounted to the base of the kicking tee to get the punctuated sound of the kickoff.

Miking is not all that the sound crew has to deal with. In the remote truck, the sound sources must be assigned and mixed. Figure 13-28 shows one approach to the audio on a network-level football broadcast.

13-28 Sound source assignments in mixing audio for a network professional football game using a 48-channel console.

Channel	Source Assignment
1–6	Returns from limiters and effects devices
7–8	Two wireless interview mics on the field
9–14	Left and right of three routers for video playback
15	Wireless field mic for sideline reporter (if not the same person doing interviews)
16–17	Two handheld microphones in the announcers' booth for the game announcers on-camera open
18–20	Three headset mics for the game announcers and any guest who comes by
21	Open
22	Feed from the house public-address system
23	Referee mic, feed from stadium
24–27	Shotgun mics on the sideline handheld cameras
28	Umpire's mic (to pick up sound from the break of the huddle to the snap of the ball, including the linebackers' calling out defensive signals)
29	Feed from the submix of the sideline parabolic mics
30–31	Left and right crowd mix from X-Y shotguns set up high at the 50-yard line
32	Surround channel crowd mics located high in the stadium
33–36	Submasters for the left, center, right, and surround sends to the Dolby encoder
37	Announce submaster
38	Send to the stereo synthesizer
39–44	Music and sound-effect playback devices, such as CD players
45–46	Feeds from incoming remotes of other football games
47–48	Return loops for cueing and updating announcers

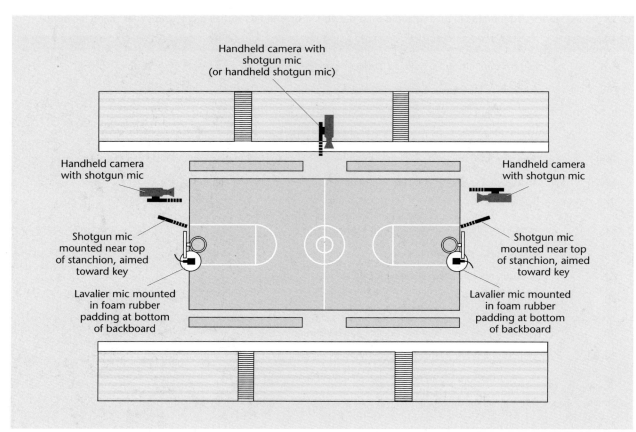

13-29 Miking basketball. Lavalier microphones are mounted to the foam rubber padding at the bottom of each backboard to pick up the sounds of the ball hitting the basket and swishing through the net. Shotgun mics aimed at the key pick up the ball-bouncing and sneaker sounds, grunts and chatter of the players, and calls from the referees. Shotgun mics on handheld cameras also pick up court sounds as well as the cheerleading and chatter from the benches. As the action moves up and down the court, the mics at either end are opened and closed to avoid undue concentration of crowd sound and the pickup of out-of-shot sounds. A shotgun mic at midcourt, either camera-mounted or handheld, helps fill the transitions as the endcourt mics are opened and closed. The midcourt shotgun is kept open throughout the up- and down-court action. There is no dedicated crowd mic because the array of microphones courtside is usually adequate to pick up more-than-sufficient crowd sound due to the highly reflective acoustics in most indoor arenas. There may be an additional shotgun mic behind the backboard (not shown) to pick up the band; but due to the possible copyright infringement of music rights, music-licensing agencies such as ASCAP (American Society of Composers, Authors, and Publishers) and BMI (Broadcast Music, Inc.) require a fee from the performing organization or its sponsor to broadcast the music. Therefore miking for such a music pickup should be cleared in advance. The same is true for similar situations in other sports.

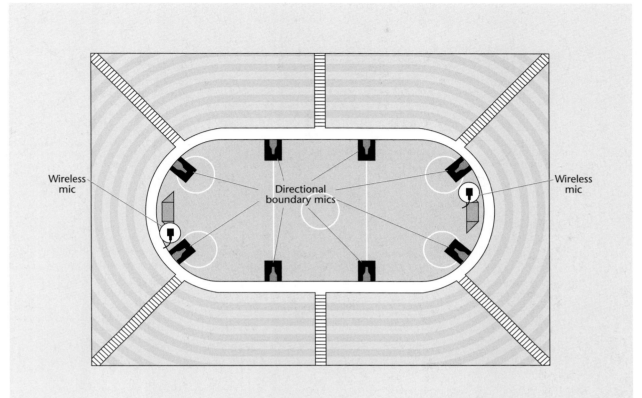

13-30 Miking ice hockey. In hockey the sound of the game itself is vital to the excitement of the pace of the action: skate sounds, puck slaps, players crashing against the boards, and stick sounds hitting the ice, the puck, and other sticks. These sounds come through in person, but unless the microphones pick them up they will not come through on television, which may be one reason why hockey is not a draw on TV. For the main-action and crowd mics, one approach uses eight directional boundary mics on transparent plastic plates mounted on the inside of the glass that surrounds the rink. The mics are positioned on either end of the blue lines and at the end of the rink in the corners, on either side, to pick up the skating and impact sounds. They also pick up sufficient crowd sound due to the concentrated acoustics in enclosed arenas. There may be additional audio pickup from handheld shotgun mics or from the shotguns on handheld cameras. Wireless mics are also placed on one bar of each goal post to pick up action sounds from near the goal. A handheld shotgun may also be assigned to the penalty box. In the American Hockey League, permission is often given to put wireless mics on the goalies, players, and/or coaches. These mics and the penalty box mic are used for replay in case something interesting happens and to screen foul language. Mics (not shown) are embedded in the ice to pick up skating, puck, and stick sounds.

In mixing hockey audio, the board operator must be adept at following the play-by-play on the monitor and riding levels accordingly because hockey is so unpredictable. When an action is anticipated, such as a goal or a body slam against the boards, the operator will boost the level to enhance the sound of the play action or the crowd reaction.

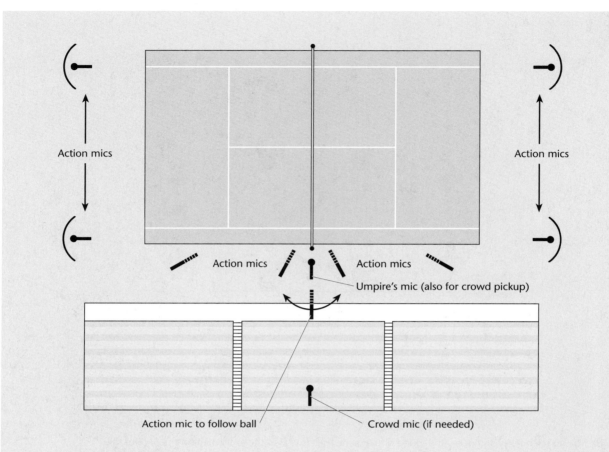

Action mics

Action mics

Action mics

Action mics

Umpire's mic (also for crowd pickup)

Action mic to follow ball

Crowd mic (if needed)

13-31 Miking tennis. In tennis sound is critical because the announcers do not talk when the ball is in play, and the crowd must be quiet. Microphones must therefore be strategically placed to pick up the court action. An omnidirectional mic is set up next to the umpire to hear his calls, the players talking to him, and the crowd sound. Two directional mics are positioned on either side of the net, pointing at the court, to pick up the sounds of the ball when it hits the net on a service, the ball hitting the strings of the tennis racket, and players' comments near midcourt. Directional mics are aimed at the service lines to pick up the whopping sound when the racket connects with the ball. A directional mic that follows the ball movement is positioned at midcourt. Parabolic mics placed behind each baseline pick up the string sound on the racket when the ball is hit deep and the players' grunts when they hit the ball. If the crowd mic at the umpire's location does not pick up enough crowd sound, another crowd mic is mounted from an overhang in the stands.

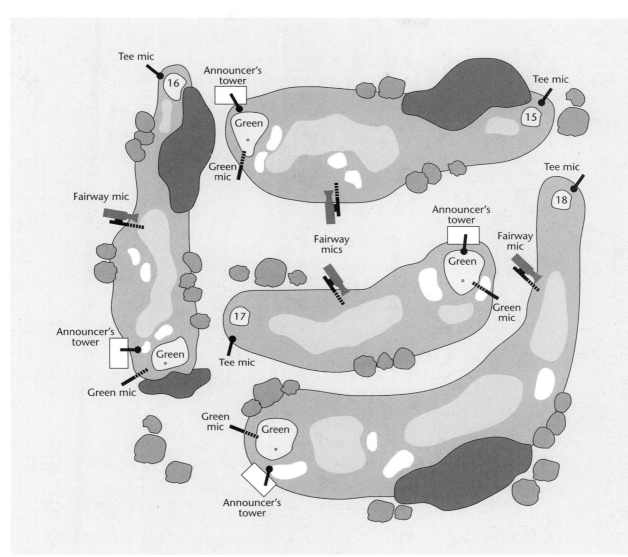

13-32 Miking golf. Omnidirectional or directional microphones are placed near the tees to pick up the sounds of the drive and the crowd. In the fairways directional mics, either handheld or mounted on mini cams, pick up fairway shots and conversation among golfers. At the greens directional mics pick up the sound of the putt and the crowd. Wireless mics are placed in the cup, with the transmitter aerial wrapped around the outside, to pick up the sound of the ball falling into the cup. At each hole is an announcer's tower with an omnidirectional mic outside to pick up crowd sound and general ambience, or the crowd sound pickup is through the mics already arrayed at the hole. Other wireless operators cover shots where balls are in difficult locations.

Recording and mixing golf presents a unique challenge in that while play at one hole is on the air, play at other holes is being recorded. This requires separate audio effects mixes for the play at each hole.

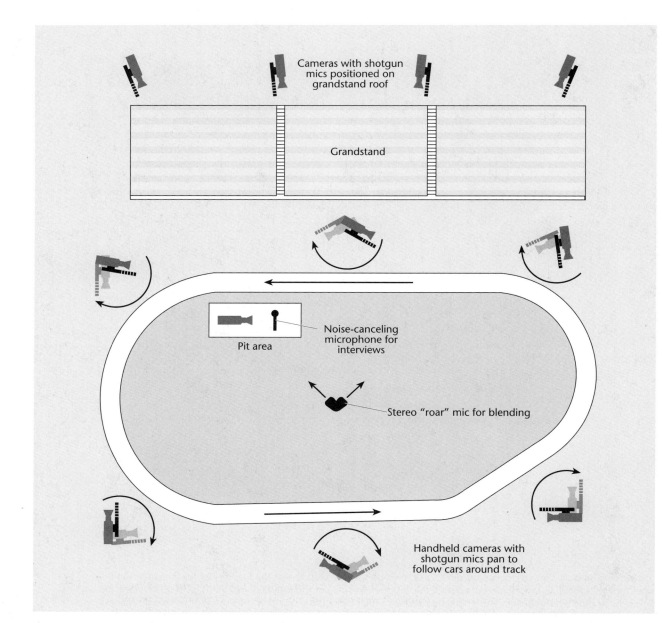

13-33 Miking auto racing. The main audio problem in auto racing is that it is essentially a one-sound sport—the cars as they careen around the track. Announcers' commentary and interviews break up the constancy of the car sounds, but the challenge is to vary the racing sounds to make them as interesting as possible. Handheld cameras with shotgun mics are positioned at strategic points on the racetrack—at the curves and the straightaways. The camera and the mics pick up the cars as they come toward the camera position and follow the cars as they race to the next camera position, where that camera picks up the action and the sound, and so on around the track. With the mics in these locations, the Doppler effect (see Chapter 15) of the pitch changes as the cars come toward the camera and move away from it. The shifting gears, the slowing down and the speeding up of the engines, the screeching brakes, and, unfortunately, the crashes—all vary the audio and help create sonic perspective. To provide a different perspective, one or more lavaliers are mounted in the cab of selected racecars. Additional pickups come from shotguns mounted on cameras positioned on the roof of the grandstand. A stereo "roar" mic is positioned in the infield of the racetrack and used in the overall mix for blending. Crowd sound is not the factor in auto racing that it is in other sports. Even when a microphone is placed in the stands, crowd reaction may not be audible above the engine roar. Due to the high levels of track noise, a noise-canceling microphone is usually employed for interviews in the pit area.

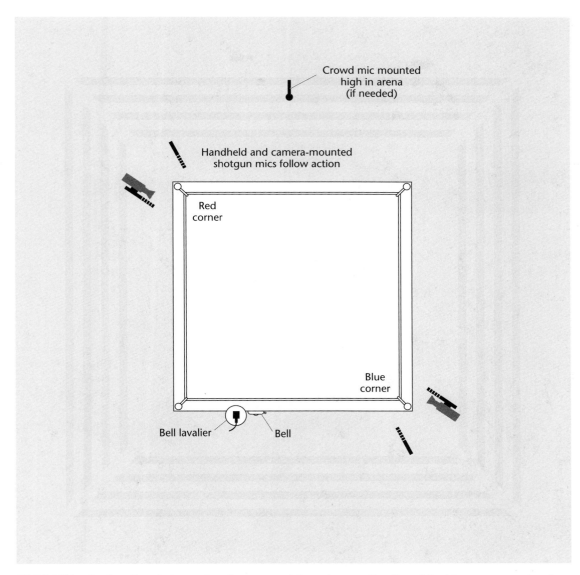

13-34 Miking boxing. Two shotgun microphones, one at the red corner, the other at the blue corner, are aimed into the ring to pick up the fight sounds. As the fighters move around the ring, the shotguns follow the action and are opened and closed (although not fully closed) as the fighters move closer to and farther from the mics. Shotgun mics on handheld cameras or on fishpoles in the red and blue corners are used between rounds to pick up the exchanges between the fighters and their handlers. Because fights usually take place indoors and the crowd is close to the ring, the shotgun mics are usually adequate to pick up crowd sound as well. If not, directional crowd mics that can also pick up ring action are spaced above the ring out of the cameras' sightlines. A lavalier picks up the sound of the bell. The ringside announcers almost always use headset mics for their commentary and handheld mics for interviews.

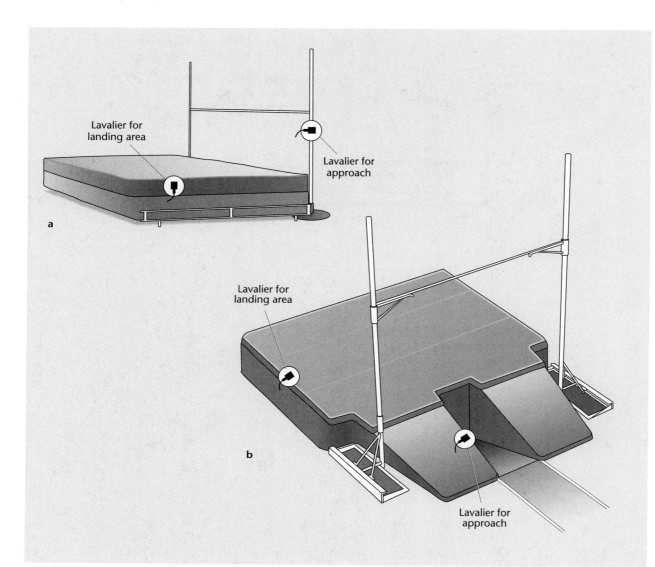

13-35 Miking track and field and gymnastics. Because the action takes place in various locations in the same venue and each event requires a different apparatus, producing audio for track and field and for gymnastics requires inventiveness in miking and coordination in mixing. To pick up the action sounds, place a mic anywhere you can put one. When action is moving from one point to another, as in the hurdles, mics should be spaced evenly on side stands between the starting and finish lines to pick up the sound oncoming and passing. With continuous events, such as hurdles and other types of racing, mics should be opened and closed as the action dictates; otherwise the sonic density will mask the audio due not only to the action sounds but also to the pickup of crowd sound. Music to accompany gymnastic routines is usually picked up by the action mics. Examples of selected track and field and gymnastic events are shown above and on the next page.

(a) High jump and (b) pole vault. Wireless lavaliers placed at the approach and the landing area pick up the sounds of the pole vault or jump, the landing, and any sounds the athlete makes. The mics are opened only for the action they cover. The approach mic opens for the approach and closes after the leap; and the landing mic, which is closed for the approach, opens after the leap. Of course, the mixer must coordinate the levels for a smooth transition.

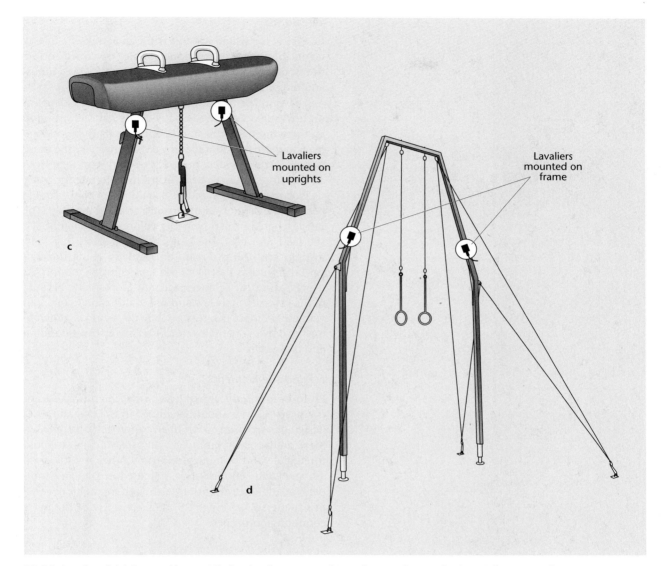

13-35 *(continued)* **(c) Pommel horse.** Wireless lavaliers mounted near the top of one or both uprights are usually sufficient to pick up the gymnast's sounds. Two mics are used to ensure that hits on the left and right sides of the pommel horse are heard, to reinforce the action sounds, or both. Mics mounted directly on the underside of the horse could produce a muffled sound because of its padding.

(d) Rings. Wireless lavaliers mounted on one or both sides of the frame pick up not only the action sounds of the gymnast but also any squeaking or metallic creaking sounds. Placing the mics between the middle and the top of the frame helps pick up the sounds of ring attachments. It is wise to place thin padding between the lavalier and the metal frame to prevent the mic from slipping or from being audibly jarred by the frame's movement.

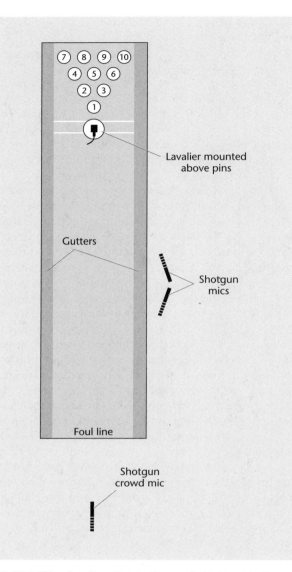

13-36 Miking bowling. Due to the usually high ambient levels in bowling alleys, directional microphones are the mics of choice. Either two shotguns or directional boundary mics are positioned at the side of the lane, one facing toward the foul line, the other facing toward the pins. This technique captures the sounds of the ball drop, the roll down the alley, and the pin strike. A lavalier may be mounted above the pin pit to reinforce the pin strike and the pin fall and, if wanted, the initial action of the pin setup mechanism. If the action mics are insufficient to deal with crowd sound, an additional mic, usually directional, is aimed toward the crowd from above and in front.

The bowlers may have wireless mics to pick up their chatter. The keys to selecting wireless mics, especially for bowlers, are to make sure that their pickups do not have low-end rumble, that the mics have sufficient headroom so the signal does not clip, and that they can handle the transient sounds.

The Bands

In events for which a band is present, mike it. In any venue microphones positioned to pick up crowd and action sounds are usually not adequate to pick up a robust and present band sound.

The number of mics and their positioning depends on how spread out the band is. If the band is sitting in and playing from the stands, it can usually be covered by a stereo pair. On a playing field, however, the band is spread more widely and may require coverage from an additional stereo pair or from the field mics or both.

Pickup from the stands is usually more concentrated because the band is stationary and grouped together. The music, therefore, can be better balanced in the mix. On the field, however, the band is more spread out—left-to-right and front-to-rear—and usually going through various routines that keep the musicians in motion. As it plays, musical balances become problematic because of the inverse square law and sound diffusion in open-air venues. These are two reasons why the sound of a marching band in an open-air venue is relatively thin-sounding and quavery.

Mixing the Elements

Philosophies vary about how crowd, action, and announcers' sounds should be mixed in the overall sound design of a sporting event. In any approach, the play-by-play and the color commentary must always be clear and intelligible and not encumbered by other sounds, such as crowd and action sounds, that are too loud and compete for audience attention. Although mixing is covered in Chapters 21 through 23, here are a few of the more common approaches:

- Using the *imaging concept*—focusing on the positioning of the various sonic elements

- Using the *immersion concept*—placing the listener-viewer in the venue

- Keeping crowd level lower during periods of inaction and increasing crowd sound during exciting plays to add to the drama of an event's natural pace

- Keeping crowd level constant throughout the broadcast to maintain interest

- Burying the announcers' voices in the crowd sound to make the announcers part of the event and to unify overall intensity

- Keeping the announcers' voices out in front of the crowd sound to avoid masking the play-by-play and the color commentary and to reduce listener fatigue engendered by too much sonic intensity over a long period; sometimes done by compressing crowd sound

- Compressing the sounds of the announcers, crowd, and action to control their dynamic ranges and to give each element more punch

- Compressing one or more sonic elements to create a layering effect

- "Producing" crowd sound (see below)

Just as audience reaction is often sweetened in game, quiz, and variety shows (see Chapter 12), it is also enhanced in sports broadcasts. Recordings of various crowd and fan reactions are archived before and during an event and mixed with live reactions to heighten the dynamics of the overall excitement. In doing this, however, the important caveat to remember is that the sweetening must sound realistic and not hokey.

Stereo Sound

As with stereo TV in general, producing stereo sports involves providing sonic spaciousness or depth while dealing with localization and stereo-to-mono compatibility (see Chapter 23). Of the three audio components involved—announcers, crowd, and action—the crowd and, depending on the sport, the action are usually the only stereo elements.

Announcers present the smallest problem. Because they are the primary source of information and are stationary during an event, it is natural that they be positioned in the center of the stereo image, although their voices may be fed through a stereo synthesizer or panned so that they sound more a part of the overall sonic setting instead of separate from it.

The crowd is miked and mixed in stereo. Primary crowd pickup comes from a main microphone array and assigned full left and right. The fan at home must feel that he or she is "sitting in one seat" and close to the action—not moving around with the shot. If additional crowd mics are used, they are for fill, not for emphasis to coincide with a shot.

Action sounds are handled in two ways: either straight down the middle or somewhat localized. Sound panned to the center gives an up-front feeling to coincide with the generally tighter shot it accompanies. Localized sounds are picked up by one mic and panned slightly to the left or right to coincide with their relative positions in the playing area. This means that the action mics must be directional and precisely aimed to make stereo imaging easier for the mixer. But even in ideal circumstances, trying to localize sound, especially moving sound, with shot changes is difficult. The mixer must constantly anticipate a director's shot change. Even if synchronization is achieved, camera angles may cut across the 180-degree axis, creating "reverse angle" audio.

In sports where movement from one end of the playing surface to the other or around a track is constant, as it is in basketball, hockey, and auto racing, the approach usually taken with stereo is to provide width to the aural imaging rather than movement. In fact, the *width-versus-movement approach* is generally taken in the stereo mix of most sports because, as noted earlier in this chapter, trying to deal with movement in many sports becomes disconcerting to the listener-viewer (see 13-37).

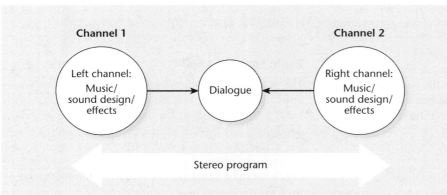

13-37 An approach to mixing stereo to help achieve width in imaging the various sound feeds.

Channel 1

Left channel:
Music/
sound design/
effects

Dialogue

Channel 2

Right channel:
Music/
sound design/
effects

Stereo program

13-38 Using a stereo simulator to facilitate the mix of mono and stereo feeds.

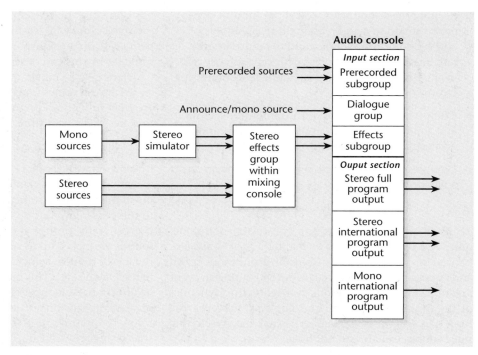

Another consideration in dealing with stereo is that some audio sources are monaural, and it is necessary to process them to help create seamless stereo imaging. To this end a stereo simulator is employed to facilitate the mix of mono and stereo feeds (see 13-38).

Surround Sound

Although producing surround sound for sporting events is more expensive and logistically involved, with the ever-increasing number of surround-sound television systems in home use it has become a regular part of most network sports telecasts.

The essential difference between stereo and surround sound in sportscasts is that it provides a greater sense of event attendance to the home viewer; it is more effective in creating the "seat in the arena" perspective. With stereo, crowd and effects sounds are in front of the viewer, imaged left to right, with the panning emphasis toward the sides of the stereo field. Surround sound puts the listener-viewer in the middle of the crowd. The announcers' sound still comes from the front-center, with maybe some slight left-to-right panning to open the space somewhat. The action sounds are pretty much handled as they would be in stereo. The key guideline in surround sound is the same as it is in stereo: avoid dislocation.

Figure 13-39 shows one example of audio coverage in surround sound (see also 13-26 caption).

As noted in Chapter 8, although the 5.1 surround-sound format has become standard for the time being, other surround-sound formats are in use. Sports broadcasts are being done in 6.1 by adding a rear-center surround channel (see 13-40). Among other things, this helps bring the front stereo portions to the rear channels without the problem of dealing with the differences in information, in the 5.1 format, between the left-, center-, and right-front loudspeakers and the left and right surround loudspeakers. Moreover, the 6.1 approach facilitates a better blend of the sonic elements so they are less speaker-identifiable.

Radio Sports Audio

The main difference between radio and TV sports audio, apart from the obvious absence of the visuals, is that radio is less dependent on the action sounds and more dependent on the announcers' word pictures. Because the playing area is not visible in radio, except for a few pronounced and recognizable game sounds like the crack of the bat in baseball, action sounds are more distracting than they are dynamic.

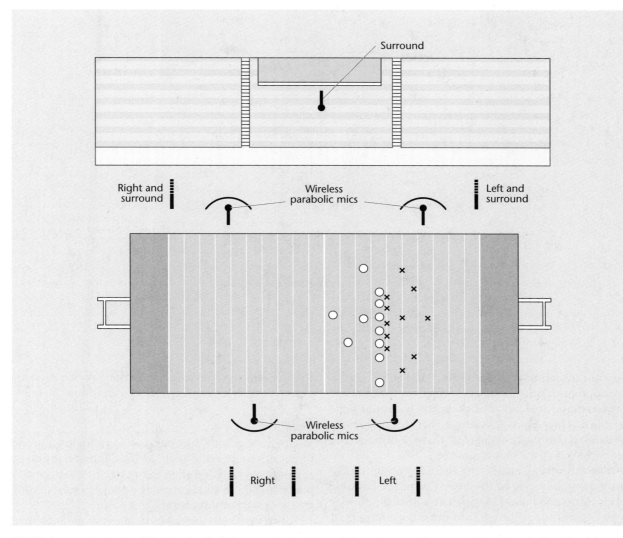

13-39 Surround-sound miking for football. For overall crowd sound, four shotgun mics are positioned on the far side of the field—across from the press box—spaced in pairs on the 20- and 40-yard lines for the main left and right pickups. The nearside shotgun mics are for more-immediate left and right crowd sound and, along with the directional mic at press box level, are fed into the surround channel. The wireless parabolic mics are used to capture field sounds.

Calling the Game

It is up to the announcers to create word pictures of the event—the sonic excitement being provided by their voices and the crowd sound. Good radio sportscasters add their own action descriptors when it is appropriate to do so, by describing the crushing board slam; piercing fast ball; slow fast ball traveling at stealth velocity; ball rattling around the rim; sky-high pop-up as a silo shot; first and goal at point-blank range to the end-zone, and so on.

Too often radio sportscasters call a game as if they were doing TV by just calling the play or only the results of the play instead of setting it up, with the color commentator filling in the space between calls. Except for the crowd sound, the broadcast is usually dull and vague. But these matters are the purview of the producer.

That said, an example from a radio broadcast of golf may make the point best. Of all the sports, few can be as difficult to call on radio as golf. Except for the ball

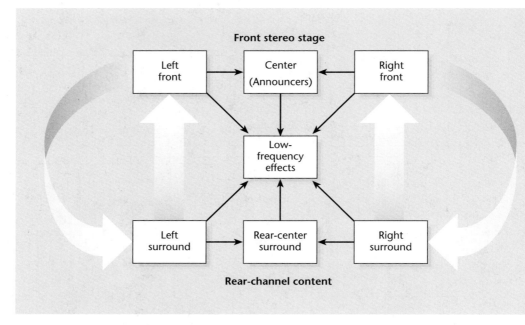

13-40 Content steering in 6.1 surround sound.

being hit, its landings in the fairway, the green, and in the cup, there is little else to call. Moreover, the intervals between these "actions" are considerable by typical game standards. Therefore it is essential that descriptions be substantive and vivid enough so that the listener can "see" as much of the play as possible.

"The right-hand rough. The ball's sitting up nicely. He's got a good angle to the hole. Cut in the backside of this thirteenth hole. 434-yard, Par-4. [Golfer] now set to play, sends the ball high into the air, working right to left. Lands 5 feet from the hole and pulls back 7 feet. What a nice shot for [golfer]! He's got 7 feet for birdie to get to 4-under. Right here at 13!"[3]

Compare that illustration to the type of call too frequently heard during, for example, football broadcasts: "Ball on the 40-yard line. Handoff to [name of running back]. He picks up three yards."

The call gives no information about the formation, defensive setup, which part of the line the back runs through, or how he is brought down. Clearly, not every play requires, nor may there be time for, all or most of

this information. The point is that play-by-play on radio should furnish what television provides—the "picture."

Miking

Miking sportscasters depends on what is logistically and physically comfortable and practical. In radio it usually comes down to either the headset mic or the desk mic: directional if the announcers' booth or the surrounding area is noisy; omnidirectional if it is not.

For crowd sound the variety of microphone arrays and techniques used in TV are also suitable for radio, although they usually do not have to be as elaborate. In some instances the crowd mics do double duty as action mics, particularly those positioned close to the playing area.

When handling crowd sound in relation to the announcers' sound, compression is often used to keep them sonically proportional. When the announcer is speaking, the compressor is set to automatically reduce the level of the crowd sound. When there are pauses in the commentary, crowd sound level is triggered to increase. Take care when setting compression ratios and thresholds. When they are not set correctly, the give-and-take of announcer and crowd sounds results in annoying rushes of increases and decreases in crowd sound level.

---

3. Donna Ditota, "Golf on Radio Is Unique Experience," *Syracuse Post Standard,* October 4, 2008.

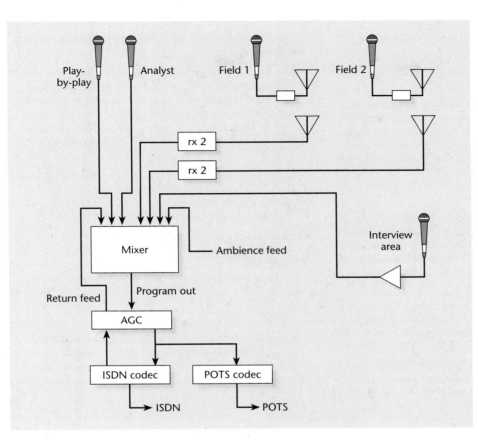

13-41 Signal flow of a sports program chain. With the exception of the radio announcers' microphones, the rest of the radio audio feed is taken from the TV audio.

When a radio and a TV sportscast are carried by the same network or by cooperating stations, the radio audio may take part or all of the effects feed—crowd and action sounds—from the TV sound, including the field mics used for interviewing (see 13-41).

▶ Producers go on-location to cover news and sports, to do a disc jockey program, to heighten realism in a drama, to add authenticity to a setting, or to provide surroundings that are difficult or impossible to reproduce in a studio.

▶ Live and live-to-recording field productions for radio and television can be grouped into two basic categories: electronic news gathering (ENG) and electronic field production (EFP). The main difference between ENG and EFP is that ENG covers news events whereas EFP is employed with the types of productions that take more time to plan and produce.

▶ Thanks to small, lightweight equipment—such as portable microphone mixers, consoles, handheld cameras, recorders, editors, high-quality headphones, mobile and cellular telephones, remote pickups, WiFi, WiMAX, and microwave transmission from a mobile unit—it is relatively easy to transmit from the field to the radio or TV station for recording or direct broadcast.

▶ When a story has immediacy, today's technology makes it possible to edit it in the field and transmit it to the newsroom server broadcast-ready. If more-elaborate production is required, the unedited files can be sent to the station for the necessary additional processing.

▶ Many broadcasters have guidelines for the submission of news reports from the field or from affiliates.

▶ Field production often presents the problem of background sounds' interfering with the intelligibility of the on-mic/on-camera reporters. In news, however, many producers believe that some sonic sense of locale is important to reports from the field.

▶ Mix-minus refers to a program sound feed without the portion supplied by the source that is receiving the feed.

▶ Recording background sound on a separate track is useful in postproduction to bridge transitions and cover awkward edits.

▶ When possible, preproduction planning is essential for most on-location broadcasting and recording. Preparation involves drafting a remote, or site, survey; confirming where the power will come from; deciding who will take care of the equipment, program, and administrative details; planning the interruptible foldback (IFB) system; and bringing to the production site the essential tools and backup supplies.

▶ As in studio productions, intercommunication systems are vital in the field, particularly because crew and facilities are usually more widely dispersed. Among the intercom systems used in the field are IFB, program sound receiver, paging, intercom, cellular telephone, and walkie-talkie.

▶ Three ways to record someone speaking from a podium are to: set up and use your own microphones, patch into the public-address (PA) system, or patch into a multiple pickup (also called a press bridge, press mult box, or presidential patch).

▶ When several speakers have to be miked, using an automatic microphone mixer may be more convenient than having one operator try to control all the mic levels.

▶ Miking sporting events requires sound pickup from the announcers, the crowd, the action, and sometimes the band and the players.

▶ In miking and mixing sporting events in stereo, the announcers are centered, action sounds are either centered or somewhat localized, and crowd sound is assigned full left and right. In surround sound announcers and action sounds are usually delegated as they are in stereo, with the crowd sound assigned to the left, right, and surround channels.

▶ In radio sports broadcasts, the announcers' word pictures, their action descriptors, the sonic enthusiasm in their voices, and the crowd sound—all contribute to the excitement and the drama of the event.

▶ Be careful of overly compressing crowd sound in relation to the announcers' sound so that the triggering of crowd sound when there are pauses in the announcers' commentary does not create excessive surges, up or down, in crowd level.

▶ Philosophies vary about how crowd, action, and announcers' sounds should be mixed in the overall sound design of a sporting event. In any approach, the announcers' play-by-play and commentary must always be intelligible and not encumbered by other sounds, such as crowd and action sounds, that are too loud and compete for audience attention.

14
Sound Design

Sound design is ongoing throughout the production process—in preproduction planning, during production, and in postproduction. In one respect it is a continuous process that "covers the spectrum from music on one end to dialogue at the other end with sound effects in between. The key to integrating it all is that the concept of sound design is to make sure these various elements work together and don't step on each other's toes."[1] But in another respect, it is more than plugging in dialogue, sound effects, and music. *Sound design* is the vision that harmonizes the various elements with the visual story by creating the overall sonic character of a production.

SOUND DESIGN AND THE SOUND DESIGNER

In terms of film and video, sound design is to producing the sound track what production design is to producing the picture. The production designer is responsible for the overall look of a production; the sound designer is responsible for the overall sound—both, of course, with the director's approval. Dialogue is entirely in the director's hands.

Responsibility for a sound design falls to a designated sound designer, who advises the audio team and, ordinarily, has a hands-on role during one or more stages of the sound track's production. The term *sound designer* was first used as a professional craft designation in theatrical film in 1979 when an academy award for sound design was

---

1. Walter Murch, "The Chase," *Music Behind the Scenes,* Bravo, August 18, 2002.

given to Walter Murch for *Apocalypse Now.* Over the years the term has been diluted to include just about anyone on the audio production team, particularly creators of sound effects and sound-effect editors, who has a hand in producing the audio. Using the preferred meaning, the **sound designer** is the one person responsible for creative control of the audio. It is the sound designer's function to put a coherent sonic stamp on the production—and the one member of the audio team who, like the production designer and the image editor, has the director's ear.

Regardless of whether there is a designated sound designer, all members of the audio team contribute creatively to the sound in a production. Hence the material in this chapter applies to sound design in general and the various components of audio in particular rather than to a specific role carried out by an individual member of the audio production team.

Whatever an audio team member's function (or anyone in sound production for that matter), there are two overriding qualifications: having the ability to listen perceptively and knowing how to effect what the audience is to perceive. Or, in the parlance of audio, having "ears."

"EARS"

For the audio professional, one fundamental requirement is having educated ears; that is, the ability to listen with careful discrimination to style, interpretation, nuance, and technical quality in evaluating the content, function, characteristics, and fidelity of a sound. (To have educated ears, however, it is essential to have healthy ears; see Chapter 1.)

Most day-to-day aural stimuli we take for granted if not actively tune out. We may pay attention to a particular song or follow a conversation, or some sound might catch our attention—an alarm, a barking dog, breaking glass—but most sound registers as little more than background to our comings and goings. To the person in audio, however, such a lack of awareness is a liability. An audio professional must be sensitive to all sound. Innate sensitivity to sound varies, and not everyone has the same perceptual acuity.

You can acquire certain skills, however, through training in audio and music courses. Ear-training resources also help (see Bibliography). Study the sounds of the environment—both natural and built. Listen to the **soundscape** with its myriad voices, textures, and rhythms. Go for a **listening walk** or a **soundwalk,** where you focus your attention on disciplined, active listening. Take advantage of the vast and rich resources from the audio worlds of film sound tracks, TV, radio, and music. When you don't listen, sound remains part of the landscape—it does not become part of your consciousness.

Developing an ear involves *discrimination,* the ability to shut out all sounds but the one you are listening to, to hear one sound among many. This is known as "putting your ear to it."

It can be argued that many sounds offer so little aesthetic satisfaction that they are not worth listening to. Many sounds even annoy, such as sirens, leaf blowers, blaring horns, music in an elevator, a loud TV from an adjacent apartment, and the sonic assault from sound systems in seemingly every public space—from airports to shopping malls to restaurants. It is enough to desensitize aural acuity and make it difficult to enjoy worthwhile sound. Hence it seems reasonable to conclude that listening should be selective. Such a conclusion might be appropriate for most people, but it does not apply to the audio professional.

Listening

Training the ear takes time. It comes with years of perceptive listening. You begin by learning *how* to listen, paying attention to sound wherever and whenever it occurs: in traffic, in conversation, at sporting events, at a concert or movie, or when dining, walking, showering, getting dressed, watching television, or just lying in bed. Remember, exposure to sound goes on during every waking hour and even during sleep.

You learn what to listen for by studying a sound both in context and by itself. That means acquiring the ability to listen analytically and critically. "Analytical listening is the evaluation of the content and function of the sound.… Critical listening is the evaluation of the characteristics of the sound itself [its technical integrity]."[2]

Analytical Listening

Words may denote meaning in speech, but sound often defines it. On paper the meaning of the phrase *Have a nice day* is clear, but the meaning changes when the stress on certain words changes or when the words are spoken with a lilt; in a monotone, whine, or drawl; or by an old man, a young woman, or a child. Sound in speech conveys such qualities as confidence, fear, anxiety, arrogance,

---

2. William Moylan, *Understanding and Crafting the Mix: The Art of Recording,* 2nd ed. (Boston: Focal Press, 2007), p. 90.

humor, and concern. In an interview a person may appear confident, but if there are unnatural pauses between words or phrases, or if there is a parched quality to the speech, the person's sound will belie the appearance. In dialogue a charming, good-looking character conveys a sense of menace when his words are delivered in a harsh and guttural voice. A character whose voice rises at the end of sentences conveys vulnerability, regardless of what is being said. *Analytical listening* is the evaluation of such sound, the interpretation of the nuances and the connotations of the sound quality in addition to—or in spite of—the words being spoken.

Take the sound of a dog barking. A bark is generally harsh and abrupt. But barks vary widely in pitch, loudness, rhythm, and context. For example, low-pitched barks last longer than high-pitched barks, and some barks begin with a gurgling-type sound rather than with a sharp attack. Within a bark may be a whine, yelp, growl, howl, or boom. Also some barks have regular rhythms, whereas others shift beats and produce irregular tempos. Each of these sounds tells you something about the dog and the situation.

The sound a chick makes while hatching may seem obvious: gradual cracking of the eggshell and then peeping. But listening to a hatching reveals more: the chick peeps inside the egg before cracking it; the peeping is muffled. The shell begins cracking slowly with short, tentative splitting sounds that increase in force. With the increase in force and slightly longer cracking sounds, peeping increases in clarity, loudness, and rapidity. The final cracks of the shell sound more like crunches as the chick stumbles into the world. Once the chick is out of the shell, the peeping is unmuffled, steady, and strong but not quite so loud as it was just before emergence.

In television, sound varies from program to program, even of the same genre. In sitcoms laughter may come from a live audience or a recorded laugh track. It may be more robust, or less, with a preponderance of elderly female or young male voices. In football there are different approaches to mixing the announcers' sounds with crowd sounds (see Chapter 13). Some audio operators like to keep the level of crowd sounds and the announcers' voices nearly the same to maintain excitement. Others prefer to keep the level of crowd noise relatively low so that, when the action justifies it, the level can be increased to accent the excitement.

Music presents the greatest challenge in listening. Its sonic combinations are infinite, and its aesthetic value fulfills basic human needs. Musical taste is intensely personal; two people listening to the same music may respond in two different ways, both valid.

Take two recordings of, say, Carl Orff's *Carmina Burana.* Keep constant as many factors as possible, such as the quality of the digital discs, the recording format (stereo, surround sound, digital), the audio system, and the room. You may be surprised at the differences in sound and interpretation. You may prefer the sound in one recording and the interpretation in another. That does not mean that one recording is necessarily better; it means that, based on your perceptions, one is preferable to another for certain reasons. Someone else may disagree.

Do not listen to music based only on taste and mood. Go beyond recreational listening. Disengage your preferences; explore all types of music, whether or not you like and enjoy it.

Critical Listening

In listening to those two recordings of Orff's *Carmina Burana,* you may prefer the sound of one recording to the other because of its technical quality: the clarity of detail, the inflection of a particular range of frequencies, the balance of orchestral instruments and chorus, or the spatial imaging. Or in listening to a song, you may decide that it is darker sounding than it should be because the bass drum is muddying the mix, there is a buildup of too many frequencies in the low midrange, or there is an absence of color in the treble range.

Critical listening is the evaluation of the characteristics of the sound itself: when the vocalist enters a bit early or late to counterpoint the lyric against the accompaniment; when a sound effect has too much wheeze and not enough whine; music underscoring that fades up at the wrong time, masking dialogue; the polyrhythms that play off one another to enhance the rhythmic excitement of an action scene; the annoying surges in crowd sound during pauses in a sportscaster's game call because the ratio and/or threshold settings on a compressor are set too severely; the sonic differences between an acoustic bass and an electric one or acoustic drums and a drum machine; the unique sound of a Zildjian® cymbal or a Telecaster® electric guitar; a concert grand piano with a percussive tonality or a tonality that "sings"; the musicians' technical proficiency; the acoustics that enrich sound or dull it; stylistic differences among artists; or the sonic difference between analog and digital sound, between 16-bit and 24-bit mastered CDs, between 48 kHz and 96 kHz sampling rates, and between a CD and a DVD-Audio.

Critical ears hear differences in sound between microphones, changes in tone color from different microphone placements, coloration of a microphone preamplifier, the difference between +3 dB at 1,000 Hz and +6 dB at 3,000 Hz, between preamplifier overload and loudspeaker distortion, subtle phase cancellation, and the right frequency or frequency range to fix an equalization problem.

This is not to overwhelm you with detail or suggest that serious listening is entirely clinical. Feeling the sound and sensing what works are also critical to active analysis as is being aware of the relationship between your taste and mood and your response to sound.

Reading reviews also provides insight into why critics think a work does or doesn't succeed. In fact, it is equally instructive to know why a recording or film sound track does not work as it is to know why it does, perhaps even more so.

Develop a sound vocabulary. Sound is nonverbal; it is difficult to describe. Coining words that are descriptive of the effect you are trying to achieve not only hones your own perceptions but also provides others on the sound team with an indication of what you are going for. There are hundreds of such terms used for sound effects, such as *twung, squidge, whibble, wubba, boink, kabong, zuzz,* and so on. In music there are terms such as *honky, mellow, warm, bright, hollow, and zitsy* (also see Chapter 22). Or, consider scientists who have come up with a variety of descriptors for the vocalizations of seals, including *chi-chi-chi, chirrup, eeyoo, chug, what-chunk, chnk-chnk, too-loo, rrwhmp* and *seitz.*[3] Such terms are inexact, of course, and need objective association to make them clear to others, but they do have a sonic texture and, in some examples, a pointed "visual" impact by themselves.

Take an audio recorder with you wherever you go. Record sounds to study and to discover their sonic characteristics. Manipulate them in the studio for their potential to be processed into other sounds. Sound designers have been doing this for years so they do not miss the opportunity of recording new and unusual sounds to add to their sound-effect libraries. They bring their recorders to toy stores to take advantage of the rich array of sounds that toys generate; on vacations to document that unique sound of a wave that does not crash but laps against the shore; into bathrooms to capture the swirling, sucking sound of water whirlpooling down a bathtub drain; and around a neighborhood, marketplace, or public square to capture its particular sonic personality.

Because response to sound is personal, standards and guidelines are difficult to establish, so listening is the key to improving aural discrimination. The ear is capable of constant improvement in its ability to analyze sound. As your aural sensitivity improves, so will your level of auditory achievement. "Listening with the ear is inseparable from listening with the mind."[4]

ELEMENTS OF SOUND STRUCTURE AND THEIR EFFECTS ON PERCEPTION

Creating a sound design involves sound effects (covered in Chapter 15) and music underscoring (Chapter 16). Paradoxically, silence (Chapter 15) and the ability of sound to evoke a picture in the mind's eye may be considered two other domains. This may not seem to be an impressive arsenal, especially when compared with the number of elements available in pictorial design—color, light and shadow, composition, scenery, costumes, physical dimension, focal length, camera angle, depth of field, and so on. Few though these aural elements are, they are powerful agents in creating, supplementing, and complementing cognitive and affective information.

All sound—speech, sound effects, and music—is made up of the same basic elements: pitch, loudness, timbre, tempo, rhythm, attack, duration, and decay. During audio production everyone involved is dealing with these elements, consciously or subconsciously, and assessing their effects on perception. Because each element contains certain characteristics that affect our response to sound, understanding those effects is fundamental to sound design.

Pitch refers to the highness or lowness of a sound. High-pitched sound often suggests something delicate, bright, or elevated; low-pitched sound may indicate something sinister, strong, or peaceful.

Loudness describes the relative volume of sound—how loud or soft it is. Loud sound can suggest closeness, strength, or importance; soft sound may convey distance, weakness, or tranquility.

Timbre is the characteristic tonal quality of a sound. It not only identifies a sound source—reedy, brassy, tympanic—but also sonic qualities such as rich, thin,

3. Jeanette Thomas and Valerian Kuechle, "Quantitative Analysis of Weddell Seal *(Leptonychotes weddelli)* Underwater Vocalizations at McMurdo Sound, Antarctica," *Journal of the Acoustical Society of America,* vol. 72, no. 6 (1982), pp. 1730–38.

4. Michel Chion, *Audio-Vision: Sound on Screen,* trans. and ed. Claudia Gorbman (New York: Columbia University Press, 1994), p. 33.

edgy, or metallic. Reedy tonal qualities produced by a clarinet or an oboe, for example, can suggest something wistful, lonely, or sweet. A brassy sound can imply something cold, harsh, fierce, bitter, forceful, martial, or big. A tympanic or percussive sound can convey drama, significance, or power.

Tempo refers to the speed of a sound. Fast tempos agitate, excite, or accelerate; slow tempos may suggest monotony, dignity, or control.

Rhythm relates to a sonic time pattern. It may be simple, constant, complex, or changing. A simple rhythm can convey deliberateness, regularity, or lack of complication. A constant rhythm can imply dullness, depression, or uniformity. Rhythmic complexity suggests intricacy or elaborateness. Changing rhythms can create a sense of uncertainty, vigor, or the erratic.

Attack—the way a sound begins—can be hard, soft, crisp, or gradual. Hard or crisp attacks can suggest sharpness, excitement, or danger. Soft or gradual attacks can imply something gentle, muted, or blasé.

Duration refers to how long a sound lasts. Sound short in duration can convey restlessness, nervousness, or excitation; more-sustained sounds can create a sense of peace, persistence, or fatigue.

Decay—how fast a sound fades from a certain loudness—can be quick, gradual, or slow. Quick decays can create a sense of confinement, closeness, or definiteness; slow decays can convey distance, smoothness, or uncertainty.

Other aspects of sound, such as changing pitch, changing loudness, and acoustic interactions, also affect response. Of course, these elements are not heard individually but in combination.

Someone speaking in a loud, high-pitched voice at a rapid rate conveys excitement, whatever meaning the words may have. Lowering pitch, reducing loudness, and slowing tempo may also convey excitement, but this combination of sounds suggests something more profound and deeply felt. Words spoken at a deliberate tempo in a reverberant—that is, acoustically live—room may suggest a weightier content than those same words spoken in an acoustically drier environment.

These same factors can be applied to music and sounds. A trumpet or violin played loudly and rapidly at a high pitch could also suggest excitement, agitation, or gaiety—perhaps agitation in drier acoustics and gaiety in livelier acoustics.

Striking a wooden door or a metal barrel loudly and rapidly can also suggest agitation or gaiety. Again,

lowering pitch, reducing loudness, and slowing tempo change the response to something more serious, whether the sound source is a trumpet, violin, wooden door, or metal barrel.

That these characteristics are elemental in sonic structure is not to suggest that sound design is prescriptive or developed by applying formulas; the basic components of sound structure do not occur separately but together in myriad forms. Rather, it is to introduce and define the building blocks of sound from which the sound designer shapes aural structure and meaning.

Sound designer Randy Thom commented that, for the filmmaker, "Sound, musical and otherwise, has value when it is part of a continuum, when it changes over time, has dynamics, and resonates with other sound and with other sensory experiences."[5] In thinking about the character of a sound, the key is to ask yourself: *Is it interesting? Is it engaging? Does it do any good?*

THE VISUAL EAR

For more than four decades, the sounds of radio drama created pictures in the audience's "theater of the mind" (a characterization coined by poet Stephen Vincent Benét). Understood in the context of synesthesia, this is not so unusual a reaction. *Synesthesia* is the phenomenon whereby a sensory stimulus applied in one modality causes a response in another. For example, hearing a particular sound creates a distinct mental image or seeing a certain color mentally triggers a specific sound. (There are other synesthetic reactions not relevant to this discussion, such as a certain smell stimulating the mental image of a particular color, or a certain sound stimulating a specific taste.) For our purpose the synesthetic phenomenon demonstrates that *the ear sees and the eye hears.*

The implications of the power of sound to stimulate visual images is another formidable consideration in sound design. Among other things, it allows expanding the screen's dimensions. Sound is not bound by screen size as picture is. Off-screen sounds can evoke additional images to what is seen on-screen, such as atmosphere, environment, and action, especially with surround sound. Even on-screen sound can add greater visual dimension to a shot. The on-screen shot shows a man sitting in a chair being questioned, but in the off-screen audio heavy footsteps shuffle by the interrogation room, people are

---

5. Randy Thom, *Designing a Movie for Sound,* Filmsound.org, 1999; *www.filmsound.org/articles/designing_for_sound.htm.*

heard screaming, and a volley of distant gunshots rings out (see also "Strategies in Designing Sound" later in this chapter).

FUNCTIONS OF SOUND IN RELATION TO PICTURE

When picture is present, the sound/picture relationship creates certain dynamics that affect overall meaning. As essential as sound is, in relation to picture its "great power is conditional. It places the image in an emotional and physical context, helping us to decide how to take the image and how it integrates itself into everything else."[6] The sound/picture relationship is not a contest of superiority. It is a symbiotic relationship; they are two different "organisms" that are mutually beneficial to the whole. In general, there are five basic relationships: sound parallels picture, sound defines picture, picture defines sound, sound and picture define effect, and sound counterpoints picture.

Sound Parallels Picture

When sound parallels picture, neither the aural nor the visual element is dominant. This function of audio in relation to picture may be the best known because it is often misunderstood to be sound's *only* function. In other words, what you see is what you hear. A character drops a glass, and you hear it. A jazz combo plays in a bar, and you hear the music. On-screen a raging fire is consuming a building, and in the sound track are the sounds of metal warping, pipes creaking, puffy explosive whomps, and the roaring crackle of the fire itself.

This sound/picture relationship should not be dismissed as unworthy just because it is familiar and expected; not all shots require sonic augmentation.

Sound Defines Picture

When sound defines picture, audio not only is dominant but also determines the point of view—the subjective meaning of the image(s). Take a scene in which prison guards are standing battle-ready in front of a cellblock. A sound track consisting of crashing, breaking, yelling sounds suggests a prison riot and casts the guards as "good guys," as protectors of law and order. If the same scene were accompanied by the song "Freedom," the

music then casts the prisoners sympathetically and the guards as their oppressors. The same scene augmented by a dissonant, distorted rendering of "The Star-Spangled Banner" not only conveys the idea of the guards as oppressors but also adds an element of irony.

Consider a picture showing a man apologizing to a woman for his many wrongs. Her look is stern and unforgiving. The music underscoring the scene is gentle and sympathetic, indicating her true feelings. In the same scene, if the music were light and farcical, both his past wrongs and his pleading would be conveyed as not very serious. Change the music to dissonant and derisive sound, and the woman's stern, unforgiving look becomes nasty and gloating.

Picture Defines Sound

Picture helps define sound by calling attention to particular actions or images. In a scene where a person walks down a city street with traffic sounds in the background, cutting to close-ups of the traffic increases the impact of the sounds. The sound of metal wheels on a horse-drawn wagon clattering down a cobblestone street is intensified all the more when the picture changes from a medium shot of the carriage to a close-up of one of the wheels.

Sound and Picture Define Effect

When sound and picture define effect, the aural and visual elements are different yet complementary. Together they create an impact that neither could alone. Take the obvious example of a wave building and then breaking on a beach, accompanied by the swelling and crashing sounds. Separately, neither sound nor picture conveys the overall impact of the effect. Together they do. Neither sound nor picture is dominant, and although they are parallel they are reinforcing each other to produce a cumulative effect. Another example would be an elderly man sitting on a park bench, watching a mother playing with her child, lovers walking hand-in-hand, and teenagers playing touch football, accompanied by a music track that evokes a feeling first of pleasure, then of loneliness, and finally of futility. Sound and picture are complementary, with both contributing equally to an effect that would not be possible if one element were dominant or absent.

Sound Counterpoints Picture

When sound counterpoints picture, both contain unrelated elements that together create an effect or a mean-

---

6. Kevin Hilton, "Walter Murch: The Sound Film Man," *Studio Sound,* May 1998, p. 77.

ing not suggested by either sound or picture alone—a *tertium quid*. For example, the audio conveys the sounds of different groups of happy, laughing people, while the picture shows various shots of pollution. The audio/video counterpoint suggests an insensitive, self-indulgent society. Or consider the shot of an empty hospital bed, with the music evoking a sense of unexpected triumph. The audio/video counterpoint creates the idea that whoever had been in the bed is now, by some miracle, recovered. Change the music to sound spiritual and ascending, and the person who had been in the bed will have died and "gone to heaven."

STRATEGIES IN DESIGNING SOUND

Sound influences how we react to picture. Try watching television or a film first with the sound off and then with the sound but without the picture. Usually, you will find that more information comes from the sound than from the images. Two different sound tracks for the same picture will produce two different meanings. In a very real sense, creating a sound design is often tantamount to defining a production's conceptual and emotional intent.

There is no set procedure for designing sound. At the outset the most important thing to do is study the script and analyze the auditory requirements line by line to determine the overall sonic approach to various scenes, for an entire work, or both. When there is a director, of course it is necessary to consult. There is no right or wrong method in this type of creative decision-making. For the director or sound designer, or both, decisions are often made on the intuitive basis of what feels best—of what "works" in serving the aesthetic intent of the whole. This is not to suggest that sound design is simply "touchy-feely." Reasoned bases should underlie determinations.

Script Analysis

Script analysis involves two things: determining the overall sound design to various scenes or to an entire work and *spotting*—deciding on the placement of sound effects and music (see "Spotting" in Chapters 15 and 16).

In deciding on a sound design, the overriding questions are: How is the audience to think or feel about a particular story, scene, character, action, or environment? And from what point of view? Moreover, is the sound design to be carried out mainly in the sound effects, the music, or both?

Here are some examples:

■ In a story about a reclusive, paranoid, unsuccessful writer, his environment, where there should be various sounds of life and living things, has only a few sounds, and those are spare, disjointed, reverberant, and mechanical.

■ In a documentary about tango dance styles, tango music is woven throughout the scenes of the story—from a dance hall to street scenes in Buenos Aires.

■ In a story about the Amish, who eschew synthetic, manufactured products, backgrounds and ambiences are devoid of any sounds that would be generated by such items.

■ In a story about a completely self-involved person, a lack of background sounds wherever he is, regardless of the locale, underscores his psychic isolation.

■ In a story that takes place in the 1930s, using audio equipment from that time to produce authentic effects and music tracks sonically frames the story in that period.

■ In a story set in Elizabethan England, using musical instruments and styles from that period in the underscoring adds to the story's authenticity.

■ In a scene showing a raging typhoon at sea, designing the sonic effect of a ship's being lashed by howling winds, masts and rigging snapping and straining, waves crashing on deck, the vessel heaving and groaning intensifies the scene.

■ In a scene taking place on a neighborhood street on the hottest day of the year, the ambience is dense and the sounds of sparse traffic, people strolling, and children playing halfheartedly are muted and slowed slightly.

■ In a scene attempting to provide the emotion of being in a vast, empty desert that is sterile and lifeless and where there is little sound, making a sonic fabric from insect-like sounds, such as faint clicking and scratching noises, and grains of sand rubbing against one another conveys a palpable sense of place.[7]

■ In a scene about building a car, tying the rhythm of the machines to the rhythm of the music underscoring creates a unifying gestalt.

---

7. From Michael Ondaatje, *The Conversations: Walter Murch and the Art of Editing Film* (New York: Alfred A. Knopf, 2002), p. 118.

■ In a jail scene, to convey the hard, tough, cold world of the prison, use the sound of iron doors closing with a metallic scrape and slamming shut with a sharp report; the hard sound of heels on concrete when walking; the hollow, reverberant, oppressive ambience; and orders being barked in harsh monotones.

■ In tight shots of a couple arguing as their marriage is falling apart, the ambience (air) is taken out of the sound track to convey the claustrophobic relationship as its life is being squeezed out.

■ In a scene meant to convey the sensory assault of information overload and the inundation of communication devices, the sound design is produced with layers of audio that include primary and secondary dialogue coming from different locations in a room, with some people talking on cell phones, a nearby television blaring the news, an answering machine playing back a message to vote for a particular candidate, and a radio in the next room hawking a commercial.

■ In a social gathering of friends meant to depict the characters' insincerity and emotional detachment from one another, their dialogue is reproduced more through a conversational hubbub than through understandable speech. Voices can be understood without words; it's not what is being said but how the voices are saying it that communicates.

■ In a scene creating the point-of-view (POV) transitions of a sightless person, the sonic environment changes as the camera shots and angles change so that what is seen is not only heard but magnified in sharpness and detail.

■ In a drama meant to have the feel of a documentary, the sounds are kept focused and austere and do not include all the sounds that would normally be heard if the approach to the design were typical. This helps prevent distraction and focuses concentration on what is being said and done on-screen.

■ In a harrowing war scene, one character is used as a focal point. To create the POV of his taking psychological refuge from it all, he witnesses all the mayhem of the battle but hears the weaponry, explosions, and screams of the wounded muffled and at a distance. Another approach is to underscore the entire action with gentle, deliberate, melodic, harmonious music to create a counterpoint between picture and sound.

■ In a story about love and lust, passion and jealousy, tragedy and betrayal, involving characters whose mutual interest is opera, arias whose lyrics express those emotions and conditions are used for the underscoring. Such an approach to sound design can be taken with any genre of music so long as it is consistent with the story and the characterizations.

Influence of Sound Design on Meaning

The following are two examples of how sound design can affect the meaning of the picture. For the first example, let's use one simple shot:

FADE IN

INTERIOR. BEDROOM. NIGHT. A LITTLE GIRL IS LYING ON A BED LOOKING AT THE CEILING. A SHAFT OF MOONLIGHT COMES IN THROUGH AN OPEN WINDOW ILLUMINATING ONLY PART OF HER FACE. THE CAMERA SLOWLY ZOOMS IN.

Clearly, the script's story and the director's choices would govern the sound design for this shot. But the intent of this example is to demonstrate sound's significant influence on picture. Consider the shot with the following sound patterns and how each pattern influences its meaning and feel.

■ The thrum of an air conditioner and the polyrhythmic din of insects

■ Gentle breaking of waves and a distant foghorn

■ The sounds of conversation and revelry coming from another room

■ The sounds of a man and a woman arguing in an adjacent room and a sudden crash

■ The whine of air raid sirens, the rumble of airplanes, and the dull thudding of distant bombs

■ The girl breathing, humming softly—almost imperceptibly—to herself

■ A single dog howling, building to a scattered chorus of baying hounds in the distance

■ The creaking of floorboards and the sound of a door latch being opened

■ The distant sounds of a playground with children laughing and singing

■ Street traffic, the occasional car horn, and the booming bass of music from a passing car

These examples have other thematic possibilities, of course. Instead of using organic sounds, nonorganic sounds processed electronically could create different textures, moods, and environments. Nonorganic sounds are less realistic and have an otherworldly detachment; they tend to make a sound track less emotional. Conversely, organic sounds are more realistic and tend to make a sound track more emotional.

Now consider what underscoring does to the meaning of each of the previous examples, with or without the sound effects. With music that is, say, celestial, mysterious, sinister, playful, comedic, romantic, melancholy, blissful, animated, and threatening, notice how the idea and the feel of each shot changes yet again.

For the second example, let's use this short scene: Mike and Paula, a couple in their midtwenties, are on the third day of a camping trip; they are emerging from dense woods into a wide clearing.

FADE IN

1. EXTERIOR, WOODS—LATE AFTERNOON ON A SUMMER DAY. MIKE AND PAULA HAVE BEEN BACKPACKING AND ARE EMERGING FROM DENSE UNDERBRUSH INTO A CLEARING.

2. MIKE STOPS AT THE EDGE OF THE CLEARING TO LOOK AROUND.

   MIKE: Wow! This looks like a perfect place to camp for the night.

3. PAULA, FOLLOWING FROM THE UNDERBRUSH, STANDS NEXT TO MIKE.

   PAULA: It sure is. [BEAT] Seems kind of unusual though, doesn't it?

   MIKE: What?

   PAULA: To have such a large clearing with no trees or plants in the middle of such dense woods. We've been hiking for almost two days and have barely seen a trail. Now all of a sudden, this. I mean, look at how well manicured it is. Almost as if someone's been caring for it.

4. MIKE TURNS TO PAULA AND SMILES. HE WALKS FARTHER INTO THE CLEARING, REMOVES HIS BACKPACK, AND DROPS IT TO THE GROUND.

   MIKE: Are you complaining? For the first time in two days we can pitch the tent and not have to sleep in the woods on dead leaves—to say nothing of the cozier advantages.

5. PAULA WALKS TO MIKE AND THEY KISS. SUDDENLY, A HOWL SOUNDS IN THE DISTANCE.

   MIKE: What was that?!

   PAULA: I don't know! Never heard anything like it before!

6. THEY LOOK AROUND SLOWLY, STARING INTO THE WOODS.

   PAULA: *Brrr.* [BEAT] I don't know whether I'm frightened or just getting chilly.

   MIKE: It's the wind. Starting to blow up a bit. [LAUGHS NERVOUSLY] That's all we need—wind, then thunder and lightning. The only thing missing is the dark castle on the hill.

7. AS MIKE SAYS THE LAST LINE, THUNDER SOUNDS IN THE DISTANCE.

This scene is brief, ordinary, and uncomplicated, yet its many sound cues can be handled in a number of ways to enliven it and give it impact. Let's explore a few possible approaches to the sound design to convey some idea of the creative possibilities.

The scene opens in woods with dense underbrush in the late afternoon of a summer day. Among the elements to consider are the sounds coming from the woods and the sounds of walking through woods and on underbrush—whether they will be natural and benign or unnatural and foreboding.

One function that sound performs is to create an unseen environment. Woods exude a close atmosphere, a thickness of air that should be present in the sound. Woods are filled with sounds in summer: birds twittering, insects buzzing, perhaps frogs croaking and, at night, an owl hooting or crickets chirping. By adding such sounds to the audio track, it is possible to picture the woods and provide a sense of density without actually showing it.

In this case, walking through woods and the underbrush requires a few different sounds: clothes scraping against branches, the crunch and the crackle of stepping on twigs or dry leaves, two pairs of footsteps—one lighter than the other—and, perhaps, increased rates of breathing or panting. The weight, rhythm, and sharpness of the sounds can detail the amount of underbrush and the characters' level of fatigue.

If the purpose of these effects is to provide a contextual sonic complement to the picture, they should sound natural. If they are to suggest the frightening experience to come, they should be unnatural in some way, taking on a narrative function.

Any number of narrative approaches might work. The animal sounds could be edged, harsh, or screechy. Their rhythms could be chattering and nervous. The buzzing could increase or decrease in loudness, as opposed to a more natural steady drone, to reflect a sense of impending attack. The animal sounds could take on a nonorganic, not-of-this-world quality. Or there could be silence—perhaps the most unnatural and ominous sound effect of all.

The footsteps could sound bigger than life, setting the stage for the theme of Man, the intruder; or they could sound smaller to convey the characters' vulnerability. The snap of the branches could sound more like a whip, the crackle and the crunch of the twigs and the leaves underfoot like bones breaking or squooshy like the crushing of an insect—sonic foretelling of events to come.

Emergence from the underbrush requires a change in ambience, footsteps, and animal sounds (assuming they were present during the previous scene). The change from the closed-in woods to the large expanse of the clearing would be accompanied by a more open-sounding ambience. The sound of the footsteps would have to reflect the difference between the dry leaves and the firmer but cushioned meadow. The animal sounds may not be so intense, underscoring the difference between being in the woods and in the clearing. They may also sound more distant to further emphasize the change.

When Mike removes his backpack, it calls for the scrape of the straps on his shirt, maybe a grunt of relief, a sigh of satisfaction, or a slight "ahh" of anticipated pleasure. There are a few possibilities for the sound of the backpack hitting the ground: a bigger-than-life thud to emphasize its weight; a metallic thud to give a sense of what is inside; a jangly crash to sharply punctuate the quieter, open ambience, to provide a sense of what is in the backpack, and perhaps to foretell the jarring events to come.

Sonically, the kiss could be used to set the stage for the first howl. Before the kiss, background sound could diminish to silence, then subtly become more intense, climaxing with the howl; or the background sound could change, again subtly, from natural to unnatural.

The howl suggests a number of possibilities, not only as a sound but also as a narrative expression. Of course, any determination about it has to be made within the context of the story line. Let's assume the howl is from a creature—half man, half beast—who is looking for revenge after being severely wounded by hunters. The howl should convey these facts. It should sound like a wail to establish the pain but be guttural enough to project the idea of a dangerous animal. The wail could embody human characteristics and vacillate expressively to convey both a sense of pain and a cry for help. The guttural edge would also provide a counterpoint to the wail by sounding angry and menacing.

A nonorganic approach could be taken using electronically generated sounds. This approach creates an alien creature, perhaps changing the half-man part to something more fantastic. In any case, not only the condition but also the personality of the creature would be conveyed by the sound.

The wind sound could be designed to convey a number of moods and conditions: mysterious, gloomy, empty, gentle, stormy, cold, and so on. As its frequency increases, wind becomes more active and turbulent.

In this scenario Paula says *"Brrr,"* so the wind should be pitched high enough to convey chill; because it has just come up, it should have some low-end sound as well to convey mystery or danger. A gradually increasing shrillness or whistle would suggest the impending storm.

Thunder has several sonic characteristics: ripping attack; sharp, deep-throated crack; rolling, continuous rumble; and gradually increasing and decreasing loudness as it moves closer and then farther away. In this case, because the thunder sounds in the distance, the sound design calls for a low-throated, continuous rumble. As it comes closer with the storm, its other sonic characteristics would be added.

The wind and the thunder also could be generated electronically. This would give the environment an alien quality, particularly if the animal sounds in the woods were also synthesized to suggest the presence of some unworldly beast.

These are only a few possible approaches to the sound design of this brief scenario. Music provides even more alternatives to the informational and emotional content; the possibilities are infinite. On the other hand, an absence of music could enhance the sense of isolation and threat. The role of music in providing and enhancing meaning is covered in Chapter 16.

Another important factor in the sound design of this shot is how the audio cues are mixed. Mixing layers the sonic elements and establishes their balance and perspective, aspects of sound that are discussed at length in Chapters 21, 22, and 23.

Achieving Effects in Selected Program Materials

The point of the previous examples was to demonstrate the power of sound to change the impact and the meaning of given content. The discussion assumed that the sound designer had the mandate to originate such changes. In reality this rarely happens because interpretation of material is up to the director. Even so, a sound designer still has creative leeway in affecting the overall outcome of program material.

The following examples are common types of assignments a sound designer is called on to handle. Because context and content of the audio in these examples are prescribed, it is up to the sound designer simply to produce it, always with the director's final approval, of course. The challenge is to see how imaginative the sound designer can be and still remain true to the director's vision.

Spot Announcement

Some audio materials are produced by one person who, in effect, is both the director and the sound designer. This is often the case in radio and with spot announcements—commercials, promos, and public service announcements (PSAs). With spot announcements, particularly commercials and promos, the "message" is often in the dynamics of the audio design and less in what is actually said, as in this illustration of a promo for an all-news station.

SFX: HARD PAN—EFFECT WITH DRONE

ANNOUNCER 1: Keeping the commitment…

MUSIC: STAGER INTO AMBIENT SOUND

ANNOUNCER 1: With detailed coverage, this is news radio 1060…

MUSIC: STAGER IN AND FADE UNDER ANNOUNCER

ANNOUNCER 1: (PAN LEFT TO RIGHT WITH RISING EFFECT) W… Z… Y… X.

MUSIC: DRAMATIC MUSIC BED IN AND UNDER

ANNOUNCER 1: For complete coverage of the day's news, keep your ears planted here.

SFX: SPLAT

ANNOUNCER 2: (High-pass filter) Apparently, that's what being planted sounds like.

SFX: DRUMBEAT SOUND OVER LAUGH, SEGUE TO…

MUSIC: PULSING BEAT THEN UNDER

ANNOUNCER 1: These days news is not funny. (PAN LEFT TO RIGHT WITH RISING EFFECT) W… Z… Y… X (EFFECT OUT) Keeping the commitment.

MUSIC: PULSING BEAT OUT… SEGUE TO THREE STINGERS

ANNOUNCER 1: News radio 1060.

Action Drama

The action takes place on a deserted city street, just after a brutal, late-night assault and robbery. The battered victim lies unconscious on the pavement. The assailant, Joe Badd, is running to his car and making his getaway.

The scene calls for the following sounds: ambience of a city street at night, footsteps, a car door opening and closing, the engine starting, and the car speeding off. These are common sounds easily recorded and even more easily obtained from prerecorded sound libraries (see Chapter 15). A typical, unimaginative sonic approach would be to produce the scene on a what-you-see-is-what-you-hear basis.

But without changing the action or the designated sounds, the audio can do more than just be there. The ambience, instead of simply being present, could be processed to sound dense and oppressive. The footsteps, instead of being those of ordinary shoes hitting the pavement, could be sonically fitted with sharp, lacerating, almost metallic attacks at each footfall. The car door handle could be snapped, the car door wrenched open, then sharply slammed shut with a report sonically similar to a high-pitched gunshot. The ignition could start with a grind, followed by a guttural revving and rasping acceleration of the engine. The drive-off could be punctuated by a piercing, brazen screech of tires. After all, these are not just any sounds; they are the sounds of nasty Joe Badd.

Cinéma Vérité Documentary

The school of documentarists producing in the cinéma vérité style record life without imposing on it; production values do not motivate or influence content. Whatever is recorded has to speak for itself. Music, produced sound effects, and narration are renounced. Deciding what is recorded and edited are the only "manipulative" elements in the production process. Even within these guidelines, however, an imaginative sound designer still has creative leeway.

A documentary producer is doing a program about poverty in America. There are shots of various locales in which the poor people live, interviews with various families in their living quarters, and interviews with selected officials responsible for carrying out programs that theoretically help the underprivileged.

Urban and rural neighborhoods where the poor exist are usually depressed, dilapidated, and depleted. One approach to recording the ambient sound reflecting such conditions might be to produce an empty, forsaken, desolate quality. Conveying such an ambient quality isn't a matter of simply sticking a microphone in the air and turning on the recorder. The imaginative sound designer will select a mic that produces a thin, transparent sound. Placement will be far enough away from reflectant surfaces so that the sound is diffused rather than concentrated and stable. On the other hand, a dense ambience created by placing a microphone with midrange coloration near reflectant surfaces might produce a more saturated, suffocating effect.

Interviews inside the living quarters could be miked to include room reflections, creating an overall hollowness to the sound. The microphone could be one that is flat through the upper bass and low midrange so as not to enhance the frequencies that produce a warm sound. Or the mic could be one with a peaky midrange response to create a tinny, spare sound.

Interviews with the officials who are dragging their bureaucratic feet could be miked to create a warm, close, secure sound, thereby contrasting the officials' comfortable lifestyle with that of the underclass. Or mic selection and placement could be designed to a harsh, cutting sound, suggesting an insensitivity to poverty. Miking at a distance might suggest an official's remoteness from the problem. All these approaches to the sound design enhance overall impact and meaning without compromising the style of cinéma vérité.

Animation

Sound in animated material is especially critical because it defines not only the action but the characters as well. This is particularly true in most TV cartoons produced today in which animated facial expressions and body movements are minimal. "Many experienced animators credit sound with contributing as much as 70 percent of the success of a project."[8]

Chasing, stopping, falling, crashing, bumping, digging, and so on—all are defined by sound effects, music, or both. In animation, sound is created in ways that often exaggerate and accelerate the action; practitioners call it *tune time*. "You try to create ambiences, atmospheres, and sounds so that if you turned the picture off, you would probably think you were listening to a live action film."[9] Although animation is a world unto itself, the audio design team has to keep in mind that the audience has expectations about what things should sound like.

That said, because sounds in animation are frequently exaggerated and accelerated, sound, more than appearance, gives most animated characters their delineation and personality. Think of Donald Duck, Daffy Duck, Scooby-Doo, Bugs Bunny, Roger Rabbit, Ariel *(The Little Mermaid)*, Simba *(The Lion King)*, and WALL-E to name a few.

Mr. Burns, in *The Simspons*, is a corporate antagonist—power hungry, evil, deceitful, and scheming. His sound, appropriately, is somewhat low in pitch and at times raspy and sibilant. Huckleberry Hound has a slow, evenly paced, low-pitched southern drawl to suggest the sense of control that is central to his characterization.

There can be sonic counterpoint as well. Tweety Bird is also in control, but his high-pitched voice and small size suggest victimization. Wile E. Coyote's sound suggests sophistication, wit, and culture, yet his actions indicate just the opposite.

Defining the sonic personality of a nonhuman character is usually not the purview of the sound designer, but the "ear" a designer brings to such a determination is invaluable to the director with sense enough to seek such assistance.

DESIGNING SOUND FOR MOBILE MEDIA

The audience viewing and listening to content on pocket- and handheld portable media players, such as cell phones and iPods, to say nothing of mediocre desktop and laptop computer sound systems, is burgeoning. In fact, a generation of users sees and hears media as much, if not more, on these small, mobile players than on conventional TV, film, radio, and music systems.

The Paradox in Listening to and Producing Audio Today

The quality of produced and reproduced sound today in film, radio, and high-definition television, and in recorded materials on DVD, Blu-ray, SACD, and high-density optical discs, is extraordinary and readily accessible to the consumer. The paradox is that with the potential to hear great sound through great systems, with too many listeners the opposite is happening: they are hearing their digital audio in compressed form, much of which reduces sound quality. And to exacerbate the situation, they are listening through inferior headphones

---

8. Robin Beauchamp, *Sound for Animation* (Boston: Focal Press, 2005), p. 17.

9. Bryant Frazer, "What Randy Thom Hears," *Film and Video*, April 2005, p. 53.

or earbuds, often in noisy ambient environments, or through a less-than-sonorous computer speaker or computer loudspeaker system. If your goal is to become a professional in audio production, it is difficult to develop analytical and critical listening skills with such deficient exposure to sound.

This has also influenced the way audio is handled in production, depending on the intended distribution medium. Instead of being able to take advantage of audio's potential for excellence, recordists and mixers are having to use broader sonic canvases: less detail and subtlety and reduced frequency response and dynamic range because the small, portable reproducing systems cannot handle the sound otherwise (see Chapters 19 and 23).

That said, and like it or not, the reality is that more and more audio (and video) is being produced with the mobile-media audience in mind. Therefore, designing sound for small, portable receivers involves considerations that are somewhat different from designing sound for traditional receivers. There are also limitations in how materials are produced for mobile media. (Production for mobile media is covered in Chapter 19.)

Considerations in Sound Design for Mobile Media

By their very nature, ***mobile media***—portable devices capable of storing and playing digital audio, video, and images, such as cell phones, iPods, cameras, and laptop computers—can reproduce only so much; so to avoid pitfalls in realizing a sound design, it is necessary to consider what receivers cannot handle.

Detail is limited. Whereas in, say, conventional film, sound can consist of layers of information provided through vocal intonations, enhanced sound effects, and subtle, nuanced underscoring, or some combination of these components, the size (or lack thereof) of the speaker or the limitations of the earphones and earbuds cannot reproduce that type of detail to any worthwhile degree.

Because detail is reduced, so is perspective. There are constraints on creating proportional or subtle near-to-far and side-to-side aural imaging. There is only so much that can be done with a limited sonic palette. Picture also has the same problem with perspective due to the very small screen size.

Frequency response is limited. Many systems in mobile media essentially reproduce midrange because they cannot handle bass and treble frequencies. Midrange-only sound can be harsh and annoying. Even though the intelligibility of most sound resides in the midrange, there are many sounds in which the bass or treble are part of their recognizability and impact. In music, bass and treble are essential for an aesthetically pleasing experience.

Dynamic range is limited. Most mobile-media systems cannot handle anywhere close to a wide dynamic range. To reproduce sound with any effectiveness, it must first be compressed. Even the best compression schemes adversely affect some sound quality. A reduced dynamic range limits the strength, effectiveness, and impact of many types of sound effects. It certainly reduces the overall dynamics of music, particularly in larger ensembles.

With all that said, the sound designer also has to consider mobile-media systems that produce comparatively good sound through headphones and earbuds. This creates the challenge of the sound's being too good and too high-energy for the tiny video image. The disproportional sound tends to separate from the video because the audio is oversized compared with the video. This is comparable to the aesthetic disconnect due to the sound from a small, monaural speaker in a TV receiver but in reverse—the video being oversized compared with the audio.[10]

The concepts developed in a sound design are realized in the actual production and postproduction of the audio materials: sound effects, music underscoring, editing, premixing, and rerecording. These subjects are discussed throughout the rest of the book.

---

10. For more information about audio/video balance, see Herbert Zettl, *Sight Sound Motion: Applied Media Aesthetics,* 5th ed. (Belmont, Calif.: Thomson Wadsworth, 2008), pp. 334–35.

MAIN POINTS

▶ Sound design is the process of creating the overall sonic character of a production and is ongoing throughout the production process.

▶ The sound designer is responsible for creative control of the audio—for putting a coherent sonic stamp on a production—although all members of the audio team make creative contributions to the soundscape.

▶ In the parlance of audio, having "ears" means having healthy hearing and the ability to listen perceptively.

▶ Having educated ears means the ability to listen with careful discrimination to style, interpretation, nuance, and technical quality in evaluating the content, function, characteristics, and fidelity of sound.

▶ Learning how to listen begins with paying attention to sound wherever and whenever it occurs.

► Analytical listening is the evaluation of the content and the function of sound.

► Critical listening is the evaluation of the characteristics of the sound itself.

► There are three domains to work with in creating a sound design: speech, sound effects, and music. Paradoxically, silence and the ability of sound to evoke a picture in the mind's eye may be considered two other domains.

► All sound is made up of the same basic components: pitch, loudness, timbre, tempo, rhythm, attack, duration, and decay.

► Sound also has a visual component in that it can create pictures in the "theater of the mind."

► Sound has several functions in relation to picture: sound can parallel picture, sound can define picture, picture can define sound, sound and picture can define effect, and sound can counterpoint picture.

► There is no set procedure for designing sound. At the outset the most important thing to do is study the script and analyze the auditory requirements line by line to determine the overall sonic approach to various scenes, for an entire work, or both.

► Determining a sound design involves consideration of how the audience is to think or feel about a particular story, scene, character, action, or environment; from what point of view; and whether that is to be carried out mainly in the sound effects, the music, or both.

► Determining a sound design also requires the awareness that doing so is often tantamount to defining a production's conceptual and emotional intent.

► The paradox in listening to recordings today is that with the potential to hear high-quality sound through great systems, with too many listeners the opposite is happening: they are listening to compressed audio through mediocre headphones or earbuds on mobile media or through a less-than-sonorous computer speaker or computer loudspeaker system.

15

Sound Effects

ound effects (SFX) can be classified as anything sonic that is not speech or music. They are essential to storytelling, bringing realism and added dimension to a production. It is worth noting that the art of sound-effect design is about not only creating something big or bizarre but also crafting subtle, low-key moments. Good effects are about conveying a compelling illusion. In general, sound effects can be contextual or narrative. These functions are not mutually exclusive; they allow for a range of possibilities in the sonic continuum between what we listen for in dialogue—namely, sound to convey meaning—and what we experience more viscerally and emotionally in music. With film and video, sound effects are indispensable to overall production value. In early "talking pictures," it was not uncommon to have no more than a handful of sound effects, whereas *WALL-E* included a palette of 2,600 sound effects.

CONTEXTUAL SOUND

Contextual sound emanates from and duplicates a sound source as it is. It is often illustrative and also referred to as *diegetic sound*. The term derives from the Greek *diegesis*, meaning to tell or recount and, in the context of film, has come to describe that which comes from within the story space. (*Extra-sound*, or *nondiegetic sound*, comes from outside the story space; music underscoring is an example of nondiegetic sound.) If a gun fires, a car drives by, or leaves rustle in the wind, what you see is what you hear; the sound is naturalistic in structure and perspective. In other words, contextual sound is like direct narration.

NARRATIVE SOUND

Narrative sound adds more to a scene than what is apparent and so performs an informational function. It can be descriptive or commentative.

Descriptive Sound

As the term suggests, *descriptive sound* describes sonic aspects of a scene, usually those not directly connected with the main action. A conversation in a hot room with a ceiling fan slowly turning is contextual sound. Descriptive sound would be the buzzing about of insects, oxcarts lumbering by outside, and an indistinguishable hubbub, or *walla,* of human activity. A young man leaves his apartment and walks out onto a city street to a bus stop. You hear descriptive sounds of the neighborhood: the rumble of passing cars, a horn, a siren, one neighbor calling to another, a car idling at an intersection, and the hissing boom of air brakes from an approaching bus.

Commentative Sound

Commentative sound also describes, but it makes an additional statement, one that usually has something to do with the story line. For example: An aging veteran wanders through the uniform rows of white crosses in a cemetery. A wind comes up as he pauses before individual markers. The wind is infused with the faint sound of battle, snippets of conversations, laughter, and music as he remembers his fallen comrades. Or behind the scene of a misty, farm meadow at dawn, the thrum of morning rush hour traffic is heard—a comment on encroaching urban sprawl.

FUNCTIONS OF SOUND EFFECTS

Sound effects have specific functions within the general contextual and narrative categories. They break the screen plane, define space, focus attention, establish locale, create environment, emphasize and intensify action, depict identity, set pace, provide counterpoint, create humor, symbolize meaning, create metaphor, and unify transition. Paradoxical as it may seem, silence is also a functional sound effect.

Breaking the Screen Plane

A film or video without sounds, natural or produced, detaches an audience from the on-screen action. The audience becomes an observer, looking at the scene from outside rather than being made to feel a part of the action—at the center of an acoustic space. In some documentary approaches, for example, this has been a relatively common technique used to convey the sense that a subject is being treated objectively and so there is less possible distraction. The presence of sound changes the audience relationship to what is happening on-screen; it becomes part of the action in a sense. The audience becomes a participant in that there is no longer a separation between the listener-viewer and the screen plane. Therefore it can also be said that sound effects add realism to the picture.

Defining Space

Sound defines space by establishing distance, direction of movement, position, openness, and dimension. Distance—how close to or far from you a sound seems to be—is created mainly by relative loudness, or *sound perspective.* The louder a sound, the closer to the listener-viewer it is. A person speaking from several feet away will not sound as loud as someone speaking right next to you. Thunder at a low sound level tells you that a storm is some distance away; as the storm moves closer, the thunder grows louder.

By varying sound level, it is also possible to indicate direction of movement. As a person leaves a room, sound will gradually change from loud to soft; conversely, as a sound source gets closer, level changes from soft to loud.

With moving objects, frequency also helps establish distance and direction of movement. As a moving object such as a train, car, or siren approaches, its pitch gets higher; as it moves away or recedes, its pitch gets lower. This phenomenon is known as the *Doppler effect* (named for its discoverer, Christian J. Doppler, an early nineteenth-century Austrian physicist).

Sound defines relative position—the location of two or more sound sources in relation to one another, whether close, distant, or side-to-side (in stereo) or to the rear-side or behind (in surround sound). Relative position is established mainly through relative loudness and ambience. If two people are speaking and a car horn sounds, the loudness and the ambience of the three sound sources tells you their proximity to one another. If person A is louder than person B with less ambience than person B, and person B is louder than the car horn with more ambience than person A and with less ambience than the car horn (assuming monaural sound), person A will sound closest, person B farther away, and the horn farthest away. If the aural image is in stereo, loudness will influence relative position in panning left to right, assuming the sound sources are on the same plane. Once lateral perspective is established, a further change in loudness and ambience moves the sound closer or farther away.

Openness of outdoor space can be established in a number of ways—for example, thunder that rumbles for a longer-than-normal period of time and then rolls to quiet; wind that sounds thin; echo that has a longer-than-normal time between repeats; background sound that is extremely quiet—all these effects tend to enhance the size of outdoor space. Dimension of indoor space is usually established by means of reverberation (see Chapters 2 and 7). The more reverb there is, the larger the space is perceived to be. For example, Grand Central Station or the main hall of a castle would have a great deal of reverb, whereas a closet or an automobile would have little.

Focusing Attention

In shots, other than close-ups, in which a number of elements are seen at the same time, how do you know where to focus attention? Of course directors compose shots to direct the eye, but the eye can wander. Sound, however, draws attention and provides the viewer with a focus. In a shot of a large room filled with people, the eye takes it all in, but if a person shouts or begins choking, the sound directs the eye to that individual.

Establishing Locale

Sounds can establish locale. A cawing seagull places you at the ocean; the almost derisive, mocking cackle of a bird of paradise places you in the jungle; honking car horns and screeching brakes place you in city traffic; the whir and the clank of machinery places you in a factory; the squeak of athletic shoes, the rhythmic slap of a bouncing ball, and the roar of a crowd place you at a basketball game.

Creating Environment

Establishing locale begins to create an environment, but more brush strokes are often needed to complete the picture. Honky-tonk saloon music may establish the Old West, but sounds of a blacksmith hammering, horses whinnying, wagon wheels rolling, and six-guns firing create environment. A prison locale can be established in several ways, but add the sounds of loudspeakers blaring orders, picks and shovels hacking and digging, grunts of effort, dogs barking, and whips cracking and you have created a brutal prison work camp. To convey a sense of alienation and dehumanization in a high-tech office, the scene can be orchestrated using the sounds of ringing telephones with futuristic tonalities, whisper-jet spurts of laser printers, the buzz of fluorescent lights, machines humming in monotonous tempos, and synthesized Muzak in the background.

Emphasizing Action

Sounds can emphasize or highlight action. A person falling down a flight of stairs tumbles all the harder if each bump is accented. A car crash becomes a shattering collision by emphasizing the impact and the sonic aftermath—including silence. Creaking floorboards underscore someone slowly and methodically sneaking up to an objective. A saw grinding harshly through wood, rather than cutting smoothly, emphasizes the effort involved and the bite of the teeth.

Intensifying Action

Whereas emphasizing action highlights or calls attention to something important, intensifying action increases or heightens dramatic impact. As a wave forms and then crashes, the roar of the buildup and the loudness of the crash intensify the wave's size and power. The slow, measured sound of an airplane engine becoming increasingly raspy and sputtery heightens the anticipation of its stalling and the plane's crashing. A car's twisted metal settling in the aftermath of a collision emits an agonized groaning sound. In animation, sound (and music) intensifies the extent of a character's running, falling, crashing, skidding, chomping, and chasing.

Depicting Identity

Depicting identity is perhaps one of the most obvious uses of sound. Barking identifies a dog, slurred speech identifies a drunk, and so on. But on a more informational level, sound can also give a character or an object its own distinctive sound signature: the rattle sound of a rattlesnake to identify a slippery villain with a venomous intent; thin, clear, hard sounds to convey a cold character devoid of compassion; labored, asthmatic breathing to identify a character's constant struggle in dealing with life; the sound of a dinosaur infused into the sound of a mechanical crane to give the crane an organic character; or the sound of a "monster" with the conventional low tonal grunting, breathing, roaring, and heavily percussive clomping infused with a whimpering effect to create sympathy or affection for the "beast."

Setting Pace

Sounds, or the lack of them, help set pace. The incessant, even rhythm of a machine creates a steady pace to underscore monotony. The controlled professionalism of two detectives discussing crucial evidence becomes more vital if the activity around them includes such sonic elements as footsteps moving quickly, telephones ringing, papers being shuffled, and a general walla of voices. Car-chase scenes get most of their pace from the sounds of screeching tires, gunning engines, and shifting gears. Sounds can also be orchestrated to produce a rhythmic effect to enhance a scene. In a gun battle, bursts can vary from *ratta tat tat* to *ratta tat,* then a few pauses, followed by *budadadada*. Additionally, sounds of the bullets hitting or ricocheting off different objects can add to not only the scene's rhythm but also its sonic variety.

Providing Counterpoint

Sounds provide counterpoint when they are different from what is expected, thereby making an additional comment on the action. A judge bangs a gavel to the accompanying sound of dollar bills being peeled off, counterpointing the ideal of justice and the reality of corruption; or a smiling leader is cheered by a crowd, but instead of cheers, tortured screams are heard, belying the crowd scene.

Creating Humor

Sounds can be funny. Think of *boings, boinks,* and *plops;* the swirling swoops of a pennywhistle; the *chuga-chugaburp-cough-chuga* of a steam engine trying to get started; and the exaggerated clinks, clanks, and clunks of a hapless robot trying to follow commands. Comic sounds are indispensable in cartoons in highlighting the shenanigans of their characters.

Symbolizing Meaning

Sound can be used symbolically. The sound of a faucet dripping is heard when the body of a murder victim killed in a dispute over water rights is found. An elegantly decorated, but excessively reverberant, living room symbolizes the remoteness or coldness of the occupants. An inept ball team named the Bulls gathers in a parking lot for a road game; as the bus revs its engine, the sound is infused with the sorry bellow of a dispirited bull, comedically symbolizing the team's incompetence. A condemned prisoner walks through a steel gate that squeaks when it slams shut. Instead of just any squeak, the sound is mixed with an agonized human groan to convey his anguish.

Creating Metaphor

Sound can create a metaphorical relationship between what is heard and what is seen. A wife leaving her husband after enduring the last straw in a deeply troubled marriage walks out of their house, slamming the door. The sound of the slam has the palpable impact of finality and with it there is a slowly decaying reverberation that reflects a married life that has faded into nothingness. Or a person in a state of delirium hears the constant *rat tat tat* of a bouncing basketball from a nearby driveway. The repeated rhythm of the sound infiltrates his consciousness and takes him back to a time when, as a musician, that rhythm was part of a song he had made famous.

Unifying Transition

Sounds provide transitions and continuity between scenes, linking them by overlapping, leading-in, segueing, and leading out.

Overlapping occurs when the sound used at the end of one scene continues, without pause, into the next. A speech being delivered by a candidate's spokesperson ends one scene with the words "a candidate who stands for…"; the next scene begins with the candidate at another location, saying, "equal rights for all under law." Or the sound of a cheering crowd responding to a score in an athletic contest at the end of one scene overlaps into the next scene as the captain of the victorious team accepts the championship trophy.

A *lead-in* occurs when the audio to the next scene is heard before the scene actually begins and establishes a relationship to it. As a character thinks about a forthcoming gala event, the music and other sounds of the party are heard before the scene changes to the event itself. While a character gazes at a peaceful countryside, an unseen fighter plane in action is heard, anticipating and leading into the following scene, in which the same character is a jet pilot in an aerial dogfight.

A *segue*—cutting from one effect (or recording) to another with nothing in between—links scenes by abruptly changing from a sound that ends one scene to a similar sound that begins the next. As a character screams at the discovery of a dead body, the scream segues to the shriek of a train whistle; a wave crashing on a beach segues to an explosion; the sound of ripping cloth segues to the sound of a jet roar at takeoff.

Lead-out sound is audio to an outgoing scene that carries through to the beginning of the following scene but with no visual scene-to-scene relationship. A cop-and-robber car chase ends with the robber's car crashing into a gasoline pump and exploding, the repercussions of which carry over into the next scene and fade out as the cop walks up the driveway to his home. Wistful, almost muted sounds of the countryside play under a scene in which boy meets girl, with love at first sight, and fade out under the next shot, showing them in a split screen sitting in their cubicles in different office buildings, staring into space.

Silence

A producer was once asked why he chose to show the explosion of the first atomic bomb test with no sound. He replied, "Silence was the most awesome sound that I could find." Silence is not generally thought of as sound per se—that seems like a contradiction in terms. But it is the pauses or silences between words, sounds, and musical notes that help create rhythm, contrast, and power—elements important to sonic communication.

In situations where we anticipate sound, silence is a particularly powerful element. Thieves break into and rob a bank with barely a sound. As the burglary progresses, silence heightens suspense to an oppressive level as we anticipate an alarm going off, a tool clattering to the floor, or a guard suddenly shouting, "Freeze!" A horrifying sight compels a scream—but with the mouth wide open there is only silence, suggesting a horror that is unspeakable. Birds congregate on telephone wires, rooftops, and TV aerials and wait silently; the absence of sound makes the scene eerie and unnatural. A lone figure waits for an undercover rendezvous in a forest clearing. Using silence can enlarge the space and create a sense of isolation, unease, and imminent danger.

The silence preceding sound is equally effective. Out of perfect quiet comes a wrenching scream. In the silence before dawn, there is the anticipation of the new day's sounds to come.

Silence is also effective following sound. An explosion that will destroy the enemy is set to go off. The ticking of the bomb reaches detonation time. Then, silence. Or the heightening sounds of passion build to resolution. Then, silence.

PRODUCING SOUND EFFECTS

There are two sources of sound effects: prerecorded and produced. Prerecorded sound effects are distributed on digital disc or can be downloaded from the Internet (see Chapter 19). Produced SFX are obtained in four ways: they can be created and synchronized to picture in post-production in a studio often specially designed for that purpose, recorded on the set during shooting, collected in the field throughout production or between productions, and generated electronically using a synthesizer or computer. Sound effects are also built using any one or a combination of these approaches. In the interest of clarity, each approach is considered separately here. Regardless of how you produce sound effects, an overriding concern is to maintain sonic consistency.

Prerecorded Sound-effect Libraries

Sound-effect libraries are collections of recorded sounds that can number from several hundred to many thousand, depending on the distributor. The distributor has produced and recorded the original sounds, collected them from other sources and obtained the rights to sell them, or both.

Advantages of Sound-effect Libraries

A major advantage of sound-effect libraries is that for one buyout fee you get many different sounds for relatively little cost compared with the time and the expense it would take to produce them yourself (see Figure 15-1). *Buyout* means that you own the library and have unlimited, copyright-cleared use of it. The Internet provides dozens of sources that make available copyright-cleared sound effects for downloading either free or for a modest charge.[1]

Most broadcast stations and many production houses use libraries because they have neither the personnel nor the budget to assign staff to produce sound effects. Think of what it would involve to produce, for example,

---

1. Whether purchasing a sound effect or sound-effect library or downloading material free of charge, be sure to read the contract or license agreement that most sound-effect distributors require. For example, sound effects may be free to obtain, but there may be restrictions related to commercial, personal, and ring tone use; there may be licensing modes related to intended use on a per-track or subscription basis; and loops may carry different usage options than do conventional sound effects.

CD Number	Track/In	Description	Time
Digi-X-01	05-01	Town square—people and birds—environment—hum of voices	1:42
Digi-X-01	06-01	Road junction—squealing brakes	1:30
Digi-X-01	07-01	Rain—heavy—railway station	1:04
Digi-X-01	08-01	Vacuum cleaner—on/off	:55
Digi-X-01	09-01	Washing dishes by hand—kitchen	1:05
Digi-X-01	10-01	Door—creaking—large—small	:31
Digi-X-01	11-01	Door bell—ding-dong	:07
Digi-X-01	12-01	Knocking on door—repeated twice	:06
Digi-X-01	13-01	Shower—person showering—bathroom	:36
Digi-X-01	14-01	Fire—in open fireplace	:46
Digi-X-01	15-01	Roller blind—down/up—flapping round	:14
Digi-X-01	16-01	Wall clock—ticking—strikes 12—fly against window—insect	:55
Digi-X-01	17-01	Toilet—flushing—old—gurgling—bathroom	:21
Digi-X-01	18-01	Tap running—in sink—kitchen	:18
Digi-X-01	19-01	Ticking alarm clock—mechanical	:17
Digi-X-01	20-01	Lambs—two—outdoors—flies—birds—mammal—insect	1:00
Digi-X-01	21-01	Creek—rushing—water	:58
Digi-X-01	22-01	Dogs barking—two—indoors—mammal	:15
Digi-X-01	23-01	Milking cow by hand—metal bucket—farm	1:02
Digi-X-01	24-01	Cows in barn—restless—mammal	1:39

a

Boats — Section 6

Catalog Number	Subject	Description	Time
6-046	Ship's deck	Large type—anchor chain down quickly	:05
6-047	Coast Guard cutter	Operating steadily—with water sounds	:41
6-048	Water taxi	Start up—steady run—slow down	:47
6-049	Water taxi	Steady run—slow down—rev ups—with water sounds	1:25
6-050	Fishing boat	Diesel type—slow speed—steady operation	:36
6-051	Tugboat	Diesel type—slow speed—steady operation	:38
6-052	Tugboat	Diesel type—medium speed—steady operation	:38
6-053	Outboard	Fast run-by	:32
6-054	Naval landing craft	Medium speed—steady operation	:50

b

15-1 Sound-effect libraries. (a) Examples of sound effects in one recorded sound-effect library. (b) Example of a detailed list of sound effects by category from another library.

the real sounds of a jet fly-by, a forest fire, a torpedo exploding into a ship, or stampeding cattle. Moreover, SFX are available in mono, stereo, and surround sound, depending on the library.

Sound quality, or the absence thereof, was a serious problem with prerecorded sound effects before the days of digital audio, when they were distributed on tape and long-playing (LP) record. The audio was analog, dynamic range was limited, tape was noisy, vinyl LPs got scratched, and too many effects sounded lifeless. Frequently, it was easy to tell that the SFX came from a recording; they sounded "canned." The sound effects on digital disc have greatly improved fidelity and dynamic range, that is, those that were digitally recorded or transferred from analog to digital with widened dynamic range and sans noise. Be wary, however, of analog SFX transferred to digital disc without noise processing. Two other benefits of sound effects on digital disc are faster access to tracks and the ability to see a sound's waveform on-screen.

The great advantage of libraries is the convenience of having thousands of digital-quality sound effects at your fingertips for relatively little cost. There are, however, disadvantages.

Disadvantages of Sound-effect Libraries

Sound-effect libraries have three conspicuous disadvantages: you give up control over the dynamics and the timing of an effect; ambiences vary, so in editing effects together they may not match one another or those you require in your production; and the effect may not be long enough for your needs. Other disadvantages are imprecise titles and mediocre sound and production quality of the downloadable materials.

Dynamics and Timing   One reason why sound editors prefer to create their own effects rather than use libraries is to have control over the dynamics of a sound, particularly effects generated by humans. For example, thousands of different footstep sounds are available in libraries, but you might need a specific footfall that requires a certain-sized woman walking at a particular gait on a solidly packed road of dirt and stone granules. Maybe no library can quite match this sound.

Timing is another reason why many sound editors prefer to create their own effects. To continue our example, if the pace of the footfall has to match action on the screen, trying to synchronize each step in the prerecorded sound effect to each step in the picture could be difficult.

Ambience   Matching ambiences could present another problem with prerecorded sound effects. Suppose in a radio commercial you need footsteps walking down a hall, followed by a knock on a door that enters into that hallway. If you cut together two different sounds to achieve the overall effect, take care that the sound of the footsteps walking toward the door has the same ambience as the knock on the door. If the ambiences are different, the audience will perceive the two actions as taking place in different locales. Even if the audience could see the action, the different ambiences would be disconcerting.

To offset this problem, some sound-effect libraries provide different ambiences for specific applications:

footsteps on a city street, with reverb to put you in town among buildings and without reverb to put you in a more open area; or gunshots with different qualities of ricochet to cover the various environments in which a shot may be fired. Some libraries provide collections of ambient environments, allowing you to mix the appropriate background sound with a given effect (see 15-2). In so doing be sure that the sound effect used has little or no ambient coloration of its own. Otherwise the backgrounds will be additive, may clash, or both.

Fixed Length of Sound Effects   Library SFX have fixed lengths. You need a sound to last 15 seconds, but the effect you want to use is only seven seconds long. What to do?

If the effect is continuous, crowd sound or wind, for example, it can be looped (see "Looping" later in this section). If it is not continuous, such as a dog barking and then growling, you are stuck unless you can find two separate effects of the same-sounding dog barking and growling. If it is possible to edit them together to meet your timing needs, be careful that the edit transition from bark to growl sounds natural.

Choosing Sounds from the Titles

Titles in sound-effect libraries are often not precise enough to be used as guides for selecting material. For example, what does "laughter," "washing machine," "window opening," or "polite applause" actually tell you about the sound effect besides its general subject and application? Most good libraries provide short descriptions of each effect to give an idea of its content (see 15-1b). Even so, always listen before you choose because nuance in sound is difficult to describe in words.

Sound and Production Quality of Downloadable Sound Effects

Although many Web sites provide easy access to thousands of downloadable sound effects, many free of charge, care must be taken to ensure that high-quality sound and production values have been maintained. Be wary of SFX that are compressed and that have low resolutions and sampling frequencies—anything with less than 16-bit resolution and a 44.1 kHz sampling rate. Make sure that the sound effects are clean and well produced and do not carry any sonic baggage such as low-level noise, unwanted ambience, brittle high frequencies, muddy bass, and confusing perspective.

15-2 Ambience sound effects.

Description	Time	Class	Category	File Name	Disc ID
Ambience Air Conditioner Hotel Room	01:35:42	General	Ambience	00001_SFX	Disc 2
Ambience Airplane Interior	01:34:08	General	Ambience	00002_SFX	Disc 2
Ambience Airport	01:34:08	General	Ambience	00003_SFX	Disc 2
Ambience Airport Runway Work Crews Tru...	01:35:17	General	Ambience	00004_SFX	Disc 2
Ambience Alley City	01:34:14	General	Ambience	00005_SFX	Disc 2
Ambience Animal Tent At Fair	01:35:07	General	Ambience	00006_SFX	Disc 2
Ambience Arcade	01:29:54	General	Ambience	00007_SFX	Disc 2
Ambience Arcade	01:35:04	General	Ambience	00008_SFX	Disc 2
Ambience Auto Repair Shop	01:34:05	General	Ambience	00009_SFX	Disc 2
Ambience Auto Repair Shop With Interco...	01:38:00	General	Ambience	00010_SFX	Disc 2
Ambience Auto Work Shop	01:39:18	General	Ambience	00011_SFX	Disc 2
Ambience Auto Work Shop Light Ambience	01:33:49	General	Ambience	00012_SFX	Disc 2
Ambience Bakery Kitchen	01:34:05	General	Ambience	00013_SFX	Disc 2
Ambience Band Tuning Up	02:02:27	General	Ambience	00014_SFX	Disc 2
Ambience Band Warming Up	00:25:51	General	Ambience	00015_SFX	Disc 2
Ambience Band Warming Up	01:41:36	General	Ambience	00016_SFX	Disc 2
Ambience Barber Shop	01:37:48	General	Ambience	00017_SFX	Disc 2
Ambience Beach Children Playing	01:59:54	General	Ambience	00018_SFX	Disc 2
Ambience Beach Children Playing Lifeguar...	01:36:23	General	Ambience	00019_SFX	Disc 2
Ambience Bus Stop	01:23:51	General	Ambience	00020_SFX	Disc 2
Ambience Cafe	01:34:14	General	Ambience	00021_SFX	Disc 2
Ambience Camp Fire	01:34:55	General	Ambience	00022_SFX	Disc 2
Ambience Car Manufacturing Plant	01:34:11	General	Ambience	00023_SFX	Disc 2
Ambience Carnival	01:45:44	General	Ambience	00024_SFX	Disc 2
Ambience Cave	01:34:05	General	Ambience	00025_SFX	Disc 2
Ambience Chicken House At Fair	01:41:24	General	Ambience	00026_SFX	Disc 2
Ambience City	01:42:33	General	Ambience	00027_SFX	Disc 2
Ambience City Courthouse	01:34:08	General	Ambience	00028_SFX	Disc 2
Ambience City Large	01:34:02	General	Ambience	00029_SFX	Disc 2
Ambience City Large Downtown Area	01:36:26	General	Ambience	00030_SFX	Disc 2
Ambience City Large Downtown Area Con...	01:34:39	General	Ambience	00031_SFX	Disc 2
Ambience City Night Distant Traffic	01:34:08	General	Ambience	00032_SFX	Disc 2
Ambience City Night With Crickets Distant...	01:34:11	General	Ambience	00033_SFX	Disc 2
Ambience City Night With Light Crickets D...	01:34:08	General	Ambience	00034_SFX	Disc 2
Ambience City Park Day	01:34:27	General	Ambience	00035_SFX	Disc 2
Ambience City Park Night	01:34:36	General	Ambience	00036_SFX	Disc 2
Ambience City Park Night	01:34:27	General	Ambience	00037_SFX	Disc 2
Ambience City Small Downtown Area	01:31:28	General	Ambience	00038_SFX	Disc 2
Ambience City Small Downtown Area	01:30:07	General	Ambience	00039_SFX	Disc 2
Ambience City Small Downtown Area	01:34:18	General	Ambience	00040_SFX	Disc 2
Ambience City Small Downtown Area With...	01:34:11	General	Ambience	00041_SFX	Disc 2
Ambience City Traffic Light	01:33:43	General	Ambience	00042_SFX	Disc 2
Ambience City With Clock Tower Ringing	01:07:04	General	Ambience	00043_SFX	Disc 2
Ambience Coffee Shop	01:34:52	General	Ambience	00044_SFX	Disc 2

Manipulating Recorded Sound Effects

Once a sound effect has been recorded, whether it's originally produced material or from a prerecorded library, any number of things can be done to alter its sonic characteristics and thereby extend the usefulness of a sound-effect collection.

Altering Playing Speed

Because pitch and duration are inseparable parts of sound, it is possible to change the character of any recording by varying its playing speed. This technique will not work with all sounds; some will sound obviously unnatural—either too drawn out and guttural or too fast and falsetto. But for sounds with sonic characteristics that do lend themselves to changes in pitch and duration, the effects can be remarkable.

For example, the sound effect of a slow, low-pitched, mournful wind can be changed to the ferocious howl of a hurricane by increasing its playing speed. The beeps of a car horn followed by a slight ambient reverb can be slowed to become a small ship in a small harbor and slowed yet more to become a large ship in a large harbor.

Hundreds of droning bees in flight can be turned into a squadron of World War II bombers by decreasing the playing speed of the effect or turned into a horde of mosquitoes by increasing the playing speed.

Decreasing the playing speed of cawing jungle birds will take you from the rain forest to an eerie world of science fiction. A gorilla can be turned into King Kong by slowing the recording's playing speed. The speeded-up sound of chicken clucks can be turned into convincing bat vocalizations. The possibilities are endless, and the only way to discover how flexible sounds can be is to experiment.

Playing Sound Backward

Another way to alter the characteristics of a sound is to play it backward. Digital audio workstations usually have a reverse command that rewrites the selected region in reverse, resulting in a backward audio effect. This is a common technique used in action films and many film trailers. A reverse bloom or slow attack followed by a sudden decay and release in a sound provides moments of sonic punctuation and emphasis for on-screen action.

Looping

Sometimes you may need a continuous effect that has to last several seconds, such as an idling car engine, a drum roll, or a steady beat. When the sound effect is shorter than the required time, you can use **looping** to repeat it continuously. In hard-disk systems, the looping command will continuously repeat the selected region.

Make sure that the edit points are made so that the effect sounds continuous rather than repetitious. Care must be taken to remove any clicks, pops, or other artifacts that may draw attention to the loop and distract from the illusion. Cross-fading loops can help ameliorate some problems when it is difficult to render a seamless loop. That said, even well-edited loops run the risk of sounding repetitious if they are played for too long.

Another looping technique that can sometimes be used to lengthen an effect is to reverse-loop similar sounds against themselves. When done correctly this technique also has the advantage of sounding natural.

Loops can also be designed to create a sound effect. For example, taking the startup sound of a motorcycle before it cranks over and putting it into a half-second repeat can be used as the basis for the rhythmic sound of a small, enclosed machine area.

Using Signal Processing

By signal-processing a sound effect using reverb, delay, flanging, pitch shifting, and so on, it is possible to create a virtually infinite number of effects. For example, flanging a cat's meow can to turn it into an unearthly cry, adding low frequencies to a crackling fire can make it a raging inferno, and chorusing a bird chirp can create a boisterous flock.

Signal processing also helps enhance a sound effect without actually changing its identity—for example, adding low frequencies to increase its weight and impact or beefing it up by pitch-shifting the effect lower and then compressing it (bearing in mind that too much bottom muddies the overall sound and masks the higher frequencies). Other signal-processing techniques are discussed in the following section.

LIVE SOUND EFFECTS

Although prerecorded sound libraries are readily available—some are quite good—most audio designers, particularly for theatrical film and television, prefer to produce their own effects because doing so allows complete control in shaping a sound to meet a precise need.

In addition, if the effect is taken from the actual source, it has the advantage of being authentic. Then too sound designers are sometimes called on to create effects that do not already exist, and they prefer to build these from live sources.

Live sound effects are collected in three ways: by creating them in a studio, by recording them on the set during shooting, and by recording them directly from the actual source, usually in the field, sometimes during production.

Producing Sound Effects in the Studio

Creating sound effects in the studio goes back to the days before television, when drama was so much a part of radio programming, and many ingenious ways were devised to create them. Sound effects were produced vocally by performers and also by using the tools of the trade: bells, buzzers, cutlery, cellophane, doorframes, telephone ringers, water tubs, car fenders, coconut shells, panes of glass—virtually anything that made a sound the script called for. These effects were produced live and were usually done in the studio with the performers. (Effects that were difficult to produce were taken from recordings.) These techniques are still useful and can be further enhanced when combined with the infinite variety of signal-processing options available today.

Vocally Produced Sound Effects

Many types of sound effects can be produced vocally. Some performers have the ability to control their breathing, manipulate their vocal cords and palate, and change the size and the shape of their mouth to produce a variety of effects, such as animal sounds, pops, clicks, and honks.

There are many notable voice artists. A few of the better known are Joe Siracusa, who was the voice of Gerald McBoing Boing in the 1951 Academy Award–winning cartoon. The story, by Dr. Seuss, relates the adventures of a six-year-old boy who communicates through sound effects instead of using words. Among the hundreds of films to his credit, Frank Welker has done the sounds of the dragon, parrot, and raven in *The Page Master,* the snake in *Anaconda,* the gopher in *Caddyshack 2,* the gorilla in *Congo,* Godzilla and the junior Godzillas in *Godzilla,* the insects in *Honey, I Shrunk the Kids,* and the Martian vocals in *Mars Attacks!* Fred Newman is probably best known as the sound-effect artist on *The Prairie Home Companion.* His repertoire of vocal effects not only can be heard on the program but are cataloged, with ways to produce them, in his book *Mouth Sounds: How to Whistle,*

Pop, Boing, and Honk for All Occasions and Then Some (see Bibliography).

Among the keys to effectively producing vocal sound effects are to make sure they do not sound like they come from a human voice and to infuse into the sound the sonic identity or personality that creates the "character."

Foley Sound Effects

The term now applied to manually producing sound effects in the studio is *Foley recording,* named for Jack Foley, a sound editor with Universal Pictures for many years. Given the history of radio drama and the fact that other Hollywood sound editors had been producing effects in the studio for some time, clearly Jack Foley did not invent the technique. His name became identified with it in the early 1950s when he had to produce the sound of paddling a small survival raft in the ocean. Instead of producing the effect separately and then having it synced to picture later, which had been the typical procedure, he produced the effect in sync with picture at the same time. The inventiveness and efficiency he showed in simultaneously producing and syncing sound effects and picture—saving the sound editor considerable postproduction time—impressed enough people that Foley's name has become associated with the technique ever since.

Today the primary purposes of Foley recording are to produce sound effects that are difficult to record during production, such as for far-flung action scenes or large-scale movement of people and materiel; to create sounds that do not exist naturally; and to produce controlled sound effects in a regulated studio environment.

This is not to suggest that "Foleying" and sonic authenticity are mutually exclusive. Producing realistic Foley effects has come a long way since the days of radio drama and involves much more than pointing a microphone at a sound source on a surface that is not a real surface in an acoustic space that has no natural environment. A door sound cannot be just any door. Does the scene call for a closet door, a bathroom door, or a front door? A closet door has little air, a bathroom door sounds more open, and a front door sounds solid, with a latch to consider. In a sword fight, simply banging together two pieces of metal adds little to the dynamics of the scene. Using metal that produces strong harmonic rings, however, creates the impression of swords with formidable strength. A basketball game recorded in a schoolyard will have a more open sound, with rim noises, ball handling, and different types of ball bounces on asphalt, than will a basketball game played in an indoor gymnasium, which will differ still from the sound of a game played in an indoor arena.

Generally, Foley effects are produced in a specially designed sound studio known as a *Foley stage* (see 15-3). It is acoustically dry not only because, as with dialogue rerecording, ambiences are usually added later but also because reflections from loud sounds must be kept to a

15-3 A Foley stage. The two Foley walkers are using the various pits and equipment to perform, in sync, the sounds that should be heard with the picture.

minimum. That said, Foley recording is sometimes done on the actual production set to take advantage of its more realistic acoustic environment.

Foley effects are usually produced in sync with the visuals. The picture is shown on a screen in the studio, and when a foot falls, a door opens, a paper rustles, a floor squeaks, a man sits, a girl coughs, a punch lands, or a body splashes, a Foley artist generates the effect at the precise time it occurs on-screen. Such a person is sometimes called a *Foley walker* because Foley work often requires performing many different types of footsteps. In fact, many Foley artists are dancers.

Important to successful Foleying is having a feel for the material—to become, in a sense, the on-screen actor by recognizing body movements and the sounds they generate. John Wayne, for example, did not have a typical walk; he sort of strode and rolled. Other actors may clomp, shuffle, or glide as they walk.

Also important to creating a sound effect is studying its sonic characteristics and then finding a sound source that contains similar qualities. Take the sound of a growing rock. There is no such sound, of course, but if there were, what would it be like? Its obvious characteristics would be stretching and sharp cracking sounds. One solution is to inflate a balloon and scratch it with your fingers to create a high-pitched scraping sound. If the rock is huge and requires a throatier sound, slow down the playing speed. For the cracking sound, shellac an inflated rubber tube. Once the shellac hardens, sonically isolate the valve to eliminate the sound of air escaping and let the air out of the tube. As the air escapes, the shellac will crack. Combine both sounds to get the desired effect.

There are myriad examples of Foley-created effects, many carryovers from the heyday of radio drama. This section presents just a sampling of the range of possibilities.

Door sounds have been a fundamental aspect of Foley recording since its beginnings. The principal sound heard on a door close or open comes from the lock and the jamb. There are numerous ways to achieve this effect for different types of doors:

■ Squeaky door—twist a leather belt or billfold, turn snug wooden pegs in holes drilled in a block of wood, or twist a cork in the mouth of a bottle

■ Elevator door—run a roller skate over a long, flat piece of metal

■ Jail door—the characteristic sound of an iron door is the noise when it clangs shut: clang two flat pieces of metal together, then let one slide along the other for a moment, signifying the bar sliding into place

■ Other iron door—draw an iron skate over an iron plate (for the hollow clang of iron doors opening); rattling a heavy chain and a key in a lock adds to the effect

■ Screen door—the distinctive sound comes from the spring and the rattle of the screen on the slam: secure an old spring, slap it against a piece of wood, then rattle a window screen

■ Swinging doors—swing a real door back and forth between the hands, letting the free edge strike the heels of the hands

Punches, slaps, and blows to the head and body are common Foley effects, as are the sounds of footsteps, falling, and breaking bones. These sounds have broad applications in different genres, from action-adventure to drama and comedy. As effects, they can be created using an imaginative variety of sources and techniques:

■ Creating blows on the head by striking a pumpkin with a bat, striking a large melon with a wooden mallet or a short length of garden hose—add crackers for additional texture—or striking a baseball glove with a short piece of garden hose

■ Creating blows on the chin by lightly dampening a large powder puff and slapping it on the wrist close to the mic, holding a piece of sponge rubber in one hand and striking it with the fist, slipping on a thin leather glove and striking the bare hand with the gloved fist, or hanging a slab of meat and punching it with a closed fist

■ Cracking a whip to heighten the impact of a punch

■ Pulling a fist in and out of a watermelon to produce the sound of a monster taking the heart from a living person

■ Creating various footsteps: on concrete—use hard-heeled shoes on composition stone; on gravel—fill a long shallow box with gravel and have someone actually walk on it; on leaves—stir cornflakes in a small cardboard box with fingers; on mud—in a large dishpan containing a little water, place several crumpled and shredded newspapers or paper towels and simulate walking by using the palm of the hand for footsteps; on snow—squeeze a box of cornstarch with the fingers in the proper rhythm or squeeze cornstarch in a gloved hand; on stairs—use just the ball of the foot, not the heel, in a forward sliding motion on a bare floor

◼ Dropping a squash to provide the dull thud of a falling body hitting the ground (to add more weight to the body, drop a sack of sand on the studio floor)

◼ Crushing chicken bones together with a Styrofoam cup for bone breaks

◼ Breaking bamboo, frozen carrots, or cabbage for more bone crunching

◼ Using string to suspend wooden sticks from a board and manipulating the board so that the sticks clack together to create the effect of bones rattling

◼ Creating the effect of breaking bones by chewing hard candy close to the mic, twisting and crunching a celery stalk, or snapping small-diameter dowels wrapped in soft paper

◼ Inserting a mini-mic up the nose to create the perspective of hearing breathing from inside the head

◼ Twisting stalks of celery to simulate the sound of tendons being stretched

◼ Bending a plastic straw to simulate the sound of a moving joint

The sounds of guns and other weaponry can be made from a wide range of other sources when the real thing is not available.

◼ Snapping open a pair of pliers, a door latch, or briefcase catch to cock a pistol

◼ Closing a book smartly; striking a padded leather cushion with a thin, flat stick or a whip; or pricking a balloon with a pin to create a pistol shot

◼ Striking a book with the flat side of a knife handle for a bullet hitting a wall

◼ For the whiz-by ricochet of a passing bullet, using a sling shot with large coins, washers, screws—anything that produces an edge tone—and recording close miked

◼ Whipping a thin, flexible stick through the air and overdubbing it several times to create the sound of whooshing arrows

◼ Piling a collection of tin and metal scraps into a large tub and then dumping it to simulate a metallic crash (for a sustained crash, shake and rattle the tub until the cue for the payoff crash)

◼ Dropping debris or slamming a door for an explosion

◼ Using a lion's roar without the attack and some flanging to add to an explosion

◼ Recording light motorcycle drive-bys, then pitch-shifting, and reshaping their sound envelopes to use as building material for an explosion

◼ Flushing a toilet, slowed down with reverb, to simulate a depth charge

◼ Banging on a metal canoe in a swimming pool and dropping the canoe into the water above an underwater mic to produce the sounds of explosions beating on the hull of a submarine

◼ Using the venting and exhaust sounds from a cylinder of nitrogen as the basis for a freeze gun

While nothing will substitute for a high-quality ambience recording, the following are ways to both enhance and approximate sounds of the elements and of various creatures:

◼ Folding two sections of newspaper in half, then cutting each section into parallel strips and gently swaying them close to the mic to create the effect of a breeze

◼ Using a mallet against a piece of sheet metal or ductwork to sound like thunder

◼ Letting salt or fine sand slip through fingers or a funnel onto cellophane, or pouring water from a sprinkling can into a tub with some water already in it, for simulating rain

◼ Blowing air through a straw into a glass of water for the effect of a babbling brook (experiment by using varying amounts of water and by blowing at different speeds)

◼ Blowing into a glass of water through a soda straw for a flood

◼ Using the slurpy, sucking sound of a bathtub drain as the basis for a whirlpool or someone sinking into quicksand

◼ Discharging compressed air in a lot of mud to create the dense bubbling sound of a molten pit

◼ Crumpling stiff paper or cellophane near the mic or pouring salt from a shaker onto stiff paper to create the sound of fire; blowing lightly through a soda straw into liquid at the mic for the roar of flames; breaking the stems of broom straws or crushing wrapping paper for the effects of a crackling fire

■ Crumpling Styrofoam near the mic for the effect of crackling ice

■ Twisting an inflated balloon for the effect of a creaking ice jam

■ Scraping dry ice on metal to create the sound of a moving glacier

■ Clapping a pair of coconut shells together in proper rhythm to create the clippety-clop sound of hoofbeats on a hard road

■ Running roller skates over fine gravel sprinkled on a blotter for a horse and wagon

■ Pushing a plunger in a sandbox to simulate horses walking on sand

■ Using a feather duster in the spokes of a spinning bicycle wheel to create the sound of gently beating wings—or flapping a towel or sheet to generate a more aggressive wing sound

■ Taking the rubber ball from a computer mouse and dragging it across the face of a computer monitor to create the sound of a bat

■ Wiping dry glass to use as the basis for a squeak from a large mouse

■ Lightly tapping safety pins on linoleum to simulate a mouse's footsteps

Often it takes two, three, or more sounds plus signal processing to come up with the appropriate sound effect. When a sound effect is built in this way, numerous strategies and techniques are employed to achieve the desired impact (see Chapter 20). Every decision informs the whole: selecting source material, layering and combining sounds, editing, (re)shaping sound envelopes, speeding up or slowing down a sound, reversing and looping, and applying reverb, delay, flanging, chorusing, or other processing:

■ The helicopter sound at the beginning of *Apocalypse Now*—the blade *thwarp,* the turbine whine, and the gear sound—was created by synthesizing the sounds of a real helicopter.

■ The sound of the insects coming out of the heat duct in *Arachnophobia* was produced by recording Brazilian roaches walking on aluminum. The rasping sound a tarantula makes rubbing its back legs on the bulblike back half of its body was created from the sound of grease frying mixed with high-pressure air bursts.

■ In *Back to the Future III,* the basic sound of galloping horses was created using plungers on different types of surfaces. The sound was then rerecorded and processed in various ways to match the screen action.

■ In *WALL-E* the howling wind of Earth at the beginning of the film was made from a recording of Niagara Falls. The sound was processed using reverb, slight feedback in the upper frequency range, and some equalization.

■ The sound blaster weapon in *Star Wars* was made from recording the sounds of tapping on a radio tower high-tension guy-wire. The characteristic, sweeping, "pass-by feeling" of the sound envelope is a result of higher frequencies traveling along the wire faster than lower frequencies. Similarly, the sound of Eve's laser in *WALL-E* was made from striking an extended Slinky.

■ The sounds of the spaceship *Millennium Falcon* in *Star Wars* included tiny fan motors, a flight of World War II torpedo planes, a pair of low-frequency sine waves beating against each other, variably phased white noise with frequency nulls, a blimp, a phased atom bomb explosion, a distorted thunderclap, an F-86 jet firing afterburners, a Phantom jet idling, a 747 takeoff, an F-105 jet taxiing, and a slowed-down P-51 prop plane pass-by. Various textures were taken from each of these sounds and blended together to create the engine noises, takeoffs, and fly-bys.

■ In *Jurassic Park III* the sounds of velociraptors were created from a variety of sources, including the hissing of a house cat, snarls and cackles from vultures, ecstatic calls from emperor and Adelie penguins, as well as marine mammals and larger cats. Building on the repertoire of the first two films, the tyrannosaurus sounds were composed of the trumpeting sound of a baby elephant, an alligator growl, and the growls of 15 other creatures, mostly lions and tigers. The inhale of T. Rex's breathing included the sounds of lions, seals, and dolphins; the exhale included the sound of a whale's blowhole. The smashing, crashing sound of trees being cut down, particularly Sequoias, was used to create the footfalls of the larger dinosaurs. The sounds of the reptilian dinosaurs were built from the sounds of lizards, iguanas, bull snakes, a rattlesnake (flanged), and horselike snorts. A Synclavier was used to process many of these sounds, including some of the dinosaur footsteps and eating effects.[2]

---

2. A Synclavier is a highly sophisticated synthesizer, but unlike most synthesizers a Synclavier is not preprogrammed; sounds have to be fed into a Synclavier before they can be programmed, processed, and sampled.

■ In the film *The PageMaster,* the dragon's sound was produced vocally and reinforced with tiger growls to take advantage of the animal's bigger and more resonant chest cavity.

■ The spinning and moving sounds of the main character going from place to place in *The Mask* were created by twirling garden hoses and power cables to get moving-through-air sounds, layering them in a Synclavier, routing them through a loudspeaker, waving a mic in front of the loudspeaker to get a Doppler effect, and then adding jets, fire whooshes, and wind gusts.

■ The multilayered sound of the batmobile in *Batman and Robin* comprised the sounds of an Atlas rocket engine blast, the turbocharger whine of an 800-horsepower Buick Grand National, a Ducati motorcycle, and a Porsche 917 12-cylinder racer.

■ In *St. Elmo's Fire,* which is a phenomenon caused when static electricity leaps from metal to metal, signal-processing the sound of picking at and snapping carpet padding emulated the effect.

■ For the final electrocution scene in *The Green Mile,* the sound of metal scraping, human screams, dogs barking, pigs squealing, and other animals in pain were integrated with the idea of making the electricity's effect like fingernails on a chalkboard.

■ In *Star Trek Insurrection,* there are little flying drones, basically robots with wings. Their sound was created by running vinyl-covered cable down a slope, tying a boom box to it on a pulley, and putting a microphone in the middle to get the Doppler effect. A series of different-quality steady-state tones was played back from the boom box's cassette to create the basic effect. All the sounds were then processed in a Synclavier.

■ Many different processed sounds went into creating the effects for the hovercraft *Nebuchadnezzar* in *The Matrix.* To help create the low metal resonances heard inside the ship, the sound of a giant metal gate that produced singing resonances was pitch-shifted down many octaves.

■ In *Master and Commander,* to simulate the sound of a nineteenth-century British frigate in a storm at sea, a large wooden frame was built and put in the bed of a pickup truck. A thousand feet of rope was strung tightly around the frame. The truck was then driven at high speed into a formidable headwind in the Mojave Desert. Acoustic blankets deadened the motor and truck sounds. The sound of the air meeting the lines of rope approximated the shriek of the wind in the frigate's rigging. A group of artillery collectors provided authentic cannons and cannon shot for the ship-to-ship cannonading. Chain shot (two cannonballs connected by a 2-foot piece of chain, used to take out rigging and sails) and grapeshot (canisters with a number of smaller balls inside, used to kill the opposition) were recorded at a firing range.[3]

Components and Context of a Foley Sound Effect

Being ingenious in creating a sound effect is not enough. You also have to know the components of the effect and the context in which the effect will be placed. Let us use two examples as illustrations: a car crash and footsteps.

The sound of a car crash generally has six components: the skid, a slight pause just before impact, the impact, the grinding sound of metal, the shattering of glass just after impact, and silence.

The sound of footsteps consists of three basic elements: the impact of the heel, which is a fairly crisp sound; the brush of the sole, which is a relatively soft sound; and, sometimes, heel or sole scrapes.

But before producing these sounds, you need to know the context in which they will be placed. For the car crash, the make, model, and year of the car will dictate the sounds of the engine, the skidding, and, after impact, the metal and the glass. The type of tires and the road surface will govern the pitch and the density of the riding sound; the car's speed is another factor that affects pitch. The location of the road—for example, in the city or the country—helps determine the quality of the sound's ambience and reverb. A swerving car will require tire squeals. Of course, what the car crashes into will also affect the sound's design.

As for the footsteps, the height, weight, gender, and age of the person will influence the sound's density and the heaviness of the footfall. Another influence on the footfall sound is the footwear—shoes with leather heels and soles, pumps, spiked heels, sneakers, sandals, and so on. The choices here may relate to the hardness or softness of the footfall and the attack of the heel sound or lack thereof. Perhaps you would want a suction-type or squeaky-type sound with sneakers; maybe you would use a flexing sound of leather for the sandals. The gait of the walk—fast, slow, ambling, steady, or accented—will

---

3. From Ben McGrath, "Wicked Wind," *New Yorker,* October 20, 2003, p. 80.

direct the tempo of the footfalls. The type of walking surface—concrete, stone, wood, linoleum, marble, or dirt—and whether it is wet, snowy, slushy, polished, or muddy will be sonically defined by the sound's timbre and envelope. The amount of reverberation added to the effect depends on where the footfalls occur.

Miking and Perspective in Foley Recording

The capacitor microphone is most frequently used in recording Foley effects because of its ability to pick up subtleties and capture *transients*—fast bursts of sound, such as door slams, gunshots, breaking glass, and footsteps—that constitute so much of Foley work. Tube-type capacitors help smooth harsh transients and warm digitally recorded effects.

Directional capacitors—super-, hyper-, and ultracardioid—are preferred because they pick up concentrated sound with little ambience. These pickup patterns also provide more flexibility in changing perspectives. Moving a highly directional microphone a few inches will sound like it was moved several feet.

Factors such as dynamic range and the noise floor require a good microphone preamp. Recording loud bangs or crashes or soft nuances of paper folding or pins dropping requires the capabilities to handle both a wide variety of dynamics and considerable gain with almost no additional noise. Many standard in-console preamps are not up to the task. Limiting and compression are sometimes used in Foley recording; except for noise reduction, processing is usually done during the final stages of postproduction.

Microphone placement is critical in Foleying because the on-screen environment must be replicated as closely as possible on the Foley stage. In relation to mic-to-source distance, the closer the microphone is to a sound source, the more detailed, intimate, and drier the sound. When the mic is farther from a sound source, the converse of that is true—but only to a certain extent on a Foley stage because the studio itself has such a short reverberation time. To help create perspective, openness, or both in the latter instance, multiple miking is often used. Nevertheless, if a shot calls for a close environment, baffles can be used to decrease the room size. If the screen environment is more open, the object is to operate in as open a space as possible. Remember, do not confuse perspective with loudness. It is hearing more or less of the surroundings that helps create perspective.

It is important to know how to record sound at a distance. Equalization and reverb can only simulate distance

and room size. Nothing is as authentic as recording in the appropriately sized room with the microphones matching the camera-to-action distance.

A critical aspect of Foley recording cannot be overstated: make sure the effects sound consistent and integrated and do not seem to be outside or on top of the sound track. When a sound is recorded at too close a mic-to-source distance, in poor acoustics, or with the wrong equipment, it is unlikely that any signal processing can save it.

Production Sound Effects

Directors may prefer to capture authentic sounds either as they occur on the set during production, by recording them separately in the field, or both. These directors are willing to sacrifice, within limits, the controlled environment of the Foley stage for the greater sonic realism and authenticity of the actual sound sources produced in their natural surroundings. Or they may wish to use field sound as a reference for Foley recording or to take advantage of a sound's authenticity and use it as the basis for further processing. Still, a number of factors must be taken into consideration to obtain usable sounds.

If sounds are recorded with the dialogue as part of the action—a table thump, a match strike, a toaster pop—getting the dialogue is always more important than getting the sound effect; the mic must be positioned for optimal pickup of the performers.

When a director wants sound recorded with dialogue, the safest course of action is to record it with a different mic than the one being used for the performers. If the dialogue mic is a boom, use a plant (stationary) mic for the sound effect; if the dialogue is recorded using body mics, use a boom or plant mic for the sound. This facilitates recording sound and dialogue on separate tracks and therefore provides flexibility in postproduction editing and mixing.

If for some reason only one mic is used, a boom would be best. Because its mic-to-source position changes with the shot, there is a better chance of capturing and maintaining perspectives with it than with a body or plant mic. Moreover, in single-camera production a scene is shot at least a few times from different perspectives, so there is more than one opportunity to record a usable sound/dialogue relationship.

This point should be emphasized: it is standard in single-camera production to shoot and reshoot a scene. For each shot time is taken to reposition camera, lights, and crew; to redo makeup; to primp wardrobe; and so on. During this time the sound crew also should be repositioning mics. Take advantage of every opportunity to record audio on the set. The more takes of dialogue and sound effects you record, the greater the flexibility in editing and mixing. Even if dialogue or effects are unusable because of mediocre audio quality, it is still wise to preserve the production recording because it is often useful in dialogue rerecording and Foleying as a reference for timing, accent, and expressiveness.

You never want to mask an actor's line with a sound effect, or any other sound for that matter, or to have a sound effect call attention to itself (unless that is the intent). If sound effects are recorded on the set before or after shooting rather than with the action, try to do it just before shooting. Everyone is usually in place on the set, so the acoustics will match the acoustics of the take. If an effect must be generated by the actor, it can be. And all sounds should be generated from the sound source's location in the scene.

When recording the effect, there must be absolute quiet; nothing else can be audible—a dog barking far in the distance, an airplane flying overhead, wind gently wafting through trees, crockery vibrating, lights buzzing, crew shuffling, actors primping. The sound effect must be recorded "in the clear" so that it carries no sonic baggage into postproduction.

This brings us back to the question: If all these added concerns go with recording sound effects on the set, why bother? Why not save time, effort, and expense and simply Foley them? Some directors do not care for the controlled acoustics of the Foley stage or for artificially created sound. They want to capture the flavor, or "air," of a particular location, preserve the unique characteristic of a sound an actor generates, and fuse the authenticity of and interaction among sounds as they occur naturally.

This poses considerable challenges in moving-action scenes, such as chases, that take place over some distance. Such scenes are usually covered by multiple cameras; and although multiple microphones may not be positioned with the cameras, using them will capture the sounds of far-flung action. The mics can be situated at strategic spots along the chase route, with separate recorder/mixer units at each location to control the oncoming, passing, and fading sounds. In addition, a mic mounted on the means of conveyance in the chase can be of great help in postproduction editing and mixing. For example, on a getaway car, mics can be mounted to the front fender, level with the hubcaps, and aimed at a 45-degree angle

toward where the rubber meets the road; or a fishpole boom can be rigged through the rear window and rested on a door for support. In a horse chase, a mic can be mounted outside the rider's clothing or fastened to the lower saddle area and pointed toward the front hooves.

Another advantage of multiple-miking sound effects is the ability to capture various perspectives of the same sound. To record an explosion, for example, positioning mics, say, 25, 50, 100, and 500 feet away provides potential for a number of sonic possibilities when editing and mixing. Another reason for recording extremely loud sound from more than one location is that the sound can overmodulate a recorder to the point that much of it may not record. With a digital recording, remember that there is no headroom. That is why, for example, the sound of loud weaponry is compressed—to create a more percussive sound that otherwise might be distorted or sound thinner and weaker than the actual sound.

The obvious microphone to use in many of these situations may seem to be the wireless because of its mobility. As good as wireless systems can be, however, they are still subject to interference from radio frequencies, telephone lines, and passing cars, which causes spitting and buzzing sounds. A directional capacitor microphone connected to a good mic preamp is the most dependable approach to take here. In these applications use very strong shock mounts and tough windscreens. And do not overlook the importance of wearing ear protection when working with loud sounds. Do not monitor these sounds directly: use your eyes and peak meter instead of your ears.

Collecting Sound Effects in the Field

Live sound recorded away from the set for a specific production—or between productions to build sound-effect libraries—is usually collected in the field. As with most field recording, utmost care should be taken to record the effect in perspective, with no unwanted sound—especially wind and handling noise. It is helpful to use a decibel level meter to measure ambient noise levels when working on-location. Like a cinematographer using a light meter, this can inform a range of decisions from mic selection to placement. It cannot be overemphasized that any recording done away from the studio also requires first-rate, circumaural headphones for reliable monitoring.

As with most sound-effect miking, the directional capacitor is preferred for reasons already noted. That said, the parabolic microphone system, using a capacitor mic, is also employed for recording sounds in the field for a long-reach, highly concentrated pickup. This is particularly important when recording weaker sounds, such as insects, certain types of birdcalls, and rustling leaves. Parabolic mics are essentially midrange instruments, so it is probably unwise to use them on sound sources with significant defining low or high frequencies.

For stereo, the middle-side (M-S) and stereo mics are most common because they are easier to set up than coincident or spaced stereo microphones and are more accurate to aim at a sound source. In fact, spaced stereo mics should be avoided because in reproducing the sound image it will jump from one loudspeaker to the other as the effect passes. M-S mics are particularly useful because it is often difficult to control environmental sounds. With an M-S mic, it is possible to keep the environmental sound separate from the principal sound and either not use it or combine the two sounds in the mix.

When recording moving stereo sound effects, be careful that the sound image does not pass across the mic in a straight line as it moves toward the center of the pickup. In certain instances it becomes disproportionately louder compared with its left and right imaging, particularly if the mic array is close to the path of the sound source. Also, the closer the stereo mic-to-source distance, the faster the image will pass the center point. Keep in mind that accurately monitoring stereo requires stereo headphones.

With any directional microphone, is it worth remembering that changing the mic-to-source angle only a few degrees will change the character of the sound being recorded. This can be advantageous or disadvantageous, depending on the effect you are trying to achieve.

Also important in field-recording sound effects is having excellent microphone preamps and the right recording equipment. Digital recorders vary in robustness and in their ability, for example, to deal with subtle sounds, percussive sounds, and dynamic range, particularly if they encode compressed audio.

A key to collecting successful live effects in the field is making sure that the recorded effect sounds like what it is supposed to be, assuming that is your intention. Placing a mic too close to a babbling brook could make it sound like boiling water or liquid bubbling in a beaker. Miking it from too far away, on the other hand, might destroy its liquidity. A flowing stream miked too closely could sound like a river; miking it from too far away could reduce its size and density. A recording of the inside of a submarine could sound too cavernous. Applause might

sound like rain or something frying. A spraying fountain might sound like rain or applause. In fact, a spraying fountain often lacks the identifying liquid sound. To get the desired audio, it might be necessary to mix in a watery-type sound, such as a river or a flowing, rather than babbling, brook. A yellowjacket flying around a box could sound like a deeper, fuller-sounding bumblebee if miked too closely or a mosquito if miked from too far away. A gunshot recorded outdoors in open surroundings sounds like a firecracker; some types of revolvers sound like pop guns.

Keep four other things in mind when recording sounds in the field: be patient, be persistent, be inventive, and, if you really want authenticity, be ready to go anywhere and to almost any length to obtain an effect.

For the film *Hindenburg,* the sound designer spent six months researching, collecting, and producing the sounds of a dirigible, including sonic perspectives from a variety of locations both inside the ship and on the ground to someone hearing a dirigible passing overhead.

In the film *Glory,* the sound designer wanted the effects of Civil War weaponry to be as close to authentic as possible, even to the extent of capturing the sound of real Civil War cannonballs and bullets whizzing through the air. Specially made iron cannonballs were shot from cannons forged for the film; this was recorded at 250 yards and at 0.25 mile downrange. These locations were far enough from the initial explosion that it would not contaminate the sound of the projectiles going by. The two distances provided a choice of whiz-by sounds and also the potential for mixing them, if necessary. Because the cannons could not be aimed very well at such distances, not one acceptable whiz-by was recorded during an entire day of taping. For the bullet whizzes, modern rifles would not have worked because the bullet velocity is not slow enough to produce an audible air whiz-by. Using real Civil War bullets, a recordist sat in a gully 400 yards downrange and taped the whiz-bys as the live rounds flew overhead. In the end the cannonball whiz-bys had to be created by playing the bullet whiz-bys in reverse and slowed down.

Finally, when collecting sounds in the field, do not necessarily think literally about what it is you want to capture. Consider a sound's potential to be built into another effect. For example, the sound of the giant boulder careening toward the frantically running Indiana Jones in *Raiders of the Lost Ark* was the processed audio of a car rolling down a gravel road, in neutral, with the engine off. The sound was pitch-shifted down and slowed with the lower frequencies boosted in level. In the Well of Souls scene, the sounds of seething and writhing in the snake pit were made from recordings of sponges and a cheese casserole. A toilet seat was used for the sound of the opening of the Ark of the Covenant, and marine mammals and synthesized sounds evoked the voices of the souls within. Other examples of transforming sound effects are cited throughout this chapter.

ELECTRONICALLY GENERATED SOUND EFFECTS

High-quality sound effects can be generated electronically with synthesizers and computers and by employing MIDI. This approach is also referred to as *electronic Foley*. Its advantages are cost-efficiency, convenience, and the unlimited number of sounds that can be created. Its main disadvantage is that electronically generated sound effects sometimes lack the "reality" that directors desire.

Synthesized Sound Effects

A *synthesizer* is an audio instrument that uses sound generators to create waveforms. The various ways these waveforms are combined can synthesize a vast array of sonic characteristics that are similar to, but not exactly like, existing sounds and musical instruments. They can also be combined to generate a completely original sound. In other words, because the pitch, amplitude, timbre, and envelope of each synthesizer tone generator can be controlled, it is possible to build synthesized sounds from scratch.

In addition to synthesized effects, preprogrammed sound from libraries designed for specific synthesizer brands and models is available. These collections may be grouped by type of sound effect—such as punches, screams, and thunder—or by instrument category, such as drum, string, brass, and keyboard sounds (see 15-4). These libraries come in various formats, such as hard disk, compact disc, plug-in memory cartridge, and computer files available as separate software or via downloading.

One complaint about synthesized sound has been its readily identifiable electronic quality. With considerably improved synthesizer designs and software, this has become much less of an issue. But take care that the synthesizer and the sound library you use produce professional-quality sound; many do not, particularly those available through downloading, because of the adverse effects of data compression.

The operational aspects of synthesizers and their programs are beyond the purview of this book. Even if they were not, it is extremely difficult to even begin to describe the sonic qualities of the infinite effects that synthesizers can generate. Suffice it to say that almost anything is possible. The same is true of computer-generated sound effects.

Computer-generated Sound Effects

A principal difference between the synthesizer and the computer is that the synthesizer is specifically designed to create and produce sounds; the computer is not. The computer is completely software-dependent. With the

15-4 One synthesizer's soundfiles in the drum category, shown mapped across a keyboard.

appropriate software, the computer, like the synthesizer, can also store preprogrammed sounds, create them from scratch, or both. Most computer sound programs make it possible not only to call up a particular effect but also to see and manipulate its waveform and therefore its sonic characteristics (see Chapter 20).

Sampling

An important sound-shaping capability of many electronic keyboards and computer software programs is *sampling*, a process whereby digital audio data representing a sonic event, acoustic or electroacoustic, is stored on disk or into electronic memory. The acoustic sounds can be anything a microphone can record—a shout, splash, motor sputter, song lyric, or trombone solo. Electroacoustic sounds are anything electronically generated, such as the sounds a synthesizer produces. The samples can be of any length, as brief as a drumbeat or as long as the available memory allows.

A *sampler*, basically a specialized digital record and playback device, may be keyboard-based, making use of musical keyboard controllers to trigger and articulate sampled audio; or it may be a rack-mountable unit without a keyboard that is controlled by an external keyboard or a sequencer. A *sequencer* is an electronic device that stores messages, maintains time relationships among them, and transmits the messages when they are called for from devices connected to it. The sampler may also be computer-based.

With most sampling systems, it is possible to produce an almost infinite variety of sound effects by shortening, lengthening, rearranging, looping, and signal-processing the stored samples. A trombone can be made to sound like a saxophone, an English horn, or a marching band of 76 trombones. One drumbeat can be processed into a thunderclap or built into a chorus of jungle drums. A single cricket chirp can be manipulated and repeated to orchestrate a tropical evening ambience. The crack of a baseball bat can be shaped into the rip that just precedes an explosion. The squeal of a pig can be transformed into a human scream. A metal trashcan being hit with a hammer can provide a formidable backbeat for a rhythm track.

Here sound effects become additional instruments in the underscoring—which, in turn, becomes a form of electroacoustic *musique concrète*. Consider the music for the film *Atonement*. The central character is an author, and at the beginning of the story we are introduced to her

as a child, writing on a manual typewriter. The clacking punches of the keys, the thud of the spacebar, and the zip of the carriage return create a leitmotiv establishing her identity and bringing us into her immediate soundscape—both literally (i.e., her bedroom) and figuratively, in the internal space of the writer's mind. Gradually, these sounds become part of the rhythmic and textural fabric of the underscoring. Another example of sound effects being treated as musical material is found in *Henry V*. In the film the pitched percussive clashes of swords from the epic battle scene were tuned to the minor key signature of Patrick Doyle's score. The sonic texture of the battle provides a tonal complement to the music.

In solid-state memory systems, such as *ROM (read-only memory)* and *RAM (random-access memory)*, it is possible to instantly access all or part of the sample and reproduce it any number of times. The difference between ROM- and RAM-based samplers is that ROM-based samplers are factory-programmed and reproduce only; RAM-based samplers allow you to both reproduce and record sound samples. The number of samples you can load into a system is limited only by the capacity of the system's storage memory.

The Samplefile

After a sample is recorded or produced, it is saved to a storage medium, usually a hard disk, compact disc, memory card, or DVD. The stored sound data is referred to as a *samplefile*. Once stored, of course, a samplefile can be easily distributed. As a result, samplefiles of sounds are available to production facilities in the same way that sound-effect libraries are available. Other storage media are also used for samplefile distribution, such as CD-ROM, erasable and write-once optical discs, and Web sites.

Sample libraries abound, with samples of virtually any sound that is needed. Here is a short list of available samples from various libraries: drum and bass samples including loops, effects pads, and bass-synth sounds; Celtic instrument riffs; arpeggiated synth loops and beats; nontraditional beats and phrases from ethnic folk instruments; violin section phrases and runs; a cappella solo, duet, and choral performances from India, Africa, and the Middle East; otherworldly atmospheres; assortments of tortured, gurgling beats; reggae and hip-hop beats; electronic sound effects and ambiences; multisampled single notes on solo and section brasses, saxophones, and French horns; and acoustic bass performances in funky and straight-eighth styles at various beats per minute.

You should take two precautions before investing in a samplefile library. First, make sure that the samplefiles are in a format that is compatible with your sampler and with the standards and the protocols of the postproduction editing environment you plan to work in. There has been increased standardization of samplefile formats for computer-based systems, with two common types being Waveform Audio Format (WAV) and *Audio Interchange File Format (AIFF)*. Second, make sure that the sound quality of the samples is up to professional standards; too many are not, particularly those obtained online. For most audio applications, mono or stereo sounds files recorded at 16-bit depth and 44.1 kHz sampling rate are standard; 24-bit at 48 kHz are optimal for film and video.

Tips for Recording Samples

Before recording a sample, plan ahead (see 15-5). It saves time and energy and reduces frustration. When recording samples from whatever source—acoustic or electronic—it is vital that the sound and the reproduction be of good quality. Because the sample may be used many times and in a variety of situations, it is disconcerting (to say the least) to hear a bad sample again and again. Moreover, if the sample has to be rerecorded, it might be difficult to reconstruct the same sonic and performance conditions.

Miking

The same advice that applies to miking for digital recording (see Chapter 17) applies to miking for sampling. Only the highest-quality microphones should be used, which usually means capacitors with a wide, flat response; high sensitivity; and an excellent self-noise rating. If very loud sound recorded at close mic-to-source distances requires a moving-coil mic, it should be a large-diaphragm, top-quality model with as low a self-noise rating as possible.

The challenge is to avoid tonal coloration of the sample. A noisy sample audibly shifts in pitch as you play different keys on the keyboard. Close miking with a directional mic helps reduce any room sound. Any recorded ambience, as with any unwanted noise, becomes part of the sample.

In recording samples in stereo, imaging and room size are significantly affected by the miking technique because the interchannel delay varies with the pitch shift. The only way to know which technique will work best for a given application is to experiment with the various

15-5 One approach to devising a workable strategy when creating a sample.

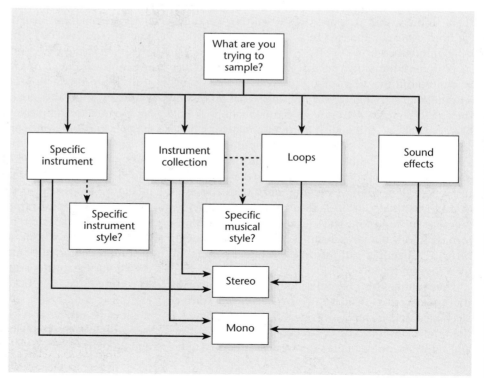

From *Electronic Musician*, January 2002, p. 40. © 2002 Primedia Musician Magazine and Media, Inc. All rights reserved. Reprinted with permission of Prism Business Media, Inc. Copyright © 2002. All rights reserved.

stereo microphone arrays—coincident, near-coincident, and spaced—before deciding.

ORGANIZING A SOUND-EFFECT LIBRARY

It is not unusual for an audio facility to have thousands of sound effects in its collection. Although prerecorded libraries come with an index, timing information, and, often, descriptions of the cues, and sound effects produced in-house are also cataloged, it can be time-consuming to locate and audition an effect. Database systems and software programs facilitate searching, locating, and auditioning a sound effect in seconds.

Generally, the search feature provides four ways to find an effect: by category, word, synonym, or catalog number. A system can be interfaced with a multidisc player so that once an effect has been located it can be auditioned from the start of the track or cued to within a split second anywhere in the track. For example, by punching in "thunder," the user finds out that there are 56 versions of thunder available, the time of each version, and a short description of what type of thunder it is. In some systems the computer will unload the disc and play back the thunder effects called for (see 15-6).

Plug-in programs are also available that can read tracks and indexes directly from a sound-effect CD and apply names and manufacturers' descriptions for almost every sound-effect (and music) library available (see 15-7). Some can rip a CD in relatively short time. *Ripping* (also referred to as *digital audio extraction*) is the process of

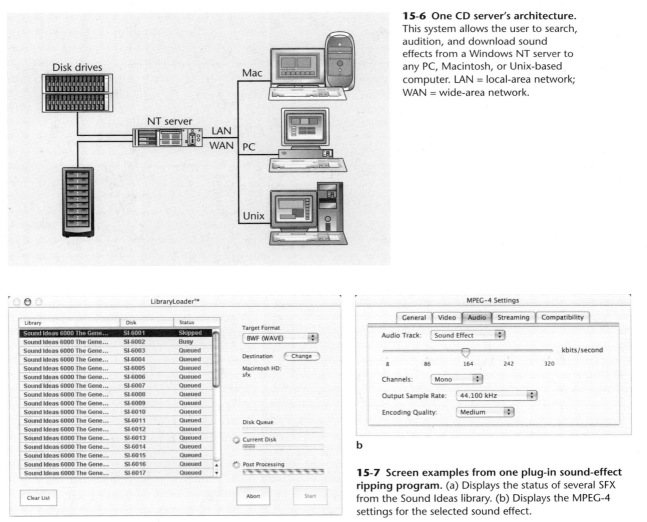

15-6 One CD server's architecture. This system allows the user to search, audition, and download sound effects from a Windows NT server to any PC, Macintosh, or Unix-based computer. LAN = local-area network; WAN = wide-area network.

15-7 Screen examples from one plug-in sound-effect ripping program. (a) Displays the status of several SFX from the Sound Ideas library. (b) Displays the MPEG-4 settings for the selected sound effect.

copying audio (or video) data in one media form, such as CD or DVD, to a hard disk. To conserve storage space, copied data are usually encoded in a compressed format, such as MP3, WMA (Windows Media Audio), MPEG-2, or MPEG-4.

SPOTTING

Spotting—going through a script or work print and deciding on the placement of music and sound effects—takes place at different times in the production process because sound effects can be produced during and after shooting, whereas music is usually spotted after the picture is edited (see Chapter 16). Regardless, its purpose is the same: to decide on the placement of sound effects and music in a production.

Spotting Sound Effects

Spotting sound effects involves going through the script or edited work print and specifically noting on a *spotting sheet* each effect that is called for; a spotting sheet indicates not only the sound effect but also whether it is synchronous or nonsynchronous, its in- and out-times, and its description. If the sounds have been recorded, notes about their dynamics, ambience, the way they begin and end, and any problems that require attention are also noted (see 15-8).

Spotting also has to take into consideration how the effects should be "played." If there are surf sounds in a beach scene, how active and dense-sounding are the waves? In a love scene, how much clothes rustle is to be heard? At a dance, is the background walla—ambient crowd sound—to be murmured, lively, or punctuated

15-8 Spotting sheet listing the sound effects required for a production.

SPOTTING SHEET

Project Title ___The Event___   Page Number __4 of 6__

Spotter ___A.M.___   Date Prepared __10/21__

Item	Syn/Nonsync	In-time	Out-time	Description
1	NS	01:42:15:10	01:43:12:09	Airplanes taking off
2	NS	01:45:26:29	01:46:15:12	Muddled voices
3	S	01:49:52:12		Door slamming
4	NS	01:49:52:12	01:53:05:05	Traffic noises
5	NS	01:54:03:27	01:56:22:17	Restaurant noises
6	S	01:56:13:25		Gunshot
7	NS	02:03:14:23	02:04:03:10	Phone ringing
8	NS	02:10:52:12	02:11:01:24	Glass breaking
9	NS	02:11:27:03	02:12:04:19	Dog barking
10	S	02:12:46:18		Glass breaking
11	NS	02:15:33:16		Thunder
12	NS	02:16:12:15	02:19:22:04	Rain, wind, and thunder
13	S	02:21:45:23		Car backfiring
14	NS	02:21:50:20	02:23:47:04	Children playing
15	NS	02:23:47:04	02:26:33:12	Ocean waves
16	NS	02:24:55:23		Thunder
17	NS	02:26:10:10		Thunder
18	S	02:30:12:14		Hit glass

with shouts? In a dinner scene, do the sounds of plates, glasses, and cutlery continue through the scene and the various shot changes from long, to medium, to close-up? If not, to what extent do they change?

MAIN POINTS

▶ Sound effects (SFX) can be classified as anything sonic that is not speech or music. They help amplify the reality created in a production.

▶ Sound effects perform two general functions: contextual and narrative. Contextual sound emanates from and duplicates a sound source as it is. It is also known as diegetic sound—coming from within the story space. (Nondiegetic sound comes from outside the story space; music underscoring is an example of nondiegetic sound.) Narrative sound adds more to a scene than what is apparent.

▶ Narrative sound can be descriptive or commentative.

▶ Sound effects can break the screen plane, define space, focus attention, establish locale, create environment, emphasize and intensify action, depict identity, set pace, provide counterpoint, create humor, symbolize meaning, create metaphor, and unify transition.

▶ Silence can be used to enhance sonic effect, particularly in situations where sound is expected or anticipated.

▶ The two primary sources of sound effects are prerecorded and produced.

▶ Prerecorded sound effects that can number from several dozen to several thousand are available in libraries. The major advantage of sound-effect libraries is that for relatively little cost many different, perhaps difficult-to-produce, sounds are at your fingertips. The disadvantages include the lack of control over the dynamics and the timing of the effects, possible mismatches in ambience and the possibility that the effects may sound canned, and the effect's not being long enough for your needs.

▶ Sound-effect libraries (and any recorded sound) can be manipulated by a variety of methods, such as varying a sound's playing speed, playing it backward, looping a sound, and altering it through signal processing.

▶ Producing live sound effects in the studio goes back to the days of radio drama. Producing SFX in synchronization

with the picture is known as Foleying, named for former film soundman Jack Foley.

▶ The keys to creating a sound effect are analyzing its sonic characteristics and then finding a sound source that contains similar qualities, whatever it may be.

▶ The capacitor microphone is most frequently used in recording Foley effects because of its ability to pick up subtleties and capture transients (fast bursts of sound). Tube-type capacitors help smooth transients and warm digitally recorded effects.

▶ A critical aspect of Foley recording is making sure that the effects sound consistent and integrated and do not seem to be outside or on top of the sound track.

▶ Some directors decry the use of studio-created effects, preferring to capture authentic sounds either as they occur on the set during production, by recording them separately in the field, or both.

▶ Sound effects can also be generated electronically with synthesizers and computers and by employing MIDI—an approach called electronic Foley. A synthesizer is an audio instrument that uses sound generators to create waveforms. Computer sound effects can be generated from preprogrammed software or software that allows sounds to be produced from scratch.

▶ An important sound-shaping capability of many electronic keyboards and computer software programs is sampling, a process whereby digital audio representing a sonic event, acoustic or electroacoustic, is stored on disk or into electronic memory. It can then be signal-processed into a different sound or expanded to serve as the basis for a longer sonic creation.

▶ In recording samples it is important to take your time and record them with the highest fidelity; if a sample has to be rerecorded, it might be difficult to reconstruct the same sonic and performance conditions.

▶ Database systems and software programs facilitate searching, locating, and auditioning a sound effect in seconds.

▶ Ripping, also referred to as digital audio extraction, is the process of copying audio (or video) data in one media form, such as CD or DVD, to a hard disk. To conserve storage space, copied data are usually encoded in a compressed format.

16

Music Underscoring

usic is elemental. Its sonic combinations are infinite, and its aesthetic values fulfill basic human needs. It is a tonal analogue to forms of human response, bearing "close logical similarity to conflict and resolution, speed, arrest, terrific excitement, calm, dreamy lapses."[1] Therein lies its power in *underscoring*—adding background music that enhances the content of a scene by evoking a particular idea, emotion, point of view, or atmosphere.

Music is generally thought of as an art form that evokes emotion. That is true, of course. It provides *affective information*—information related to feeling and mood. But it also provides *cognitive information*—information related to mental processes of knowledge, reasoning, memory, judgment, and perception.

USES OF MUSIC IN A PRODUCTION

Music in a production can have three uses: as production source, as source, and for underscoring. *Production source music* emanates from an on-screen singer or ensemble and is produced live during shooting or in postproduction. *Source music* is background music from an on-screen source such as a stereo, radio, or jukebox; it is added during post. *Underscore music* is original or library music. Underscore music is the focus of this chapter.

Underscoring serves picture in a number of ways. As composer Aaron Copland observed many years ago, and

1. Susanne K. Langer, *Feeling and Form* (New York: Scribner's, 1953), p. 27.

which still holds true today: underscoring creates a more convincing atmosphere of time and place; it underlines psychological refinements—the unspoken thoughts of a character or situation; it serves to fill pauses between conversation; it builds a sense of continuity; it underpins dramatic buildup and gives finality to a scene.[2]

Film composer Ennio Morricone put it another way: the underscore "must say all that the dialogue, images, and [sound] effects cannot say."[3]

Consider the following scene:

Opening shot: A man is walking down the street in an obviously small, rural town.

What is the story about? The music underscoring can tell you. Accompany the shot with skittish, galumphing music, and you have a comedy. Romantic music tells you it's a love story. Dissonant, high-pitched, staccato strings convey the unsettling imminence of threat and danger. A bright, upbeat harmonica tells you that the story is lighthearted and folksy. Change the harmonica's musical line to something slow, simple, and repetitive, and it foreshadows a story about the man's tiresome life. Accompany the shot with a large, full-bodied, contemporary symphonic score, and it counterpoints the setting against something epochal that is to occur.

MUSIC CHARACTERISTICS

Music has the same basic structural elements common to all sound, such as pitch, loudness, tempo, tone color, and envelope. It also contains other characteristics that broaden its perceptual and aesthetic meaning, such as melody and tonality; harmony and its qualities of consonance, dissonance, and texture; tempo; dynamic range that is quite wide compared with speech and sounds; and style in limitless variety.

The characteristics of music are both more and less complex than those of verbal language. Unlike speech (and sound effects), musical structure is both horizontal and vertical and therefore at once linear and simultaneous. That is, linear sound provides melody and rhythm; simultaneous sound provides harmony and texture. The entire audible spectrum of sound can be used in an infinite variety of combinations. It is difficult, however,

---

2. Aaron Copland, *Our New Music* (New York: McGraw-Hill, 1941).

3. Harlan Kennedy, "The Harmonious Background," *American Film*, vol. XXVII, no. 2 (February 1991), p. 40.

to be objective about the semantics of music, whereas with verbal language the problem of semantics is not nearly so acute.

Melody

Melody is a succession of pitched musical tones of varied durations. Because each tone has duration, melody also establishes rhythm. Hence melody has both a tone quality and a time quality and cannot be separated from rhythm. Generally, if a melody moves in narrowly pitched steps and ranges, it tends to be expressive and emotional. If it moves in widely pitched steps and ranges, it tends to be conservative and unexpressive.

Melodies are usually written in keys or tonalities, designated as major and minor. Subjectively, keys in the major mode usually sound positive, happy, bright, and vigorous; keys in the minor mode usually sound darker, tentative, wistful, and melancholy.

Although not explicitly defined as such, a melody is also considered to be a recognizable pattern of notes that can be characterized in terms useful to the sound designer, such as simple, sad, plaintive, sentimental, romantic, and so on.

Harmony

Harmony is a simultaneous sounding of two or more tones, although three or more tones are usually necessary to be classified as a chord. *Chords* are categorized as consonant or dissonant, and they are important to musical texture.

Consonance in music is produced by agreeable, settled, balanced, stable-sounding chords. *Dissonance* is produced by unsettled, unstable, unresolved, tense-sounding chords.

Texture, as the term suggests, is the result of materials interwoven to create a fabric. In music, melody and harmony are those interwoven materials. Undoubtedly, the infinite variety of musical textures that can be designed is a major reason for music's universal appeal and role in human communication. Subjectively, musical texture can be described as delicate, coarse, dense, airy, brittle, and so on.

In this regard various musicologists and sound therapists have ascribed emotional characteristics to harmonic intervals (see Figure 16-1). The table does not suggest, however, that a formulaic approach be taken to using music for dramatic purposes. It is simply to illustrate one of the many ways in which music can influence response.

16-1 The relationship of harmonic intervals to emotional characteristics.

Interval	Ratio	Emotional Characteristic
Unison	1:1	Strength, solidity, security, calmness
Octave	1:2	Completeness, openness, togetherness, circularity
Perfect fifth	2:3	Power, centering, comfortable, completeness, feeling of home
Perfect fourth	3:4	Serenity, clarity, openness, light, angelic
Major third	4:5	Hopeful, friendly, resolved, comfortable, square, characterless
Minor sixth	5:8	Soothing but delicate and sad
Minor third	5:6	Elated, uplifting
Major second	8:9	Happiness, openness, lightness, though irritating
Minor seventh	4:7	Suspenseful, expectant, rich but unbalanced
Major seventh	5:9	Strange, discordant, eerie
Major second	9:10	Anticipatory, unsettled
Minor second	15:16	Tense, uneasy, mysterious
Diminished fifth	5:7	Malevolent, demonic, horror

From David Sonnenschein, *Sound Design: The Expressive Power of Music, Voice, and Sound Effects in Cinema* (Studio City, Calif.: Michael Wiese Productions, 2001), p. 121. Reprinted with permission of Michael Wiese Productions; www.mwp.com. *Sound Design* copyright © 2001 David Sonnenschein.

Tempo

Tempo provides the pulse and the drive in music. A quick tempo tends to intensify stimulation; a slow tempo tends to allay it. Speeding up—*accelerando*—and slowing down—*ritardando*—influence response by heightening, sustaining, or diminishing it.

Dynamic Range

Because the *dynamic range* of music can be much wider than the dynamic ranges of speech and sounds, it is possible to create a greater variety of loudness-related effects. Three such effects commonly used are crescendo, diminuendo, and tremolo.

Crescendo changes sound level from quiet or moderate to loud. It is effective in building tension, drawing attention to a character or an action, and increasing proximity, intensity, force, or power.

Diminuendo (or *decrescendo*) changes sound level from loud to soft. It de-emphasizes importance and presence and helps shift attention, make transitions, and decrease intensity and power.

Tremolo is a rapidly repeated amplitude modulation—encoding a carrier wave by variation of its amplitude—of a sound usually used to add dramatic expression and color to music. Subjectively, it can heighten the sense of impending action or suggest hesitancy or timidity. (Tremolo should not be confused with *vibrato,* which is a frequency modulation—encoding a carrier wave by variation of its frequency.)

Style

Style is a fixed, identifiable musical quality uniquely expressed, executed, or performed. It is that combination of characteristics that distinguishes the Beatles from the Rolling Stones, Beethoven from Brahms, Thelonious Monk from Oscar Peterson, Chopteeth from Blitzen Trapper, chamber music from jazz, and an eighteenth-century symphony from a nineteenth-century symphony. Like texture, style is a source of infinite musical variety.

Musical Instruments and Their Associations

Coincident with determining what musical characteristics to use to evoke a particular idea, emotion, point of view, or atmosphere is deciding what musical instrument or combination of instruments is best suited for their expression. Figures 16-2 and 16-3 list the moods and the qualities associated with the more common orchestral instruments. Again these tables are not to suggest that underscoring is formulaic, akin to painting by numbers. They are intended to provide a convenient reference for what is within the scope of an instrument's performance.

FUNCTIONS OF MUSIC UNDERSCORING

Music underscoring performs many of the same functions in audio design that sound effects do but does so more broadly and diversely. One essential difference between sound effects and music is that *sound effects are generally associated with action and music with reaction.* This can be

Adapted from Martin Skiles, *Music Scoring in TV and Motion Pictures* (Blue Ridge Summit, Penn.: Tab Books, 1976), pp. 70–71.

16-2 Selected musical instruments and their associations with dramatic mood categories.

Quality	Instruments
Drama	Low strings French horn or trombone Low woodwinds English horn (low register) Bass flute (low register) Piano
Mystery	Low flute Strings (tremolando) French horn Hammond organ Electronic organ Synthesizer
Romance	Violin (middle and high registers) Oboe Flute (middle register) French horn (middle and high registers) Clarinet (low register) Viola, cello (middle and high registers) Vibraphone Piano Guitar
Humor	Bassoon (middle and low registers) Oboe (middle and high registers) Clarinet Xylophone Trombone
Scenic (pastoral)	Flute (middle and high registers) Horn (middle and high registers) Trumpet (middle register) Clarinet (middle register) English horn (middle register) Oboe (middle and high registers) Violin (high register) Harp (middle and high registers) Piano (middle and high registers)
Science fiction	Synthesizer Electronic organ Female soprano voice Vibraphone Many percussion effects Strings (harmonics) Flute (high register) Electronic instruments
Horror	Bassoon Tuba Low trombone Electronic instruments Piano (low, bass clef) French horn (low register) Tympani Bass drum

argued, of course, but it serves to provide insight into their different roles and effects. There are also the unique language, vast vocabulary, and universal resonance of music that make it so powerful and so widely applicable in aural communication.

Establishing Locale

Many musical styles and themes are indigenous to particular regions. By recalling these styles and themes or by simulating a reasonable sonic facsimile, music can establish a locale such as Asia, the American West, old Vienna, Mexico, Hawaii, the city, the country, the sea, outer space, and other environments.

Emphasizing Action

Music emphasizes action by defining or underscoring an event. The crash of a chord defines the impact of a fall or collision. A dramatic chord underscores shock or a moment of decision. A romantic theme highlights that flash of attraction between lovers when their eyes first meet. Tempo increasing from slow to fast emphasizes impending danger.

Intensifying Action

Music intensifies action, usually with crescendo or repetition. The scariness of sinister music builds to a climax behind a scene of sheer terror and crashes in a final, frightening chord. The repetition of a short melody, phrase, or rhythm intensifies boredom, the threat of danger, or an imminent action.

Depicting Identity

Music can identify characters, events, and programs. A dark, brooding theme characterizes the "bad guy." Sweet music indicates a gentle, sympathetic personality. Strong, evenly rhythmic music suggests the relentless character out to right wrongs. A particular theme played during an event identifies the event each time it is heard. Themes also have long served to identify radio and television programs, films, and personalities.

Setting Pace

Music sets pace mainly through tempo and rhythm. Slow tempo suggests dignity, importance, or dullness; fast tempo suggests gaiety, agility, or triviality. Changing tempo from slow to fast accelerates pace and escalates

16-3 Associated qualities of selected musical instruments.

Instruments	High Register	Middle Register	Low Register
Flute	Panoramic Scenic Bright and gay	Romantic Subtle	Mysterious Subtle
Alto flute **Bass flute**		Dramatic Mysterious Ominous	Dramatic Weak Ominous
Oboe	Thin Plaintive	Assertive Impressive Humorous	Dramatic Suspenseful
English horn	Thin Appealing	Strong Lonesome Foreboding	Dark Vivid
Bassoon	Thin Plaintive	Forceful Melodic Mysterious Dramatic	Dramatic Humorous
Clarinet	Strong Assertive	Melodic Romantic	Dark Warm
French horn	Assertive Forceful	Warm Appealing	Dramatic
Trumpet	Heroic Strong Independent Assertive	Melodic Forceful Individualistic	Dramatic Nostalgic
Trombone	Melodious Heavy	Strong Dramatic	Dark Melodramatic Somber
Violin	Spirited Melodic Arresting	Warm Romantic Compassionate	Dark Dramatic Morose
Viola	Thin Melodic	Warm Mellow Nostalgic	Dark Dramatic
Cello	Tense Romantic	Warm Sonorous	Dramatic Assertive

Adapted from Martin Skiles, *Music Scoring in TV and Motion Pictures* (Blue Ridge Summit, Penn.: Tab Books, 1976), pp. 70–71.

action; changing from fast to slow decelerates pace and winds down or concludes action. Regular rhythm suggests stability, monotony, or simplicity; irregular (syncopated) rhythm suggests complexity, excitement, or instability. Using up-tempo music for a slow-moving scene accelerates the movements within the scene and vice versa.

Providing Counterpoint

Music that provides counterpoint adds an idea or a feeling that would not otherwise be obvious. Revelers flitting from party to party are counterpointed with music that is monotonous and empty to belie their apparent good cheer. Football players shown blocking, passing, and running are counterpointed with ballet music to under-score their grace and coordination. A man proposing to a woman is accompanied by skittish music to counterpoint the seriousness of the occasion with the insincerity of the man's intent.

Creating Humor

A sliding trombone, clanking percussion, or a galumph-ing bassoon can define a comic highlight or underscore its humor. For example, a bumbling jungle explorer is made all the more ridiculous by the mocking cackle of a heckelphone, or a fight is made silly, instead of violent, by adding tympanic boings or cymbal hits with each punch.

Unifying Transition

Music is used to provide transitions between scenes for the same reasons that sounds are used: to overlap, lead in, segue, and lead out. *Overlapping* music provides continuity from one scene to the next. *Leading-in* music establishes the mood, atmosphere, locale, pace, and so on of the next scene before it actually occurs. *Segued* music changes the mood, atmosphere, pace, subject, and so on from one scene to the next. By gradually lowering and raising levels, music can also be used to *lead out* of a scene. A complete fade-out and fade-in makes a definite break in continuity; hence the music used at the fade-in would be different from that used at the fade-out.

Smoothing Action Scenes

In kinetic action scenes that may be filled with quick cuts and rapid-fire sound effects, the soundscape is typically not wall-to-wall; that is, it does not fill every instant. An underscore is often used to help the flow by smoothing the abruptness of the shots and the sounds.

Fixing Time

Among the many uses for musical style is fixing time. Depending on the harmonic structure, the voicings in the playing ensemble, or both, it is possible to suggest the Roman era, Elizabethan England, the Roaring Twenties, the Jazz Age, the future, morning, noon, night, and so on.

Recalling or Foretelling Events

If music can be used to fix a period in time, it can also be used to recall a past event or foretell a future occurrence. A theme used to underscore a tragic crash is repeated at dramatically appropriate times to recall the incident.

A character begins to tell or think about the first time she saw her future husband at a party as the music that was playing during that moment is heard. A soldier kisses his girl good-bye as he goes off to war, but the background music indicates that he will not return. A budding com-poser looks wistfully at a secondhand piano through a pawnshop window as the strains of his most famous composition, yet to be written, are heard.

Evoking Atmosphere, Feeling, or Mood

Perhaps no other form of human communication is as effective as music in providing atmosphere, feeling, or mood. There is a musical analogue for virtually every condition and emotion. Music can evoke atmospheres that are thick, unsavory, cold, sultry, and ethereal. It can evoke feelings that are obvious and easy to suggest, such as love, hate, and awe, and also subtle feelings such as friendship, estrangement, pity, and kindness. Music can convey the most obvious and the subtlest of moods: ecstasy, depression, melancholy, and amiability.

MUSIC IN SPOT ANNOUNCEMENTS

Because of the effects of music on memory and emo-tion, it is a staple in *spot announcements*—commercials, public service announcements (PSAs), promotional an-nouncements *(promos),* and jingles. The majority of *spots* incorporate music in some way. But too often, due to lack of imagination, time, or understanding of its potency, music for spots is chosen or composed carelessly to the detriment of the message. For example, a producer using a music bed will simply grab a CD, start it playing at the beginning of the copy, and fade it out when the copy ends. Such shortsightedness is a particular handicap in a medium like radio, which has one primary sensory channel to exploit.

Well-selected music can enhance the effectiveness of a spot announcement in a number of ways:

■ Music creates mood and feeling. The purpose of most spots is to have emotional appeal. Nothing reaches the emotions as quickly or as comprehensively as music.

■ Music is memorable. Music in spots should have a short, simple melodic line, lyric, or both—something that sticks in the mind and can be easily, even involun-tarily, recalled.

■ Music gets the audience's attention. A musical spot should grab attention at the start with a compelling musical figure. It can be a catchy rhythm or phrase, percussive accents, an electronic effect, a sonic surprise, or a lyrical statement that impels an audience to listen to its resolution.

■ Music is visual—it provokes visual images. It can set scenes on shipboard, in the country, at the seashore, on the ski slopes, and so on. By so doing, music saves precious copy time spent evoking such scenes verbally.

■ Music can be directed to the taste of a specific demographic group or audience viewing or listening to a particular type of program or format. In radio, for example, the type of music in a spot announcement can be suitable both to the audience to which the message is aimed and, if appropriate, to the station's musical format. This makes the sound of the spot at once comfortable and familiar.

■ Music style can be matched with the product. Music for an airline can be open and spacious and establish a floaty feeling; for a car commercial, it can evoke the feeling of power, speed, or luxury; for a perfume it can be romantic, sensuous, or elegant.

■ Music unifies. In a series of spots emphasizing different copy points about a single product or message, the same music can be used as a thematic identifier to unify the overall campaign. Music also bonds the various elements in spots with, say, multiple copy points and two or more voices.

All that said, music in spot announcements is not always recommended—for a few reasons: more copy points can be covered in a spoken announcement than in one that is sung; a spot with music usually has to be aired several times before the music is remembered; and music can place an announcement in a less serious light than can the spoken word.

CREATIVE CONSIDERATIONS IN UNDERSCORING

The key to underscoring is capturing the tone of a scene or story. For example, it is not enough to look at a scary shot and use tremulous, agitated strings and pulsating rhythm to say, "This is scary." Anyone can do that. What should be considered is the intention and the significance of the action. It may be that the subtext of the scary shot is hoax or parody, not menace. In other words, resolve the creative considerations before deciding what the function of any underscoring is to be. (Keep in mind throughout this discussion that the director, of course, has the final say about the underscoring.)

Tone

In defining the underlying tone of a scene or story, first determine its intent and then decide what that intent requires to help articulate it. Suppose it is a love story. There are many kinds and shades of love: the love of a parent for a child, a child for a parent, a man for a woman, a woman for a man, a subject for his queen, a boy for his dog, and so on. Each requires a different musical motif. For example, a love theme for a subject in relation to his queen would not be romantic in the same way it would for a young couple courting. In the former instance, the theme would convey a sense of admiration and devotion whereas in the latter instance it would be more tender and amorous.

Style

Decide what musical style best suits the story, such as symphonic, jazz, country, blues, rock, afro-funk, and so on. Also determine whether the music should be played using acoustic, electric, or electronic instruments or some combination of the three. A war story does not necessarily call for patriotic music played by a military band. If the war story is treated as an epic, it may require a full symphonic sound to enhance the scope of the saga. If it focuses on a hero who comes from humble beginnings in a farming community, a small ensemble made up of such instruments as harmonica, mandolin, banjo, fiddle, and the like may be appropriate to counterpoint his simple, rustic life with the complexities of life and death in war.

Role

Resolve what role the underscoring should play in telling the story. Will it be fully involved, restrained, expansive, used to carry most of the action, or used sparingly? If the story has little dialogue, chances are the music (and the sound effects) will play a large role in its telling. If there is a great deal of action, music may be necessary to smooth the quick cutting of shots and the hurly-burly within the shots. A low-key story may need underscoring only to highlight certain scenes.

Genre or Non-genre

Decide whether stories that can be categorized—such as mystery, comedy, science fiction, romance, film noir, or western—will be underscored in their conventional musical genres or with different thematic material. The conventional approach to a science fiction story may call for electronic music. But if the story has more emphasis on personal relationships in a world of the future rather than, say, the use of advanced technology to conquer new vistas, the electronic sound may not be as appropriate as music that sounds more acoustic and organic. A typical western could justify a traditional western-sounding musical score. But if the story revolves around a character who had a modern sensibility in his approach to life, although the time period may be the late nineteenth century, the underscoring could have an early-twenty-first-century sound.

Original or Compiled

Whether the underscoring is original or compiled is another consideration. An *original score* molds audience reaction. It manipulates emotion, characterization, expectation, and point of view. It conditions identification. The music becomes a language without the audience's knowing it. For example, music in a historical drama becomes associated with that period even though the time may be so far in the past that nobody living could have any idea what it actually sounded like. You see love, a wedding, a battle, and a chase, and you hear it in the underscoring, thereby identifying the music with the event.

A *compiled score,* that is, music taken from already-existing recordings, is familiar. Its identifications are affiliated, tied to experiences outside the story. The music tends to trigger memories associated with it, which could compete with or distract from the main information. Familiar music usually does not compel the attention on the part of the listener that unfamiliar music does, which could reduce the overall impact of the scene or story.

Sometimes using a compiled music sound track is justified and effective, however. For example, in a story set in the 1950s, music from that era can set the appropriate tone; or in a drama about the social upheavals caused by the Vietnam War, incorporating music from the late 1960s can have additional impact. Several of Woody Allen's films incorporate well-known songs to great advantage. TV series such as *The Sopranos* and *Six Feet Under* also use familiar popular music to establish a contemporary feel or because the lyrics provide informational supplement or counterpoint.

But the decision to use familiar music should come only after careful consideration. It should not be used simply because it is an easier way to provide informational or emotional enhancement. That said, some film and TV producers are less concerned with familiar music's furthering the storyline or adding to the drama than they are with its commercial potential and taking advantage of the opportunity to sell more CDs with sound tracks comprising popular or potentially popular songs.

Another problem with using familiar music, for the budget conscious, is that it usually comes from commercially released recordings, so obtaining copyright clearance could be costly. The copyright fee may be higher than the cost of commissioning and recording original music and is definitely much more expensive than using library music (see "Prerecorded Music Libraries" later in this chapter).

Whatever the advantages and the disadvantages of using a compiled music sound track, most directors generally prefer original to derivative music. It can be more carefully crafted to serve the story and fulfill a production's dramatic goals.

Spotting

Recall from Chapters 14 and 15 that *spotting* consists of going through a script or work print and deciding on the placement of music and sound effects. In deciding when and where to spot music, there are several questions to consider:

- How much music is there in the production?

- Where is it used? How is silence used?

- Where does the music enter?

- What is the dramatic motivation for each cue?

- Is the music used to play scenes that have important dramatic or psychological text or subtext, or is it used as filler to keep scenes from seeming too empty?

- How does it enter—does it sneak in softly or enter loudly?

- How does it end? What is the dramatic motivation for ending the music?[4]

In the process of spotting music in a production, decisions are made about the music design overall and in various segments and scenes. Overall, is the music to complement, supplement, or counterpoint the production? In action and romantic films, music generally plays a major role in underscoring events. In fact, to generate the impact in action stories, there is often more reliance on music (and sound effects) than on dialogue.

---

4. From Fred Karlin, *Listening to Movies* (New York: Schirmer Books, 1994), p. 77.

In a love story, is the music to be emotionally "hot" and aggressive or "cool" and restrained? By what type of an ensemble—orchestral, jazz, chamber—is it to be played and therefore colored?

In choosing to use music from commercial recordings that are already familiar to an audience, for example, for the sake of the story it is wise to have an aesthetic rationale. Familiar music carries with it the baggage of association, which can detract from a drama's impact. Of course, as mentioned, the rationale to use popular music may be motivated solely by the financial prospect of selling CDs of the sound track, which does not necessarily serve the story.

This can also work in reverse. If the commercial music is unfamiliar to an audience, its association is then to the picture and not to any previous experience.

Regardless, when familiar music is used, songs in particular, it makes a big difference to the success of the storytelling when the music is interpretive and not just an embellishment for commercial purposes.

In spotting individual scenes, decisions are made about whether music should enter before or after a character says a line, whether it should carry through the scene or punctuate its most dramatic aspects, and whether it should be stirring, romantic, heroic, melancholy, threatening, or convey some other mood.

Placement

Decisions about where music cues should start, fade under, and stop are perhaps the most challenging of all. There are no rules in underscoring music—there are only guidelines—so decisions about when and where to incorporate music are as varied as the productions that use it and the creativity of spotting teams. With that caveat, in the most general way spotters have made certain observations about when and where to place music:

■ It is better to bridge into a scene from a previous line of dialogue, or come into the scene a bit later under a line of dialogue or under an action from a character, than it is to start music on a scene change.

■ If music starts within a scene, usually it should not be fragmented; it should play through the scene. There are, however, scenes in which stopping the music can heighten a dramatic action, after which the underscoring may continue, not continue, or change.

■ It is less obvious, less intrusive, and more effective to start music at the moment when emphasis shifts, such as a camera movement or a reaction shot.

■ To cover the entrance of a music cue so that it is unobtrusive, it can be sneaked in or distracted from by some visual action.

■ In action scenes with music and considerable sound effects, either the sound effects should play over the music or vice versa to avoid sonic muddle and confusing the action's emphasis and point of view.

■ Perhaps music is easiest to spot when it covers scenes without dialogue. Simplified, this means: music up when they kiss and down when they talk.

■ Trust your instincts. View the piece many times until you have some kind of response—cerebral or emotional. If after many viewings nothing occurs to you, maybe instinct is suggesting that the scene does not need music.

It is always best to spot music with the composer, music editor, and director present. Whether the score is original or taken from a music library, underscoring is so much a matter of intuition, taste, and biases that final decisions are better made in consultation than individually. Even when one person has the final say, the ideas, reactions, and perspectives of the other spotters provide a far more wide-ranging basis for decision-making.

APPROACHES TO UNDERSCORING

Underscoring has been used for just about every picture produced in film and television since sound was added to movies in 1927. And even before "talkies," silent films were accompanied by scores played on an organ or a piano by a live musician in the movie house.

The following are some examples of approaches to underscoring. There are myriad choices available, and what follows does not necessarily imply the best illustrations; they are good examples, however, of the creative approaches film composers bring to their art. The examples are drawn from films because they are still more readily available on DVD, Blu-ray, and videotape than are materials produced for television. That said, some major television programs and series are now released on DVD, and several fine underscores have been composed for, among others, the *CSI* series, *24*, *Band of Brothers*, and *John Adams*. Although they use mostly library music, infomercials, sports features, and documentaries on the History, Learning, Travel, and National Geographic channels, for example, consider underscoring important to the impact of their programs.

It is understood that in the following list a particular illustration may not be completely apprehensible if you are unfamiliar with the film, but it may serve as a reference for future viewing.[5]

■ *The Age of Innocence* is a violent film—not in the physical sense but in its emotional and psychological treatment. Composer Elmer Bernstein designed the score to the refined yet stifling atmosphere of the late-nineteenth-century upper-class society in which the characters live. In one scene two of the main players are at the opera. The music of the opera is heard, and then, in the underscoring, a thin, nervous motif calls attention to a sense of discomfort.

■ The intense, quirky, dark comedy *American Beauty,* centered around one man's midlife crisis, is filled with contradictory moods, embarrassment, and discord that are unsettling and indefinable. Composer Thomas Newman complements the emotional shifting with a propulsive, percussion-based score that, as director Sam Mendes wanted, "hammered and thwacked."

■ The main title theme in *The American President,* scored by Marc Shaiman, accompanies a sequence of images of the White House and past presidents. The music adds to the sequence a sweeping, admiring grandeur that has the character of an anthem.

■ In *Apocalypse Now* Richard Wagner's "The Ride of the Valkyries" underscored the assault scene. In one shot the view is looking down from a helicopter to an acidic blue ocean. Sound designer Walter Murch decided to use a recording conducted by Georg Solti because in it the brass highlighted the appropriate section in the music that he felt went with the shot. Whereas other conductors had highlighted the strings during the same section, Murch felt that the coloration of the metallic brass synergized with the blue of the ocean better than the strings which, compared with the brass, were "too soft and pillowy."

■ *Atonement* is a film that is visually decorous, photogenic, and lavish, and Dario Marianelli's lush, haunting, hypnotic underscore complements its look. The music

5. Some of the examples are based on material from Michael Ondaatje, *The Conversations: Walter Murch and the Art of Editing Film* (New York: Alfred A. Knopf, 2002); Mark Russell and James Young, *Film Music: Screencraft* (Boston: Focal Press, 2000); John Burlingame, *Sound and Vision* (New York: Billboard Books, 2000); Walter Murch, "The Chase," *Music Behind the Scenes,* Bravo, August 18, 2002; and the Film Music Magazine Web site at *www.filmmusicmag.com.*

is also tinged with a melancholy that foreshadows the twist at story's end. There are several different themes whose basic instrumentations include some combination of piano, strings, woodwinds, harmonica, and, in one theme, chorus. The sound and the rhythm of a typewriter, important to the storyline, become musically percussive and imbue a sense of foreboding. Yet the various themes and their orchestrations incorporate a similar emotional feel that provides the continuity through the film's four parts and the scenes within these parts that are shown from different perspectives; the underscore holds the film together.

■ *Basic Instinct* is a film that elevates mystery and intrigue to terror. Composer Jerry Goldsmith used silences throughout the underscoring to heighten the terror, which he felt was essential to the structure of the narrative. In his words, "It gave the music a chance to breathe."

■ *Breach* is a low-key but taut suspense film about the FBI mole responsible for the biggest security breach in U.S. history. Mychael Danna's music is tailored to the film's approach and "atmosphere." It uses a hauntingly beautiful piano theme and an overall underscore that is subdued and somber, reflecting the traitor and his world of stealth and evasion. The music is tailored to individual scenes, of course, but one scene in particular illustrates Danna's sensitivity to the story's "feel." An FBI computer and surveillance expert wishing to become an agent is assigned to shadow one of the bureau's top Russian intelligence experts for sexually perverse activities. Becoming frustrated that there is no justification for such suspicion, the surveillance expert, in one of the film's climactic scenes, is told that in fact he has been assigned to shadow a traitor. The underscore is spare and effective, consisting of subtle, deliberate low-end tympani in even beats not overly punctuated yet dramatic in that it creates ominousness and tension.

■ In *Dangerous Liaisons,* a story of intrigue, scheming, and doom, George Fenton composed a score that helps the audience relate to the idea that the conspirators are not saying what they really mean.

■ In *Defiance,* a movie about the bravery of Eastern European Jews who stood up to the Nazi invaders, composer James Newton Howard uses a powerful, moving, violin-driven underscore that complements the film's heroic story, impact, and action.

■ *Dirty Harry* composer Lalo Schifrin used rhythm rather than themes in a number of sequences to provide the story with a pulse. The rhythm also played under the music for the Scorpio character, which included voices at an unusual interval (the distance in pitch between two notes) to build tension.

■ In *Emma* the main character has the potential to create disaster because of her irrepressible penchant for match-making and her blindness to her own emotions. There are elements of tragedy, destiny, and satire in Emma's character. Composer Rachel Portman's score guides the audience through the romantic game playing and the changing emotions. In one scene, during which Emma is trying to manipulate a misguided match for one of her friends, Portman uses separate instruments to paint the right colors in representing the emotions each character is feeling: the sneaky, conniving sound of a clarinet for Emma, and a quivering violin to underscore her friend's anxiety.

■ In *Gladiator,* instead of taking a conventional blood-and-guts approach to the music to underscore the violence in the story, composer Hans Zimmer wanted to treat the internal, spiritual side of the hero. Part of the score speaks *to* the farmer who loses his family and his "voice" and speaks *for* the hero amid the performance of his heroics during which he hardly speaks at all.

■ In *The Godfather,* after Michael Corleone kills the corrupt police captain McCluskey and the mafia family rival Sollozzo in the Italian restaurant, it raises the question: is Michael a bad guy or is he the young ex-Marine and war hero whose outrage at the attempt on his father's life drives him to take revenge on his father's enemies? Nino Rota's music after the shooting clarifies the moment. It says that Michael, of his own volition, has descended into the dark, corrupt, murderous world of the mob. He has lost his idealism and his innocence.

■ *The Grey Zone* is based on a true story about a group of Jewish Sonderkommandos working in the crematoria at Auschwitz who plot and succeed in destroying two of the camp's four crematoria. The subplot is about how far a person will go to survive. In the film a young girl survives the gas chamber and is rescued and cared for by the Jewish doctor who wrote the book on which the film is based. After the crematoria are destroyed and the plot's survivors are shot, the girl, who is forced to watch the executions, is allowed to flee toward the main gate only to be shot before she can get very far. The film closes with a voice-over by the dead girl as she describes the horrors of the camp and what is happening to her as she is cremated

and turned to ashes. The music composed by Jeff Danna serves as a wrenching counterpoint to the monologue. It is virtually a sustained tone—spare, ethereal, choir-like. Infused in it is the feel of wind, perhaps the wind that blows the ashes of the dead from the crematorium's smokestack. It also conveys a sense of release from the horrors of Auschwitz, where life has no value, to the next life, where it does.

■ One of the hallmarks of Bernard Herrmann's music, evident in such films as *North by Northwest, Psycho,* and *Taxi Driver,* is using patterns in the underscoring that do not go anywhere; they do not lead to resolution. This helps articulate the subtext of obsession that runs through the stories. In *Psycho,* for example, his discordant, high-pitched, repetitive motifs anticipate waiting terror or accompany it. As Janet Leigh is driving through the torrential rainstorm looking for a place to stay, the music foreshadows the horror she is about to encounter. If she had heard that music, she never would have gone near the Bates Motel. The 45-second shower scene is another classic instance of an underscore—Herrmanns's shrieking violins—underpinning picture—Alfred Hitchcock's deliberate shot progression.

■ In the James Bond films, music tells the audience that the hero is a fantastic character—that despite all the killing and the mayhem, he is not to be taken seriously. His theme has a mysterious, throbbing, ruthless intensity that is leavened with flamboyance. (Monty Norman composed the James Bond theme. John Barry, followed by David Arnold and others, wrote the films' scores.)

■ John Williams's theme for *Jaws* captures in a few minutes the shark's character and domain. The indelible theme establishes the shark's presence even without seeing it. The bass conveys its size and power; the tempo moving from slow to fast establishes the shark's relentlessness; the music going from soft to loud conveys the growing and ever faster menace coming at you; and the figure in the French horns suggests the grace of the shark as it swims.

■ *Letters from Iwo Jima,* despite being about one of World War II's bloodiest battles, is both intimate and claustrophobic. The Japanese soldiers set to defend the island are ordinary guys who long to be home; they spend much of their time plotting strategy, digging out tunnels and caves, sitting in foxholes, and crawling through terrain. Music is used sparingly, but when it is composers Kyle Eastwood and Michael Stevens produce an underscore that is melancholy and plaintive, evoking sadness and futility. Its main theme is simple, played on solo piano; it is later augmented by light strings and then solo trumpet and snare drums to interject a military feel. To give it a sense of place and culture, the music sounds Eastern, although it is played on Western instruments.

■ *Love Story* composer Francis Lai wanted the audience to feel the same sense of loss that Oliver was to feel about Jenny, the girl he had grown to love and who would soon die. Another feature of the underscoring played to Jenny's being a music student. Some of the score is played on a piano, and variations of the main theme are arranged in the styles of music that Jenny adored, such as Mozart and the Beatles.

■ In *Nurse Betty* the score is essential because it helps clarify the relatively complex and schizophrenic nature of the film. Parallel stories run throughout most of the picture, shifting between reality and fantasy. Composer Rolfe Kent uses two thematic strands for Betty in the underscoring: a theme for her as she is—lively, upbeat, and buoyant—and a mushy emotional theme to depict her obsession with a character in a soap opera whom she thinks is real, which evolves into a love theme as the story brings the two characters together.

■ *Out of Africa* composer John Barry wrote a lyrical, melodic, sweeping score. It had two main purposes: to connect the audience emotionally to the story and to produce thematic material based on the love relationship of the two leading characters and of their interaction with the landscape surrounding them.

■ In *The Perfect Storm,* James Horner composed an appropriate main theme that is sonorous, positive, hopeful, propelling, and nautical in its repetitive wavelike swells.

■ In *Saving Private Ryan,* most of the sound track's impact is supplied by the sound effects; there is not much music. What music there is, however, makes a significant contribution to the film's overall effect. John Williams's score is hymnal, both in the orchestral passages and especially with the chorus. It underscores the contrast of the people lost in the war and those who survived. This is established in the opening scene when the now middle-aged Ryan, thankful, reflective, and deeply moved, visits the gravesite of the ranger captain, killed in action, who found him and by so doing saved his life.

■ In *Seven,* referring to the seven deadly sins being carried out by a sadistic murderer, composer Howard Shore's underscore, rather than being typically suspenseful or frightening, is more "stark, cold, and relentlessly grim."

■ In *Silence of the Lambs,* Howard Shore focused the music on the Jodie Foster character, Clarice Starling. From the opening, where she is shown going for a run, the music is dramatic and intended to focus on her emotional side. In a sense it is a foreshadowing of her relationship with Hannibal Lecter, and it follows her throughout the film.

■ *A Simple Plan* is a film about greed destroying friendship. To underscore the deteriorating relationships of the main characters, composer Danny Elfman created an unsettling tone by using detuned instruments, particularly pianos and banjos; he used strings and flutes to establish eeriness.

■ Although the continuity of *Slumdog Millionaire*'s story is obvious, the feel of the film is episodic with varying intensities. A. R. Rahman's underscore is a major influence on the film's "feel." The main segments are "characterized" by thematic music, in both the melodic lines and the rhythmic structures that either support the action or "express" personal emotion. In fact, the music in each segment is titled to help define its distinctiveness. To provide a sonic sense of place and predicament, the music segments resonate with Eastern tonalities yet they do not sound foreign to the Western ear. The aggressive, thumping percussiveness in much of the score adds to the film's almost relentless energy and pace.

■ *Speed* composer Mark Mancina replaced all orchestral percussion with actual sounds for the bus "music." The bus sounds of metal banging, hubs rattling, telephone wires being hit, and telephone poles being struck became the percussion to bring the bus into the orchestra, so to speak.

■ Elmer Bernstein's score for *The Ten Commandants* has the rich, inspiring, and magisterial orchestral music appropriate for this epic. But it also has tailored themes for characters and situations. For example, in the Exodus sequence as Moses leads the Jews out of Egypt, the music is joyful and buoyant, bringing life to and accelerating the pace of a scene that without such music is visually slow-moving, even plodding.

■ Instead of using conventional military action music in the war film *The Thin Red Line,* composer Hans Zimmer's score creates atmospheres that are hypnotic and elegiac in keeping with the story's exotic visuals and studied, introspective plot line.

■ In *To Die For,* a woman entices some wayward teens to murder her husband. The film is a quirky comedy, however, and Danny Elfman composed a subtly nuanced theme to convey a character who was wicked but not evil.

■ In *Tootsie,* when we first see Dustin Hoffman in a crowd, walking toward us dressed as Dorothy Michaels, composer Dave Grusin's music has a bouncy rhythm and a positive theme that underscore Hoffman's confidence in his newfound purpose.

■ For *Valkyrie,* composer John Ottman originally planned a minimal score. Because the film is dialogue-heavy, however, it became clear that the absence of music took away from the story's progressive dramatic action. To maintain tension without making the music expository or melodramatic, Ottman created a running, subliminal pulsation throughout the film that underscored its progression from thriller to tragedy.

■ Music in the animated feature *WALL-E* comes from either popular songs or Thomas Newman's underscore. Music plays a vital part in the film not only for the obvious reasons but because there are long stretches without dialogue, including the film's first half hour. The underscore renders a toon tone using a melodic blend of strings and samples that serve as the title character's other "voice." There is longing and loneliness, whimsy and wonder, humor and rapture in the music that complement scenes or infuse personality traits. At times the underscore has an inorganic, electronic, futuristic, feel and at other times it is organic and familiarly emotional.

■ In *Young Frankenstein* John Morris composed a typical Gothic horror score, but the film is not a typical Gothic horror story—it is a parody. He wrote a lovely, romantic lullaby to foster in the audience an emotional attachment for the monster.

PRERECORDED MUSIC LIBRARIES

Prerecorded music libraries, like prerecorded sound-effect libraries, are convenient and less expensive alternatives to commissioning the music to be composed and recorded. Music libraries are used for commercials, promos, bumpers, and drama. They provide original music composed to evoke a wide range of human emotions and information: happiness, conflict, melancholy, liveliness, danger,

the future, the eighteenth century, the Far East, the bustling city, and countless others.

Music libraries are available in scores of different categories, such as sports, drama and suspense, motivation, high tech, romantic, family, corporate, country, industrial, ambience, and so on. And they provide music in a variety of styles and textures. Compositions are arranged for orchestras of various sizes, dance and military bands, rock and jazz groups, solo instruments, synthesizers—virtually any voicing or combination of voicings necessary to evoke an idea or emotion. Music cues are also subdivided by length and version. A disc may have cuts of 0:29, 0:59, 1:30, and 2:30 minutes, and tag edits, each with a full orchestral mix and just a rhythm track for underscoring an announcer (see 16-4).

Also available are entire music libraries recorded with reduced dynamic range for the sole purpose of music underscoring. The reduced dynamic range enables use of the music to accompany an announcement or a narration without overwhelming or competing with it.

Avoiding the "Canned" Music Sound

The problems with sound quality that used to plague analog music libraries have for the most part been eliminated with digital-quality audio. Those problems resulted in the "canned" sound—deficiencies such as thin, raspy sound; not enough presence or brilliance; too much midrange; limited dynamic range; and so on.

Although those characteristics of canned sound have been largely eliminated in today's music libraries, you still have to be wary of another facet of the canned sound: stilted and mechanical performances and mediocre composing and arranging, which obviously have nothing to do with the analog or digital format. In addition to sound quality, good performance, and creative composing and arranging, also listen for true stereo imaging, realistic acoustics or ambience, and music that is not so invasive that it could draw attention away from the narrative or dialogue, or so predicable that it adds little to either.

When considering libraries from online providers, be mindful of music that has been compressed. The inherent sound quality of digital audio notwithstanding, compression can have a detrimental effect on a recording. Cost is also a factor; despite the temptation to use music libraries that allow free downloads, inexpensive buyout plans, and other low-cost features, the paramount considerations in choosing a music library should be originality and sound quality.

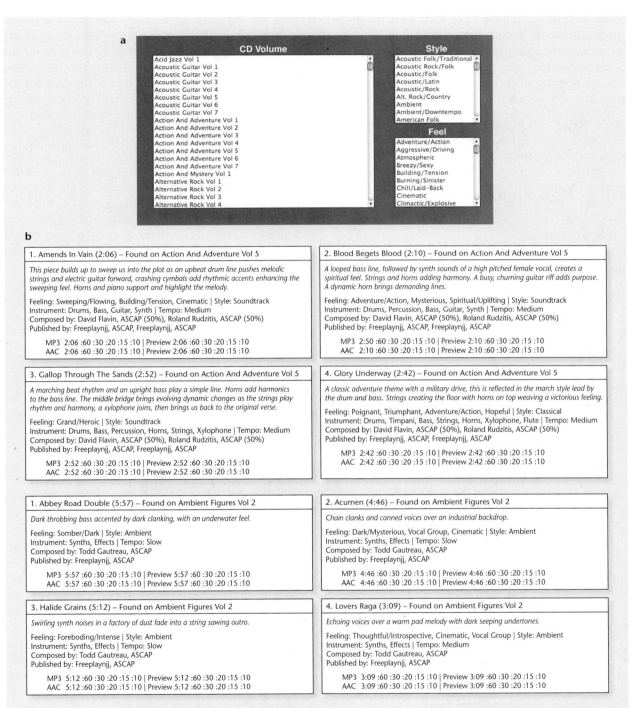

16-4 Selected contents in one CD music library. (a) Library listings by CD volume, style, and feel. (b) Descriptions of music examples, possible applications, instrumentation, tempo, number of cues per example and their times, and availability with MP3 or AAC (Advanced Audio Coding) compression.

Because music libraries vary in creative and sonic quality, listen to examples of the product before you buy. Avoid making a decision on the basis of a demo disc. A demo disc is produced to make the sale and usually consists of an impressive montage of samples. The reality may be that the overall library does not provide sufficient usable content to make a purchase worthwhile. Reputable music libraries have evaluation copies for short-term loan that can be retained with a purchase or returned if the decision is not to buy.

CUSTOMIZED MUSIC PROGRAMS

Prerecorded music libraries have the same limitations as sound-effect libraries: fixed cues, times, and dynamics.

Computer programs are available that allow you to customize music cues and assemble a jingle or sound track in a number of ways, by designating openers, finales, accents, and backgrounds to times that can be specified to tenth-of-a-second accuracy. These automated score generators also make it possible to choose from a variety of musical styles and describe the effect you want the music to have. The editing function breaks soundfiles into movable blocks for positioning in any order. It may also be possible for the nonmusician to "compose" music; if assembled pieces do not fit together musically, the system may convey a warning and provide a function for smoothing transitions between blocks.

Figure 16-5 displays one example of an automated score-generating program, Cinescore. Another product,

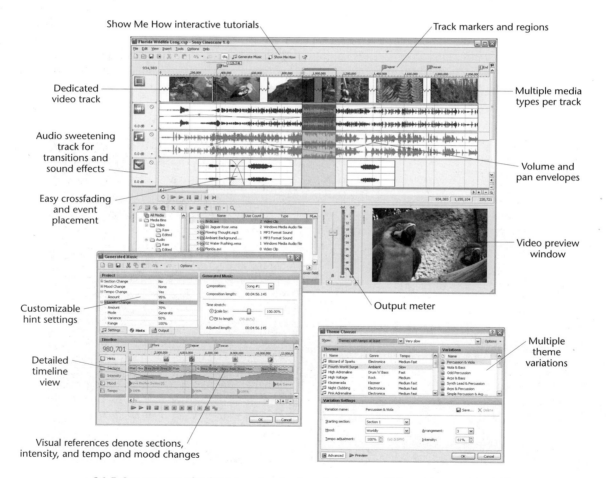

16-5 Screen examples from a customized music program. This program automatically generates music to fit project length; includes 20 customizable themes in multiple genres; generates hint markers to control changes in tempo, mood, and intensity; and has one video track and three audio tracks. There are volume and pan controls, audio time stretching, real-time editing during playback, and audio sweetening.

called Smart Sound, includes a video window to precisely synchronize the music to the picture; multi-instrument layers to change musical textures; mood mapping to adapt the music to different moods; control of transition times; timing control of beats and beat alignment; hit files with such effects as cymbal swells, crashes, and whooshes; spotting to mark the in- and out-points of cues; and length adjustment of music.

CUSTOMIZED MUSICAL INSTRUMENT PROGRAMS

Customized programs can be used to orchestrate anything from a short music cue to an underscore, using samples of musical instruments. The sounds of individual instruments can be built into just about any combination of voicings and size of ensemble, from a solo or duo to a full orchestra (see 16-6).

Some libraries are capable of playing orchestrations directly from supported notation programs. For example, they can read and interpret performance indications such as articulation marks, playing techniques, and slurs and dynamics.

COPYRIGHT AND LICENSES

By law any recorded material with a copyright may not be played over the air, copied (dubbed), or used for most nonprivate purposes without permission from the licensor—that is, the company or individual(s) holding the rights to the recorded material. Broadcasters, for example, pay fees to such major licensors as Broadcast Music, Inc. (BMI) and the American Society of Composers, Authors, and Publishers (ASCAP) for the right to play commercially recorded music on the air. The rights to music libraries, however, usually belong to the companies that distribute the libraries, and fees are paid to these companies. The main rights to consider are listed in Figure 16-7.

A variety of payment and licensing options are usually available, and a company may offer one or more of them. One option is to lease the music library for a set period of time, usually one year, and pay a fee for that lease, which is renewable annually. If the licensee does not renew, the discs must be returned. If the licensor offers a buyout plan acceptable to the licensee, any discs that are purchased may be retained.

16-6 Screen of a customized orchestral program. Content of this program is provided on three double-layer DVDs that include more than 1,200 instruments that reproduce the articulations, expressive playing techniques, and dynamic ranges of strings, brass, woodwind, and percussion. Other features include adjustable ambience and a variety of styles from Baroque to contemporary popular music.

16-7 Music licenses
and copyrights.

Audiovisual work This is an industry term for film, television, or any other audiovisual production, such as presentations, Flash animation, QuickTime and other Internet visual formats, videos, CDs, and DVDs.

Copyright This is the exclusive right, granted by law for a stated period, usually until 70 years after the death of the surviving author of the work, to make, dispose of, and otherwise control copies of literary, musical, dramatic, pictorial, and other copyrightable works.

Synchronization rights This is the right to use the music in timed relations with other visual elements in a film, video, television show/commercial, or other audiovisual production. In other words, it is the right to use the music as a sound track with visual images. Synchronization licenses are obtained from the publisher (or composer if no publisher) or the music library.

Master use rights When you hear music on the radio or TV, this recording is known in the music industry as the master recording. This is what is produced after all the musicians have played their parts and those parts have been mixed for release. The recording of the master is also protected by copyright. A record label or music library owns the copyright and can grant the right to use the sound recording on a compilation album, film sound track, or other audiovisual medium.

Performing rights Public performance right is the exclusive right that U.S. copyright law gives to the creator of a musical work or other copyrighted material, authorizing the use in public. Every time a song is performed on a broadcast, there is a public performance. This public performance is licensed by performing rights organizations (such as BMI and ASCAP) or directly from the copyright holder as a direct license.

Mechanical rights This license grants the right to record and release a specific composition at an agreed-upon fee per unit manufactured and sold. It is the right to use on a recording a musical piece owned by someone else.

Grand rights This term describes "dramatic" performing rights, which includes musical comedies (Broadway and off-Broadway), operas, operettas, and ballets, as well as renditions of musical compositions in a dramatic setting where there is narration, a plot, and/or costumes and scenery. The copyright owner has the exclusive right to issue licenses and collect fees for grand rights. Performance rights organizations do not collect performing-rights royalties for this use; the license is granted directly by the composer or publisher.

Direct license A license obtained directly from the copyright owner or publisher where the performing rights are paid directly to the copyright owner by the licensee. With a direct license, no royalties are collected by, or paid to, the performing rights organizations.

Source: IAMUSIC.com

In addition to the leasing fee, there are fees for usage rights determined on the basis of *needle,* or *laser, drops*—the number of times the licensee uses music from any selection or any portion of a selection in a given production; there is also a fee that gives the licensee unlimited usage rights for one or a number of years (see 16-8). (*Needle drop* was the term coined when music libraries were available on vinyl.)

Paying on the basis of laser drops requires filling out a clearance form and listing all the laser drops used in your production (see 16-9). You pay whatever fee the licensor's rate card indicates. The licensor then sends you written permission to use its music, for profit, in your production. If you use any of the same music in another production, you usually have to pay another laser-drop fee.

Often a production contains so many laser drops that the copyright fee is prohibitive. In such cases many licensors charge a flat rate, which has become the most common way of charging usage fees.

Some organizations, such as educational institutions, small production companies, and many broadcast stations, do not generate enough in copyright fees to make the rental of a music library worthwhile to the licensor. Therefore many licensors rent their libraries to such organizations for a lower, flat annual rate. This clears the music for royalty-free blanket use. Such an arrangement may be renewed each year; when it terminates, most licensors require return of the library.

Leasing to own is another option whereby the money paid for each year's lease is applied to the cost of buying

TV Broadcast (Local, Regional, Non-licensed National, International, Educational, or Pay-per-view)
Rates are for each 4 minutes of use per year.

Per Episode	Per Freeplay Title	Opening or Closing Theme	Blanket Production 30 minutes	Blanket Production 60 minutes
National	$ 250	$ 350	$1,300	$2,400
Regional	$ 150	$ 250	$ 900	$1,200
Local	$ 85	$ 150	$ 500	$ 700
Pay-per-view	$ 250	$ 350	$1,200	$2,400
International (per country)	$ 150	$ 250	$1,000	$1,800
Educational	$ 50	$ 100	$ 250	$ 500

Advertising and Promos
Rates are per project for each 4 minutes of use per Freeplay title.

One Commercial Spot	TV Rights	Radio
Worldwide—one year	$1,500	$1,400
Worldwide—13-week cycle	$1,200	$1,100
National—one year	$ 900	$ 800
National—13-week cycle	$ 300	$ 250
Regional— one year	$ 600	$ 500
Regional—13-week cycle	$ 200	$ 150
Local—one year	$ 300	$ 200
Local—13-week cycle	$ 100	$ 100

Intranet and Internet—Web Use
Rates are per project for each 4 minutes of use per Freeplay title.
Unlimited use within the same domain. Worldwide.

Per Freeplay Title	1 Year	3 Years	5 Years	7 Years
Corporate intranet only	$ 150	$ 300	$ 450	$ 600
Small-business intranet only	$ 75	$ 150	$ 300	$ 375
Corporate Internet	$ 250	$ 500	$ 750	$1,000
Small-business Internet	$ 125	$ 250	$ 375	$ 500
Personal (individual, noncommercial) Internet	$ 100	$ 200	$ 300	$ 400

Podcasting/Blogs/Personal Videos (Viral Videos—i.e., YouTube, MySpace)
Rates are per podcast episode for each 4 minutes of use per year.

Per Freeplay Title	
Personal onetime background use	$ 25
Personal onetime opening and closing use	$ 50
Business onetime background use	$ 50

16-8 Music licensing fees from Freeplay Music. Other categories not shown here are "Audio Productions for Distribution," such as audiobooks, CDs, games, electronics, and toy use; "Corporate Conferences, Trade Shows, Live Events, and PowerPoint Presentations"; "E-mail Greeting Cards/E-mail Brochures"; student and non-student "Film Festivals"; and "Wireless Content," including ring tones, blogs, and shareware/freeware.

Name of program/production _____

Name of program/production _____

Episode number/name _____   First airdate _____

Length of program/spot _____ Production year _____ Country of origin _____

Name of production company/distributor/religious organization _____

Title of musical work	Composer(s)	Publisher	ASCAP/BMI	Segment length	Production music library	CD/Track Number

16-9 Clearance form.

out the library discs already received. After so many payments, the music library belongs to the lessee with no further charge for leasing. There may or may not be continued royalty fees for use.

There are a number of options in lease-to-own contracts. For example, in one program, if after a one-year lease a lessee does not wish to renew, the money paid for the year's lease may be applied to a onetime buyout price for each disc the lessee wants to keep, with no further synchronization fees to pay for the music on those discs. If after, say, three years, the decision is made not to renew, credit for the three years of lease payments may be used to convert the discs of choice to a onetime buyout price with no further leasing fees to pay. Depending on the number of discs involved, continued synchronization fees may remain in effect.

Straight buyout is a third option. For a single payment, you own the library discs with no further leasing fees required. In many straight buyouts, after purchase the music may be used royalty-free. With some companies, however, even though you own the discs, usage fees may still apply for a limited period of time or for as long as the library is used.

To provide pricing flexibility, most companies offer options on the number of library discs you care to lease or purchase.

USING MUSIC FROM COMMERCIAL RECORDINGS

Using music from commercial recordings, such as CDs and DVDs, for underscoring should be carefully considered. In theatrical film and television, it is expensive, usually more so than producing original music or using a music library. And as pointed out earlier in relation to its potential dramatic effect, familiar music carries affiliated identifications.

USING MUSIC FROM SAMPLE CDs AND THE INTERNET

Sample CDs of music are available in all types of styles and instrumentations. Musical style may be hip-hop, rap, general purpose, pop, rock, and so on. Samples may be of drum loops, bass and voices, funky guitar, synthesizer, keyboards, or music indigenous to a particular region. A bank of samples may have several variations, such as short release, darker, and octave stacks. Rhythm samples come in a variety of *beats per minute (bpm)*.

Samples are also designed for use with particular synthesizer platforms. Accompanying manuals provide instructions for sample manipulation, which may include ways to produce alternative envelope shapes, velocity curves, equalization balances, phase shifts, and stereo imaging.

Countless samples are also available online. As with any audio material that is downloaded, acceptable sound quality cannot be assumed. It depends on how the samples were produced, the data compression scheme used, and the quality of your retrieval and sound system. The convenience and often-nominal cost of downloading data cannot be disputed, but the sheer volume of audio available on the Internet means the range of sound quality is very wide. Caveat emptor!

Music Sampling and Copyright

The issue of sampling and copyright is thorny because a sample is so easy to produce and hide in a recording and samples are so easy to acquire from sample libraries and the Internet.

Suppose a production company leases a music library and in that library are portions of selections—accents, phrases, beat combinations—that are particularly suitable for sampling. The company redesigns them to make a new music cue. The new music cue sounds nothing like the work from which it was taken, and the samples used were only fractions of a second. Has copyright been violated? If so, who pays what to whom?

The letter of the law is straightforward: *it is illegal to make derivative works of another person's copyrighted material without express permission.* In this example clearing usage of a sample requires the permission of the copyright owner of the original composition (the composer or publishing company) and the owner of the copyright of the master (record company, music library, or other distributor).

There are other considerations in negotiating a sample clearance as well: the territory of your authorized use of the sample, cost of the sample, whether there will be an ongoing royalty for as long as the sample is in use, what credits are to be given to the original copyright holder, who owns the new work, and whether new permissions must be given for other uses of the sample.

Sampling has made it possible to take any recorded sound, process it, and use it for one's own purposes. The practice is so widespread that it has created a major controversy about royalty and copyright infringement, and millions of dollars have already been awarded for such infringement.

Using the copyrighted work of others without their permission for your own financial gain, no matter how little of that material you use, is unethical and illegal. If you use it, you have to pay for it. Consider your reaction if someone took credit for and profited from material *you* created without sharing any of the earnings with you.

ORGANIZING A MUSIC LIBRARY

To better organize and more speedily retrieve the thousands of selections an audio facility may have in its music collection, server systems are available similar to those used for sound-effect collections. Depending on the management system, a user can call up a music cue by library, genre, keyword, instrumentation, tempo, version, style, attitude, and so on.

Systems vary, but they generally facilitate almost instant auditioning and editing to time or dynamic need any number of musical segments, saving the preferred segments, adding remarks and classifications of how the music is to be used, and creating a cue sheet. Systems also vary in the number of discs they can support. For example, one system can provide up to 300 discs requiring a system size of 250 GB to 5,000 discs requiring 4 TB.

MAIN POINTS

▶ Music underscoring consists of adding background music that enhances the content of a scene by evoking a particular idea, emotion, point of view, or atmosphere.

▶ A production may have three types of music: production source, source, and underscore.

▶ Production source music emanates from a primary on-screen source. Source music is background music from an on-screen source. Underscore music is original or library music added to enhance a scene's content.

▶ Music has the same basic structural elements common to all sound, such as pitch, loudness, tempo, tone color, and envelope. It also contains other characteristics that broaden its perceptual and aesthetic meaning, such as melody and tonality; harmony and its qualities of consonance, dissonance, and texture; tempo; dynamic range that is quite wide compared with speech and sounds; and style in limitless variety.

▶ Melody is a succession of pitched musical tones of varied durations. Harmony is a simultaneous sounding of two or more tones, although three or more tones are usually necessary to define a chord. Tempo provides the pulse and the drive in music. The dynamic range of music can be much wider than the dynamic ranges of speech and sounds. Style is a fixed, identifiable musical quality uniquely expressed, executed, or performed.

▶ Coincident with determining what musical characteristics to use to evoke a particular idea, emotion, point of view, or atmosphere is deciding what musical instrument or combination of instruments is best suited for their expression.

▶ Music underscoring provides such functions as establishing locale, emphasizing action, intensifying action, depicting identity, setting pace, providing counterpoint, creating humor, unifying transition, smoothing action scenes, fixing time, recalling or foretelling events, and evoking atmosphere, feeling, and mood.

▶ Well-selected music in spot announcements can enhance the effectiveness of the message in a number of ways. There are instances, however, when music in spots can detract from the message.

▶ Among the creative considerations in underscoring are tone, style, role, genre or non-genre, original or compiled, spotting, and placement.

▶ There are myriad approaches to underscoring that call for the collaborative efforts of the director and the composer and their vision of how they want the music to enhance the meaning and the impact of the story.

▶ Music for productions can be obtained in three ways: by having it composed and recorded for a particular piece, by choosing it from a prerecorded music library, or by selecting it from a commercial music recording.

▶ Prerecorded music libraries provide a relatively inexpensive way to use original music to underscore the ideas and the emotions in a script.

▶ When using prerecorded music libraries, beware of the "canned" music sound.

▶ Computer programs are available that allow you to customize music cues and assemble a jingle or sound track in a number of ways, by designating openers, finales, accents, and backgrounds to times that can be specified to tenth-of-a-second accuracy.

▶ Customized musical instrument programs can be used to orchestrate anything from a short music cue to an underscore, using samples of musical instruments.

▶ Most recordings are copyrighted and may not be used unless a fee is paid to the licensor. In the case of music libraries, various types of contracts are available in relation to leasing, buyout, and usage options.

▶ Using music from commercial recordings, such as CDs and DVDs, for underscoring should be carefully considered either because of their expense or affiliated identifications, or both.

▶ Sampling has made it possible to take any recorded sound—including copyrighted material—process it, and use it for one's own purposes. Using any copyrighted material without permission is unethical and illegal.

▶ Be wary of downloading samples, or any audio material for that matter, from the Internet. Acceptable sound quality cannot be assumed.

▶ Like sound libraries, music library servers facilitate cataloging, locating, and auditioning cues.

17

Music Recording

Music recording is foremost about the music. Recording technique and technology are the means to the end, not the end in themselves; they are employed only to serve. Although great music and great musicianship cannot be defined, you have to know when it is there. If they are not part and parcel of a recording, there is little you can do with the microphone selection, placement, and mixdown that will bring about an aesthetically successful recording.

Assuming the music and musicians can "cut it," there are general guidelines that can serve as starting points to help smooth the recording session. There are no rules. The guidelines are just that. It is not possible to predict that by selecting a specific mic for a given instrument and placing it in a particular position that it will produce a certain sound. There are as many approaches to microphone selection and placement on various instruments as there are recordists. The reasons are understandable. Every situation has different variables: the studio acoustics; what the instrument is made of; how it is played; the combination of voicings and their interaction; the quality of the equipment; personal knowledge and taste; and, of course, the music itself; to name a few.

The focus of this chapter is studio-based music recording, as opposed to music recording in live venues, such as concert halls and theaters. There are four basic ways to record musical instruments: close miking, distant miking, accent miking, and ambient miking. Depending on the music, size of the ensemble, room acoustics, mixer, and software program, one or more of these techniques may be employed in a given session.

CLOSE MIKING

Close miking places a microphone relatively close to each sound source or group of sound sources in an ensemble—generally at a distance of about an inch to a foot. Close miking is the technique of choice in studio recording for most popular music genres for a number of reasons: greater control can be achieved in recording the nuances of each musical element; the sound from each instrument, and leakage from other instruments, is better contained; in popular music the difference in loudness between electric and acoustic instruments can be very difficult to balance with distant miking; and much of pop music is played loudly, and in even relatively live acoustics close miking helps prevent the music from being awash in reverberation. Reverberation, spatial positioning, and blend are added in the postproduction *mixdown*.

Generally, directional mics are used in close miking for better sound control of each instrument and to reduce leakage of one instrument into another instrument's microphone. Most of the discussion of close-miking techniques that follows assumes the use of directional microphones. If acoustics and recording logistics permit, however, there are three good reasons why omnidirectional mics should not be overlooked: the better omni capacitors have an extraordinarily wide, flat response, particularly in the lower frequencies, and little or no off-axis coloration; omni mics are not as subject to proximity effect, sibilance, plosives, and breathing sounds as are directional mics; and, because of the inverse square law (see Chapter 13), it is possible to close-mike with an omni and still reduce leakage if the instrument's sound-pressure level is high enough.

DISTANT MIKING

Distant miking places a microphone(s) from about three feet to several feet from the sound source. It picks up a fuller range and balance of an instrument, or a group of instruments, and captures more of the studio acoustics for a more open and blended sound.

Distant miking is employed when all sounds or voicings, or groups of sounds or voicings, are recorded at the same time and it is important to preserve the ensemble sound, or a sonic sense of it. Orchestral and choral music and certain types of jazz are examples of genres that use distant miking. The technique is also used along with close miking to enhance a recording by adding natural acoustics.

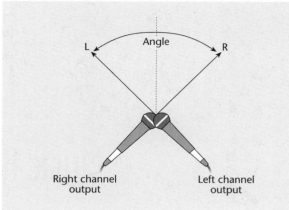

17-1 Coincident miking technique.

Distant-miking Stereo Arrays

As previously noted, the purpose of distant miking, especially when mixed with sound from close mics, is to add airier, more ambient sound to the overall recording. The microphone arrays used are often stereo arrays. They are mainly coincident, near-coincident, and spaced.

Coincident Miking

Coincident miking, also called *X-Y miking,* employs two matched, directional microphones mounted on a vertical axis—with one mic diaphragm directly over the other—and angled apart to aim approximately toward the left and right sides of the sound source. The degree of angle, the mics' pickup pattern, and the distance from the sound source depend on the width of the stereo image you want to record (see Figure 17-1).

A stereo pair must be matched to ensure a uniform sound, and the mics should be capacitors. Miking at a distance from the sound source, particularly with classical music, requires high-output, high-sensitivity microphones; capacitors are the only type of mic that meets this requirement. Moreover, the microphone preamps should be high gain, low noise.

The stereo mic provides the same coincident pickup as the stereo pair but with two directional microphone capsules housed in a single casing. The upper element can rotate up to 180 or 360 degrees, depending on the model, relative to the lower element. Some stereo mics enable control of each capsule's polar pattern (see 3-30 and 3-31).

Coincident microphone arrays produce level (intensity) differences between channels and minimize differences in arrival time. This has the advantage of being

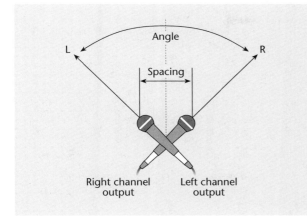

17-2 Near-coincident miking technique.

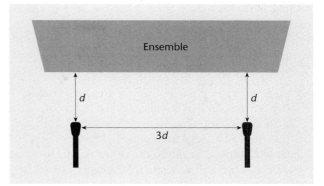

17-3 Spaced miking technique. This technique positions the mics at a distance *(d)* of 3 feet or more. It allows the full range and balance of an instrument or ensemble and captures the room sound as well. If the spaced mics are relatively close to the source, to prevent phase anomalies remember the three-to-one rule: the mics should be placed at least three times as far apart as the distance between the sound source and microphone (see 9-3).

mono-compatible because the two mics occupy almost the same space, meaning their signals are in phase at all frequencies.

Middle-side (MS) miking is another coincident technique (see 3-33 and 3-34). You will recall that an M-S microphone is housed in a single casing combining a cardioid mic—the mid—with a side-facing bidirectional mic. The middle mic faces the sound source and, depending on the mic-to-source distance, picks up more direct than indirect sound; the null of the bidirectional mic faces the sound source, so it picks up mostly indirect sound from the left and right of the sound source. By increasing the level of the mid, the stereo image narrows; by increasing the level of the side, the stereo image widens.

It is also possible to employ the MS technique with two multipattern microphones or with a cardioid and a bidirectional mic. With multipattern mics, set one pickup pattern to cardioid and the other to bidirectional. Position one above the other, almost touching, with the cardioid mic facing the sound source and the bidirectional mic pointed at a 90-degree angle away from the sound source (see 17-32).

Near-coincident Miking

Near-coincident miking angles two directional microphones, spaced horizontally a few inches apart (see 17-2). It is also referred to as *X-Y miking*. The few inches' difference between the near-coincident and the coincident arrays adds a sense of warmth, depth, and air to sound compared with the coincident array. The mics are close enough to retain intensity differences between channels at low frequencies yet far enough apart to have sufficient

time delay between channels for localization at high frequencies. The stereo spread can be increased or decreased with the angle or space between the mics. The time delay between channels creates a problem, however: the greater the delay, the less the chance of stereo-to-mono compatibility.

Spaced Miking

Spaced miking employs two matched microphones at least three to several feet apart, perpendicular to the sound source and symmetrical to each other along a centerline (see 17-3). They reproduce a lusher, more spacious sound than any of the near-coincident arrays—but at a cost. Stereo imaging is more diffused and therefore less detailed. And because so much of the sound reaching the mics derives its directional information from time differences (in addition to intensity differences), stereo-to-mono compatibility is unreliable.

If studio acoustics and the music permit, spaced omnidirectional mics are preferred to directional mics because they have less off-axis coloration and flatter overall response, especially in the low frequencies. Capacitors are almost always used. Spacing is determined by the desired width of the stereo image. With omni mics, of course, spacing must be wide enough to reproduce a stereo image. If it is too wide, however, separation may be exaggerated; if spacing is too narrow, the stereo image may lack breadth.

Spaced cardioid mics are arrayed similarly to spaced omni mics, but their directionality produces a different sonic outcome. Used with an ensemble, spaced cardioids tend to emphasize the voicings that are most on-axis. They also show the effects of coloration, particularly from any studio ambience. Placement is critical to producing acceptable results with any spaced miking but is even

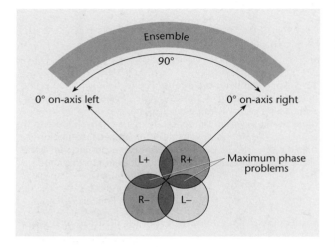

17-4 Blumlein miking technique. This technique uses two coincident bidirectional mics positioned at a 90-degree angle. It is designed to reproduce accurate representation of the original stereo sound stage, a sense of the ambience surrounding the primary sound source, and the room's reverberance.

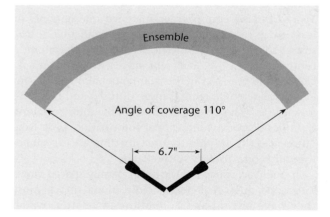

17-5 ORTF microphone array. The *ORTF array* (named for the Office de Radiodiffusion-Television Française, the French broadcasting system) mounts two cardioid microphones on a single stand spaced just under 7 inches apart at a 110-degree angle, 55 degrees to the left and the right of center. This technique is designed to produce a clean, clear, often bright sound with a sense of openness while still maintaining mono compatibility.

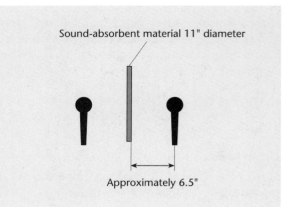

17-6 Jecklin disk. Also known as the *optimal stereo signal (OSS),* this technique separates two omnidirectional mics with a sound-absorbing disk or baffle. It is designed to produce a big, spacious sound with good low-frequency response. Localization is adequate but not precise.

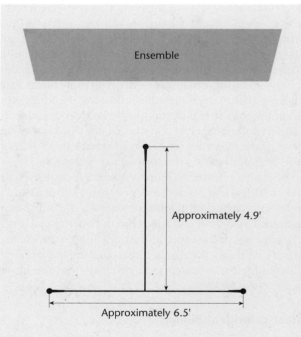

17-7 Decca Tree. This technique mounts three spaced omni mics at the ends of a T-shaped frame. It is designed to reproduce good stereo imaging with an open, spacious sound. It is favored in recording film scores because it produces a pleasing and stable stereo image that holds up throughout the application of Dolby and other surround-sound matrix systems.

more so with cardioids than with omnis. Spaced cardioids do provide a better chance for mono compatibility, however, because each mic is picking up less common information, reducing the chance of phase cancellations.

Spaced nondirectional boundary microphones used for off-miking, particularly in relatively dry studios, are another possibility. Their pickup is similar to that of omni mics, although around the boundary surface the polar pattern is hemispheric.

Other Types of Stereo Microphone Arrays

There are several variations of the three basic stereo microphone arrays. Figures 17-4 to 17-7 display four of the more commonly employed (see also 17-8).

Stereo-miking an Ensemble

When a stereo microphone array—coincident, near-coincident, or spaced—is used for the primary pickup, the configuration affects the image location of the sound source. Figure 17-8 illustrates examples of those effects.

ACCENT MIKING

Accent miking, also known as *off-miking,* is used to pick up instruments in an ensemble when they solo. It is, in effect, a relatively close-miking technique but is used when distant microphones are picking up the ensemble's overall sound and a solo passage needs to stand out. A mic

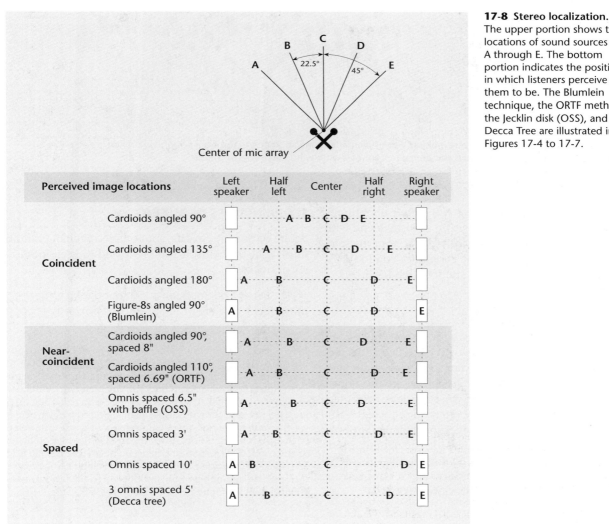

17-8 Stereo localization. The upper portion shows the locations of sound sources A through E. The bottom portion indicates the positions in which listeners perceive them to be. The Blumlein technique, the ORTF method, the Jecklin disk (OSS), and the Decca Tree are illustrated in Figures 17-4 to 17-7.

From Bruce and Jenny Bartlett, *On Location Recording Techniques* (Boston: Focal Press, 1999).

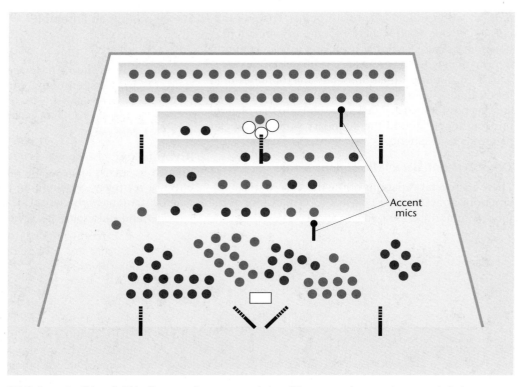

17-9 Accent miking. In this diagram of one approach to miking a symphony orchestra and choir, accent mics positioned in front of a woodwind and a chorus soloist.

placed too close to the soloist will sound unnaturally present because there is little or no acoustic blend with the ensemble sound; a mic placed too far from the soloist will pick up so much of the ensemble's sound that it competes with or overpowers the solo (see 17-9).

AMBIENCE MIKING

Ambience miking, used along with distant miking, attempts to reproduce the aural experience that audiences receive in a live venue by recording in an acoustically suitable studio or concert hall. Microphones are positioned far enough from the ensemble, where the later reflections are more prominent than the direct sound (see 17-10). In the mixdown, the ambient pickup is blended with the pickup from the closer mics, making the natural reverb part of the recording, and not adding it artificially in the mixdown, which may be necessary with distant miking and is definitely necessary with close miking.

SIX PRINCIPLES OF MIKING

Before getting into specific applications of miking various musical instruments, it will be helpful to keep in mind six principles:[1]

■ The closer a microphone is to a sound source, the drier, more detailed, more intimate, and, if proximity effect is

---

1. As noted earlier there are almost as many approaches to miking instruments as there are recordists. The following sections on miking instruments are intended to show some of the basic techniques. Decisions about microphone preference and positioning are personal. Therefore drawings rather than pictures are used to avoid showing a specific mic placed in a particular way on an instrument, thereby implicitly suggesting a preference or recommendation. As for the myriad other approaches to microphone selection and placement, magazines such as *Mix, Electronic Musician, EQ, Sound on Sound,* and *Recording;* the Internet; and a number of the books cited in the Bibliography abound with examples.

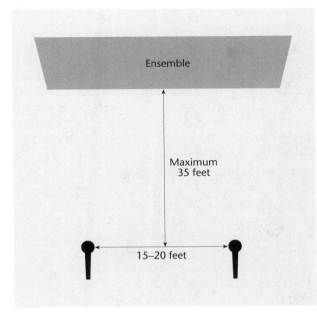

17-10 Ambient miking. Spaced omnidirectional microphones situated toward the rear of the room. The success of this technique is dependent on a studio or hall with appropriate acoustics. In rooms of some size, to minimize echoes that could result from mixing the direct signal with the signal from the acoustically delayed ambient mics, the distance between the ensemble and the ambient mics should not exceed 35 feet. The distance between the spaced mics should be limited to 15 to 20 feet to minimize comb filtering.

a factor, bassier the sound. The farther a mic is from a sound source, the more diffused, open, less intimate, and ambient the sound.

■ Regardless of a directional microphone's pickup pattern: the higher the frequency, the more directional the sound wave and therefore the mic pickup; the lower the frequency, the more omnidirectional the sound wave and the mic pickup.

■ Although close miking may employ a number of microphones, more is not always better. Each additional mic adds a little more noise to the system, even in digital recording, and means another input to keep track of and control, to say nothing of possible phasing problems.

■ With most moving-coil mics, the farther from the sound source they are placed, the more reduced the high-frequency response.

■ Generally, large-diaphragm microphones are more suitable in reproducing low-frequency instruments; small-diaphragm mics are more suitable in reproducing high-frequency instruments.

■ Do not confuse perspective with loudness. Loudness aside, in considering mic-to-source distance, it is hearing more or less of the ambience that helps create perspective.

DRUMS

Perhaps no other instrument provides as many possibilities for microphone combinations, and therefore presents as much of a challenge, as the drums. Several different components make up a drum set—at least a bass drum, a floor (low-pitched) tom-tom, medium- and high-pitched tom-toms, a snare drum, a hi-hat cymbal, and two overhead cymbals.

Characteristics

Drums consist of at least one membrane (drumhead) stretched over a cylinder and, usually, a second membrane that resonates with the struck head. Drums produce loud sound levels and steep transients. They are not considered pitched instruments, although drumheads can be tuned to a musical pitch; and the pitch relationships of the floor, medium, and high tom-toms must be maintained. Also, various sonic effects can be achieved by tuning the top and bottom heads to different tensions relative to each other.

It is important that tension be uniform across the head to produce a single pitch. When several pitches are produced simultaneously, the sonic result is dissonance.

Drums radiate sound perpendicularly to the heads, particularly the top head. High-frequency transients are most pronounced on-axis, perpendicular to the point where the stick hits the drumhead. This is the sound responsible for most of the drum's "kick." Harmonics and overtones are produced from the tension rings, the shell, and the bottom head.

Bass (Kick) Drum   The bass drum is the lowest pitched. Its fundamental frequencies range from 30 to 147 Hz, with harmonics extending from 1 to, in some drums, as high as 5 kHz. Hence its energy is in the very low end, which provides the transient energy bursts that help establish the primary rhythm pattern. Its higher-end frequencies provide the sharpness of the attack.

It is commonly called the *kick drum* because it is struck with a beater controlled by the drummer's foot. The drum stands on its side with the rear "top," or beater, head facing the drummer. The front "bottom" head is usually removed or has a hole cut into it because of the low-frequency resonances and very steep transients that the drum can generate and for ease of mic placement. Most of the drum's low frequencies are emitted omnidirectionally, though vibrations from the shell and the heads resonate throughout the instrument.

Tom-toms   Tom-toms come in a variety of sizes and pitches and usually have two heads. They produce the steep transients and the radiating characteristics common to most drums. Lower-pitched toms generate more-omnidirectional waves; higher-pitched toms generate more-directional waves. They are tuned to have more sustain than the kick and snare drums. Although tom-toms are often used for fills to accent a piece, they are part of the rhythmic structure.

Snare Drum   The snare can be characterized as a tom-tom tuned to a higher pitch, with little or no sustain, and steep transients. Its sound cuts through that of the other drums and usually establishes the tempo. Fundamental frequencies range from 100 to 200 Hz, with attack energy in the 4 to 6 kHz range and harmonics extending from 1 to 15 kHz. What produces the drum's crisp signature sound and cutting power, and gives it its name, is the chainlike snares stretched across the bottom head of the instrument.

Cymbals   Cymbals are usually round, metal plates shaped like a flattened bell. They may be struck with a hard wooden drumstick, a soft mallet, or brushes. The type of striker used is largely responsible for the sound produced. Unlike drums, cymbals have a long decay. The harder the striker, the more high frequencies of the transients are produced. A cymbal tends to radiate sound perpendicularly to its surface, with a ringing resonance near its edge.

A cymbal's pitch is determined by, among other things, size and thickness. Cymbals are also designed to produce different textures; the ring of the ride cymbal and the splash of the crash cymbal are two common examples. Generally, their fundamentals range from 300 to 587 Hz. Harmonics extend from 1 to 15 kHz.

Hi-hat Cymbal   The hi-hat cymbal is actually two cymbals with the open ends of the bells facing each other. A foot pedal, controlled by the drummer, raises and lowers the top cymbal to strike the bottom cymbal, or the top cymbal is struck with a drumstick, or both. Varying the pressure and the distance between the two cymbals generates different timbres. Striking the cymbal when it is opened changes the sound from tight to more sustained and shimmery. For these reasons the high-frequency transients perpendicular to the contact point and the shimmer from the edges are important. The hi-hat is integral to the drum sound not only for its different timbres but as a timekeeper.

Overhead Cymbals   As the name implies, the overhead cymbals are positioned above the drum kit, usually to the left center and the right center of the drummer. The most commonly used overhead cymbal is the *ride cymbal*. It produces a shimmery or sizzly sound, depending on how it is struck. Usually, its function it to provide a steady rhythmic pattern, known as a *ride pattern,* rather than accents. The *crash cymbal* may also be used, mainly for accents. It produces a sharp, splashy sound.

Tuning the Drums

A good drum sound begins with the musicianship of the drummer and the quality and the tuning of the drum set. No miking technique will save the drum sound of an incompetent drummer or a low-quality kit.

Before drums are miked, they must be tuned. Tuning the drum set is important to the sound of individual drums and also to their overall sound because it brings out the fundamental resonances and enhances the overtones. Many studios have an in-house drum set always tuned and ready to go, not only to ensure the desired drum sound but also to avoid having this necessary and time-consuming procedure cut into recording time.

Although the drummer usually does the tuning, it helps to know what is involved and what to look and listen for. Before tuning begins, check for heads that should be changed. Look for holes or cuts (other than the hole that may have been cut into the front head of the bass drum); dents or indentations; a coated head that has lost a significant amount of its top layer; an overstretched head; or a head with too wide a difference in sound between its middle and sides.

There are many ways to tune a drum set: in fifths and octaves; in thirds; by tapping on the sides of the drum, finding its fundamental pitch, and then tuning the head to it; and by pitching the bass drum low enough to leave room in the upper bass and the midrange for the tom-toms and the snare. If the bass drum is pitched too high, it pushes too close to the toms, which in turn get pushed too close to the snare, making the drum sound smaller.

A common interval between tom-toms is fourths. Some drummers use a fifth between the lowest tom and the bass drum. Moreover, by not separating the individual drum sounds, little room is left for such instruments as the bass and the guitar.

One problem with even the best drum sets is resonance, such as ringing and buzzing. Damping the drums helps reduce these sounds—and undesirable overtones as well. Placing a pillow, blanket, foam rubber cushion, or the like inside the bass drum helps dampen offending sounds (see 17-17). To dampen a tom-tom and a snare drum, specially made gel-type stick-ons are available that are removable and do not leave residue (see 17-21). Remember to place any damper out of the way of the drumstick. Before dealing with the snare drum, first check for problems with the snares off. Make sure the damping does not muffle the drum sound.

To reduce cymbal ringing, apply masking tape from the underside of the bell to the rim in narrow radial strips or use specially made cymbal silencers. If the cymbals sound dead, they may need cleaning. Copper or metal cleaner usually does the job.

Where the drum set is placed in a studio also affects its sound. Isolated in a drum booth (to reduce leakage into other instruments' microphones), the overall sound takes on the acoustic properties of the booth: if the booth is live, the drums will sound live; if the booth is absorptive, the drums will sound tight or dull. On a hard floor, the drums sound live and bright; on a carpet they sound tighter and drier. In a corner they sound boomier because the dominant lower frequencies are more concentrated. Often drums are put on a riser that can resonate to reduce low-end leakage.

Miking

Although the drum kit consists of several different-sounding instruments, it must be miked so that they sound good individually yet blend as a unit. That said, drums are miked in many ways. The approach to take depends on the desired sound control and the type of music being recorded.

Explaining how to deal with sound control is relatively easy: the more components to regulate, the more mics you use (although this can have its drawbacks—possible phasing, for one). Achieving a particular drum sound for a certain type of music involves many variables and is more difficult to explain.

Generally, in rock-and-roll and contemporary pop music, producers like a tight drum sound for added punch and attack. Because this usually requires complete control of the drum sound, they tend to use several microphones for the drums. In jazz many styles are loose and open, so producers are more likely to use fewer drum mics to achieve an airier sound. Figures 17-11 to 17-15 illustrate a few basic approaches to miking a drum kit.

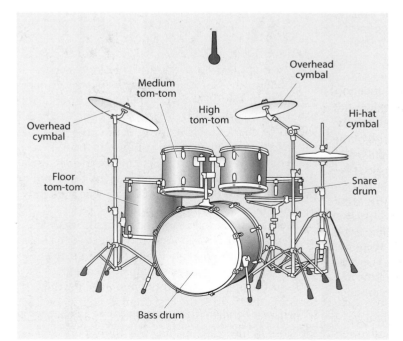

17-11 One cardioid capacitor microphone overhead. The mic hears essentially what the drummer hears. The cardioid pattern is usually wide enough to pick up the blend of drum sounds. If it is not, the wide-angle subcardioid should do. The capacitor mic is best suited to reproduce the spectrum of frequencies the drums emit. The problems using one overhead mic are: (1) it may not pick up an adequate bass drum sound; (2) to get a decent blend, it may have to be positioned far enough overhead so that the closer drums and the cymbals will not be too loud; (3) if the mic is positioned too close to the overhead cymbals, their sound and possibly the snare drum's sound will be disproportionately louder than the rest of the kit; (4) the balance and the blend of the drum kit is entirely dependent on the recording, so there is little that can be done in the mixdown; and (5) the drums can be recorded only in mono.

Using two spaced overhead mics provides a stereo pickup and a better blend, but the recording still lacks an adequate bass drum and other low-end drum sounds.

17-12 Three microphones. This setup uses two cardioid capacitor microphones overhead and one directional or non-directional moving-coil mic in the bass drum. Using two overhead mics helps with the blend and the balance and provides a stereo image. The coincident, near-coincident, and spaced arrangements will yield different acoustic results (see "Distant Miking" earlier in this chapter). The mic in the bass drum allows separate control of its sound. The directional mic concentrates its impact; the nondirectional mic opens the sound somewhat without picking up much if any of the other drum sounds due to the inverse square law—sound levels increase (or decrease) in inverse proportion to the square of the distance, in this case, from the mic to the drum head. This arrangement produces an open, airy drum sound. Using high-quality microphones is essential.

Bass (Kick) Drum   The bass drum is the foundation of the drum set because, as noted earlier, it provides the primary rhythm pattern with transient punctuations. In much of popular music, it also works with the bass guitar to provide the bottom sound that supports the other musical elements. Because the bass drum also produces high levels of sound pressure and steep transients, large-diaphragm moving-coil microphones usually work best, although there are a few large-diaphragm capacitor mics that also work well, particularly by adding some midrange coloration. As noted in Chapter 3, there are dual-diaphragm mics designed especially for the bass drum. One model uses a moving-coil element for the low frequencies and a capacitor element to better reproduce the higher frequencies (see 3-7a and 3-7b).

A device called the KickPad™ can be used with a directional microphone to provide, as the manufacturer

17-13 Four microphones. Three mics are placed as suggested in Figure 17-12. The fourth is usually placed on the snare drum but sometimes between the snare and hi-hat to obtain a better hi-hat pickup. It can be a moving-coil or capacitor mic, depending on the desired sound, and it is almost always a directional mic (see "Snare Drum" and "Hi-hat Cymbal" later in this section). The overhead mics, however, may pick up enough of the snare sound so that the sound from the fourth mic may be used only for fill in the mix.

17-14 Five microphones. Four mics are placed as suggested in Figure 17-13. The fifth is positioned between the medium and high tom-toms for added control of these drums.

17-15 Miking each drum. For the drum kit in this illustration, eight microphones are required. The advantages of this technique are that it provides the recordist with optimal control of each drum and cymbal sound in the recording and in the mixdown. The disadvantages are that there may be phasing, leakage, or too dense a sound, or some combination of these factors.

17-16 KickPad.™ This device requires no phantom power and plugs directly into the mic line.

states, an "instant, repeatable kick drum sound." It is a passive device, requiring no phantom power, and it plugs directly into the mic line (see 17-16).

The common technique for mic placement is to use the hole often cut in the front drumhead or to remove the head entirely and place the mic inside. This gives the sound of the bass drum more punch. Pointing the mic perpendicular to the beater head produces a fuller sound (see 17-17). If the mic is too close to the head, it will pick up more click and attack than fullness and maybe the action of the beater head as well. Pointing it to the side of the drum picks up more of the drum's overtones, creating a rounder sound with more definition but less attack (see 17-18). Placing the mic outside the open head deepens the drum sound but decreases clarity and attack and could pick up leakage from other instruments.

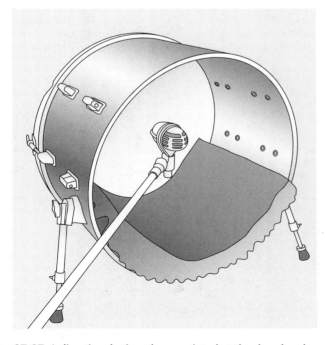

17-17 A directional microphone pointed at the drumhead produces a fuller sound. Foam rubber padding is placed in the drum to reduce vibrations.

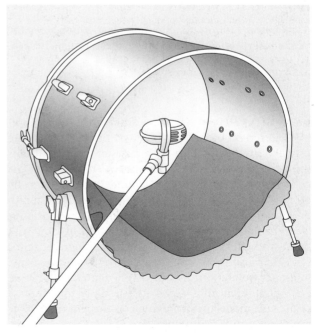

17-18 A microphone pointed to the side of the drum produces more of the drum's overtones.

Getting the desired sound from the bass drum is essential not only to the surrounding drum set but also to the overall recording and mix. It provides the music's downbeat.

Drum mics are usually directional to increase sound separation and reduce leakage from the rest of the drum set, though an omnidirectional mic can be effective in a bass drum. Placing the mic in close proximity to a loud sound source usually prevents leakage from the other drums (remember the inverse square law). To separate the bass drum even more, use a low-pass filter, shelving, or a parametric equalizer to cut off or reduce frequencies above its upper range. Be careful, though—the perceived punch of the bass drum goes into the midrange frequencies. In fact, boosting in the 2,500 to 5,000 Hz range adds a brighter attack to the bass drum sound. The dull, thuddy, cardboard sound the bass drum tends to produce can be alleviated by attenuating between 300 Hz and 600 Hz.

A word about equalizing during recording: First, equalization (EQ) should not be used as a substitute for good microphone technique or to correct poor mic technique. Second, if you must equalize, make sure you know exactly what you are doing. Even if mistakes in equalizing during recording can be undone in the mixdown, it may not be possible to undo the additional noise and the possible distortion created in passing a signal through an electronic device.

Tom-toms Tom-toms come in a variety of sizes and pitches. Typical drum sets have three toms: the low-pitched, fuller-sounding floor tom; the middle-pitched medium tom; and the higher-pitched, sharper-sounding high tom.

Although toms produce loud transients (all drums do), they are not as strong as those the bass drum produces; you can therefore mike them with moving-coil, capacitor, or the more rugged ribbon mics. Placement, as always, depends on the sound you want. Generally, the mic is placed from 1 to 10 inches above the tom and is aimed at the center, or slightly off-center, of the skin. It is usually mounted just over the edge of the rim to avoid interfering with the drummer's sticks (see 17-19 and 17-20).

The mic-to-source distance depends on the low-frequency content desired from the drum sound itself. If it has little low-frequency content, try placing a directional mic with proximity effect close to the drum skin to boost the lower frequencies. Placing a mic inside a single-headed tom gives the best isolation, but it could also produce a closed, dull sound and may require an EQ boost in the range of 5,000 Hz to bring the attack back to life. With two-headed toms, placing a second mic underneath the drum can add dimension and depth to the instrument's overall sound. If the top and bottom mics are recorded on the same channel, switch the polarity of the bottom mic; otherwise they will be out of phase—the top mic is picking up the drum sound as the head moves in, and the bottom mic is picking up the drum sound as the head moves out. For the sake of flexibility, many producers prefer to record the top and bottom mics on separate channels. Whatever technique

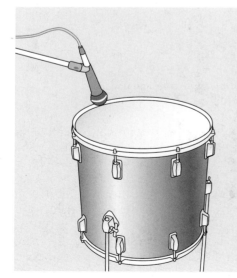

17-19 Miking a floor tom.

17-20 Miking a medium tom (left) and a high tom (right).

you use, remember that the sonic relationships of the toms must be maintained; using the same make and model of microphone on each tom helps.

Snare Drum Of all the components in a drum set, the snare usually presents the biggest problem in miking. Most producers prefer a crisp snare drum sound. Miking the snare too closely tends to produce a lifeless sound, whereas miking it too far away tends to pick up annoying overtones, ringing, and leakage from the other drums.

Another problem is that the snare drum sometimes sounds dull and thuddy. In this instance the problem is most likely the drum itself. Try rolling off from 50 Hz or pulling out some of the frequencies between 300 and 700 Hz, or both. Two ways to add crispness to the sound are to use a mic with a high-frequency boost or to equalize it at the console. Boosting in the 4,000 to 6,000 Hz range adds crispness and attack. Some boost between 7,000 Hz and 10,000 Hz can add airiness to the highs. If these EQ adjustments still do not enhance the sound, the better alternatives are to retune the drum set and, if that doesn't work, to replace the drumhead(s).

Another potential problem with the snare sound is that the levels may be difficult to control because the drum is forcefully played. Some compression can help. Ratios of 2:1 or 3:1 with a high threshold should bring the levels under control without crushing the snare sound.

Moving-coil or capacitor mics work well on the snare drum; the moving-coil mic tends to give it a harder edge, and the capacitor mic tends to make it sound richer or crisper. To find the optimal mic position, begin at a point 6 to 10 inches from the drumhead and aim the mic so that its pickup pattern is split between the center and top edge of the drum (see 17-21). This picks up the sounds of the snares and the stick hitting the head. To get the snares' buzz and the slight delay of their snap, use two mics: one over the drum and one under it. Remember to take the same precautions as when double-miking a two-headed tom (see 17-22).

Hi-hat Cymbal The hi-hat cymbal produces two sounds: a clap and a shimmer. Depending on how important these accents are to the music, the hi-hat can either share the snare drum's mic or have a mic of its own. If it shares, place the mic between the hi-hat and the snare and adjust the sound balance through mic placement (see 17-23).

If the hi-hat has a separate mic, the two most common positions for it are 4 to 6 inches above the center

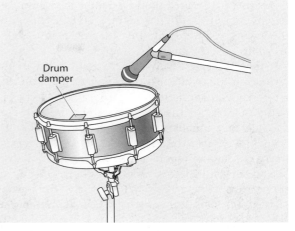

17-21 Miking a snare drum. The pad on the skin of the drum reduces vibrations.

17-22 Miking a snare drum over and under.

stem, with the mic pointing straight down (see 17-24), and off the edge (see 17-25). Sound is brightest over the edge of the cymbal. Miking too closely off the center produces ringing, and miking off the edge may pick up the rush of air produced each time the two cymbals clap together (see 17-26). Equalize by rolling off the bass to reduce low-frequency leakage—but only if the hi-hat is miked separately. If the mic is shared with the snare drum, rolling off the bass adversely affects the low-end sound of the snare.

17-23 Miking a hi-hat cymbal and a snare drum.

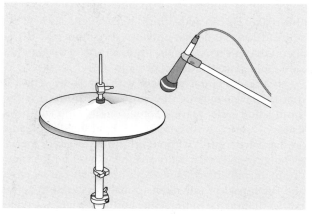

17-24 Miking over a hi-hat cymbal.

Overhead Cymbals In miking either the ride or the crash cymbal, the definition of the characteristic sounds must be preserved. To this end capacitors usually work best; for stereo pickup the coincident (see 17-1), near-coincident (see 17-2), or spaced pair (see 17-3) can be used. When using the spaced pair, remember to observe the three-to-one rule to avoid phasing problems.

Because the overhead microphones usually blend the sounds of the entire drum set, they must be at least a few feet above the cymbals. If they are too close to the cymbals, the drum blend will be poor and the mics will pick up annoying overtones that sound like ringing or gonging, depending on the narrowness of the mic's pickup pattern. If blending the drum sound is being left until the mixdown and it is important to isolate the cymbals, roll off the low frequencies reaching the cymbal microphones from the other drums.

Sometimes, regardless of the miking technique, the sound of the overhead cymbals is disproportionately loud and washes over the drum track. There are two ways to reduce the problem: have the drummer hit the cymbals with less force and, if the cymbals are thick, use thinner cymbals, which are not so loud.

17-25 Miking at the edge of a hi-hat cymbal.

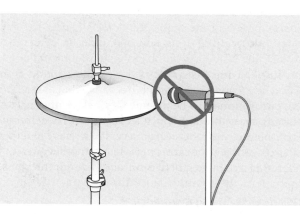

17-26 A mic aimed at the point where the cymbals clap may pick up the rush of air as they come together.

Reducing Drum Leakage

Drums produce loud sound levels. If leakage from one drum's microphone to other drums' mics or from the drums to the mics of other instruments being recorded is unwelcome, there are techniques to employ that can considerably reduce the problem.

■ Close-mic each drum. The greater the mic-to-source distance, the greater the chance of leakage as well as ambience and background noise.

■ Use highly directional mics, super- and hypercardioid pickups, instead of cardioids, for example.

■ Record the drums separately and then overdub the other voicings. (**Overdubbing** is a technique used in much of popular music recording. One or a few instruments are recorded first, usually the rhythm instruments, and the other voicings are added separately or in groups to the previously recorded tracks.)

■ If the electric instruments are being recorded, they can be recorded with the drums by "going direct"; plugging them directly into the mixer instead of miking their amplifiers.

■ Use a noise gate on each drum track. The potential problems here, however, are that it requires time to set up; it adds electronic processing in the signal path; and the gating must be precise or some of the drum sound can be lost, or the gating action can be heard, or both.

■ Enclose the drum area with portable gobos to help isolate the sound or, if one is available, use the isolation booth that some facilities have for drums.

■ If it does not adversely affect the drum sound or the overall music blend, have the drummer play more softly.

■ Before reducing the leakage, consider whether it, in fact, adds something to the drum and/or ensemble sound, such as openness, liveness, or cohesion.

ACOUSTIC STRING INSTRUMENTS

Acoustic string instruments derive their sound from stretched strings, held taught in a frame, that are set into vibratory motion by being bowed, plucked, or struck. As strings do not produce much loudness, the frame, which also vibrates with the strings, serves to amplify and radiate sound. Three variables help determine the pitch of a vibrating string: length, tension, and mass (or thickness).

Plucked String Instruments

Plucked string instruments include the guitar, the banjo, and the mandolin.

Characteristics

Because the six-string guitar is clearly the most popular of the plucked string instruments, it is considered here. The guitar's six strings are stretched across a hollow body with a flat top and a sound hole that resonates the fundamental frequencies and the harmonics of the vibrating strings. Fundamental frequencies range from 82 to 988 Hz, with harmonics extending from 1 to 13 kHz.

The guitar has a fingerboard with raised metal frets that divide the effective length of the strings into exact intervals as the strings are pressed down onto the frets. Where the guitar string is plucked affects sound quality because of the relationship of the distance from the point of contact to the ends of the strings. For example, a string plucked close to the bridge contains more high-frequency energy due to the relatively short distance between the point of contact and the bridge. A string plucked farther from the bridge produces a warmer sound due to the presence of longer wavelengths and therefore lower frequencies.

Overall most high frequencies are near the bridge. The joint between the neck and the body produces more lower frequencies. Most lower frequencies are resonated by the back of the guitar and are generated from the sound hole.

What the strings are made of and what is used to pluck them also affect a guitar's sound quality. For example, metal strings tend to sound brighter than nylon, and a string plucked with a pick will be brighter than one plucked with a finger.

Miking

Most of a guitar's sound radiates from the front of the instrument, so centering a microphone off the middle of the sound hole should, theoretically, provide a balanced sound. But the mic has to be at least a foot or more from the instrument to pick up the blend of radiated sound. If a mic is too close to the hole, sound is bassy or boomy. Also, because the sound hole resonates at a low frequency, the mic could pick up those vibrations. If it is moved closer to the bridge, detail is lost. If it is moved closer to the neck, presence is reduced; if it is moved too far away, intimacy is affected and, if other instruments are playing, there could be leakage.

If it is necessary to mic close to the sound hole, roll off some of the bass for a more natural sound, but be careful not to adversely affect the sound of the instrument. If a guitar lacks bottom, mike closer to the sound hole but slightly off-axis to avoid picking up low-end vibrations.

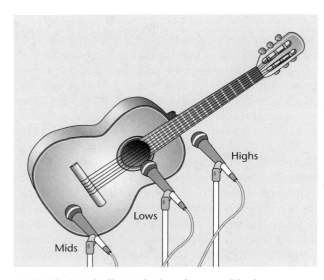

17-27 The tonal effects of microphone positioning on an acoustic guitar.

17-28 Miking an acoustic guitar. A microphone placed about 6 inches above the bridge and even with the front of the guitar brightens the instrument's natural sound.

If it lacks highs, aim a mic at the neck; to increase midrange, mike closer and (facing the guitar) to the left of the bridge (see 17-27).

One way to achieve a natural, balanced sound is to position the mic 2 to 3 feet from the sound hole. To set a more high- or low-frequency accent, angle the mic either down toward the high strings or up toward the low strings. To brighten the natural sound, place the mic above the bridge and even with the front of the guitar because most high-frequency energy is radiated from a narrow lobe at right angles to the top plate (see 17-28). Miking off the twelfth fret, across the strings, produces a sound rich in harmonics.

Another way to achieve natural sound is to place a mic 8 to 12 inches above the guitar, 1 to 2 feet away, aimed between the sound hole and the bridge. A good-quality capacitor mic reduces excess bottom and warms the sound.

A microphone about 4 to 8 inches from the front of the bridge creates a warm, mellow sound, but the sound lacks detail; this lack is beneficial if pickup and string noises are a problem.

Clipping a mini-mic outside the sound hole facing in toward the center yields a natural, balanced, slightly bright sound. Clipping a mini-mic inside the sound hole gives good isolation and added resonance but also reproduces a more closed, bassier sound and less string noise.

Sometimes two microphones are used on an acoustic guitar to add body or dimension to the sound. Common

placements include close-to-far, sound hole/neck, and stereo. In the close-to-far technique, the close mic picks up the essential guitar sound, and the far mic is used to pick up ambience (see 17-29). Placing one mic off the sound hole and another off the neck captures a more detailed low- and high-frequency sound blend (see 17-30). Stereo miking adds size to the guitar sound; be careful, however, not to space the mics too far apart or it will create a hole in the middle of the sound (see 17-31). Stereo imaging can also be achieved using middle-side miking, either with an M-S mic or two mics, one cardioid and one bidirectional (see 17-32).

The stereo miking technique requires matching microphones. For the close-to-far and sound hole/neck approaches, either matching mics can be used for a uniform sound or two different mics can be employed to capture different tonal nuances.

For a classical guitar, which requires favorable room acoustics for interaction with the instrument's sound, the mic should be placed at least 3 feet from the sound hole. Make sure mic-to-source distance is not too great, or the subtleties of the instrument will be diminished by too much reverberation. Another approach is to use a primary mic or stereo pair closer in for the main guitar sound and a secondary mic, or stereo pair, higher and farther off-instrument for the ambience.

Plucking creates quick attacks. Using a dynamic microphone, which has slower transient response than a capacitor mic, can slow the attacks and diminish de-

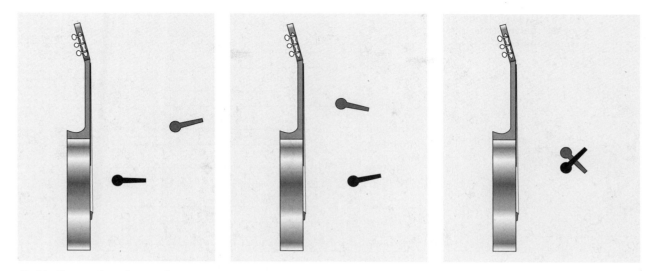

17-29 Close-to-far miking technique on an acoustic guitar.

17-30 Sound hole/neck miking technique on an acoustic guitar.

17-31 Stereo miking technique on an acoustic guitar.

tail, particularly in the guitar's bass frequencies. But if a capacitor mic brings out too much crispness, a good moving-coil mic can reduce it.

A natural part of the sound of most plucked string instruments is the screechy, rubbing noises called *fret sounds* caused by the musician's fingering. Fret noises usually bring to the fore the issue of whether they should be part of the recording. Personal taste is the determining factor. If you do not care for fret sounds, mike farther from the instrument or use a super- or hypercardioid mic placed at a slight angle to the neck of the instrument. This puts the mic's dead side facing the frets. Make sure the mic's angle is not too severe, or the sound from the instrument will be off-mic. There are also strings specially designed to reduce fret sounds and sprays to reduce friction.

Bowed String Instruments

The well-known bowed string instruments are the violin, the viola, the cello, and the bass.

Characteristics

Bowed string instruments are similar to plucked string instruments in that their strings are stretched across a fingerboard and a hollow body, which resonates the vibrating strings. But bowed instruments have only four strings and no metal frets on the fingerboard; intervals are determined by the placement of the musician's fingers on the fingerboard. Another difference is that the strings are vibrated by a bow drawn across them, thereby

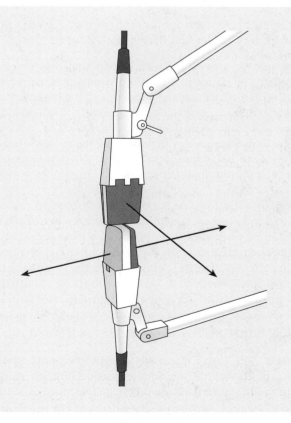

17-32 Middle-side miking using two multidirectional mics—one set for cardioid pickup and the other set for bidirectional pickup.

17-33 Dynamic ranges of selected musical sound sources.

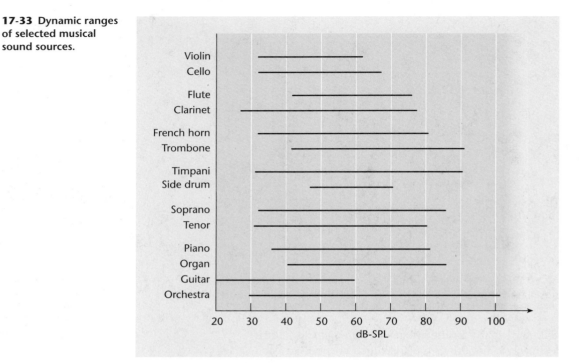

generating a smoother attack than that of a plucked string. The bridge in a bowed instrument is connected to a top plate through a sound post to the back plate. It is important to overall sound, as are the F-holes in the top plate that allow the air inside the body to resonate. The dynamic range of bowed string instruments is not as wide as that of most other orchestral instruments, nor is their projection as strong (see 17-33).

Violin The four violin strings are tuned to perfect fifths and have a fundamental frequency range of 196 to 3,136 Hz, with harmonics that extend from 4 to 13 kHz. The violin radiates lower frequencies in a roughly spherical pattern. As frequencies get higher, the violin radiates them about evenly in the front and the back, as both the top plate and the back plate are designed to resonate with the strings. The highest frequencies are radiated upward from the top plate.

Viola The viola is essentially a larger, lower-pitched version of the violin. The strings are tuned a fifth lower than the violin's; their fundamental frequency range is 131 to 1,175 Hz, with harmonics that extend from 2 to 8.5 kHz. The radiating pattern is similar to that of the violin but is less directional due to its lower frequency range.

Cello The cello's strings are tuned a full octave below the viola's, with a fundamental frequency range of 65 to 698 Hz and harmonics that extend from 1 to 6.5 kHz. The cello's radiating pattern is more omnidirectional than directional, but it is affected by the playing position. The cello rests on a rubber- or plastic-tipped spike that is set on the floor. Hence vibrations are transmitted to the floor, which reflects and absorbs the sound waves to some degree, depending on the sound absorption coefficient of the flooring material.

Bass The bass strings are tuned in fourths rather than fifths and have a fundamental range from 41 to 294 Hz, with harmonics extending from 1 to 5 kHz. It radiates sound omnidirectionally; and because it is positioned like the cello, the sound is affected by the flooring material.

Miking

Because the dynamic range of bowed string instruments is not wide, sound must be reinforced by using several instruments, multiple miking, or both, depending on the size of the sound required. Overdubbing is another method used to reinforce string sound. The need for reinforcement is compounded by the dearth of competent string players in many communities, to say nothing of

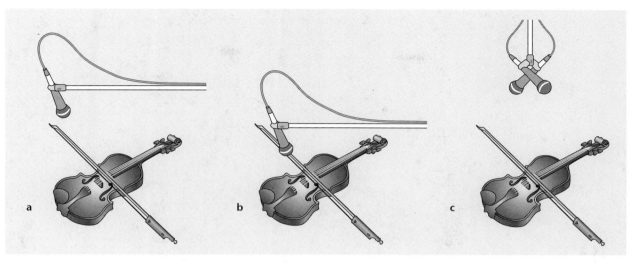

17-34 Miking a violin or viola. (a) Placing the microphone several feet above the instrument, aimed at the front face, tends to produce an open, natural sound. (b) To produce a country fiddle sound, place the mic closer to the bridge but not close enough to interfere with the bowing. (c) With stereo miking, a coincident or near-coincident pair produces a fuller, more open sound compared with using a single microphone. The angle between the mics and their distance from the instrument should be such that the highs, mids, and lows blend and the stereo imaging is not so wide that it creates a larger-than-life sound (and mental picture)—unless that is the intention.

the cost of hiring very many of them where they do exist in sufficient numbers.

Individually, miking a violin or viola a few feet above the instrument, aiming the mic at the front face, produces an open, natural sound, assuming fairly live acoustics, which are essential to recording a good string sound (see 17-34). Although sound radiation is uniform up to 500 Hz, depending on the microphone a single mic may not hear sufficient low end and therefore not reproduce a robust sound. Miking "over and under" ensures that the highs, which are concentrated above 500 Hz and radiate perpendicularly to the sounding board, are picked up from above the instrument and the lows are picked up from both above and below. This technique also tends to make one instrument sound like a few and a few sound like several (see 17-35). Assuming that the acoustics are drier than what is usually required to record a good string sound, overdubbing will accomplish this, usually with greater effectiveness.

Miking a few inches from the side or above the strings of a violin produces a country fiddle sound; the closer a microphone is to the strings, the coarser or scratchier the sound. But take care not to interfere with the musician's bowing when close-miking over bowed instruments (see 17-34b).

Generally, for either the cello or the acoustic bass, miking off the bridge 2 to 3 feet produces a brighter sound and miking off the F-hole produces a fuller sound. The right contact mic placed behind the bridge produces a tight, robust sound (see 17-36). The wrong contact mic can yield a closed, dull sound.

With a plucked bass, used in jazz, some producers like to clip a mic to the bridge or F-hole for a more robust sound. A danger with this technique is getting a thin, midrange-heavy sound instead. Close-miking a plucked bass picks up the attack. If close miking also produces too boomy a sound, compress the bass slightly or roll off some of the low end, but beware of altering the characteristic low-frequency sound of the instrument.

Capacitor and ribbon mics work particularly well with bowed string instruments. Capacitor mics enrich the string sound and enhance detail. Ribbon mics produce a resonant, warm quality, although there may be some loss of high-end detail. For plucked strings, capacitors are preferred because of their excellent transient response.

Mini clip-on and contact mics are other alternatives for miking bowed string instruments.

Assuming the musician does not mind having a mic attached to the instrument (and many do), a clip-on or contact mic attached between the bridge and the tailpiece

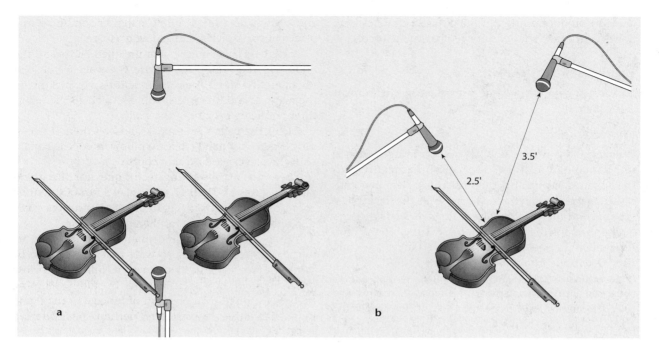

17-35 Enlarging the sound of a violin or viola. (a) Place one microphone several feet above the instrument(s) and one below the instrument(s). This tends to make one instrument sound like a few and a few sound like several. (b) Another approach to layering parts from a single player is to set up mics at different angles and distances from the instrument.

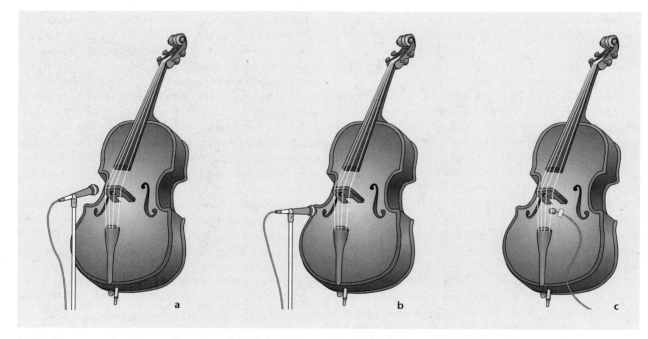

17-36 Three ways to mike a cello or bass. (a) Off the bridge produces a brighter sound. (b) Off the F-hole produces a fuller sound. (c) A contact mic behind the strings, near or at the bridge, taped to the body of the instrument produces a more resonant sound, which could also be dull and devoid of harmonics.

tends to produce a bright, resonant sound. Be careful, however, that the sound is not too harsh or closed.

Struck String Instruments: Piano

The best-known example of a struck string instrument is the piano.

Characteristics

The piano's strings are stretched across a bridge attached to a sounding board that resonates in sympathy with the vibrating strings after they are struck. Hammers controlled by the keys on the keyboard strike the strings. The strings continue to vibrate until the key is released and a damper stops the vibration of the string. The piano's fundamental frequency and dynamic ranges are quite wide (see inside front cover and Figure 17-33).

Radiation is generally perpendicular to the sounding board, primarily upward in a grand piano. The lower-frequency strings are more omnidirectional; the higher-frequency strings are located closer to an axis perpendicular to the sounding board. The lid is also a factor in a piano's sound radiation, but directionality depends on the angle at which the lid is open.

Because of the percussive nature of the key striking the string, timbre is affected by how hard the string is struck. Higher harmonics are more present in strings that are struck hard. Strings struck more gently produce a warmer sound.

Miking

The piano offers almost unlimited possibilities for sound shaping. More than with many other instruments, the character of the piano sound is dependent on the quality of the piano itself. Smaller grand pianos may have dull, wooden low-end response. Old or abused pianos may ring, thump, or sound dull. Steinways, generally, are built to produce a lyrical sound. Yamahas produce crisp sound with more attack. The Bösendorfer aims for additional sonority by adding semitones in the bass range. Mic technique and signal processing cannot change a piano's voicing from dull to bright, from thin to rich, or from sharp to smooth, but they can alter a piano's existing sound. That said, unless the piano is nicely voiced and well tuned, the most savvy recordist with the best equipment has little chance of producing acceptable sound.

Another factor in piano miking is the music. Classical music and jazz generally require a more open sound, so mic placement and pickup should capture the full sonic radiation of the instrument. Popular music, such as rock and country, usually requires a tighter sound, so mic placement and pickup are generally closer.

Regardless of the music, aim the open lid toward the middle of the room, not toward the wall. If you aim the open lid toward the wall, in addition to picking up the piano sound, the mic(s) will also pick up the reflections bouncing back from the wall.

Check the pedals for squeaks, and oil them if necessary. If oil is not handy, place a pillow under the pedals, with the player's approval of course.

There are many miking techniques for the grand piano. Figures 17-37 to 17-41 display a few of the more common approaches.[2] Figure 17-42 illustrates basic microphone positioning for the upright piano.

When miking the grand piano, keep in mind its dynamic range; it can be so wide that you have to be some distance from the piano to get its full sound—close distances yield only partial sound. In studio recording there is the additional problem of leakage in the piano mics from other instruments, perhaps necessitating

---

2. Some of the techniques displayed are suggestions from the *Shure, Earthworks,* and *DPA* miking guides.

17-37 Middle-side–miking a grand piano. An M-S microphone about 12 to 18 inches above the middle strings, 8 inches horizontally from the hammers, produces a natural, balanced sound and a relatively spacious low-end to high-end stereo image (assuming appropriate acoustics). Best results are achieved with the piano lid off. Otherwise the lid should be at full stick. At full stick there will be a more concentrated sound with less ambience pickup.

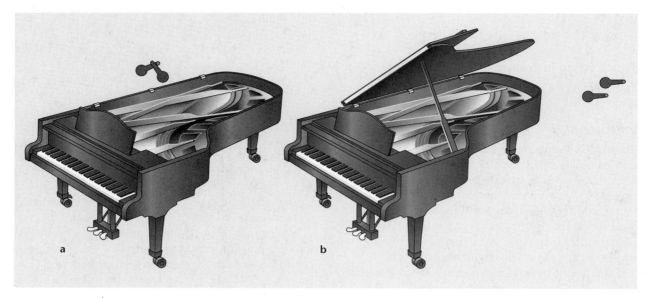

17-38 Near-coincident microphone array. (a) This illustration employs an X-Y pair of directional mics about 12 to 18 inches above the middle strings using the ORTF technique (see 17-5). It spaces the array just under 7 inches apart at a 110-degree angle, 55 degrees to the left and the right of center. Stereo imaging is wide and, in good acoustics, spacious, with the mids spread somewhat wider across the aural frame than the low and high ends. Best results are achieved with the lid off. (b) When the piano lid remains attached, it should be at full stick. (At short stick the sound can be too closed and muddy.) Because the pickup usually will be more concentrated and less spacious, use a near-coincident or spaced pair of distant mics to pick up more of the blended radiations and ambience to add openness, regardless of whether close-miking is used over the sound board.

17-39 PianoMic™ system. This approach uses two omnidirectional microphones mounted to a telescoping bar that spans over the strings and is supported at the ends by the piano case. The telescoping bar allows the mics to be positioned in a variety of recommended ways: one-third of the way in from each side of the piano, 3 inches in front of the hammers, and 3 inches above the strings; closer together for a fuller midrange sound; father apart for wider low-to-mid-to-high-frequency stereo image; and closer to the hammers for a more percussive sound. The telescoping bar can also be turned to position the mics at various distances farther from the hammers and strings for more open-sounding pickups. The system can be used with the piano lid up or down. With the lid up, the sound is airier; with the lid down, it is more condensed. In addition to producing an open, rich, spacious sound, omni mics are not subject to proximity effect in close-miking situations.

PianoMic is a trademark of Earthworks.

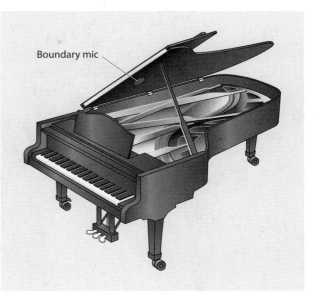

17-40 Side-positioned microphones. Two omnidirectional mics are placed at each side of the piano, pointed directly at each other. Begin at about 4 feet and experiment with the height that yields the preferred sound. One mic is over the high C note and the other is over the low A note. The recorded sound is close to what the pianist hears.

17-41 Using boundary microphones. A number of techniques are possible using boundary microphones. Two of the more commonly used are (1) mounting one boundary mic on the piano lid to pick up a blended monaural sound (shown here), or (2) mounting two directional boundary mics on the piano lid, one toward the low strings and the other toward the high strings for a balanced, open stereo pickup.

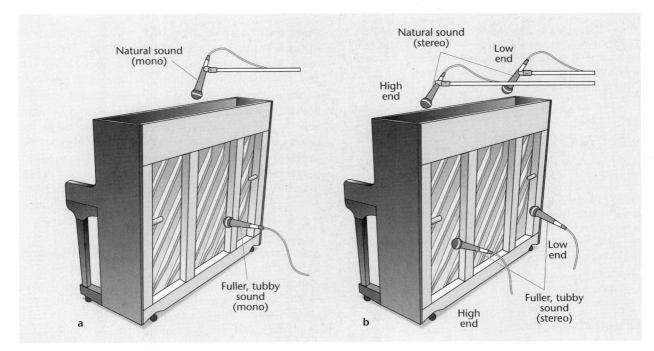

17-42 Miking an upright piano. (a) For mono, position a microphone over an open top for a natural sound or behind the sounding board for a fuller, tubby sound. (b) For stereo, position two mics, one for low-end pickup and the other for high-end pickup, over an open top or behind the sounding board, or use a stereo boundary mic. Mics can also be placed inside the piano to pick up the hammer sounds. When spacing the mics, remember the three-to-one rule.

17-43 Miking across the bridge/rail axis. This produces a spacious, full-bodied sound but at the expense of low-end/high-end stereo imaging.

closer mic-to-source distances. Because there is more piano sound across the bridge/rail axis than horizontally along the keyboard, miking along the piano instead of across it reproduces a more spacious, full-bodied sound (see 17-43); a clear low-end/high-end stereo image is sacrificed, however, because the sound is more blended.

Any microphone mounted on a floor stand should be equipped with a shock mount. A large instrument with significant low-end response such as the piano can vibrate the floor, and those vibrations can carry to the floor stand.

WOODWINDS

Just as the vibrating string is the acoustical foundation of string instruments, a vibrating column of air is the foundation of woodwind (and brass) instruments. All wind instruments have in common a tube or cone through which air is blown, generating a standing wave of vibrating air within. In woodwinds the vibrations are produced in the clarinet and the saxophone using one reed, in the oboe and the bassoon using a double reed, and in the flute and the piccolo by blowing across the air hole.

Characteristics

The sounds of woodwinds are determined by the length of the tube, by whether the tube is open at one end

(clarinet) or at both ends (flute), and by the opening and closing of the holes in the tube. A tube open at one end has odd-number harmonics: third, fifth, seventh, and so on. A tube open at both ends, and flared or conical tubes (oboe and bassoon), has the normal harmonics: second, third, fourth, fifth, et cetera. The vibrating reed and the sound holes generate their own overtones. In general, higher frequencies radiate from the bell, and lower frequencies radiate from the holes.

Flute   The flute is a tube that is held horizontally. The musician blows air across a sound hole and controls pitch and timbre by varying the blowing force. Opening and closing the holes in the side of the instrument also determine pitch. Sound radiates from the sound hole, the side holes, and the end of the flute. Fundamental frequencies range from 261 to 2,349 Hz, and harmonics extend from 3 to 8 kHz. Its dynamic range is limited.

Clarinet   The clarinet is a single-reed tube played almost vertically, with the bell pointed toward the floor. Its fundamental frequency range is 165 to 1,568 Hz, with harmonics extending from 2 to 10 kHz. Sound is generated from the mouthpiece and the reed, the side holes, and the bell. Reflections from the floor also may affect the clarinet's sound.

Oboe and Bassoon   The fundamental frequencies of the oboe and the bassoon are 261 to 1,568 Hz and 62 to 587 Hz, with harmonics extending from 2 to 12 kHz and 1 to 7 kHz, respectively. Despite their relatively narrow frequency response and limited dynamic range, both instruments are comparatively rich in harmonics and overtones. The oboe's sound emanates from the mouthpiece and the reed, sound holes, and bell. Like the clarinet, it is played aimed at the floor and may also be affected by sound that is absorbed by and/or reflected from the floor. The bassoon curves upward at its bottom, pointing toward the ceiling. If the ceiling is high enough, the bassoon's overall sound is usually not affected.

Saxophone   The family of saxophones includes the soprano, alto, tenor, and baritone. Saxophones have a conical shape with a bell that curves upward (except for the soprano sax, which may be straight). The saxophone's sound radiates mostly from the bell, but the sound holes also generate significant detail. Fundamental frequency ranges are roughly as follows: soprano—200 to 1,100 Hz; alto—138 to 820 Hz; tenor—100 to 600 Hz; and baritone—80 to 400 Hz. Depending on the instrument, harmonics can extend into the 8,000 Hz range.

Miking

Woodwinds such as the flute, clarinet, and oboe are among the weaker-sounding instruments and have a limited dynamic range. Alto, tenor, and baritone saxophones are stronger sounding. But the higher-pitched woodwinds—flute, clarinet, and soprano saxophone—can cut through the sound of more-powerful instruments if miking and blending are not properly managed (or if the sound designer intends it).

Because most woodwinds are not powerful instruments, the tendency is to close-mike them, but, due to their sound radiation, this results in an uneven pickup. They should be miked far enough away so that the pickup sounds blended and natural. Also, keep in mind that with woodwinds most of the sound radiates from the holes, not from the bell.

The flute and the piccolo (a smaller, higher-pitched version of the flute) radiate sound in shifting patterns sideways and from the instruments' end holes. Therefore, miking too close tends to miss certain frequencies and emphasize others. Moreover, dry, less reverberant sound can distort some tonalities. Attaching a mini-mic, usually omnidirectional, produces a tight sound with reduced breath noise and ambience.

Selecting a microphone that can reproduce the high frequencies of these very high-pitched instruments is, of course, critical. Otherwise the sound can be brittle, hard, or distorted, and the instruments' higher harmonics may not even reproduce. Capacitors are almost always the mics of choice.

For the flute, mic-to-source distance depends on the music. For classical it should be about 3 to 8 feet; for pop, about 6 to 24 inches. For a natural sound, microphone positioning should start slightly above the player, a few inches from the area between the mouthpiece and the first set of finger holes. To add the breathy quality of the blowing sound, mike more toward the mouthpiece—how close depends on how much breath sound you want. Using a mic with a windscreen or pop filter should help. If breath noise is a problem regardless of the mic or where it is placed and you want to eliminate it, try placing the mic behind the player's head, aiming it at the finger holes (see 17-44). This technique also reduces high-frequency content. A windscreen or pop filter reduces unwanted breath noise, too. In miking a flute or any woodwind, be careful not to pick up the sound of the key action.

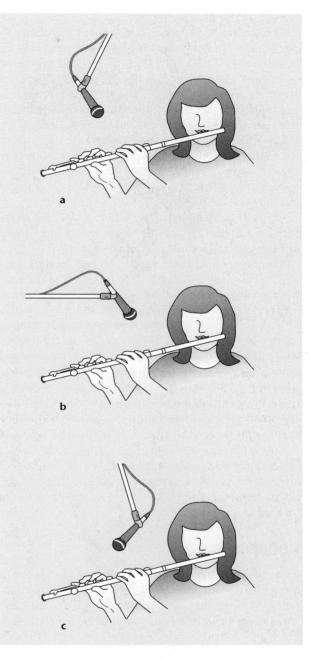

17-44 Miking a flute or piccolo. (a) Placing a microphone over the finger holes near the end of the instrument picks up most of the sounds these instruments emit and does not pick up the breathy sounds that miking the mouthpiece produces. (b) Some producers feel that these sounds are part of the instruments' overall aural character, however, and mike the mouthpiece to produce a thinner-textured sound. (c) If unwanted breath sounds persist, place the mic behind the musician's head, aimed at the finger holes.

Microphone positioning for the clarinet and the oboe must take into account the narrowing of high frequencies radiating in the vertical plane in front of the player, as well as floor reflections from the bell's being aimed downward. Miking too close tends to emphasize these disparities. If close miking is unavoidable, position the mic slightly to the side of the bell rather than straight at it. This should smooth most of the sonic anomalies. Miking a few inches from the bell tends to reduce leakage and makes the sound brighter. Another possibility is to mike toward the bottom third of the instrument and far enough away to blend the pickup from the finger holes and the bell (see 17-45).

Classical music solos require an airy sound. Assuming good acoustics, mic about 4 to 12 feet away. Using a stereo pair can give the sound added spaciousness.

Saxophones distribute sound between the finger holes and the bell fairly well, but the proportion of sound radiating from the holes and the bell changes constantly as the keys open and close. The best sound can be obtained with a mic placed at about the middle of the instrument, pointed toward the horn. Point the mic toward the bell for a fatter sound. Some producers or players want the sound of the keypads and the keys; others don't. The more the mic is pointed at the bell, the less key noise is apparent. Sometimes a clip-on instrument mic is used in live situations. This is an easy setup to adjust. Simply clip

the mic onto the outside edge of the bell and adjust it. Some players prefer a dynamic mic close to the bell and a condenser mic farther away, pointed toward the keys, which achieves rather the best of both sounds.

Generally, miking saxophones off the bell produces a bright sound that, depending on the instrument, can be thin and hard. Miking too close to the bell further accentuates the high frequencies, making the sound piercing or screechy. Miking off the finger holes adds fullness, presence, and warmth. Aiming a mic at the holes from above the bell produces a natural, more blended sound (see 17-46). Mounting a mini-mic on the bell yields a sound that is bright and punchy.

BRASS

Brass instruments—trumpet, trombone, baritone, tuba, and French horn—generally are conical and have a cup-shaped mouthpiece that acts as a vibrating "reed" when the musician blows into it. They are the loudest acoustic musical instruments with the widest dynamic range (see 17-33).

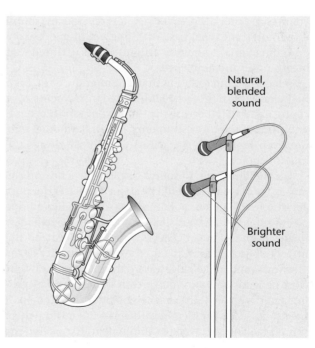

17-46 **Miking a saxophone.** Aiming a microphone at the finger holes from above the bell produces a natural, blended sax sound. Aiming a mic off the bell produces a bright sound. Miking too close to the instrument may pick up blowing or key sounds.

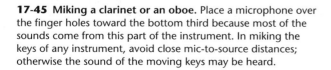

17-45 **Miking a clarinet or an oboe.** Place a microphone over the finger holes toward the bottom third because most of the sounds come from this part of the instrument. In miking the keys of any instrument, avoid close mic-to-source distances; otherwise the sound of the moving keys may be heard.

Characteristics

Trumpet   The fundamental frequency range of the trumpet is 165 to 988 Hz, with harmonics extending from 1 to 7.5 kHz. In addition to the sound control by lip pressure and tension at the mouthpiece, a series of three valves is used to vary the tube length and therefore the pitches. Most of the sound radiates from the bell, with higher frequencies located on an axis closer to the center of the bell.

Trombone   The trombone is the orchestra's most powerful instrument. Its distinctive feature is a slide that is moved in and out to vary the length of the tube and change pitches. (Some trombone models use valves instead of a slide.) The fundamental frequency range is 87 to 493 Hz, with harmonics and a radiation pattern similar to those of the trumpet.

Baritone   The baritone has roughly the same range as the trombone, although its harmonics do not go as high—from about 980 to 4,000 Hz. Its low-frequency power is greater than that of the trombone because of the amount and the size of tubing and the wider circumference of the bell. It uses valves to vary its effective length and emits sound upward. Higher-frequency harmonics are present at the axis of the bell, although to a live audience they are not a recognizable component of the baritone's sound because they are generated upward. Most of a baritone's distinctive bass sound is radiated omnidirectionally.

Tuba   The tuba is a larger version of the baritone and is the lowest-pitched of the brass instruments. Its fundamental frequency range is about 40 to 330 Hz, with harmonics that extend from about 500 to 3,500 Hz.

French Horn   The French horn is a curved, conical tube with a wide bell and valves that is played with the bell pointed to the side of or behind the musician, often with the musician's hand inside the bell for muting. The instrument's sound is therefore not closely related to what the live audience hears. Its fundamental range is relatively narrow—87 to 880 Hz, with harmonics extending from 1 to 6 kHz—but the French horn's sound can cut through the sound of louder instruments with wider frequency response.

Miking

Because of their loudness, dynamic range, and rich harmonics, brass instruments are best recorded in a relatively live room. Reverberation can be used in the mixdown, of course, but regardless of how good the reverb unit is, it can rarely match the sound of brass instruments playing in a fine acoustic environment.

Brass instruments require care in microphone placement and careful attention in adjusting levels. They emit the most directional sound; high-frequency harmonics radiate directly out of the bell. But the most distinctive frequencies of the trumpet and the trombone are around 1,200 Hz and 700 Hz, respectively, which are radiated from the sides of the bell. Below 500 Hz radiation tends to become omnidirectional, so close-miking brass instruments with a directional microphone does not quite produce their full frequency response. A directional mic close to and in front of the bell produces a bright, biting quality. Miking at an angle to the bell or on-axis to the side of the bell produces a mellower, more natural, horn-like sound (see 17-47).

About 1 to 5 feet is a starting point for capturing a good working mic-to-source distance. Closer placement gives a tighter sound, although miking too close to a brass

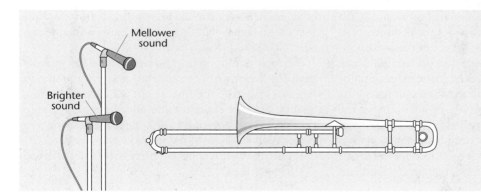

17-47 Miking off the bell. Mike trumpets, trombones, baritones, and tubas at an angle to the bell for a natural, mellower sound, being careful to avoid close mic-to-source distances so that airflow and spit sounds are not heard. Miking in front of the bell produces a brighter sound.

Mellower sound

Brighter sound

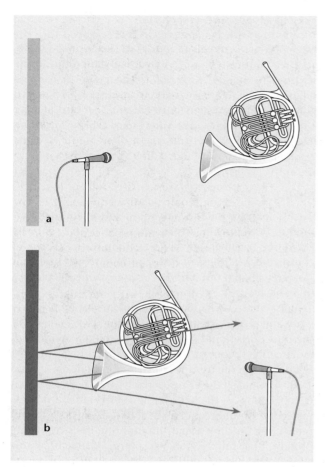

17-48 Miking a French horn. (a) To control leakage place the musician away from the ensemble and the microphone near a soft baffle pointing at the bell. (b) If this arrangement creates a blending problem due to the horn's lack of presence, placing a hard baffle a few feet from the bell should carry the sound to the mic in sufficient proportions.

17-49 Miking a baritone or tuba from above the bell.

horn could pick up spit and valve sounds. More-distant placement makes the sound fuller and more emphatic.

For the French horn, a mic-to-source distance of at least 3 to 5 feet is recommended. It is not the most powerful brass instrument, but, as noted previously, it can cut through and overwhelm louder instruments, and its levels fluctuate considerably. For a natural sound, aim the mic toward the bell. If leakage is a problem, move the instrument away from the ensemble (see 17-48).

In miking brass sections, trumpets and trombones should be blended as a chorus. One mic for each pair of instruments produces a natural, balanced sound and provides flexibility in the mixdown. If you try to pick up more than two trumpets or trombones with a single mic, it has to be far enough from the instruments to blend them, and the acoustics have to support the technique. Of course, leakage will occur. Mike baritones and tubas individually from above (see 17-49).

The type of mic you use also helps shape the sound of brass. The moving coil can add transparency and smooth transient response; the ribbon can add a fuller, warmer tonality; and the capacitor can add sizzle and produce accurate transient response. Be careful when using a capacitor with brass instruments, however. Their on-axis sound off the bell has peaky, high harmonics that can overload the mic.

17-50 Direct box. This unit converts unbalanced signals from guitar amps, stereo keyboards, CD and tape players, and computer sound cards. There are two sections; each includes an XLR connector, ¼-inch parallel wired in/out jacks, ground lift switch to help eliminate hum and buzz, and a 20 dB pad switch for connection to inputs with overly loud signal levels.

ELECTRIC INSTRUMENTS

Electric instruments—bass, guitar, and keyboards—generate their sounds through an electric pickup that can be sent to an amplifier or directly to the mixer. Three techniques are generally used to record an electric instrument: plugging the instrument into an amplifier and placing a mic in front of the amp's loudspeaker; *direct insertion (D.I.)*, or plugging the instrument directly into the mic input of the mixer through a direct box; or both miking the amp and using D.I.

Electric instruments are usually high impedance, whereas professional-quality audio equipment is low impedance. Not surprisingly, high- and low-impedance equipment are incompatible and produce sonic horrors if connected. The direct box matches impedances, making the output of the instrument compatible with the console's input (see 17-50).

Although this chapter deals with the miking techniques, it is important to know the difference between miking an amp and going direct. Deciding which method to use is a matter of taste, practicality, and convenience (see 17-51 and 17-52).

17-51 Advantages and disadvantages of miking an amplifier loudspeaker.

Advantages	Disadvantages
Adds interaction of room acoustics to sound	Could leak into other mics
Captures more midbass for added punch	Could be noisy due to electrical problems with amp
Creates potential for different sound textures	Level of amp can make it difficult for musicians to hear less powerful instruments
Gives musician greater control over an instrument's sound output	Distortion
Allows other instrumentalists more chance to hear what the electric instruments are playing so that the acoustic players can better interact with the electric instruments	The amplifier is another "instrument," with its own range of sonic characteristics
The amplifier is another "instrument," with its own range of sonic characteristics	

17-52 Advantages and disadvantages of direct insertion.

Advantages	Disadvantages
Has a cleaner sound	Has a drier sound—no room ambience
Captures more high and low frequencies	May use a transformer, which adds another electronic device to the sound chain
Allows more sound control at the mixer	Too present
Eliminates leakage	
Does not require an amp	

Miking the Amplifier Loudspeaker

A single amplifier loudspeaker emits directional sound waves whose sonic characteristics change depending on the angle of the microphone and its distance from the amp. A mic on-axis at the center of the speaker tends to produce more bite compared with the mellower sound of a mic positioned off-axis to the center or at the edge of the speaker. An amp cabinet with bass and treble speakers produces a more complex output and usually requires a greater mic-to-source distance to capture a blended sound.

Placement of the cabinet also affects sound. On a carpet, brightness is reduced. On a hard surface, depending on the amp, sharpness or brightness is increased. On a riser off the floor, low end is reduced.

When miking an amp loudspeaker, the moving-coil mic is most often used because it can handle loud levels without overloading. With the bass guitar, the directional moving coil is less susceptible to vibration and conductance (especially with a shock mount) caused when the instrument's long, powerful wavelengths are amplified. Due to its powerful low end, the bass is usually recorded direct to obtain a cleaner sound. The fundamental frequency range of the electric bass is 41 to 300 Hz, with harmonics extending from 1 to 7 kHz.

Leslie Loudspeaker Cabinet

The Leslie amplifier loudspeaker, most often used with an electric organ, is almost an instrument in itself (see 17-53). It is not a loudspeaker in the normal sense but is designed especially to modify sound. It contains a high-frequency loudspeaker (the tweeter) in the upper portion and a low-frequency loudspeaker (the woofer) in the lower portion. The two loudspeaker systems rotate, creating a vibrato effect. (*Vibrato* is short and repeating fluctuation in the pitch of a sound, not to be confused with tremolo, which is a rapid fluctuation in the amplitude of a sound.)

In the absence of an actual Leslie amplifier loudspeaker, Leslie simulators are available. Depending on the design, they can be used by directly connecting the output of an electric organ into the simulator or by connecting the simulator to a patch panel and connecting the organ through it. With Leslie simulators, as with electronic simulators in general, how close they come to producing the actual sound of the instrument varies.

Recording Electric Bass

Recording electric bass presents a particular challenge. If there is too much bass, the mix will sound muddy. This

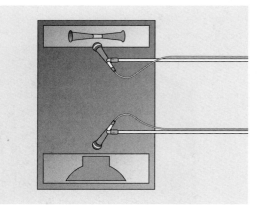

17-53 Miking a Leslie amplifier loudspeaker. One way is with two directional mics: one to pick up the highs and the other to pick up the lows. The greater the mic-to-source distance, the less the chance of picking up the rotor sounds and the increased vibrato and the better the sound blend. To record stereo use either a top and bottom pair of mixed mics left and right, or just single mics panned toward the left and the right. If the sound of the rotating horn is desired, place a boundary mic inside the cabinet.

could mask the fundamentals of other instruments and result in a thickening and a weighing down of the overall sound. Among the ways to improve clarity are to have the bassist increase treble and reduce bass on the guitar or to equalize in the control room by attenuating around 250 Hz and boosting around 1,500 Hz.

Compression is commonly used in recording the electric bass. It helps reduce noise, smooth variations in attack and loudness, and tighten the sound. Be careful in setting the compressor's release time. If it is too fast in relation to the decay rate of the bass, the sound will be organlike. A slower release time maintains the natural sound of the instrument; too slow a release time muddies the sound.

Recording Electric Guitar

When recording an electric guitar, a directional moving-coil mic adds body to the sound. But if it is necessary to reproduce a subtler, warmer, more detailed sound, try a capacitor or one of the more rugged ribbon mics. The fundamental frequency range of the electric guitar is 82 to 1,319 Hz. When amplified the harmonics extend from 1 to 3.5 kHz; when going direct the harmonics range from 1 to 13 kHz.

As for placement, the main challenge is understanding the dispersion pattern of the amplifier's loudspeakers (see 17-54). Miking close to the amp and head-on

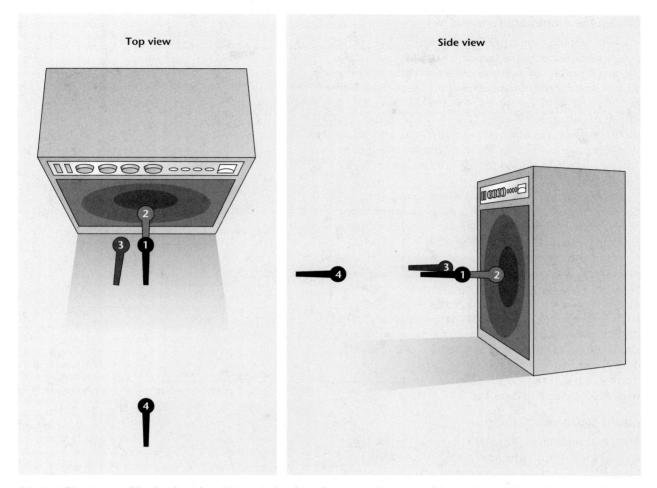

17-54 Miking an amplifier loudspeaker. (1) Four inches from the amp at the center of the speaker cone produces a natural, balanced sound. (2) One inch from the center of the speaker cone produces a bassy sound but minimizes feedback and leakage. (3) Off-center to the speaker cone produces either a dull or a mellow sound, depending on the acoustics and the microphone, but reduces amplifier noise. (4) Three feet from the center of the speaker cone produces a thinner sound with reduced bass but picks up more ambience and leakage.

produces a strong central lobe that has considerable high-frequency content within the bandwidth of the instrument itself. Off-axis miking reduces high-frequency content, and backing the mic farther from the amp produces a more blended, balanced sound. Also, the decrease in highs gives the impression of a heavier, bassier sound. Hanging a small mic over the amp emphasizes a guitar's midrange and reduces leakage. If leakage is not a problem, and even if it is, close miking with an omni works well.

An omnidirectional microphone has no proximity effect—its response is uniform. It will therefore pick up various aspects of the loudspeaker dispersion pattern, and the inverse square law takes care of the leakage problem because you are essentially force-feeding the mic from

an amp that is producing a high sound-pressure level at a short mic-to-source distance. Use an omni capacitor or ribbon mic with a fast response.

Producers also record both amp loudspeaker and D.I. feeds simultaneously. This technique combines the drier, unreverberant but crisp sound of direct insertion with the acoustic coloring of the amplified sound. The amp and D.I. signals should be recorded on separate tracks. This provides more flexibility in the mixdown when the two sounds are combined or if you decide to not use one of the tracks.

It should be noted that direct recording of guitars does not necessarily guarantee a leakage-free track. If a guitar pickup is near or facing a loud instrument, it will "hear"

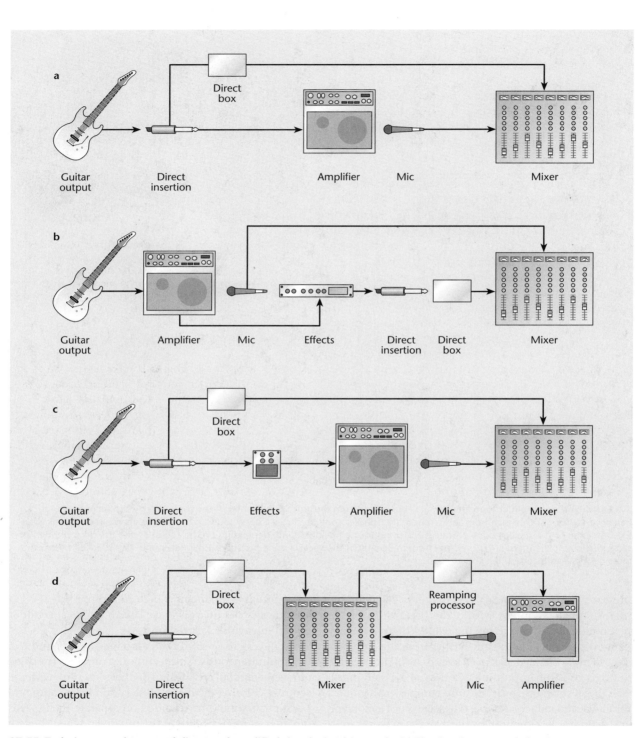

(d) Adapted from Mike Levine, "Direct Results," *Electronic Musician*, December 2006, p. 31.

17-55 Techniques used to record direct and amplified signals simultaneously. (a) The signals are recorded on separate tracks. Special-effect boxes can be used for (b) the usual technique or (c) an alternative technique. (d) A technique employing reamplification. The techniques illustrated in this figure can also be achieved with modeling plug-ins (see 17-56). The sonic results will be different, however, which may not necessarily be unwanted.

the vibrations. By turning the musician away from the direct sound waves or by putting a baffle between the instruments, leakage is reduced.

With the electric guitar, special-effect boxes are often used to add to the sonic possibilities (see 17-55). Here too the various signals should be recorded on separate tracks, if possible, to allow flexibility in the mixdown.

Musicians' Amplifiers

An amp often produces annoying hum. Using a mic with a *humbuck* circuit can help reduce hum but not always enough. It also helps to turn up the loudness control on the guitar and turn down the volume on the amp and to use guitar cables with extra shielding. Another solution is to move the musician around the studio until a spot is found where the hum is reduced or disappears. If possible, convince the musician to use a smaller, lower-powered amp than is used in live concerts. There may be a problem here, however, because the change in amp produces a change in sound.

An alternative to using amplifiers for an electric guitar or bass is modeling technology that simulates the sounds of various makes and models of speaker cabinets or electric guitars and basses. Instead of plugging the instrument into an amp, it is plugged into the modeling device (see 17-56).

The array of modeling devices available continues to grow, providing ever-increasing sources for sonic emulation of amplified guitar sounds—so much so that the days of speaker cabinets may be numbered.

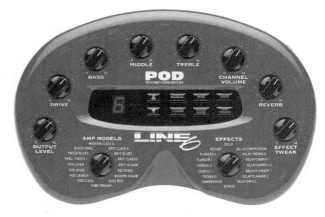

17-56 Guitar modeler. This device is designed to capture the tone and the feel of guitars heard through a variety of speaker cabinets and microphones and in various studio acoustics. It includes 36 memory locations, stereo balanced and unbalanced outputs, and a chromatic tuner. This device is a desktop model; pocket-sized models are also available.

VIRTUAL INSTRUMENTS

A variety of software programs make it possible to manipulate and record the sound of traditional acoustic and electric instruments in the virtual domain. Figures 17-57 and 17-58 display windows from two such programs.

The idea of using virtual instruments in place of the real thing has raised differences of opinion in the music and production worlds. There are those who feel that virtual instruments, regardless of their sound quality, are artificial and that artificiality does not do justice to the

17-57 Virtual rhythm guitar. This program plays acoustic and electric guitar. It includes guitar parts tracked by professional guitarists and riffs for many different styles of music. It plays in any key, plays automatically in time with a song's tempo, and can adapt parts to MIDI.

17-58 Virtual drums.
This program creates, controls, and produces drum performances, using a range of different types of drum kits and styles. It provides real-time control of the virtual drummer's intensity, complexity, timing, and dynamics. The preset drum patterns and performances are editable.

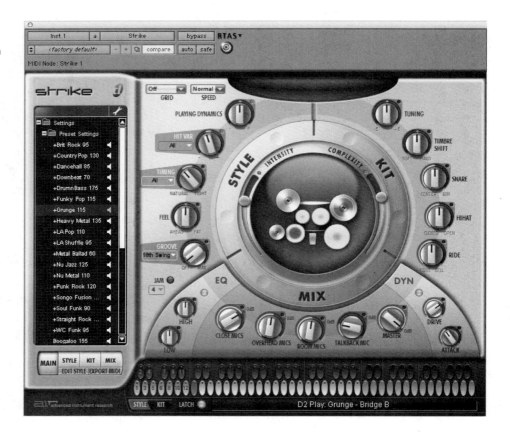

music or its sonic authenticity; that virtual instruments cannot take advantage of the differences in sound created by the types of materials that go into the manufacture of conventional instruments; and that there is an almost clinical, too perfect, tonality to their sound and an absence, or at least a reduction, of the human factor in how they are "played." This affects the ability to infuse individual subtle colorations and dynamics into a performance.

Those who have no problem using virtual-instrument programs cite their almost unlimited reservoir of new and different types of sound—that they should not be considered competition for, or replacements of, traditional instruments but simply additions to the choices of how to play music. After all, many of the instruments taken for granted in today's orchestra did not begin appearing until the mid-1700s. Electric instruments did not become a major part of the music scene until the 1950s. Although the first synthesizer was invented in 1876, it was not until the 1960s that it became commercially viable. Development of the synthesizer helped bring about *MIDI (Musical Instrument Digital Interface)* in the early 1980s. Then

there are *hyperinstruments*—large-scale musical systems that enable the control of complex musical events by a performer. Virtual, or hyper-, instruments are simply another advance that diversifies the musical soundscape.

VOCALS

At its most basic level, the human voice acts like a wind instrument. The lungs expel air through the vocal cords, which vibrate and act like a double reed. The voice is then radiated through the larynx and the mouth and out into the air. Sound is modified by the movement of the tongue, jaw, and lips and the rate of exhalation. Pitch is determined primarily by the vocal cords and the larynx, but mouth, lip, and tongue movements change timbre. The wide-ranging and complex harmonics and overtones of the human voice are a product of the mouth, nasal cavity, and chest cavity.

Although the speaking voice has a comparatively limited frequency range, the singing voice does not, and it can place a severe test on any microphone (see 17-59). The singing voice is capable of subtle and almost unlim-

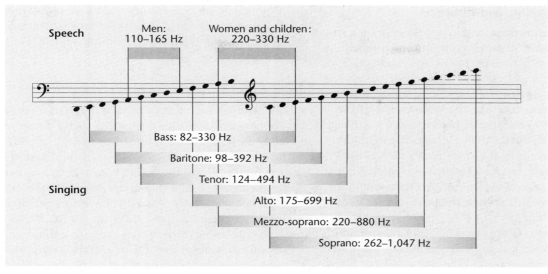

17-59 Fundamental frequency ranges for speech and singing in the human voice. Harmonics in the male singing voice extend from 1 to 12 kHz and in the female singing voice from 2 to 12 kHz.

ited variations in pitch, timbre, and dynamic range. There are also plosives and sibilance—annoying popping and hissing sounds—to deal with.

Timbre

In choosing a vocal mic, the most important consideration is the singer's timbre—how edged, velvety, sharp, mellow, or resonant the voice sounds. The microphone should enhance a voice's attractive qualities and minimize the unattractive. Usually, assuming there are no serious problems with tone quality, most producers prefer to use capacitor mics for vocals. They are far more sensitive to subtle changes in sound-pressure waves than are dynamic mics, they can better handle the complicated pattern of harmonics and overtones in the human voice, and overall sound quality is the most natural.

Dynamic Range

Controlling the dynamic range—the quietest to loudest levels a sound source produces—is another tricky problem. Well-disciplined singers can usually control wide fluctuations in the dynamic range themselves. But many cannot—their voices barely move the peak meter during soft passages and put it in the red during loud ones. In miking these vocalists, a producer has three alternatives: ride the level, adjust the singer's mic position, or use compression. There is a fourth alternative: record the vocal on two tracks. Noise gating may also be an alternative, but it is more often than not time-consuming and requires precise settings to be effective so that its action is not heard.

Riding the level works, but it requires an engineer's full attention, and this may be difficult if other voicings are being recorded at the same time. Also, less gifted singers may handle dynamic range differently each time they sing, which means that riding the level is more a matter of coping than of aiding.

The preferred methods are to use mic technique to adjust for irregularities in a vocalist's dynamic range, use compression, or use both. In pop music, vocals are often compressed 10 to 13 dB. But to do so requires that a recordist know how to compensate after compression.

One placement method is to situate the vocalist at an average distance from the mic relative to the loudest and softest passages sung; the distance depends on the song, the power of the singer's voice, and the acoustics. From this average distance, you can direct the vocalist how closely to move toward the mic during quiet passages and how far for the loud ones. The success of this method depends on the singer's mic technique—the ability to manage the song and the movements at the same time.

If these approaches don't work, try recording the vocal on two tracks with one track down 10 dB. If there is overload or a problem with the noise floor, the undistorted or less noisy sections of each recording can be intercut during editing.

Breathing, Popping, and Sibilance

The closer to a microphone a performer stands, the greater the chance of picking up unwanted breathing sounds and plosives from *p*'s, *b*'s, *k*'s, and *t*'s and sibilance from *s*'s. If the singer's vocal projection or the type of music permits, increasing the mic-to-source distance significantly reduces these noises. Windscreens also help, but some tend to reduce the higher frequencies, although clearly some high-frequency loss is preferable to sibilance, plosives, or breathiness. If a windscreen is used, the stocking (fabric) windscreen works best (see 3-57d). It is not as dense as most other windscreens, and therefore it does not inhibit most of the high frequencies from getting through to the mic.

Other ways to reduce popping and sibilance are to have the singer work slightly across mic but within the pickup pattern or to position the mic somewhat above the singer's mouth (see 17-60). If this increases nasality, position the mic at an angle from slightly below the singer's mouth. If leakage is no problem, using an omnidirectional mic permits a closer working distance because it is less susceptible to popping, sibilance, and breathing sounds. The sound may be less intimate, however, because an omni mic picks up more indirect sound waves than does a directional mic; but the closeness of the singer should overcome the larger amount of indirect sound picked up.

Although capacitors are almost always the microphone of choice for vocals, they do tend to emphasize sibilance because of the mid- to treble-range response of

many models. In such cases, and when other techniques fail to eliminate sibilance, a first-rate moving-coil mic with a built-in pop filter, or a ribbon mic, usually takes care of the problem.

Acoustics

Studios in which high-energy popular music is recorded usually have dry acoustics so that the sound does not become awash in reverberation. This can be disconcerting to a singer who is used to hearing a natural acoustic environment as part of the overall vocal sound. To compensate, recordists feed a comfortable amount of reverb through the foldback system so that the singer hears the vocal in a more familiar acoustic setting. If there is too much reverb coming through the headphones, however, it can wash out detail and throw off intonation and phrasing. If the reverb is too loud, a singer may tend to lay back in the performance; if it is too soft, a singer may overproject. For these reasons, some recordists try to avoid putting any reverb in the foldback so long as it does not inhibit performance.

Reflections

Be aware that when a music stand (or any hard surface) is near the singer's microphone, sound waves reflect off the stand and into the mic. This can cause phase cancellations, adversely coloring tone quality. Remembering that a sound's angle of incidence is equal to its angle of reflectance, position the music stand so that reflections from it do not reach the mic (see 17-61), or cover the stand with material to absorb the reflections.

Mic-to-source Distance Versus Style

Generally, the style of the music sets the guidelines for mic-to-source distance. In popular music vocalists usually work close to the mic, from a few inches to a few feet, to create a tight, intimate sound. Classical and jazz vocalists work from a couple feet to several feet from the mic to add room ambience, thereby opening the sound and making it airy.

When close miking be careful of proximity effect. Rolling off the unwanted bass frequencies may be one solution, but it almost certainly will change the delicate balance of vocal harmonics unless it is carefully and knowledgeably effected. Note that unless a mic is specifically designed for it, positioning the mic just about touching the lips, as some vocalists are seen doing on television and which unfortunately is imitated in the

17-60 Eliminating unwanted vocal sounds. Positioning the microphone slightly above the performer's mouth is a typical miking technique used to cut down on unwanted popping, sibilance, and breathing sounds.

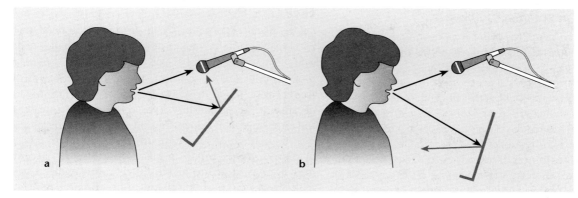

17-61 **Preventing reflections from a music stand from entering a microphone.** (a) Problem. (b) Solution.

recording studio, rarely produces ideal sound. Indeed, if the mic is not up to it, such a technique rarely produces usable sound. If the distortion does not get you, the oppressive lack of air will.

Isolating the Vocalist

To record as clean a vocal sound as possible, many studios use an isolation booth to prevent leakage from instruments or acoustics from reaching the vocal mic. In the absence of such a booth—or because it may color sound or a vocalist may find it difficult to work in a claustrophobic environment—there are other ways to isolate a microphone (see 17-62).

Backup Harmony Vocals

Once the lead vocal is recorded, the accompanying backup harmony vocals are overdubbed. This may involve a singer overdubbing the harmonies one or more times, or it may involve a few vocalists singing at the same time. With the latter technique, if each has a microphone, mic-to-source distances are easier to balance, but it also means more mics to control and requires extra tracks. Another technique groups the vocalists around a bidirectional or an omnidirectional microphone. This reduces the number of mics and tracks but requires greater care in balancing and blending harmonies. Backup vocalists must be positioned to prevent any one voice or harmony from being too strong or too weak. It also reduces flexibility in signal processing and positioning in the mixdown.

Virtual Harmony

Vocal software programs can process an original vocal track and harmonize it, creating a backup vocal track or tracks. The harmonies can be programmed to follow a specified scale. Other features may include voice panning, interval and level controls, glide, pitch, timing, and vibrato. One program has a "throat length" parameter that can change the character of a harmony from loose to tight and vice versa.

17-62 **Portable sound filter for recording with reduced room ambience.** The filter's main function is to help obtain a dry vocal (or instrumental) recording. It has six main layers, which both absorb and diffuse the sound waves hitting them, so progressively less of the original source's acoustic energy passes through each layer. The filter also helps prevent reflected sound from reaching the back and the sides of the mic.

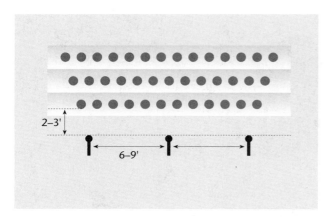

17-63 Miking a choir. Large choir using spaced miking. With spaced miking, remember to observe the three-to-one rule. Ambient mics may or may not be needed, depending on the acoustics and the amount of reverb desired in the final mix.

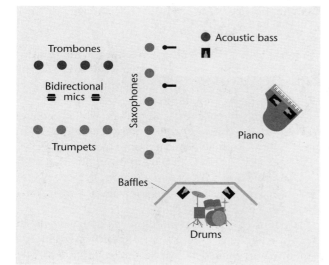

17-64 Miking a jazz band when all voicings are recorded at the same time. Notice that trumpets and trombones are miked with bidirectional microphones and that the piano, acoustic bass, and drums are miked with boundary mics. Bidirectional mics are particularly useful in reducing leakage. For example, by facing the mic straight down in front of each saxophone, each mic's nulls are directed toward sound coming from the sides and the rear. This is especially effective when woodwinds or other weak instruments are in front of brass or other strong instruments. A high ceiling is necessary for this technique to work.

Choirs

Choirs are usually recorded all at once, so it is vital to have microphones situated to pick up each section—soprano, alto, tenor, and bass—for a balanced, blended pickup; you also need ambient mics for acoustic fill (see 17-63). Capacitors are almost always employed because of their suitability in reproducing the sound of the singing voice. Depending on the size of the choir, near-coincident or spaced miking is usually used. If one or more soloists remain in place while singing, accent mics are positioned to pick up their sound—unless the main arrays can do the job and still maintain balances.

MIKING STUDIO ENSEMBLES

The discussion so far in this chapter has centered mainly on the individual instrument. There are studio situations, however, in which ensembles record as a group but are divided into smaller sections to control leakage. This requires isolating them as much as possible to avoid sonic confusion yet blending them so that they sound cohesive. Figures 17-64 to 17-68 illustrate a few ways to mike studio ensembles.

MIKING MUSIC FOR DIGITAL RECORDING

As clear and noise-free as digital sound can be, there are valid complaints about digital recordings: that the high end is strident, thin, and shrieky, or that there is too much unwanted noise from amplifiers, pedals, keys, bows, tongues, teeth, lips, and so on. Many of these problems can be traced to two causes: the microphones and the miking techniques that were used.

Microphones in Digital Recording

Many microphones that were used in analog recording were selected for their rising high-end response; these mics helped deal with problems associated with analog reproduction, the most serious being the potential loss of high-frequency information during disc mastering and copying. There is little such loss in digital recording, copying, or mastering. (Uneven quality in the manufacture of CDs is, alas, another story altogether.) Therefore using such mics for digital recording only makes the high frequencies more biting and shrill. To avoid this problem, use mics with smooth high-end response. Recordists have

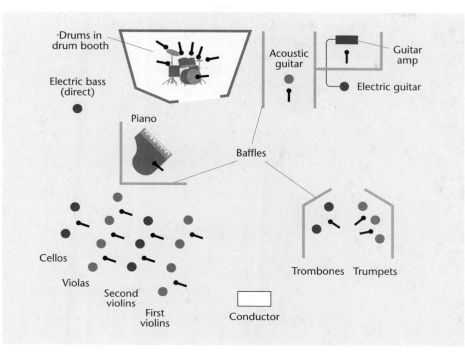

17-65 One way to position and mike a mixed ensemble when all voicings are recorded simultaneously.

From Rusty Cutchin, "Bring 'Em Back Alive," *Electronic Musician,* January 2007, p. 36.

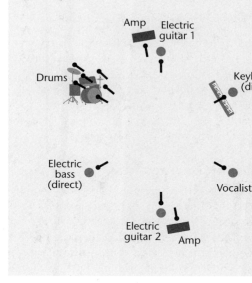

17-66 A circular studio setup. This approach positions the musicians facing one another, with all microphones pointing outward so that their nulls are pointing inward. The arrangement makes it easier for band members to communicate and minimizes the likelihood of leakage.

returned to tube-type equipment in the signal chain—microphones, amplifiers, and equalizers—and plug-ins that simulate the warmth of tube-type sound to offset the edge in digital reproduction.

Capacitor mics have preamplifiers, which generate noise. In analog recording, this noise is usually masked. In the digital format, if preamp noise is loud enough, it will be audible. Digital, high-definition, and other high-quality capacitors are therefore preferred because of their superior sound quality and very low-level self-generated preamp noise.

Modern ribbon microphones are popular in digital recording. Their response is inherently nontailored, smooth, warm, and detailed without being strident. Mics used in digital recording should be linear—that is, output should vary in direct proportion to input. The mic should not introduce unwanted sonic information because, in digital sound, chances are it will be audible.

Furthermore, mics used in digital recording should be not only of the highest quality but also carefully handled and kept in clean, temperature- and humidity-controlled environments. The dust, moisture, and rough handling that may not have perceptibly affected mic response in an analog recording may very well sully a digital one.

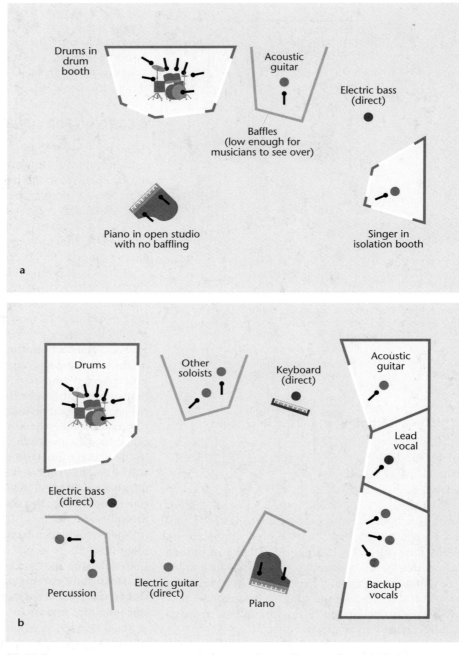

17-67 Two more ways to arrange musical groups for studio recording. (a) Musicians are isolated from one another to prevent sound from one instrument from leaking into the mic of another instrument, yet they are still able to maintain visual contact. It is possible in this arrangement that the acoustic guitar sound will leak into the piano mics and vice versa. Leakage can usually be reduced, however, by supercardioid mics' on both instruments rejecting sound from the sides and the rear, the piano lid's blocking of sound coming from the front guitar baffle, and the guitarist's body blocking the piano sound coming from the back of the studio. (b) Another example of arranging a musical group in a studio to control leakage.

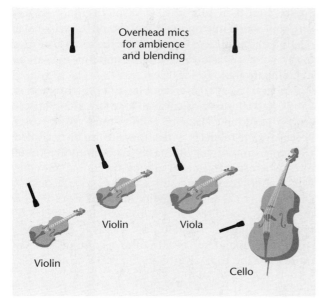

17-68 Miking a string quartet. In this example all microphones are capacitors with a cardioid pickup. The main microphones are positioned to pick up each instrument's sound. Three are placed just above the two violins and viola and the fourth is placed off the bridge of the cello. The overhead mics are positioned to pick up ambience and used for overall blending in the mix.

Microphone Technique in Digital Recording

In analog recording, close miking was employed virtually pro forma because vinyl records usually smoothed its rough spots by burying some of the harshness in background surface noise. In digital recording, no such masking occurs. For example, when close-miking an acoustic guitar in analog recording, there was little concern about noise that might be generated by the guitarist's shirt rubbing against the instrument; in digital recording, on the other hand, the rubbing sound may be audible if the guitar is not carefully close-miked. In addition, in analog recording, noise from a musician's amplifier may have gotten lost in tape hiss; that is not the case in digital recording, regardless of the mic used.

Even if mic-to-source distance is acceptable in digital recording, microphone placement may not be. For example, the upper harmonics of a violin radiate straight up in two directions. If a mic is placed directly in one of these paths, the digital sound could be too crisp and shrieky, even though the mic is at an optimal distance from the violin. By placing the mic more in the path of the lower-frequency radiations, the digital sound should flatten.

High frequencies of brass instruments are radiated straight ahead in a relatively narrow beam. Placing a mic directly in front of the bell may produce a harsh digital recording. Placing it at more of an angle to the bell to pick up a better blend of the lower frequencies should smooth the sound.

RECORDING FOR SURROUND SOUND

There are a few ways to handle a music recording for surround sound.[3] One is to use the miking techniques already discussed in this chapter and apply the surround-sound imaging during the mix through panning. Another is to mike for surround sound in the recording session. Using a combination of the first two approaches may be considered a third technique. (Mixing music for surround sound is covered in Chapter 22.)

Generally, there are differences in how popular and classical/jazz music are handled in surround recording. Because pop music is usually looking for impact and presence, the common approach is to close-mic the voicings with directional microphones and do the surround panning and the delay in the mixdown. In classical music and much of acoustic jazz, the idea is to record the sound as naturally as possible using surround miking arrays.

It is worth noting that in the music industry, recordings miked for surround sound are also miked for stereo. The main reasons are economic. Stereo releases are still where record companies make most of their sales. It is also less expensive to set up and record both the stereo and the surround microphone arrays in one session than in two. To simplify coverage this section deals only with surround techniques. (See "Distant-miking Stereo Arrays" earlier in this chapter for coverage of stereo microphone methods; also see "Downmixing to Stereo" in Chapter 22.)

In miking for surround sound during recording, there are two basic means of handling selection and placement. One is to use direct and ambient miking; the other is to take the direct approach.

Direct/Ambient Surround-sound Miking

With *direct/ambient surround-sound miking,* either one of two stereo arrays—near-coincident or spaced—will do as a basis for the left-right frontal pickups; then add a center mic for the center channel. Because of the center

---

3. This discussion assumes the 5.1 surround-sound format.

mic, the angle or space between the stereo mics should be wider than usual. The surround microphones are typically used for ambience and are pointed away from the sound source to the rear or rear-side of the studio or hall. The surround mics can be used for principal voicings, however, depending on the type of music being recorded and the size and the acoustics of the room.

In addition to the surround-sound microphones, accent mics may be used on selected instruments to help fill in the overall pickup. Balancing is done in the mixdown.

Figure 17-69 illustrates a basic surround-sound miking technique. Figures 17-70 to 17-78 display other variations of surround-sound microphone arrays to provide a sense of the ongoing experimentation with surround miking techniques. None of these examples is intended to suggest that any one approach is preferred to or better than another, nor are they necessarily the most common

approaches; there are other workable techniques. Any surround-sound microphone array should be evaluated in relation to the music being recorded, the room acoustics, the amount of spaciousness desired, and how the various instruments are to be localized.

For example, large ensembles, such as orchestras, bands, and choruses, usually call for more widely spaced arrays than do small jazz and country-music groups. Also, because of the rooms in which they are usually recorded, the larger ensembles ordinarily take omnidirectional mics, whereas with smaller groups directional mics may work better. These generalities assume good acoustics. Omnidirectional surround mics may not work in very live venues, and directional surround mics may pick up too concentrated a sound in drier rooms.

Direct/ambient surround-sound recording may use more than the three front and the two surround mics;

17-69 A basic approach to direct/ ambient surround-sound miking. The mics can be either cardioid or wide-angle cardioid, depending on the breadth of the ensemble. The left, center, and right mics face forward. The left and right surround mics may face toward the ceiling (assuming suitable ceiling height and proper acoustics) or may be angled slightly toward the rear.

From Jason Corey and Geoff Martin, "Surround Sound Miking Techniques," *Broadcast Engineering,* March 2004, p. 42. © 2004 Mondo Code.

17-70 Decca Tree surround-sound techniques. Mic 1 is a supercardioid X-Y stereo array, mics 2 and 3 are a near-coincident supercardioid stereo pair, and mics 4 and 5 are a spaced subcardioid stereo pair. For a quasi-traditional Decca Tree, use mics 1, 2, and 3 (the traditional Decca Tree uses three omnis—see Figure 17-7); for an ambient Decca Tree, use mics 1, 4, and 5.

From Ron Streicher and F. Alton Everest, *The New Stereo Soundbook,* 3rd ed. (Pasadena, Calif.: Audio Engineering Associates, 2006), p. 13.18.

17-71 Delos VR (virtual reality) surround microphone technique. This method uses a coincident stereo mic in the center flanked by omnidirectional mics left and right. The distance between the left and center mics and the center and right mics depends on the size of the ensemble and the room acoustics. The surround mics face the rear of the room and are either omnis or cardioids. The distance between the front and surround mics depends on the length of the room.

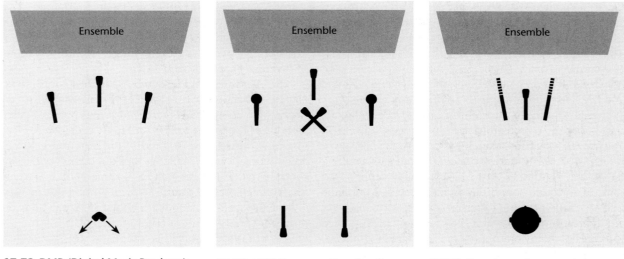

17-72 DMP (Digital Music Products) surround microphone technique. The front mics are cardioids arranged in a quasi–Decca Tree. The surround mics aimed toward the rear of the room can be a coincident stereo array (shown here), another quasi–Decca Tree, or a pair of cardioids spaced to match the distance between the outer pair of frontal mics.

17-73 NHK (Japanese Broadcasting Corporation) surround microphone technique. A cardioid mic is centered between and slightly in front of a near-coincident stereo array in a quasi–Decca Tree configuration. Cardioids are also used for the surround mics. Widely spaced omni mics are flanked to the left and right of the center and near-coincident mics.

17-74 Five-channel surround microphone technique using a binaural head. The center mic is a cardioid, the left and right mics are supercardioids, and the surround pickup is through a binaural microphone head.

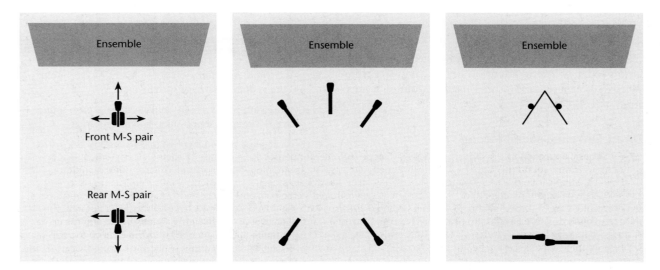

17-75 Double middle-side surround microphone technique.

17-76 Multichannel microphone array (MMA). Also known as the *Williams Five Cardioid Mic Array,* this setup arranges one cardioid mic to the front and the others to the sides and the rear.

17-77 Woszcyk surround microphone technique. Two hard baffles are arranged in a wedge shape. A mini omni mic is flush-mounted on each baffle. The surround mics are a coincident pair of cardioids in opposite polarity, aiming left and right and angled 180 degrees apart.

17-78 Adjustable surround-sound microphone array for small ensembles. This approach uses five capacitor omnidirectional mics positioned horizontally 30 degrees toward the floor. When recording a jazz trio, for example, the array is positioned 6 feet from the ensemble and 12 feet from the floor. For a string quartet, the array is 18 feet from the ensemble and 13 feet high.

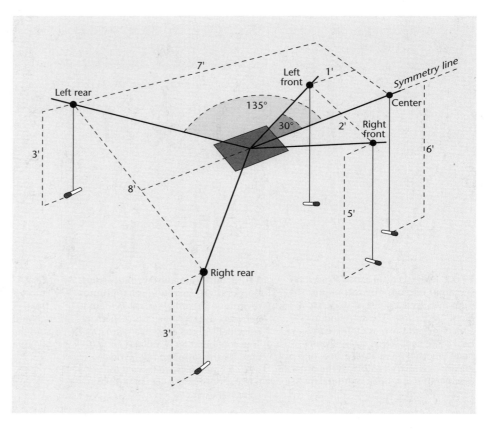

From K. K. Profitt, "The Resolution Project," *Mix*, October 2005, p. 74. © 2005 Mix Magazine.

whatever configuration is needed, do what it takes to get the optimal sound pickup. However many mics are employed, pay careful attention to how their signals are delegated; otherwise the sonic results could be a mishmash (see 17-79).

Direct Surround-sound Miking

The *direct surround-sound miking* approach uses microphone arrays especially designed for surround-sound pickup. The array may be used to record individual instruments or groups of instruments or to pick up the sound of an entire ensemble (see 17-80 and 17-81). Direct miking tends to center the listener more "inside" the music by placing the voicings side-to-side across the front and from the front speakers to the surrounds. Or the spatial imaging may be in a horseshoe shape, with the listener centered at or somewhat inside its base. Among the direct surround-sound microphone arrays available are the SoundField 5.1 microphone system, the Atmos 5.1 system, and the Holophone (see Chapter 3).

MAIN POINTS

▶ Music recording is foremost about the music; technology is not the end; it is the means to the end.

▶ Close miking places a mic relatively close to each sound source or group of sound sources in an ensemble.

▶ Because close miking involves miking most of the instruments in an ensemble, it means that the three-to-one rule, or an appropriate variation of it, should be observed to avoid phasing problems.

▶ Distant miking places a microphone(s) from about three feet to several feet from the sound source. It picks up a fuller range and balance of an instrument, or a group of instruments, and captures more of the studio acoustics for a more open and blended sound.

▶ Generally, the three distant stereo arrays are coincident, near-coincident, and spaced miking.

▶ Coincident miking, also called X-Y miking, employs two matched directional microphones mounted on a vertical axis—with one mic diaphragm directly over the other—

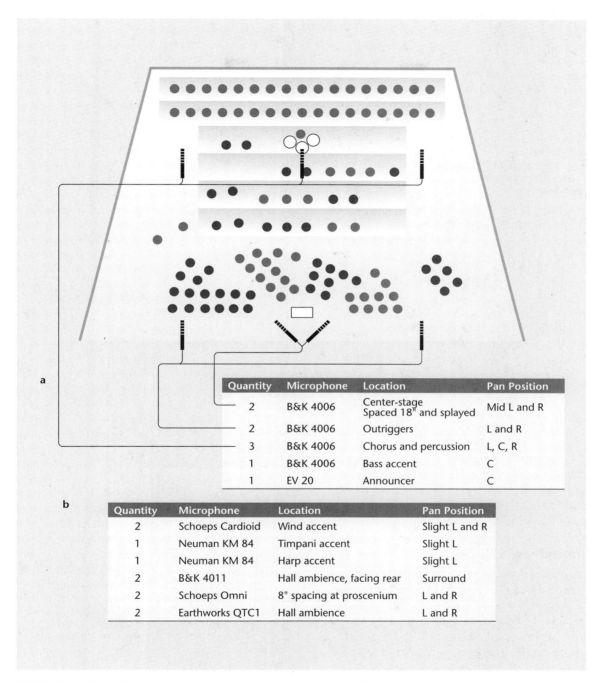

Quantity	Microphone	Location	Pan Position
2	B&K 4006	Center-stage Spaced 18" and splayed	Mid L and R
2	B&K 4006	Outriggers	L and R
3	B&K 4006	Chorus and percussion	L, C, R
1	B&K 4006	Bass accent	C
1	EV 20	Announcer	C

Quantity	Microphone	Location	Pan Position
2	Schoeps Cardioid	Wind accent	Slight L and R
1	Neuman KM 84	Timpani accent	Slight L
1	Neuman KM 84	Harp accent	Slight L
2	B&K 4011	Hall ambience, facing rear	Surround
2	Schoeps Omni	8" spacing at proscenium	L and R
2	Earthworks QTC1	Hall ambience	L and R

17-79 Signal delegation for a symphony orchestra in (a) stereo and (b) surround sound.

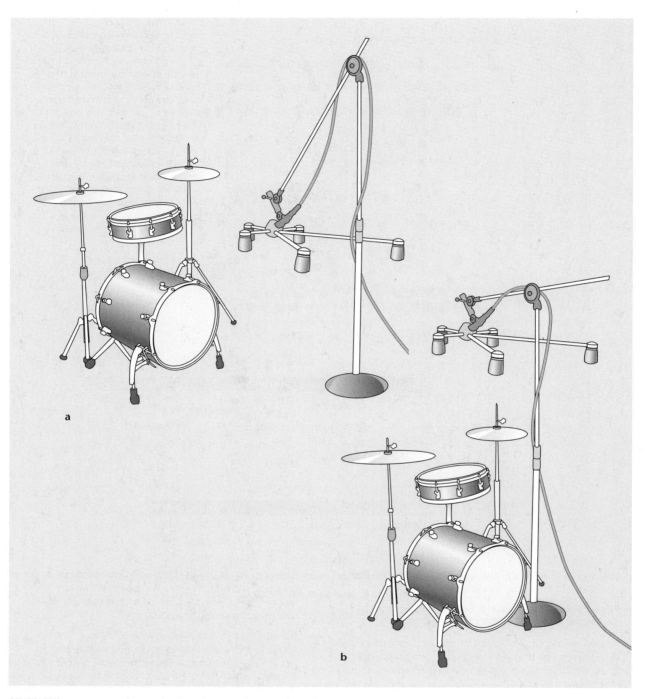

17-80 Using a surround-sound microphone system on drums.

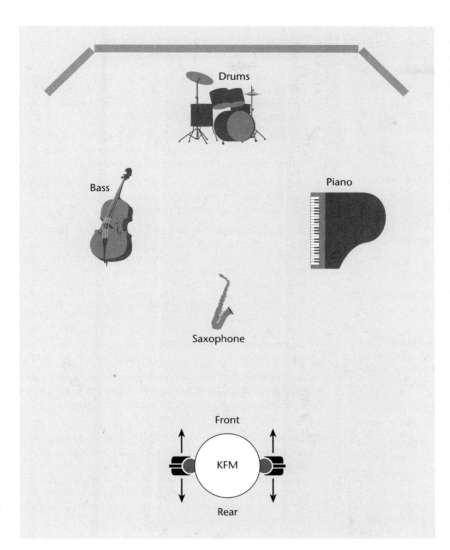

17-81 Miking a jazz combo with the KFM 360 surround microphone system. Two modified Schoeps KFM omnidirectional mics are mounted on opposite sides of a 7-inch sphere. Two bidirectional mics are mounted on either side of the sphere next to the omni mics, facing front and rear. In recording, the omni and bidirectional mics are summed to produce a frontal cardioid pickup and differenced to produce a rear cardioid pickup. The front and rear separation is controlled by adjusting the relative levels of the front and rear signals.

and angled apart to aim approximately toward the left and right sides of the sound source.

▶ Near-coincident miking angles two directional microphones, spaced horizontally a few inches apart.

▶ Spaced miking employs two matched microphones—uni- or omnidirectional—several feet apart, perpendicular to the sound source and symmetrical to each other along a centerline.

▶ There are a number of stereo microphone arrays, including the Blumlein technique, the ORTF method, the OSS or Jecklin disk, and the Decca Tree.

▶ Accent miking, also known as off-miking, is used to pick up instruments in an ensemble when they solo.

▶ Ambience miking, used along with distant miking, attempts to reproduce the aural experience that audiences receive in a live venue by recording in an acoustically suitable studio or concert hall.

▶ The closer a mic is to a sound source, the drier, more detailed, and, more intimate, and, if proximity effect is a factor, bassier the sound. The farther a mic is from a sound source, the more diffused, open, less intimate, and ambient the sound.

▶ Regardless of a directional microphone's pickup pattern: the higher the frequency, the more directional the sound wave and therefore the mic pickup; the lower the frequency, the more omnidirectional the sound wave and the mic pickup.

▶ Although close miking may employ a number of microphones, more is not always better. Each additional mic adds a little more noise to the system, even in digital recording, and means another input to keep track of and control, to say nothing of possible phasing problems.

▶ With most moving-coil mics, the farther from the sound source they are placed, the more reduced the high frequency response.

▶ Generally, large-diaphragm microphones are more suitable in reproducing low-frequency instruments; small-diaphragm mics are more suitable in reproducing high-frequency instruments.

▶ Do not confuse perspective with loudness. Loudness aside, in considering mic-to-source distance, it is hearing more or less of the ambience that helps create perspective.

▶ In recording drums, tuning the drum set is critical if the individual elements are to sound good together.

▶ Although the drum set consists of several different-sounding instruments, it must be miked so that they sound good individually and blend as a unit.

▶ Because most of an acoustic guitar's sound radiates from the front of the instrument, centering a microphone off the middle of the sound hole should, theoretically, provide a balanced sound. But if a mic is too close to the hole, sound is bassy or boomy. If it is moved closer to the bridge, detail is lost. If it is moved closer to the neck, presence is reduced. If it is moved farther away, intimacy is affected.

▶ Because the dynamic range of bowed string instruments is not wide, sound must be reinforced by using several instruments, multiple miking, or both, depending on the size of the sound required.

▶ The piano offers almost unlimited possibilities for sound shaping. More than with many other instruments, the character of the piano sound is dependent on the quality of the piano itself.

▶ Because most woodwinds are not powerful instruments, the tendency is to close-mike them. Due to their sound radiation, however, this results in an uneven pickup. They should be miked far enough away so that the pickup sounds blended and natural.

▶ The loudness and the dynamic range of brass instruments require care in microphone placement and careful attention in adjusting levels at the console.

▶ Some electric instruments, such as the bass and the guitar, can be recorded by miking their amplifier loudspeaker; by direct insertion (D.I.), or plugging the instrument into the console; or by a combination of both.

▶ An alternative to using amplifiers for an electric guitar or bass is modeling technology that simulates the sounds of various makes and models of speaker cabinets.

▶ A variety of software programs make it possible to manipulate and record the sound of traditional acoustic and electric instruments in the virtual domain.

▶ Recording a vocalist is a test for any microphone because the mic must be able to handle the nuances of the singer's timbre and dynamics as well as any popping, sibilance, and breathing sounds. Mic selection and placement depend on voice quality, style of music, and microphone presence.

▶ Recording music digitally requires the highest-quality microphones because unwanted noise and other quiet sounds that are masked in analog recording may be audible in the digital format.

▶ Because digital recording often reproduces sounds not audible in analog, the mics used for digital recording must be of very high quality, generate very low self-noise, be carefully handled, and be kept in clean, temperature- and humidity-controlled environments.

▶ Generally, there are two approaches to handling a music recording for surround sound: direct/ambient surround-sound miking, using conventional techniques during recording and applying the surround-sound imaging during the mix; and the direct surround-sound approach, miking for surround sound during recording and feeding the signals directly to the surround-sound channels.

▶ Among the arrangements used for direct/ambient surround-sound miking are the Decca Tree surround, Delos VR (virtual reality), DMP (Digital Music Products), NHK (Japanese Broadcasting Corporation), five-channel surround using a binaural head, double middle-side (M-S), multichannel microphone array (MMA), and Woszcyk surround microphone techniques.

18

Audio for Interactive Media: Game Sound

Although interactive media and more-traditional linear media share a number of fundamental audio production processes, approaches and techniques between the two often differ substantially. Many involve levels of computer hardware and software integration as well as programming that are beyond the purview of this book. To provide an idea of what is involved in producing audio for interactive media, this chapter covers the basic concepts of sound design and production, with a focus on game sound.

INTERACTIVE MEDIA

Interactive media allow a user to be a participant in the viewing and listening experience instead of just being a passive spectator. A user can directly manipulate and control the picture and the sound. Conventional linear media, such as film and television, sequence visual and aural events in a precise order at predetermined times. The audience has no control over these events.

Types of Interactive Media

Interactive media include a number of genres, such as simple Web pages, dynamic Web sites, informational CD-ROMs, and educational software. Video games are an advanced form of interactive media employing high-end sound (as well as video and graphics). In fact, they do more with sound than many feature films, and they tend to use sound more effectively than most other genres of interactive media. That said, in general the principles of creating and producing game audio discussed here are applicable to the other genres of interactive media as well.

Video Games

A video game is not as easy to characterize as it may seem. Educational software, for instance, sometimes takes on gamelike aspects. Some computer programs, although not games themselves, include mini games or game elements. And even programs that are obviously games—computerized card games, computerized board games, or computer versions of chess or checkers—are not necessarily what people think of first when they envision video games.

For the purposes of this chapter, *video games* are any interactive media in which the focus is on entertainment rather than on productivity, instruction, or information dissemination. More specifically, the subject is those games that utilize the latest advances in computer hardware and software. Using state-of-the-art games as a model of the most advanced of the interactive media genres allows discussion of many techniques and technologies not used by less complex interactive media.

DESIGNING AUDIO FOR INTERACTIVITY

Little is predictable in interactive-sound design. The best video games give users complete control, allowing them to go where they want, to go when they want, to do what they want. This means that nothing, including sound, can play back linearly. From sound effects to music to dialogue, game sound design must be able to seamlessly accommodate all conceivable user actions, giving users the freedom to explore the game without experiencing poor-quality sound, poorly designed sound, or sound dropouts.

This is in stark contrast to sound design for linear media, where the sound designer is working with a fixed picture. In the linear environment, everything in the completed audio track occurs exactly as the sound designer and the creative crew intended, at all times, every time, with no exceptions.

In both modes of working—linear and interactive—effective sound design should serve to enhance both the realism and the subjective or emotional depth of the viewer or player experience.

Sound Design for Linear Media

Sound design based on a fixed picture involves a range of considerations, approaches, and techniques suited to the linear nature of the experience. For instance, music has a definite formal structure and relationship to picture and story arc. Music cues can be accurately timed to occur at specific moments in the sound track, and sound effects can be made to play in sync with picture events. A fixed picture also allows a designer to create a precise sound mix, with dynamics, equalization, and other signal-processing effects adjusted to achieve sound clarity and a reasonably predictable viewer response.

The sound designer can rely on the picture to help guide creative choices within a linear construct. If an action or event occurs in the picture—such as a door closing—the designer can easily determine the kind of sound effect required. If the door shown in the picture ominously swings shut, the designer may choose to use a long creaking sound. If the door is slammed, the designer can easily tell that a whoosh of air and a loud bang will be more realistic. To a great extent, the fixed picture dictates sonic choices and their structuring.

Sound Design for Interactive Media

In creating an interactive-sound design, the sound designer has to develop a coherent audio package that will never play back in the same way twice. It is a **stochastic process** whereby the sound track is not deterministic; rather it is a probability-based expression of variable and predictable user actions and random elements. Sound must anticipate user input and, where this is not possible, react to changing user actions. This is referred to as **interactive sound**, also known as *dynamic sound*.

Creatively, an interactive-sound designer is faced with decisions similar to those of a designer for linear media: consideration of the overall mood and tone of the production, the musical choices and styles to be used, and the types of sound effects to be incorporated. Implementing these creative decisions into an interactive production, however, presents different complexities and challenges.

As in a linear sound design, an interactive-sound designer might be presented with a picture event, such as a closing door, which will require a sound effect. In an interactive production, however, there is no obvious correct choice for this sound. One user might slam the door and another might close it softly. A third user might close the door quickly but not loudly, and a fourth might not even close the door at all. An interactive-sound designer cannot merely choose one of these options and create an effect for it or create a sound effect that works pretty well for any of them. In the first case, the sound will simply be wrong for a significant proportion of users; in the second, users will experience a poorly matched sound that weakens their game experience.

The interactive-sound designer must find ways to handle all these possibilities and eventualities so that each user experiences the appropriate sound mix for individual actions being performed. This is known as *dynamic mixing*. The challenge of a game mixer involves composing the numerous sonic variables into a continuum that balances the need for realism with a visceral emotional experience—the thrill of the game.

Interactive productions rarely have a picture to use as a guide for audio production. Most game sound is under development early in the production process, before picture is available, and, in any case, what picture there is will change from user to user. Because many user actions are to be considered, the interactive-sound designer must generate many different audio effects to cover the range of possibilities.

Interactive-sound designers contend with long run times. Many video games have as many as 200 hours of game-play time. Designing a 200-hour sound track is a formidable challenge that presents difficult creative and logistical hurdles to even the best sound designers.

All these creative roadblocks are made more challenging because interactive productions in general and video games in particular are relatively new types of media that have come into widespread existence within the past 30 years. Unlike audio production in film and television, there is no long-established methodology for creating interactive-sound tracks.

Video game companies handle their sound production process differently; and because interactive media are so technology dependent, many sound designers find themselves inventing new technologies and processes simply to keep up with the expanding possibilities of interactive design.

In addition to tackling the enormous creative and technical challenges posed by user interaction, lack of a formal picture edit, and long run times, the end result is that interactive-sound designers must also be able to work with new technologies, have technical and computer skills, and develop a firm understanding of how interactive media and video games work (see Figure 18-1).

Audio Potential in Interactive Media

An effective interactive-sound design creates an immersive environment through which a user can travel and explore. The sound in such an environment can be designed and programmed to change based on such elements as the user's physical location, time of day, atmospheric and environmental conditions, and the distance from the sound source.

For example, a video game may feature a section with a flowing river and a waterfall. The sound may be programmed so that when the user stands in close proximity to the falls, the audio is loud, crashing, and full of clear, crisp high-frequency splashing sounds. When the user stands farther away, the sound shifts to lower frequencies (lower-frequency sounds travel farther than higher-frequency sounds because higher frequencies more quickly dissipate over distance) and favors the deep rumbling of the distant falls. Sounds of trees swaying in the wind, the rushing stream, and the calls of birds can be programmed to bring the scene more to life.

In a conventional production, the user is unable to explore a location at will. In an interactive design, the sounds can change dynamically as a user moves through the environment. Instead of merely *seeing* the space, the user can actually *experience* it.

18-1 Differences between linear and interactive sound design.

Linear Sound Design	Interactive Sound Design
Based on a fixed picture	Picture is not fixed
Sound track will play back in exactly the same way every time it plays	Sound track will never play back in exactly the same way
Fixed picture can help designer determine what sounds to use	Picture is often not helpful when designing sound
Relatively short run times	Relatively long run times
Many traditions and standards for proper design and production	Few traditions and standards for proper design and production
Knowledge of linear sound design is critical	Technical and computer knowledge are required in addition to sound design expertise

An interactive-sound design also allows the same actions to carry a variety of effects. For example, a sword fight in a video game may feature a variety of crashing and clanging noises even though the image of the different sword strikes is much the same. This randomization of sound allows sound designers to create more-realistic sonic environments in which users can explore and interact.

Interactive media and games also allow music to affect mood and pacing in a dynamic way. In linear media an underscore is fixed. Interactively, a user's actions can dictate changes in speed, pacing, and style. For example, a user who races through one level[1] of a video game may hear a fast-paced, action-oriented score, whereas a user who favors exploration may experience a softer, eerier music track. These two tracks could be blended for yet a third user, who perhaps starts a level slowly but intensifies the mood and accelerates the pace.

Sometimes the music in a video game can be chosen by a user. Some games take advantage of DVD, Blu-ray, and online delivery that allows users to substitute the game music with their own music selections. Instead of listening to music composed for the game, users can choose to listen to their own favorite mix.

The technology of video game sound also offers interactive-sound designers unique possibilities not present in linearly produced media. For example, sound can be used to provide aural cues to help users figure out where to go or what to do next. Certain items may have sounds associated with them that let a user know to pick them up or manipulate them in some way. Switches and doors may use clicking or creaking noises to encourage users to open them. Sound becomes more than illustration or background; it influences actions and choices within the gaming environment.

Dialogue can also be used to instruct users; many games feature a talkative companion who delivers instructions or advice when needed. Game menus use sound to indicate which choices can be clicked; and in-game options, such as switching weapons or changing characters, may use sound effects as a cue to users about what actions they are performing.

In addition to allowing users to interact with a video game through a mouse, keyboard, or game controller, some games allow users to communicate with the game or with other users through sound. Headset and microphone systems are a popular accessory for a variety of games, especially those that allow online play through a network or Internet connection. This technology, called *Voice over Internet Protocol (VoIP),* allows users who have a headset and a microphone to speak with one another, give and receive instructions, and play in a team environment against others using the same technology. VoIP can add a whole new level of realism to a game as users work as a team to complete group tasks.

Although video game technology allows for myriad creative uses for audio, the sound crew also has to deal with a variety of restrictions and technological hurdles. Primary among these technological constraints is the challenge of managing shared system resources.

SYSTEM RESOURCES

System resources may be either dedicated or shared depending on the architecture and the design of a given game. Allocating *dedicated system resources* often offers advantages in terms of computing power and asset (data and file) management and, therefore, a potentially wider range of creative and sonic possibilities. Sharing system resources may make more sense in terms of cost and streamlining, depending on the scope of the game.

Shared system resources refers to the need for all parts of a video game—sound control and playback, picture display, game-play and game control, and control of various hardware components—to use simultaneously the same finite set of system resources (see 18-2). Rather than use one specific system to play sound, another entirely separate system to accept user input, and a third system to display video, interactive media applications use the same hardware and software resources to perform these tasks at the same time. Such competition dictates, to a certain extent, what sound designers can and cannot do when designing video game sound.

Adapting to Shared System Resource Limitations

The processing power of the central processing unit (CPU) and the system memory are the two major inhibitors in producing interactive sound. In the earliest days of video game development, these elements were so limited that most games didn't incorporate sound at all. As computer systems (and video game–specific console systems) improved, however, more processing power and more system memory became available, and sound soon made its way into interactive design.

---

1. Many video games are subdivided into sections, or levels, where users are presented with different tasks and unique environments in which to complete them. Often the division of a game into levels is necessary so that the computer need not run the entire game all at once.

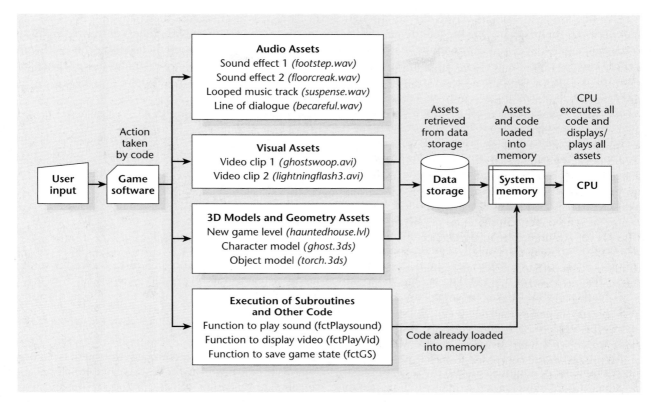

18-2 Shared system resources and responses to user input.

Early interactive-sound designers often came from a technical or programming background rather than a sound design background. In fact, in many early games the sound track and the sound effects were programmed rather than recorded. Sound designers would utilize programming code to force the sound hardware on these early systems to reproduce a variety of beeps in sequence to create simple, looped melodies and sound effects.

Whether programmed or recorded, sound has always faced the challenge of having too little memory and processing power allocated for its use. In the past, game sound was relegated to perhaps only a few kilobytes of memory, forcing designers to find creative ways to get the most out of their sound design with limited resources. The mark of a true interactive designer was—and still is—the ability to impress a user while consuming as little of the system resources as possible. In the past, sound designers looked for efficient programming techniques and clever tricks to make game sound better without adversely affecting playback. Today's designers have a larger set of tools and a richer set of system resources, but the challenge remains essentially the same.

Today's more powerful computing systems help alleviate some of the technical challenges presented by sharing system resources. Hardware has improved dramatically from the early days of video game development, and now most home computers and video game consoles have the CPU processing power, speed, system memory, and storage space to allow for advanced graphics and improved sound design. Instead of dealing with beeps and boops of mere kilobytes, interactive-sound designers are now able to record high-quality digital sound, process it, and manipulate it in highly creative and advanced ways. Instead of restricting themselves to a few kilobytes of storage, sound designers can now store thousands of high-quality audio files in a variety of formats.

DVD, Blu-ray, and online technologies have also helped improve sound tracks while limiting the load placed on processors and memory. Some games feature professionally recorded musical orchestrations, collections of pop songs, or other complied source music. These scores can often be considerably lengthy and of high quality. This is achievable because many computer systems can play high-quality audio without using the

CPU or memory; the sound is played directly through a **sound card**—essentially playing the sound track through a separate audio player and eliminating the need to use other shared system resources for the music. Sound effects still require the use of the CPU and the memory, and external playback also prevents interactive or dynamic manipulation or adjustment of the score during gameplay. But it does allow games to have vibrant, high-quality musical scores without hampering or slowing play. This method also allows game sound tracks to be played in regular audio players.

File compression technology is commonly used to reduce the file size of audio files, improving performance and playback though sometimes at the expense of sound quality. File compression is a technique in which sound is sampled in regular intervals at a certain *resolution* (the amount of information stored per sample, measured in *bits*). This allows fewer bytes of data to be saved for any given audio file while keeping the overall sound quality of the audio as high as possible. Remember that the higher the sample size and resolution, the better the sound quality will be but the larger the resulting file size.

An interactive-sound designer's goal is to achieve the highest amount of compression and the smallest file size possible without reducing audio quality to unacceptable levels. Common sampling-rate values are 44,100 Hz and 48,000 Hz for high-quality digital audio, although reduced sampling frequencies of 22,000 Hz are not uncommon; 16-bit resolution is used mostly, but 8-bit resolution also serves at times. Lower sampling rates and resolutions result in smaller file sizes and may sometimes be preferable, but audio designers must always take care that higher levels of compression do not have an adverse impact on quality.

Different audio files offer different compression **codecs**—different methods of calculating and performing compression and decompression (reading a compressed sound) on an audio file. A wide variety of codecs are in use. Some are associated only with a particular type of audio file, whereas others can be used with a variety of file types.

Interactive-sound designers need to be familiar with various audio file formats—the different file types used to store sound data, regardless of the codec used. A few common formats used for interactive-sound design include MP3, WAV, and WMA, but there are many others. Audio file formats are often chosen because they work well across many different computer systems, because they work well on specific types of computers (PC, Mac, or Linux), or even because they happen to work well in specific sound-editing environments or software applications. In a digital environment, it is usually not difficult to convert audio files from one format to another based on need.

THE PRODUCTION PROCESS

The production process for interactive-sound design can be roughly divided into the standard phases of preproduction, production, and postproduction. There are significant differences, however, among these phases as they pertain to interactive media compared with conventional linear media.

Preproduction

One of the first steps during interactive-sound development is to assemble the creative crew, which includes game producers, artists, programmers, and sound designers.

The Creative Crew

Most video game production environments include four distinct teams, which take the game from concept to completion: design, artistic, programming, and testing. The *design team* is responsible for the overall game concept and the game elements. The sound design crew is part of the *artistic team,* which also includes visual developers who create the artwork and the 3D models for the game. The *programming team* writes the software that makes the game function. The *testing team* is responsible for quality assurance and debugging to ensure that everything in the game, including the sound, works correctly. Unlike in linear production, sound designers are typically brought into production early to provide input, and they produce audio throughout the development process rather than toward the end of the production pipeline.

The sound crew comprises five principal areas of endeavor: design, engineering, composition, recording engineering, and recording support. Although these are distinct responsibilities, individuals on the sound crew may undertake several roles during production. The *sound designer* is responsible for the overall sound design and audio production. The *sound engineer* deals with the operational details of working with and manipulating the audio components—sound effects, dialogue, and music. The *composer* underscores the music for the game. The *recording engineer* is responsible for recording the audio components. Sometimes there is also a *recording support specialist,* who handles logistics, scheduling, and other organizational duties.

Proof-of-concept Development

Video games sometimes go into limited development during what would normally be considered the preproduction phase. Many games benefit from a limited type of production known as *proof-of-concept,* or *demo* (demonstration), production. During development a sample game level or two are created using limited staff and reduced resources. These levels serve as a prototype of how the game will eventually look and sound and how it will be played. Proof-of-concept can often highlight production challenges and spark new design ideas.

Unlike scratch tracks or other types of temporary development in linear production, the proof-of-concept development for a video game is intended to be relatively complete. In fact, as with the actual game development that takes place during the production phase, the preproduction development often goes through phases, from a rough concept to a nearly finished design. Likewise the sound design of the sample levels often progresses from rough filler audio to a polished product that can be incorporated into the finished game.

Though the early stages of video game development, including sound design, can be thought of as a preproduction stage, there is no standardized way that game production is addressed. Production companies approach development in different ways; and because interactive media and video games are a relatively new genre of entertainment, most developers are continually seeking new and better ways to streamline the production process.

Development for Different Platforms

Most creative decisions made during preproduction have technical ramifications that must be considered. One is the game's release platform. *Platform* refers to what type of computer system the game will be played on—personal computers, console systems, or mobile media such as cell phones and PDA devices.[2] The term *platform* also refers to the computer's operating system, which is usually Microsoft Windows or Apple Macintosh.

Platform is important to the interactive-sound designer because different platforms are capable of sup-

porting different audio technologies and complexities. For example, a game developed for a Windows system will use audio file formats appropriate to Windows, such as Microsoft's WMA audio file format. A game developed for a Macintosh might use Mac-appropriate audio files such as those in the Audio Interchange File Format (AIFF).

Computer hardware configurations are also important. Console systems from a specific manufacturer are configured in a standardized way, assembled to be exactly the same. This means that sound developed to run on one console system may not function perfectly on another. Sound designers must consider the console to be used before development and during production to ensure that the sound design will function properly on the chosen console. If the video game is to be *ported* to another console (redeveloped for use on another system), often technical changes to the sound design will result.

Personal computer systems are not built in a standardized way. Home users often modify, augment, or remove components from their systems at will. A game developed for a PC can likely take advantage of technologies and the hardware not present in most console systems, but it will also have to adapt to much more variation in hardware quality. Some PCs are advanced, capable of playing back sound that draws heavily on shared system resources, but most are not. Game sound must be conceptualized and developed to run on a wide variety of systems no matter what their quality. This is why many PC video games offer users the option to modify both video and audio settings prior to playing the game.

Although platforms for mobile media such as PDAs and cell phones offer environments for interactive-sound designers, they are limiting. They have less processing power, system memory, and data storage than personal computers or consoles. Any sound designed for mobile media must be carefully planned and produced so that it does not tax the system too heavily. This often means that sound designs for handheld games are much simpler than designs for other platforms. Sound designs for mobile media may use fewer sounds; audio may be compressed to a lower resolution with less dynamic range and timbral richness; and many handheld video games still utilize electronically generated scores and sound effects because of their low demand on system resources.

The speaker systems in mobile media have limited dynamic range and frequency response. Most reproduce high-frequency sounds well but have significant reduction in performance when reproducing midrange or low frequencies. Additionally, these speakers are often

---

2. *PDA* stands for *personal digital assistant.* A PDA may include such features as a calculator, clock, and calendar and the ability to record audio and video, access the Internet, send and receive e-mail, and play computer games.

designed to be held close to the ear and are usually inadequate for reproducing wide dynamic ranges. Sound for handheld devices is often highly compressed to compensate for the more-limited dynamic range. These factors place further limitations on what is possible from the standpoints of both design and intelligibility.

Such a design might favor higher-pitched sounds—beeps, clicks, and the like—and will avoid audio requiring wide frequency response, such as voices. Many popular music tunes are compressed for playback on the radio, and these tend to reproduce better than, for example, a classical music track with a wide dynamic range. Subtle, quiet sounds are also likely to be excluded from mobile media sound design because they will not reproduce well and may even be inaudible. The end result is generally a simpler sound design.

Production

The production stage in interactive media differs from linear media in a number of ways. Producers must deal with such matters as assets, basic and complex interactivity, and the wide flexibility necessary to shape the sound effects, music, and speech cues. The one area of similarity between interactive audio and linear audio production is the collection and the recording of sound.

Collecting and Recording Audio

As with a linear production, an interactive-sound crew gathers the audio through traditional methods. If a video game requires gunshot sounds, for example, the sound crew may spend a day at a shooting range, recording a variety of sounds using an array of field recording equipment. Likewise, the sound effects for an off-road racing game may be recorded at a racetrack using authentic dirt bikes, four-wheelers, and racecars.

Dialogue too is usually recorded in the studio using standard microphones, recording equipment, and studio practices (see Chapter 11); prerecorded sound effects and music can be gathered from libraries online and on CD and DVD (see Chapters 15 and 16).

Once the audio is collected and recorded, the similarity ends: the interactive-sound crew handles it differently from the sound crew on a film or television show because game sound must be dynamic. The overall sound design must conform to the technical limitations of dedicated or shared system resources yet take advantage of the many creative opportunities that interactive sound affords.

Assets

In a video game or any interactive production, every piece of sound is referred to as an *asset*. Assets are data that can be referenced and used at various points in the game. Some assets, such as a specific piece of dialogue, may be used only once. Others, such as a gunshot sound, may be referenced repeatedly throughout the game. During play, a video game is constantly utilizing a multitude of assets, which, in combination, present the user with the overall audiovisual experience. The assets are controlled by the game software—the computer code written by the programming team to make the game function properly (see 18-3).

```
i = 1; //loop increment variable
textx = 95; //x startposition for text
descx = 102; //x start position for description
imagex = 35; //x startposition for image
yspace = 0; //y start position for vertical placement of
    name and image
yincrement = 75; //y increment value for vertical spacing
ydesc = 17; //y drop value for positioning description
    below name
textwidth = 100; //value for width of text box
namewidth = 120; //value for width of name box

    NameTextFormat = new TextFormat();
    NameTextFormat.font = "arialtitle";
    NameTextFormat.size = 11;
    NameTextFormat.bold = true;
    NameTextFormat.color=OxFFFFFF;//white

    DescTextFormat = new TextFormat();
    DescTextFormat.font = "arialtext";
    DescTextFormat.size = 9;
    DescTextFormat.bold = false;
    DescTextFormat.color=OxFFFFFF;//white

//hide hit state
hitarea.visible = false;

for (var parttype:XMLNode = partlist.firstChild; parttype
    != null; parttype = parttype
nextSibling) {

//create an empty button to select items
eval(_global.path).createEmptyMovieClip("bufton"+i,
    400+i);

    eval("button"+i)._x = imagex;
    eval("button"+i)._y = yspace;
    eval("button"+i).width = 150;
    eval("button"+i).height = 65;
```

18-3 Computer code that controls a game's audio assets.

Courtesy of Nathan Prestopnik.

At their most basic level, sound assets are individual audio files. An asset such as *gunshot.wav* or *footstep.wav* would consist of a simple gunshot or footstep sound effect. In more-complex sound designs, assets might be composed of several audio effects or even a series of effects coupled with instructions for how they should be played. Complex sound assets can take on the nature of software and include programming code that controls how and when a host of audio files play. Whatever the level of complexity, a sound asset is a discreet piece of data that is referenced by the game software and made to execute at the appropriate time and with the proper dynamics.

Video games may reference thousands of sound assets during game-play. This can create an organizational headache for the sound designer even under the best circumstances. To maintain the required level of organization, most sound assets and individual audio files are stored in an organized structure called a *sound library.* Such a library may be a simple hierarchical structure that organizes audio files by type, by the levels of the game in which they are used, and by their version number (if more than one version of a sound is used). Many interactive development companies use file management software or proprietary sound library software, which, in addition to organizing audio files, can be used to more extensively manage and control their integration into a game.

Basic Interactivity

Basic interactivity, one of two types of interactive-sound design, is characterized by a simple relationship between user actions and audio playback. For example, in a baseball video game, when a user presses a certain button or key, the batter on-screen will take a swing. This swing will always be accompanied by the characteristic whooshing sound as the bat passes through the air. In a sound design using basic interactivity, a user action—a button press or a mouse click—results in specific sound playback. Such sound effects are often referred to as *audio sprites,* and the audio file to be played is usually in a standardized format such as MP3 or WAV.

A simple instruction for basic interactivity might look like this:

```
on (release) { _root.sound.attachsound("batswing.wav");
  _root.sound.start(0,10); }
```

This instruction waits for the user to click the mouse; this action establishes and plays the *batswing.wav* sound.

Basic interactivity has the advantage of allowing sound to play interactively based on user actions, but it does not always allow for the most creative use of sound. If, for instance, a user performs the same action repeatedly, such as swinging the baseball bat many times in a row, the sound gets repetitive as the same audio sprite is played over and over with each click. Repetition can take a user out of an otherwise immersive experience and underscore the fact that he is simply playing a video game.

That said, basic interactivity can be acceptable and even desired because it is impossible to predict how long a user will take to move through a section of a game. Interactive music, for example, can be composed to adjust for varying run times. A simple way to do this is to compose a score that is able to loop endlessly, so as a user plays, the score continues until the user finishes, even if it takes hours to complete the game.

Within the game itself, basic interactivity may be appropriate if a user can perform a certain action only once or only occasionally. There is little need to create variation when the action occurs in the same way every time. Large games employ basic interactivity using simple audio sprites because they require fewer system resources and are simpler to create and implement.

Many games include status bars, menus, or other in-game information to help the user navigate. Audio used in a status bar often employs basic interactivity because it sounds consistent and provides the user with aural information that is easy to become familiar with and understand (see 18-4).

When applied well, basic interactivity is a useful tool. But many high-end games are progressing toward a more advanced type of interactive-sound design called complex interactivity.

Complex Interactivity

Complex interactivity, also called *adaptive*, or *interactive, sound,* is a more complex and dynamic way of handling interactive audio. In a video game that employs complex interactivity, user actions result in more than just simple audio sprite playback. When a user clicks on or otherwise manipulates something within the game, a complex sound asset will execute. The complex sound asset will then run stored algorithms or functions that can play back sound in a variety of dynamic ways. Such functions may play several audio files simultaneously or in sequence, or they may apply digital signal-processing (DSP) effects to force the sound to play back with reverb,

18-4 Codes screen.

pitch modulation, time compression, or other modifications. Playback of complex sound assets can be based on both user actions and the current game state.

Game state is a collection of all useful information about the game at any given point during play. It includes information about the user, such as the level at which the user is playing; the simulated environmental conditions within the current level; the elapsed time of the game; the location of objects and characters within the game; and the game's sound environment. Game state is essentially a snapshot of the video game that describes where a user has come from, where he is now, and where he is going.

Game state information is accessed by complex sound assets to control and manipulate audio in different ways. The location of objects can be used to create reverb or echo effects. The location of characters can dictate the relative volume and quality of their voices. The amount

of elapsed time can be used to accelerate music and urge the user to move faster through a level.

In the baseball scenario, a user might click repeatedly and cause a bat to swing, but complex sound assets will cause the bat to make different whooshing sounds with each swing. The game state might also indicate the number of swings or the amount of time at bat and modify the crowd to sound increasingly irritated that the user is swinging and missing.

The game state of a basketball video game might keep track of the amount of time left in the game and the closeness of the score. As the amount of time ticks down during a close game, a complex sound design could use game state information to play progressively more excited crowd noises, culminating in either loud applause or stunned silence, depending on whether the player wins or loses. If the user's score is significantly below or above the computer score, on the other hand, a complex sound design could use game state to play the sounds of a bored crowd (if the player is winning) or even boos and catcalls (if the player is losing). Complex sound designs of this kind are able to achieve a high level of realism with many opportunities to involve users in the game by bringing the virtual environment to life.

Complex sound designs offer technical advantages over basic interactivity. They are built using specialized software that is entirely under the control of the sound designer. In a more basic design, sound designers must work closely with programmers to ensure that the proper audio files are being called and that the game software is playing back the sound correctly. In the past this has sometimes meant that programmers, rather than sound designers, had the final say over the game sound. In a complex sound design, however, the sound designer can modify, manipulate, and adjust the audio as much as necessary, often while the game is well into production. This puts control back into the hands of the designer and provides a much more efficient and productive development environment for both the artistic and programming teams.

Creating Complex Interactivity

Complex sound development applications allow designers to work with audio in a variety of ways. They allow sound designers to import individual or multiple audio files, process them, mix them, apply programming instructions to them, and export them as a sound asset ready for use in a completed video game. Such complex applications allow designers to apply numerous signal-processing effects to sounds, such as pitch-shift effects, reverberation, flanging, and distortion. They also allow a designer to include instructions about when and how a sound is to be played.

In a boxing game, for example, a user's character might have the option of wearing boxing gloves or fighting with bare fists. A punch sound asset for this game might include this simple instruction: "If the user is wearing a glove, play the 'glove' sound; otherwise, play the 'bare fist' sound." Ultimately, this instruction is written in computer code:

```
On (release) {
_root.playpunchsoundasset(punchtype); }
```

This instruction waits for the user to click the mouse and then executes a section of code known as a *function*. In this case, the function is called *playpunchsoundasset,* and it is sent a variable called "punchtype," which con-

tains information about what type of punch is being delivered. The function code that handles sound playback may look like this:

```
Function playpunchsoundasset(punchtype) {
If (punchtype = "glove") {
_root.sound.attachsound("glovepunch.wav");
_root.sound.start(0,1);
} else if (punchtype = "barefist") {
_root.sound.attachsound("fistpunch.wav");
_root.sound.start(0,1); } }
```

This function looks at the incoming sound type and then plays either a gloved punch or a bare-fist punch effect. This is a relatively straightforward complex sound asset, but already the code is becoming more involved than the purview of many traditional sound designers.

To simplify the process, complex sound applications use a *graphical user interface (GUI)* that allows sound designers to drag and drop files and create instructions using prebuilt menus and visual tools. Instead of writing computer code to control a limiting effect, for example, a complex sound design application will include an interface showing controls similar to those found on a studio limiter. Instead of compelling a sound designer to type computer code, a complex sound design application provides sets of precoded instructions, which can be applied to a sound asset.

Logical instructions used to control complex sound assets are called *parameters*. In the boxing example, the "glove" sound would be referred to as the glove parameter, and the "bare fist" sound would be referred to as the bare-fist parameter. A third parameter in the boxing game might be controlled by the game's simulated weather conditions. If a boxing match takes place in rainy weather, the dampness parameter might be used to augment the punch to sound more like it is hitting a wet surface. There may also be a strength parameter to make a punch sound harder or weaker depending on the strength of the character.

Complex sound assets are sometimes referred to as *sounds with knobs*. Here the term *knobs* refers to the GUI controls that a sound designer uses to apply parameters to a sound.

The entire sound design of a video game is created by combining hundreds or thousands of complex sound assets so that they fill the game with appropriate sound at all times. The complex sound assets are played at specified sound cues throughout the game, according to the instructions written in their individual sound functions. The combined effect of these sound assets and the levels of instruction that control the game sound is referred to as the game's **audio engine**—the software/asset combination that controls the entire sound design for a game.

Once a complex sound asset is completed, it is made available to the programming team for incorporation into the game. If a change is made to the sound asset during production, the programming code that orders the asset to play generally remains unchanged. Changes to the asset are usually made by the sound designer and (ideally) will be automatically reincorporated into the latest version of the game as it progresses through production.

An example of complex sound design can be seen in high-end automobile racing games. In early computer racing games, car sounds were handled by a few simple sound effects. Engine noises were recorded or created within the computer at a few different speeds. A few tire squeals and the sounds of shifting played during the transition between engine pitches were thrown into the mix to emphasize the speed of the car. These few sounds combined to create a reasonably convincing basic interactive-sound design. Development of such designs was relatively simple and usually did not adversely affect game performance or infringe on shared system resources.

High-end racing games take advantage of the opportunities afforded by faster computer hardware and complex sound theory. A car in a state-of-the-art racing game may have as many as 40 or 50 distinct sounds attached to it. Instead of merely recording the sound of the car at different speeds, the sound crew may record the engine pistons, exhaust, wheel spins, rushing air, hard braking, slow braking, tires squealing at different speeds, and fast acceleration sounds. These sounds can be combined into a sound asset that mixes them into an appropriate overall car sound for playback during a racing sequence.

Parameters of these sounds can be dynamically mixed based on the user's viewpoint from the car. If the viewpoint is close to the back of the car, the sound asset may be programmed to emphasize the exhaust and rear-wheel sounds, lowering the volume and the clarity of the other sounds. If the view is from farther away, the sounds may be mixed more evenly, with subtler sounds, such as engine piston noises, being reduced because they would be overwhelmed by louder sounds.

The sound asset for the car is programmed to change playback based on user actions. Because the car is in motion during most of the race, its sounds change based on the environment through which the user is driving. If the user drives through a tunnel, the car sounds become reverberant; if in the open, the sound is airier. If the car

crashes, in addition to playing a crash sound asset, the game engine modifies the car effects to sound damaged. Some complex sound designs are advanced enough to register specific kinds of damage to the car and modify only the required sounds.

For example, if the user's car is rear-ended, the exhaust and rear-wheel sounds may change. A flat tire may result in a noticeable flopping sound or even the grinding sound of the rim on the pavement. If the engine is damaged in a front-end collision, the piston noises may become irregular. Damage to the body of the car could result in changes to the wind sound effects. Instead of the sounds of air rushing over the car's smooth body, the user may hear roaring as air roils around the damaged parts of the car. The damaged areas themselves may now begin emitting creaking, groaning, or flapping sounds as they are shaken by the car's movement.

Producing Sound Effects

A key step in interactive-sound production is the establishment of mood and style. Typically, the game's sound designer will discuss its overall feel with the game producer and the rest of the creative crew. If the game is meant to be an edgy, fast-paced action shooter, the sound design may reflect this with pounding electronic sound tracks, high-energy laser sounds for the weapons, and cold, metallic sound effects for the various environments. In a game designed for children, the sound might favor more cute and funny sound effects. Such decisions are made early and, with occasional exceptions, are adhered to throughout the remainder of production. A proof-of-concept, if developed, can be useful as a means of auditioning the sound design. Such demo levels can often highlight changes that will be required in the design for either creative or technical reasons.

As the game proceeds into full production, the sound design crew begins recording appropriate sound effects using standard studio and field recording techniques. Generally, sound is recorded at the highest quality. Even though files will be down-sampled to a reduced file size using compression, it is always a good practice to start with the highest-quality audio possible.

Sound effects are recorded based on established sound cues or events within a game. A *sound cue* is a significant event that occurs within the game and which requires a corresponding sound. A door opening or closing, footsteps, vehicles passing, spoken dialogue, dripping water, and countless other greater or lesser events—all are sound cues that require the sound crew to record or create appropriate sounds to accompany them. A video game may contain thousands of sound cues.

If not managed carefully, the recording and the subsequent storage and organization of these effects can become overwhelming. To alleviate this difficulty, recorded sounds are often saved using a *naming convention,* which is a standardized method of naming files. Water sounds, for example, may all have file names beginning with *WA,* engine sounds may start with *EN,* and so on. Recorded sounds are cataloged in the sound library, discussed previously.

Once sound effects are cataloged, they can be referenced as assets and used in the game. In a basic interactive design, the files are often accessed directly by the game programming code, usually by file name, and any changes or updates to a given sound can sometimes require programming changes as well. In more-complex sound design, complex sound assets, rather than the files themselves, are referenced in the programming code. These assets can contain one, several, or many different audio files. Because sound designers will be modifying a complex sound asset's content but usually not the

reference name that identifies it in code, they are free to add, remove, or edit sound within the asset, knowing that their adjustments will not require any programming changes or complications for the programming team. This separation of sound design from programming is a key advantage of complex sound assets (see 18-5).

Producing Music

Music, of course, has long been a mainstay for creating mood and feeling in linear media and to some extent this is no different in interactive production. But with interactive media, using music presents a unique set of challenges that are not factors in conventional film and television production.

Unlike individual sound effects, music is usually meant to play for a specific period of time and in a linear fashion. When working in a linear medium, composers take advantage of this fact by writing the musical score to be precisely timed with the picture. In a horror movie, for example, the score can emphasize or intensify the action by establishing an eerie mood and then startle with a loud chord crash or percussive downbeat as something

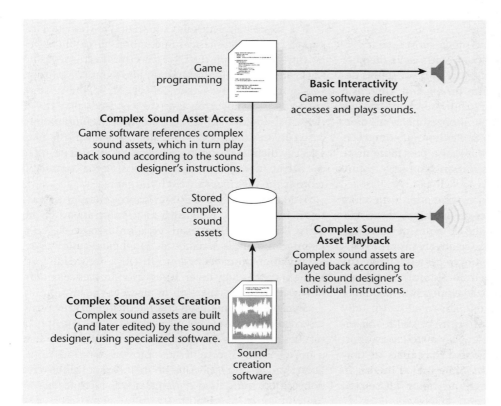

18-5 Differences between basic and complex interactivity and how complex interactivity can be separated from game programming.

frightening happens—the rush of a killer across the screen, a ghost or zombie appearing from the dark, or a menacing figure launching an attack. In action movies a fast-paced score may shift into a slow, dramatic section to emphasize a hero shot of the main character. For these techniques to work effectively, the music must play in precise timing with the visual it is meant to underscore.

Interactive media does not have a precisely defined run time. Some users progress quickly through part of a video game; others linger to explore for a time or even reverse course and head backward through the game. Some games are not structured with a linear storyline at all, allowing users to choose their actions at will. This means that the music must accommodate nonlinear sequences of events, unpredictable user actions, and undefined run times.

In many interactive development environments, the composer is part of the sound crew itself rather than an outsider contracted for the specific purpose of scoring a project. In fact, interactive-sound designers have the talent to handle both sound-effect design and music composition. This is because the earliest games generally relied on one person to handle all sound development. This has changed somewhat as games have increased in complexity.

As games increase in size and scope, most interactive-sound crews are becoming larger, with each member specializing in one or a few distinct areas of sound development. As with feature film production, there is a growing need for specialization, and video game productions are increasingly turning to professional composers for the music. Some high-profile Hollywood composers are underscoring video games. It is also becoming more common for game composers to transition into feature film composition as well.

In the past, video game scores were often little more than single electronic tones sequenced into a melodic pattern. This had the advantage of requiring relatively few system resources. It was also relatively simple to program such note sequences to loop repeatedly while the user was playing the game. Such simple scores, however, left most composers and game developers wanting more.

New games are advanced enough to allow for fully orchestrated scores using a vast array of styles and instrumentations. Instead of finding a way to loop a short sequence of single notes, interactive composers are now challenged with looping a fully orchestrated theme. In addition, complex sound designs are rarely well served

by simple looping techniques, and composers are constantly seeking new ways to write and create completely dynamic scores.

One such method is to write a score based on a few strong melodic themes. A sound designer can build a music asset that plays these themes in a looped fashion but with more variety than a simple repeating loop. For example, a composer may write four variations of the same theme: a soft version, a melancholy version, a suspenseful version, and an action version. These variations may be composed at the same tempos and in the same key so that they can be inserted one after another in virtually any order. Shifting among these different versions makes the score more interesting. Instead of looping the same theme over and over, the score can now loop randomly through several different variations.

Moreover, the sound designer may create a music asset that looks to the game state for information about the user's actions. Based on the game state information, different versions of the theme can be played. If the user is fearful, the suspenseful version of the theme will play. If the user is hurt, the melancholy version will play. If the user is doing well and moving quickly through a level, the action theme could play.

It is possible in a complex sound design to write a dynamic score using solo instrumentation tracks and "composing" the score on the fly. To do this a variety of solo tracks are recorded in the same key and tempo—a bassoon version of the theme, a trumpet version, a flute version, and so on. A complex music asset is created to play any of these instruments, either individually or in combination. Based on user actions and the game state, the music asset selects which instrument tracks and which variations of the theme to play, essentially composing the completed score as the user plays through the game.

Video games can use music as more than just a tool to establish effect. Some use it as an integral part of the game. Dance games, for example, allow users to select different music tracks to dance to. Other games allow users to play an instrument in concert with a recorded score. These games usually determine a user's success based on how well or poorly they follow along to the music.

Some video games use a compiled score of previously recorded music instead of a composed score. The opportunities for a truly dynamic score are more limited when using a compiled score because most current radio hits, library music, and other off-the-shelf compositions were not written to be used dynamically. Sometimes clever music editing can prep a composition to be more useful in a dynamic setting, and sometimes truly dynamic music is not required in a video game.

In games that use current pop music as a selling point, a compiled score may play back much like a radio show, with a variety of songs by different artists intermixed into a complete playlist. Compiled scores of this kind may use specific genres of music to emphasize the style of the game. An off-road racing game may feature heavy rock-and-roll selections; a football video game featuring all-time great players might play the themes used in past football television broadcasts.

Racing games and other driving-oriented games have taken this technique a step further. While playing the game, users can click through different "radio stations" and listen to whichever style of music suits them. Different compiled scores are used to generate, for example, contemporary hit, country, jazz, or classical radio stations. The music on each station is frequently interrupted by appropriate advertising spots, jingles, and DJ chatter to add to the feeling that the user is listening to an actual radio program.

Producing Dialogue and Narration

Dialogue was added to video games fairly late in the development of interactive media and remained problematic until computer technology had advanced enough to overcome shared resource limitations and the inability of computers to play back high-quality sound without choppiness, stuttering, or hesitation.

Simple systems that could reproduce an electronic melody or electronically generated sound effects were not powerful enough to handle sounds at the resolutions and the sampling frequencies required for clear and intelligible speech. Attempts were made to reproduce dialogue using electronically generated tones, but this fell well short of simulating human speech. Until computer systems could handle spoken dialogue, "speech" in games was limited to text printed on the screen. Today computers have more than enough power to play back high-quality audio, and dialogue is now as common in games as are music and sound effects.

Most video game dialogue starts out as a script, not unlike in film and television. The nature of the script may vary from game to game; often, instead of scripted dialogue, guided scenarios are created and the dialogue is improvised. In a story-driven game with fully developed characters and a clearly defined plot arc, the script is often written in a conventional format, including dialogue. In a less-story-driven game—a sports game, for example—the script may be in the form of a list of required sound assets and their appropriate locations in the game. Many games also include other important information in the script, such as scene descriptions and audio cues. Interactive productions often use a *node map* to describe the different sections of the production. The node map, in addition to describing the game's structure, includes information about the dialogue required in each section (see 18-6).

A video game script must accommodate a game's lack of linearity. Unlike conventional scripts, which read sequentially, an interactive script may read something like a choose-your-own-adventure book, with dialogue written conditionally so that two different user actions result in the playback of two different dialogue lines. Sometimes dialogue is written and recorded even though some users may never hear it. Game scripts also include dialogue that plays randomly or intermittently, such as comments of passersby on a city street or epithets yelled by drivers in a racing game. Because much of this dialogue is not part of the story, it cannot be written into a story-driven script format, so interactive dialogue scripts often appear as large lists of sound assets that are collected like any other sound effect.

Once the script is written, the dialogue is recorded. Many video game producers hire voice actors to deliver the dialogue, and some producers have begun hiring higher-profile film actors for leading parts. The dialogue-recording process can be compared to the recording process for animated movies: actors record a variety of styles and takes for each line and, later, the best takes are used to create the dialogue assets. Video games can include a great deal more dialogue than can films. Often this dialogue is disconnected, seemingly unrelated, and used randomly throughout the game.

Recorded dialogue is carefully cataloged in the sound library for later use within either basic or complex sound assets. Individual pieces of dialogue can be combined into a single sound asset, which plays different lines based on user actions. A dialogue sound asset may include a friendly greeting, an annoyed greeting, and an angry greeting. During game-play a user may encounter a character to which this sound asset is assigned. Depending on that character's current attitude toward the user (as defined by the game state), the appropriate greeting is played.

Sports games offer an interesting example of how interactive dialogue is used to create a realistic sound

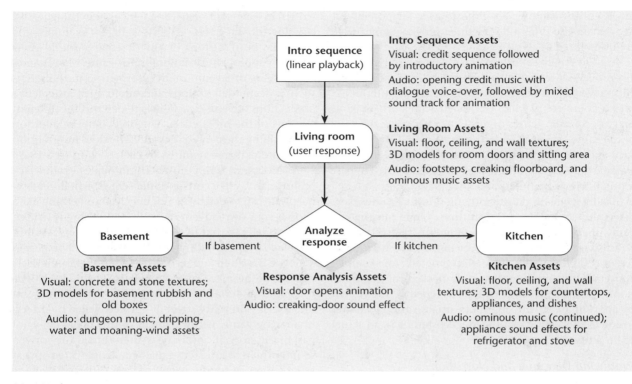

Intro Sequence Assets
Visual: credit sequence followed
by introductory animation
Audio: opening credit music with
dialogue voice-over, followed by mixed
sound track for animation

Living Room Assets
Visual: floor, ceiling, and wall textures;
3D models for room doors and sitting area
Audio: footsteps, creaking floorboard, and
ominous music assets

Basement Assets
Visual: concrete and stone textures;
3D models for basement rubbish and
old boxes
Audio: dungeon music; dripping-
water and moaning-wind assets

Response Analysis Assets
Visual: door opens animation
Audio: creaking-door sound effect

Kitchen Assets
Visual: floor, ceiling, and wall
textures; 3D models for countertops,
appliances, and dishes
Audio: ominous music (continued);
appliance sound effects for
refrigerator and stove

18-6 Node map.

design. Most real-life athletic events feature play-by-play announcing. Complex sound assets can be designed to handle a variety of game state information—which team is winning, which players are performing well or poorly, the time remaining in the game, the closeness of the score, and events that happened during the course of the game. A complex dialogue asset that tracks this game state information essentially knows what is going on within the game at any point.

Play-by-play dialogue—literally thousands of lines—can be recorded, stored in the sound library, and used in the complex sound assets. The lines of dialogue cover virtually any possible action within the game and are sometimes recorded in pieces so that different segments of dialogue can be combined to create complete sentences. The lines of dialogue can also be recorded in a variety of styles, tones, and excitement levels so that the appropriate tone of dialogue can be played back no matter what is happening in the game.

As the game progresses and the game state changes, the complex sound asset accesses and plays the appropriate dialogue lines. Different lines of play-by-play dialogue

are triggered based on specific game state information and audio cues. Though the programming for such an asset is complex and the organizational tasks associated with such large amounts of dialogue can be daunting, the end result is a level of realism in the play-by-play that is appropriate to the game's action and mood.

Postproduction

Postproduction in interactive media is the production phase least like its counterpart in linear media. Instead of editing and mixing in a postproduction environment, interactive-sound designers create complex sound assets—the audio engine—that edit and mix the sound automatically during production according to programmed sets of instructions. The audio engine constantly tracks changing game state and user actions and instructs different sound assets to play at different times and in different ways. When these sound assets play simultaneously according to the audio engine's instructions, the full audio track is automatically created, mixed, and played back. Editing and mixing processes are not required because the audio engine and the complex sound assets are already programmed to play back sound no matter what happens in the game.

A detailed analysis of a hypothetical video game sequence illustrates how the final audio track is built from individual sound assets.

EXAMPLE OF A VIDEO GAME SEQUENCE

This sequence is part of a war game. It encompasses a variety of sound assets that include enemy soldiers yelling and firing different types of weapons, shouted commands from the user's character, an orbiting observation helicopter, rain and wind effects, and different intensities of reverberation from the city street on which the scene takes place. There is also music to underscore the action.

In this sequence linear sound editing and mixing is not possible. There is no way to know if the helicopter will be close to the user or far away. The number of soldiers in the scene will change based on the game level that the user has completed. Enemy gunfire will occur at different times and for changing intervals because the enemy soldiers are programmed to fire only when they have a clear shot at the user's character. This game also features dynamic weather effects, so for some users the sequence may take place in sunny, calm weather instead of in rain and wind.

Transient Sound-effect Assets

The gunfire sound effects in the scene are transient; they have a quick attack and a short decay. As such they must be synced with specific sound cues within the sequence—in this case the enemy soldiers who are firing on the user's character.

The gunfire assets will be created from multiple recordings of different firearms sound effects. They will have parameters that identify the type of weapon used (pistol, machine gun, rifle) and that modify the sound effect slightly so that each burst of gunfire is consistent with the weapon being fired.

The game state can record the weapon's physical location in the scene and determine its distance from the user. The gunfire asset will have a parameter that uses this distance measurement to modify sound playback. Gunfire assets that are distant will be fainter and will emphasize lower frequencies. They will also be filtered to sound thinner. Gunfire assets that are close will be louder, denser, and crisper.

Each gunfire asset will also have a parameter to determine the overall level of reverb required. If the fired weapon is in the open, less reverb will be applied. If the shooter is hiding in an alley, more reverb will be appropriate.

The sound cues in the game instruct the completed gunfire assets to play. In this case, the sound cues are firing actions taken by the soldiers. These cues tell the audio engine, "I'm firing a weapon. Play the gunfire asset." When the audio engine receives this instruction, it plays the gunfire asset based on the described parameters.

With the gunfire assets completed and in place, the sequence takes on its first dimension of sound. Instead of silence, the user will now hear sporadic gunfire as the enemy soldiers attack. A clever user will advance under cover, and the sounds of gunfire will slacken because fewer enemy soldiers have a clear shot. A brave or foolish user will charge into the open and be confronted with a cacophony of rifle, machine-gun, and pistol shots as the gunfire sound assets are instructed to play.

Moving Sound Effects

To sound realistic, the orbiting helicopter requires sound effects that change as the helicopter moves. These effects must play from the beginning of the sequence until it is complete and adapt to the changing position of the helicopter as it moves through the level geometry.

A sound asset will be created for the helicopter, including the swish of rotors spinning through the air, the engine sound, the high-pitched fast tail rotor sound, and the sound of air rushing around the airframe. Other sounds may be recorded for this asset to play if the helicopter is damaged from gunfire or a collision. These effects might include rough engine noises, a choppy rotor, a stall, and engine failure.

A second set of parameters to create proximity—near to far—and differences in reverberation—wet to dry—are also added to further modify these sounds according to the helicopter's sonic behavior.

The helicopter sound asset will play simultaneously with the gunfire sound assets, creating a second layer of sound. The helicopter sound layer may sometimes play over the gunfire effects (if the helicopter is very close) but will usually play underneath them because the helicopter is programmed to stay away from the shooting when possible. A user who enters the sequence at this point hears sporadic gunfire and a helicopter orbiting the scene.

Instead of playing based on a specific sound cue, the helicopter sound asset will be attached to the helicopter object in the game. That is, the sound asset will play continuously, but because of the way it is designed, the sound effects are modified continuously so long as the helicopter remains in the sequence. If the helicopter crashes, the sound asset will be instructed to stop playing altogether (see 18-7).

Intermittent Dialogue

In this sequence certain dialogue will be played intermittently. The sound design calls for enemy soldiers to yell to each other and to the user during the course of the fighting. This dialogue is meant to add detail and realism to the scene but is not intended to be heard with much clarity. It is also not intended to follow the scene's action too closely or to add much to the storyline. It is designed

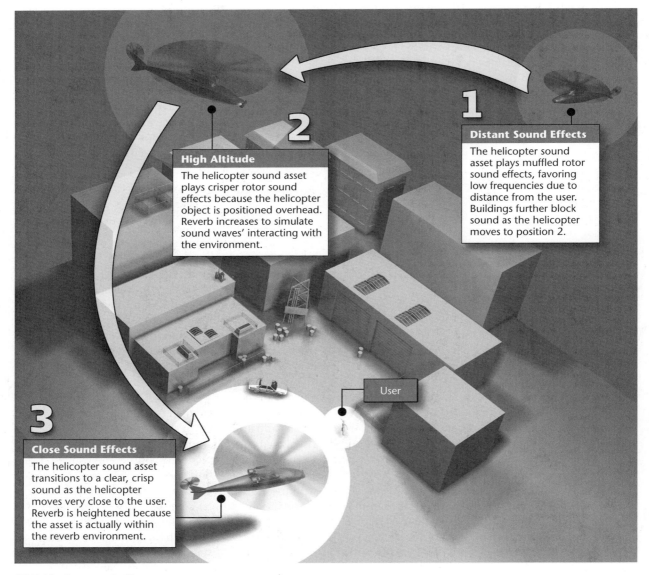

1 Distant Sound Effects

The helicopter sound asset plays muffled rotor sound effects, favoring low frequencies due to distance from the user. Buildings further block sound as the helicopter moves to position 2.

2 High Altitude

The helicopter sound asset plays crisper rotor sound effects because the helicopter object is positioned overhead. Reverb increases to simulate sound waves' interacting with the environment.

3 Close Sound Effects

The helicopter sound asset transitions to a clear, crisp sound as the helicopter moves very close to the user. Reverb is heightened because the asset is actually within the reverb environment.

User

18-7 Moving sound-effect assets.

to play throughout the sequence based on game state information and user actions, almost like a second set of sound effects.

This dialogue asset will include different utterances. Some of them are friendly and are meant to be called to other enemy soldiers: "Keep low!" and "Watch yourself!" and "Try to pin him down!" Others are hostile or taunting, intended for the user, whom the enemy soldier attacks, such as "Go back where you came from, coward!" and "Stop hiding and come out to fight!"

Some intermittent dialogue is specific and played with particular sound cues. It may include angry shouts when a soldier is fired on, screams of pain if he is hit, fearful mutterings if the user is advancing and attacking, and triumphant taunts if the user is injured and retreating.

Like the gunfire assets, the dialogue assets play based on audio cues in the scene. These cues occur when the game software instructs one of the enemy soldiers to speak and the audio engine receives a command: "I am speaking. Play my dialogue asset." Intermittent dialogue assets add a third layer of sound to this sequence as the battle unfolds (see 18-8).

Specific Dialogue

Specific dialogue consists of shouted commands, which a user can give to friendly soldiers, such as "Go left" and "Attack!" The user plays these commands by pressing different buttons or keys. When a command is played, the friendly soldiers obey it.

A parameter will be added to the user dialogue asset to monitor the user's actions. If the user's character is running through the game environment, dialogue will be played from the "running" effects, whereby all lines are delivered to include the character's exertion. If the user's character is wounded, the dialogue will be played from the "wounded" takes, delivered to convey pain.

A set of parameters will be created to handle user input by monitoring the keyboard and playing a sound when

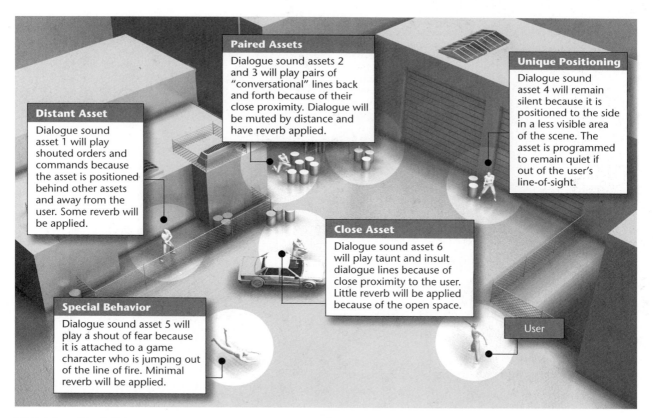

Paired Assets

Dialogue sound assets 2 and 3 will play pairs of "conversational" lines back and forth because of their close proximity. Dialogue will be muted by distance and have reverb applied.

Unique Positioning

Dialogue sound asset 4 will remain silent because it is positioned to the side in a less visible area of the scene. The asset is programmed to remain quiet if out of the user's line-of-sight.

Distant Asset

Dialogue sound asset 1 will play shouted orders and commands because the asset is positioned behind other assets and away from the user. Some reverb will be applied.

Close Asset

Dialogue sound asset 6 will play taunt and insult dialogue lines because of close proximity to the user. Little reverb will be applied because of the open space.

Special Behavior

Dialogue sound asset 5 will play a shout of fear because it is attached to a game character who is jumping out of the line of fire. Minimal reverb will be applied.

User

18-8 Intermittent dialogue assets.

a key is pressed. Pressing the R key causes the dialogue asset to play the line "Go right!" Pressing the C key plays the line "Take cover!" Another set of parameters will add spatial and acoustic effects to play back lines of dialogue.

Specific user dialogue adds a fourth layer of sound to the sequence. Because the user dialogue is tied to game functionality and is meant to sound like the user is speaking, the user dialogue layer is usually louder and more prominent than most of the other sounds in the sequence. Now a user entering the sequence hears the other layers of sound and is able to trigger specific dialogue using the keyboard (see 18-9).

Environment

The environmental sound asset is critical to the realism of this interactive sequence. Layered sound effects will

sound disconnected and unrealistic until an ambient sound layer playing underneath supports them. This sequence calls for interactive environmental effects to play wind, rain, thunder, and different spatial and acoustic assets.

Parameters will be created to check the game state for weather information. A wind parameter will check the wind strength and play back one of several appropriate wind sounds. This sound effect can be augmented further by pitch and level adjustment. A rain parameter will similarly check for rain information, playing back a variety of looped rain sound effects based on the heaviness of the rainfall. A thunder parameter will look for specific lightning sound cues that have been programmed into the game's weather simulation. Every time a lightning event occurs, the thunder parameter will trigger one of

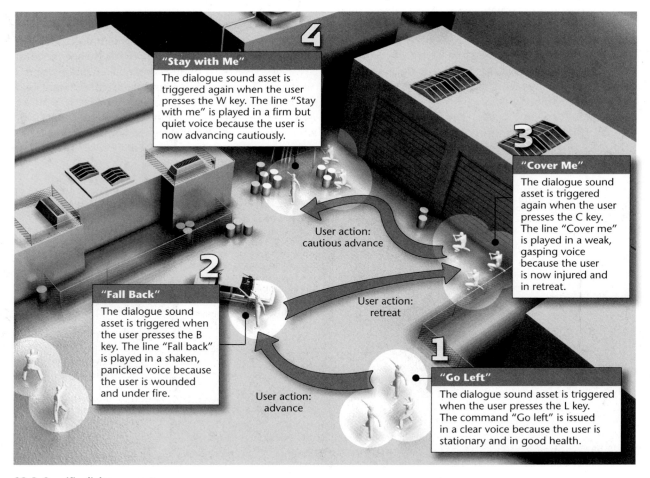

"Stay with Me"
The dialogue sound asset is triggered again when the user presses the W key. The line "Stay with me" is played in a firm but quiet voice because the user is now advancing cautiously.

"Cover Me"
The dialogue sound asset is triggered again when the user presses the C key. The line "Cover me" is played in a weak, gasping voice because the user is now injured and in retreat.

"Fall Back"
The dialogue sound asset is triggered when the user presses the B key. The line "Fall back" is played in a shaken, panicked voice because the user is wounded and under fire.

"Go Left"
The dialogue sound asset is triggered when the user presses the L key. The command "Go left" is issued in a clear voice because the user is stationary and in good health.

User action: cautious advance

User action: retreat

User action: advance

18-9 Specific dialogue assets.

several interesting thunderclap sound effects. These will be played in sync with lightning streaks and quick lighting changes in the scene geometry. Depending on the severity of the simulated lightning storm, the thunder parameter will create a greater or lesser delay between a visual lightning bolt and a thunderclap sound effect.

The audio engine will instruct the environmental sound asset to play during the entire sequence. This environmental sound asset is a fifth sound layer in the sequence (see 18-10).

Music Underscoring

Music is the sixth and final layer for this sequence. The underscore is designed to highlight the dramatic moments in the action and to provide quiet, suspenseful passages to build intensity.

A parameter will be created to control the looped music. Most of the time, quieter themes will be randomly looped to provide sonic interest and maintain continuity among the various actions without detracting from them. Certain user actions will trigger the parameter to play a more dramatic section of music if, for example, the user advances suddenly toward the enemy. If the user retreats under fire, the music will become somber and melancholy. If the user succeeds in defeating the enemy soldiers, a triumphant victory theme will trigger. If the user dies in combat, a tragic theme will play (see 18-11).

DEBUGGING

The *debugging* or *testing* phase is the stage of video game development during which the testing team—professional video game players—check for errors and problems that must be fixed before the game can be released. There are always errors—sometimes simple, sometimes complex—caused by bad code, poor system resource management, problems with the game's audio engine, and incorrect sounds playing at an audio cue, to name a few. Working out a bug may be the responsibility of the sound crew or the programming team, depending on the nature and the source of the problem. Regardless of their scope, all bugs must be fixed before a game is released, and sound designers spend much of what is in essence postproduction resolving them.

USER PLAYBACK

The wide variation in computer sound playback equipment is yet another concern to the sound design crew. Many professional users and game addicts have the most advanced desktop computers available, including sound cards capable of playing sound in 5.1 or 7.1 surround sound. Some users connect their computer to a stereo system or use a pair of computer speakers. Others play on a laptop, with its usually poor sound quality. Users may employ headphones, an ear bud, or a headset/

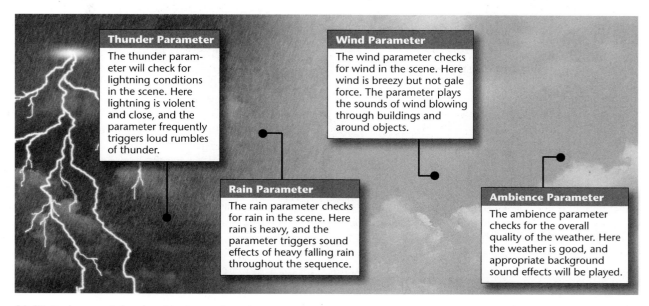

18-10 Environmental and ambient sound assets.

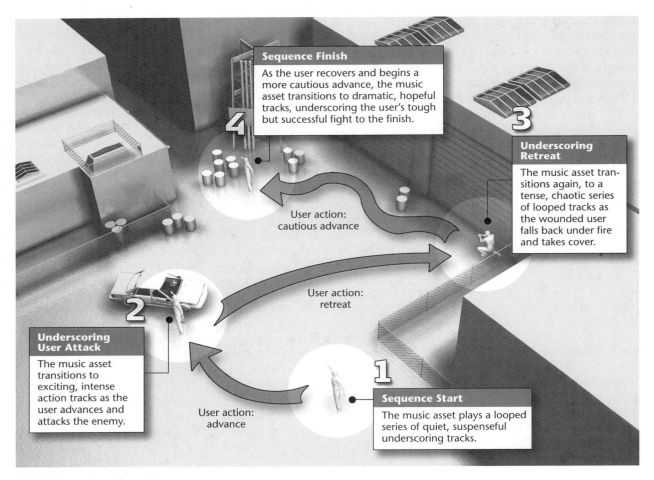

Sequence Finish

As the user recovers and begins a more cautious advance, the music asset transitions to dramatic, hopeful tracks, underscoring the user's tough but successful fight to the finish.

Underscoring Retreat

The music asset transitions again, to a tense, chaotic series of looped tracks as the wounded user falls back under fire and takes cover.

User action: cautious advance

User action: retreat

Underscoring User Attack

The music asset transitions to exciting, intense action tracks as the user advances and attacks the enemy.

User action: advance

Sequence Start

The music asset plays a looped series of quiet, suspenseful underscoring tracks.

18-11 Dynamic music assets.

microphone combination. Some console users have their system hooked to a television and listen through the built-in TV speakers. A video game developed for mobile media may play audio through headphones or a low-quality built-in speaker or earpiece. In all these cases, there are three critical questions for a sound designer: What is the system capable of? What is its frequency response? What is its dynamic range?

As frustrating as it may seem to try to accommodate these widely differing playback possibilities, interactive media actually have an advantage in this regard over linear media. Many video games offer users the option of defining their sound output settings. Sound assets and the game engine can be programmed to handle audio playback in different ways. A user who adjusts the game to play in 5.1 or 7.1 hears the game in surround sound.

A user who chooses a stereo setup hears the game in that format, and so on. Remember, however, that a computer system's sound playback capabilities are determined by the sound card (see Chapter 5).

The sound quality of the loudspeakers being used is also important—the frequency response and the dynamic range in particular. Most games do not give users the option of adjusting the audio settings, primarily because few users understand how to optimize frequency response to improve their aural experience.

Instead a sound designer considers during preproduction what kind of frequency response a game should support. In a high-end game, the designer will likely opt for a wide frequency response, assuming that users willing to invest in such a game have the appropriate audio equipment to handle it. Sound designed for a game targeted to more-casual users may assume lower-quality loudspeakers and make some concessions in frequency response to reach a wider market.

Dynamic range is handled in the same way—wider dynamic range for high-end games and upscale gamers, limited dynamic range for the broader array of games targeted to the average user. Games targeted at mobile media users are designed to have quite limited dynamic range and frequency response due to the amount of compression necessary to accommodate those systems.

Some games allow users to pick from a few (usually two or three) sound-quality settings typically defined as low, medium, and high. Choosing high quality plays back the best audio available in the game; the file sizes, however, will be larger, increasing the potential for slower game playback, stutters, and crashes. Choosing low quality plays back highly compressed audio files that use fewer system resources; users with lower-end computer systems may find that the trade-off in sound quality is essential if a game is to run correctly.

MAIN POINTS

▶ Interactive media allow a user to be a participant in the viewing experience instead of just a spectator.

▶ Interactive media include a number of genres, such as simple Web pages, dynamic Web sites, informational CD-ROMs, and educational software. Video games are an advanced form of interactive media employing high-end sound as well as video and graphics.

▶ Video games include any interactive medium in which the focus is on entertainment rather than on productivity, instruction, or information dissemination.

▶ In creating an interactive-sound design, the sound designer has to develop a sound track that will never play back in the same way twice. It is a stochastic process whereby the sound track is not deterministic; rather it is a probability-based expression of variable and predictable user actions and random elements. It has to react to changing user input and be able to accommodate all conceivable user actions seamlessly. This is referred to as interactive sound, or dynamic sound.

▶ An effective interactive-sound design creates an immersive environment through which a user can travel and explore.

▶ In a conventional production, the user is unable to explore a location at will. In an interactive design, the sounds can change dynamically as a user moves through the environment. Instead of merely seeing the space, the user can actually experience it.

▶ Voice over Internet Protocol (VoIP) allows users who have a headset and a microphone to speak with one another, give and receive instructions, and play in a team environment against others using the same technology.

▶ Shared system resources refers to the need for all parts of a video game—sound control and playback, picture display, game-play and game control, and control of various hardware components—to use simultaneously the same finite set of system resources.

▶ Most video game production environments include four distinct teams who take the game from concept to completion: design, artistic, programming, and testing.

▶ The design team is responsible for the overall game concept and the game elements. The sound design crew is part of the artistic team, which also includes visual developers who create the artwork and the 3D models for the game. The programming team writes the software that makes the game function. The testing team is responsible for quality assurance and debugging to ensure that everything in the game, including the sound, works correctly.

▶ Video games sometimes go into limited development during what would normally be considered the preproduction phase, a stage known as proof-of-concept, or demo (demonstration), production.

▶ Platform refers to what type of computer system the game will be played on—personal computers, console systems, or mobile media such as cell phones and PDA (personal digital assistant) devices. Platform is important to the interactive-sound designer because different platforms are capable of supporting different audio technologies and complexities.

▶ In production, producers must deal with such matters as assets, basic and complex interactivity, and the wide flexibility necessary to shape the sound effects, music, and speech cues.

▶ In a video game or any interactive production, every piece of sound is referred to as an asset. A sound asset is a discreet piece of data that is referenced by the game software and made to execute at the appropriate time and with the proper dynamics.

▶ Basic interactivity is one of two types of interactive-sound design. The other is complex interactivity. Basic interactivity is characterized by a simple relationship between user actions and audio playback. Complex interactivity, also called adaptive, or interactive, sound, is a more complex and dynamic way of handling interactive audio; user actions result in more than just simple audio sprite playback.

▶ Game state is a collection of all useful information about the game at any given point during play.

▶ Sound effects are recorded based on established sound cues or events within a game. A sound cue is an important event that occurs within the game and which requires a corresponding sound.

▶ Music in interactive media does not have a precisely defined run time. Some users progress quickly through part of a video game; others linger. This means that the music must accommodate nonlinear sequences of events, unpredictable user actions, and undefined run times.

▶ A video game script must accommodate a game's lack of linearity and may vary from game to game. In a story-driven game with fully developed characters and a clearly defined plot arc, the script is often written in a conventional format, including dialogue. In a less-story-driven game, the script may be in the form of a list of required sound assets and their appropriate locations in the game. Many games also include other important information in the script, such as scene descriptions and audio cues.

▶ Postproduction in interactive media is the production phase least like its counterpart in linear media. Instead of editing and mixing in a postproduction environment, interactive-sound designers create complex sound assets—the audio engine—that edit and mix the sound automatically during production according to programmed sets of instructions. Editing and mixing processes are not required because the audio engine and the complex sound assets are already programmed to play back sound no matter what happens in the game.

▶ The debugging or testing phase is the stage of video game development during which the testing team—professional video game players—check for errors and problems that must be fixed before the game can be released.

19

Internet Production

Computer and digital technologies in general and the Internet in particular have provided the means to produce and disseminate audio on an unprecedented scale. What was once a relatively closed medium—the purview of professionals in studio-based environments—is now accessible to practically anyone, with the potential to reach a worldwide market at the touch of a button.

Opportunities abound. They include producing audio for an online company, recording online sessions interactively, promoting and selling your own work, hiring out your production services to others, podcasting, producing sound for Web pages, and creating audio just for the fun of it. In producing sound for professional purposes, however, it serves to rephrase avant-garde writer Gertrude Stein's famous line "A rose is a rose is a rose is a rose": audio production is audio production is audio production.

As the methods of producing sound change, the wisdom of that proverb is sometimes forgotten. How audio is produced is only the means to an end. The basic principles related to that end are similar regardless of where production is carried out—in a major production facility with state-of-the-art gear or in a project studio with only a personal computer. The end is always to produce a high-quality product, technically and aesthetically. The point can be made in another way: whether writing with a pen, a typewriter, or a computer, it is not the medium that creates the poetry; it is the poet.

Because the world of computers and the Internet changes continuously, the approach to this chapter is generic, dealing with the processing of audio in a general way and avoiding as much as possible proprietary references and detailed operational information. This material also assumes some experience with computers and the Internet.

DATA TRANSFER NETWORKS

The delivery and the playback of audio over the Internet differ from the traditional methods used in the conventional audio studio. They involve, in computer parlance, a *network*—a system of computers configured and connected in a way that allows them to communicate with one another. Such a system allows the transfer of information among computers. The Internet is simply an extremely large computer network comprising many smaller networks.

Local-area Networks

A *local-area network (LAN)* is configured for a small, localized area such as a home or business. Generally, a LAN is more controllable than a wide-area network because it is small enough to be managed by only a few people. LANs often feature fast data transfer speeds because the connection types and the hardware of all computer systems on the network can be controlled. One concept and approach using LANs is *Audio over Ethernet (AoE)*.

In some measure AoE is similar to *Voice over Internet Protocol (VoIP)*, which was discussed in Chapters 3 and 18. The difference lies in greater bandwidth that can accommodate the higher sampling rates and bit-depth resolution associated with uncompressed, high-quality digital audio. When developing AoE for use on a LAN, an audio or broadcast engineer may take full advantage of low latency—a short delay of usually no more than 6 ms—and fast connectivity, within a stable and reliable transmission environment. Depending on configuration and cabling, AoE protocols can transmit anywhere from 32 to 64 channels of audio at a 48 kHz sampling rate at 16- or 24-bit. While other sampling rates and bit-depth rates may be accommodated, there may be a trade-off in channel capacity. Overall, LAN and Ethernet-based networking is geared to produce high-quality audio not possible on less controlled wide-area networks.

Wide-area Networks

A *wide-area network (WAN)* is configured for a large geographical area. Often a WAN is composed of several interconnected LANs. The Internet is the largest and best-known example of a WAN. A WAN is generally less controllable than a LAN because it comprises too many computers and individual LANs for any one person or group to manage. Some computers on a WAN may be quite fast, whereas others may be quite slow. When producing audio for the Web, a designer must take into consideration that WANs are extremely sizable and multifaceted.

Servers

A *server* is a computer dedicated to providing one or more services to other computers over a network, typically through a request-response routine. Users of the Internet are familiar with the practice of visiting various Web sites. Web sites are stored on a server, which receives Web page requests from users and transmits the desired page. Any audio associated with that page (or requested by a user in other ways) is likewise sent from a server across the network to the user. A network usually has one or several servers serving a large number of client computers. A server can be configured for specific tasks, such as managing e-mail, printing, or Web pages, or to store and serve audio files, for example, on a radio station's Web site.

Clients

A *client* is a computer connected to a network configured to make requests to a server. A client could be a personal home computer, an office workstation, or another server. Client computers are often the limiting factor when developing audio (or anything else) for use on the Internet. Whereas servers are fast, robust, and capable of quickly processing large amounts of data, clients come in all shapes and sizes. A video gamer might have an extremely fast computer connected to the Internet over a high-speed connection, whereas a casual Internet user, on the other hand, may use an older PC connected through a telephone modem and a dial-up connection at a very slow speed. Therefore, when designing audio for the Web, the limitations of the client computers must be considered. When developing audio to be used over a LAN, however, clients are often configured and controlled by the same team that manages the servers, so LAN clients are often more capable than the typical client computers found on a WAN or the Internet.

AUDIO FIDELITY

Networks, including the Internet, have a variety of limiting factors that reduce the speed at which data can be transmitted. Large amounts of data can take a great deal of time to be fully transmitted from a server to a client.

Such large transfers of information can also interfere with or impede other transmissions across a network. The overall time it takes for information to move from a server to a client is known as the *connection speed*.

We are all familiar with the experience of clicking on a Web link and waiting for endless minutes as an audio file opens. Because audio files are often quite large, transmitting them from server to client can take a long time. To reach the largest audience possible, a Web sound designer must design audio for the slowest likely connection. The slower the connection speed, the poorer the sound quality. If a designer has the advantage of creating sound to be used in a very fast LAN application, higher-quality sound can be used because of the greater bandwidth and faster connection speeds. A Web designer creating audio for a Web site likely to be viewed by users on slow connections would do well to reduce audio file size so that the sound is accessible to users with slower connections.

It is worthwhile to remember that, unlike telephone or radio sound transmission, the transfer of data over a network does not require that sound be sent in real time (although it can be, if desired). Sound sent by a server via the Internet can and often does take longer to reach its intended client than it takes for the client to play it back. Waiting for long periods of time to download audio over a network is frustrating. A number of solutions have been developed to address this problem, such as improvements in connection speed, reducing file size by manipulation, and data compression. These techniques allow information to flow faster across a network but in some cases not without a tradeoff in audio quality.

Connection Speed

The greater the connection speed, the faster a network can transmit information, including audio information.

Connection speed is measured in *kilobits per second (Kbps)*. For example, a connection speed of 150 Kbps can allow a bandwidth of 20,000 Hz and stereo CD-quality sound if played in real time. If sound is transmitted in real time, a connection speed of 8 Kbps produces a bandwidth of 2,500 Hz and mono telephone-quality sound (see Figure 19-1).

In fact, most Internet audio is not transmitted in real time, so connection speed is viewed as a limitation on the speed of transmission rather than as a means of determining a transmission's sound quality. A 150 Kbps connection transmits 150 kilobits per second, so with a bit rate of 150 kilobits you can transfer an audio file of 18.85 *kilobytes (KB)* in one second. The file could be a short clip of high-quality audio or a lengthy clip at reduced audio quality. In either case, the file would still take one second to travel to the client. This is known as *latency*. Obviously, a faster connection speed allows the same audio file to transfer more quickly.

File Manipulation

Another way to improve Internet sound is by reducing the size of audio files because size reduction facilitates file transfer between computers. This can be done through manipulation and compression (compression is covered later in this section).

There are different ways to handle file size reduction by manipulation, such as reducing the sampling rate, reducing the word length, reducing the number of channels, reducing playing time by editing, and, with music, using instrumental rather than vocal-based tracks (see 19-2).

Often these reductions in file size result in a loss of sound quality because many of them actually remove information from the file. Because the Internet is a huge,

19-1 Changes in audio quality in relation to connection speed.

Connection Speed (Kbps)	Mode	Audio Quality	Bandwidth (kHz)	Application
128–150	Stereo	CD quality	20	Intranets
96	Stereo	Near CD quality	15	ISDN, LAN
56–64	Stereo	Near FM quality	12	ISDN, LAN
24–32	Stereo	Boombox FM quality	7.5	28.8 modem
16	Mono	AM quality	4.5	28.8 modem
12	Mono	SW quality	4	14.4 modem
8	Mono	Telephone sound	2.5	Telephone

ISDN = Integrated Services Digital Network; LAN = local-area network

19-2 Approximate file sizes for one minute of audio recorded at differing sampling rates and resolutions.

Word Length/Sampling Rate	44.1 kHz	22.05 kHz	11.025 kHz
16-bit stereo	10 MB	5 MB	2.5 MB
16-bit mono/8-bit stereo	5 MB	2.5 MB	1.26 MB
8-bit mono	2.5 MB	1.26 MB	630 KB

1,000 KB = 1 MB

varied, and sometimes slow network, most audio distributed across the Web is reduced in file size to improve transmission speed, and therefore most Web audio is of reduced quality. That said, if longer download times are acceptable, audio quality does not have to suffer.

Reducing the Sampling Rate

Some sounds, such as a solo instrument, a sound effect, and a straight narration, to name just a few, do not require a high sampling rate of, say, 44.1 kHz. For these sounds 32 kHz may suffice. Be aware, however, that reducing the sampling rate may have unintended consequences with regard to the fidelity of a complex sound with a rich overtone or harmonic structure.

Reducing the Word Length

Audio with a narrow dynamic range, such as speech, simple sound effects, and certain instruments (see 17-33), does not require longer word lengths. An 8-bit word length should support such sound with little difficulty. Of course, wider dynamics require longer word lengths—16-bit and higher. But a given audio recording does not comfortably fit into either a narrow or a wide dynamic range; it almost always includes both. One technique used to counter the adverse effects caused by having too short a word length to handle a changing dynamic range is to use a *sliding window*—selecting an 8-bit format that moves up and down on the 16-bit scale, depending on whether the sound level is high or low.

Reducing the Number of Channels

Stereo audio uses twice as much data as mono. If an audio file can be handled in mono, it makes sense to do so. Sound effects are usually produced in mono; effects in stereo do not provide as much flexibility to the editor, mixer, and rerecordist in postproduction because the spatial imaging has already been committed. Speech and vocals can be monaurally imaged because they are usually centered in a mix. Music is the one sonic element that requires fuller spatial imaging and therefore stereo. But

on the Web, music is ordinarily distributed in a mono format to reduce file size and improve transmission speed.

Reducing Playing Time by Editing

Obviously, reducing playing time reduces file size. Of course, this is not always feasible or desirable, but when the opportunity does present itself editing the file will help. In this case, *editing* refers to eliminating extraneous bits of data (as opposed to conventional editing discussed in Chapter 20). Three ways to handle such editing is through compression, noise reduction, and equalization.

Compression (in relation to dynamic range) reduces the distances between the peaks and the troughs of a signal. This raises the level of the overall signal, thereby overriding background noise.

Noise reduction is best handled by listening to the silent parts of a file to check for unwanted noise. If it is present, that section of the file can be cleaned, taking care to retain all desirable sound.

Equalization comes in handy to add the high frequencies that are usually lost in compression (data reduction).

Using Instrumental Music Instead of Vocal-based Tracks

Reducing the data of instrumental music is easier than that of vocal-based music backed by an accompanying ensemble. Therefore it is another way to eliminate unwanted bits so long as production requirements make it feasible to do so.

Compression

Compression is the most common way to reduce the size of large audio files by removing psychoacoustically unimportant data. The process is facilitated by a *codec*, a device that computes enormous mathematical calculations (called *algorithms*) to make data compression possible.

Compression can be either lossless or lossy. In **lossless compression** the original information is preserved; in **lossy compression** it is not. Lossless compression preserves binary data bit-for-bit and does not compress data at very high ratios. Historically, the codec does not articulate audio data as well because its operations are based on strict mathematical functions that are more conducive to handling video. But, this is changing with open source solutions such as *Ogg* and *Free Lossless Audio Codec (FLAC)*.

Lossy compression delivers high compression ratios. The lossy codec compression approximates what a human ear can hear and then filters out frequency ranges to which the ear is insensitive.

There are several compression formats in use today: adaptive differential pulse code modulation, a-law and μ-law, RealAudio, MPEG, MPEG-2 layer 3 technology, MPEG-2 AAC, MPEG-4 AAC, Ogg, and FLAC.

■ *Adaptive differential pulse code modulation (ADPCM)* uses the fact that audio is continuous in nature. At thousands of samples per second, one sample does not sound much different from another. ADPCM records the differences between samples of sound rather than the actual sound itself. This technique reduces the sampling rate from 16-bit to 4-bit, compressing original data to one-fourth its size.

■ *A-law* and *μ-law* constitute an 8-bit codec format developed for sending speech via digital telephone lines. It uses the principle of redistributing samples to where sound is loudest—during speech—from where it is softest, during pauses in speech. μ-law is used in North America and Japan; a-law is used in the rest of the world.

■ *RealAudio* is a proprietary system using a compression method called *CELP* at low bit rates for speech. For music it uses the Dolby Digital codec with higher bit rates. The Dolby system is known as *AC-3* (the *AC* stands for *audio coding*) (see Chapter 22).

■ *MPEG* stands for the *Moving Picture Experts Group*. It was established by the film industry and the International Standards Organization (ISO) to develop compression software for film. MPEG uses an analytical approach to compression called *acoustic masking*. It works by establishing what the brain perceives the ear to be hearing at different frequencies. When a tone, called a *masker*, is at a particular frequency, the human ear cannot hear audio on nearby frequencies if they are at a low level. Based on this principle, MPEG developers determined various frequencies that could be eliminated. They use perceptual coders that divide the audio into multiple frequency bands, called *filterbanks*, each assigned a masking threshold below which all data is eliminated.

■ *MPEG-2 layer 3 technology* is commonly known as *MP3*. It is considered an excellent system for speech, sound effects, and most types of music. It ranges from 16 to 128 Kbps. MP3 is among the most commonly used codecs because of its ability to dramatically reduce audio file size while retaining fairly good sound quality. It supports a variety of sound applications and Web authoring environments.

■ *MPEG-2 AAC (Advanced Audio Coding)* is a compression format from MPEG. It is approximately a 30 percent improvement over MPEG-2 layer 3 technology and 100 percent better than AC-3.

■ *MPEG-4 AAC with SBR (Spectral Bandwidth Replication)*, or *MP4*, is the most recent coding system from MPEG. It offers near-CD-quality stereo to be transmitted over connection speeds as low as 48 Kbps. A data rate of 96 Kbps for a 44.1 kHz/16-bit stereo signal is also possible. MP4 compression is replacing the popular MP3 format because it offers higher-quality audio over the same connection speeds. In addition to mono and stereo, MPEG-4 AAC with SBR supports various surround-sound configurations, such as 5.1 and 7.1.

Most AAC encoder implementations are real-time capable. AAC supports several audio sampling rates ranging from 8 to 96 kHz. This makes it suitable for high-quality audio in applications with limited channel or memory capacities.

■ *Ogg* is an open-source multimedia container format, comparable to MPEG program stream or QuickTime. Its suite of video, audio, and metadata compression formats and solutions, however, are designed as nonproprietary—that is, free—alternatives and are attractive to individuals as well as third-party audio and media developers. *Ogg Vorbis* is a professional audio encoding and streaming technology. The encoder uses *variable bit rate (VBR)* and can produce output from about 45 to 500 Kbps for a CD-quality (44.1 kHz/16-bit) stereo signal, improving the data compression transparency associated with lossy compression.

■ *Free Lossless Audio Codec (FLAC)* is an open-source, cross-platform file format that achieves lossless compression rates of 40 to 50 percent for most musical material. It can handle a wide range of sampling rates, bit-depth resolutions from 4- to 32-bit, and between one and eight channels, making stereo and 5.1 groupings possible. The format is popular among groups sharing music and also for those who are interested in archiving music recorded on vinyl and CD. Unlike MPEG formats, FLAC has the advantage of storing exact duplicates of original audio, including metadata from a recording such as track order, silences between tracks, cover art, and text.

File Formats

Because programs that play digital audio need to recognize the files before they can play them, files that are converted into digital audio must be saved in a particular format. The process adds an *extension* (a period followed by a two- to four-letter descriptor) to the file name, identifying it as an audio file. It also adds *header information,* which tells the playback program how to interpret the data. File identifiers specify the name of the file, file size, duration, sampling rate, word length (bits), number of channels, and type of compression used.

A large number of formats are available on the Internet, and they come and go; a few, however, have been in relatively widespread use for a while (see 19-3). These include MPEG formats (.mpa, .mp2, .mp3, .mp4), Windows Media Audio (.wma), WAV (.wav), RealAudio (.ra), OGG (.ogg), FLAC (.flac), and Flash (.swf).

Downloadable Nonstreaming Formats

Downloadable nonstreaming formats require that the user first download the entire file and store it on the computer's hard disk. A plug-in then plays the file. No specific server (transmitter) software is needed.

The difference between nonstreaming and streaming is that streaming allows audio data to be sent across a computer network so that there are no interruptions at the receiving end for what appears to be continuous audio playback. In practice, however, interruptions do occur with slower connections.

Downloading nonstreaming data is usually slow when the files are even relatively large. Because a WAV file with one minute of digital-quality sound—44.1 kHz/16-bit stereo—will occupy roughly 10 MB of disk space, these formats are generally used for audio of a minute or so. Figure 19-4 provides an idea of the various formats' ease of use, quality versus size, and portability.

Nonstreaming formats are easily portable and useful for file-sharing applications. Because the file downloads to the computer before playback, it can be easily copied, saved, manipulated, and redistributed (note, however, that copyrighted material should not be distributed without express permission of the copyright holder).

Nonstreaming formats are not useful if the desire is to have audio play automatically within a Web browser

19-3 Common file formats and their associated extensions.

Lossless File Formats	Extensions
WAV	.wav
AIFF (Audio Interchange File Format)	.aif, .aiff
RealAudio	.ra
Broadcast Wave Format	.wav
Windows Media Audio	.wma
Free Lossless Audio Codec	.flac

Lossy File Formats	Extensions
MPEG Audio	.mpa, .mp2, .mp3, .mp4
ATRAC (used with mini disc™)	
Flash	.swf
Sun	.au
Ogg	.ogg

Metafile Formats	

(Metafile formats are designed to interchange all the information needed to reconstruct a project.)

AES-31 (AES is the Audio Engineering Society)

OMF (open media format)

or Web page. Nonstreaming files often need to be started manually by the user and often take some time to download before playback can begin.

Downloadable Streaming Formats

The principle behind streaming technologies is *buffering.* As the *player,* which is built into or added onto a user's Web browser, receives data, it stores it in a buffer before use. After data builds a substantial buffer, the *player* (such as RealPlayer) begins to play it. All incoming data is first stored in the buffer before playing.

Thus the player is able to maintain a continuous audio output despite the changing transmission speeds of the data. Sometimes the buffer runs empty, and the player has to wait until it receives more data, in which case the computer displays the message "Web congestion, buffering." Data is sent over the Internet in *packets*. Each packet bears the address of the sender and the receiver. Because the Internet is lossy and non-deterministic, packets may get lost and arrive at different times. One company has developed a system that allows audio to flow even if packets are lost or appear later. Nonetheless, streaming technologies come closest to approximating traditional broadcast.

19-4 Common downloadable formats in relation to ease of use, quality versus size, and portability (its support across different platforms, such as Windows, Macintosh, and Unix).

	Ease of Use	Quality Versus Size	Portability
AU*	Good	Good	Excellent
MPEG (MP3)	Fair	Excellent	Good
MPEG-4 AAC	Fair	Excellent	Good
WAV/AIFF	Excellent	Poor	Good
WMA	Excellent	Excellent	Good
Flash	Fair	Good	Excellent
FLAC	Good	Excellent	Good
Ogg	Good	Excellent	Excellent

	Strengths
AU	Can be used across all platforms
MPEG (MP3)	High compression ratios that can shrink CD files to one-tenth their size with no apparent loss of quality
MPEG-4 AAC	Higher quality than MP3; small file sizes
WAV/AIFF	Because these are the default audio type for all operating systems, they are extremely easy to use on all systems and applications
WMA	Native to Windows environment so it plays on any Windows machine; good sound quality
Flash	Due to widespread plug-ins, Flash files are playable on 90 percent of computers; format also allows the creation of interactivity not available in other formats
FLAC	High-quality compression; open source; fast streaming
Ogg	High-quality compression; open source; can be used across many platforms

	Recommendation: Use in...	Reasons
AU	Short audio clips (<30 seconds), background sound tracks, sound effects, and voice clips	High portability; good sound with small file sizes
MPEG (MP3)	Audio that requires CD quality	Highly compressible; extremely popular
MPEG-4 AAC	Audio that requires CD quality	Will replace MP3 eventually
WAV/AIFF	Short audio clips of voice and solo instrumental music	Files too large; non-portable if compressed
WMA	Short to medium-length clips intended for Internet playack	Works well in Windows Media Player embedded into a Web page
Flash	Audio that needs to be interactive or features integrated user controls	Allows the inclusion of programming artwork and other nonaudio elements
FLAC	Audio that requires CD quality	Lossless compression and flexibility
Ogg	Audio that requires CD quality	Highly efficient compression

*AU is a simple audio file format developed by Sun Microsystems.

Streaming formats cannot be permanently saved and are purged from the buffer after playback. This is sometimes desirable when distributing copyrighted material, for instance. At other times the inability to save material is a limitation. Streaming formats also tend to be of lower sound quality than downloadable formats. Often users experience choppiness or stuttering during playback as well as dropouts and artifacts, especially with slower connection speeds.

Transmission of Streaming Formats

With streaming technology the transmission process passes through the encoder, the server, the Internet, and the player. The *encoder* is responsible for translating the original audio signal into one of the data compression formats. The compressed audio bitstream is then sent to a server. Sometimes the encoder and the server can run on the same computer, but this is not usually the case for high-capacity servers or encoders running at high bit rates. The server is responsible for repackaging the bitstream for delivery over the Internet, sending the same bitstream to multiple users. This link is the weakest in the chain because the Internet was not designed with real-time streaming applications in mind. At the receiving end is the user's computer with the appropriate applications software to play the audio file. This player unpacks the streaming data from the server, recovers the compressed audio bitstream, and decodes it back into an audio signal.

Progressive Download Formats

Web developers working with sound also take advantage of *progressive download formats*. These files download like a nonstreaming file, allowing users to save them for later use. They buffer like a streaming format, however, allowing playback to begin before the entire file has been completely saved. This improves performance and playback over the Web while retaining the advantages of a nonstreaming format.

ONLINE COLLABORATIVE RECORDING

Integrated Services Digital Network (ISDN) made it possible to produce a recording session—from a radio interview to music—in real time between studios across town or across the country (see Chapter 5). Various software applications allow multiple users to connect to one another in real time and record or perform together. These systems generally require very fast connection speeds and robust server and client setups.

The Internet has seen an explosion in social networking sites, where audiophiles and music lovers form online communities. Audio—especially music—can be created, performed in virtual venues, and distributed or shared online.

For many years it has been possible for individuals to collaborate by sharing files to produce audio materials such as spot announcements, radio programs, music recordings, film sound tracks, and more. An entire project can be posted to a secure server and downloaded by one or more members of the production team, who can provide additional audio and then edit and mix the project. All the updating can then be posted back to the server. The process can be repeated as many times as necessary from anywhere in the world with an Internet connection. Often these systems can be configured to pass audio files back and forth automatically, reducing the likelihood that various team members will accidentally work on different versions of a file or overwrite each other's work. Some companies have developed in their online software the features of a virtual studio, facilitating fast, convenient ways to collaborate with others synchronously and in real time.

The possibilities of this technology seem limitless. With recent innovations in online collaborative recording, it is possible to assemble a team of musicians from around the globe without requiring travel, relocation, or adjustments to personal schedules. Musicians from different cities, countries, or continents can be engaged for a recording session in a virtual online studio. These musicians report to studios near their own homes, or work from home, yet still perform together as a group just as they would in a single studio. The key elements that make such collaboration possible involve access to adequate bandwidth, as well as the development of data-thinning schemes and algorithms that ameliorate latency and delay issues that hinder real-time musical interaction.

It is also becoming easier to arrange a recording session in one country but monitor and mix it elsewhere. Wireless technology makes it possible to record sound effects in the field and transmit them to a studio. As Internet technology and connection speeds improve, the sound quality to be found in such collaborative experiences will equal that of the best studios.

Currently, however, Internet technology is still somewhat limited in making online collaborative recording viable for many potential users. Within a LAN, connection speeds and client performances are high enough to make these techniques practical and sometimes beneficial, although LANs usually do not cover a wide geographical area. Across the Internet, where slow connections and outdated technology still abound, online collaborative recording techniques are still in their infancy.

But online collaboration is happening in the production of commercials and bona fide programs, as Thomas Friedman points out in his book *The World Is Flat.* He tells of a program called *Higglytown Heroes* and how this

> all-American show was being produced by an all-world supply chain.... The recording session is located near the artist, usually in New York or L.A., the design and direction is done in San Francisco, the writers network in from their homes (Florida, London, New York, Chicago, L.A., and San Francisco), and the animation of the characters is done in Bangalore (India).... These interactive recording/writing/animation sessions allow [recording] an artist for an entire show in less than half a day, including unlimited takes and rewrites.[1]

Although not interactive, there is online collaborative recording, of sorts, available from services that make professional musicians available for personal recording projects. Using the Internet, the client submits an MP3 example of the music and indicates the type of musical support needed. The service then discusses the musical direction to take, the musicians it has available, and the fee. Working in their own studios, the hired musicians record their individual parts. As each instrument recording is completed, the service compiles an MP3 rough mix and sends it to the client for approval. The process is repeated until completion, at which point the client receives the edit master files for final mixing. If the client prefers, the service can provide a professional engineer to handle the final mix.

PODCASTING

Podcasting is an ever-increasingly popular mode of media production and distribution. Through rapid advances, Internet technology allows users to create and distribute their own audio (and video) productions over the Web. The term *podcasting* is a combination of the words *pod,* referring to the iPod sound player, and *casting,* short for *broadcasting.* It points to the essential idea behind podcasting: to create a media broadcast suitable for playback on mobile media, more often than not an MP3-compatible player like the iPod, a cell phone, or a personal digital assistant (PDA).

From a technical perspective, there are three reasons why podcasting is more related to Internet technology than to audio production. First, the pioneers of podcasting tended to be Web designers and developers rather than audio professionals. Much has gone into the development and the deployment of the various Web technologies that make podcasting possible, but less attention has gone into the good use of sound in a podcast.

Second, podcasters hope to reach large audiences, but the emphasis is on achieving a widespread distribution through *RSS feeds*—a method of distributing data about a podcast to a widespread group of Internet subscribers—and other Web technologies (see discussion later in this section).[2] Less attention is given to sound production technique and sound quality as a means of increasing audience size.

Third, the medium's surging popularity has tended to dilute the emphasis on sound quality. As in any field, a relatively small group of professionals can better implement and control high production standards. The large and ever-growing group of novices getting into podcasting is more intent on learning how to create a podcast and (because of inexperience) not necessarily on producing one that is professional sounding. Typical podcasts feature poor-quality audio and amateurish production values. That said, there are also many well-done podcasts, usually on large, heavily trafficked Web sites that feature professionally produced audio—narration, music, and sound effects. They are essentially professional radio broadcasts distributed via the Internet.

Though the current emphasis in podcasting is with Web technology and Web distribution, the podcaster is still faced with many of the same limitations as any other developer who distributes audio over the Internet. File size is still of paramount concern. Though fast connections make the download of podcasts relatively speedy, it is still advantageous for a podcaster to compress audio and reduce file sizes to reach as wide an audience as possible. It is also important for the podcaster to consider that users may not be willing to upload a large podcast to an iPod or other portable MP3 player that is already full of other media. A smaller file size leaves a smaller

---

1. Thomas L. Friedman, *The World Is Flat* (New York: Farrar, Straus, and Giroux, 2005), p. 72.

2. RSS is a family of Web *feed* formats used to publish frequently updated digital content, such as a podcast, blog, or news feed. The initials *RSS* are variously used to refer to *Really Simple Syndication, Rich Site Summary,* and *RDF Site Summary.* RSS formats are specified in XML (a generic specification for data formats). RSS delivers its information as an XML file called an *RSS feed, Webfeed, RSS stream,* or *RSS* channel. (From Wikipedia.)

footprint on an MP3 player, making storage and playback easier for the listener.

Most audio podcasts are distributed in MP3 format, which is playable on virtually all computers and MP3 players, although some MP3 players require a specific type of encoding for certain MP3 files to be played. Despite this limitation MP3 is still the file type of choice for podcasting.

Creating a podcast MP3 is relatively straightforward. Computer technology notwithstanding, the equipment required is the same used in conventional radio broadcasting. What accounts for differences in sound quality is whether the podcaster employs consumer-grade equipment with no signal-processing capability or any of the higher-quality podcasting equipment packages available.

Conceptually, a podcast can take any number of forms. Some are released in sequence or on a schedule—daily, weekly, or monthly audio blogs or "webisodes." Many are simply experiments or onetime releases. It is becoming increasingly common for news outlets, both print and broadcast, to create podcast versions of some content (both audio and video) so that users can listen or watch on the go, using mobile media. Whatever the format, if the podcaster is serious about the product and building an audience, it pays to keep good Internet sound production practices in mind.

There are many technical details involved in placing a podcast on the Web. Some Web sites offer free or paid services that allow users to handle this with relative ease. More-ambitious podcasters and professional Web developers generally learn how to distribute a podcast manually. Whatever the approach, there are certain requirements for a podcast to become more than an audio file sitting in a user's home computer.

First, the audio file must be uploaded to a Web server, via *File Transfer Protocol (FTP),* where it is accessible to anyone with an Internet connection. The file is now available, but a user may not know it exists. Linking to the file from a Web site can help, as can including useful metatag data in the header of the Web page. Successful podcasting requires a more robust approach to distribution, however. One popular method of getting one's work out there makes use of the RSS feed.

An *RSS feed* is specified using XML (Extensible Markup Language) that facilitates sharing data over the Internet. The feed format lends itself to frequent updates and may include a range of metadata about the podcast: from content summary, to transcript, to dates and authorship. The feed is a computer file in a standardized format that lists addresses and information about the various podcasts available on a particular server. The feed is also made available on the server in a semi-permanent location known as the *feed URI* or *feed URL*.[3] Ideally, this feed is made available in a variety of places across the Internet. Users who find the feed can look through it using a software application called an ***aggregator,*** or *podcatcher,*[4] and select various podcasts to which to subscribe.

A feed of this kind is more advantageous than a simple link because as the feed is updated with new podcasts or changed information, the aggregator on the user's computer will see the changes and bring them to the user's attention automatically. Some services will also download to the user's MP3 player so that new podcasts are always available.

AUDIO PRODUCTION FOR MOBILE MEDIA

Producing audio for ***mobile media*** such as iPods, MP3 players, cell phones, and PDAs involves numerous considerations, especially where they intersect with multiple platforms and the parameters of Internet delivery (see Chapters 14, 18, and 23). Unlike production for a state-of-the-art cinema experience, home entertainment center gaming or film environment, or multichannel playback system geared to the highest fidelity, producing audio for mobile media presents particular technical and aesthetic challenges that are generally without historical precedent.

You will recall that mobile devices are designed to handle compressed audio—based on the need to manage access speed and sound quality according to available

---

3. A *URI,* or *Uniform Resource Identifier,* is a compact string of characters used to identify or name a resource. The main purpose of this identification is to enable interaction with representations of the resource over a network, typically the World Wide Web, using specific protocols. URIs are defined in a specific syntax and associated protocols. A URI can be classified as a locator, a name, or both. A *URL,* or *Uniform Resource Locator,* is a URI that, in addition to identifying a resource, provides means of acting on or obtaining a representation of the resource by describing its primary access mechanism or network "location." (From Wikipedia.)

4. An *aggregator* is client software that uses a Web feed to retrieve syndicated Web content such as blogs, podcasts, and mainstream mass media Web sites and, in the case of a search aggregator, a customized set of search results. Aggregators reduce the time and the effort needed to regularly check Web sites for updates, creating a unique information space or "personal newspaper." (From Wikipedia.)

bandwidth and storage capacity. Although this may seem to be purely a technical matter, the implications affect creative and aesthetic decision-making at every stage of production. The full range and power of a symphony orchestra or the subtle sonic complexity of nature's dawn chorus may not be possible to render in a compressed audio format; too much would be lost. Other music and voices may fare better from a listener's perspective. To some extent, form follows function in relation to what is possible.

Playback through mobile media is often through small piezoelectric loudspeakers with a limited frequency response and dynamic range (such as inboard and outboard computer speakers of varying quality and cell-phone speakers). The latter are designed with the human voice in mind and therefore have a correspondingly narrow frequency response, ranging from around 100 Hz to 8 kHz. Earbuds are capable of handling a broader spectrum, from 10 Hz to 20 kHz, but they too are limited in playing back acoustically rich and detailed audio because of their size and unnatural positioning as a sound source at the outer edge of the ear canal. Headphones, particularly those with noise-canceling capability, offer the better sound option for individual listening.

Editing and mixing audio for mobile media generally requires careful and selective equalization in the upper and lower ranges of the program material; highs and lows are rolled off, and the midrange is emphasized. Dynamics usually must be compressed so that program material is heard clearly through tiny loudspeakers.

Apart from the technical challenges, the conditions for listening to mobile media for those on the go are not necessarily conducive to focused, attentive listening. People are more likely to listen to an iPod on the bus, while riding a bicycle, or while walking down a city street than in the solitude of a quiet room. These environments are often acoustically competitive and many sounds are masked by ambient din. To compound the situation, a listener may be engaged in any number of other activities—reading, texting, exercising, and so on. In a word: *multitasking.* The listening experience is therefore compromised on many levels and exists in a multisensory continuum of stimulation.

From a sound design perspective, there is also a need to consider how program audio associated with picture functions with regard to scale in small mobile-media devices. While it is possible to download a feature film or television episode to an iPod or a cell phone, much is lost in translation. These materials were designed with a larger picture and acoustic image space in mind and the experience was, more often than not, a collective one: a cinema or living room where people gathered together. Consider watching a film like *Lawrence of Arabia* with its sweeping, epic desert scenes and a cast of thousands on a screen that is 2 inches wide. Individuals are rendered in little more than a few pixels. Although the sound track, even though it is compressed audio, can be turned up and experienced with much of its drama and grandeur intact through headphones, the essential relationship of sound to picture no longer exists with regard to scale and appropriate, meaningful perspective.

As more and more content is created specifically for mobile media, from short-form webisodes, to audio/video blogs, podcasts, and games, a new aesthetic is emerging. With a viewing area reduced to a few inches, production designers are tending to adjust their scene and shot compositions to accommodate more-elemental information: the massing of bold and simple shapes; bright color schemes using primary and secondary colors; light and shadow relationships that need to stand out on an LCD screen being pushed into higher contrast ratios; and close-ups being favored over long and medium camera shots. For the sound designer working with mobile media, the sonic palette remains somewhat restricted and the production parameters limited, at least until the technical means afford greater possibilities with respect to aesthetic ends.

All this is not to forget the aesthetic challenge created by the disproportionate "sizes" of the sound and the picture. Compared with the video, in sonically good reproducing systems the sound heard through headphones or earbuds can be enveloping, overwhelming the video image and therefore dominating it, if not separating from it entirely (see Chapter 14).

MAIN POINTS

▶ Computer technology in general and the Internet in particular have provided the means to produce and disseminate audio on an unprecedented scale.

▶ The delivery and the playback of audio over the Internet differ from the traditional methods used in the conventional audio studio. It involves, in computer parlance, a network—a system of computers configured and connected in a way that allows them to communicate with one another.

▶ A local-area network (LAN) is configured for a small, localized area such as a home or business. A wide-area network (WAN) is configured for a large geographical area.

▶ A server is a computer dedicated to providing one or more services to other computers over a network, typically through a request-response routine. A client is a computer connected to a network configured to make requests to a server.

▶ Achieving digital-quality sound transmission over the Internet depends on several factors, not the least of which are a computer and loudspeakers capable of delivering the high-quality audio.

▶ Among the factors relevant to high-quality audio are the connection speed and the file size.

▶ Reducing file size can be done by file manipulation or data compression.

▶ File manipulation includes reducing sampling rate, word length, number of channels, and playing time and, with music, using instrumental instead of vocal-based tracks.

▶ Playing time can be reduced by editing through compression of the dynamic range, noise reduction, and equalization.

▶ Compression can be either lossless, preserving the original information, or lossy, with high compression ratios where some data is filtered out.

▶ Protocols used for data compression include adaptive differential pulse code modulation (ADPCM); a-law and μ-law; RealAudio; MPEG; MPEG-2 layer 3 technology (MP3); MPEG-2 AAC (Advanced Audio Coding); MPEG-4 AAC with SBR (Spectral Bandwidth Replication), or MP4; Ogg; and FLAC (Free Lossless Audio Codec).

▶ File formats facilitate the saving of digital audio files.

▶ The difference between streaming and nonstreaming is that streaming allows audio data to be sent across a computer network with no interruptions at the receiving end, although, in practice, interruptions do occur with slower connections.

▶ Downloading nonstreaming data is usually slow and therefore limited to small files.

▶ The principle behind streaming technologies is buffering.

▶ With streaming technology the transmission process passes through the encoder, the server, the Internet, and the player.

▶ Using secure file servers, it is possible to do collaborative audio production online by uploading and downloading such audio materials as music, voice-overs, and sound effects. An entire project can be posted to a server and then downloaded by one or more members of the production

team, who can provide additional audio and then edit and mix the project.

▶ Podcasting involves Internet technology that allows users to create and distribute their own audio (and video) productions over the Web.

▶ File size is of paramount concern to the podcaster. Though fast connections make the download of podcasts relatively speedy, it is still advantageous to compress audio and reduce file sizes to reach as wide an audience as possible.

▶ Most audio podcasts are distributed in MP3 format, which is playable on virtually all computers and MP3 players.

▶ Sound quality in podcasts varies widely for several reasons: the emphasis is more on achieving widespread distribution than on audio production values; equipment runs from consumer-grade to professional; and many podcasters have little or no experience with audio production techniques.

▶ The RSS feed is a robust computer file in a standardized format that lists addresses and information about the various podcasts available on a particular server.

▶ Unlike production for a state-of-the-art cinema experience, home entertainment center gaming or film environment, or multichannel playback system geared to high-fidelity, producing audio for mobile media presents particular technical and aesthetic challenges that are generally without historical precedent.

▶ Playback through mobile media is often through small piezoelectric loudspeakers with a limited frequency response and dynamic range.

▶ Editing and mixing audio for mobile media generally requires careful and selective equalization in the upper and lower ranges of the program material; highs and lows are rolled off, and the midrange is emphasized. Dynamics usually must be compressed so that program material is heard clearly through tiny loudspeakers.

▶ The conditions for listening to mobile media for those on the go are not necessarily conducive to focused, attentive listening.

▶ For the sound designer working with mobile media, the sonic palette remains somewhat restricted and the production parameters limited, at least until the technical means afford greater possibilities with respect to aesthetic ends.

▶ There is also the aesthetic challenge in mobile media when listening to good audio-reproducing systems through headphones or earbuds that the audio imaging compared with the video imaging will be disproportionately greater.

IV

Postproduction

20
Editing

The results of good production for picture are readily perceptible to the viewer—lighting, cinematography, composition, transitions, special effects, and so on. Not so with audio. When audio is well produced, it goes unnoticed, as it should. If audience attention is drawn to the dialogue, sound effects, or music, at the expense of the overall dramatic intent, it detracts from the viewing experience. Nowhere in audio production is "invisibility" more important than it is with editing.

Editing is indispensable to the production process. Program segments may need to be rearranged, shortened, or cut out altogether. Directors commonly record elements of a program out of sequence; editing makes this possible. It also makes it possible to transpose parts of words; "recompose" music; change the character of a sound effect; improve the quality of dialogue; take out noises such as clicks and pops; eliminate mistakes, long pauses, coughing, "ahs," "ers," "ums," and other awkwardness; record a segment several times and choose the best parts of each take; change the relationship of characters in a drama; create the pace; establish timing; and even redirect an entire storyline. The art of editing requires the ability to see a whole and build toward it while it is still in parts. The best editors have a first-rate ear and an innate sensitivity to the aesthetics of sound.

DIGITAL EDITING

Digital editing allows the assembly of disk-based material in or out of sequence, taken from any part of a recording, and placed in any other part of the recording almost instantly. It is therefore also referred to as *nonlinear edit-*

ing. Nonlinear editing is not new. Film and audiotape have always been edited nonlinearly; that is, a sound (or shot) is accessed in one part of a recording and added to another part of the recording, or deleted, in whatever order the editor chooses.

Today nonlinear editing is done using software in disk-based editing (and recording) systems that provide tools that are far beyond anything that an editor could envision in the days before computers. With a *nonlinear editor (NLE)*, it is possible to "see" a sound in its waveform; audition an edit at any stage in the procedure; cut, paste, and copy; adjust levels; add signal processing; and restore any change in the edited material to its original waveform at any time, quickly and seamlessly—all without endangering the master audio.

Because it is possible to see the waveform of any sound being edited, it is much easier to deal with sound in general and with sustained sounds having no attack, such as vowels and legato strings, in particular. If needed, most editing software programs can display video in sync with the audio using QuickTime or another audio/video interface.

Digital editing affords the convenience of allowing any recording from almost any source to be transferred and coded (or recoded, if necessary) in the process. In performing such transfers, however, it is critical that frame rates between the input source and the NLE are compatible (see Chapter 6). Also, file conversion must be considered. With so many different audio formats out there, it's important to know which ones can be supported and the extent of a system's file conversion capability. Once editing and mixing at the computer are completed, the audio may be sent on for mastering or transferred back to the distribution medium if video is involved.

There are two main types of NLEs: two-track and multitrack. *Two-track editors* are typically used in radio for news, call-ins, and various types of less complex stereo production. They are suitable for any production and on-air situation in which speed is important. *Multitrack editors* are used for more-complex productions that require the layering of multiple segments of audio, such as commercials, music recording, and sound tracks.

Functions of Editing Software

Many excellent audio-editing software programs are available. Although they vary in price and sophistication, they all perform functions similar to word processing, such as cut, paste, delete, insert, and overtype. They also perform a variety of other functions, depending on the program's complexity.

Given the number of editing programs available, it would be unwieldy to list and explain their many features here. As with all computer software, each editing program comes with an instruction manual. The following section is a distillation of the basic functions found in most NLEs. It is intended to provide an operational overview of digital editing. Although all the terms are explained, some are more common than others and their familiarity may depend on your knowledge of a particular editing system.

BASIC FUNCTIONS IN DIGITAL EDITING

With a nonlinear editor, audio that is encoded onto the disk takes the form of a *soundfile*, which contains information about the sound such as amplitude and duration. When the soundfile is opened, that information is displayed as a waveform on the monitor, usually within the overall features of the edit screen.

The *waveform* displays the profile of a sound's amplitude over time. By being able to see a representation of a sound, it is easy to spot its dynamics (see Figure 20-1). It is also possible to see greater detail in a waveform by zooming in, a feature that facilitates extremely precise

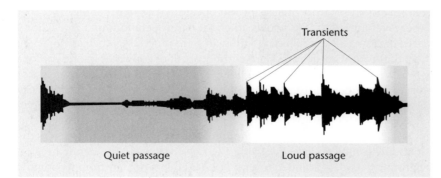

20-1 Dynamics of a waveform.

Transients

Quiet passage   Loud passage

20-2 Spectrum editing display. This example shows a surgical edit within a waveform.

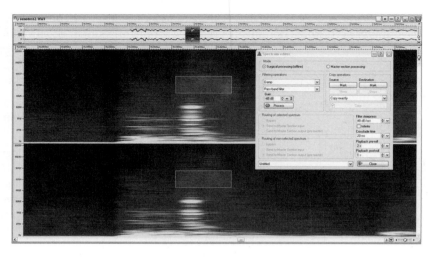

editing. Once the soundfile is retrieved and its waveform is displayed, it can be auditioned to determine which of its sections is to be defined for editing.

For a more refined view of an audio file, some programs include **spectrum editing.** The spectrum display provides a sonogram view of an audio file, facilitating ultrafine surgical editing of such elements as noise, ambience, and unwanted frequencies (see 20-2).

As a sound is played, a *play cursor* (also known as a *playbar* or *play head*), scrolls the waveform, enabling the editor to see precisely the part and the shape of the sound that is playing at any given moment. When the soundfile is longer than the screen can display, as the scroll moves to the end of the visible waveform, approaching the off-screen data, the screen is either redrawn, or refreshed, showing the entire updated waveform, or it continues scrolling to the end of the track.

When the editor determines the part of the sound to be edited, the segment is highlighted as a *defined region.* Once a region is defined, the selected edit is performed only in that section of the waveform (as shown in Figure 20-4). The region can be cut from the waveform display or moved and/or copied to another part of the waveform or to another waveform. It can also be inverted or changed in level, envelope, frequency, and so on, up to the limits of the system.

A *marker,* or *identification flag,* can be placed anywhere in the waveform to facilitate jumping the play cursor to the desired marker points. The marker can be a graphic identifier using a number, a letter, or text (see 20-3).

Anytime in the editing process, the soundfile can be auditioned in a number of ways: from beginning to end,

from the defined region, from marker to marker, and at increased or decreased speed in either direction. This latter operation is called scrubbing.

Scrubbing lets you move, or *rock,* the play cursor through the defined region at any speed and listen to the section being scrubbed. With scrubbing you can audibly and visibly locate the in- and out-points of a defined region. Many NLEs have jogging and shuttling functions. ***Jogging*** allows direct control of an audio track by moving the mouse from side to side. ***Shuttling*** changes speed in response to mouse movements.

Suppose the task is to pinpoint a chord located in one section of a soundfile and use the same chord at the end of the soundfile to end the song. By moving the play cursor to an area just before the chord, you can slowly scrub the area until you find the precise location at the beginning of the first sound. This will be the first point in the defined region. Continue scrubbing until you locate the precise end point of the chord's decay and mark it as the end of the defined region. Then, as you would in word processing, copy the defined region and paste it at the precise location near the end of the song.

As noted earlier, the basic operations in digital editing are similar to those in word processing, such as when you delete a word entirely or cut or copy it from one part of a sentence and paste it elsewhere in the same sentence or into another context. Once a region is defined, the *Cut command* removes it from its original location and copies it to the computer's memory for temporary storage. This section of computer memory is usually referred to as the *clipboard.* Using the *Copy command,* the defined region is added to the clipboard but is not cut from its original

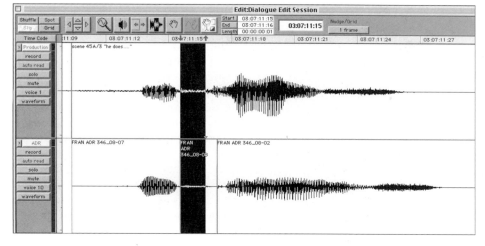

position. The *Paste command* copies the defined region from the clipboard and inserts it into the waveform immediately after the position of the play cursor. Additional paste functions facilitate how a defined region is placed in any part of the waveform. *Undo/Redo* allows reversing the previous edit or applying the edit (or change) again.

Snapping appends a defined region to another region like a magnet, with no gap or overlap between them. *Slipping* moves a defined region freely with spaces preceding or following it, or it can overlap a portion of another region. *Spotting* places a defined region into a specific location displayed in time code, minutes and seconds, bars and beats, or feet and frames. It may also allow the defined region to be automatically lined up at a precise interval; in a music recording, for example, if quarter-note increments are set, dragging a defined region to a new location in a track will cause it to spot to the nearest quarter-note location.

There are also commands in digital editing that are similar to the insert and overtype operations in word processing. *Insert* moves the audio that originally followed the play cursor to a point immediately following the newly inserted segment. *Overtype* or *replace* overwrites the audio immediately following the play cursor.

Scaling and *zooming* allow adjustments of the track view; that is, the waveform can be made taller or shorter, expanded to the right or left, widened to show more of its duration, or tightened to better display a more concentrated duration.

Trim or *crop* shortens or expands a defined region to a desired length. On most NLEs it provides a quick way to remove noise or silence from the head or tail of an audio clip. There may also be a *delete silence* command that removes unwanted silences between words and sentences or on music tracks. A *limit silence* command determines the length of the silence to be removed.

Time compression and *expansion* decrease or increase the length of a soundfile so that it plays for a shorter or longer period of time. With most editing programs, this is accomplished without changing the sound's pitch.

Looping allows soundfiles to be repeated exactly at the touch of a button as many times as desired. A looping program may also facilitate the creation of synthetic sounds and pitch shifting.

Track grouping moves two or more tracks when they have to retain a direct time relationship; in a music recording, for example, this function is used when one track contains the vocal, another track contains the accompanying piano, and other tracks contain the supporting rhythm instruments.

Time displays include: the *start display*, which gives the start point of the current selection; the *end display*, which gives the end point of the current selection; *length display*, which gives the duration of the current selection; and *current time*, which indicates the present point of the play cursor in a track. Data indicators can be displayed in time code, minutes and seconds, bars and beats, or feet and frames.

Crossfades are used to smooth the transition between edits (see "Crossfade" later in this chapter).

Still another advantage of digital editing is that the edits you make can be nondestructive. **Nondestructive editing** changes only the pointers, not the data on the disk. The original soundfile is not altered regardless of what editing or signal processing you apply. ***Destructive editing***, on the other hand, changes the data on the disk by overwriting it.

This raises the question: why employ destructive editing when you can process a soundfile in any way you wish and still preserve the original? There are three answers: the editing program itself may be destructive, that is, changes to the files on the disk are temporary until the file is saved; destructive editing may be necessary when memory is limited—it is easier to save a single soundfile than both the original and the duplicate soundfiles; and it may be necessary when the edited soundfile has to be downloaded to another system.

To use a specific example, some effects plug-ins can operate in real time (that is, their intended effect is added at the same time the audio track being processed is playing back) and therefore are nondestructive. On the other hand, some effects plug-ins may be too processor-intensive for a real-time effect and necessitate destructive editing to free up memory for additional signal processing.

Editing Example

Let's go through a short editing procedure with a specific example: the guitar strums in Figure 20-4. The peaks in the waveform are where the volume goes up; the valleys are where the volume goes down. Different types of sounds produce different types of waveforms. Vowel sounds in speech and wind sounds, for example, produce waveforms with less pronounced peaks and valleys because they have softer attacks and longer decays (see 20-5).

Notice in Figure 20-4 that the accents in the fifth beat, which begins at roughly 02:45, are played more strongly compared with the accents in the previous four beats. The challenge is to move this stronger strum from the fifth beat to the first and still maintain the 4/4 time. Whenever possible define a region precisely before a volume peak and end it immediately before another volume peak. In this case, that would be from the instant before the fifth beat begins, at about 02:45, to the tail end of the beat sequence at what would be about 04:00.

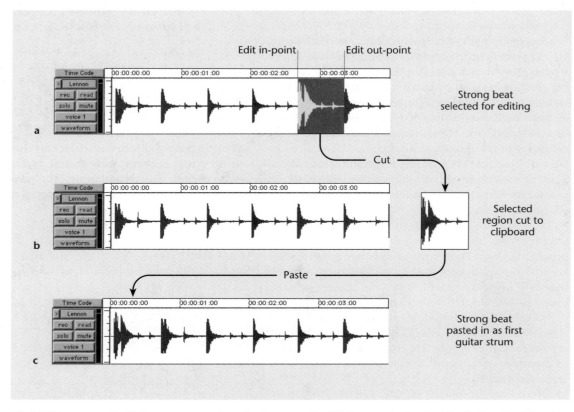

20-4 Editing example. Guitar strums must be edited to move the fifth beat to the first by (a) selecting the defined region to edit, (b) cutting it to the clipboard, and (c) pasting it to the first position.

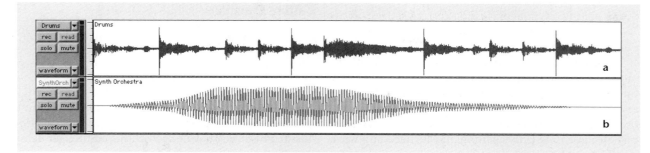

20-5 Waveforms showing percussive and sustained sounds. Editing percussive sounds (a) is easier than editing sustained sounds (b) because percussives usually have distinct breaks in the audio.

The editing procedure would be as follows: Scrub the region to be edited until you are sure of the in and out edit points. If necessary, use the *zoom* magnification tool for a more precise look at the in- and out-points. These points can be verified using the current position indicator. Click on the selector and drag the cursor from the in-point to the out-point, thereby defining the region to be edited. Once the region is defined, clicking on the Edit menu Cut command removes the edit and places it on the clipboard.

To replace the edited region at the beginning of the track, position the cursor there and click on the Edit menu Paste command. Another method of making the move is to select the shuffle mode, assuming the edit has to snap to another region, and use the grabber tool to actually move the defined region. If placement of the edit is critical to maintaining the beat, the grid mode may be the one to use.

This example is quite basic and generalized. Techniques specific to editing dialogue, sound effects, and music are discussed later in this chapter.

GENERAL EDITING GUIDELINES

As with any creative activity, there are about as many approaches as there are players. From the various techniques used in digital editing, the following are a few generally accepted guidelines. Editing tips specific to dialogue, sound effects, and music are listed in the appropriate sections later in this chapter.

■ It is physically easier and sonically cleaner to select the in and out edit points at silent spots in the track.

■ If there is no silent spot, listen and look for the attack of a dynamic, such as a hard consonant, a percussive hit, or other transient sound. The best place to edit is just before the dynamic. The quick burst of its onset usually provides enough separation from the preceding sound (see 20-6).

■ If it is not possible to find a silent or well-defined point in the track, start and end the edit at zero crossings. A *zero crossing* is the point where the waveform crosses the centerline. It denotes a value of zero amplitude and

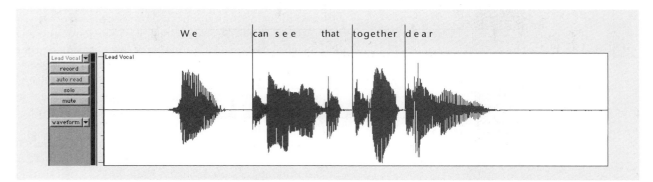

20-6 Editing before the dynamic. The best places to edit in this example are just before the hard consonants in the words "can," "together," and "dear."

divides the positive (upper) and negative (lower) parts of the waveform. This technique brings little unwanted audio to the edit when segments are pasted together.

■ If the zero-crossing technique still yields too much unwanted sound at the edit point, crossfading smoothes the edit. A *crossfade* fades out one segment while fading in another and requires sufficient material on either side of the edit point with which to work (see 20-7). Crossfades can vary in length from a few seconds to a few milliseconds. The audibility of a crossfade of a few milliseconds is virtually imperceptible.

■ Editing during a continuous sound tends to be obvious because it usually interrupts the sustain. It is better to move the edit to the beginning of the next sound, particularly if the subsequent sound is loud, because the new sound distracts the ear.

■ In performing a *fade-in*, when a signal increases in amplitude from silence to the desired level over a period of time, or a *fade-out*, when a signal gradually decreases to silence, the rates of increase or decrease can vary. The rate of a fade's curve can be *linear*—constant over the length of the fade; *logarithmic*—starting quickly and then slowly tapering off at the end; or *S-type*—starting quickly, slowing toward the middle, and then speeding up toward the end.

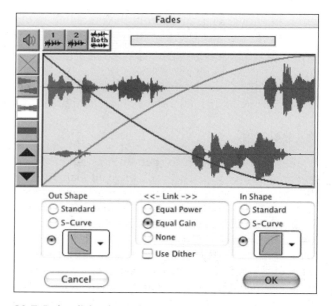

20-7 Fades dialog box. This command allows several different fade-out/fade-in curves from which to choose in crossfading between two adjoining regions.

■ Avoid using time-based effects, such as reverb and delay, during recording. It makes pasting sections from different tracks difficult because they may not match. Dry tracks are far easier to edit because they provide a more uniform sound.

Edit Decision List

An essential part of editing is the *edit decision list (EDL)*. This step-by-step list, generated during editing, contains the in and out edit points of a shot or an audio segment, the nature of the transitions, the duration of the edit, and, if needed, the source reel numbers or addresses. The format of an EDL may be charted in whatever arrangement is most functional to a production and editing system (see 20-8). Coding is usually in time code, but with film it can also be in film frame numbers. EDLs are computer-generated but can be handwritten if need be.

Produce an EDL at the outset of editing to serve as the guide to subsequent editing sessions, during which it is revised and refined until the final edit. As an accurate record of all editing events, the EDL is indispensable both for control and as a timesaver.

ORGANIZING THE EDIT TRACKS

The approach to organizing edit tracks obviously depends on the number of individual sound tracks involved. If only a few tracks are to be edited, which may be the case in, say, an interview, the procedure is apparent: intercut the questions and the answers so the continuity is logical. But when numerous sound tracks are involved, which is likely in drama and music recording, it is necessary to devise a system whereby they are organized to facilitate editing and mixing. There is no definitive way of doing this; audio editors use various approaches. The point is: before any editing begins, catalog all the sounds and keep a running log throughout the editing process; otherwise mix-ups—or worse—are inevitable. List each sound and include appropriate information, such as its content; time code address; film frame number; scene and take number; any special instructions for editing, signal processing, or mixing; and any problems with the sound, such as noise, change in ambience, sudden dropout, a fluff in pronunciation, and so on.

In productions with dialogue, music, and sound effects, first group the sound by category (often referred to, appropriately enough, as the *DME tracks*). Then further group them in each category. For example, the dialogue tracks may be arranged by character and then divided

20-8 Edit decision list.

No.	Reel	Source	Type	A time in	A time out	Comment	Cue name	Track	Time in	Time out
0			C			In court with the defense	Scene 1	0		
2	012	4	C	07:00:10:24:20	07:01:22:05:16		fill	4	02:00:00:03:40	02:00:00:28:24
3	008	4	C	07:00:10:24:20	07:01:22:05:16		fill	4	02:00:00:28:20	02:00:01:02:76
2	006	1	C	06:12:24:10:00	06:12:30:14:00			1	02:00:01:12:00	02:00:01:25:62
3	006	2	C	06:12:24:10:00	06:12:30:14:00			2	02:00:01:12:00	02:00:01:25:62
3	006	1	C	06:07:08:18:00	06:07:12:00:00			1	02:00:01:25:62	02:00:02:09:04
4	006	1	C	06:06:12:22:00	06:06:22:12:00			1	02:00:02:09:44	02:00:02:23:26
5	006	1	C	06:24:10:23:00	06:24:15:00:00			1	02:00:02:23:26	02:00:03:07:08
9	004	4	C	07:00:15:04:40	07:00:43:09:36	If Mr. Kipner wishes to	Lawyer	4	02:00:06:16:00	02:00:16:01:48
7	020	3	C	07:00:24:02:00	07:00:48:25:36	Sustained, …	judge	3	02:00:14:04:20	02:00:30:15:36
11	028	5	C	07:00:38:14:60	07:00:58:23:16		mvmnt	5	02:00:30:15:40	02:00:38:29:00
12	000	15	C	07:00:21:00:00	07:01:55:04:76	Intro music	7M1	15	02:00:30:17:20	02:01:44:18:14
13	016	16	C	07:00:21:00:00	07:01:55:04:76	Intro music	7M1	16	02:00:30:17:20	02:01:44:18:14
6	013	1	C	07:00:45:26:00	07:00:58:19:36	Hi, Carolyn, where have	MIKE@	1	02:00:38:19:40	02:00:39:27:21
7	019	1	C	07:00:45:28:00	07:00:58:12:36	Mike, what happened to	Carolyn	1	02:00:38:28:60	02:00:39:24:15
8	011	1	C	07:00:45:28:00	07:00:58:29:36	Where is Brad	MIKE@	1	02:00:38:29:20	02:00:40:04:10
9	010	1	C	07:00:45:28:00	07:00:58:19:36	He disappeared from…	Carolyn	1	02:00:41:00:40	02:00:42:19:37
10	005	1	C	07:00:45:28:00	07:00:58:12:36	Oh! My god	MIKE@	1	02:00:41:05:20	02:00:42:21:26
11	031	1	C	07:00:45:26:00	07:00:58:29:36		MIKE*	1	02:00:41:05:60	02:00:42:26:50

into dialogue from the production recording and dialogue from the automated dialogue replacement (ADR). Sound effects can be categorized as Foley, background, ambience, location, hard (or cut), soft, and design. A ***design sound effect*** does not exist in nature; it must be created. A ***hard**, or *cut, sound effect,* such as a car ignition, door slam, or pistol shot, begins and ends cleanly, requiring little adjustment in editing to remain in sync with the picture. A ***soft sound effect,*** such as crowd noise, buzzing, and oceans waves, does not have a defined beginning and end and does not explicitly synchronize with the picture.

Another way that production sound tracks can be grouped is by microphone pickup. In a multicamera program, for example, the sound pickup may be from two boom, two plant, and four audience mics, each recorded on a separate track.

In music recording, takes can be grouped by passage; for example, the first 32 measures, the final section of a movement, or a song verse. In noting each take, it saves time to indicate whether the take is worth considering for editing or should be rejected.

Once sounds have been grouped, assign them to individual tracks, determining to the extent possible those sounds that do and do not have to overlap. This not only facilitates editing but also affects a sound's placement in a track. For example, if a transition from one scene to another calls for a *dissolve* (gradually fading one scene out while fading the next scene in) and the accompanying music has to crossfade from one theme into another, the two different pieces of music must be on separate tracks. On the other hand, a cut sound effect can be placed on one track.

In editing a music selection, the best parts of several music takes are usually combined to make the composite final version, a practice called *comping*. Each take is therefore assigned to a separate track (see "Comping" later in this chapter).

FILE NAMING

As already noted, organize soundfiles using whatever system works for you. That said, there are naming systems that have become relatively common and it may be helpful to describe a few here. To make file naming as simple and easy to reference as possible, use single or few word phrases.

In projects with few soundfiles, naming them is relatively straightforward. For example, a voice-over for a commercial can be noted by talent name, take, and whether the performance is or is not a keeper. For example: Smith 1 No. The announcer's name is Smith, it is the first take, and it is not a keeper.

In more-complex productions, there are a number of approaches, depending on the components involved. The *category-based system* groups a soundfile's content under an inclusive descriptor, then names the file's other features and numbers it. For example, a dialogue soundfile may be categorized under an actor's name, say Jane Jones, followed by the scene and take numbers, the date of recording, where the scene was recorded, any notation about performance, and a reference number if a larger operating system or search engine is involved in the postproduction process. The reference number should be zero-filled (01, 02, 03, et cetera) to avoid placing the numbers out of order based on the first digit. So this particular file name might look like this: *Jones 4-3 09/12/10 Living room Swallows 3rd word 04.*

For a sound-effect file name: *Foot Concrete Scrape EXT Joe's Bar 32* indicates that the sound-effect category is Footsteps, the footstep is on concrete, it scrapes, it was recorded outside of Joe's Bar, and the search number is 32.

For a music recording, the category name might be ensemble- or song-based. If the ensemble's name is the category, it probably would be followed by the song title, then, perhaps, the take number and a note about an individual's performance and/or the overall performance. For example, using the song title as the category, the file name may be: *"Love You" 2 vocal pops OK ensem.* Or the soundfiles of individual voicings can be named and described, such as *Snare 5 sizzly&misses beats,* indicating that it is the snare drum track, take 5, and that the sound is too sizzly and the drummer misses some beats.

When a search engine and metadata are involved, a numbering scheme is essential. For example, the soundfile containing the underscore of a chase scene on a mountain road could read: *Chase Mtn Rd 0017* or simply *0017*.

DRIVE MANAGEMENT

Just as file management is essential to avoid chaos in maintaining production details, so is drive management. With the ability of disk drives to process and store an ever-increasing magnitude of data, it is imperative to also catalog the information they hold. Devise whatever recordkeeping system works for you, but keep track of which disk drives contain which files and what soundfiles are where. It seems like obvious advice, but too frequently the obvious is overlooked.

DIFFERENCES BETWEEN EDITING SOUND AND EDITING PICTURE

Editing picture is one-dimensional: one shot is cut, dissolved, or faded out and in to another shot. Once the transition has been made, in terms of editing little happens until the next transition.

Editing sound, on their other hand, is multidimensional. Sounds are layered within each shot, so editing audio becomes more than attending to transitions. In a scene an actor may be speaking to another actor with traffic outside, a clock ticking, a bath running in another room, footsteps moving back and forth, and music underscoring the action. All these elements must be edited so that the various sonic layers are properly matched and synchronized and the perspectives are maintained.

EDITING SPEECH

Among the considerations basic to editing speech are recognizing the sounds that make up words, cutting together similar and dissimilar sounds, handling emphasis and inflection, matching ambience, and taking corrective action with problem tracks.

Identifying Sounds That Make Up Words

Editing speech more often than not requires dealing with the sounds that make up a word rather than with the entire word. These sounds are called *phonemes*—the smallest unit of speech capable of conveying a distinction in meaning, such as the *p* and the *b* in the words "pat" and "bat" or the *m* and the *d* in the words "mark" and "dark."[1]

In scrubbing a sound, some sounds are easier than others to recognize. The easiest are those consonants with striking power, such as *d, k, p,* and *t*—sounds with a pronounced attack identified sonically by a click or pop and visually by a spike in the waveform. Consonants are either voiced or unvoiced. A voiced consonant, such as the *g* in "gap" or the *v* in "vary," is formed of vocal tone (resonating the vocal cords) and breath. An unvoiced

---

1. The International Phonetic Alphabet uses characters to indicate spoken sounds; but because many do not resemble letters in the alphabet, listing and explaining them here is beyond the scope of this book. Instead this discussion uses the familiar symbols of the alphabet.

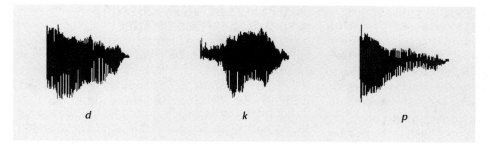

20-9 Waveforms of the consonants *d, k,* and *p*. These waveforms were generated by a female alto voice delivering them with emphasis. Waveforms of the same consonants will look different with other types of voices and deliveries.

consonant, such as the *p* in "put" or the *h* in "hot," is formed only of breath.

Voiced and unvoiced consonants can be further categorized for editing as to how their sounds are generated. The five categories are stop, friction, nasal, glide, and diphthong.

Stop consonants (also called *plosives*) are produced by stopping air in your mouth at some point and then releasing it. Voiced, they are *b* as in "bat," *d* as in "dog," and *g* as in "got." Unvoiced, they are *p* as in "pat," *t* as in "tog," and *k* as in "cot."

Friction consonants are produced when the air stream is not totally stopped but is obstructed to a narrow area, such as between the lips or between the tip of the tongue and the back of the teeth, causing friction. Voiced, they are *v* as in "vary," *z* as in "zinc," *zh* as in "seizure," and *th* as in "there." Unvoiced, they are *f* as in "fool," *s* as in "size," *sh* as in "shot," *th* as in "think," and *h* as in "host."

There is no phoneme for *c* because it can be emitted as a stop consonant, *k,* or a friction consonant, *s.*

Nasal consonants are produced through air coming out of the nose instead of the mouth. Voiced, they are *m* as in "mind," *n* as in "name," and *ng* as in "hung." There are no unvoiced nasal consonants.

Glide consonants (or *semiconsonants*) are sounds that have the quality of high-pitched vowels, such as *e* or *u,* but that serve as a consonant before or after the vowel, as in the initial sounds of "yell" and "well" and the final sounds of "coy" and "cow."[2] In other words, adjacent words influence a glide and change its sound as it is pronounced. Voiced glide consonants are *w* as in "weather," *y* as in "yawn," *l* as in "lie," and *r* as in "rug." There are no unvoiced glides.

2. Definition from *The American Heritage Dictionary of the English Language,* 4th edition (Boston: Houghton-Mifflin, 2006).

A *diphthong* is a glide in speech that begins with one sound and changes to another sound within the same syllable. Diphthongs are usually associated with vowels rather than consonants, even though they commonly occur with both types of phonemes. A voiced example of a consonant diphthong is *d-zh* as in "judge." An unvoiced example is *t-sh* as in "choose."

Figure 20-9 shows how selected consonants appear in a waveform to illustrate why understanding how they look in relation to how they sound facilitates editing speech.

The vowels *a, e, i, o,* and *u* are the most difficult to identify and separate because they lack any attack. In Figure 20-9 notice in the consonants *d* and *p* that after the initial attack the trailing *ee* sound is relatively legato as is the trailing *aa* sound after the transient *k.* Vowels usually blend with the other sounds in a word. This is particularly the case when they occur in a diphthong, such as *ay-ih* in "stay," *i-ih* in "sigh," and *aw-ih* in "boy." When vowels begin or are embedded in phrases in connected speech, their sound is more readily apparent when scrubbed at a slower speed.

One way to locate vowels, or any sound that is difficult to perceive, is to listen for differences in pitch or look for a change in the waveform, however slight. Suppose you had to cut between the *o* and the *i* in "anoint." In pronouncing the word, the *oi* combination is usually sounded as "aw-ih" (as in "boy" or "toy"), with the pitch going from lower to higher. Therefore the cut can be made just before or at the pitch change (see 20-10).

Sometimes sounds are run together and cannot be separated in the usual way. If the word *deem* were mispronounced "dreem," you would have to delete the *r.* But scrubbed forward, the sound of the *r* runs into the sound of the *e* and is difficult to hear clearly. The waveform might show a slight rise at the *r,* but by scrubbing the sound backward the point where the "ee" changes

20-10 Waveform of the word "anoint."

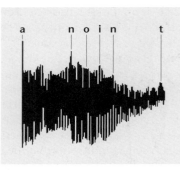

to the lower-pitched and more guttural "r" may be more apparent. If cutting between sounds is still a problem, try the crossfade technique.

Editing Similar and Dissimilar Sounds

Editing dissimilar sounds in speech is easier than editing similar sounds because they are usually distinct and flow more naturally. Consider the sentence "Sound is both challenging and creative." If we delete *both*, the edit will be made after *is* and before *challenging*. The *s* will be pasted to the *ch* and, because they are different sounds, the rhythmic transition between *is* and *challenging* is natural and distinct.

Such is not the case with speech sounds that are similar. Suppose a speaker says, "I am, as you already know, more than happy to be here" and you want to remove *as you already know*. At first glance, after the *am* and before *more* appear to be the edit points. But this could alter natural speaking rhythm because most people do not pronounce separately adjacent words that begin and end with the same letter, such as "am more." The tendency is to slur them together so, in effect, one *m* serves both the "a" and the "ore": "amore." (Test this by saying "and Donna" or "Joe's soda.") Therefore one of the *m*'s should be dropped to maintain the natural sound and rhythm. Probably the best place to edit is in the word *am*, just after the "a" and before the lips come together to form the "m" sound. Cutting between the *m* and the *o* in *more* would be difficult and awkward.

This example assumes that the speaker enunciated the "I" and "am" distinctly. What if the two words were run together and the beginning of the "a" sound is inaudible? So long as it does not change the speaker's style, cut the *m* in "am," making the contraction "I'm" sound more natural.

You can think of this technique as editing on, or to, the same sound. Another way to handle similar sounds that are adjacent is to cut within a sound. Suppose some-one says, "Nothing means more to me than my muse, or, I should say, music." Obviously, the intention was to say, "Nothing means more to me than my music." A quick look at the problem points to a cut between *my* and *muse* as the simplest edit. For the sake of illustration, let's assume "my muse" is so slurred that there is no way to cut between the words. By editing within the sound common to both words—"zi"—you can maintain the natural sound and rhythm. Cut through the *s*'s in *muse* and *music,* and paste "mus" to "sic." Clearly, the "mu" sound in both words helps make this edit possible.

If that approach doesn't work, another would be to listen if the speaker made a "zi" sound somewhere else in the recording. Assuming inflection, ambience, and tonal quality match the "s" sound in "muse" and "music," this may be a suitable alternative.

Slurring can be a problem with non-professional speakers. When possible, slightly extending a consonant that has some sonic attack can give a word added bite and clarity.

You can also edit by taking advantage of the mind's ability to hear what it expects to hear, rather than what is actually there. For example, if you continually repeat the word "tress"—the old name for a lock of hair—other words start to appear, such as "stress" and "rest"; and even though there is no "d" sound, you also hear "dress" and "stressed." Suppose a speaker says, "products and," but slurs the two words so there is no space between them and it comes out "productsand." The audio cue must end on the word "products." If there is not another us-able "s" sound to edit in, by taking, say, a final "f" sound from a word like "belief," the edit will work. The reason is that both the "s" and "f" sounds are produced in the same way—by forcing air through a constricted mouth and teeth (see "Changing Words" later in this section). This technique was developed years ago by the late audio pioneer Tony Schwartz, who called it *mnemonic editing.*

These examples of editing on, or into, the same sound involve relatively short sounds. If the sound is long, cutting away from it, once it begins and before it stops, into silence or into the middle of another sound is not recommended because the edit will be obvious. What does work, however, is cutting from a long sound that is soft to a sound with a hard attack. These guidelines also work with editing sound effects and music.

Emphasis and Inflection

Another common problem for the sound editor is dealing with emphasis and inflection. Suppose the speaker says, "How are you?" with the emphasis on "you" to express concern. For some reason the "you" is garbled, and without this word it is not possible to use the phrase. If it is unimportant, there's no problem; but if it must be kept, there are three alternatives: ask the person to deliver the line again, which may be impractical if not impossible; go through the recording to hear whether the person said "you" elsewhere with the same or almost the same inflection; or construct the word from similar sounds the speaker uttered.

To construct the word, you would have to listen for a "yoo" sound. Perhaps, with luck, the speaker may have said the word "unique," "unusual," or "continue." The "yoo" sound is part of each word; and if the emphasis, audio level, and ambience match, one of these "yoo's" may suffice.

As for inflection, suppose two characters exchange these lines:

> *Character 1:* Does it have to be that way? It doesn't have to.
>
> *Character 2:* I just don't know.
>
> *Character 1:* Well, it shouldn't have to be that way.

The director decides that character 1 should not ask a question first but make a definite statement: "It doesn't have to be that way." Character 1 has already said, "It doesn't," so we need a "have to be that way." Character 1 says "have to" three times. To take it from character 1's question and add "be that way" would mismatch the intended inflection and keep the statement a question—and an awkward one. To take the second "have to" would also sound unnatural because the *to* would probably be pronounced "tu." The third *to* would most likely be pronounced "t," which is more natural. So the final edit would butt the "It doesn't" from character 1's first statement and the "have to be that way" from character 1's second statement.

Ambience

Ambience is background sound. Other terms used synonymously are *room tone* and *presence*. The British call it **atmos**, short for *atmosphere*. Some people draw a distinction between these terms: *ambience* being any background sound that is part of a recording or has been added in postproduction; and *room tone* or *presence* being background sound recorded during actual production to provide the sound editor with the material to assemble sonically consistent backgrounds.

Editing speech recorded in different acoustic environments requires not only maintaining continuity of content but also matching the background sounds. For example, in the sentence "Good evening [breath] [cough] [breath], ladies and gentlemen," the cuts should be made after the first breath and before "ladies." Why not cut after "evening" and before the second breath? A breath would still be there to preserve the rhythm. Does it matter which breath we use?

The difference is in the ambient sounds of the two breaths. For one thing, the cough is percussive whereas "evening" is not. Thus the reverberation after the first breath sounds different from the reverberation after the second breath. If "evening" were pasted to the breath after the cough, it would sound unnatural; the ambience does not match.

In editing two statements from the same speech when one was delivered over applause and the other over silence, or when one was delivered in a room full of people and the other was delivered after most of the audience had left, the edit will be obvious unless something is done to match the different backgrounds.

One technique used to make the transition from one statement/background to the other is by diverting the listeners' attention. In the second of the preceding examples, if the ambience during one statement was quiet when the room was filled with people, and the ambience during the second statement was reflectant when the room was almost empty, you could try to locate in the recording a cough, a murmur, someone accidentally hitting the microphone, or some other distraction. Paste the distracter between the two statements (the distracter would also contain some room background) so attention is called to it momentarily instead of to the obvious change in background sound.

Another technique used to match backgrounds is to mix one background with another to even them out. This assumes that they were recorded "in the clear" before or after the event, which, by the way, should be standard procedure.

Still another approach that works well in dialogue editing is the *backfill technique*. Assume that a scene cuts from a *close-up (CU)* of character 1 to a CU of character 2, then back to a CU of character 1, with a noticeable change in background sound in the second CU. Say the drone of a plane, audible in shots 1 and 3, drops out in shot 2. The in-and-out effect of the edit will draw attention to the change in sound.

To remedy this problem, you could go through the dialogue tracks until you find the same sound with no one talking. Use time compression or expansion so that it conforms to the length of shot 2. Take a modulated section of a soundfile and paste it to the beginning and the end of the noise track for shot 2 so that the total track length equals that of the three shots. Take the original dialogue track containing the background sound and paste an unmodulated section of a track the exact length of shot 2 between shots 1 and 3. Paste a third "strip" of unmodulated track for shot 1, the dialogue without the background sound for shot 2, and a blank track for shot 3. Then mix all three tracks with picture so that the same background sound is continued through the scene (see 20-11).

If there are rhythmic sounds in the background, such as a motor or a clock, take care to preserve these rhythms when editing. You may need a *chug* or a *tick* from another part of the recording to prevent a noticeable break in the background rhythm or, if it is possible, loop the sound (addressed later in this discussion). Again, try to record the background sound separately to provide flexibility in editing.

A technique frequently used to smooth a potentially awkward transition between two ambiences is to have the sound and the picture cut at slightly different places in the shot change. For example, a man and a woman in two different rooms (say, a bathroom and an adjoining bedroom) are talking to each other. Cutting the audio

and the picture from the man to the woman at the same time would sound abrupt, if not jarring, given the obvious differences in ambience between the two rooms. To smooth the transitions, the shot of the man can begin slightly before the woman stops talking, and the dialogue of the woman can begin slightly before she is shown (see 20-12). This technique is referred to as **split editing** (see also Figures 20-13 and 20-22).

Another technique used to handle background sound is **looping**. A *loop* is a section of audio that is repeated, with its start and end having no perceptible edit point. When background sound, such as crowd, wind, or room tone, is continuous, particularly through lengthy scenes, running a continuous track could be unwieldy, take up unnecessary memory, or both. Using the automatic loop function in an NLE solves this problem. But remember: *to be effective a loop must sound continuous, not repetitive.* To help eliminate a perceptible edit point, start and end the waveform on the zero crossing.

In broadcasting, field reporting is so common that the audience has grown used to abrupt changes in levels and background sound within the same program. Nevertheless, change should be motivated and not unnecessarily jarring. With dialogue, however, audiences are more

20-11 Backfill editing technique.

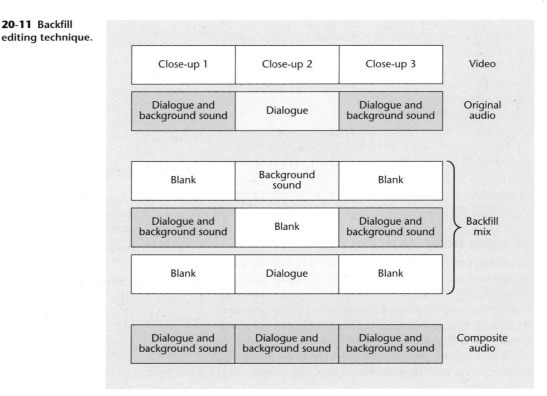

Close-up 1	Close-up 2	Close-up 3	Video
Dialogue and background sound	Dialogue	Dialogue and background sound	Original audio

Blank	Background sound	Blank	
Dialogue and background sound	Blank	Dialogue and background sound	Backfill mix
Blank	Dialogue	Blank	

| Dialogue and background sound | Dialogue and background sound | Dialogue and background sound | Composite audio |

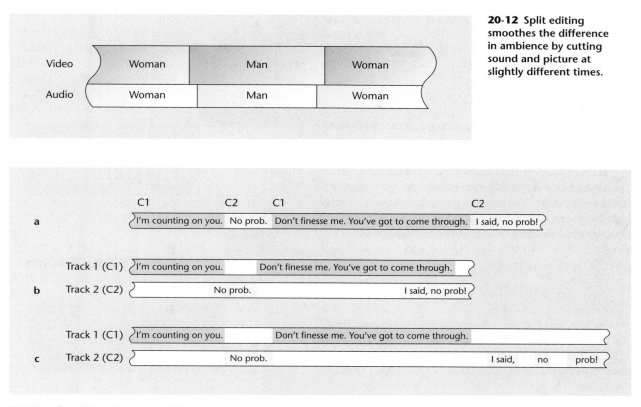

20-12 Split editing smoothes the difference in ambience by cutting sound and picture at slightly different times.

20-13 Split-editing dialogue. (a) The dialogue of characters 1 and 2 as recorded during production recording. (b) Splitting off their dialogue to facilitate overlapping the lines. (c) Splitting off their dialogue to extend a line.

apt to be annoyed by uneven background sound. The best thing to do during the recording is to anticipate the editing.

Ambience is a concern not only in editing speech; it is also an important factor when editing sound effects and music. In all three domains, ambience—background sound—is usually not effective without foreground sound. The two together bring to a scene perspective, environment, and size.

Changing Words

When dialogue is dubbed to English from another language or when films shown on television have dialogue changed to eliminate profanity or for legal reasons, trying to match lip movements to the word changes is a challenge. Too often it is obvious that they are not consistent with the words being heard. One technique to help remedy the problem is to look for labials, dentals, and fricatives because within each group lip movements are interchangeable.

Labials—m, b, and *p*—you close your lips to say. *Dentals—c, d, s,* and *t*—you speak through the teeth. *Fricatives—f, v, s,* and *z*—are produced by forcing air through a constricted mouth and teeth.

EDITING DIALOGUE

When dialogue, sound-effect, and music tracks are to be edited for a production, the dialogue tracks should be edited first. Dialogue is the most important of the three components with effects and music referenced to it.

General Guidelines for Editing Dialogue to Picture

As with so much of audio production, there are no rules for editing dialogue to picture, but there are guidelines that have evolved over the years that can make the process easier.

■ Set up a reference tone to ensure standard and uniform levels throughout dialogue editing using the signal generator provided in many software programs or in a plug-in.

■ When setting level remember that with digital sound there is no headroom. Anything above 0 level distorts. A working level of –20 dBFS provides a headroom of 20 dB before overload distortion occurs.

■ Before the actual dialogue editing begins, delete any extraneous sounds, such as clicks, pops, and background noise; unwanted or unusable dialogue; and other interferences. Put them on separate tracks, depending on their purpose, in case any may be of use later on. For example, background noise that may have been undesirable at first may become useful to smooth a dialogue transition that has different ambiences and therefore calls attention to the edit.

■ Cut any sound effects that are in the clear—with no dialogue—and paste them onto a separate track in case they may be of use when editing the sound-effect track.

■ Cut dialogue recorded in production that is specified for dialogue rerecording and paste it to a separate track reserved for this purpose. Leave in any noises, such as lip smacks, breaths, sighs, inhales, and exhales, that may be useful to the director and the actor for interpretive reference during ADR.

■ Note any gaps created by transfers from the production track(s) and, where necessary, indicate what needs to be filled with matching background; what the nature of that background should be; and, if available on any production track, its location.

■ Make sure that any replacement dialogue from other production takes—words, syllables, or phonemes—matches the tone of the performance as well as the perspective, pitch, and level.

■ If there is a noticeable change in the loudness of the dialogue when cutting from one shot to the next, move the edit point of the incoming dialogue to just before the shot change. The relative loudness of the incoming dialogue will distract from the abruptness of the otherwise awkward transition (see "Audio-leading-video and Video-leading-audio" later in this chapter).

■ When a picture cut occurs during a dialogue line, edit the audio slightly off the cut. If audio and video change at the same time, it may create an abruptness that calls attention to the cut (see 20-14).

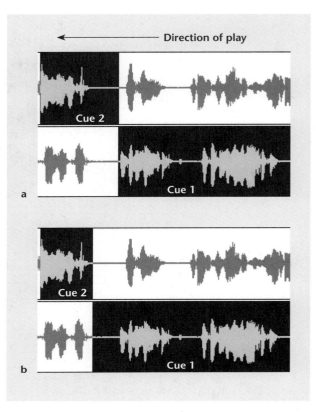

20-14 Shifting audio so that it doesn't emphasize a video cut. (a) Original edit position. (b) Incoming dialogue moved to just behind the video cut.

■ To smooth background ambience from one take to another, it helps to extend the outgoing ambience under the incoming dialogue instead of fading it out beforehand (see 20-15).

■ In editing an ADR track, it is easier to shorten one that is too long than it is to lengthen one that is too short (even using expansion or alignment software). It is usually quicker and easier to begin by dealing with the obvious sync points—those with hard consonants—than it is to tackle the ones with little or no audible striking power. Edits should be straight cuts, adjusting for sync with the production recording by using compression, expansion, or alignment rather than by employing a crossfade, which would create a doubling of the actor's voice.

■ In preparing the edited dialogue tracks for the mix, unused tracks should be laid out in sync against the main

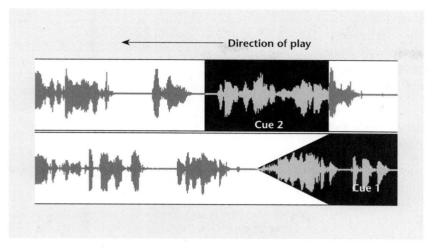

20-15 Smoothing a transition in ambience by crossfading the incoming audio under the outgoing audio before the first shot ends and the second shot begins. This type of transition also works well with sound-effect and underscoring transitions.

tracks so that the mixer can easily access them by just using the fader. Tracks should be split to facilitate any necessary changes in perspective; they should also be split if the various elements are different enough to require separate adjustments in equalization. Place dialogue requiring special effects—such as reverb, pitch shifting, phasing, or telephone equalization—on separate tracks assigned for each particular purpose (see 20-16).

■ Keep a record of the dialogue takes of every scene. Note what works and does not work dramatically as well as any background sound or other noises, and, if possible, rate the takes in terms of acceptability. In refitting a dialogue line, you never know what interpretation of a phrase, emphasis of a phoneme, hard or soft breath, or quieter or louder background sound from an unused take will come in handy.

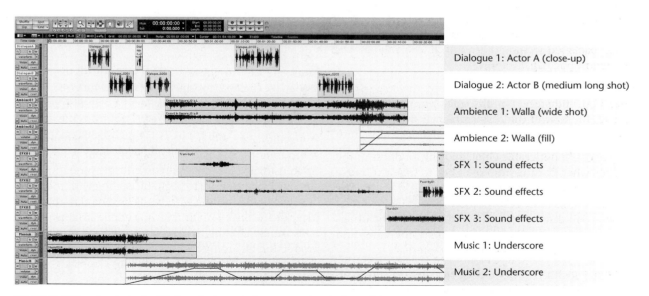

Dialogue 1: Actor A (close-up)

Dialogue 2: Actor B (medium long shot)

Ambience 1: Walla (wide shot)

Ambience 2: Walla (fill)

SFX 1: Sound effects

SFX 2: Sound effects

SFX 3: Sound effects

Music 1: Underscore

Music 2: Underscore

20-16 Splitting tracks to facilitate adjustments in perspective during mixing.
For greater ease in editing, it is better to group the tracks, if possible, as shown here.

Composite Dialogue

It is not unusual for a line of dialogue to be built from different takes in the production recording, from the ADR, or both. A director may prefer three words from take 4, one word from take 7, two from take 8, and a breath from take 11. These "best" takes are then combined into what becomes the optimal dialogue track. Of course, this technique assumes that the various takes, when combined, flow naturally in relation to delivery, synchronization with picture, and ambience (see also "Comping" later in this chapter).

Dialogue Database

Because of the obvious importance of dialogue, to say nothing of the inconvenience and the expense of having to redo any of it once production recording and ADR are completed, creating a database of every line recorded and putting it on hard disk is a boon to the editor.

Once the dialogue takes are chosen, printed, and cataloged, add to the catalog all the remaining unselected dialogue by date and time recorded, scene and take numbers, and word content. It also helps to note the reason(s) why unselected dialogue was not used. Then, during editing, if there is a problem in the working dialogue that escaped detection, such as an almost imperceptible background sound, a slight mispronunciation, or a bit too much emphasis on a word, the editor can search the dialogue database for a suitable replacement that is intact or fabricate a replacement from appropriate sounds in the dialogue recording.

Dialogue Processing

In processing production dialogue, four problems typically occur: ring-off, additive ambience, defective or unusable dialogue, and synchronizing dialogue to picture.

Ring-off occurs when a dialogue line ends with the ambient ring of a room, and another line begins with that ring decaying under it. This can be a problem, for example, when someone is entering a room and the ring-off is decaying under the line of the entering actor. In editing, cut the ring-off and either mix it with digital reverb on a controlled basis, thereby blending the ambient qualities of the two dialogue lines so that continuity is maintained underneath, or drop the ring-off and create the appropriate background values using digital reverb only. If when cutting to the entering actor, ring-off of the old word is still perceptible under the new word, even after doctoring with digital reverb, use a sound effect to cover the transition or use the crossfade technique, with the director's concurrence of course.

Additive ambience occurs when several actors are recorded at the same time on separate tracks of a multitrack recorder and the multiple room tones become cumulative when the tracks are mixed. To avoid additive ambience, cut from one track to another to keep the single room sound on each track. In the case of overlapping dialogue, try to close down the room sound through digital reverb. Failing that—or if too many voices overlap, making the digital reverb processing sound too unnatural—dialogue rerecording is the likely alternative.

Defective or unusable dialogue occurs when, for example, actors are body-miked and stand very close to one another or hug, covering words; or when an unwanted sound, such as clothes rustling, an object being bumped, or voice cracking, masks a word. If there is no time to retake a scene, or if these problems go unnoticed and reediting the material is not worth the time or expense, there are solutions. Editing in the same syllable(s) or word(s) from another part of the track is one alternative. Another is to expand the syllable(s) or word(s) so that they overlap the defect. In both cases, ambience must be processed so that it matches the original. If the dialogue track was produced in ADR, ambience, of course, is not a problem.

To facilitate editing dialogue, split-edit the dialogue track into two or more separate tracks. This makes it easier to extend lines that may have been cut too short during picture editing, to compress lines that are too long to sync with picture, to overlap voices, and to carry over lines from one scene to the next. Such splitting off of dialogue also makes it easier to adjust levels in the mix (see 20-13).

Synchronizing dialogue to picture is a common problem when the dialogue being edited is not from the production recording but from ADR. Frequently, when the ADR recording is matched against the picture, it is not always in sync with the lip and mouth movements of the actors. Therefore ADR tracks must be processed to be brought in sync with the tracks of production dialogue, which, of course, are in picture sync.

Various techniques are used to synchronize dialogue. One of the more common is digital time compression or expansion to shorten or lengthen a dialogue line without affecting its pitch, loudness, or timbre (refer back to Figure 7-20). Another is to use a dedicated alignment program that can automatically synchronize two audio signals. For example, in working with a dialogue line from a production recording that has been edited with

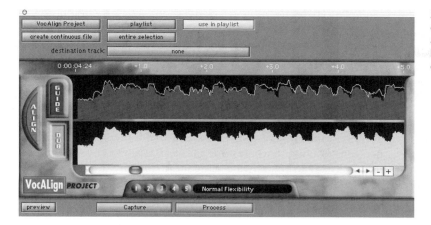

20-17 Adjusting the timing of one audio signal to match that of another. This software program can be used with ADR, foreign-language dialogue, sound effects, and music.

words that are in different parts of a sentence, alignment software can guide how to cut the ADR take so that it is in sync with the line from the production recording and therefore the picture (see 20-17).

Alignment programs have applications in other types of audio production as well. In music recording, for example, such software is used to tighten background vocals, double lead vocals, accompany instrumental tracks, and line up tracks against a dominant beat.

EDITING SOUND EFFECTS

Many of the techniques used in dialogue editing are also used in editing sound effects. If there is an essential difference between the two, dialogue editing mostly involves fixing, whereas sound-effect editing also involves creating. Among the typical challenges an SFX editor faces are building backgrounds, building effects, and matching perspective.

Building Backgrounds

In shooting picture or producing material for radio, segments are usually recorded out of order. In the various takes, background sound may change. For example, in film and video a scene may be recorded in a master shot and in several cutaways. Even if the location stays the same, background sound may change over time, however slightly, so it may not match a particular shot. Or a scene may be recorded in different areas of the same location. Or a required background sound may not be easily obtained during production and must be created in the studio. Or it may be less costly to produce a background on a computer than to hire people to perform

and record it. In such cases it is the editor's role to build the appropriate background sound.

For example, a scene requires the sound of a storm. This particular storm requires several different sonic components—wind, rain, thunder claps, and thunder rumble—and each component must have a certain texture: wind that is fierce and howling, rain that pelts down, and thunder that tears and booms and then rolls into a long rumble. By processing and layering various prerecorded tracks of wind, rain, and thunder, an editor can build the appropriate storm effect.

If a restaurant scene calls for typical background sounds, instead of hiring a loop group to do the voices and a Foley artist to produce the other effects, an editor can build the background with sound effects of glasses clinking, cutlery clattering, and conversational hubbub with, perhaps, a laugh or two to complete the layering.

When building a background of traffic sounds, an editor can use the motor hum of cars moving, a horn sounding here and there, the screech of brakes, and a siren in the distance. If the scene has a particular visual rhythm, the editor can cut the sound effects to complement it, adding yet another sonic dimension to the background.

Building Effects

An SFX editor is often called on to create a specific sound effect by building it. The effect may be needed because it does not exist in the natural world, is unavailable due to poor production planning, to save the expense of paying for sound personnel and studio time to produce it, or because it is simply easier to create on a computer.

The sound of fire, for example, may require the components of crackle to convey the licking sound of its mounting threat, roar to enhance its intensity, and the whoosh of small explosions to add punctuated impacts. To build the sound of a fierce cannon firing, an editor can use the sounds of a nitro blast to give it a heavy black-powder feel, an old-fashioned cannon shot to give it bite, and a mortar shell whiz-by to add reality to the flight of the projectile.

Another example of building an effect is re-creating the sound of a dam bursting. There are the crackling sounds of the dam beginning to come apart; the deep-throated, fuller, more intense sound of the dam breaking; the roar of the onrushing water, first in a torrent and then leveling off to an intense rush; and, finally, the crash, roar, and boom of the dam crumbling. Soundfiles for each of these components can be created, manipulated, and processed by the sound editor to create the overall effect.

Matching Perspective

In dealing with different but related or connected sounds in the same locale, an editor must make sure that perspectives match. For example, in editing the screech of tires to a car crash, the crash has to sound as though it came out of the screeching tires. It sometimes happens that the screech is heard close up and the crash far away, as if the sounds, though related, occurred in two different locations. The same thing happens in editing a police siren to the sounds of a screech and a stop. The siren is heard in one perspective and the screech and the stop are heard in another because either the levels or the ambiences differ.

There is also the problem of ensuring that the sound effect is coming from the shot's environment. If the ambience of the effect sounds as though it is coming from outside the shot, or, in the parlance of audio, *on top of the film,* the editor has to mix the effect into the appropriate background sound.

Guidelines for Editing Sound Effects

Here are some other guidelines that may prove helpful in editing sound effects:[3]

■ Digitize sound effects at full level, even the quieter ones. When signal processing is used, this helps prevent noise buildup and aids in masking noise. Level can always

---

3. A few of these guidelines are based on Marvin A. Kerner, *The Art of the Sound Effects Editor* (Boston: Focal Press, 1989) and Jay Rose, *Producing Great Sound for Film and Video,* 3rd edition (Boston: Focal Press, 2008).

be lowered when called for. When editing SFX, however, do it at the average level relative to their intended release format. Not only do effects sound different at high and low levels, but, remembering the equal loudness principle, effects (and music) processed at a higher-than-normal level and played back at a lower-than-normal level affect the lowest and highest frequencies by reducing their loudness. Conversely, if the audio level is too low when playing back, the bass and treble frequencies could be too loud when set at a normal level and overwhelm the SFX's midrange.

■ It is easier to edit the SFX tracks after the dialogue and music tracks are in place. That way the editor has a better sense of determining how to adjust levels so that an effect is neither too loud nor too quiet; whether an effect is needed to fill a sonically sparse section of the sound track; or whether an effect planned for a particular shot becomes unnecessary because it would be masked by the music or ambience.

■ Recall from Chapter 15 that a single sound effect may be composed of several different sounds. For example, opening a door may include the rattle of the doorknob, the turn of the knob, the click of the bolt, perhaps a squeak and a scrape of the door opening, the click of the knob release, and the squeak, scrape, and thud of the door closing.

■ Cut the effect as close to the first point of sound as possible. The effect may be preceded by low-level ambience or noise, the audible rush of a channel being opened, or some extraneous sound associated with the effect.

■ Sound effects are ordinarily recorded and placed in a track in mono because most are single-source sounds. Ambience, however, is ordinarily not a single-source sound and is therefore handled in stereo or surround.

■ Most sounds have a natural decay, or tail. A sound may start at once but does not stop that way; even transient sounds have some trail-off. Cutting into the tail will be noticeable unless another sound comes in over it and "washes it out," it is crossfaded with another sound, or if the cutoff occurs with a shot change to an entirely different scene. If the decay is too long for a shot, try making the cut somewhere in the middle of the effect (see 20-18).

■ When editing in a sound effect that occurs off-screen, it is usually distracting to lay it over dialogue. Spot the effect between two lines of dialogue.

■ Some sounds, such as a horse's hoofbeats, are difficult to sync with picture. All four hooves cannot be synched. Generally, editors follow the first front leg and then establish the horse's rhythm.

■ In "Editing Music to Picture" later in this chapter, it is suggested that an abrupt sound cut will not be as jarring if it is covered by an equally abrupt picture cut. Some SFX editors prefer to avoid such a sharp change in sound by overlapping a split second or two of background on either side of the transition.

■ In fight scenes it is not uncommon to see an actor's head-jerk occur before the attacker's fist is close enough to the face. The choice is to match the sound of the chin-sock to the head-jerk or at the point where the fist is closest to the chin. Neither choice will be completely satisfactory, so the sound effect should simply be placed where it looks best. Also, the sound of the hits should vary: a punch to the face sounds different from a punch to the head, upper body, lower body, and so on.

■ If when looping an effect it is difficult to achieve a seamless loop, try a very short crossfade at the audible loop point. It should smooth the apparent beginning point of the repetition each time the sound is repeated.

■ Increasing the speed of an effect can add excitement; decreasing the speed can make the effect sound bigger. Be careful that pitch is not sufficiently altered to change the sound's character.

■ Using pitch shifting on one channel of a stereo effect can make it sound bigger. Doing the same with hard effects can make them sound wider.

■ Organize the SFX tracks so that they are grouped: the mono effects on, say, tracks 1 through 8, the stereo tracks on 9 through 16, the ambience tracks on 17 through 20, tracks that require special signal processing on 21 through 24, and so on.

EDITING MUSIC

A music editor is usually a trained musician. This is particularly helpful in working with the composer. That said, editing music is difficult to discuss in any detail because it involves using one language—the printed word—to explain another language—the notes, chords, rhythms, and other features of abstract, temporal sound. Although there is some similarity between editing speech and

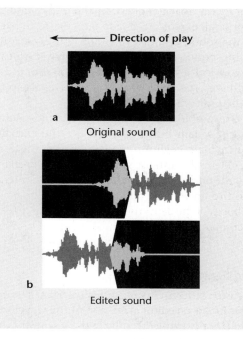

20-18 Cutting out the middle to shorten an effect.
(a) Original sound. (b) Shortened effect smoothed with a crossfade.

editing music, such as consideration of space, rhythm, loudness, and inflection (intonation), there are also differences. Music contains so many simultaneous sonic elements that matching sounds is more complex, and slight editing mistakes are more easily detected. In music editing, you have to consider cutting on the right accent to maintain rhythm, tonality, relative loudness, and style. If any of these elements are aurally incompatible, the edit will be obvious.

Generally, edits that heighten intensity cut together well, such as going from quiet to loud, slow to fast, or nonrhythmic to rhythmic. A transition from a seemingly formless or meandering phrase to one that is obviously structured and definite also tends to work.

Cutting to Resolution

Perhaps one of the most useful guidelines is to cut before an accent, a downbeat, or a resolution. Think of the final chord in a musical phrase or song. Although it resolves the music, it is the chord before it that creates the anticipation of and the need for resolution; it sets up the last chord. Edit on the anticipatory note—the one requiring some resolution, however brief—so that it leads naturally to the note being joined.

For example, if the music's progression is: *da, da, da, da-da* and the edit is to be made to "ta tum," the cut would be made just after the third "da" because it sets up the final "da-da." So the progression would be: *da, da, da, ta tum.*

Preserving Tempo

Most Western music has a *time signature*—2/4 ("two-four"), 3/4, 4/4, 3/8, 6/8, and so forth. The first numeral indicates the number of beats in each measure; the second indicates the value of the note that receives each beat. For example, in 4/4 time there are four beats to a measure and each quarter-note receives a whole beat; in 3/8 time there are three beats to the measure and each eighth-note receives a beat. In editing music, you have to preserve the beat, or the edit will be noticeable as a jerk or stutter in the tempo. If you cannot read music or no sheet music exists, pay close attention to the waveform of the music to discern the tempo (see 20-4). Listen to the beat and look for the resulting spike in the waveform.

Regardless of the number of beats in a measure, some beats are strong and others are weak. When you tap your foot to a song, it usually comes down on the strong beat, or *downbeat,* and lifts on the weak beat, or *upbeat.* A song in 3/4 time, known as waltz time, is characterized by a strong beat followed by two weak beats—*one,* two, three, *one,* two, three. Beats in 2/4 time follow a *one,* two, *one,* two, strong beat/weak beat pattern. This is a rudimentary explanation of a complex subject, to be sure. The point is that when editing tempo, you have to be aware of preserving the number of beats per measure as well as the accents. In a piece in 3/4 time, if you cut after the first beat in a measure, the beat you cut to should be a weak beat, and another weak beat should follow; if you cut after the third beat in a measure, you would cut to a strong beat with two weak beats to follow.

Repetitive Measures

One way to shorten or lengthen audio material through editing is to use repetitive measures in the music. These measures can be cut out to shorten material, which is obvious. Lengthening the audio using a digital system is relatively straightforward: repetitive measures can be extended by digital time expansion or by copying, pasting, and sliding them.

Preserving the tempo in music editing is not an isolated consideration. There are other factors, such as looping, key signature, comping, and musical style and texture.

Looping

Looping is often used in dealing with tempo in music. Unlike dealing with sound effects, where the concern is making sure the loop sounds continuous and not repetitive, with music the concerns are making sure that the loop both serves the score and, if necessary, can be adjusted to changes in tempo. Although most NLE systems have a looping function, many require additional software that makes it possible to adjust the loop's tempo without altering pitch or sacrificing sound quality. Although the available programs go about the procedure in different ways, generally the software looks for transients in the loop, breaks the loop into slices at the selected transients, and then adds markers. In changing the loop's tempo, the start point of each slice shifts to conform to the change. For example, if there are slices at, say, every eighth-note and the original loop is changed from 120 beats per minute (bpm) to 130 bpm, the software moves the slice points closer to retain the eighth-note relationships at the new tempo.

When editing loops, keep in mind the following tips:

- Cut at the beginning of the first beat in the measure or bar, preferably immediately before the first cycle of the attack.

- Edit immediately before the attack begins. Cutting into the transient could alter the envelope of the voicing and change its character.

- The start and end points of the loop should start at the zero crossing.

- If the edit point is perceptible, perform a very small fade-in at the beginning of a loop and a very small fade-out at the end of the loop, or do a very small crossfade.

- Be sure to assign a file name to a loop and note the tempo and the number of measures in the loop's file name.[4]

---

4. From Todd Souvignier, "Closing the Loop," *Electronic Musician,* April 2003, p. 39.

Key Signature

Just as most music has a time signature to regulate its tempo, it also has a *key signature*—E major or B minor, for example—that determines its overall tonality. Some keys are compatible: when you change from one to the other, it sounds natural, or "in tune" (see 20-19). Other keys are not, and pasting them together is jarring, or "out of tune." Unless it is for effect, or if the picture justifies the change (discussed later in this chapter), edited music should sound consonant so as not to be noticed.

Another way to cover a bad key change in an edit is with pitch shifting. It is usually easier to bring one of the offending keys into musical compatibility with the other key than it is to look for a sonic compromise between the two. Using an attention-grabber in the dialogue such as a cough or a distracting sound effect can also cover an unmusical edit, but consider this approach only when there is no alternative.

Comping

Comping takes the best part (or parts) of each recorded track and combines them into a composite final version. In theory comping music seems straightforward: edit together all the best takes of every note, phrase, section,

lyric, or whatever. In practice, however, that approach often does not work because, overall, the music may lack coherence, sound too mechanical, or result in a part from one take not making sense when played next to a part from another take. There could also be problems in matching pitch—the segments may not be in tune; in the timing—performances may not have quite the same tempo or phrasing; in delivery—one segment may have a more impassioned performance than the another; or in recording quality—segments may not have the same sonic fidelity. Maintaining perspective is critical if comping is to be aesthetically successful. It is analogous to a painter who must work close to a canvas on a detail but must step back to view the entire painting to determine if the detail works (see 20-20).

Planning in the recording session for the possibility of later comping can save time and reduce aesthetic problems when trying to edit together the best takes. Any one or combination of three approaches can be taken: the vertical, the horizontal, and the layered.

In the *vertical approach*, tracks are set up in relation to their specific console and processing settings and are labeled, say, 01, 02, 03, et cetera. Take 1 is 01, take 2 is 02, and so on. In laying out the tracks, keep one track empty, above or below the recorded tracks. In a 20-track

20-19 Compatible or consonant music keys.

Music in this key will segue with →	First Choice	Second Choice	Third Choice	Fourth Choice
A	A	D	E	F♯/G♭ minor
A♯ (B♭)	A♯ (B♭)	D♯ (E♭)	F	G minor
B	B	E	F♯	G♯/A♭ minor
C	C	F	G	A minor
C♯ (D♭)	C♯ (D♭)	F♯ (G)	G♯ (A♭)	A♯/B♭ minor
D	D	G	A	B minor
D♯ (E♭)	D♯ (E)	G♯ (A)	A♯ (B♭)	C minor
E	E	A	B	C♯/D♭ minor
F	F	B♭	C	D minor
F♯ (G♭)	F♯ (G♭)	B	C♯ (D♭)	D♯/E♭ minor
G	G	C	D	E minor
G♯ (A♭)	G♯ (A♭)	C♯ (D♭)	D♯ (E♭)	F minor

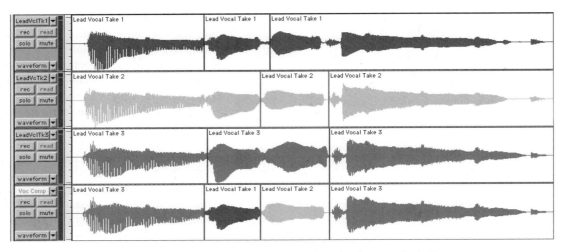

20-20 Comping. Fragments from takes 1 and 2 have been combined with most of take 3 to create the final product.

recording, the *open,* or *comp, track* would be 01 or 21. After identifying the best segments within each take, it is just a matter of dragging them to the appropriate part of the comp track.

The *horizontal approach* is used mainly for dealing with tempo. Choose the tempo that is called for, then set up the beginning of the material to become bar 1. Create a *click track* using MIDI or an audio sample and determine how many count-off bars will be used to cue the start of the audio. Record take 1 at bar 101, take 2 at bar 201, and so on. If the recording is a song, for example, note when the intro, verse, and chorus occur in each take by numbering the intro of each take 101, 201, et cetera. Assuming the structure of the song does not change from take to take, if the verse starts at bar 12, the verse numbering for each take would be 112, 212, and so on. If the chorus starts at bar 25, the successive takes would be numbered 125, 225, et cetera.

In the *layered approach,* the same track or group of tracks is used to record individual takes. This creates a new virtual playlist each time a recording is made. In comping, switch between the playlists to audition the takes and identify the preferred section to be selected and copied. Then paste it either onto a clean playlist on the same track or to a new vertical track.[5]

Regardless of the approach to comping, it helps to color-code takes or parts of takes by quality. This makes it easier later on to recall the judgments made at the

time of the recording. It also helps to use as few source tracks as possible. Having too much material can slow the creative process considerably—to say nothing of how assessing and reassessing many tracks can dull aesthetic perspective.

Style and Texture

Each type of music and musical group has a unique style and texture. This distinguishes the style of jazz from rock, the texture of one voice from another although both may have identical registers, or one group from another although both may play the same instruments and music.

Editing from the same piece of music usually does not present a problem in matching style and texture so long as you follow the other guidelines for editing. But if the music is from different sources, matching elements can be a problem. Normally, you would not edit different styles—a piece of classical music to rock music just because they had the same tempo, or a dance band to a military band just because they were playing the same song. The differences in sound would make the edits conspicuous and distracting.

Editing Music to Picture

In editing music to picture, the edits must make musical sense and have an identifiable purpose. Here are a few guidelines.

■ Editing loud, fast symphonic music to that of a soft, quiet trio seems disconcerting, but if a picture cuts from a scene of violent destruction to one of desolation, the

---

5. Approaches to comping from Tal Herzberg, "Comping as a Way of Life," *EQ,* September 2002, p. 38.

edit makes sense. In fact, it would also make sense to cut from loud, jarring music to silence.

■ Changing from a dull tonality to a bright one, or vice versa, within the same scene or shot is not recommended generally. But if the edit is played behind, say, a change from night to day or day to night, or from the anticipation of sad news actually being good news, the picture would justify it.

■ Editing together two different styles, perhaps the most awkward type of change, is acceptable if the picture covers it. Cutting from Mozart to wall-of-sound rock would normally offend our sensibilities—but not if the picture cuts from a shot of an elegant palace ball in eighteenth-century Vienna to the rebellious protests at the 1968 Democratic convention in Chicago.

■ When editing music to picture, do not mask dialogue and sound effects. Sometimes, however, a smooth music edit is difficult to make. A common technique to hide the obvious edit is to mix the music level under a louder sound in the mix, such as a sound effect.

■ Keep edits and crossfades on the beat, or the beats will be out of sync and heard as double beats.

■ Because of the multitrack nature of drum recording, when moving tracks around keep them grouped and edit them simultaneously. Cutting off the extended decay of the overhead cymbals at the edit point may make this difficult, however. Extending the cymbals' decay region by crossfading it slightly past the edit point is one way to disguise the transition.

■ When shortening a musical cue, retain any transitional phrase(s) between any key change(s), or the edit will sound "out of tune."

■ Editing song lyrics to play under dialogue (or any speech) creates the potential of bifurcating audience attention by forcing the listener-viewer to concentrate on one set of words or another. It could also compromise intelligibility. If possible, establish the lyrics in the clear long enough for the audience to get their gist before lowering their level for the entry of dialogue; or use lyrics the audience would be familiar with so that they provide meaning and "tone" without its being essential to concentrate on them.

Automatic Music Editing

Prerecorded music libraries are a source of underscoring material for many. Even when a selection suits the sound/ picture relationship aesthetically, it is often a problem finding one that also has the exact timing required for a cue. Software can handle the problem. Generally, it breaks down the music selections into phrases of various lengths; these phrases can even be linked to more precisely contour a timing requirement. Be wary, however, of programs with music that sounds stylized and stereotypical and is played mechanically.

TRANSITIONS

Sequencing two sounds (or shots) involves creating a *transition,* which helps establish pace. In audio four techniques are used to make transitions: segue or cut, crossfade, soft cut, and fade-out/fade-in.

Segue and Cut

Segue (pronounced "seg-way") is a musical term that means "follow on." In radio it refers to the playing of two or more recordings with no live announcing in between or live announcing over the segue. In a broader sense, segue is analogous to the term *cut* used to describe transitions in TV and film. In this context cutting from one element to another means establishing a picture or sound immediately after the previous picture or sound stops, and doing it at once, not gradually. In discussing the effects of this particular type of transition, we use the broader term *cut.*

The *cut* is standard language for a small related change within the same time, place, or action, such as cutting from someone waking up, to washing, to eating breakfast, or cutting from a striking match and the eruption of a flame to an alarm sounding at a fire station. Cutting creates transitions that are sharp and well defined, picking up the rhythm of sequences and giving them a certain briskness. Cutting also tightens the pace of a production because the change from one sound (or picture) to another is quick. Due to its aesthetic value, the cut is also used for larger transitions, such as cutting from a person walking out the door in the morning to coming back in at dinnertime, or from the eruption of flames to the charred remains.

The cut, in effect, butts two different sounds or groups of sounds together; in that regard it is like an edit. Like with the edit, you have to give some thought to whether the effect is natural. Cutting from a fast, loud sound to one that is very slow and quiet, or vice versa, may be too abrupt; segueing two songs in keys that are incompatible may create a transition that has unwanted dissonance; or cutting from a program about folks living in poverty to a commercial for a disinfectant may raise questions of taste.

Dramas and documentaries provide more of an opportunity to make unnatural cuts because the action or picture can cover the transition, like cutting from a furious storm to the quiet calm of its aftermath, or from a deeply moving love scene to a raucously funny bachelor party. The cut has both an informational and an aesthetic function, and either purpose justifies its use.

Crossfade

The *crossfade,* in addition to its corrective uses in editing, is another type of transition for smaller changes in time, locale, and action, although you can vary the length of these changes somewhat by increasing or decreasing its duration (see 20-21). The crossfade accomplishes the same thing as the fade-out/fade-in, but aesthetically it is softer, more fluid, and more graceful. It also maintains, rather than breaks, rhythmic continuity and pace.

You can produce a crossfade in a number of ways, depending on the crossfade times and the loudness levels of the sounds when they cross. Usually, it is more aesthetically satisfying to cross the sounds at the moment they are at full and equal loudness. This keeps audience attention "stage-center" with no loss of focus or gap in continuity, which could occur if the crossfade were made at lower levels. Crossfading at too low a level could sound like a sloppy fade-out/fade-in. These suggestions assume that the crossfade is not being used for the type of corrective purposes discussed earlier in this chapter.

Soft Cut

A *soft cut* is a term used with picture when a shot change is brief but not quite as abrupt as a cut nor as deliberate as a dissolve. In audio, a soft cut can be used for transitions that need a quick yet aesthetically graceful change; to cover a minor technical apparency without appreciably affecting rhythm, tempo, pace, or dramatic intent; or to provide, as the term suggests, a somewhat gentler way of moving from one shot or scene to another.

Fade-out/Fade-in

The *fade-out/fade-in* transition is used to make a clearly defined change from one time, place, and action to another. Aesthetically, it is gentler than the cut; it gives a stronger sense of finality to a scene that is ending and a sense of new possibilities to the scene that is beginning.

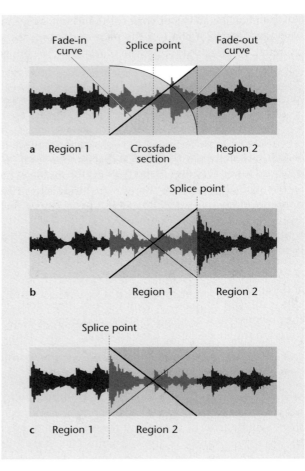

20-21 Common types of crossfades. (a) *Standard,* or *centered, crossfade* on both sides of the splice point. In this example the fade-in curve is linear and smooth, and the fade-out curve is gradual, reducing level steadily. (b) *Pre-crossfade* creates a crossfade before the splice point, thus maintaining the level of the beginning of region 2 instead of fading across it. Pre-crossfade is useful if there is a strong percussive downbeat or a loud sound at the beginning of region 2. (c) *Post-crossfade* generates the crossfade after the splice point. It is useful in maintaining the level of region 1 until it ends, to keep, for example, a strong upbeat or an exclamatory sound that occurs at the end of region 1.

In TV and film, the rate of the fade-out/fade-in depends on the picture. Generally, the type of fade used provides not only an aesthetic effect but an informational one as well. A slow fade-out and fade-in with silence between suggests a complete break from one action to another. The change is rather marked because it so obviously and deliberately stops one scene and starts another and also because it changes the pace or rhythm of the material. You could use this type of transition to bridge the time between a student's going off to college as a freshman and her graduation, or to link a police car's hot pursuit of bank robbers and the thieves' being booked at the police station. Faster fades suggest shorter lapses of time, smaller changes of location, or fewer events in a series of actions. They still provide a definite break in the presentation, but their quicker rate implies that less has happened. You should not, however, consider these guidelines as prescriptive. There are no formulas for how long transitions should be relative to the scenes they bridge; it is a matter of what feels right.

Audio-leading-video and Video-leading-audio

Transitions involving sound and picture often do not occur at the same time for dramatic or technical reasons. When there is a picture transition, the sound transition may not be simultaneous or vice versa; the audio or video leads or lags a portion of the previous edit (see 20-22). These are split-editing techniques known as *audio-leading-video* and *video-leading-audio,* which are also called *L-cuts.*

When the sound of the incoming scene starts before the corresponding picture appears, the audio is leading the video. For example, the picture shows a boy building a model airplane as the sound of a jet fighter fades in. The picture then cuts to a shot of the grown-up boy as the pilot.

When the picture of a new scene starts before the sound of the old scene has finished, the video is leading the audio; for example, the audio of a romantic song in a scene showing a couple who has just met carries into the next scene, showing the couple dancing on their honeymoon.

LISTENING FATIGUE

Editing for long periods of time can cause *listening fatigue*—the reduced ability to perceive or remember the nuances of sound. In computer editing the problem can be compounded by eyestrain and physical discomfort (see Chapter 2). If listening fatigue sets in during editing, such features of sound as tempo, inflection, and tonality are continually mismatched, cuts are slightly off, and it is difficult to keep track of what should be edited to what.

One way to defer listening fatigue is to work in a quiet acoustic environment with no predominance of mid-range frequencies because they tend to tire the listener faster. If a recording or loudspeaker system has too much midrange, equalize the monitor playback by slightly boosting the lower frequencies anywhere between 50 Hz and 150 Hz and the frequencies above 10,000 Hz. This balances the sound and reduces its harshness and intensity. You can also attenuate the frequencies between 1,000 Hz and 3,500 Hz, although this may reduce intelligibility. It is also important to remember to bring down playback gain after turning it up, as is often required to better hear an edit point. Finally, take regular breaks to rest the ears and anything else that needs relaxation.

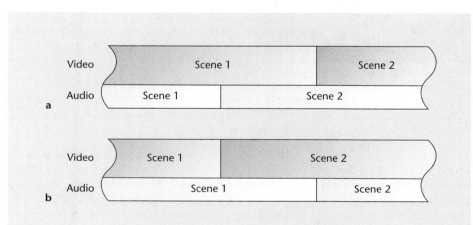

20-22 (a) Audio-leading-video split edit and (b) video-leading-audio split edit.

MAIN POINTS

▶ Editing permits the rearranging, shortening, deleting, and recomposing of elements in a production. It allows elements to be recorded out of sequence and as often as necessary.

▶ Digital editing allows the retrieval, assembly, and reassembly of disk-based material quickly and in any order, regardless of the order in which the material was recorded and its location on the disk.

▶ A nonlinear editor (NLE) makes it is possible to audition an edit at any stage in the procedure, adjust levels, add signal processing, and restore any change in the edited material to its original waveform without endangering the master audio.

▶ Audio encoded on an NLE takes the form of a soundfile, which is displayed in a waveform. A waveform displays the profile of a sound's amplitude over time.

▶ For a more refined view of an audio file, some software programs include spectrum editing, which provides a sonogram view of an audio file, facilitating ultrafine surgical editing of such elements as noise, ambience, and unwanted frequencies.

▶ Basic functions in digital editing include: scrubbing, jogging, and shuttling; cut, copy, paste, delete, insert, and overtype; undo/redo; snapping, slipping, and spotting; scaling and zooming; trim or crop; time compression and expansion; looping; track grouping; time displays; and crossfades.

▶ Nondestructive editing does not alter the original soundfile regardless of what editing or signal processing you apply. Destructive editing permanently alters the original soundfile by overwriting it.

▶ An essential part of editing is the edit decision list (EDL), a step-by-step list, generated during editing, of the in and out edit points of a shot or an audio segment, the nature of the transitions, the duration of the edit, and, if needed, the source reel numbers or time code addresses.

▶ Before editing begins, organize the edit tracks by cataloging all the sounds and keep a running log throughout the editing process.

▶ As part of the organization, name each file.

▶ Employ drive management: keep track of which disk drives contain which files and what soundfiles are where.

▶ Editing picture is one-dimensional: one shot is cut, dissolved, or faded out and in to another shot; little happens until the next transition. Editing sound is multidimensional: sounds are layered within each shot, so editing audio becomes more than attending to transitions.

▶ Among the considerations basic to editing speech are recognizing the sounds that make up words, cutting together similar and dissimilar sounds, handling emphasis and inflection, matching ambience, and taking corrective action with problem tracks that raise such issues as ring-off, additive ambience, defective or unusable dialogue, and synchronizing dialogue to picture.

▶ When dealing with dialogue it is a good idea to keep a database of every recorded line on hard disk to facilitate editing.

▶ Among the challenges a sound-effect editor deals with are building backgrounds, building effects, and matching perspective.

▶ When editing music, attention must be paid to cutting to resolution, preserving tempo, repetitive measures, looping, key signature, comping, style and texture, and editing music to picture.

▶ Generally, edits that heighten intensity will work, such as cutting from quiet to loud, nonrhythmic to rhythmic, slow to fast, formless to structured, or atonal to tonal.

▶ Comping takes the best parts of each recorded track and combines them into a composite final version.

▶ Mismatching of sound makes an edit obvious, unless the sound is being edited to a picture and the picture justifies the edit.

▶ Transitions used in audio editing include the segue or cut, the crossfade, the soft cut, and the fade-out/fade-in.

▶ Transitions involving sound and picture may employ the audio-leading-video or video-leading-audio technique, where sound and picture transitions do not occur at the same time.

▶ Editing for long periods of time can cause listening fatigue. Take regular breaks.

21

Mixing: An Overview

Until now the elements that go into producing audio have been considered separately. But audiences are usually not aware of ingredients; they hear only the final product, the result of the last phases in the production process—mixing and rerecording. The procedure in getting to the final stages in production may differ among the media, but the purpose is the same: to combine the parts into a natural and integrated whole.

Mixing is the final opportunity to take care of any unsolved problems. Inevitably, each stage of production leaves problems for the next stage. Issues that may not be resolvable in one phase can often be taken care of later on. But mixing is usually the last stop, and any problems created there either are there for good or have to be corrected by going back into an earlier production stage or, with music recording, in *mastering*—the final preparation of audio material for duplication and distribution.

The term *mixing* is used generally in radio, television, and music recording to describe the process of combining individual audio tracks into two (stereo) or more (surround sound) master tracks. In theatrical film and television, the dialogue, music, and sound-effect (DME) tracks are *premixed* and then rerecorded. *Rerecording* is the process of combining the DME tracks into their final form—stereo or surround sound. Regardless of terminology, mixing, premixing, and rerecording have the same purposes:

- To enhance the sound quality and the style of the existing audio tracks through signal processing and other means

- To balance levels

447

- To create the acoustic space, artificially if necessary
- To establish aural perspective
- To position the sounds within the aural frame
- To preserve the intelligibility of each sound or group of sounds
- To add special effects
- To maintain the sonic integrity of the audio overall, regardless of how many sounds are heard simultaneously

MAINTAINING AESTHETIC PERSPECTIVE

The general purposes of mixing and rerecording notwithstanding, the overriding challenge is to maintain aesthetic perspective. The ears have an uncanny ability to focus on a single sound in the midst of many sounds. You may have noticed that in a room with several people talking in separate conversations at once, you can focus on hearing one conversation to the exclusion of the others. This capability is known as the *cocktail party effect*. In mixing and rerecording, it can be both a blessing and a curse.

Mixing and rerecording require that as you pay attention to the details in a recording, you never lose aesthetic perspective of the overall sound balance and imaging. This is easier said than done. Aural perception changes over time. What sounds one way at the outset of a mixing session often sounds quite another way an hour or so later, to say nothing of the listening fatigue that inevitably sets in during a long session. To make matters worse, the ear tends to get used to sounds that are heard continuously over relatively short periods of time. Then there is "the desire to make things sound better [that] is so strong that one does not actually need it to sound better in order for it to sound better."[1]

These effects are manifested in several ways. In what sensory researchers call *accommodation,* the ear may fill in, or resolve, sounds that are not actually there. The ear may also tune out certain sounds and therefore not hear them. This is particularly the case when the focus is on another sound. Because all the sounds are competing for your attention as a mixer, it becomes necessary to concentrate on those that require processing at any given time. While attending to the details, it is possible to lose the perspective of how those details fit into the overall

mix. The more you listen to the fine tunings, the greater the danger of drifting from the big picture. What to do?

- Begin mixing sessions rested, including the ears. Do not listen to anything but the quiet for several hours before a mix.
- Do not take anything that can impair perception and judgment.
- Keep the problem of perspective always in mind.
- Take a checks-and-balances approach: after attending to a detail, listen to it within the context of the overall mix.
- Seek another opinion.
- As with any lengthy audio session, take regular and frequent "ears" breaks. When there are no union regulations in place that prescribe break times and if a client balks, tactfully explain the problem of listening fatigue: that trying to use every second of studio time just because it is paid for will reach a point of diminishing aesthetic returns.

MIXING FOR VARIOUS MEDIA

Another purpose of the mix (and rerecording) to add to those listed earlier is to keep all essential sonic information within the frequency and dynamic ranges of the medium for which it is being made. In other words, you have to take into consideration what type of delivery system will be used to reproduce the audio because it is difficult to create one mix suitable for all systems.

Radio

The foremost considerations in doing a mix for radio are the frequency response of the medium (AM or FM), dynamic range, whether the broadcast is in analog or digital sound, and the wide range of receivers the listening audience uses, from the car radio to the high-end component system.

Although conventional AM radio may transmit in stereo and play music from compact discs, its frequency response is mediocre—roughly 100 to 5,000 Hz. The frequency response of FM is considerably wider, from 20 to 20,000 Hz. Dynamic range for AM is 48 dB; for FM it is 70 dB. Therefore it would seem that mixing for AM requires care to ensure that the essential sonic information is within its narrower frequency band and dynamic range and that in mixing for FM there is no such problem.

---

1. Alexander U. Case, *Sound FX* (Boston: Focal Press, 2007), p. 85.

Both statements would be true were it not for the broad assortment of radio receivers that vary so greatly in size and sound quality and for the variety of listening conditions under which radio is heard.

There is also the additional problem of how the levels of music CDs have changed over the years. Compact discs produced 25 years ago had an average (root mean square) level of –18 dB. In 1990, as the pop music industry entered the "level wars," it was –12 dB. In 1995 average level was raised to –6 dB. Since 2000 the average level of many CDs is between zero-level (0 dBFS) and –3 dB. As the average level is raised using compression, the music gets louder and has more punch, but dynamic range is reduced and there is a greater loss in clarity.

There is no way to do an optimal mix, for either AM or FM, to satisfy listeners with a boom box, a transistor radio, and car stereos that run the gamut from mediocre to excellent and are played against engine, road, and air-conditioner noise. To be sure, car stereo systems have improved dramatically, and surround systems are increasingly available, but unless the car itself is built to lower the noise floor against sonic intrusions, the quality of the sound system is almost moot.

The best approach is to mix using loudspeakers that are average in terms of frequency response, dynamic range, size, and cost and to keep the essential sonic information—speech, sound effects, and music—within the 150 to 5,000 Hz band, which most radio receivers can handle. With AM radio's limited frequency response, it often helps to compress the sound to give it more power in the low end and more presence in the midrange. For FM mixes a sound check on high-quality loudspeakers is wise to ensure that the harmonics and the overtones beyond 5,000 Hz are audible to the listener using a high-quality receiver.

But be careful here. Extremes in equalization should be avoided because of FM broadcast pre-emphasis. **Pre-emphasis** boosts the treble range by 6 dB per octave, starting at 2.1 kHz (in the United States) or 3.2 kHz (in Europe). In receivers there is a complementary de-emphasis to compensate for the treble boost. The result of all this is a flat response and a reduction of high-frequency noise but also a considerable reduction in high-frequency headroom. Therefore, if a mix is too bright, the broadcast processing will clamp down on the signal.

As for dynamic range, given the wide variety of sound systems used to hear radio and under different listening conditions, music with a wide dynamic range is usually a problem for most of the audience. To handle dynamic range, broadcast stations employ processing that controls the dynamics of the signal before transmission, thereby bringing it within the usable proportions of a receiver.

Another factor that may influence a music mix, if not during the mixdown session then in the way it is handled for broadcast, is a *tight board*—radio parlance for having no dead air and playing everything at a consistent level. Because most radio stations compress and limit their output, running a tight board tends to raise the level of music with soft intros, back it off as the song builds, and then let compression and limiting do the rest. Songs ending in a fade are increased in level as the fade begins, until the music segues evenly into the next song or spot announcement.

Because of this it is a good idea to keep a mix for radio on the dry side. Compression can increase the audibility of reverb. In broadcast signal processing, quieter elements, such as reverb tails, are increased in level so they are closer to that of the louder elements. Also, avoid limiting and compression in the mix for the sake of loudness because the broadcast processing will reduce the music level to where the station's engineers want it to be anyway.

Monaural compatibility, that is, how a stereo mix sounds in mono, is yet another factor to consider (see "Stereo-to-mono Compatibility" in Chapter 23).

Hybrid Digital (HD) Radio not only provides the capability of offering multiple programs on a single channel but also produces CD-quality sound and reduced interference and static. Frequency response is 20 to 20,000 Hz, and dynamic range is 96 dB. These parameters greatly improve the sonic fidelity of programs compared with conventional AM and FM broadcasts. This is particularly advantageous to both producers and listeners of music. But, again, the only way to get the full benefit of HD Radio is to have the receiver capable of reproducing its full-frequency and wide-dynamic-range signal.[2]

Mixing stereo in radio usually means positioning speech in the center and music across the stereo field without its interfering with the intelligibility of the speech. If there are sound effects, they can be positioned relative to their dramatic placement so long as they do not distract from the focus of the material. Because there is no picture to ground the sound effects, and because radio is a "theater of the mind" medium, there is more

---

2. Note that with television, *HD* refers to *high-definition*, whereas with radio *HD* is a brand name for a method of digital audio transmission developed by iBiquity Digital Corporation.

freedom in positioning effects than there is in TV and film. A lot of movement of SFX across the stereo field, however, should be done only as a special effect and if it is compatible with the production style and the message.

As for surround sound, many of the same mixing techniques that apply to music, TV, and film also apply to radio and are covered in Chapters 22 and 23.

Television

Frequency response in standard television (STV) audio transmission goes to 15,000 Hz and has a dynamic range of 60 dB. Frequency response in *high-definition television (HDTV),* which transmits digital audio, is 20 to 20,000 Hz, with a dynamic range of at least 85 dB. But in television as in radio, mixing must conform to the capabilities of the home TV receiver.[3]

There is also the reality that TV viewing does not usually take place in a quiet, focused environment: one parent is getting the meal together, another is talking on the phone, and the kids are playing. To ensure that subtle or low-level sounds are heard, it is necessary to bring the levels above the noise floor. But TV has a comparatively narrow signal-to-noise ratio because many models of conventional television sets still cannot play very loud without distortion, though this limitation has improved considerably with the upgraded receivers to accommodate HDTV.

To be safe, and until the majority of home receivers in use improve in quality and catch up with HDTV transmission, it would be wise to mix the essential information (dialogue and effects as well as music) between roughly 150 Hz and 5,000 Hz. Boosting around 700 Hz should tighten the bass and at around 4,000 to 5,000 Hz should enhance clarity and presence. Gentle limiting (to prevent overmodulation) and compressing overall sound are often a good idea, especially with digital sound, which has no headroom. Dynamic range should not exceed 60 dB. These parameters can be widened considerably when mixing for HDTV home receivers capable of reproducing the dynamic range and the full frequency of digital audio.

Keep in mind that although a TV set is capable of receiving HDTV, it may be due to a converter, which means that it can handle the HDTV signal but the set

itself may be only marginally able to take full advantage of its superior sound and picture quality.

As for monitoring, it is still a good idea to hear the audio on different-quality loudspeakers. Monitor on average-type bookshelf speakers most of the time. For overall referencing, occasionally switch to the big loudspeakers and small mono loudspeakers. For television the mono loudspeaker mix is essential for the audience still listening in mono. Also make sure that the quality and the imaging of a surround-sound mix are suitable for reproduction on home entertainment systems. This requires more-discriminating mixing on higher-end loudspeakers.

In mixing for surround sound, consideration must be made for home systems with and without a center loudspeaker. When there is a center channel, dialogue is usually mixed to it. Care must be taken, however, to ensure that the audio in the center channel does not overwhelm material mixed to the front-left and front-right channels because of the center channel's proximity to the listener. To be safe, it is a good idea to mix some of the dialogue to the left and right channels for home reception that does not include a center-channel loudspeaker.

In the absence of a center channel, or when downmixing from surround sound to stereo, the dialogue must be mixed so it is phantom-imaged to the center of the space between the front-left and front-right loudspeakers (see "Spatial Imaging of Stereo and Surround Sound in Television and Film" in Chapter 23).

Mixing for television and radio is different from mixing for digital disc (discussed later in this chapter). Fewer people listen to TV and radio on decent stereos compared with those who use higher-quality playback systems for CDs and DVDs (although this too is changing because of HD Radio and HDTV). It is still wise to avoid going for a big, deep low end or for tingly, shimmery high-end sounds because many viewers will not hear them. Make sure the essential sonic information is clear on both stereo and mono loudspeakers.

For TV and also for radio, keep the stereo mix mono-compatible by not hard-panning anything to the extreme left and right. If reverb is used, make it wetter than normal because TV transmission diminishes reverb.

The top priority in television is what is on the screen. If there is a close-up of a singer or a lead guitarist, this is what the audience expects to hear front and centered; do not be afraid to exaggerate these or other featured elements. In surround sound the audio usually carried in the surround channels is supplementary to the principal

---

3. Do not confuse HDTV with *digital television (DTV).* All HDTV is digital, but not all digital TV is high-definition. The same bandwidth for DTV broadcasting can be used to either supply a video signal (or signals) and other services or to transmit a single HDTV signal.

audio, such as ambience, crowd sound, environmental sound effects, and so on.

Film

In mixing for film, a premix of dialogue, music, and sound effects is done first, and final adjustments are made later. To this end a flexible approach is to not restrict too severely low-end and high-end roll-offs and to leave some play for adjustments in processing. In surround sound very-low-frequency audio is typically mixed to the subwoofer. In mixes that assume the reproducing system will not use a subwoofer, only essential low-end information is mixed to the full-frequency surround channels in appropriate proportions.

Even though the frequency response and the dynamic range in movie theater sound systems can be extraordinary, most home systems do not have the capability of reproducing that level of sound quality. The highest-end home systems, however, do have impressive sound reproduction. A safe way to handle a mix is to start with the "unisound" approach; that is, keep all essential sonic information within certain sonic bounds. For example, by cutting out all sound below 100 to 150 Hz and above 5,000 to 6,500 Hz, problems with rumble and hiss are considerably reduced and the frequency response is sufficient to keep dialogue, sound effects, and music intelligible. Then for high-end systems, fill out the lower and higher frequencies.

As for sound level, unlike the disparities in television sound and among CDs, in film it is fairly consistent because monitoring gain during mixing has been standardized. It has been found that 83 dB-SPL is an optimal level because it is not too loud or too soft. It permits a wide dynamic range, and it is also where the ear's frequency response is most linear in relation to the equal loudness curve.

Digital Disc

In mixing an album for compact disc, three important factors are digital edge, distortion, and total playing time. There may be other considerations as well, such as applying the Red Book and Orange Book standards (see Chapter 5).

Digital edge is the overly bright sonic byproduct of the digital recording process that too often spoils the sound quality on a CD. It is usually the result of such factors as improper miking and recording techniques, poor analog-to-digital conversion, inappropriate equalization

during mixing that makes certain midrange and treble frequencies overly apparent, and signal processing that is unmusical. It may also be the result of poor CD mastering, but that is another discussion.

Distortion can be another problem in mixing digital sound. As pointed out previously, there is no headroom in digital recording; levels must be watched carefully. Once you reach zero-level, you have run out of headroom—there is no place to go.

Trying to pack too much program material onto a music CD can create problems in mastering and reproduction. A CD can hold more than 70 minutes of data, and many discs sell on the basis of length as well as content. On a CD that has much more than 60 minutes of material, the spiral traces of the data track are pushed closer together, which makes laser tracking more difficult and can cause skipping.

Generally, a compact disc is mixed with one of three types of playback systems in mind: a high-quality system with an amplifier and loudspeakers capable of reproducing wide dynamic range and frequency response; a medium-quality system capable of reproducing a fairly wide dynamic range and frequency response; or a low-quality system with limited dynamic range and frequency response.

For CDs being prepared for radio airplay, another consideration is doing a radio-friendly mix. In an album mix, most important are the integrity of the song, how the song fits within the CD, and the artist's vision. What's important in doing an alternative mix for radio is making sure it takes into consideration the particular conditions of broadcast processing and having the music loud and punchy.

Music on audio DVDs and Super Audio Compact Discs (SACDs) is qualitatively superior to music on CDs (see Chapter 5). But here again the improved data storage and sonic fidelity can be realized only with an excellent sound-reproducing system. It can be said, however, that the music mixed for DVD-A and SACD, in particular, assumes the audiophile as the primary market.

Multimedia

Even though digital sound has extremely wide dynamic range and most of it is mastered in 16-, 20-, or 24-bit, the reproducing medium remains a factor. Mixing for multimedia is like mixing for any consumer medium: you do not know what the end user has for playback.

Multimedia usually means that the product is heard (and seen) on a computer, cell phone, iPod, and the like.

Because these mobile-media systems generally have limited frequency response and bit depth—dynamic range and signal-to-noise ratio—the essential information must therefore be mixed and mastered so that it can be heard within the ranges that mobile media can accommodate.

Another factor is the data compression and expansion that is so much a part of multimedia signal processing. Even with higher-end mobile media capable of 16-bit audio, computers for example, the consideration is still the quality of the loudspeaker being used for playback. This could mean that audio information below 100 or 200 Hz and above 7 or 8 kHz might not be heard.

MIXING VERSUS LAYERING

Not to quibble about semantics, but *mixing* suggests a blend in which the ingredients lose their uniqueness in becoming part of the whole. Although such blending is important, in relation to a mix the term *layering* may be more to the point.

When sounds are combined, there are four essential objectives to keep in mind:

- Establish the main and supporting sounds to create focus or point of view.

- Position the sounds to create relationships of space and distance and, in music, cohesion.

- Maintain spectral balance so that the aural space is properly weighted.

- Maintain the definition of each sound without losing definition overall.

These considerations come closer to the definition of layering than they do of mixing. The following discussion notwithstanding, *mixing* is the term used to refer to the process and the one that is used in the following chapters.

Layering involves some of the most important aspects of aural communication: balance, perspective, and intelligibility. When many sounds occur at once, unless they are layered properly it could result in a loud sound drowning out a quiet sound; sounds with similar frequencies muddying one another; sounds in the same spatial position interfering with focus; and sounds that are too loud competing for attention—in short, a mishmash. Usually, when elements in a mix are muddled, it is because too many of them are sonically alike in pitch, tempo, loudness, intensity, envelope, timbre, style, or positioning in the aural frame; or there are simply too many sounds playing at once.

Layering: Sound with Picture

Imagine the sound track for a Gothic mystery thriller. The scene: a sinister castle on a lonely mountaintop high above a black forest, silhouetted against the dark, starless sky by flashes of lightning. You can almost hear the sound: rumbling, rolling thunder; ominous bass chords from an organ, cellos, and double basses; and the low-pitched moan of the wind.

The layering seems straightforward, depending on the focus: music over wind and thunder to establish the overall scariness; wind over thunder and music to focus on the forlorn emptiness; and thunder over wind and music to center attention on the storm about to break above the haunting bleakness. But with this particular mix, setting the appropriate levels may be insufficient to communicate the effect. The sounds are so much alike—low pitched and sustained—that they may cover one another, creating a combined sound that is thick and muddy and that lacks clarity and definition. The frequency range, rhythm, and envelope of the sounds are too similar: low pitched, continuous, weak in attack, and long in sustain.

One way to layer them more effectively is to make the wind a bit wilder, thereby sharpening its pitch. Instead of rolling thunder, start it with a sharp crack and shorten the sustain of the rumble to separate it from any similar sustain in the music. Perhaps compress the thunder to give it more punch and better locate it in the aural space. These minor changes make each sound more distinctive, with little or no loss in the overall effect on the scene.

This technique also works in complex mixes. Take a far-flung battle scene: soldiers shouting and screaming, cannons booming, rifles and machine guns clattering, jet fighter planes diving to the attack, explosions, and intense orchestral music dramatically underscoring the action. Although there are multiple elements, they are distinctive enough to be layered without losing their intelligibility.

The pitch of the cannons is lower than that of the rifles and the machine guns; their firing rhythms and sound envelopes are also different. The rifles and the machine guns are distinct because their pitches, rhythms, and envelopes are not the same, either. The explosions can be pitched lower or higher than the cannons; they also have a different sound envelope. The pitch of the jets may be within the same range as that of the rifles and the machine guns, but their sustained, whining roar is the only sound of its kind in the mix. The shouting and the screaming of the soldiers have varied rhythms, pitches, and tone colors. As for the music, its timbres, blend, and intensity are different from those of the other sounds. Remember too that the differences in loudness levels and positioning in a stereo or surround-sound frame will help contribute to the clarity of this mix. Appropriate signal processing is employed as well.

In relation to loudness and the frequency spectrum, two useful devices in maintaining intelligibility are the compressor and the equalizer. Compressing certain sounds increases flexibility in placing them because it facilitates tailoring their dynamic ranges. This is a more convenient and sonically better way to place sounds than by simply using the fader. Through modest and deft equalization, attenuating, or boosting, sounds can cut or fill holes in the aural frame, thereby also facilitating placement without affecting intelligibility.

Some scenes are so complex, however, that there are simply too many sonic elements in the SFX and the music to deal with separately. In such instances try grouping them and playing no more than three or four groups at the same time, varying the levels as you go. For example, in the previous battle scene the different elements (other than the voices) could be put into four groups: mortars, guns, planes, and music. By varying the levels and positioning the groups in the foreground, background, side-to-side, and front-to-rear and moving them in, out, or through the scene, you avoid the sound track's collapsing into a big ball of noise. (The movements cannot be too sudden or frequent, however, or they will call attention to themselves and distract the listener-viewer.) In dealing with several layers of sound, the trick is to use only a few layers at a time and to balance their densities and clarity.

Another approach to scenes densely packed with audio effects is to use only the sounds that are needed—perhaps basing their inclusion on how the character perceives them or to counterpoint intense visual action with relatively spare sound. For example, it is opening night at the theater: there is the hubbub of the gathering audience, the last-minute preparations and the hysteria backstage, and the orchestra tuning up; the star is frightfully nervous, pacing the dressing room. By dropping away all the sounds except the pacing, the star's anxiety becomes greatly heightened.

Focusing sonically on what the audience is seeing at the moment also works. In the battle scene described earlier, in a tight shot of, say, the cannons booming, play to that sound. When the shot is off the cannons, back off their sound. In a wider shot with the soldiers firing their rifles in the foreground and explosions bursting in the background, raise the levels of the soldiers' actions to be louder than the explosions.

Another reason not to play too many sounds at once, particularly loud sounds, is that if they stay constant, the effect is lost; they lose their interest. Contrast and perspective are the keys to keeping complex scenes sonically interesting.

It is also unwise to play too many loud sounds at the same time because it is annoying. In a hectic scene with thunderclaps, heavy rain, a growling monster rampaging through a city, people screaming, and cars crashing, there is no sonic relief. It is loud sound on loud sound; every moment is hard. The rerecording mix can be used to create holes in the din without diminishing intensity or fright and can provide relief from time to time throughout the sequence. For example, the rain could be used as a buffer between two loud sounds. After a crash or scream, bring up the rain before the next loud sound hits. Or use the growl, which has low-frequency relief, to buffer two loud sounds.

Be wary of sounds that "eat up" certain frequencies. Water sounds in general and rain in particular are so high-frequency-intense that they are difficult to blend into a mix, and the presence of other high-frequency sounds only exacerbates the problem. Deep, rumbly sounds like thunder present the same problem at the low end of the frequency spectrum. One means of handling such sounds is to look for ways to change their perspectives. Have the rain fall on cars, vegetation, and pavement and in puddles. Make the thunder louder or quieter as the perspective of the storm cloud changes in relation to the people in the scene.

Layering: Music

In music recording, an ensemble often has a variety of instruments playing at once. Their blend is important to the music's structure but not to the extent that violins become indistinguishable from cellos, or the brass drowns out the woodwinds, or a screaming electric guitar makes it difficult to hear the vocalist. Layering also affects blend—positioning the voicings front-to-rear, side-to-side, or (with surround sound) front-to-back (or back side).

For example, in an ensemble with, say, a vocalist, lead and rhythm guitars, keyboard, and drums, one approach to layering in stereo could place the vocalist in front of the accompanying instruments, the guitars behind and somewhat to the vocalist's left and right, the keyboard behind the guitars panned left to right, and the drums behind the keyboard panned left to right of center.

With an orchestra in surround, the frontal layering would position the ensemble as it usually is, front-to-rear and left-to-right—violins left to center and right to center; basses right, behind the violins; and so on. Ambience would be layered in the surround channels to define the size of the space.

A jazz ensemble with piano, bass, and drums might be layered in surround to place the listener as part of the group. One approach could be to position the piano in the middle of the surround space, the bass toward the front, and the drums across the rear.

With music, however the voicings are layered it is fundamental that the sounds coalesce. If the blend is lacking, even layering, well done, will not produce an aesthetically satisfying sound.

Perspective

In layering, some sounds are more important than others; the predominant one usually establishes the focus or point of view. In a commercial the announcer's voice is usually louder than any accompanying music or effects because the main message is likely to be in the copy. In an auto-racing scene, with the sounds of speeding cars, a cheering crowd, and dramatic music defining the excitement, the dominating sound of the cars focuses on the race. The crowd and the music may be in the middleground or background, with the music under to provide the dramatic support. To establish the overall dramatic excitement of the event, the music may convey that point of view best, in which case the speeding cars and the cheering crowd might be layered under the music as supporting elements.

In music recording, it is obvious that a vocalist should stand out from the accompaniment or that an ensemble should not overwhelm a solo instrument. When an ensemble plays all at once, there are foreground instruments—lead guitar in a rock group, violins in an orchestra, or a piano in a jazz trio—and background instruments—rhythm guitar, bass, woodwinds, and drums.

Whatever the combination of effects, establishing the main and supporting sounds is fundamental to a good mix, indeed, to good dramatic technique and musical balances. *Foreground does not mean much without background.*

But because of the psychological relationship between sound and picture, perspectives between what is heard and what is seen do not necessarily have to match but rather complement one another. In other words you can cheat in handling perspective.

For example, take a scene in which two people are talking as they walk in the countryside and stop by a tree. The shot as they are walking is a long shot (LS), which changes to a medium close-up (MCU) at the tree. Reducing the loudness in the LS to match the visual perspective could interfere with comprehension and be annoying because the audience would have to strain to hear, and the lip movements would be difficult to see.

When people speak at a distance, the difficulty in seeing lip movements and the reduced volume inhibit comprehension. It may be better to ride the levels at almost full loudness and roll off low-end frequencies because the farther away the voice, the thinner the sound. Let the picture also help establish the distance and the perspective.

Psychologically, the picture establishes the context of the sound. This also works in reverse. In the close-up there must be some sonic change to be consistent with the shot change. Because the close-up does not show the countryside but does show the faces better, establish the environment by increasing ambience in the sound track. In this case, the ambience establishes the unseen space in the picture. Furthermore, by adding the ambience, the dialogue will seem more diffused. This creates a sense of change without interfering with comprehension because the sound is louder and the actors' lip movements are easier to see.

METERING

The importance of using meters to help identify and avoid sonic problems is discussed in Chapters 4, 6, 8, and 23. It is useful to reinforce their value in relation to mixing. In producing audio our ears should always be the final arbiters. There are instances, however, when a problem may be evident but its cause is difficult to identify. In such cases the ear may be better served by the eye.

Metering tools can perform many different types of analyses and are readily available in stand-alone models and plug-ins. They can display, in real time, waveforms, spectrograms, and scopes with attendant alphanumeric information and keep a history of an event. The array of metering programs available can deal with just about any problem—loudness, distortion threshold, frequency, signal and interchannel phasing, monitoring anomalies, stereo and surround-sound imaging and balances, transfer function, and signal correlation, to name a few.

Keep in mind that the useful data that meters provide are just that: data. Meters are not intuitive about sound. Rely on the information they provide, but do not be seduced by it, especially when an aesthetic value is involved.

MIXING AND EDITING

It is worthwhile to note that although this and the following two chapters focus on the mixer and mixing, the boundary between the two operations is blurring. Today's technology allows mixers to cross over into the editorial realm and vice versa.

So long as it does not conflict with union regulations, the decision an editor makes may also involve some mixing and a mixing procedure may also require some editing. For example, in editing two tracks of, say, dialogue or music for continuity or timing, it may also make sense to use signal processing at that stage to achieve a blend. Or to more precisely contour a sound effect in a mix may involve rebuilding it for proper impact. When unions are involved, however, be clear about the guidelines defining what an editor and a mixer may and may not do.

MAIN POINTS

▶ Mixing and rerecording are the phases of postproduction when the separately recorded elements are combined into a natural and integrated whole.

▶ The term *mixing* is used generally in radio, television, and music recording to describe the process of combining individual audio tracks into two (stereo) or more (surround sound) master tracks. In theatrical film and television, the dialogue, music, and sound-effect (DME) tracks are premixed and then rerecorded.

▶ Rerecording is the process of combining the DME tracks into their final form—stereo or surround sound.

▶ Mixing, premixing, and rerecording have the same purposes: to enhance the sound quality and the style of the existing audio tracks through signal processing and other means; to balance levels; to create the acoustic space, artificially if necessary; to establish aural perspective; to position the sounds within the aural frame; to preserve the intelligibility of each sound or group of sounds; to add special effects; and to maintain the sonic integrity of the audio overall, regardless of how many sounds are heard simultaneously.

▶ The general purpose of mixing and rerecording notwithstanding, the overriding challenge is to maintain aesthetic perspective.

▶ In proceeding with a mix, it is necessary to know on what type of delivery system it will be reproduced. Radio, television, film, digital disc, and multimedia—all have different sonic requirements.

▶ In layering sound it is important to establish the main and supporting sounds to create focus or point of view; position the sounds to create relationships of space and distance and, in music, cohesion; maintain spectral balance so that the aural space is properly weighted; and maintain the definition of each sound without losing definition overall.

▶ To help maintain definition as well as intelligibility in a mix, the various sounds should have different sonic features. These features can be varied in pitch, tempo, loudness, intensity, envelope, timbre, style, and so on.

▶ In layering sounds it is also important to establish perspective. Some sounds are more important than others; the predominant one usually establishes the focus or point of view.

▶ It is important to use meters to help identify and avoid sonic problems. There are times when they can indicate an issue that the ear cannot perceive.

▶ The boundary between editing and mixing is blurring. Today's technology allows mixers to cross over into the editorial realm and vice versa.

22

Music Mixdown

There is a common misunderstanding about the music mixdown, namely, that it is the stage in music production where everything that went wrong in the recording session is put right. No doubt this unfortunate notion has been nurtured in recording sessions that have not met expectations, when producers have glibly reassured clients, "Don't worry, we can fix it in the mix." The mixdown certainly is very important to the finished product, but keep its significance in perspective.

The *mixdown*—when all the separately recorded audio tracks are processed, positioned, and combined into stereo or surround sound—cannot change a mediocre performance into a good one, compensate for poor microphone technique, or make a sloppy recording precise. In most instances the quality of the recording session determines the overall quality of the mix.

That said, the mixdown should not be taken lightly. A good mix cannot salvage a bad recording, but a poor mix can ruin a good one.

Keeping the significance of the mixer's role in perspective is also important to the outcome of a recording. Whatever the mixer does should be music driven; a mixer's responsibility is to serve the music, not the other way around. It is always about the music.

PREPARING FOR THE MIXDOWN

It is poor practice to do a mix on the same day that you finish the recording. Regardless of what you may think it sounds like immediately after the session, in a day or so it will sound different. Taking some time to regain perspective and renew "ears" is essential. Therefore before beginning a mix or making any final decisions about approach, signal processing, positioning, special effects, and so on, refamiliarize yourself with the recording by auditioning it as often as necessary to get a handle on what to do.

Ideas about the mix usually begin forming during recording and crystallize during mixing. However your vision develops, its outcome should be appropriate to the music. Different types of music employ different instrumentation and blends of that instrumentation. The handling of foreground, background, side-to-side, and front-to-back voicings vary with musical styles.

For example, in music with lyrics, the vocal is usually the defining element. But in heavy rock, it is sometimes mixed as another lead "instrument" rather than in front of the accompaniment. Country music is mixed with the vocal prominent; no other instrument can detract from it. Generally, the vocal is handled in the same way in pop music but with the tendency to give other elements in the ensemble more-discernible roles.

Characteristics of a Successful Mix

Regardless of the musical genre, there are basic elements that distinguish a successful mix.[1]

■ **Balance** This is the arrangement, loudness level, and relationships among the musical instruments. Many mixers think that balance is the single most important element in mixing. Using headphones is a good double-check to make sure that nothing unwanted stands out or distracts.

■ **Frequency range** Have all appropriate frequencies properly represented. The lows should be strong yet tight and controlled, not boomy, overwhelming, or muddy. The midrange should be blended to avoid any of its unpleasant characteristics from predominating, such as honkiness, tinniness, and abrasiveness. The highs should have clarity, brightness, and airiness, not the harsh, edgy, piercing sound that results from overemphasis.

■ **Spatial positioning** Suitably place the musical elements in the soundfield.

---

1. Some of this material is based on Bobby Owsinski, *The Mixing Engineer's Handbook,* 2nd edition (Boston: Thomson Course Technology, 2006), p. 10, and Bill Gibson, *Mixing and Mastering Audio Recordings* (Boston: Thomson Course Technology, 2006), pp. 76–80.

■ **Dimension** Add the appropriate acoustic space to the music. Reverberation and delay should be appropriate to the music and the type of venue in which it usually heard.

■ **Depth and width** Proper distribution of left-to-right and front-to-rear (or back) sounds creates the frontal two-dimensional imaging or the deeper front-to-back dimensional imaging.

■ **Dynamics** Control the volume envelopes of the instruments. Do not use the maximum available headroom—let the mix "breathe." Vary intensity and texture so that the music has sonic variety; too much of the same thing wears out its welcome.

■ **Context** Mix each track so that it sounds wonderful, then play it against the other tracks to keep checking how the mix sounds overall. Remember that distribution formats have only so much bandwidth and dynamic range.

■ **Focus** The lead elements should be easy to follow. A lead vocal, for example, is the focal point, but during breaks in the vocal the other lead voicing (or voicings) should be apparent.

■ **Interest** Make the mix compelling; get a vibe from the music.

Characteristics of an Amateur Mix

Various characteristics can reduce the effectiveness of a mix and make it sound amateurish.

■ Lack of contrast in the musical texture of the song

■ Overall sound that is dull, uninteresting, and lifeless

■ No center of attention to focus the listener

■ Overproduction of effects that detract from the music

■ Edgy and harsh sound

■ Too much compression that makes sound squishy or becomes irritating and fatiguing

■ Lack of intimacy that distances the listener from the song

■ Insufficient detail

■ Stereo or surround-sound imaging with inappropriate or unbalanced depth and width

■ Disproportionate spectral balance whereby certain frequencies or groups of frequencies are too thin or too boomy

■ Inappropriately wide dynamic range

■ Level-dominating outbursts and levels that are too low or inconsistent in one or more voicings or overall

■ Extraneous noise such as a sigh, lip smack, mic hit, hum, or crackle

■ Lack of clarity and intelligibility that reduces the distinctiveness and the definition of instruments and makes lyrics difficult to understand

Setting Up

Before getting down to the mix, following certain procedures helps avoid operational and technical problems during the mixdown. If an engineer handles some of the following operations, verify that they have been done.

1. Check that all the equipment is in working order.

2. Set the mixer and any outboard equipment controls intended for use to *off, zero,* or *flat.* If the mixer takes a SmartMedia card, use it to put the system in its default configuration.

3. Set up a reference tone to ensure standard and uniform levels throughout the mixdown.

4. Calibrate the meters in the signal path—mixer, recorder, and so on. With digital audio workstations (DAWs), use a meter-measuring plug-in. A signal generator with several types of noise and waveforms in the appropriate bit resolution is also helpful in making sure that no sonic anomalies are present in the DAW.

5. Establish a working level with headroom; –20 dBFS (0 VU), for example, provides a headroom of 20 dB before overload distortion occurs (with digital sound).

6. Test the monitoring system with a sound-pressure-level meter and a pink-noise source to make sure that the stereo and surround-sound loudspeaker distributions are what they should be (see Chapter 8). Test measurement discs are available to help with this procedure (see Bibliography).

In refamiliarizing yourself with the recording, resist the temptation to make detailed adjustments. Focus on the big picture first. Set relative levels and basic panning. Before any mixing begins, it is usually obvious that in the final mix certain voicings will be louder than others and that some elements in the ensemble will be positioned toward the front, rear, left-side, and so on. These basic adjustments allow the opportunity to evaluate what you have without the influence of additional processing. In other words simply set the relative level and the location of each voicing to achieve approximate but satisfactory overall loudness and positional balances.

Working with a console, all tracks are visible and accessible at the touch of a fader. With a DAW avoid clutter and confusion by having on-screen only the tracks with which you are working. If the software program supports it, color-code the tracks to facilitate visual identification of the instruments or groups of instruments.

Here is one approach:

1. Set the level of the loudest or most prominent sound first, leaving plenty of headroom on the peak meter. For example, if the loudest sound is a support instrument, such as a snare drum, set the level at, say, –27 dBFS (–7 VU); if the sound is a prominent lead voicing, such as a vocal, the level can be set higher at, say, –24 dBFS (–4 VU). Leaving headroom is vital not only because there is none in digital audio but because mixing almost always involves adding level during signal processing through equalization (EQ), reverb, and so on. Note that too much boosting without compensating attenuation creates a number of sonic problems (discussed later in this section).

2. Turn up the monitor level so that it is comfortably loud; 85 dB-SPL is usually considered optimal. Because what is considered comfortably loud depends on personal taste, musical style, and hearing acuity, however, 85 dB-SPL is at least a good place to start. It is critical to not set the monitor level too loud. Loud levels desensitize hearing or, in the vernacular of audio, "fry" ears, to say nothing of the potential for hearing loss. Some mixers prefer to keep the monitor level low not only to preserve hearing acuity but also to better hear quiet detail and subtlety.

Once the monitor loudness is set, avoid changing it; if you do, the reference you are using to determine sonic values and proportions will change as well. That said, there are mixers who prefer to change monitor loudnesses throughout the mix to hear how different levels affect certain voicings and balances.

3. Add all other tracks relative to the level of the first voicing. If you started with drums, add bass guitar, the rest of the drum set, the other accompanying instruments, and the vocal(s). If you started with the lead or most prominent instrument, bring in the other tracks

one at a time, starting with the rhythm instruments, followed by the rest of the accompaniment. Another approach is to set all instruments equally loud, then increase levels of the lead voicings and decrease levels of the support instruments.

4. Position each instrument in the stereo or surround-sound space approximately where you plan to put it in the final mix.

5. Readjust fader levels to compensate for loudness changes resulting from these positional alignments.

6. If something is not working, don't force it. Maybe it is not needed. That applies, for example, to parts of a song, control settings, signal processing, and, if necessary, even an entire instrumental track. Let the music tell you what it wants.

7. Mix with the highest resolution possible.

Once you have refamiliarized yourself with the recording and have reconfirmed its design, you are ready to do the actual mixdown. It is likely that during the mix, as various sonic alterations are made, many of the original decisions will change. This is natural. Do not be afraid to experiment. Be flexible. When you get a vibe, go with it. Trust your instincts. But remember: anything that is done must always be in relation to the musicians' vision and the music.

Recordkeeping

Obvious though the importance of recordkeeping may be, it is an often underestimated or, worse, overlooked part of the mixing (and recording) process. Keeping good records is essential to the success of the final product because it helps avoid confusion, disorder, wasted time, and added expense.

The number of details in a mix can be daunting. It often takes several sessions to complete a mix, and any adjustments previously made must be reset precisely. Computer-assisted mixers and DAWs automatically store much essential internally configured data. Such systems may include software functions that facilitate keeping a record of each track's processing and a field for comments. They may or may not provide the flexibility needed for all the necessary documentation, such as impressions of takes, individual performances, recommendations for corrections and improvements, results of various approaches to signal processing, and so on. Therefore it would be necessary to devise a form either

in hard copy or computerized. In such cases, each studio makes up its own forms. Choose the template that works best for you.

Regardless of whether the means for recordkeeping is provided by the software program, there is generally agreed-upon information that should be at hand and easy to reference. Such information includes the following:

■ Session particulars on a so-called *track sheet,* such as band and song name, session date(s), producer, engineer, assistant engineer, instrument on each track, recording medium, sampling frequency, bit depth, frame rate (if necessary) and, sometimes, or on a separate sheet, microphones used and their positioning during recording

■ Pertinent information about each take, such as what worked and did not work in the performance and what the mix did or did not accomplish in relation to those factors

■ EQ settings and levels; compression and reverb send/return settings; pan positions; submaster assignments; special effects; tempo changes; song key; time code settings; a lyric sheet with notations about interpretation, dynamics, vocal noises, or fluctuations in level on a particular phrase or word that need attention; any other signal processing data necessary for reference; and perceptions of the results of each mix

SIGNAL PROCESSING

Signal processing is so much a part of music recording that sound shaping seems impossible without it.[2] Yet overdependency on signal processing has created the myth that just about anything can be done with it to ensure the sonic success of a recording. These notions are misleading. Unless special effects are required, or MIDI is involved, or there are particular surround-sound needs, signal processing in the mixdown should be used to touch up the aural canvas, not repaint it. The greater the reliance on signal processing in the mixdown, the poorer the recording session is likely to have been. Nevertheless, signal processing is important—and often critical. Mixers who proudly proclaim that they can do without it are foolish. The purpose of this section is only to suggest possibilities and techniques. It is not intended to imply

---

2. It may be useful to remember that the techniques discussed in this chapter can be achieved in the virtual domain and by using outboard equipment.

that these are preferred approaches to signal processing or that because signal processing offers so many options most of them should be used. Remember: *less is more.*

Equalization

One question often asked of a mixer is "What kind of a sound will I get on this instrument if I equalize so many decibels at such and such a frequency?" The question suggests that there are ways to predetermine equalization. There are not! Consider the different things that can affect sound. For example, with a guitar you might ask: What is it made of? Is it acoustic or electric? Are the strings steel or nylon, old or new, played with a metal or a plastic pick or with the fingers? Is the guitarist heavy- or light-handed? Are there fret sounds? Is the guitar miked and, if so, with what type of microphone? How are the acoustics? What type of song is being played? What is the spatial placement of the guitar in the mix? These influences do not even include personal taste, the most variable factor of all.

EQ: How Much, Where, and When?

The best way to approach equalization is to know the frequency ranges of the instruments involved, know what each octave in the audible frequency spectrum contributes to the overall sound, listen to the sound in context, have a good idea of what you want to achieve before starting the mixdown, and decide whether EQ is even needed on a particular sound.

Also remember the following:

■ Equalization alters a sound's harmonic structure.

■ Very few people, even under ideal conditions, can hear a change of 1 dB or less, and many people cannot hear changes of 2 or 3 dB.

■ Large increases or decreases in EQ should be avoided.

■ Equalization should not be used as a substitute for better microphone selection and mic placement.

■ Equalization often involves boosting frequencies, and that can mean more noise, among other problems. Be careful with digital sound when increasing some of the unpleasant frequencies in the midrange and the high end.

■ Beware of *cumulative equalization.* Only a certain number of tracks in the same frequency range should be increased or decreased. For example, on one channel you may increase by 4 dB at 5,000 Hz the sound of a snare drum to make it snappier; then on another channel, you increase by 2 dB at 5,000 Hz to make a cymbal sound crisper; on a third channel, you increase by 3 dB at 5,000 Hz to bring out a vocal. If you consider each channel separately, there has been little equalization at 5,000 Hz, but the cumulative boost at the same frequency, which in this example is 9 dB, could unbalance the overall blend.

■ Because boosting frequencies on one track often necessitates attenuating frequencies somewhere else, consider *subtractive equalization* first. For example, if a sound is overly bright, instead of trying to mellow it by boosting the appropriate lower frequencies, reduce some of the higher frequencies responsible for the excessive brightness.

■ Be aware of the effects of additive and subtractive equalization (see Figure 22-1).

■ Frequencies above and below the range of each instrument should be filtered to reduce unwanted sound and improve definition. Be careful not to reduce frequencies that are essential to the natural timbre of an instrument, however.

■ To achieve a satisfactory blend, the sounds of individual elements may have to be changed in ways that could make them unpleasant to listen to by themselves. For example, the frequencies between 1,000 Hz and 3,500 Hz make most vocals intelligible. One way to improve the clarity of a vocal and make it stand out from its instrumental accompaniment while maintaining the overall blend is to boost it a few decibels in the 1,000 to 3,500 Hz range and decrease the accompaniment a few decibels in the same range. Separately, the vocal will be somewhat harsher and thinner and the accompaniment will sound a bit dense and lifeless; together, however, they should sound quite natural.

■ If a voice is powerful and rich with harmonics in the 5,000 Hz range, the sound is usually clear and full. Male singing voices, particularly in opera, have this sonic characteristic; female vocals usually do not.

Voices deficient in the 5,000 Hz range can be enhanced by a boost of several decibels in this area. Not only is the definition of such sounds as "t," "s," "ch," and "k" increased but a 6 dB increase at 5,000 Hz gives an apparent increase of 3 dB to the overall mix. When mixing digital sound using these EQ values, be wary of *digital edge*—that overly bright sonic byproduct of digital recording that too often spoils sound quality on a CD.

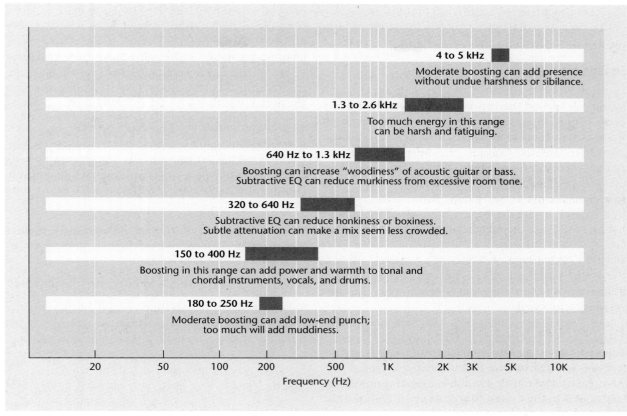

From Myles Boisen, "Space Is the Place, Part II," *Electronic Musician*, January 2009, p. 26.

22-1 Additive and subtractive effects of equalization in key frequency ranges.

■ Use *complementary equalization* to help define instruments and keep masking to a minimum. Many instruments have comparable frequency ranges, such as the bass guitar and the kick drum, or the keyboard, guitar, and female vocal. Because physical law states that no two things can occupy the same space at the same time, it makes sense to equalize voicings that share frequency ranges so that they complement, rather than interfere with, one another (see 22-2 and 22-3).

■ An absence of frequencies above 600 Hz adversely affects the intelligibility of consonants; an absence of frequencies below 600 Hz adversely affects the intelligibility of vowels.

■ Equal degrees of EQ between 400 Hz and 2,000 Hz are more noticeable than equalizing above or below that range, especially in digital sound (remember the equal loudness principle; see Chapter 1).

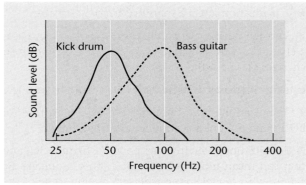

22-2 Complementary EQ for bass instruments.

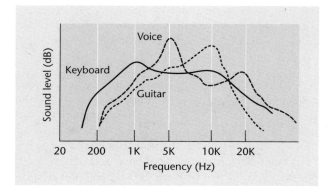

22-3 Complementary EQ for midrange instruments.

■ Most amplified instruments do not have ranges higher than 7,500 Hz; boosting above that frequency usually adds only noise.

■ Each sound has a naturally occurring peak at a frequency or band of frequencies that contains more energy than the surrounding frequencies and which, by being boosted or cut, enhances or mars the sound. In other words, the naturally occurring peak can become a sweet spot or a sore spot. The peaks are caused by natural harmonics and overtones or by a *formant*—an individual frequency or range of frequencies that is consistently emphasized because it contains more energy and loudness than adjacent frequencies.

To find the resonance area, turn up the gain on the appropriate section of the equalizer and sweep the frequency control until the voicing sounds noticeably better or worse. Once you find the sweet or sore spot, return the equalizer's gain to zero and boost or cut the enhancing or offending frequencies to taste.

Equalization and Semantics

A major problem in equalization is describing what it sounds like. What does it mean, for example, when a producer wants "sizzle" in a cymbal sound, "fatness" in a snare sound, "brightness" in an alto saxophone sound, or "edge" to a vocal? Not only is there a problem of semantics but you must identify the adjustments needed to achieve the desired effect. Then too one person's "sizzle" and "fatness" may be another person's "bite" and "boom." The following may be of some help in translating the verbal into the sonic.

■ Twenty to 50 Hz is considered the "rumble zone," and a subwoofer or full-range loudspeaker is required to

reproduce it accurately. Even so, it does not take much of a boost in this range to add unwanted boom to the sound, which also eats up headroom.

■ The range from about 60 to 80 Hz adds punch to sound. It can also give sound impact, size, power, and warmth, without clouding, depending on the instrument and the amount of EQ. The range is also bassy enough to eat up headroom with too much of a boost.

■ A boost between 200 Hz and 300 Hz can add warmth and body to a thin mix, but too much of an increase makes sound woody or tubby. It can also cloud sound, making the bass, in particular, indistinct.

■ Generally, boosting below 500 Hz can make sound fat, thick, warm, or robust. Too much can make it muddy, boomy, thumpy, or barrel-like.

■ Flat, extended low frequencies add fullness, richness, or solidity to sound. They can also make sound rumbly.

■ Low-frequency roll-off thins sound. This can enhance audio by making it seem clearer and cleaner, or it can detract by making it seem colder, tinnier, or weaker.

■ Mid-frequency boost between 500 Hz and 7 kHz (5 kHz area for most instruments, 1.5 to 2.5 kHz for bass instruments) can add presence, punch, edge, clarity, or definition to sound. It can also make sound muddy (hornlike), tinny (telephonelike), nasal or honky (500 Hz to 3 kHz), hard (2 to 4 kHz), strident or piercing (2 to 5 kHz), twangy (3 kHz), metallic (3 to 5 kHz), or sibilant (4 to 7 kHz). Between 500 Hz and 800 Hz, too much boost can cause a mix to sound hard or stiff.

■ Flat mid-frequencies sound natural or smooth. They may also lack punch or color.

■ Mid-frequency boost (1 to 2 kHz) improves intelligibility without increasing sibilance. Too much boost in this range adds unpleasant tinniness.

■ Mid-frequency dip makes sound mellow. It can also hollow (500 to 1,000 Hz), muffle (5 kHz), or muddy (5 kHz) sound.

■ The 2 to 4 kHz range contains the frequencies to which humans are most sensitive. If a sound has to cut through the mix, this is the range with which to work; but too much boosting across these frequencies adds a harshness that brings on listening fatigue sooner rather than later.

■ High-frequency boost above 7 kHz can enhance sound by making it bright, crisp, etched, or sizzly (cymbals).

It can also detract from sound by making it edgy, glassy, sibilant, biting, or sizzly (voice). Most vocal sibilance is in the range of 5 to 10 kHz.

◼ Extended high frequencies in the range of roughly 10 kHz and higher tend to open sound, making it airy, transparent, natural, or detailed. Too much boost makes a mix sound brittle or icy.

◼ High-frequency roll-off mellows, rounds, or smoothes sound. It can also dull, muffle, veil, or distance sound.[3]

In relation to specific instruments, the EQ values in Figure 22-4 may help refine the semantics.

Note that frequencies and frequency ranges listed in the table are general and intended only to provide a point of departure for more-refined sound shaping.

Approaches to Equalizing Selected Instruments

It is unwise to predetermine EQ values before a mixdown. Every session is different, to say nothing of the differences among music genres and the compositions involved. Moreover, ideas and perceptions change; being flexible is vital to the creative process. That said, over the years mixers in the popular idioms have found that certain approaches to equalizing are reasonable places to begin sound shaping. With that in mind—and with the understanding that the following suggestions are not intended to be prescriptive; that equalizing any one instrument during the mix must ultimately be assessed in relation to how it blends with the entire ensemble; and that other factors, such as compression and reverberation, also have an effect on equalization—here are some guidelines for equalizing a few of the most commonly used instruments in popular music.

Drums

◼ **Bass drum** The defining sounds of the bass drum are its low-frequency punch and higher-frequency attack. These frequencies reside in the 50 to 60 Hz and 1.5 to 2.5 kHz ranges, respectively. The muddiness, or boominess, that is an unwanted part of the bass drum's sound is in the bandwidth between 200 Hz and 500 Hz. Attenuating the offending frequencies in this range helps clarify and tighten the punch. Be careful not to attenuate these frequencies too much or the bass drum will sound

too thin. Also, in dealing with the low end, remember complementary equalization to leave room for the bass guitar so that together the sounds are not muddied, masked, or too dense.

◼ **Snare drum** Mixing the snare drum presents a unique challenge because of its broad range of frequencies, the complex tonal relationship between the top and bottom heads, and, depending on how it is played, the different tonal centers. In general, the snare has three main areas of sound: body, crispness or presence, and snap or buzz. Boosting somewhere between 100 Hz and 400 Hz provides more body; boosting between 3 kHz and 5 kHz adds crispness or presence; and boosting from 10 kHz and up helps with the snap or buzz. Boosting between 500 Hz and 1,000 Hz can adversely affect clarity.

◼ **Toms** Regardless of what flavoring of EQ you bring to the toms, remember to maintain the pitch relationships among the floor, medium, and high toms. Broadly, the very low frequencies may need attention to reduce rumble. Fullness is in the 200 Hz area, but make sure there is enough of a boost; otherwise an insufficient increase can produce a thuddy sound. If a boost at 200 Hz adds muddiness, try some attenuation. Be careful not to take out too much of the low-frequency character of the instrument, however, or it will sound flat. Boosting about 5 to 8 kHz adds crispness or brightness to the attack. If there is a tubby, muffled sound, the offending frequencies can usually be found between 400 Hz and 1,500 Hz.

◼ **Overhead cymbals** Handling the overhead cymbals depends on whether the cymbal tracks are being processed for the cymbal sound alone or are being integrated into the overall drum mix.

In the first approach, to etch their sound, roll off the frequencies below their fundamental range of about 300 to 600 Hz. (The larger the cymbal, the lower its fundamental.) This cuts off or reduces the lower-end pickup from the snare, toms, and bass drum and helps set apart the cymbals' sound from that of the rest of the kit. Add crispness between 1.2 kHz and 6 kHz, and add shimmer from 8 kHz and up, to taste.

In the second approach, to bring the entire drum kit into focus, shelving from 8 kHz and up brings out the cymbals' shimmer; adding some bottom at 100 to 200 Hz integrates more of the lower-end sound from the toms, bass drum, and snare.

With either approach, adding too much boost in the midrange can bring undesirable clang or gong. Regardless

---

3. Some of this material is adapted from Bruce Bartlett, "Modern Recording and Music," *Modern Recording and Music Magazine,* November 1982. Used with permission.

22-4 Approximate EQ values for selected instruments.

Instrument	Equalization Values
Bass drum	Bottom ranges between 60 Hz and 125 Hz. Attenuating below 80 Hz reduces boominess; attenuating between 300 Hz and 600 Hz reduces dullness, thuddiness, or floppiness (600 Hz) and cardboardlike sound (400 Hz). Boosting between 1,600 Hz and 5,000 Hz adds brightness, attack, and snap.
Low (floor) tom-tom	Fullness ranges between 80 Hz and 120 Hz. Attenuating around 300 Hz reduces boominess. Boosting around 2,500 Hz adds slap; brightness and attack are in the 4,000 Hz range.
High (rack) tom-tom	Fullness ranges between 220 Hz and 240 Hz. Brightness and attack are in the 5,000 Hz range.
Snare drum	Bottom ranges between 120 Hz and 160 Hz. Fullness ranges between 150 Hz and 200 Hz. Fatness ranges between 220 Hz and 240 Hz. Tinniness or harshness is around 1,000 Hz. Crispness begins above 2,000 Hz and ranges to 5,000 to 6,000 kHz.
Cymbals	Dullness—clank and gong—ranges between 200 Hz and 240 Hz. Harshness is around 1 kHz. Sparkle, brilliance, shimmer, and brightness range from 5,000 Hz and up.
Bass guitar	Bottom ranges between 60 Hz and 80 Hz. Reducing around 60 Hz increases overtones and recognition. Cutting around 250 Hz adds clarity. Boominess boosting around 600 Hz adds growl. Attenuating around 600 Hz makes the sound hollow. Boominess is around 200 Hz. Attack ranges between 700 Hz and 1,200 Hz. String noise is around 2,500 to 3,500 Hz. Fret sounds are around 5,000 Hz.
Electric guitar	Fullness ranges between 210 Hz and 240 Hz. Muddiness is 80 Hz and below. Bottom is around 125 Hz. Clarity is around 3,000 Hz. Edge or bite ranges between 2,500 Hz and 3,500 Hz. Upper harmonic limits do not range much beyond 6,500 Hz.
Acoustic guitar	Bottom ranges between 80 Hz and 140 Hz. Boominess is around 200 Hz. Fullness and body range between 220 Hz and 240 Hz. Clarity ranges between 1,600 Hz and 5,000 Hz, but too much boost between 2,000 Hz and 3,000 Hz increases tinniness. Sound becomes thinner as upper midrange frequencies get higher. Steel strings are 5 to 10 dB louder than nylon strings.
Piano	Bass ranges between 80 Hz and 120 Hz. Body ranges between 65 Hz and 130 Hz. Boosting around 100 Hz adds warmth. Tinniness is around 1,000 Hz to 2,000 Hz. Clarity and presence range between 2,000 Hz and 5,000 Hz, with sound becoming thinner as these frequencies get higher. The most robust sound is obtained from a concert grand; sound is less robust in a baby grand and least robust in an upright.
Strings	Generally, sound from the bridge of a violin, viola, cello, or acoustic bass is brighter compared with sound coming from the F-holes, which is fuller. Bowing close to the bridge produces a gentler, less brilliant tone. Muddiness is below 120 Hz. Fullness ranges between 220 Hz and 240 Hz. Too much boost between 3,000 Hz and 10,000 Hz adds edge or scratchiness; just enough boost adds lushness at 400 to 600 Hz and clarity above 2,000 Hz.

of the approach taken, in the final drum mix it is the overhead cymbal tracks that bring the drum kit together.

Other Instruments

■ **Bass guitar** The challenges in mixing the bass are to control its low-end spread, which muddies the sound and inhibits definition yet gives it power and presence in the attack. You must also make sure that the bass guitar and kick drum do not inhabit the same spectral space, which would result in a muddled, often lifeless sound with either instrument dominating the other or rendering both instruments undefined. The bass's impact resides between 40 Hz and 250 Hz. Too much boost in this area adds boominess; not enough boost thins the sound. Clarity can be increased with some attenuation in the 200 to 800 Hz range. A boost between 800 Hz and 6 kHz adds presence; boosting between 1.2 kHz and 4 kHz adds attack.

To deal with a bass guitar/kick drum conflict, it is difficult to suggest frequency ranges because these instruments can vary considerably in sound quality. An example should suffice, however. If, say, the kick drum is defined in the 65 to 100 Hz range, some attenuation of the bass in that range would complement both instruments' sounds while maintaining the punch, power, and definition essential to each and to the mix overall.

■ **Guitar** Acoustic and electric guitars are central to much of popular music. The problem is that they share many of the same frequencies as other voicings in an ensemble, which can create sonic interferences. Therefore, equalizing may be as much a matter of attenuating as boosting to allow the other tracks to come through with clarity and definition. Generally, the body or punch is between 100 Hz and 200 Hz. Sound becomes boomy or muddy with too much of a boost in this range. Attenuating between 80 Hz and 300 Hz can add clarity not only to the guitar but to other voicings whose fundamentals reside in this range. Boosting or attenuating in the 400 Hz to 1.8 kHz range is usually not recommended: increased levels can create a honky or woody sound; decreased levels can hollow out the sound. Assuming it does not adversely affect the overall blend, and depending on the amount of increase, boosting between 2.1 kHz and 6 kHz adds presence, boosting from 3 kHz to 5 kHz adds attack, and boosting from 6 kHz on up adds sheen and air. Too much upper-midrange boost makes guitars sound brittle. With the electric guitar, be wary of noise that level increases from 7.5 kHz and above often bring out.

■ **Piano** As noted in Chapter 17, the piano sound begins with the instrument itself. Regardless of how it is recorded and mixed, its sound is anchored to its inherent tonality. Beyond that, how it is handled in the mix depends on whether it is a grand, baby grand, or upright and the role it plays—frontline or supporting. As a supporting instrument, it should complement the timbre and the overall feel of the mix. If the mix is airy, bright, dark, punchy, sparkly, and so on, the piano's sound should be similar. Generally, airiness is in the upper mid- and treble range; brightness is in the upper midrange; darker tonalities are in the low end; punch is in the upper bass and lower midrange; and sparkle is in the upper treble range. This assumes that any boost in these frequencies does not conflict with other voicings.

For example, if a darker lower end is called for, take care that the piano sound does not interfere with the kick drum, toms, and bass guitar and vice versa. If the piano sound must be equalized, it may be necessary to attenuate frequencies in its lower octaves. If brightness or sparkle is required, listen for a boost in the appropriate frequencies that brings out unwanted hardness, harshness, or brittleness as a cumulative effect from other voicings in the same frequency range and attenuate the offending frequencies in either the piano or in one or more of the other instruments.

For example, if the piano and the guitar are playing similar parts and conflicting sonically in, say, the 250 to 400 Hz range, attenuating or high-pass-filtering one or the other of these instruments may be necessary to bring about a satisfactory blend. Which instrument to equalize, of course, depends on the music and the arrangement. All this seems straightforward enough, but to add to the challenge of mixing piano is the fact that its complex harmonics change over time. The sound you hear while listening to one pass of a song may be not the sound you hear during a subsequent pass. Mixing piano takes skill and "ears."

■ **Vocal** Almost always the vocal is the lead "instrument." It is where the focus in a mix should be. Whatever the ensemble's various EQ settings (and compression, reverb, and other signal-processing settings as well), the vocal must be processed to fit in without being too far out in front of or too far inside the mix (unless those are the intentions). So as you shape the vocal, continue to reference it in the context of the accompanying instruments.

Although the fundamental range of the singing voice is not wide, the harmonics are complex. In general, fullness in the male voice is between 100 Hz and 150 Hz; in the female voice, it is between 200 Hz and 250 Hz. A slight boost in these ranges and up to 350 Hz also adds warmth. Boosts between 1.2 kHz and 8 kHz add presence; boosting between 900 Hz and 3.5 kHz brings out intelligibility; and boosting from 10 to 12 kHz adds airiness. Be careful with the amount of boost in these ranges; unwanted qualities can result, such as muddiness and density in the lower frequencies and nasality and sibilance in the upper frequencies.

Compression

Sounds are compressed to deal with the dynamic ranges of certain instruments so that they better integrate into the overall mix. Like any other signal processing, it is not a panacea for corrective action; it is more a sound-shaping tool and, as such, is to be used only when aesthetically justified. The type of voicing with which compression is generally used is one tending to have a transient attack, a wide dynamic range, or a frequency response that can cut through a mix, such as drums, vocals, bass guitar, French horn, and piano.

Certain styles of music have also developed a tradition as to the amount of compression that is employed. For example, much of pop music has more compression than most country music and punk rock. Jazz generally uses light compression. In classical music, compression varies widely, depending on dynamic range.

Chapter 7 covers a number of reasons why compression is used in sound shaping and offers some tips for its implementation. Here are some additional general guidelines for applying compression to selected areas of the frequency spectrum and to instruments that are commonly compressed. These are only a point of departure and should not be followed without careful listening and experimentation. It is worth repeating that some compression effects are subtle and take experience to handle. Bear in mind that no one effect in mixing should be evaluated in isolation: the outcome of equalization, compression, reverberation, delay, spatial placement, and so on—all are interrelated.

■ **Bass (80 to 150 Hz)** To tighten the low end: *ratio*—2.5:1; *attack time*—20 ms; *release time*—150 ms; *threshold*—fairly low. Makeup gain should be just enough to compensate for the gain lost in compression.

■ **Low midrange (150 to 600 Hz)** To tighten the mix: *ratio*—3:1; *attack time*—20 ms; *release time*—150 ms; *threshold*—set to trigger regularly. Makeup gain should be just enough to compensate for the gain lost in compression or a bit more for added warmth.

■ **Midrange (600 to 1,500 Hz)** To add punch to a mix: *ratio*—6:1; *attack time*—10 ms; *release time*—150 ms; *threshold*—set fairly low. Add 4 to 6 dB makeup gain for lost gain and to add solidity.

■ **Upper midrange (1,500 to 6,000 Hz)** To add clarity and presence: *ratio*—3:1; *attack time*—10 ms; *release time*—150 ms; *threshold*—set to trigger regularly. Add 1 to 3 dB of gain for clarity and presence.

■ **High end (6 to 14 kHz)** To reduce harshness without losing brilliance: *ratio*—2:1; *attack time*—10 ms; *release time*—150 ms; *threshold*—set high enough to trigger when harshness is present. Add 1 to 2 dB makeup gain to compensate for brilliance lost in compression.[4]

Here are some specific applications of compression on selected instruments:

■ **Drums** *Ratio*—2:1 to 3:1 or 4:1 to 8:1; *attack time*—fast; *release time*—medium to fast; *threshold*—set to compress loudest peaks 4 to 6 dB or 6 to 8 dB. Compressing drums allows you to mix them at a lower level and still retain their impact.

■ **Bass guitar** *Ratio*—4:1; *attack time*—medium; *release time*—medium to fast; *threshold*—set to compress loudest peaks 2 to 4 dB. One main reason why recordists compress the bass is because its low-frequency energy tends to eat up much of the mix's overall headroom. One cautionary note: watch out for distortion that can be introduced by overly quick release times.

■ **Rhythm instruments (guitar, saxophone, and synthesizer)** *Ratio*—4:1 to 6:1; *attack time*—medium; *release time*—medium; *threshold*—set to compress loudest peaks 3 to 5 dB. Moderate compression can enrich texture and help make rhythm instruments forceful without dominating the mix.

■ **Vocals** *Ratio*—3:1 to 4:1; *attack time*—fast to medium; *release time*—medium to fast; *threshold*—set to compress loudest peaks 3 to 6 dB. The amount of compression on a vocalist depends on the singer's technique; that is, does the singer back off slightly when hitting loud notes and lean in slightly to compensate for softer ones—which is good technique—or does the singer not compensate

---

4. From Rob McGaughey, "Using a Multi-band Compressor on a Mix," *Keyboard,* June 1999, p. 64.

for dynamic range or, worse, eat the microphone? If the music track is dense and the vocals need to be heard, compression will have to be more aggressive. For delicate singers use more-sensitive threshold levels and smaller ratios. For screamers you may need to compress 6 to 8 dB to get the proper texture. Beware that high compression levels bring out sibilance and background noise.

Here are some other effects of compression on selected instruments:

- **Drums** A medium-to-long attack time reduces the percussive effect. A short release time and a wide ratio create a bigger or fuller sound.

- **Cymbals** Medium-to-short attack and release times and an average ratio reduce excessive ringing.

- **Guitar** Short attack and release times and a wide ratio increase the sustain.

- **Keyboards** A medium-to-long attack time, a medium-to-short release time, and a wide ratio give a fuller sound.

- **Strings** Short attack and release times and an average ratio add body to the sound.

- **Vocals** Medium-to-short attack and release times and an average ratio reduce sibilance.

There are many other approaches to compression. The suggestions listed here are not intended to imply that compression should be used just because it is available or that most voicings should be compressed. If you do employ compression, these suggestions may be good starting points.

Reverberation: Creating Acoustic Space

Due to the common practice of miking each sound component separately (for greater control) and closely (to reduce leakage), many original multitrack recordings lack a complementary acoustic environment. In such cases the acoustics are added in the mixdown by artificial means using signal-processing devices such as reverb and digital delay (see Chapter 7).

If you add acoustics in the mixdown, do it after equalizing (because it is difficult to get a true sense of the effects of frequency changes in a reverberant space) and after panning (to get a better idea of how reverb affects positioning). Avoid giving widely different reverb times to various components in an ensemble, or it will sound as though they are not playing in the same space, unless that is your intention for special effect.

The quality of the reverberation depends on the musical style. Most types of popular music work well with the sound of digital reverb, a reverb plate, or equivalent plug-ins. Jazz usually requires a more natural-sounding acoustic environment; classical music definitely does.

In determining reverb balance, adjust it one track at a time (on the tracks to which reverb is being added). Reverb can be located in the mix by panning; it does not have to envelop an entire recording. Reverb in stereo mixes should achieve a sense of depth and breadth. In surround sound it should not overwhelm or swallow the mix, nor if there is reverb from the front loudspeakers should it be the same as it is from the rear-side (or rear) loudspeakers. In acoustic conditions the listeners sitting closer to an ensemble hear less reverb than do the listeners sitting farther away.

With reverberation some equalization may be necessary. Because plates and chambers tend to generate lower frequencies that muddy sound, attenuating the reverb between 60 Hz and 100 Hz may be necessary to clean up the sound. If muddiness is not a problem, boosting lower frequencies gives the reverb a larger and more distant sound. Boosting higher frequencies gives the reverb a brighter, closer, more present sound.

Less-expensive reverberation devices and plug-ins tend to lack good treble response. By slightly boosting the high end, the reverb will sound somewhat more natural and lifelike. If any one voicing is inevitably assigned to reverb, it is the vocal. Try to give the vocal its own reverb so that any changes to the vocal track do not affect the other voicings.

Be wary of the reverb's midrange interfering with the harmonic richness of the vocal's midrange. Attenuating or notching out the reverb's competing midrange frequencies can better define the vocal and help make it stand out.

Other effects, such as *chorusing* and *accented reverb*, can be used after reverberation is applied. By setting the chorus for a delay between 20 ms and 30 ms and adding it to the reverb, sound gains a fuller, shimmering quality. Sending the reverb output into a noise gate and triggering the noise gate with selected accents from a percussive instrument such as a snare drum, piano, or tambourine can heighten as well as unify the rhythm.

Before making a final decision about the reverb you employ, do an A-B comparison. Check reverb proportions using large and small loudspeakers to make sure the reverb neither envelops sound nor is so subtle that it defies definition.

Digital Delay: Enhancing Acoustic Space

Sound reaches listeners at different times, depending on where a listener is located relative to the sound source. The closer to the sound source you are, the sooner the sound reaches you and vice versa. Hence a major component of reverberation is *delay*—the time interval between a sound or signal and each of its repeats. To provide more-realistic reverberation, therefore, many digital reverbs include *predelay*, which is the amount of time between the onset of the direct sound and the appearance of the first reflections. If a reverb unit or plug-in does not include predelay, the same effect can be generated by using digital delay before reverb.

Predelay adds a feeling of space to the reverberation. In either case, predelay should be short—15 to 20 ms usually suffices. (A millisecond is equivalent to about 1 foot in space.) With some outboard delays the longer the delay time, the poorer the signal-to-noise ratio.

Post-delay—adding delay after reverb—is another way to add dimension to sound, particularly to a vocal. In the case of the vocal, it may be necessary to boost the high end to brighten the sound, to avoid muddying it, or both.

Synchronizing delay to tempo is another effect that can heighten sonic interest. This technique involves adjusting the rate of delay to the music's tempo by dividing the tempo into 60,000—the number of milliseconds per measure to which the digital delay is set.

It is also possible to create *polyrhythms*—simultaneous and sharply contrasting rhythms—by using a plug-in capable of creating the effect or by employing two delays and feeding the output of one into the input of the other. Varying delay time of the second unit generates a variety of spatial effects.

In using delay there is one precaution: make sure the device or plug-in has a bandwidth of at least 12 kHz. Given the quality of sound being produced today, however, 15 kHz and higher is recommended.

Two features of digital delay—feedback and modulation—can be employed in various ways to help create a wide array of effects with flanging, chorusing, doubling, and slapback echo. *Feedback*, or *regeneration,* as the terms suggest, feeds a proportion of the delayed signal back into the delay line, in essence, "echoing the echo."

Modulation is controlled by two parameters: width and speed. Width dictates how wide a range above and below the chosen delay time the modulator will be allowed to swing. You can vary the delay by any number of milliseconds above and below the designated time. Speed dictates how rapidly the time delay will oscillate.

Electronic Sounds

There are three basic kinds of electronic sounds: samples or emulations of music; samples or emulations of real-world (nonmusical) sounds; and completely artificial sounds. It is inappropriate to place these elements in an acoustic environment using the same rationale you would in placing musical instruments. There are no templates. Because an electronic sound is used for its own uniqueness and not as an attempt to replicate the sound of a musical instrument, it can be manipulated in any way and placed anywhere in a mix so long as it makes sense aesthetically.

SPATIAL IMAGING OF MUSIC IN STEREO AND SURROUND SOUND

Almost from the beginning of recorded sound, attempts have been made to increase the dimensionality of sonic reproduction. Years before stereo, recordists were experimenting with miking techniques to make sound more spacious and realistic. Binaural recording has been around for decades, but it still requires playback through headphones to appreciate its extraordinary three-dimensional effect. A number of years ago, the commercially failed quadraphonic sound increased the depth of sonic space by using loudspeakers to the rear as well as in front of the listener. Formats are available that augment the stereo image by effectively bringing the depth and the width of the aural frame to the outermost edges of the soundfield on a plane with the listener. In short, a number of approaches applied during recording or mixing have been, or are being, used to bring sound reproduction closer to the live listening experience. Of those stereo and surround sound have so far proved to be the most commercially viable.

Stereo

In multitrack recording, each element is recorded at an optimal level and on a separate track. If all the elements were played back in the same way, it would sound as though they were coming from precisely the same location, to say nothing about how imbalanced the voicings would be. In reality, of course, this is not the case. Each musical component has to be positioned in an aural frame by setting the levels of loudness to create front-to-rear perspective, or depth, and panning to establish left-to-right perspective, or breadth. In setting levels, the louder a sound, the closer it seems to be; and, conversely, the quieter a sound, the farther away it seems.

Frequency and reverb also affect positioning. In panning stereo there are five main areas: left, left-center, center, right-center, and right. There are many options in positioning various elements of an ensemble in an aural frame, but three factors enter into the decision: the aural balance, how the ensemble arranges itself when playing before a live audience, and the type of music being played. Keep in mind that each musical style has its own values.

Pop music is usually emotional and contains a strong beat. Drums and bass therefore are usually focused in the mix. Country music is generally vocal-centered with the accompaniment important, of course, but subordinate. Jazz and classical music are more varied and require different approaches. The mixer must have a clear idea of what the music sounds like in a natural acoustic setting before attempting a studio mix, unless the sonic manipulations are such that they can be produced only in a studio.

Sounds and where they are placed in aural space have different effects on perception. In a stereo field, these effects include the following: the sound closest to the center and nearest to the listener is the most predominant; a sound farther back but still in the center creates depth

and a balance or counterweight to the sound that is front and center; sound placed to one side usually requires a similarly weighted sound on the opposite side or else the left-to-right aural space will seem unbalanced and skew listener attention; and the more you spread sound across the aural space, the wider the sound sources will seem.

This is not to suggest that all parts of aural space must be sonically balanced or filled at all times; that depends on the ensemble and the music. A symphony orchestra usually positions first violins to the left of the conductor, second violins to the left-center, violas to the right-center, and cellos to the right. If the music calls for just the first violins to play, it is natural for the sound to come mainly from the left. To pan the first violins left to right would establish a stereo balance but would be poor aesthetic judgment and would disorient the listener, especially when the full orchestra returned and the first violins jumped back to their original orchestral position.

To illustrate aural framing in a stereo field, see Figures 22-5 to 22-12.

Surround Sound

Sound is omnidirectional; our natural acoustic environment is 360 degrees. Surround sound provides the opportunity to come far closer to reproducing that experience

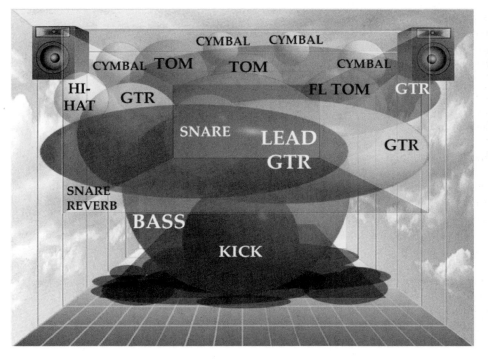

22-5 Rock mix. Quite full with lots of fattening and overlapping sounds. The lead guitar is spread in stereo with a rhythm guitar behind it and another stereo guitar in the background. The low end is clean, with a strong kick drum and bass. (In this figure and in Figures 22-6 to 22-12, the size of the globes indicates the relative loudness of the voicings.)

22-6 Heavy metal mix.
A full, busy mix yet with a clear low end (kick and bass). The hi-hat, snare, and lead guitar are out in front. There are multiple guitar parts, with a few panned in stereo. The overall effect is a wall of sound.

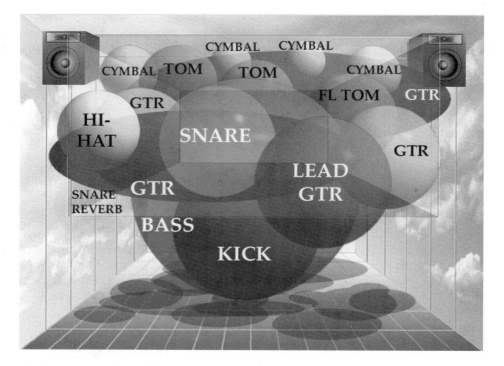

22-7 Jazz mix. Overall, a clean, clear mix, with the guitar, piano, and hi-hat in front and the kick drum atypically loud for a jazz mix.

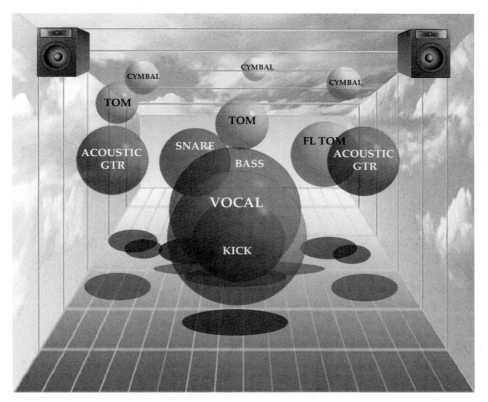

22-8 Country mix. A loud vocal in front of a clean, clear, spacious mix of the ensemble.

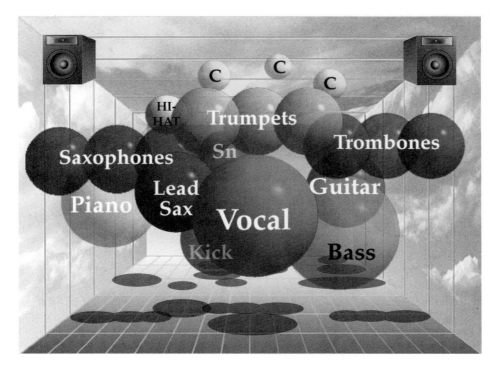

22-9 Big-band mix. The vocal and the horns are the prominent features of this mix.

22-10 The mix on the song "She Blinded Me with Science" from the album *Wireless* by Thomas Dolby.

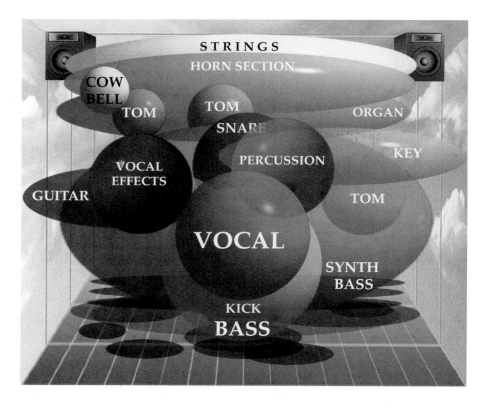

22-11 The mix on the song "Babylon Sisters" from the album *Gaucho* by Steely Dan.

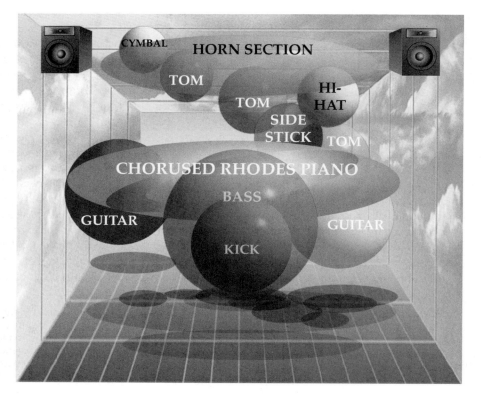

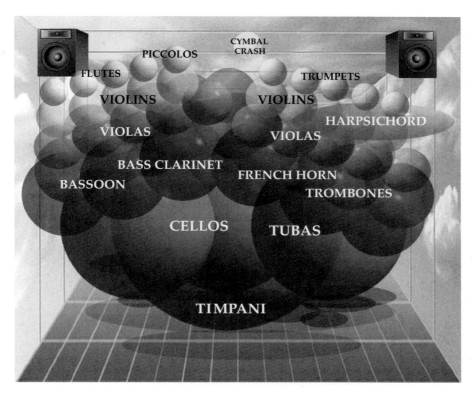

22-12 A mix of "The Four Seasons" by Antonio Vivaldi.

than stereo by enabling the music and the listener to occupy the same space.[5] With stereo the audio is localized wide and deep in front of the listener, whereas ***surround sound*** increases the depth of the front-to-rear and side-to-side sound images, placing the listener more inside the aural event. In stereo two discrete channel signals are reproduced separately through two loudspeakers, creating phantom images between them. In surround sound discrete multichannel signals are reproduced separately, each through a dedicated loudspeaker.

There are two basic ways of handling surround sound. One is to take two-channel stereo and synthesize it to multichannel pseudo-surround. This is known as ***upmixing***. An upmix can be done using any of several different stand-alone hardware devices or plug-ins. Generally, the operation involves feeding the stereo signals to the upmix processor or program for encoding and then decoding the signals into 5.1 surround sound. Typically, this results in

imaging that still positions the principal voicings in front of the listener but extends the depth of the aural space so that the overall sound is more immersing. Depending on the quality of the device or software employed, sonic results can vary from stable surround imaging, to imaging that lacks positional clarity or that sounds obviously electronically processed, or both.

Upmixing is useful in broadcasting, for example, where a signal can be transmitted in stereo but not in surround. The quandary that faces broadcasters is the cost of processing surround sound at the station for the relatively few listeners capable of reproducing it at home or in the car versus allowing the consumer to handle it with surround-capable equipment. With CDs, upmixing provides a way to get the feel of surround sound in music recordings that are available only in stereo. (*Downmixing*, discussed later in this chapter, is the process whereby the surround-sound signals are mixed to stereo.)[6]

---

5. All discussion of surround sound in this chapter assumes the 5.1 format, which is the most widely used. The 7.1 format has begun to make inroads, however; it features seven channels of full-frequency sound in the left, center, right, left surround, right surround, rear-left, and rear-right plus the low-frequency enhancement (LFE) channel (see Chapter 8).

6. *Upmix* and *downmix* in the context of surround sound should not be confused with the terms *up mix* and *down mix* used in the context of mixing. To provide more perspective in evaluating overall blend and balance, a principal voicing (or voicings) may be mixed with that part (or parts) recorded slightly louder (up mix) or slightly softer (down mix).

The other way to produce surround sound is to build a multichannel mix from the outset. Because this is the preferred method, it is considered here. The 5.1 format is in widespread use; 6.1, 7.1, and, mostly in live venues, 10.2 are also being employed. The first number refers to the discrete production channels of full-bandwidth audio—20 Hz to 20 kHz. These channels play back through the array of loudspeakers used to reproduce them.

The second number refers to a separate, discrete channel (or channels) for *low-frequency enhancement (LFE)*. (The *E* can also stand for *effects*.) The LFE production channel has a frequency response rated from 5 to 125 Hz. A subwoofer is used to play back the LFE channel. Because few subwoofers can produce sounds lower than 15 to 20 Hz, their range more realistically begins around 30 to 35 Hz.

In the 5.1 surround-sound format, audio from the five channels is sent to loudspeakers positioned frontally—left, center, and right—and to the left and right surround loudspeakers. LFE audio feeds to the subwoofer, which may be positioned between the left and center or the center and right frontal loudspeakers (see Chapter 8). Sometimes two subwoofers are used to reproduce the mono LFE signal, ordinarily positioned behind and outside the front-left and front-right speakers.

BASIC EQUIPMENT FOR MIXING SURROUND SOUND

To produce a surround-sound mix in the 5.1 format, a few basic types of equipment are required: a console or DAW with the capability to pan sounds among the six surround channels; loudspeakers and amplification to reproduce five full-bandwidth channels and one LFE channel; a recorder (hard disk or conventional) to record the six surround channels; and, depending on the intended delivery format, an encoder to compress the data.

There are two principal format specifications used in encoding and decoding surround sound: *Dolby Digital* and *Digital Theater System (DTS)*. (*Sony Dynamic Digital Sound [SDDS]* is a third format specification, but it is used with film only.) Uncompressed audio at 44.1 kHz with 16-bit resolution requires a bandwidth of about 700 Kbps. Therefore the six channels in the 5.1 format require 4.2 Mbps.

Dolby Digital uses lossy data compression and an encoding algorithm called *AC-3* (the *AC* stands for *audio coding*) to reduce the required bit rate to roughly 400 Kbps. DTS also uses lossy compression. Its compres-

sion is less extreme than Dolby's and is slightly more robust than AC-3. Its bandwidth requirements are about 1.4 Mbps. Implementing these formats for encoding is beyond the scope of this book. There are, however, articles and books available that provide this information and cover stand-alone hardware and software and built-in software programs.

MIXING FOR SURROUND SOUND

Mixing for surround sound, compared with stereo, opens up a new world of aesthetic options in dealing with the relationship of the listener to the music (see 22-13 to 22-16). But by so doing, it also creates new challenges in dealing with those options. Among them are handling the center and surround channels, reverberation, and bass management.

Center Channel

Because there is no center channel or loudspeaker in stereo, the center image is a psychoacoustic illusion; in surround sound it is not. There is a discrete center channel and speaker in surround sound, so if you are not careful about delegating the signal (or signals) there, it could unbalance the entire frontal imaging. This is particularly important in a music mix. For TV and film, the center channel must be used because it is necessary for the dialogue (see "Surround Sound" in Chapter 23).

There is no single recommended way of handling the center channel; it depends on producer preference and the music. Generally, dealing with the center channel can be divided into two broad approaches: delegating little if anything to it or using it selectively.

Those who use the center channel little or not at all believe that handling the center image is better done by applying the stereo model: letting the left and right loudspeakers create a phantom center. When too much audio is sent to the center channel, there is a greater build in the middle of the frontal sound image. This makes the voicings coming from the center speaker more dominant than they should be, thereby focusing attention there to the detriment of the overall musical balance.

Another consideration is that many home surround systems do not come with a center loudspeaker; when they do, it is often positioned incorrectly or not set up at all, so there is no way of reproducing any center-channel audio.

Producers who prefer to use the center channel take various approaches. One technique creates a phantom

22-13 Surround-sound mix using the entire space.

22-14 Surround-sound mix of an a cappella choir.

22-15 Fattened surround-sound mix of an a cappella choir.

22-16 Surround-sound mix of a vocal with reverberation.

center between the left and right loudspeakers, along with a duplicated discrete center channel several decibels down. This adds depth and perspective to the center voicings without overly intensifying their image.

In a typical pop song, the bass guitar and the kick drum are positioned rear-center to anchor the mix. If they are delegated to the center channel, it may be necessary to diffuse their center-channel impact. Their signal can be reduced in level and also fed to the left and right loudspeakers, then panned toward the center.

Producers who take full advantage of the center channel do so because they want that emphasis in the mix. Their point is that in stereo, when a voicing is put in the center, it is not really in the center—it is a phantom image created from the left and right channels. Why do the same thing with surround? Use the discrete center channel to create a truer spatial spectrum that will add more depth and power to the frontal imaging.

The type of music also has something to do with how the center channel is used. Classical music and large jazz bands, for example, take advantage of it because of the size and the breadth of the ensembles. Pop music producers tend to center such voicings as the bass guitar, snare drum, kick drum, and vocal, but they are careful not to delegate too many instruments to it or to delegate a voicing solely to the center channel without some duplication elsewhere in the mix. As for the problem with surround-sound home systems' not having a center loudspeaker, their feeling is: Why bother mixing for surround if the music is not going to be played in the medium for which it is intended? Take advantage of what surround sound provides and mix for those who have the systems to hear the music the way it should be heard.

Regardless of the aesthetic involved in using or not using the center channel, one caveat is important to remember: if a voicing is delegated only to the center channel and to no other channels, a playback system with no center loudspeaker will not reproduce that voicing.

Surround Channels

How the surround channels are used comes down to what the music calls for, producer preference, or both. It is an artistic decision—there are no rules.

Some music mixes, such as classical and live concerts, may take a more objective approach. The presentation is mainly frontal, with the surrounds used for ambience to place the listener in the venue's audience. Other types of more studio-based music, such as pop and perhaps jazz, may take a more subjective approach and place the listener more inside the music. For example, a jazz combo with a lead piano may be mixed to center the listener at or near the piano, with the rest of the ensemble and the ambience surrounding the listener. Or an approach may be a combination of the objective and the subjective.

In the previous example, instead of centering the listener inside the ensemble, the mix would arc to the listener's sides, filling out the surrounds with some signal duplication and ambience. Regardless of the approach, in any music mix, surround or otherwise, it always helps to remember that what you do should primarily serve the music.

In panning sounds between the front and surround channels, two perceptual effects are worth noting: the frequency response between the front and the surrounds is different, and sound panned halfway between the front and the surrounds draws some attention forward and some attention behind; this instability creates a separation or split in the sound.

Reverberation

The presence of the center channel calls for some precautions when using reverb. Just as putting too much of any voicing in the center channel focuses the ear on it, the same is true with reverberation. There are also the added concerns of phasing problems with the reverb in other channels, particularly the left and the right, and if the music is played back on systems without a center loudspeaker or with a center loudspeaker that is positioned incorrectly.

The current wisdom is to leave the center channel dry and put reverb in the left and right channels, continuing it in the surrounds. Any reverb placed in the center is minor and is usually different from what is in the other channels.

Bass Management

Bass management refers to the redirection of low-frequency content from each of the full-bandwidth production channels to the subwoofer, where it is combined with the LFE channel. The advantage of the LFE channel is that it provides more headroom below 125 Hz, where the ear is less sensitive and requires more boost to perceive equal loudness with the midrange. By providing this headroom, bass enhancement can be used without its eating up other frequencies. Generally, the LFE channel is for low-end effects used in theatrical film and television, such as rumbles, explosions, thunder, and gunshots. If it is used in mixing music, it is for the very lowest notes of the lowest bass instruments. Generally, however, in music mixes low-end instruments are usually assigned to the full-frequency-range channels, not the LFE, for two main reasons: the LFE channel has limited frequency response and most bass instruments have ranges that go beyond 125 Hz, and because of the potential of bass enhancement to imbalance or overwhelm the mix.

That said, some mixers use the LFE channel as a bass extender to reproduce the very low content of the main channels for emphasis. Another rationale for using the LFE channel is that taking a good deal of the bass out of the surround speakers can enhance their clarity and help reduce distortion. The success of this technique of course depends on properly proportioning the low end in the subwoofer relative to the rest of the frequency spectrum coming from the main loudspeaker array.

In working with the LFE channel, it helps to add a bass management and volume controller to the system. This assists in giving a better idea of how the low end will sound on different-quality reproduction systems, such as a typical home unit or a top-of-the-line system. For example, sounds such as plosives and breath blasts from a vocalist may be picked up by a high-quality mic but not heard through a small speaker. But if they are mixed to, say, a DVD, those sounds would be routed automatically to the LFE channel via the bass management filters in the receiver and, therefore, be quite audible. Keep in mind that with any .1 surround-sound format, the LFE is a monaural channel. Any bass that requires stereo must be delegated to the main channels or to a .2 format.

Track Assignment

Although there is no agreed-upon protocol for assigning surround-sound tracks, the International Telecommunication Union (ITU) has suggested that the track assignments be as follows: track 1, front-left; track 2, front-right; track 3, front-center; track 4, subwoofer; track 5, rear-left surround; and track 6, rear-right surround. Other groupings are also used (see 22-17). Whichever mode of assignment you use, make sure that the mix file is clearly labeled as to which tracks are assigned where.

Downmixing to Stereo

Even with the advent of multiple-channel distribution and broadcast media such as the DVD and HDTV, most listeners and viewers are still hearing sound in stereo. Hence any mix in surround-sound will be most likely downmixed to stereo.

In doing both a stereo mix and a surround mix, monitoring the stereo is more important. Getting it right in stereo first and then doing the surround mix is easier. Some mixers prefer to start with stereo and then turn to surround, going back and forth as the mixes proceed, to check for stereo-to-surround compatibility and vice versa in relation to phasing and cancellation (see "Surround-to-stereo Compatibility" in Chapter 23).

There is more aural space to work with in surround sound. Using that mix as the reference could create problems with density and balance in the stereo mix because there is less aural space in which to place the voicings. When trying to apply surround-type ideas to stereo, there may be too many extra elements thrown in which stereo cannot handle but that sound OK in surround, resulting in such sonic discomforts as clutter, muddiness, and disproportional localization. In monitoring it helps to listen for any change in the vibe of the music between the surround and stereo mixes.

All that said, there are mixers who prefer to do the surround mix first. They feel that it opens up possibilities for the stereo mix that may not have been considered had the stereo mix been done first.

Procedurally, downmixing surround sound to stereo is relatively straightforward. Center-channel audio is added equally to the front-left and front-right channels as is the audio from the left and right surrounds. In some cases, if there is LFE content, it is added to the stereo channels economically to ensure that the bass does not overwhelm the rest of the mix. In most instances the LFE channel is just dropped. For mono mixes all channels except LFE are delegated to the center loudspeaker.

As straightforward as a downmix may be, there are potential problems to watch out for. For example, if there is delay between the front-left and left-surround channels or the front-right and right-surround channels, significant phasing could occur when the channels are combined. Reverberation values may also change. A lot of high end that sounds good in a surround mix may not translate well when downmixed to stereo due to the effects of cancellation.

AESTHETIC CONSIDERATIONS IN SURROUND-SOUND MIXING

Two basic approaches to mixing surround sound have emerged: the traditional approach and the perspective approach. The *traditional approach* positions the listener in front of the musicians, with the room (or the artificial reverberation) adding the ambience. The added dimen-

Track	1	2	3	4	5	6	7	8
Mode 1	L	R	Ls	Rs	C	LFE	Lt	Rt
Mode 2	L	C	R	Ls	Rs	LFE	Lt	Rt
Mode 3	L	Ls	C	Rs	R	LFE	Lt	Rt
Mode 4	L	R	C	LFE	Ls	Rs	Lt	Rt
Mode 5	L	C	Rs	R	Ls	LFE	Lt	Rt
Mode 6	C	L	R	Ls	Rs	LFE	Lt	Rt

22-17 Six common modes of assigning surround-sound channels. Tracks 7 and 8 are the left and right stereo downmix.

sion of the ambience is what surrounds the listener. The *perspective approach* positions the listener inside the ensemble, creating the experience of being surrounded by the musical ingredients. Due to conditioning, this is not the natural way most people experience music (unless you are a musician). These approaches raise the question: because technology has made possible a different perspective in designing a musical experience, should we take advantage of that opportunity? The answer of course rests with the musicians and the music.

It is generally agreed among most recordists, however, that regardless of the mixing approach and for a number of reasons, surround sound is a far superior sonic experience compared with stereo.

◼ There is greater dimension overall in surround sound, and individual monaural tracks can be made to sound bigger by panning them across the loudspeakers.

◼ Music in surround is airier and more open. Stereo, by comparison, is more closed and focused.

◼ In stereo, with music that is dense with lots of loud instruments, parts of the frequency spectrum that are essential to hear certain instruments must be carved out so that there is space for the other voicings. There is less conflict in surround sound because there is more aural space in which to maneuver. Surround is easier to blend because it provides a broader aural canvas.

◼ Instruments sound more distinct in surround sound, and not as much equalization is required to make each instrument heard.

◼ The center channel (used properly) improves clarity because it grounds the mix by eliminating the phantom image shifts that can occur in stereo.

◼ Depth must be created artificially in stereo, whereas in surround it is almost built-in because much of the dimension is created through miking, channel/loudspeaker assignment, or both.

◼ Stereo is best listened to in the **sweet spot**—the optimal distance between and away from the loudspeakers. There is no single best listening position with surround sound. Moving around provides different perspectives of the mix without significantly changing clarity, dimension, and spatial coherence.

Additionally, observations from respected industry professionals about mixing music in surround have had some resonance in the audio world and are worth noting here. They follow in no particular order.

◼ In placing instruments in an ensemble, do not be a slave to the visual sense. We see in front and peripherally to the sides; sound comes from all around. The idea of placing the listener in front of the ensemble, whether up close or "in the eighth row" is not necessarily the best approach. Do not buy into any dogma about how voicings should be positioned on surround's aural canvas.

◼ That said, the type of music does require some consideration in how it is handled in the surround environment. An intimate song may call for more of a concentration in the center speaker, with the accompaniment folding around the vocal. A large jazz ensemble playing something upbeat may call for a more wide-open use of the front-side and rear speakers. A symphony may call for a spacious sound enveloping the listener from the front and the sides, with the hall ambience in the rear speakers. With pop/rock the listener can be "on-stage," surrounded by the musicians.

■ Keep in mind that the ITU specification for placement of the surround-sound loudspeakers and how this positioning may influence a mix was a compromise between the needs of the film sound mixer and those of the music mixer. Loudspeaker placement that serves one need does not necessarily serve the other (see Chapter 8). In fact, so long as the loudspeakers are calibrated, the sense of surround's spaciousness remains the same even though loudspeaker placement may not conform to the ITU specification.

■ Surround sound provides much more latitude than stereo in creating a sound stage that is more involving for the listener. Because it is more "cinematic" than stereo, surround sound can be more expressive and take the audience more into the music.

■ In doing a surround mix in the various genres of popular music, do not discount making the listener take notice because of what is coming from the rear loudspeakers.

■ When recording surround sound using the multimicrophone technique, the sweet spot may be tight in mixing pop in the 5.1 format. Using a dedicated surround-sound microphone array, the sweet spot is wider and more spacious.

MAIN POINTS

▶ A good mix cannot salvage a bad recording, but a poor mix can ruin a good one.

▶ Whatever the mixer does should be music driven; a mixer's responsibility is to serve the music, not the other way around. It is always about the music.

▶ The characteristics of a successful mix involve balance, frequency range, spatial positioning, dimension, depth and width, dynamics, context, focus, and interest.

▶ The characteristics of an amateur mix are lack of contrast; dull, uninteresting, and lifeless sound; lack of focus; overproduction of effects; edge and harshness; too much compression; lack of intimacy; insufficient detail; inappropriate stereo or surround-sound balance; disproportionate spectral balance; inappropriately wide dynamic range; level-dominating outbursts; extraneous noise; and lack of clarity and intelligibility.

▶ Before getting down to the mix, following certain procedures helps avoid operational and technical problems during the mixdown.

▶ In a music mixdown, one procedure is to evaluate the positive and negative attributes of the recording, working

with one track at a time but building on the tracks already processed. When each track sounds acceptable in the context of the overall mix, blend and balance the sounds together. This may involve changing individual settings in favor of the overall mix.

▶ Recordkeeping, whether handwritten or using computer software, is important in any type of mixing. The number of details in a mix can be daunting.

▶ When equalizing, avoid large increases or decreases in equalization (EQ), do not increase or decrease too many tracks at the same frequency, and do not use EQ as a substitute for better microphone selection and placement. Try subtractive, instead of additive, equalization and use complementary EQ to keep masking to a minimum. Equalizing between 400 Hz and 2,000 Hz is more noticeable than equalizing above and below that range. Be sure to equalize with an awareness of the frequency limits of the medium in which you are working.

▶ When equalizing be aware of how boosting or attenuating in particular frequency ranges affect an instrument's sound.

▶ Sounds are compressed to deal with the dynamic ranges of certain instruments so that they better integrate into the overall mix. Like any other signal processing, it is not a panacea for corrective action.

▶ The quality of reverberation added to a recording in the mix depends, to a considerable extent, on musical style. Classical, jazz, and some types of folk music usually require natural-sounding acoustics; various reverberant environments may be appropriate for pop music.

▶ Do not add artificial reverb until after signal processing and panning because it is difficult to get a true sense of the effects of frequency and positional change in a reverberant space. Also, avoid giving widely different reverb times to the various components in an ensemble unless they are supposed to sound as though they are in different acoustic environments.

▶ A major component of reverberation is delay.

▶ Factors involved in placing musical components in the stereo frame are the aural balance, the arrangement of the ensemble when performing, and the type of music being played.

▶ Surround sound comes far closer than stereo to reproducing our natural acoustic environment by enabling the music and the listener to occupy the same space. It increases the depth of the front-to-rear and side-to-side sound images.

▶ Surround sound can be produced by upmixing—synthesizing a multichannel signal from two-channel stereo—or by building the multichannel mix from the outset, which is the preferred method.

▶ The 5.1 surround format uses five full-bandwidth channels and a low-frequency enhancement (LFE) channel for sounds below 125 Hz. The 7.1 surround format adds two full-bandwidth channels to feed the left-side and right-side surround loudspeakers.

▶ In mixing for surround sound, four important elements to manage are the center channel, the surround channels, reverberation, and bass management.

▶ Two basic approaches have emerged to mixing surround sound: the traditional approach and the perspective approach. The traditional approach positions the listener in front of the musicians, with the room (or the artificial reverberation) adding the ambience. The added dimension of the ambience is what surrounds the listener. The perspective approach positions the listener inside the ensemble, creating the experience of being surrounded by the musical ingredients.

23

Premixing and Rerecording for Television and Film

The process of combining the *dialogue, music, and sound-effect (DME)* tracks for television and film is accomplished during the premixing and rerecording stages. Improving in postproduction the already-recorded audio, adding necessary material and signal processing, is also known as *sweetening*. Depending on the medium, the number of tracks involved, and the release format, the operational stages differ somewhat between television and film. Generally, if few tracks are involved, they may be mixed directly to the *edit master*—the finished program on videotape, film, or disk. In more-complex mixes involving many audio tracks, sounds are first grouped, smoothed, and combined in a *premix*. The groupings are typically dialogue, music, ambience, Foley, and production and ambience sound effects (see Figure 23-1).

The *rerecording* mix is the final stage in postproduction, when the premixed tracks or *stems*—dialogue, music, and sound effects—are combined into stereo and surround sound and sent to the edit master. The differences in technology and release formats between television and film may account for the differences in the sequence and the type of operations during mixing and rerecording, but the purposes are the same: to produce a finished sound track.

Whatever differences there may be between mixing for TV and for film, both media involve picture, so keep in mind that in most cases, regardless of the material, *what the audience sees it wants to hear.*

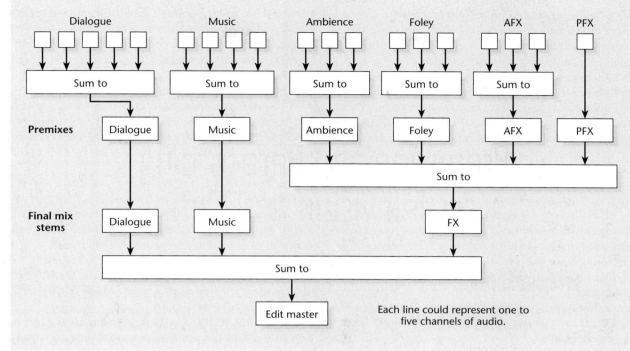

23-1 Example of a workflow for mixing.

PREMIXING FOR TELEVISION AND FILM

Because the differences in postproduction procedures between television and film are ever narrowing, in the interest of organization it makes sense to cover their mixing stages together, taking a general approach to techniques and aesthetics. Significant differences in mixing guidelines between the two media will be considered individually.

Dialogue and Narration

Speech is mixed first. The centerpiece of television and film audio is the spoken word because that is where most of the information comes from. Whether it is an announcer, a voice-over narrator, or an actor, every syllable from first to last must be delivered and heard "loud and clear." Maintaining both the sonic integrity of the voice and the intelligibility of the speech are most important.

The audience hears the dialogue or narration only once. The mixer hears it dozens, perhaps hundreds, of times and has to be wary of being so familiar with the words that they are not *listened* to. Even professional ac-

tors and narrators tend to drop syllables in their delivery, particularly the first and last syllables of a sentence. It is important that all the syllables be audible, particularly the first syllable in a sentence. It has to instantly capture the listener-viewer's ear and attention. Dropping the first syllables in a sentence can cause the listener to falter and lose a few seconds while regaining the continuity of meaning. Words in a delivery are sometimes "swallowed" or not well enunciated and must be resurrected; otherwise apprehending meaning is compromised.

Clear dialogue and narration begin with a good master recording, whether it is the production recording, the automated dialogue replacement (ADR) recording, or a combination of both. The editor should have already smoothed the tracks so that there are no surges in levels from loud to soft or soft to loud or discontinuities in ambience from one word or sentence to another within the same spoken passage or between the dialogue of two or more actors in the same ambient setting. But mixers have to do their own cleanup. This involves the familiar processing techniques of equalization, filtering, compression, limiting, noise reduction, and so on. The order in implementing these techniques is not as critical with frequency-related processing as it is with dynamic processing because dynamic processors produce different results depending on when they are used in the signal chain. The following is one approach.

Get rid of any high-end and low-end noise with low-pass and high-pass filtering, taking care not to filter out essential content. Use a notch filter to remove such sounds as hum and buzz. Broadband noise reduction can help reduce background noise from nature sounds, traffic, motors, and din. Be wary of using a noise gate on dialogue tracks because the gating action is noticeable more often than not. Reducing quieter noises, including ambience, with an expander sounds more natural.

In addition to the significance of equalization (EQ) in dialogue mixing—to make speech intelligible and agreeable sounding and to bring out the voice's timbre—it can be employed to smooth or match discrepancies between dialogue takes on different tracks. It helps overcome anomalies in frequency response due to varying microphone techniques used during production, proximity effect, the recording system, and body mics hidden under clothing.

For example, body mics usually require more equalization than do boom mics. A boom mic is positioned at mic-to-source distances that are relative to the shots' fields of view to help maintain acoustic perspective between sound and picture. The sonic perspective of a body mic, regardless of a shot's focal length, is the same, and the sound tends to be sterile. Even though the mini-mics used for body miking have a built-in high-end boost, clothing usually absorbs sufficient high frequencies to require their restoration.

To reproduce speech with more clarity, some mini-mics are designed to reduce upper bass frequencies, which could make male voices sound thinner. A slight boost in the lacking frequencies can restore a more natural timbre. Positioning a body mic in the chest area can increase frequencies around the middle 600 Hz range because of chest resonance. The offending frequencies can be attenuated to neutralize this effect. When the reverberation time in the bass is longer than it is in the midrange and the treble, equalization helps improve the imbalance in reverb by rolling off bass frequencies.

Compression and limiting are used to ensure that the dialogue stays within the dynamic range of the sound-reproducing system. Remember that in recording and mixing, the important factor is how the audience will hear the sound, not the sonic capabilities of the recording or transmitting systems. Compression is also used to

enhance the intelligibility of speech by keeping it above the ambience and the noise floor of the combined speech tracks and free from interference from other sonic elements such as music and sound effects. It is better to compress individual tracks, rather than the overall dialogue mix, because the risk of distortion, audible pumping, and a clustered, blurred sound is considerably less.

A *de-esser* smoothes the sibilance in speech, which is a boon in digital recording. As with most dynamic processing, de-essing should be applied lightly and on individual tracks, taking care to adjust the de-esser to the actor's or narrator's frequency range.

The *Aural Exciter* can add clarity to a dialogue track and help the voice stand out at a quieter level. Short delays can add depth and apparent loudness to the voice, but be careful here: it takes only a bit more delay than necessary for the delay to become obvious and, if it is inappropriate to the narrative material, ludicrous.

Given the many signal-processing tools available, in general the effectiveness of a good noise reduction program cannot be overestimated.

Once the speech tracks have been premixed, before proceeding with the ambience, sound effects, and music tracks, set up the signal feeds and the monitoring so that you can hear the speech tracks in relation to the other tracks. This procedure is known as *mix in context*.

Ambience

In addition to its familiar function of providing acoustic definition to a space, ambience helps match the characteristics of different ambiences that may be part of the various dialogue tracks. This may involve using room tone, reverberation, or slight delay. Almost all dialogue in general and ADR in particular requires ambience to sonically reflect the visual space in which a character is seen.

One way of creating ambience is known as *worldizing*, whereby a microphone and a loudspeaker are set up in a room in a way that is similar to their arrangement in an acoustic reverberation chamber. The room sound is recorded to add the sound of that space to a dry recording or to enhance or smooth ambient backgrounds that are already part of a dialogue track. Or the room sound is recorded in the same space in which the dialogue was recorded. This type of processing is particularly important in creating perspective where none exists in the original dialogue track. If a performer is 15 feet away and that was not captured in the original sound track, it is necessary for the mixer to lay in the appropriate acoustic envelope so that the performer's dialogue is in spatial perspective.

Once ambience is applied, it may require equalization to establish the appropriate tone as well as level adjustment to establish the appropriate perspective. Obviously, whatever signal processing is applied, it is vital that the dialogue and the ambience be heard in context with the picture so that audio and video are compatible.

Sound Effects

The same considerations that pertain to premixing dialogue apply to premixing sound effects, although the degree and the application of signal processing often differ. For example, it is more likely that sound effects will be manipulated to a greater extent than dialogue. Using a significant amount of EQ boost or cut on dialogue would change voice character dramatically, whereas with a sound effect dramatic alteration may be quite appropriate.

More liberties can be taken with sound effects because they are not as familiar to our ears as is the human voice, particularly effects that emanate from science fiction, fantasy, and animation—sounds that are not part of the natural world. But paying attention to sonic clarity, preventing distortion, and keeping an effect within the prescribed dynamic range are no less important for SFX mixing than they are for dialogue mixing. This is sometimes easier said than done because sound effects tend to be mixed "hot." There are other notable differences between dialogue and sound-effect premixing.

Sound-effect premixing usually includes handling most or all of the fades. It sometimes also includes setting the relative differences in level that are to occur in a final mix. Dialogue in film and television normally is centered in the stereo and surround-sound mixes, and underscored music is mixed left, center, and right. In surround it may be arced more toward the left and right sides as well. These operations are done in the rerecording mix. Sound effects are often placed in a particular screen space or, if there is no danger of dislocation, moved with the action in the picture. A sound effect is normally done in mono; it is the reverb that gives it the stereo imaging or feel. With surround sound too, mixers place and signal-process primarily with mono effects. Any panning of sound effects is done in the premix.

Music

Music in a premix is handled differently than dialogue and sound effects in that very little, if anything, is done to prepare it for rerecording. Musical knowledge is integral to mixing music, and not all sound people have

that foundation. Of the three main stems in the sound track—dialogue, music, and sound effects—music is the most structurally complex and spectrally and dynamically varied. Another reason that little premixing is done with music is that by the time a music track is ready for the premix, most of what a premix would accomplish has already been done. If the music undergoes any processing at the premix stage, it may be some high-end boosting (to compensate for high-frequency loss during subsequent processing) and compression if the music is conflicting with the dialogue that it is underscoring.

THE RERECORDING MIX

There is one thing about the rerecording process involving film that differs from mixing for TV that you cannot get around: because film is played in a large room, it is necessary to rerecord it in a large room to be sure that what is done sonically translates to a theater environment. It comes down to the acoustics; things happen in a large room that do not happen in a small room.

That said, the purpose of the rerecording mix is to blend the premixed dialogue, music, and SFX tracks into seamless stereo and surround-sound recordings. Depending on budget, market level, and union regulations, rerecording may be handled by the same people who recorded, edited, or premixed the sound or by people who have not yet heard the track or seen the picture.

On the one hand, the rerecording mix should be relatively straightforward, assuming the premix has been well produced. Gross changes should be unnecessary. On the other hand, if the rerecording mix is unsuccessful, all the previous work is just about for naught.

It is therefore particularly important that the premixed tracks are free of technical problems so that the rerecording mixer can concentrate on aesthetic points. (There may be one, two, three, or more rerecording mixers, depending on the scale and the complexity of the material. Two mixers usually divide duties between dialogue/music and effects; three mixers handle each component separately. The dialogue mixer is usually in charge of rerecording.)

All extraneous sounds should be deleted during editing and certainly no later than the premix. The three composite DME tracks should be clean at the beginning and the end of each sound or sequence. Each track should be cut as close to the beginning and the end of a sound as possible without cutting off soft attacks or decay. In addition, in- and out-points of each cue must be precise—a rerecording mixer cannot be expected to pinpoint cues.

A well-laid-out cue sheet is mandatory (see "Cue Sheets" later in this chapter).

SPATIAL IMAGING OF STEREO AND SURROUND SOUND IN TELEVISION AND FILM

Another important factor in a mix for TV and film is the spatial placement of the DME components in the stereo and surround-sound fields.

Stereo

Natural assumptions in placing elements in a stereo mix for television and film are that dialogue and SFX are positioned in relation to their on-screen locations and that music, if it is not coming from an on-screen source, fills the aural frame from the left to the right. For the most part, these assumptions are imprecise. Placement depends on the screen format, the reproduction system, and the type of material being produced.

The aesthetic demands of television and film differ because of the differences between their screen sizes and the size and the number of loudspeakers—their sonic and pictorial dimensions—and the environments in which TV and film are viewed. Clearly, film has more space in which to place and maneuver the aural and visual elements than does television.

In most film theaters, the loudspeakers are positioned to reproduce surround sound, so they are placed from left to right behind the screen and down the sides to the rear of the theater. But film mixes also have to take into account DVD and high-density optical disc distribution, which means that the mix will be played back on a TV receiver with a mono, stereo, or surround-sound loudspeaker system. Therefore the mix for theaters must be suitable for that acoustic environment and for the frequency response and the dynamic range that the loudspeaker system can reproduce. The mix for DVD has to sound decent when played back on the array of home systems out there.

That said, when it comes to *localization*—the placement of dialogue, music, and sound effects in the stereo frame—there are two aesthetic considerations in TV and film: scale and perspective.

Scale   Until the advent of stereo TV, the television loudspeaker was smaller than the screen, but together the scales of picture and sound images have seemed proportional. No doubt conditioning has had something to do with this perception.

With stereo TV, loudspeakers are either attached or built-in to the left and right sides of the set or detachable. With small-screen TVs, permanently attached speakers can be no farther apart than the width of the TV set. This is a limiting factor in creating a stereo image because the aural space is so narrow. Detachable speakers can be situated an optimal distance apart—6 feet is usually recommended to reproduce a more realistic stereo image. Built-in speakers in wide-screen TVs are usually mounted far enough apart to reproduce a decent stereo image. In fact, when sound is more spacious because of stereo, the picture seems bigger: *what we hear affects what we see.*

With film, the acceptance of proportion between picture and sound is more understandable. Both the size of the screen and the "size" of the sound system are perceived as similarly large.

Perspective   Despite the trend toward much larger screens, compared with film, television is still a small-screen medium. Regardless of a TV's screen size, the aspect ratios of the medium are not as sizeable as for film. *Aspect ratio* is the width-to-height proportions of a video image. The aspect ratio for the standard video screen is 4 × 3 (1.33:1); for HDTV it is 16 × 9 (1.78:1). For wide motion picture screens, aspect ratios are between 5.55 × 3 (1.85:1) and 7 × 3 (2.35:1). This means that whether the video screen is 19 inches or 66 inches, the shot is the same; there is no more information included in the width or height of the larger screen compared with the smaller screen. This is why television relies on close-up (CU) shots to enhance impact and to show detail that otherwise would be lost. Speech (and song lyrics) is therefore concentrated in the center.

Screen size and the left, center, right frontal loudspeaker array gives mixers a bit more leeway in film—but not much more. The three channels are necessary because of the screen width and the size of the audience area. Without a center channel, people sitting at the left and the right would hear only the loudspeaker closest to them and receive no stereo effect. The center channel anchors the sound. Trying to match sound with shot changes would be chaotic.

Localization of Talk and Dialogue

In television talk and dialogue are usually kept at or near the center of the stereo frame. Unless the shot remains the same, trying to match a performer's sonic location to that person's on-screen position can disorient the listener-viewer.

For example, if in a variety show a wide shot shows (from the viewer's perspective) the host in the center, the announcer to the left, and the band leader and the band to the right and the shot does not change, the audio can come from these locations in the stereo space. If the host and the announcer exchange remarks and the shot cuts to the host on the right and the announcer to the left in a two-shot, and the shot stays that way, the host's sound can be panned toward the right and the announcer's sound can be panned toward the left. If during their interchange, however, the shots cut back and forth between close-ups of the host and the announcer, the left and right stereo imaging becomes disconcerting because the image of either the host or the announcer is in the center of the frame when the sound is toward the left or right. When frequent shot changes occur, the best approach is to keep the overall speech toward or at the center (see 23-2).

When a performer is moving in a shot, say, from left to right, and the camera-to-source distance remains the same, the stereo image can be panned to follow the performer's movement without audience disorientation.

If the performer's camera-to-source distance changes, however, due to cutting from wider shots to closer shots or vice versa, or due to intercutting another actor into the frame even though the first performer's momentum is clearly left to right, the dialogue must be centered to avoid dislocation (see 23-3).

In film, as a general rule, on-screen dialogue is also placed in the center. If a character moves about and there are several cuts, as in television it can become an-noying to have the sound jump around, particularly if more than one character is involved. On the other hand, if characters maintain their positions in a scene, even though shots change from a wide to a medium close-up (MCU) or vice versa, so long as they are shown together stereo imaging can be effected without disorienting the audience.

Sound Effects

The handling of sound effects should be conservative in mixing for TV. Obvious motion should be selective and occur mostly with effects that make pronounced crossing movements. The extent of the movement has to be carefully controlled so that it is not greater than the physical dimension of the screen (unless it is surround sound).

Ambiences in stereo television certainly can be fuller than they are in mono TV. Undoubtedly, the significant perceptible difference between mono and stereo TV is in the fullness and the depth of the ambience.

Sound effects also tend to be concentrated toward the middle in film. If they are stationary or move across a wide distance, they may be located and panned without distraction. But too much movement muddles the sound to say nothing of disorienting, if not annoying, the audience. To create the sense that an effect is positioned relative to the action, the effect may be reverberated. Most of the dry effect is placed at or near screen-center, and the wet part is used to convey its placement in the frame. Background sounds and ambience may be mixed toward the left and the right of center to create overall tone and to add dimension.

23-2 Speech localization in a two-shot. (a) In this example, so long as the announcer and the host remain positioned left and right in a medium shot and the shot does not change, their sounds can be panned toward the left and the right, respectively, with no dislocation. (b) If the shot changes, say, to a medium close-up of the announcer followed by an MCU of the host and the stereo imaging remains the same, it will create a Ping-Pong effect. (c) If close-ups of the announcer and the host are planned, the sound in the original two-shot should be centered for both of them and carried through that way throughout the sequence. Panning the sound with the shot changes is even more sonically awkward than the Ping-Pong effect.

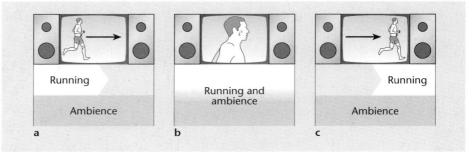

23-3 Sound localization in a moving shot. (a) If a subject is, say, running across the screen from left to right and the shot does not change, the stereo imaging can also move from left to right without dislocation. (b) If the shot cuts to a close-up to show perspiration on the runner's face, in which case the across-screen movement would be reflected in the moving background, the subject's sound would have to be centered. If the sound continued moving left to right in the CU, the difference between the visual and the aural perspectives would be disorienting. (c) When cutting from the CU back to the wide shot, the sound once again can move across the screen with the runner without disorientation because the perspectives match. If throughout the runner's across-screen movement there were a few cuts from the wide shot to the CU, however, the sound in the wide shots would have to be more centered to avoid the Ping-Pong effect.

Music

Generally, in the DME mix for TV and film, underscored music is the one element that is usually in stereo. It is typically mixed across the stereo field with the left and the right sides framing dialogue and sound effects.

Mixing Audio for the Home TV Receiver

Despite the increase in wide-screen and surround-sound home TV receivers, enough of the television audience still hears the audio through small loudspeakers to warrant its being a factor in mixing. Not only do these small TV loudspeakers reproduce little or no bass but they tend to accentuate sound that resides in the midrange, producing an unpleasant hard, raspy sound and sonically unbalancing the audio overall. To avoid potential problems caused by the small TV speakers, switch back and forth during a mix between high-end full-frequency loudspeakers and smaller TV-type loudspeakers.

Although the larger speakers are used for the bulk of the mixing, referencing the mix through the smaller ones helps ensure that essential low-frequency audio is not lost when played back through those speakers and that midrange harshness has been neutralized.

Surround Sound

Mixing surround sound for picture differs from mixing it for music. With music there is no screen to focus on, so listener attention can be directed in whatever way is consistent with the musicians' vision and the aesthetics of the music. With picture the primary information is coming from the screen in front of the audience, so it is necessary that the audience's attention be focused there and not drawn away by the surround sounds, a distraction known as the *exit sign effect*—sounds in the surround imaging that cause the audience to turn toward them.

How sonic elements are placed in a surround-sound mix for television depends to a considerable extent on the program, except for speech (and lyrics) and compensating for the home loudspeaker setup. In TV the word, spoken or sung, is delegated to the center channel. Sometimes to give the sound source some spread, to avoid too much center-channel buildup, or to adjust for the absence of a center-channel loudspeaker in signal reception, speech is panned slightly toward the left and the right of center. Surround sound notwithstanding, the two main objectives of mixing speech are still to make sure it is clear and to avoid dislocation.

As for sounds and music, taste and the program type affect placement. For example, in a talk show the audience sound may be panned to the left, right, and surround loudspeakers. In sports the crowd may be handled in the same way, or the action sounds may be mixed into the left and right imaging, with the crowd in the surrounds. Music underscoring for a drama may be handled by sending it to the left, right, and surround speakers or just to the left and right speakers and using the surrounds for ambience.

In music programs, delegating the audio is often related to the type of music being played. As noted earlier, with classical music the mix is primarily left, center, and right, with the surrounds used for ambience. Pop music may approach the mix by taking more advantage of the surrounds to place voicings. Or because it is television, with the picture showing an ensemble front and centered, the surrounds may be used for audience sound, if there is one, and ambience.

Then too with any surround-sound mix, you must consider how it will translate on a stereo or mono TV receiver, so back-and-forth monitoring is essential throughout the mixdown or rerecording session. Several years ago a music program was mixed for stereo, but the announcer was inadvertently recorded in mono. Those in the listening audience hearing the broadcast in stereo were unable to hear the announcer because his audio, being in mono, was canceled.

The traditional approach to surround sound for film has been to delegate the principal audio—dialogue, music, and sound effects—to the left, center, and right channels and the nonessential sound, such as ambience and background effects, to the surround channels. Specifically, the addition of the center and the surround channels to conventional stereo reproduction creates a stable center and background imaging. The center loudspeaker provides more-precise localization, particularly of dialogue. This is more important with television sound than it is with film sound because the TV image takes up a smaller space in the field of view. Hence the center loudspeaker helps localize dialogue toward the center of the screen.

Because audio producers have become more accustomed to working with surround sound, and audiences—film audiences in particular—have become more used to it as part of the overall viewing experience, the surround channels are being employed for more than just ambience and additional environmental effects, when the situation warrants. The thinking is that sound is omnidirectional and our natural acoustic environment puts it all around us all the time, so why not do the same thing with surround sound, the caveats being so long as it contributes to or furthers the story and does not call attention to itself, distracting the audience.

In these types of surround mixes, the dialogue of a character walking into a scene may be heard first from the side or rear and panned to the front-center as he appears on-screen. Music from a band playing behind a character seated in a venue with lots of people and hubbub may be heard in the surround speakers, with the dialogue frontally centered and the walla of the hubbub panned from the front speakers to the surrounds. A battle scene may have the sound of explosions and firing weaponry and the shouts of soldiers coming from the front and the surround speakers, placing the audience in the middle of the action.

In general, when mixing in surround sound, it may be useful to consider the following guidelines:

■ The main purpose of surround sound is to provide an expanded, more realistic sense of aural space.

■ Do not pull the audience's attention from the screen or try to overwhelm them with directional pyrotechnics in the surround-sound channels. Never try to rival what is on-screen.

■ When the surround channels consist of long arrays of loudspeakers, as they do in theaters, sounds do not localize as well as they do through discrete frontal and rear (or rear-side) loudspeaker arrays.

■ Because localization is poor at low frequencies, it is not a good idea to try to focus a sound source using the low-frequency enhancement (LFE) channel.

■ Be aware that when using the LFE channel for a discrete effect, it cannot be correlated with anything in a main channel. In a downmix the LFE channel is not used, so any information in that channel will not be retrievable. For example, a scene shows windows rattling from an off-screen explosion, the sound of which is carried in the LFE channel and heard through the subwoofer. The window rattling is heard in one or more of the main channels. Because the LFE is not used in a downmix, an audience would see and hear the windows rattling but not hear the explosion that caused it.

■ The frequency response between the front speakers and the surrounds is different.

■ Sound panned halfway between the front and the surrounds draws some attention forward and some attention behind. This instability creates a separation or split in the sound.

■ Mix to the visual perspective on the screen.

■ Keep in mind the edges of the medium for which you are mixing and place the principal elements within that frame.

■ Dialogue goes in the center channel and is usually not panned unless the on-screen action justifies it.

■ Principal sound effects may be centered, placed somewhat left and right of center, or both. Environmental or nonessential effects can be delegated to the surrounds.

■ Ambience is usually treated as fill or surround sound. Sometimes it may be music to add more dimension to the frontal music spread.

■ Before doing the surround mix, first do the left, center, and right mixes.

■ When using compression or limiting on dialogue, do not process any additional ambience signal through the same compressor-limiter. This reduces the potential for the dominant sound to cause the ambience to "pump."

■ When using signal processing, use separate processing devices for each element. Using the same processor for more than one element could, among other things, smear sonic imaging. And, as noted earlier, the order in which dynamics processors are used does matter.

■ When background sound distracts from dialogue, it helps to widen the voice by panning it toward the surround-sound position. If the material is recorded and it is possible to work with separate tracks, the best thing to do is change the mix.

■ When the visual action justifies them, moving sounds not only support on-screen elements passing by the audience but also support a moving point of view.

■ Unless it makes sense in relation to the on-screen action or it is for special effect, placing major program elements to the side and/or behind the audience is usually disconcerting. Being gimmicky only calls attention to itself and does little, if anything, to further the storyline or maintain the audience's attention. That said, although in film the general guideline has been to not put anything in the surround speakers that will distract from what is happening on-screen, as film mixers and the audience become more accustomed to surround sound, mixers are putting more in the rear and side speakers, such as music cues and sound effects. But beware of the exit sign effect.

■ In mixing surround (or stereo) for TV, it helps to use a near-field loudspeaker array because it more closely corresponds to home setups. Theater environments with far-field loudspeaker arrays are necessary for film mixing. When film surround sound is remixed for DVD

or high-density optical disc, near-field monitoring is recommended.

All in all, the advantages of multidimensional manipulation of sound far outweigh its problems:

■ Dialogue and sound effects can be accurately localized across a wide or small screen for almost any audience position.

■ Specific sound effects can be localized to the surround-sound loudspeakers.

■ Ambience and environmental sounds can be designed to reach the audience from all directions.

■ Panning of sound can occur across the front sound stage and between front and surround locations.

Encoding and Decoding Surround Sound

The handling of encoding and decoding surround sound is done through *metadata*—data that go along with the audio, describing its contents. Any number of flags can be written into the metadata that affect processing. Three of the most essential flags are dialogue normalization, dynamic range control, and downmixing.

Dialnorm (short for *dialogue normalization*) is an attenuation signal designed to normalize the loudness levels among different distribution sources such as television and DVD and from program to program, using speech as the common reference. If you are watching TV and put in a DVD, dialnorm regulates the volume of the DVD dialogue to be more or less close to that of a normal broadcast. Dialnorm does not change the mix.

Although different types of meters have been developed to measure loudness levels, there are consistency issues with the measuring standards. As engineers are apt to observe facetiously, the nice thing about standards is that there are so many of them. Audio levels can vary from channel to channel and sometimes within the same channel. Television viewers experience the differences in levels between programs or between programs and commercials. The levels of DVDs often vary not only from broadcast levels but from other DVDs as well.

To help rectify these level inconsistencies in digital television broadcasting, Dolby Laboratories developed the Broadcast Loudness Meter to measure the perceived loudness of speech, it being the essential element in most programs and films (see 23-4). The process maintains a consistent dialogue level for the listener-viewer by analyzing the input signal, which is the original dialogue level (whatever it is), and uses the metadata scheme to take care of level matching. Dialnorm objectively measures what the listener-viewer subjectively experiences.

Figure 23-5 shows the various correlations between analog and digital signal levels and their relationships to dialnorm, reference, and overload levels. Dialnorm not only adjusts speech levels to a standard but, by applying these guidelines for loudness compensation, also helps ensure that the other elements in the mix are not louder than the words.

The general dialogue normalization guidelines from Dolby Laboratories for film and various types of TV audio are shown in Figure 23-6.

Dynamic range control (DRC), also known as *dynamic range compression* and *dynamic range compensation,* is a gain control signal applied during decoding that allows different amounts of overall dynamic range. The flags set in the metadata control the type and the amount of compression that occurs when setting the dynamics control

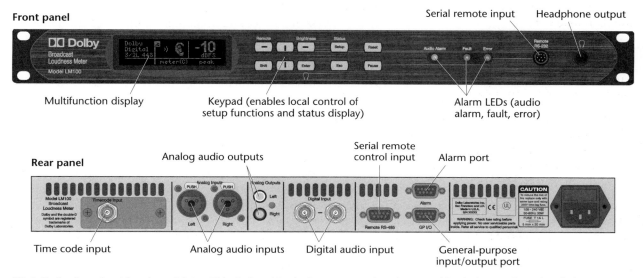

Front panel

Serial remote input   Headphone output

Multifunction display   Keypad (enables local control of setup functions and status display)   Alarm LEDs (audio alarm, fault, error)

Rear panel

Analog audio outputs   Serial remote control input   Alarm port

Time code input   Analog audio inputs   Digital audio input   General-purpose input/output port

23-4 Dolby Broadcast Loudness Meter. This device objectively measures what viewers subjectively experience in relation to the perceived loudness of speech. The unit can simultaneously display the incoming dialogue normalization (dialnorm) value of a Dolby Digital program for direct comparison with the actual measured value. Measurements are in a numerical format, thereby eliminating the variations in results often found when using volume-unit or peak program meters, neither of which is designed to measure subjective loudness.

23-5 Selected operating levels and their relationships.

From Jim Starzynski, "Managing Audio Levels," *Broadcast Engineering,* September 2005, p. 64. © 2005 Mondo Code.

Analog signal level	=	VU scale	=	Digital signal level	
–7 dBu		–11 VU		–31 dBFS	
–3 dBu		–7 VU		–27 dBFS	*Typical dialnorm level*
0 dBu		–4 VU		–24 dBFS	
+4 dBu		0 VU		–20 dBFS	*Reference level*
+8 dBu		+4 VU		–16 dBFS	
+12 dBu		+8 VU		–12 dBFS	
+16 dBu		+12 VU		–8 dBFS	
+20 dBu		+16 VU		–4 dBFS	
+24 dBu		+20 VU		0 dBFS	*Overload point*

23-6 General dialogue normalization guidelines from Dolby Laboratories for film and various types of TV audio. These standards are intended to compensate for the differences in original loudness compared with the loudness in a living room.

Audio Type	Normalization
Rock-and-roll	–10 to –20 dBFS
News	–15 dBFS
Television programs in general	–18 to –20 dBFS
Sports	–22 dBFS
Small (acoustic) music ensembles	–22 dBFS
Film	–27 dBFS
Popular music	–27 to –30 dBFS

on a home receiver or player. This allows adjustment of dynamic range based on the reproduction system being used, assuming it has such a controller, and whether the viewer wants that range to be wider or narrower.

Consumer audio systems provide two options for adjusting dynamic range: line output and RF (radio frequency) output. *Line output* sets the compression type for high-fidelity systems. *RF output* is the compression designed to match the audio levels from RF decoded audio at the receiving antenna. (RF is the signal broadcast by the station, picked up at the home receiving antenna, and then decoded.)

In dynamic range control, there are five profiles that determine how much high-level signals are cut and low-level signals are boosted (see 23-7).

Downmixing

As is the case with mixing music, a surround-sound mix for film or television may not be reproducible on a surround-sound system. To provide a compatible playback format for other types of systems, the film and TV surround mix is generally downmixed to other formats in stereo.

Downmixing to stereo can be handled either manually as a separate mix from surround or automatically through decoding. Although automatic decoding is easier and less time-consuming, it is not as reliable as doing a separate mix. There are instances when the decoder does not perform as directed.

There are two alternatives for downmixing surround sound to stereo: *Lo/Ro* and *Lt/Rt*. The **Lo/Ro** (left-only/right-only) method is the more common of the two. It adds the center channel to the front-left and front-right channels, the left surround to the left channel, and the right surround to the right channel.

The **Lt/Rt** (left total/right total) approach adds the center channel to the left and right channels. The surround channels are summed to mono and added to the left and right channels with the right channel 90 degrees out of phase. The Lt/Rt downmix enables those using Dolby Pro Logic to reproduce the left, center, right, and surround signals.

Keep in mind when producing surround sound with the intention of downmixing to stereo that no essential discrete information is in the LFE channel. The LFE channel is not transferred to the left or right stereo channel.

MIXING FOR MOBILE-MEDIA RECEIVERS

The compression factor aside, there are technical and aesthetic challenges to be mindful of when mixing for mobile-media receivers such as the iPod, cell phone, and handheld TV. Dynamic range and frequency response are limited, these receivers and their headsets or earbuds cannot handle uncompressed high-fidelity sound, and many are inadequate even to deal with compressed material. Because both sound and picture are small, there

23-7 Dynamic range compression profile parameter values. *Max boost* indicates the amount of boost in the low-level signal. *Boost ratio* is the compression ratio of low-level signals boosted. The *null bandwidth* is centered at the dialnorm setting; no compression is applied in this range. All other settings are adjusted in relation to this setting. *Early cut ratio* sets the initial compression ratio of high-level signals. *Max cut* is the maximum cut level of high-loudness signals.

Profile Name	Film Standard	Film Light	Music Standard	Music Light	Speech
Max boost (absolute range)	6 dB (−43 dBFS)	6 dB (−53 dBFS)	12 dB (−55 dBFS)	12 dB (−65 dBFS)	15 dB (−50 dBFS)
Boost ratio (absolute range)	2:1 (−43 to −31)	2:1 (−53 to −41)	2:1 (−55 to −31)	2:1 (−65 to −41)	5:1 (−50 to −31)
Null bandwidth (absolute range)	10 dB (−31 to −21)	20 dB (−41 to −21)	10 dB (−31 to −21)	20 dB (−41 to −21)	10 dB (−31 to −21)
Early cut ratio (absolute range)	2:1 (−21 to +4)	2:1 (−21 to +4)	2:1 (−21 to +4)	2:1 (−21 to +9)	2:1 (−21 to +4)
Max cut (absolute range)	24 dB (+4 dBFS)	24 dB (+4 dBFS)	24 dB (+4 dBFS)	15 dB (+9 dBFS)	24 dB (+4 dBFS)

From Dolby Laboratories, *Dolby Digital Professional Encoding Guidelines*, vol. 1, #S00/12972. Courtesy of Dolby Laboratories, Inc.

is not a great deal of aural and visual space in which to operate. Even with these sonic limitations, the audio is often bigger in "size" than the video, which imbalances the sound/picture relationship.

The sound has to be simple to work well, so that means using fewer audio sources. Simplified audio is less muddy and sounds crisper, which is necessary to maintain the intelligibility of speech and lyrics. Also, for mobile-media systems sound with less detail and subtlety is less annoying, does not demand as much attention, and is easier for the listener to assimilate. An increased number of sounds requires more processing and bandwidth to encode and transmit.

As pointed out in Chapter 14, the paradox today is that with the opportunity to produce better sound than ever before—and to hear it through great systems—too many listeners are hearing their digital audio in compressed form, much of which reduces sound quality. To exacerbate the condition, many listen through mediocre headphones or earbuds, often in noisy ambient environments, or through a less-than-sonorous computer speaker or loudspeaker system. In relation to aesthetic satisfaction from mobile-media receivers, less is definitely not more.

CUE SHEETS

Cue sheets are essential throughout any production in any medium, and they are no less indispensable during the premix and rerecording stages. They are the road maps that facilitate finding sounds on tracks. The forms vary from studio to studio; they may be handwritten or computer-generated, but they should contain at least the following information.

■ **A grid with each track forming a column and time cues laid out in a row** Time cues may be designated in time code, real time, or footage, depending on the medium and the format. By using one column to serve all tracks, it is easy to see at a glance the relationships among the time cues on a track-by-track basis.

■ **What the sound is** Each cue must be identified. Identification should be both brief to avoid clutter and precise to give the mixer certainty about what the cue is.

■ **When a sound starts** The word or words identifying a sound are written at the precise point it begins. With dialogue or narration, in-points may be indicated by a line or the first two or three words.

■ **How a sound starts** Unless otherwise indicated, it is assumed that a sound starts clean; that is, the level has been preset before the sound's entry. If a cue is faded in, faded in slowly, crossfaded with another sound, or the like, that must be indicated on the cue sheet.

■ **The duration of a sound** The point at which a cue begins to the point at which it ends is its duration. The simplest way to indicate this is with a straight line between the two points. Avoid using different-colored markers, double and triple lines, or other graphic highlights. The cue sheet or screen should be clean and uncluttered. If the cues are handwritten, pencil is better than ink in case changes must be made.

■ **When a sound ends** This can be indicated by the same word (or words) used at the entry cue accompanied by the word *out* or *auto* (for *automatically*). This tells the mixer that the end cue is clean and has been handled in the premix.

■ **How a sound ends** If a sound fades, crossfades, or the like, this should be indicated at the point where the sound must be out or crossfaded. The mixer then has to decide when to begin the out-cue so that it has been effected by the time indicated.

■ **Simple symbology** Where appropriate, accompany cues with symbols such as < for a fade-in, > for a fade-out, + to raise level, – to lower level, and Ø for crossfade.

COMPATIBILITY: STEREO-TO-MONO AND SURROUND-TO-STEREO

Anytime one format is downmixed to another format, there are considerations of compatibility that must be addressed.

Stereo-to-mono Compatibility

Although *stereo-to-mono compatibility*—ensuring that a recording made in stereo is reproducible in mono without spatial or spectral distortion—is not the problem it once was because monaural reproduction has become increasingly rare and most reception is at least in stereo, it does warrant some attention here. In surround sound, stereo-to-mono compatibility is even less of a concern because most systems in use are mono-compatible.

Stereo discs, radio, TV, film, and multimedia notwithstanding, except for home component music systems and visits to the motion picture theater, enough people still receive mediated information in mono so that mono-phonic compatibility is a consideration with much of what is stereo-mastered.

Stereo-to-mono compatibility must be checked and rechecked throughout a mix. What sounds good in stereo may be less than acceptable in mono. A wide and satisfac-torily balanced stereo recording played in mono may be too loud. For example, a 0 VU reading at the extreme left and right in stereo is equivalent to +6 in mono. Anything assigned to the center in the stereo mix may be too loud in mono and out of context with the rest of the sound. Moreover, placing voicings extreme left or right in stereo results in a 3 dB or greater loss in their level(s) relative to the rest of the spectrum when played in mono.

So the problem of stereo-to-mono compatibility is twofold: too much sound in the center and not enough at the left and the right. The reason, briefly stated, is that signals that are in phase in stereo add in mono, and signals that are out of phase in stereo cancel in mono.

Certain devices, such as the phasing analyzer and the stereo display processor, are used to indicate stereo-to-mono compatibility during a mix (see 23-8). Many of today's pan pots are designed with either a 3 dB or a 6 dB down notch that facilitates mono compatibility.

Two other techniques are also in use. One is to not put anything dead center or at the extreme left or right in a stereo mix. About 3 o'clock and 9 o'clock are usually recommended. This reduces both center-channel buildup and loss of some of the left and right information when playing stereo recordings in mono. But the stereo image may not be as wide as it should be, and center imaging could be awkward.

The better technique is to be very careful of in-phase and out-of-phase signals during recording and signal processing, especially with reverb, and to constantly make A-B comparisons between stereo and mono play-back during a mix, using both your ears and a phasing analyzer. In the A-B comparisons, always check to ensure

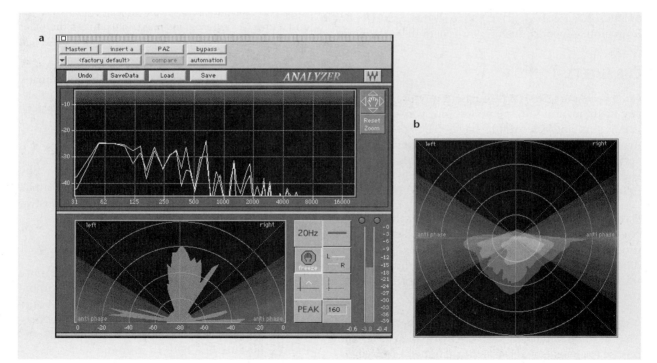

23-8 Real-time analyzer. (a) This model provides frequency analysis, a stereo position display, and loudness/peak meters. The stereo position display shows a mono-compatible stereo signal. A skewing to the left or the right indicates a left-heavy or right-heavy stereo signal, respectively. (b) Stereo position display showing a badly out-of-phase stereo signal.

that nothing is lost due to phase, that nothing stands out inordinately, and that the overall blend is maintained.

Surround-to-stereo Compatibility

As noted earlier, it is possible to have a surround mix automatically downmixed to stereo using the Dolby Digital encoder, but the results are unpredictable. Mixers prefer to do a separate downmix from the surround recording to stereo. There are a few reasons for this practice.

Mixing the information and handling the levels from the center and surround channels to the left and right stereo channels is better controlled. For example, the center and surround channels are usually attenuated by 3 dB to ensure that when they are added to the left and right stereo channels they are balanced. There is less chance of phasing, reduced intelligibility, and less imbalance of sonic elements because mixers are usually on the alert for such problems.

Successful downmixing from surround to stereo begins with a stable surround-sound sonic image. It is advantageous to double-check what you hear with an analyzer that can provide a visual position display (see 23-9).

▶ The process of combining the dialogue, music, and sound-effect (DME) tracks for television and film is accomplished, generally, during the premixing and rerecording stages.

▶ The premix is the phase during which dialogue, sound effects, and, to some extent, music are prepared for the final rerecording mix.

▶ The purpose of the rerecording mix is to blend the premixed DME tracks into a seamless stereo or surround-sound recording.

▶ Of the factors that influence mixing sound for television, three important ones are how the audio is heard in most homes, the emphasis of the television medium on the spoken (and sung) word, and how screen size and program type affect spatial imaging.

▶ Apsect ratio is the width-to-height proportions of a video image. For the standard video screen, it is is 4 × 3 (1.33:1); for HDTV it is 16 × 9 (1.78:1). For wide motion picture screens, aspect ratios are between 5.55 × 3 (1.85:1) and 7 × 3 (2.35:1).

▶ Stereo placement in film and TV usually positions dialogue and sounds in the center and music to the left, in the

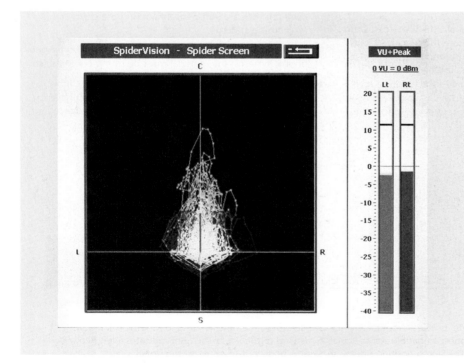

23-9 Analyzer displaying an in-phase surround-sound image.

center, and to the right. Large-screen film positions dialogue in the center with limited lateral movement, sound effects across a somewhat wider space but still toward the center, and music left, center, and right. One reason for such placement is to avoid disorienting the audience in relation to the on-screen sources of sound and image. Another reason is that in motion picture theaters the audience sitting to the left or right side of the screen will not hear a left- or right-emphasized sound image.

▶ Generally, in surround sound, the left, center, and right channels contain the principal audio—dialogue, music, and sound effects—and are reproduced by the frontal loudspeakers. The center channel is used for dialogue. The surround-sound channel is dedicated to background sound(s) and reproduced by the side or rear loudspeakers or both. As producers and the audience grow more accustomed to surround sound, the surround channels are being used for secondary audio in addition to ambience and environmental effects.

▶ However surround sound is mixed, the main imperative is to not pull the audience's attention from the screen.

▶ The handling of encoding and decoding surround sound is done through metadata—data that go along with the audio, describing its contents. Three of the most essential flags are dialogue normalization, dynamic range control (DRC), and downmixing.

▶ To help rectify inconsistencies in levels, the Broadcast Loudness Meter was developed to measure the perceived loudness of speech in television programs and films. Known as dialnorm (short for dialogue normalization), it is an attenuation signal designed to normalize the loudness levels among different distribution sources such as television and DVD and from program to program, using speech as the common reference.

▶ Dynamic range control (DRC, also known as dynamic range compression and dynamic range compensation) is a gain control signal applied during decoding that allows different amounts of overall dynamic range.

▶ Downmixing surround sound to stereo can be handled either manually as a separate mix from surround or automatically through decoding.

▶ There are two alternatives for downmixing surround sound to stereo. The Lo/Ro (left-only/right-only) method adds the center channel to the front-left and front-right channels, the left surround to the left channel, and the right surround to the right channel. The Lt/Rt (left total/right total) approach adds the center channel to the left and right channels. The surround channels are summed to mono and added to the left and right channels with the right channel 90 degrees out of phase.

▶ There are technical and aesthetic challenges to be mindful of when mixing for mobile-media receivers such as the iPod, cell phone, and handheld TV because of their limited dynamic range and frequency response. Sound with less detail and subtlety is less annoying, does not demand as much attention, and is easier for listeners to assimilate. Also, the disproportionate "size" of the audio compared with the video can imbalance the sound/picture relationship.

▶ Cue sheets are essential throughout the production process, but they are indispensable during the premix and rerecording stages.

▶ In mixing stereo sound that may be reproduced on monophonic systems, the material must be mono-compatible.

▶ To help ensure surround-to-stereo compatibility, mixers prefer to do a separate downmix rather than have it handled automatically because elements like balance and phasing are better controlled.

24

Evaluating the Finished Product

What makes good sound? Ask 100 audio specialists to evaluate the same sonic material and undoubtedly you will get 100 different responses. That is one of the beauties of sound: it is so personal. Who is to tell you that your taste is wrong? If it satisfies you as a listener, that is all that matters. When sound is produced for an audience, however, professional "ears" must temper personal taste. To this end there are generally accepted standards that audio pros agree are reasonable bases for artistic judgment.

Before discussing these standards, a word about the monitor loudspeakers is in order. Remember that the sound you evaluate is influenced by the loudspeaker reproducing it. You must therefore be thoroughly familiar with its frequency response and how it otherwise affects sonic reproduction. If a sound is overly bright or unduly dull, you have to know whether that is the result of the recording or the loudspeaker. Remember, a good way to familiarize yourself with a loudspeaker's response is to take a few test discs and well-produced commercial recordings with which you are thoroughly familiar and listen to them on the monitor system until you are confident about its response characteristics.

INTELLIGIBILITY

It makes sense that if there is narration, dialogue, or song lyrics, the words must be intelligible. If they are not, meaning is lost. But when working with material over a long period of time, the words become so familiar that it might not be apparent that they are muffled, masked, or otherwise difficult to distinguish. In evaluating intelligibility it is therefore a good idea to do it with fresh ears—as though you were hearing the words for the first time. If that does not give you the needed distance from the material, ask someone else if the words or lyrics are clear.

TONAL BALANCE

Bass, midrange, and treble frequencies should be balanced; no single octave or range of octaves should stand out. Be particularly aware of too much low end that muddies and masks sound; overly bright upper midrange and treble that brings out sibilance and noise; absence of brilliance that dulls sound; and too much midrange that causes the harshness, shrillness, or edge that annoys and fatigues.

The timbre of the voice, sound effects, and acoustic instruments should sound natural and realistic. Music and sounds generated by electric and electronic instruments do not necessarily have to sound so, unless they are supposed to.

Ensemble sound should blend as a whole. As such, solos and lead voicings should be sonically proportional in relation to the accompaniment.

SPATIAL BALANCE AND PERSPECTIVE

All sonic elements in aural space should be unambiguously localized; it should be clear where various sounds are coming from. Their relationships—front-to-back and side-to-side—should be in proper perspective: dialogue spoken from the rear of a room should sound somewhat distant and reverberant; an oboe solo should be distinct yet come from its relative position in the orchestra; a vocal should not be too far in front of an ensemble or buried in it; background music should not overwhelm the announcer; and crowd noise should not be more prominent than the sportscaster's voice.

Positional and loudness changes should be subtle and sound natural. They should not jar or distract the listener by jumping out, falling back, or bouncing side-to-side (unless the change is justified in relation to the picture).

DEFINITION

Each element should be clearly defined—identifiable, separate, and distinct—yet, if grouped, blended so that no single element stands out or crowds or masks another.

Each element should have its position in, and yet be a natural part of, the sound's overall spectral range and spatial arrangement.

DYNAMIC RANGE

The range of levels from softest to loudest should be as wide as the medium allows, making sure that the softest sounds are easily audible and the loudest sounds are undistorted.

If compressed, sound should not seem squeezed together, nor should it surge from quiet to loud and vice versa.

CLARITY

A clear recording is as noise-free and distortion-free as possible. Hum, hiss, leakage, phasing, smearing, blurring from too much reverb, and harmonic, intermodulation, and loudness distortion—all muddle sound, adversely affecting clarity.

AIRINESS

Sound should be airy and open. It should not seem isolated, stuffy, muffled, closed-down, dead, lifeless, overwhelming, or oppressive.

ACOUSTICAL APPROPRIATENESS

Acoustics, of course, must be good, but they must also be appropriate. The space in which a character is seen and the acoustic dimension of that space must match.

Classical music and jazz sound most natural in an open, relatively spacious environment. Acoustics for rock-and-roll can range from tight to open. A radio announcer belongs in an intimate acoustic environment.

SOURCE QUALITY

When a recording is broadcast, downloaded, or sent on for mastering, there is usually some loss in sound quality. This occurs with both analog and digital sound. For example, what seems like an appropriate amount of reverb when listening to a scene or a song in a studio may be barely discernible after transmission or transfer. As a general guideline, be aware that a source recording should have higher resolution than its eventual release medium.

PRODUCTION VALUES

In dealing with production and production values, director Francis Ford Coppola uses a triangle to explain what the priorities should be. The top of the triangle says "Good." The bottom-left side says "Quick." The bottom-right side says "Cheap." You can connect only two of the sides but not all three. If the production is good and quick, it will not be cheap. If is good and cheap, it will not be quick. And if the production is quick and cheap...

The degree to which you are able to develop and appraise production values is what separates the mere craftsperson from the true artist. Production values relate to the material's style, interest, color, and inventiveness.

Production values are the most difficult part of an evaluation to define or quantify because response is qualitative and intuitive. Material with excellent production values grabs and moves you. It draws you into the pro-duction, compelling you to forget your role as objective observer; you become the audience. When this happens it is not only the culmination of the production process but its fulfillment.

MAIN POINTS

▶ In evaluating a final product, factors that should be considered include intelligibility, tonal balance, spatial balance and perspective, definition, dynamic range, clarity, airiness, acoustical appropriateness, and source quality.

▶ Production values relate to the material's style, interest, color, and inventiveness.

▶ Material with excellent production values grabs and moves you, drawing you into the production and compelling you to forget your role as objective observer. When this happens it is not only the culmination of the production process but its fulfillment.

Appendix: Occupations in Audio

This list of occupations is intended to provide a sense of the breadth of available jobs in audio and audio-related fields. It is not inclusive, nor are these positions mutually exclusive. Depending on the type of production and the assignment, one or more of these functions may be incorporated. The job descriptions are generalized and differ from studio to studio.

Job responsibilities in given markets also vary. A person in a smaller audio production house may have more than one duty to perform. In a large market, union regulations may dictate that members perform a designated job and may not perform other tasks also credentialed to that union or to other unions.

In the audio marketplace, a college education; a background in production, music, engineering, computers, or some combination of the four; and "ears" are distinct advantages. Of considerable importance too is the ability to get along with people.

assistant, setup, or second engineer In music recording, sets up the studio and the control room before a session, checks and readies the equipment, and assists the engineer during production.

audio books producer/recordist Oversees production and recording of book narration.

audio designer/producer for Web services Designs and/or produces the audio for Web sites.

audio educator Teaches audio courses in a community college, university, or trade school. In colleges and universities, audio courses are located in various departments, such as broadcasting, television and radio, and film, as well as in the schools of music, engineering, and communications.

audio engineer Depending on the medium—radio, television, film, or music recording—maintains the audio equipment, operates the console and other control room gear, and performs the recording, editing, and mixing functions.

audio for video postproduction editor Edits audio material for video in television postproduction. May also do the mixing.

audio for video postproduction mixer Mixes audio material for video in television postproduction. May also do the editing.

audio lead In game sound, responsible for seeing that daily deadlines are met.

audio production engineer In radio and television, equipment operator and producer of audio material.

audio software designer/producer Creates, designs, and produces audio software for computers, games, and Internet production.

automated dialogue replacement (ADR) editor Edits the ADR recording.

automated dialogue replacement (ADR) producer In charge of the ADR recording session and postproduction editing.

automated dialogue replacement (ADR) recordist Records ADR sessions.

board operator Operates the console and the other control room equipment during a broadcast and a production session.

boom operator Operates the boom microphone during a broadcast and a production recording.

cable puller Sets up and handles power and microphone cables.

concert sound reinforcement engineer Sets up, tests, and operates the sound equipment for live concerts.

dialogue editor Edits production dialogue and postproduction ADR recordings.

director of audio   In game sound, responsible for overseeing projects, coordinating the creative and operational staffs, and dealing with contributing outside personnel.

duplication technician   Duplicates client audio recordings, determines if material is suitable for duplication, handles packaging, and checks and readies the recording and playback equipment.

entry-level trainee   Does whatever is asked in the execution of studio and control room activities and in helping during a production session; performs routine housekeeping duties; takes every opportunity to observe and learn.

Foley artist   Creates and performs sound effects in a Foley studio.

Foley editor   Edits Foley-produced sound effects. May also record and mix Foley effects.

Foley mixer   Mixes Foley-produced sound effects. May also record and edit Foley effects.

Foley recordist   Records the sound effects during Foley production. May also mix and edit Foley effects.

librarian   Receives, catalogs, files, and mails a studio's audio material; obtains appropriate authorization for recordings' release.

machine room operator   In film, loads and operates the magnetic film recorder/playback machines. In television, handles the loading and the operation of the recorders.

maintenance engineer   Maintains the audio equipment to keep it up to working specifications, including the alignment and the calibration of recorders, digital signal processing (DSP) calibration, real-time analysis of the monitor system, finding sources of noise, and performing emergency repairs.

maintenance technician   Diagnoses problems and repairs audio and other electronic equipment.

mastering engineer   Processes and records master discs from the production master recordings.

museum sound designer/producer   Designs and/or produces sound for museum exhibits.

music editor   Edits the recording of the music score.

music premixer   Mixes the music score to prepare it for the rerecording mix.

music producer   Has creative charge of the music production; may be affiliated with a record company, a film studio, or the performing artist.

playback operator   Plays any needed prerecorded music or dialogue on the set.

production recordist/mixer   Records and, if necessary, mixes dialogue on the set.

programmer   Writes the software that makes the audio in interactive media, such as games, function.

radio production engineer/producer   Operates the equipment and produces audio material, such as spot announcements, promos, jingles, and station IDs.

remote broadcast engineer   Maintains the audio equipment on-location; may also handle the recording.

remote broadcast mixer   Records the audio on-location.

rerecording mixer   Mixes the composite dialogue, sound-effect, and music tracks to stereo or surround sound; may be handled by one, two, or three mixers.

scoring mixer   Mixes the film or video music sound track.

sound assistant   Assists the principal audio production personnel in whatever ways they need, including packing and carrying equipment, setting up the studio and the control room, doing light maintenance, organizing the paperwork, and getting coffee.

sound designer   Creates, directs, and is usually involved in the production of the overall sonic character of a work, such as a film, video, television program, spot announcement, game, CD-ROM, Web page, theatrical play, or musical.

sound-effect editor   Edits the sound effects; may collect, record, and produce them as well.

sound-effect specialist   In game sound, responsible for producing user-triggered sound effects.

sound transfer engineer   Transfers audio from one recording medium to another.

speech specialist   In game sound, works with the scriptwriter to design and produce voice characterizations.

television postproduction editor/mixer   Edits and mixes the production audio plus the music and any additional sound effects in postproduction.

theater sound designer for plays and musicals Records, edits, and mixes the audio for plays and musicals; handles the audio at the theater's mixing console during performances.

writer Writes books and/or articles about audio equipment, technology, production techniques, trends, and news in the various media of the audio world.

In addition to the listed occupations in production-related audio, there are other areas of opportunity for employment in audio-related fields:

- Acoustic design
- Advertising and marketing professional products
- Aerospace, industrial, and military development and applications
- Audio equipment design, manufacturing, and distribution
- Audio forensics and consultant to law-enforcement agencies
- Audio for religious centers
- Audio in medicine and security applications
- Audiology
- Audiovisual media for industry, government, and education
- Bioacoustics
- Broadcast station and network operations
- Communications systems, such as telephone, satellite, and cable TV
- Consumer audio equipment sales and services
- Disc preparation and distribution
- Motion picture distribution and exhibition
- Professional audio equipment sales, marketing, and services
- Public relations
- Sound-effect and music library licensing
- Sound equipment rentals and installations
- Sound restoration and preservation

Selected Bibliography

Books

Adam, Thomas, and Peter Gorges. *FX: 100 Effects Settings for Sound Design and Mix.* New York: Schirmer Books, 1999.

Alburger, James. *The Art of Voice Acting,* 3rd ed. Boston: Focal Press, 2006.

Alten, Stanley. *Audio in Media: The Recording Studio.* Belmont, Calif.: Wadsworth, 1996.

Altman, Rick, ed. *Sound Theory/Sound Practice.* New York: Routledge, 1992.

Ament, Vanessa Theme. *The Foley Grail: The Art of Performing Sound for Film, Games, and Animation.* Boston: Focal Press, 2009.

Amyes, Tim. *The Technique of Audio Postproduction in Video and Film,* 3rd ed. Oxford: Focal Press, 2005.

Anderton, Craig. *Audio Mastering.* Bremen, Germany: Wizoo, 2002.

Ballou, Glen. *Handbook for Sound Engineers,* 4th ed. Boston: Focal Press, 2008.

Bartlett, Bruce, and Jenny Bartlett. *Practical Recording Techniques,* 5th ed. Boston: Focal Press, 2008.

———. *Recording Music on Location.* Boston: Focal Press, 2006.

Baskerville, David, and Tim Baskerville. *Music Business Handbook,* 9th ed. Thousand Oaks, Calif.: Sage, 2010.

Baxter, Dennis. *A Practical Guide to Television Sound Engineering.* Boston: Focal Press, 2007.

Beauchamp, Robin. *Designing Sound for Animation.* Boston: Focal Press, 2005.

Beck, Jay, and Tony Grajeda, eds. *Lowering the Boom: Critical Studies in Film Sound.* Champaign: University of Illinois Press, 2008.

Benedetti, Robert, Michael Brown, Bernie Laramie, and Patrick Williams. *Creative Postproduction: Editing, Sound, Visual Effects, and Music for Film and Video.* Boston: Pearson Allyn and Bacon, 2004.

Berendt, Joachim-Ernst. *The Third Ear: On Listening to the World.* New York: Henry Holt, 1992.

Blauert, Jens. Trans. by John S. Allen. *Spatial Hearing.* Cambridge, Mass.: MIT Press, 1983.

Borwick, John, ed. *Loudspeaker and Headphone Handbook,* 3rd ed. Oxford: Focal Press, 2001.

Brandon, Alexander. *Audio for Games.* Berkeley, Calif.: New Riders, 2005.

Bregitzer, Lorne. *Secrets of Recording: Professional Tools, Tips, and Techniques.* Boston: Focal Press, 2008.

Bregman, Albert. *Auditory Scene Analysis.* Cambridge, Mass.: MIT Press, 1990.

Brixen, Eddy Bøgh. *Audio Metering.* Denmark: Eddy Bøgh Brixen and DK Technologies, 2007.

Brophy, Philip. *100 Modern Soundtracks.* London: British Film Institute, 2008.

Brown, Royal. *Overtones and Undertones: Reading Film Music.* Berkeley: University of California Press, 1994.

Burt, George. *The Art of Film Music.* Boston: Northeastern University Press, 1995.

Cancellaro, Joseph. *Exploring Sound Design for Interactive Media.* Boston: Delmar Cengage Learning, 2005.

Carlin, Dan, Sr. *Music in Film and Video Productions.* Boston: Focal Press, 1991.

Case, Alex. *Sound FX: Unlocking the Creative Potential of Recording Studio Effects.* Boston: Focal Press, 2007.

Chandler, Heather. *Game Production Handbook.* Boston: Charles River Media, 2006.

Chappell, Jon, ed. *Digital Home Recording,* 2nd ed. San Francisco: Backbeat Books, 2002.

Chion, Michael. Trans. and ed. by Claudia Gorbman. *Audio-vision: Sound on Screen.* New York: Columbia University Press, 1994.

———. *The Voice in Cinema.* New York: Columbia University Press, 1998.

Clark, Rick. *The Expert Encyclopedia of Recording.* Vallejo, Calif.: Artistpro, 2001.

———. *Mixing, Recording, and Producing Techniques of the Pros.* Boston: Thomson Course Technology, 2005.

Collins, Mike. *Professional Audio and Music Software.* Oxford: Focal Press, 2003.

———. *Professional Guide to Audio Plug-ins and Virtual Instruments.* Oxford: Focal Press, 2003.

Connelly, Donald. *Digital Radio Production.* New York: McGraw-Hill, 2005.

Cooke, Mervyn. *A History of Film Music.* Cambridge: Cambridge University Press, 2008.

Crich, Tim. *Recording Tips for Engineers.* Boston: Focal Press, 2005.

Dagys, Andrew. *Podcasting Now! Audio Your Way.* Boston: Course Technology, 2006.

Davis, Richard. *Complete Guide to Film Scoring: The Art and Business of Writing Music for Movies and TV.* Boston: Berklee Press, 2000.

DeSantis, Jayce. *How to Run a Recording Session,* 2nd ed. Emeryville, Calif.: MixBooks, 2000.

Desjardins, Christian. *Inside Film Music: Composers Speak.* Los Angeles: Silman-James Press, 2007.

Deutsch, Diana, ed. *The Psychology of Music.* Orlando: Academic Press, 1982.

Dorritie, Frank. *Essentials of Music for Audio Professionals.* Emeryville, Calif.: MixBooks, 2000.

———. *Handbook of Field Recording.* Vallejo, Calif.: Artistpro, 2003.

Douthitt, Chris. *Voice-overs: Putting Your Mouth Where the Money Is.* Portland, Or.: Grey Heron Books, 1996.

Dowling, W. J., and D. L. Harwood. *Music Cognition.* Orlando: Academic Press, 1986.

Eargle, John. *Handbook of Recording Engineering,* 4th ed. New York: Springer-Verlag, 2005.

———. *The Microphone Book,* 2nd ed. Boston: Focal Press, 2004.

Eisenberg, Evan. *The Recording Angel: Explorations in Phonography.* New York: McGraw-Hill, 1987.

Emerick, Geoff, and Howard Massey. *Here, There, and Everywhere: My Life Recording the Music of the Beatles.* New York: Gotham Books, 2006.

Everest, F. Alton. *Critical Listening Skills for Audio Professionals.* Boston: Thomson Course Technology, 2006.

———. *Master Handbook of Acoustics,* 4th ed. New York: McGraw-Hill, 2001.

Everest, F. Alton, and Ron Streicher. *The New Stereo Soundbook,* 3rd ed. Pasadena, Calif.: Audio Engineering Associates, 2006.

Farnell, Andy. *Designing Sound: Procedural Audio for Games and Film.* Bournemouth, U.K.: Applied Scientific Press Limited, 2008.

Fisher, Jeffrey P. *Cash Tracks: Compose, Produce, and Sell Your Original Sound Track, Music, and Jingles.* Boston: Thomson Course Technology, 2005.

———. *Instant Surround Sound.* San Francisco: CMP Books, 2005.

———. *Soundtrack Success: A Digital Storyteller's Guide to Audio Postproduction.* Vallejo, Calif.: Artistpro, 2009.

Fletcher, Neville, and Thomas Rossing. *The Physics of Musical Instruments,* 2nd ed. New York: Springer-Verlag, 1998.

Geoghegan, Michael, and Dan Klass. *Podcast Solutions: The Complete Guide to Podcasting.* New York: Springer-Verlag, 2005.

Gibson, Bill. *Mixing and Mastering Audio Recordings.* Boston: Thomson Course Technology, 2006.

———. *The Sound Advice On... series* (Compressors, Limiters, Expanders, and Gates; Equalizers, Reverbs, and Delays; Microphone Techniques; MIDI Production; Mixing). Vallejo, Calif.: Artistpro, 2002.

————. *The S.M.A.R.T. Guide to Digital Recording, Software, and Plug-ins.* Boston: Thomson Course Technology, 2005.

————. *The S.M.A.R.T. Guide to Mixers, Signal Processors, Microphones, and More.* Boston: Thomson Course Technology, 2005.

————. *The S.M.A.R.T. Guide to Recording Great Audio Tracks in a Small Studio.* Boston: Thomson Course Technology, 2005.

Gibson, David. *The Art of Mixing,* 2nd ed. Vallejo, Calif.: Artistpro, 2005.

Gibson, David, and Maestro Curtis. *The Art of Producing.* Vallejo, Calif.: Artistpro, 2005.

Gorbman, Claudia. *Unheard Melodies: Narrative Film Music.* Bloomington: Indiana University Press, 1987.

Gottlieb, Gary. *Shaping Sound in the Studio and Beyond: Audio Aesthetics and Technology.* Boston: Thomson Course Technology, 2008.

Grant, Tony. *Audio for Single Camera Operation.* Boston: Focal Press, 2003.

Greenebaum, Ken, and Ronen Barzel, eds. *Audio Anecdotes: Tools, Tips, and Techniques for Digital Audio.* Wellesley, Mass.: A. K. Peters, 2004.

Gross, Lynne. *Digital Moviemaking,* 7th ed. Belmont, Calif.: Wadsworth, 2009.

Hagen, Earle. *Scoring for Films.* Sherman Oaks, Calif.: Alfred, 1989.

Handel, Stephen. *Listening: An Introduction to the Perception of Auditory Events.* Cambridge, Mass.: MIT Press, 1989.

Harris, John. *Tips for Recording Musicians,* 2nd ed. New York: Cimino, 1999.

Hatschek, Keith. *Golden Moment: Recording Secrets of the Pros.* San Francisco: Backbeat Books, 2007.

Hausmann, Carl, Philip Benoit, Fritz Messere, and Lewis O'Donnell. *Modern Radio Production,* 8th ed. Belmont, Calif.: Wadsworth, 2010.

Hayward, Philip, ed. *Off the Planet: Music, Sound, and Science Fiction Cinema.* Eastleigh, U.K.: John Libbey Publishing, 2004.

Hickman, Roger. *Reel Music: Exploring 100 Years of Film Music.* New York: W. W. Norton, 2005.

Hogan, Harlan. *VO: Tales and Techniques of a Voice-over Actor.* New York: Allworth Press, 2002.

Hogan, Harlan, and Jeffrey Fisher. *The Voice Actor's Guide to Home Recording.* Boston: Thomson Course Technology, 2005.

Holman, Tomlinson. *5.1 Surround Sound Up and Running,* 2nd ed. Boston: Focal Press, 2007.

————. *Sound for Digital Video.* Boston: Focal Press, 2005.

————. *Sound for Film and Television,* 2nd ed. Boston: Focal Press, 2002.

Howard, David, and James Angus. *Acoustics and Psychoacoustics,* 4th ed. Oxford: Focal Press, 2009.

Huber, David Miles. *The MIDI Manual,* 3rd ed. Boston: Focal Press, 2007.

Huber, David Miles, and Robert Runstein. *Modern Recording Techniques,* 7th ed. Boston: Focal Press, 2010.

Huber, David Miles, and Phillip Williams. *Professional Microphone Techniques.* Milwaukee: Hal Leonard, 1999.

Hugonnet, Christian, and Pierre Walder. *Stereophonic Sound Recording: Theory and Practice.* New York: John Wiley & Sons, 1998.

Irish, Dan. *The Game Producer's Handbook.* Boston: Thomson Course Technology, 2005.

Izhaki, Roey. *Mixing Audio: Concepts, Practices, Tools.* Boston: Focal Press, 2007.

Jackson, Blair, ed. *Classic Tracks: The Studios, Stories, and Hit Makers Behind Three Decades of Groundbreaking Songs.* Emeryville, Calif.: Mix Books, 2006.

Kalinak, Kathryn. *Settling the Score: Music and the Classical Hollywood Film.* Madison: University of Wisconsin Press, 1992.

Kamichik, Stephen. *Practical Acoustics.* Indianapolis: Prompt, 1998.

Karlin, Fred. *Listening to Movies.* New York: Schirmer Books, 1994.

Karlin, Fred, and Rayburn Wright. *On the Track: A Guide to Contemporary Film Scoring.* New York: Schirmer Books, 1990.

Kassabian, Anahid. *Hearing Film.* New York: Routledge, 2001.

Katz, Bob. *Mastering Audio,* 2nd ed. Boston: Focal Press, 2007.

Katz, Mark. *Capturing Sound: How Technology Has Changed Music.* Berkeley: University of California Press, 2004.

Kenny, Tom. *Sound for Picture,* 2nd ed. Vallejo, Calif.: Artistpro, 2000.

Kim, Casey. *Audio Post-Production in Your Project Studio.* Boston: Thomson Course Technology, 2009.

Kozloff, Sarah. *Invisible Storytellers: Voice-over Narration in American Fiction Film.* Berkeley: University of California Press, 1988.

———. *Overhearing Film Dialogue.* Berkeley: University of California Press, 2000.

Larson, Peter. Trans. by John Irons. *Film Music.* London: Reaktion Books, 2005.

Lastra, James. *Sound Technology and the American Cinema: Perception, Representation, Modernity.* New York: Columbia University Press, 2000.

Laycock, Roger. *Audio Techniques for Television Production.* Oxford: Focal Press, 2003.

LoBrutto, Vincent. *Sound-on-film: Interviews with Creators of Film Sound.* Westport, Conn.: Praeger, 1994.

Lubin, Tom. *Getting Great Sounds: The Microphone Book.* Boston: Course Technology, 2009.

MacDonald, Laurence. *The Invisible Art of Film Music.* New York: Ardsley House, 1998.

McLeish, Robert. *Radio Production,* 5th ed. Oxford: Focal Press, 2005.

Maes, Jan, and Marc Vercammen. *Digital Audio Technology.* Oxford: Focal Press, 2001.

Marks, Aaron. *The Complete Guide to Game Audio.* Boston: Focal Press, 2008.

Martin, George. *All You Need Is Ears.* New York: St. Martin's Press, 1979.

———. *With a Little Help from My Friends: The Making of Sgt. Pepper.* Boston: Little, Brown, 1995.

———. *Playback.* Surrey, England: Genesis, 2003.

Massey, Howard. *Behind the Glass: Top Record Producers Tell How They Craft the Hits.* San Francisco: Miller Freeman Books, 2000.

Mayer, Lyle V. *Fundamentals of Voice and Articulation,* 14th ed. New York: McGraw-Hill, 2008.

McCarthy, David, Ste Curran, and Simon Byron. *The Art of Producing Games.* Boston: Thomson Course Technology, 2005.

McDaniel, Drew O., Rick C. Shriver, and Kenneth R. Collins. *Fundamentals of Audio Production.* Upper Saddle River, N.J.: Allyn and Bacon, 2008.

Middleton, Chris. *Creating Digital Music and Sound.* Boston: Focal Press, 2006.

Millard, Andre. *America on Record: A History of Recorded Sound,* 2nd ed. New York: Cambridge University Press, 2005.

Molenda, Michael. *What's That Sound? The Audible Audio Dictionary.* Milwaukee: Hal Leonard, 1998.

Moore, Brian C. J. *An Introduction to the Psychology of Hearing.* San Diego: Academic Press, 1990.

Mott, Robert. *Radio Live! Television Live!: Those Golden Days When Horses Were Coconuts.* Jefferson, N.C.: McFarland & Company, 2000.

———. *Sound Effects: Radio, TV, and Film.* Boston: Focal Press, 1990.

Moulton, David. *Total Recording: The Complete Guide to Audio Production and Engineering.* Sherman Oaks, Calif.: KIQ Productions, 2000.

Moylan, William. *Understanding and Crafting the Mix: The Art of Recording,* 2nd ed. Boston: Focal Press, 2007.

Music Producers, 2nd ed. Emeryville, Calif.: MixBooks, 2000.

Music Yellow Pages. United Entertainment Media (annual).

Newall, Philip. *Project Studios.* Oxford: Focal Press, 1999.

———. *Recording Studio Design,* 2nd ed. Oxford: Focal Press, 2008.

Newman, Fred. *Mouth Sounds: How to Whistle, Pop, Boing, and Honk for All Occasions and Then Some.* New York: Workman, 2004.

Nisbett, Alec. *The Sound Studio,* 7th ed. Oxford: Focal Press, 2003.

Olsen, Keith. *A Music Producer's Thoughts to Create By.* Boston: Thomson Course Technology, 2005.

Ondaatje, Michael. *The Conversations: Walter Murch and the Art of Editing Film.* New York: Alfred A. Knopf, 2002.

Owsinski, Bobby, and Dennis Moody. *The Drum Recording Handbook.* Milwaukee: Hal Leonard, 2009.

———. *The Mixing Engineer's Handbook,* 2nd ed. Boston: Thomson Course Technology, 2006.

———. *The Recording Engineer's Handbook.* Boston: Thomson Course Technology, 2004.

Pasquariello, Nicholas. *Sounds of Movies: Interviews with the Creators of Feature Film Soundtracks.* San Francisco: Port Bridge Books, 1996.

Pohlmann, Kenneth. *Principles of Digital Audio,* 5th ed. New York: McGraw-Hill, 2005.

Purcell, John. *Dialogue Editing for Motion Pictures: A Guide to the Invisible Art.* Boston: Focal Press, 2007.

Prendergast, Roy. *Film: A Neglected Art.* New York: W. W. Norton, 1992.

Ramone, Phil, with Charles Granata. *Making Records: The Scenes Behind the Music.* New York: Hyperion Books, 2008.

Recording Industry Sourcebook. Boston: Thomson Course Technology (annual).

Reese, David, Lynne Gross, and Brian Gross. *Audio Production Worktext,* 6th ed. Boston: Focal Press, 2008.

Robair, Gino. *The Ultimate Personal Recording Studio.* Boston: Thomson Course Technology, 2009.

Rose, Jay. *Audio Postproduction for Digital Video.* San Francisco: CMP Books, 2002.

———. *Producing Great Sound for Film and Video,* 3rd ed. Boston: Focal Press, 2008.

Rossing, Thomas, Richard F. Moore, and Paul Wheeler. *The Science of Sound,* 3rd ed. Reading, Mass.: Addison-Wesley, 2001.

Rudolph, Thomas E., and Vincent A. Leonard, Jr. *Recording in the Digital World.* Boston: Berklee Press, 2001.

Rumsey, Francis. *Spatial Audio.* Oxford: Focal Press, 2001.

Rumsey, Francis, and Tim McCormick. *Sound and Recording: An Introduction,* 6th ed. Oxford: Focal Press, 2010.

Rumsey, Francis, and John Watkinson. *Digital Interface Handbook,* 3rd ed. Oxford: Focal Press, 2003.

Russell, Mark, and James Young. *Film Music: Screencraft.* Boston: Focal Press, 2000.

Schafer, Murray. *The Tuning of the World.* New York: Alfred A. Knopf, 1977.

Schelle, Michael. *The Score: Interviews with Film Composers.* Los Angeles: Silman-James Press, 1999.

Schwartz, Tony. *The Responsive Chord.* Garden City, N.Y.: Anchor, 1974.

Sergi, Gianluca. *The Dolby Era: Film Sound in Contemporary Hollywood.* Manchester, U.K.: Manchester University Press, 2005.

Shrivastava, Vinay. *Aesthetics of Sound.* Dubuque, Iowa: Kendal & Hunt Press, 1996.

Sider, Larry, ed. *Soundscape: Exploring the Art of Sound with Moving Images.* New York: Columbia University Press, 2001.

Simons, Dave. *Analog Recording: Using Vintage Gear in Today's Home Studio.* San Francisco: Backbeat Books, 2006.

Sonnenschein, David. *Sound Design: The Expressive Power of Music, Voice, and Sound Effects in Cinema.* Studio City, Calif.: Michael Wiese Productions, 2001.

Swedien, Bruce. *Make Mine Music.* Norway: MIA Musikk, 2003.

Thomas, Tony. *Music for the Movies,* 2nd ed. Los Angeles: Silman-James Press, 1997.

Timm, Larry. *The Soul of the Cinema.* Upper Saddle River, N.J.: Prentice-Hall, 2003.

Toole, Floyd. *Sound Reproduction: Loudspeakers and Rooms.* Boston: Focal Press, 2008.

Touzeau, Jeff. *Artists on Recording Techniques.* Boston: Course Technology, 2009.

———. *Careers in Audio.* Boston: Course Technology, 2008.

———. *Making Tracks: Unique Recording Studio Environments.* Atglen, Penn.: Schiffer Books, 2005.

Truax, Barry. *Acoustic Communication,* 2nd ed. Norwood, N.J.: Ablex, 2000.

Viers, Ric. *Sound Effects Bible.* Studio City, Calif.: Michael Wiese Productions, 2008.

Watkinson, John. *MPEG Handbook,* 2nd ed. Oxford: Focal Press, 2004.

Weis, Elisabeth. *The Silent Scream.* Rutherford, N.J.: Farleigh Dickinson, 1982.

Weis, Elisabeth, and John Belton, eds. *Film Sound: Theory and Practice.* New York: Columbia University Press, 1985.

Wentz, Brooke. *Hey, That's My Music.* Milwaukee: Hal Leonard, 2007. (music licensing)

Whitaker, Jerry. *Master Handbook of Audio Production.* New York: McGraw-Hill, 2003.

White, Glenn, and Gary J. Louie. *The Audio Dictionary,* 3rd ed. Seattle: University of Washington Press, 2005.

Whittington, William. *Sound Design and Science Fiction.* Austin: University of Texas Press, 2007.

Wilde, Martin. *Audio Programming for Interactive Games.* Boston: Focal Press, 2004.

Yewdall, David Lewis. *Practical Art of Motion Picture Sound,* 3rd ed. Boston: Focal Press, 2007.

Zettl, Herbert. *Sight, Sound, Motion: Applied Media Aesthetics,* 6th ed. Boston: Wadsworth, 2011.

Periodicals

The Absolute Sound

aM.MAG [*audioMIDI.com* magazine]

Audio Engineering Society [AES] Journal

Audio Media (U.K.)

Audio Technology Magazine (Australia)

AudioXPress

Broadcast Engineering

Broadcaster (Canada)

Canadian Producer

Digital Content Producer

Digital Juice

Electronic Musician

EQ

Film and Video

Home and Studio Recording

Home Recording

International Recording Equipment and Studio Directory

Millimeter

Mix

Mix Annual Master Directory of Recording Industry Facilities and Services

Mixdown

Post

Pro Audio Review

Professional Sound

Pro Sound News

Radio

Radio World

Recording

Remix

Resolution

SMPTE Journal

Sound and Communications

Sound and Video Contractor (SVC)

Sound and Vision

Sound on Sound (U.K.)

Stereophile

Studio

Tape Op

Videography

Virtual Instruments

Voice Coil

Audio- and Videotapes, CDs, CD-ROMs, DVDs, and Programs

Anechoic Orchestral Music Recording. Denon PG-6006.

Auralia: Complete Ear Training Software for Musicians. Rising Software, Australia.

Begault, Durand. *The Sonic CD-ROM for Desktop Audio Production.* San Diego: Academic Press, 1996.

Tom Dowd and the Language of Music. 2003.

Gehman, Scott. *From Tin to Gold: Train Your Ears to Golden Standards.* Houston: Gehman Music, 1996.

Hernandez, John. *Miking the Drum Set.* Claremont, Calif.: Terence Dwyer Productions, 1992.

Hollywood's Musical Moods. American Movie Channel, 1995.

Tom Lubin. *Shaping Your Sound.* Los Angeles: Acrobat, 1988–1991.

Mix Reference Disc: Deluxe Edition. Emeryville, Calif.: MixBooks.

Moulton, Dave. *Golden Ears.* Sherman Oaks: Calif.: KIQ Productions, 1995.

Music and Technology. National Public Radio (seven-part series), 2008.

Music Behind the Scenes (six-part series). Bravo Channel, 2002.

Owsinski, Bobby. *Setting Up Your Surround Studio.* San Francisco: Backbeat Books, 2003.

The Sheffield Drum Record/The Sheffield Track Record. Sheffield Lab CD-14/20.

Sides, Alan. *Alan Sides' Microphone Cabinet.* Emeryville, Calif.: EM Books, 1995.

Sound Check, vols. 1 and 2. Compiled by Alan Parsons and Stephen Court.

Sterling, Christopher, Stanley Alten, Lynne Gross, Skip Pizzi, and Joan Van Tassel (eds.). *Focal Encyclopedia of Electronic Media.* Boston: Focal Press, 1998.

Stokes, Jason. *Modern Recording and Mixing* (three DVDs). Secrets of the Pros, Inc., 2006.

Studio Reference Disc. Prosonus SRD.

Swedien, Bruce. *Recording with Bruce Swedien,* vol. 1. San Francisco: AcuNet, 1997.

TechnoPop: The Secret History of Technology and Pop Music (six-part series). National Public Radio, 2002.

TMH Digital Audio Test Discs. TMH Corporation and Tomlinson Holman (producers). Hollywood Edge.

Various compilation and test CDs, including stereo and surround sound and techniques for miking. Chesky Records.

Wadhams, Wayne. *Sound Advice: The Musician's Guide to the Recording Studio.* New York: Schirmer, 1990.

Web Sites

There are hundreds of audio-related Web sites. Those listed below are a few of the more essential.

Association of Motion Picture Sound (AMPS): *www.amps.net*

Association of Professional Recording Services (APRS): *www.aprs.co.uk*

Audio Engineering Society (AES): *www.aes.org*

Audio Publishers Association (APA): *www.audiopub.org/apa*

Canadian Academy of Recording Arts and Sciences: *www.juno-awards.ca*

Canadian Recording Industry Association: *www.cria.ca*

www.filmscoremonthly.com

www.filmsound.org

G.A.N.G. (Game Audio Network Guild): *www.audiogang.org*

H.E.A.R.: *www.hearnet.com*

Home Recording Rights Coalition: *www.hrrc.org*

Institute of Electrical and Electronics Engineers, Inc. (IEEE): *www.ieee.org*

International Radio and Television Society: *www.irts.org*

Mix Foundation for Excellence in Audio: *www.tecawards .org*

mixonline.com

Moving Picture Experts Group (MPEG): *www.mpeg.org*

Music Producers Guild of America (MPGA): *www.mpga.org*

NAMM—The International Music Products Association: *www.namm.org*

National Association of Broadcasters (NAB): *www.nab.org*

National Association of Recording Merchandisers (NARM): *www.narm.com*

National Academy of Recording Arts and Sciences: *www .grammy.com*

Recording Industry Association of America (RIAA): *www .riaa.com*

Society of Motion Picture and Television Engineers (SMPTE): *www.smpte.org*

Society of Professional Audio Recording Services (SPARS): *www.spars.com*

www.soundtrack.net

widescreenmuseum.com/sound/sound01.htm

Glossary

Ω *See* **ohm**

μ Microsecond.

μ-law An 8-bit codec compression format for sending speech via digital telephone lines; used in North America and Japan. *See also* **a-law**.

λ *See* **wavelength**

5.1 The surround-sound format incorporating five discrete full-frequency audio channels and one discrete channel for low-frequency enhancement. *See also* **7.1** and **surround sound**.

7.1 The surround-sound format incorporating seven discrete full-frequency audio channels and one discrete channel for low-frequency enhancement. *See also* **5.1** and **surround sound**.

24p The format used in high-definition video where the camera is substituting for film. The *24* refers to the standard frames-per-second rate; the *p* stands for *progressive*.

60 percent/60-minute rule Limit listening through headphones to no more than one hour per day at levels below 60 percent of maximum volume.

AC-3 The encoding algorithm used in Dolby Digital data compression. *AC* stands for *audio coding. See also* **Dolby Digital**.

ACN *See* **active combining network**

accent miking Used to pick up instruments in an ensemble when they solo. It is, in effect, a relatively close-miking technique but used when distant microphones are picking up the ensemble's overall sound and a solo passage needs to stand out. Also called *off-miking. See also* **ambience miking, close miking**, and **distant miking**.

acoustical phase The time relationship between two or more sound waves at a given point in their cycles.

acoustic masking *See* **MPEG**

acoustic pickup mic *See* **contact microphone**

acoustics The science that deals with the behavior of sound and sound control, including its generation, transmission, reception, and effects. The properties of a room that affect the quality of sound.

active combining network (ACN) An amplifier at which the outputs of two or more signal paths are mixed together before being routed to their destination.

active loudspeaker A loudspeaker that is powered internally. *See also* **passive loudspeaker**.

active microphone mixer Allows amplification control of each audio source and usually includes other processing features as well. *See also* **passive microphone mixer**.

active ribbon microphone A ribbon microphone that uses an amplifier system requiring phantom power.

adaptive differential pulse code modulation (ADPCM) Compression format that records the differences between samples of sound rather than the actual sound itself, compressing original data to one-fourth its size.

adaptive sound *See* **complex interactivity**

additive ambience When the ambience of each track becomes cumulative in mixing a multitrack recording.

ADPCM *See* **adaptive differential pulse code modulation**

ADR *See* **automated dialogue replacement**

ADSR *See* **sound envelope**

AES/EBU Internationally accepted professional digital audio interface transmitted via a balanced-line connection using XLR connectors, specified jointly by the Audio Engineering Society (AES) and the European Broadcast Union (EBU). *See also* **Sony/Philips Digital Interface (S/PDIF)**.

aggregator Client software that uses a Web feed to retrieve syndicated Web content such as podcasts, blogs, and mass media Web sites and, in the case of a search aggregator, a customized set of search results. Aggregators reduce the time and the effort needed to regularly check Web sites for updates. Also called *podcatcher*.

a-law An 8-bit codec compression format for sending speech via digital telephone lines, used worldwide, except in North America and Japan. *See also* **μ-law**.

ambience   Sounds such as reverberation, noise, and atmosphere that form a background to the main sound. Also called *room tone* and *presence* and, in Great Britain, *atmos.*

ambience miking   Used along with distant miking, attempts to reproduce the aural experience that audiences receive in a live venue by recording in an acoustically suitable studio or concert hall. Microphones are positioned far enough from the ensemble where the later reflections are more prominent than the direct sound. *See also* **accent miking, close miking,** and **distant miking.**

amp   *See* **ampere**

ampere   The basic unit of electric current. Also called *amp.*

amplifier   A device that increases the amplitude of an electric signal.

amplitude   The magnitude of a sound wave or an electric signal, measured in decibels.

amplitude processor   A signal processor that affects a signal's loudness. The effects include compression, limiting, de-essing, expanding, noise gating, and pitch shifting. Also called *dynamic processor.*

analog recording   A method of recording in which the waveform of the recorded signal resembles the waveform of the original signal.

analytical listening   The evaluation of the content and the function of sound. *See also* **critical listening**.

anechoic chamber   A room that prevents all reflected sound through the dissipation or absorption of sound waves.

artificial head stereo   *See* **binaural microphone head**

aspect ratio   The width-to-height proportions of a video image. For the standard video screen, it is 4 × 3 (1.33:1); for HDTV it is 16 × 9 (1.78:1). For wide motion picture screens, aspect ratios are between 5.55 × 3 (1.85:1) and 7 × 3 (2.35:1).

asset   In an interactive video game, a discreet piece of sound data that is referenced by the game software and made to execute at the proper time and with the proper dynamics.

assignable console   Console in which the dynamics, in addition to other functions depending on the model, are grouped in a separate module and can be assigned to individual channels selectively.

atmos   Short for *atmosphere,* the British term for ambience. *See* **ambience.**

Atmos 5.1 surround microphone system   A microphone system for surround-sound pickup consisting of an adjustable surround-sound microphone and a console for controlling the output assignment and the panning of the various surround configurations.

attack   (1) The way a sound begins—that is, by plucking, bowing, striking, blowing, and so on. (2) The first part of the sound envelope—how a sound starts after a sound source has been vibrated.

attack time   The length of time it takes a compressor to respond to the input signal.

attenuator   *See* **fader**

audio data rate   The relationship between sampling frequency and quantization. When audio is converted to digital, it becomes data. The data rate is computed by multiplying bit depth times sampling frequency.

audio engine   The software/asset combination that controls the entire sound design for an interactive video game.

audio-leading-video   When the sound of the incoming scene starts before the corresponding picture appears. Also called *L-cut. See also* **video-leading-audio.**

auditory fatigue   *See* **temporary threshold shift**

Aural Exciter   *See* **psychoacoustic processor**

automated dialogue replacement (ADR)   A technique used to rerecord dialogue in synchronization with picture in postproduction. The picture is automatically replayed in short loops again and again so that the performers can synchronize their lip movements with the lip movements in the picture and then record the dialogue. Also known as *automatic dialog recording* and *looping.*

automatic dialogue replacement   *See* **automated dialogue replacement**

automatic microphone mixer   Controls a group of live microphones in real time, turning up a mic when someone is talking and turning down the mics of the participants who are not talking.

backtiming   A method of subtracting the time of a program segment from the total time of a program so that the segment and the program end simultaneously.

balanced line   A pair of ungrounded conductors whose voltages are opposite in polarity but equal in magnitude.

band-pass filter   A filter that attenuates above and below a selected bandwidth, allowing the frequencies in between to pass.

bandwidth   The difference between the upper and lower frequency limits of an audio component. The upper and lower frequency limits of AM radio are 535 kHz and 1,605 kHz; therefore the bandwidth of AM radio is 1,070 kHz.

bandwidth curve   The curve shaped by the number of frequencies in a bandwidth and their relative increase or decrease in level. A bandwidth of 100 to 150 Hz with 125 Hz boosted 15 dB forms a sharp, narrow bandwidth curve; a bandwidth of 100 to 6,400 Hz with a 15 dB boost at 1,200 Hz forms a more sloping, wider bandwidth curve.

basic interactivity   One of two types of interactive-sound design, characterized by a simple relationship between user actions and audio playback. *See also* **complex interactivity**.

bass   The low range of the audible frequency spectrum; usually from 20 to 320 Hz.

bass management   In surround sound, the redirection of low-frequency content from each of the full-bandwidth production channels to the low-frequency enhancement channel.

bass roll-off   Attenuating bass frequencies. The control—for example, on a microphone—used to roll off bass frequencies.

bass tip-up   *See* **proximity effect**

bass trap   *See* **diaphragmatic absorber**

BD   *See* **Blue-ray Disc**

bidirectional microphone   A microphone that picks up sound to its front and back and has minimal pickup at its sides.

binaural hearing   Hearing with two ears attached to and separated by the head. *See also* **binaural microphone head**.

binaural microphone head   Two omnidirectional capacitor microphones set into the ear cavities of an artificial head, complete with pinnae. This arrangement preserves binaural localization cues during recording and reproduces sound as humans hear it: three-dimensionally. Also called *artificial head* or *dummy head (Kunstkopf) stereo*.

bit depth   *See* **word length**

blast filter   *See* **pop filter**

blocking   Plotting performer, camera, and microphone placements and movements in a production.

Blu-ray Disc (BD)   High-density optical disc format developed to enable recording, playback, and rewriting of high-definition television.

board   Audio mixing console. *See also* **console**.

boundary microphone   A microphone whose capsule is mounted flush with or close to, but a precise distance from, a reflective surface so that there is no phase cancellation of reflected sound at audible frequencies.

bpm   Beats per minute.

broadband compressor   A compressor that acts on the dynamic range of the input signal across the entire frequency spectrum. *See also* **split-band compressor**.

bus   A mixing network that combines the outputs of other channels.

calibration   Adjusting equipment—for example, a console and a recorder—according to a standard so that their measurements are similar.

camcorder   A handheld video camera with a built-in or dockable video recorder.

capacitor loudspeaker   *See* **electrostatic loudspeaker**

capacitor microphone   A microphone that transduces acoustic energy into electric energy electrostatically. Also called *condenser microphone*.

cardioid microphone   A unidirectional microphone with a heart-shaped pickup pattern.

CD-R   *See* **recordable compact disc**

CD-RW   *See* **rewritable CD**

center frequency   In peak/dip equalizing, the frequency at which maximum boost or attenuation occurs.

channel strip   One channel (usually input) of a console.

chipmunk effect   *See* **speed-up pitch-shifting**

chorus effect   Recirculating the doubling effect to make one sound source sound like several. *See also* **doubling**.

clapboard   *See* **clapslate**

clapslate   A slate used in synchronizing sound and picture during filming and editing. The slate carries such information as scene and take number, production title, location of shot—e.g., indoors or outdoors—and time code. On top of the slate is a clapstick, which is lifted and then snapped closed to produce a loud sound that is used to synchronize picture and sound. Also called *slate, clapboard,* or *sticks*.

clipping   Audible distortion that occurs when a signal's level exceeds the limits of a particular device or circuit.

close miking   Placing a microphone close to a sound source to pick up mostly direct sound and reduce ambience and leakage. *See also* **accent miking**, **ambience miking**, and **distant miking**.

cocktail party effect A psychoacoustic effect that allows humans to localize the sources of sounds around them.

codec A device that encodes a signal at one end of a transmission and decodes it at the other end. The word codec is a contraction of en*co*der/*deco*der.

coincident miking Employing two matched microphones, usually unidirectional, crossed one above the other on a vertical axis with their diaphragms. *See also* **X-Y miking**.

comb-filter effect The effect produced when a signal is time-delayed and added to itself, reinforcing some frequencies and canceling others, giving sound an unnatural, hollow coloration.

commentative sound Descriptive sound that makes a comment or an interpretation. *See also* **descriptive sound** and **narrative sound**.

compander A contraction of the words *compressor* and *expander* that refers to the devices that compress an input signal and expand an output signal to reduce noise. Also called a *noise reducer*.

companding A contraction of the words *compressing* and *expanding* that refers to wireless mics' increasing dynamic range and reducing noise inherent in a transmission system.

comping Taking the best part(s) of each recorded track and combining them into a composite final version.

complementary equalization Equalizing sounds that share similar frequency ranges so that they complement, rather than interfere with, one another. *See also* **cumulative equalization** and **subtractive equalization**.

complex interactivity One of two types of interactive-sound design, characterized by user actions that result in more than just simple audio sprite playback. Also called *adaptive sound* and *interactive sound. See also* **basic interactivity**.

compression (1) Reducing a signal's output level in relation to its input level to reduce dynamic range. (2) The drawing together of vibrating molecules, producing a high-pressure area. *See also* **rarefaction**.

compression ratio The ratio of the input and output signals in a compressor.

compression threshold The level at which a compressor acts on an input signal and the compression ratio takes effect.

compressor A signal processor with an output level that increases at a slower rate as its input level increases.

condenser microphone *See* **capacitor microphone**

console An electronic device that amplifies, balances, processes, and combines input signals and routes them to broadcast or recording. Also called *board, mixer,* or, in Europe, *mixing desk. See also* **mixer**.

constructive interference When sound waves are partially out of phase and partially additive, increasing amplitude where compression and rarefaction occur at the same time.

contact microphone A microphone that attaches to a sound source and transduces the vibrations that pass through it. Also called *acoustic pickup mic*.

contextual sound Sound that emanates from and duplicates a sound source as it is. *See also* **diegetic sound**.

contrapuntal narration Juxtaposes narration and action to make a statement not carried by either element alone.

control surface Provides tactual means of controlling various console-related functions. Generally there are no actual audio signals present inside a simple control surface, only control circuitry that sends digital instructions to the device doing the actual audio signal processing. Also called *work surface*.

converter Changes analog signals into discrete digital numbers in analog-to-digital converters, and changes discrete digital numbers into analog signals in digital-to-analog converters.

convolution reverb A sample-based process that multiplies the spectrums of two audio files, providing a virtually infinite range of acoustic spaces.

cordless microphone *See* **wireless microphone system**

coverage angle The off-axis angle or point at which the loudspeaker level is down 6 dB compared with the on-axis output level.

cps Cycles per second. *See* **hertz**.

critical listening The evaluation of the characteristics of the sound itself. *See also* **analytical listening**.

crossfade Fading in one sound source as another sound source fades out. At some point the sounds cross at an equal level of loudness.

crossover frequency The frequency at which the high frequencies are routed to the tweeter(s) and the low frequencies are routed to the woofer(s).

crossover network   An electronic device that divides the audio spectrum into individual frequency ranges (low, high, and/or middle) before sending them to specialized loudspeakers such as the woofer(s) and the tweeter(s).

cue sheet   Any type of form used in recording, editing, or mixing audio that lists dialogue, music, or sound-effect cues and their in- and out-times.

cumulative equalization   Too much boost of the same frequency in various tracks in a multitrack recording, which could unbalance the overall blend of a mix. *See also* **complementary equalization** and **subtractive equalization**.

cut   (1) An instantaneous transition from one sound or picture to another. (2) To make a disc recording. (3) A decrease in level.

cut sound effect   *See* **hard sound effect**.

cycles per second (cps)   *See* **hertz**

DAW   *See* **digital audio workstation**

dB   *See* **decibel**

dBFS   *See* **decibel full-scale**

dBm   An electrical measure of power referenced to 1 mW as dissipated across a 600-ohm load.

dB-SPL   *See* **sound-pressure level**

dBu   A unit of measurement for expressing the relationship of decibels to voltage—0.775 V. The *u* stands for unterminated.

dBv   *See* **dBu**

dBV   A measure of voltage with decibels referenced to 1 V.

DC   Direct current.

DCA   *See* **digitally controlled amplifier**

deadpotting   Starting a recording with the fader turned down all the way. Also called *deadrolling*.

deadrolling   *See* **deadpotting**

decay   How fast a sound fades from a certain loudness.

decay time   *See* **reverberation time**

decibel (dB)   A relative and dimensionless unit to measure the ratio of two quantities.

decibel full-scale (dBFS)   A unit of measurement for the amplitude of digital audio signals.

de-emphasis   Reduces the high-frequency noise at the receiver.

de-esser   A compressor that reduces sibilance.

delay   The time interval between a sound or signal and each of its repeats.

delay time   The amount of time between delays. In a digital delay, delay time regulates how long a given sound is held.

descriptive sound   Describes sonic aspects of a scene not connected to the main action. *See also* **commentative sound** and **narrative sound**.

design sound effect   An effect that must be created because it does not exist in nature.

destructive editing   Editing that permanently alters the original sound or soundfile. It changes the data on the disk by overwriting it. *See also* **nondestructive editing**.

destructive interference   When sound waves are partially out of phase and partially subtractive, decreasing amplitude where compression and rarefaction occur at different times.

dialnorm   Short for *dialogue normalization*. An attenuation signal designed to normalize the loudness levels among different distribution sources such as television and DVD and from program to program, using speech as the common reference.

diaphragmatic absorber   A flexible panel mounted over an air space that resonates at a frequency (or frequencies) determined by the stiffness of the panel and the size of the air space. Also called *bass trap*.

diegetic sound   Sound that comes from within the story space, such as dialogue and sound effects. *See also* **contextual sound** and **nondiegetic sound**.

diffraction   The spreading of sound waves as they pass around an object.

diffusion   The scattering of sound waves to a uniform intensity.

digital audio extraction   *See* **ripping**

digital audio workstation (DAW)   A multifunctional hard-disk production system, controlled from a central location, that is integrated with and capable of being networked to other devices, such as audio, video, and MIDI sources, within or among facilities. Generally, there are two types of DAW systems: computer-based and integrated.

digital clock   *See* **word clock**

digital delay   An electronic device designed to delay an audio signal.

digital editing   The assembly of disk-based material in or out of sequence, taken from any part of a recording and placed in any other part of the recording almost instantly. Also known as *nonlinear editing*.

digitally controlled amplifier (DCA) An amplifier whose gain is remotely controlled by a digital control signal.

digital microphone A microphone that converts an analog signal into a digital signal at the mic capsule.

digital multilayer disc (DMD) High-density optical format disc that can store between 22 and 32 GB of data, with the potential for 100 GB of storage space. Successor to the fluorescent multilayer disc.

digital news gathering (DNG) Reporting and gathering news from the field using digital equipment.

digital recording A method of recording in which samples of the original analog signal are encoded as pulses and then decoded during playback.

digital signal processing (DSP) Provides various manipulations of sound in a digital format. The term is generally used to refer to signal processing using computer software.

Digital Theater System (DTS) A lossy data compression format that reduces the bit rate to roughly 1.4 Mbps.

digital versatile disc (DVD) A compact disc providing massive data storage of digital-quality audio, video, and text.

direct/ambient surround-sound miking A surround-sound miking technique using a stereo microphone array for the left-right frontal pickups, plus a center mic for the center channel and a stereo microphone array for the left- and right-rear surround pickup. *See also* **direct surround-sound miking**.

directional microphone *See* **unidirectional microphone**

direct narration Describes what is being seen or heard. *See also* **indirect narration**.

direct sound Sound waves that reach the listener before reflecting off any surface. *See also* **early reflections**.

direct surround-sound miking A surround-sound miking approach that uses a microphone array especially designed for surround-sound pickup. *See also* **direct/ambient surround-sound miking**.

distant miking Placing a microphone far enough from the sound source to pick up most or all of an ensemble's blended sound, including room reflections. *See also* **accent miking, ambience miking,** and **close miking**.

distortion The appearance of a signal in the reproduced sound that was not in the original sound. *See also* **har-**monic distortion, intermodulation distortion, loudness distortion,** and **transient distortion**.

diversity reception Multiple-antenna receiving system for use with wireless microphones. *See also* **nondiversity receiver**.

DME Stands for dialogue, music, and sound effects.

DNG *See* **digital news gathering**

Dolby Digital A lossy data compression format that reduces the bit rate to roughly 400 Kbps. *See also* **AC-3**.

donut In mixing audio for a spot announcement, fading the music after it is established to create a hole for the announcement and then reestablishing the music at its former full level.

Doppler effect The perceived increase or decrease in frequency as a sound source moves closer to or farther from the listener.

double-system recording Filming sound and picture simultaneously but separately with a camera and a recorder.

doubling Mixing slightly delayed signals (15 to 35 ms) with the original signal to create a fuller, stronger, more ambient sound. *See also* **chorus effect**.

downmixing A way to handle surround sound whereby the surround signals are mixed to stereo. *See also* **upmixing**.

DRC *See* **dynamic range control**

driver A program that allows the transfer of audio signals to and from an audio interface.

dropout (1) A sudden attenuation of sound or loss of picture. (2) Sudden attenuation in a wireless microphone signal due to an obstruction or some other interference.

dry sound A sound devoid of reverberation or signal processing. *See also* **wet sound**.

DSP *See* **digital signal processing**

DTS *See* **Digital Theater System**

dub Transferring sound from tape or disk to another tape or disk. Also called *transfer*.

dummy head (Kunstkopf) stereo *See* **binaural microphone head**

duration How long a sound lasts.

DVD *See* **digital versatile disc**

DVD-Audio (DVD-A) A digital versatile disc format with extremely high-quality audio.

DVD authoring   The phase of DVD production when the user decides what goes onto the DVD and then applies the appropriate software to implement the process.

DVD-R   A DVD format allowing users to record one time but to play back the recorded information repeatedly. The format writes its data differently from DVD+R making the two record formats incompatible. *See also* **DVD+R.**

DVD+R   A DVD format allowing users to record one time but to play back the recorded information repeatedly. The format writes its data differently from DVD-R, making the two record formats incompatible. *See also* **DVD-R.**

DVD-RW   A DVD format that can be recorded on, erased, and used again for another recording. It employs a phase-change technology. A primary application for this format is authoring media for DVD-V.

DVD+RW   A DVD erasable format using phase-change technology that was developed to compete with DVD-RAM.

dynamic microphone   A microphone that transduces energy electromagnetically. Moving-coil and ribbon microphones are dynamic.

dynamic mixing   Composing the numerous sonic variables in interactive-sound design into a continuum that balances the need for realism with a visceral emotional experience so that each user experiences the appropriate sound mix for individual actions being performed.

dynamic processor   *See* **amplitude processor**

dynamic range   The range between the quietest and the loudest sounds that a sound source can produce without distortion.

dynamic range compensation   *See* **dynamic range control**

dynamic range compression   *See* **dynamic range control**

dynamic range control (DRC)   A gain control signal applied during decoding that allows different amounts of overall dynamic range. Also called *dynamic range compensation* and *dynamic range compression.*

dynamic sound   *See* **interactive sound**

early reflections   Reflections of the original sound that reach the listener within about 40 to 50 ms of the direct sound. Also called *early sound. See also* **direct sound.**

early sound   *See* **early reflections**

earset microphone   Consists only of an earpiece cable (with no headband) connected to a microphone.

echo   Sound reflections delayed by 35 ms or more that are perceived as discrete repetitions of the direct sound.

echo threshold   The point in time at which an echo is perceived, generally between 1 and 30 ms following the direct sound.

edit decision list (EDL)   A list of edits, computer-generated or handwritten, used to assemble a production.

edit master   The finished program on videotape, film, or disc.

EDL   *See* **edit decision list**

EFP   *See* **electronic field production**

eigentones   The resonance of sound at particular frequencies in an acoustic space. May add unwanted coloration to sound. More commonly known as *room modes.*

elasticity   The capacity to return to the original shape or place after deflection or displacement.

electret microphone   A capacitor microphone which, instead of requiring an external high-voltage power source, uses a permanently charged element and requires only a low-voltage power supply for the internal preamp.

electroacoustics   The electrical manipulation of acoustics.

electronic field production (EFP)   Video production done on-location, involving program materials that take some time to produce.

electronic Foley   Creating sound effects electronically using MIDI and devices such as synthesizers and computers.

electronic news gathering (ENG)   News production done on-location, sometimes recorded and sometimes live, but usually with an imminent deadline.

electrostatic loudspeaker   A loudspeaker that uses minimal moving mass and obtains its driving force by applying an electric field to a charge trapped in the diaphragm. Also called *capacitor loudspeaker.*

ENG   *See* **electronic news gathering**

enharmonic   In music two different notes that sound the same, for example, C# and D♭, G# and A♭.

EQ   Equalization. *See* **equalizer.**

equalizer   A signal-processing device that can boost, attenuate, or shelve frequencies in a sound source or sound system.

equal loudness principle   The principle that confirms the human ear's nonlinear sensitivity to all audible frequencies: that midrange frequencies are perceived with greatest intensity and that bass and treble frequencies are perceived with lesser intensity.

equivalent noise level *See* self-noise

ergonomics Designing an engineering system with human comfort and convenience in mind.

EVD Stands for *enhanced versatile disc.*

expander An amplifier whose gain decreases as its input level decreases. It increases dynamic range.

extra-sound *See* nondiegetic sound

fade-out/fade-in A transition usually indicating a marked change in time, locale, continuity of action, and other features. It is effected by gradually decreasing the loudness of a signal level to silence (or to "black" in video) and then gradually increasing the loudness of a signal level from silence (or from "black").

fader A device containing a resistor that is used to vary the output voltage of a circuit or component. Also known as an *attenuator,* a *gain* or *volume control,* or a *pot* or *potentiometer.*

far-field monitoring Monitoring sound at the listening position from large, powerful frontal loudspeakers several feet away and usually built into the mixing-room wall. *See also* **near-field monitoring.**

feed A computer file in a standardized format that lists addresses and information about the podcasts available on a server. It is also made available on the server in a semi-permanent location known as the *feed URI* or *feed URL.*

feedback When part or all of a system's output signal is returned into its own input. Feedback can be acoustic or electronic. A common example of acoustic feedback is the loud squeal or howl caused when the sound from a loudspeaker is picked up by a nearby microphone and reamplified. Electronic feedback is created in digital delay devices by feeding a proportion of the delayed signal back into the delay line. Also called *regeneration.*

filter A device that removes unwanted frequencies or noise from a signal.

FireWire A technology that enables isosynchronous service while providing the bandwidth needed for audio, imaging, video, and other streaming data. Isosynchronous service means it guarantees *latency*—the length of time between a requested action and when the resulting action occurs. FireWire offers a standard, simple connection to all types of electronics, including digital audio devices, digital VCRs, and digital video cameras as well as to traditional computer peripherals such as optical disc drives and hard-disk drives. FireWire can support up to 63 devices on a single bus.

first harmonic *See* fundamental

fixed-frequency equalizer An equalizer with several fixed frequencies usually grouped in two (high and low), three (high, middle, and low), or four (high, high-middle, low-middle, and low) ranges of the frequency spectrum.

fixed-frequency wireless microphone system A wireless system assigned to one frequency. *See also* **variable-frequency wireless microphone system.**

fixed mic *See* plant microphone

FLAC *See* Free Lossless Audio Codec

flanging Combining a direct signal and the same signal slightly delayed and continuously varying their time relationships, using a time delay.

flat Frequency response in an audio system that reproduces a signal between 20 Hz and 20,000 Hz (or between any two specified frequencies) that varies no more than ±3 dB.

flutter echoes Echoes between parallel walls that occur in rapid, even series.

FM microphone *See* wireless microphone system

foldback The system in a multichannel console that permits the routing of sound through a headphone monitor feed to performers in the studio.

Foley recording Producing and recording sound effects in the studio in synchronization with picture.

formant A frequency band in a voice or musical instrument that contains more energy and loudness than the neighboring area.

four-way system loudspeaker A loudspeaker system with three crossover networks.

fps Frames per second.

frame rate The number of film frames that pass in 1 second of real time—frames per second (fps).

Free Lossless Audio Codec (FLAC) An open-source, cross-platform file format that achieves lossless compression rates of 40 to 50 percent for most musical material.

frequency The number of times per second that a sound source vibrates, expressed in hertz (Hz); formerly expressed in cycles per second (cps).

frequency-agile system *See* variable-frequency wireless microphone system

frequency response A measure of an audio system's ability to reproduce a range of frequencies with the same relative loudness; usually represented by a graph.

full coat Magnetic film in which the oxide coating covers most or all of the film width. *See also* **stripe coat.**

fundamental The lowest frequency a sound source can produce. Also called *first harmonic* and *primary frequency.*

FVD Stands for *forward versatile disc.*

gain control *See* **fader**

game state A collection of all useful information about a video game at any given point during play.

GB *See* **gigabyte**

gigabyte (GB) 1,024 megabytes (2^{30} bytes).

graphic equalizer An equalizer with sliding controls that gives a graphic representation of the response curve chosen.

Haas effect A sound reflection arriving up to 30 ms after the direct sound must be about 10 dB louder to be audible, resulting in the direct and reflected sounds' being perceived as one. *See also* **temporal fusion** and **precedence effect.**

hard-disk recording Using a hard-disk computer system as the recording medium. Data storage and retrieval are random, quick, and nonlinear; storage capacity is considerable; and data can be nondestructive.

hard knee compression Abrupt gain reduction at the start of compression. *See also* **knee** and **soft knee compression.**

hard sound effect Begins and ends cleanly, requiring little adjustment in editing to remain in sync with the picture. Also called *cut sound effect. See also* **soft sound effect.**

harmonic distortion Nonlinear distortion caused when an audio system introduces harmonics to a signal at the output that were not present at the input.

harmonics Frequencies that are exact multiples of the fundamental.

HD High definition.

head-related transfer function (HRTF) The filtering capacities of the head, outer ears, and torso in locating a sound in three-dimensional space. *See also* **diffraction** and **reflected sound.**

headroom The amount of increase in loudness level that a recording medium, amplifier, or other piece of equip-ment can take, above working level, before overload distortion.

headset microphone A microphone attached to a pair of headphones; one headphone channel feeds the program and the other headphone channel feeds the director's cues.

Helmholtz absorber A resonator designed to absorb specific frequencies depending on size, shape, and enclosed volume of air. The enclosed volume of air is connected to the air in the room by a narrow opening, or neck. When resonant frequencies reach the neck of the enclosure, the air inside cancels those frequencies. Also called *Helmholtz resonator.*

Helmholtz resonator *See* **Helmholtz absorber**

hertz (Hz) Unit of measurement of frequency; numerically equal to cycles per second (cps).

HID *See* **human interface device**

High Definition Microphone™ A trademark of Earthworks, Inc., referring to its line of very high-quality mics and their proprietary technology.

high end The treble range of the frequency spectrum.

high-pass (low-cut) filter A filter that attenuates frequencies below a selected frequency and allows those above that point to pass.

holographic versatile disc (HVD) High-density optical disc that uses two lasers in a single beam and can hold up to 3.9 TB of data.

Holophone™ microphone system A microphone used for surround-sound pickup consisting of seven or eight miniature omnidirectional microphone elements housed in an ellipsoid shaped like a giant teardrop.

HRTF *See* **head-related transfer function**

human interface device (HID) A hands-on device, such as a mouse, keyboard, joystick, or touchscreen, that facilitates control of computer functions.

humbuck coil A circuit built into a microphone to reduce hum pickup.

HVD *See* **holographic versatile disc**

Hz *See* **hertz**

IEM *See* **in-ear monitor**

IFB *See* **interruptible foldback system**

IID *See* **interaural intensity difference**

IM *See* **intermodulation distortion**

impedance The measure of the total resistance to the current flow in an AC circuit; expressed in ohms.

indirect narration Describes something other than what is being seen or heard. *See also* **direct narration.**

indirect sound Sound waves that reflect from one or more surfaces before reaching the listener.

in-ear monitor (IEM) Used by musicians in live concerts to replace stage monitors.

infinitely variable pattern microphone A microphone that allows fine adjustments to any on-axis response from omnidirectional through bi- and unidirectional pickup patterns.

infrasonic The range below the frequencies audible to human hearing.

inharmonic overtones Pitches that are not exact multiples of the fundamental. *See also* **overtones.**

initial decay In the sound envelope, the point at which the attack begins to lose amplitude.

in-line console A console in which a channel's input, output, and monitor functions are placed in line and located in a single input/output (I/O) module. *See also* **input/output (I/O) module.**

inner ear The part of the ear that contains the auditory nerve, which transmits sound waves to the brain.

input/output (I/O) module On an in-line console, a module containing input, output, and monitor controls for a single channel.

input section On a console the section into which signals from a sound source, such as a microphone feed, are routed to the output section.

Integrated Services Digital Network (ISDN) A public telephone service that allows inexpensive use of a flexible, wide-area, all-digital network for, among other things, recording simultaneously from various locations.

interactive media Media such as computer games that allow a user to be a participant in the viewing experience—to directly manipulate and control the picture and the sound.

interactive sound A sound track that reacts to user input and is designed to never play back in the same way twice. Also called *dynamic sound* and *complex interactivity.*

interaural intensity difference (IID) The difference between signal intensity levels at each ear. Also known as *interaural level difference.*

interaural level difference *See* interaural intensity difference.

interaural time difference (ITD) The difference between signal arrival times at each ear.

intermodulation distortion (IM) Nonlinear distortion that occurs when different frequencies pass through an amplifier at the same time and interact to create combinations of tones unrelated to the original sounds.

Internet Protocol (IP) The method used to send data from one computer to another over the Internet.

Internet SCSI (iSCSI) A standard based on the Internet Protocol (IP) for linking data storage devices over a network and transferring data by carrying SCSI commands over IP networks. *See also* **Small Computer Systems Interface (SCSI)** and **Internet Protocol.**

interruptible foldback (IFB) system A communications system that allows communication from the producer or director and selected production personnel with the on-air talent. *See also* **mix-minus.**

in-the-ear monitoring Using small headphones instead of stage monitors to feed the sound blend to on-stage performers.

in the mud Sound level so quiet that it barely "kicks" the VU or peak meter.

in the red Sound level so loud that the VU meter "rides" over 100 percent of modulation.

inverse square law The acoustic situation in which the sound level changes in inverse proportion to the square of the distance from the sound source.

I/O module *See* **input/output (I/O) module**

IP ENG Stands for *Internet Protocol electronic news gathering.*

iSCSI *See* Internet SCSI

ISDN *See* **Integrated Services Digital Network**

ITD *See* **interaural time difference**

jack Receptacle or plug connector leading to the input or output circuit of a patch bay, a recorder, or other electronic component.

jitter A variation in time from sample to sample that causes changes in the shape of the audio waveform and creates adverse sonic effects such as reduced detail, harsher sound, and ghost imaging.

jogging In digital editing, moving the mouse from side to side to direct control of an audio track. *See also* **scrubbing** and **shuttling.**

Kb *See* kilobit

KB *See* kilobyte

Kbps Kilobits per second.

KB/s Kilobytes per second.

kHz *See* kilohertz

kilobit (Kb) 1,024 bits.

kilobyte (KB) 1,024 bytes.

kilohertz (kHz) A measure of frequency equivalent to 1,000 hertz, or 1,000 cycles per second.

knee The point at which a compressor starts gain reduction. *See also* **hard knee compression** and **soft knee compression**.

K-system Measurement system developed by Bob Katz that integrates measures of metering and monitoring to standardize reference loudness.

LAN *See* local area network

latency The period of time it takes for data to get from one designated point to another. In audio the signal delay through the driver and the interface to the output.

lavalier microphone Microphone that used to be worn around the neck but is now worn attached to the clothing. Also called *mini-mic*.

layering When many sounds occur at once, layering involves making sure that they remain balanced, in perspective, and intelligible in the mix.

L-cut *See* audio-leading-video and video-leading-audio

LFE *See* low-frequency enhancement

limiter A compressor with an output level that does not exceed a preset ceiling regardless of the input level.

linearity Having an output that varies in direct proportion to the input.

listening fatigue A pronounced dulling of the auditory senses, inhibiting perceptual judgment.

listening walk A walk with a concentration on listening. *See also* **soundwalk**.

local area network (LAN) A computer network configured for a small, localized area such as a home or business.

localization (1) Placement of a sound source in the stereo or surround-sound frame. (2) The direction from which a sound source seems to emanate in a stereo or surround-sound field. (3) The ability to tell the direction from which a sound is coming.

longitudinal time code (LTC) A form of SMPTE time code. A high-frequency signal consisting of a stream of pulses produced by a time code generator used to code tape to facilitate editing and synchronization. Also called *SMPTE time code*.

loop group People who provide the background sound for a crowd scene and various vocal utterances that it would be too expensive to hire an A-list actor to perform.

looping Repeating a sound continuously. *See also* **automated dialogue replacement**.

Lo/Ro Stands for *left-only/right-only*. The more common of the two methods for downmixing surround sound to stereo. It adds the center channel to the front-left and front-right channels, the left surround to the left channel, and the right surround to the right channel. *See also* **Lt/Rt**.

lossless compression A data compression process during which no data is discarded. *See also* **lossy compression**.

lossy compression A data compression process during which data that is not critical is discarded during compression. *See also* **lossless compression**.

loudness The relative volume of a sound.

loudness distortion Distortion that occurs when the loudness of a signal is greater than the sound system can handle. Also called *overload distortion*.

low bass Frequency range between roughly 20 Hz and 80 Hz, the lowest two octaves in the audible frequency spectrum.

low end The bass range of the frequency spectrum.

low-frequency enhancement (LFE) In a surround-sound system, using a separate channel and a subwoofer loudspeaker to reproduce low-frequency sounds.

low-pass (high-cut) filter A filter that attenuates frequencies above a selected frequency and allows those below that point to pass.

LTC *See* longitudinal time code

Lt/Rt Stands for *left-total/right-total*. The less common of the two methods for downmixing surround sound to stereo. It adds the center channel to the left and right channels. The surround channels are summed to mono and added to the left and right channels with the right channel 90 degrees out of phase, enabling those using Dolby Pro Logic to reproduce the left, center, right, and surround signals. *See also* **Lo/Ro**.

MADI *See* Multichannel Audio Digital Interface

magnetic film Sprocketed film containing sound only and no picture. *See also* **full coat** and **stripe coat**.

makeup gain A compression control that allows adjustment of the output level to the desired optimum. Used, for example, when loud parts of a signal are so reduced that the overall result sounds too quiet.

masking The hiding of some sounds by other sounds when each is a different frequency and they are presented together.

master fader The fader that controls the combined signal level of the individual input channels on a console.

master section In a multichannel production console, the section that routes the final mix to its recording destination. It usually houses, at least, the master controls for the mixing bus outputs, reverb send and reverb return, and master fader.

mastering The final preparation of audio material for duplication and distribution.

maximum sound-pressure level The level at which a microphone's output signal begins to distort, that is, produces a 3 percent total harmonic distortion.

Mb *See* megabit

MB *See* megabyte

Mbps Megabits per second.

MD™ *See* mini disc™

megabit (Mb) 1,048,576 (2^{20}) bits; sometimes interpreted as 1 million bits.

megabyte (MB) 1,048,576 bytes (2^{20} bytes); sometimes interpreted as 1 million bytes.

megahertz (MHz) A measure of frequency equivalent to 1 million cycles per second.

memory card A nonvolatile memory that can be electrically recorded onto, erased, and reprogrammed, such as Flash memory. It does not need power to maintain the stored information.

memory recorder A digital recorder that has no moving parts and therefore requires no maintenance. Uses a memory card as the storage medium.

MHz *See* megahertz

mic *See* microphone

microphone A transducer that converts acoustic energy into electric energy. Also called *mic*.

microphone modeler A device or plug-in that emulates the sound of various microphones.

middle ear The part of the ear that transfers sound waves from the eardrum to the inner ear.

middle-side (M-S) microphone Consists of two mic capsules housed in a single casing. One capsule, usually cardioid, is the midposition microphone. The other capsule, usually bidirectional, has each lobe oriented 90 degrees laterally.

MIDI *See* **Musical Instrument Digital Interface**

MIDI time code (MTC) Translates SMPTE time code into MIDI messages that allow MIDI-based devices to operate on the SMPTE timing reference.

midrange The part of the frequency spectrum to which humans are most sensitive; the frequencies between roughly 320 Hz and 2,560 Hz.

millimeter (mm) A unit of length equal to one thousandth (10^{-3}) of a meter, or 0.0394 inch.

millisecond (ms) One thousandth of a second.

milliwatt (mW) A unit of power equal to one thousandth (10^{-3}) of a watt.

milking the audience Boosting the level of an audience's sound during laughter or applause and/or reinforcing it with recorded laughter or applause.

mm *See* **millimeter**

mini disc™ (MD™) Magneto-optical disc 2½ inches wide that can store more than an hour of digital-quality audio.

mini-mic Short for *miniature microphone*. Any extremely small lavalier mic designed to be unobtrusive on-camera and which can be easily hidden in or under clothing or on a set.

mixdown The point, usually in postproduction, when all the separately recorded audio tracks are sweetened, positioned, and combined into stereo or surround sound.

mixer A small, highly portable device that mixes various elements of sound, typically coming from multiple microphones, and performs limited processing functions. *See also* **console**.

mixing desk *See* **console**

mix-minus A program feed through an interruptible foldback circuit minus the announcer's voice. *See also* **interruptible foldback (IFB) system**.

mobile media Any of a number of different portable devices capable of storing and playing digital audio, video, and images, such as cell phones, iPods, cameras, PDAs, and laptop computers.

mobile unit A car, van, or tractor-trailer equipped to produce program material on-location.

monitor section   The section in a console that enables the signals to be heard. The monitor section in multichannel production consoles, among other things, allows monitoring of the line or recorder input, selects various inputs to the control room and studio monitors, and controls their levels.

morphing   The continuous, seamless transformation of one effect (aural or visual) into another.

moving-coil loudspeaker   A loudspeaker with a moving-coil element.

moving-coil microphone   A mic with a moving-coil element. The coil is connected to a diaphragm suspended in a magnetic field.

MP3   *See* MPEG-2 layer 3 technology

MP4   *See* MPEG-4 AAC with SBR

MPEG   Stands for *Moving Picture Experts Group.* A compression format for film established by the film industry and the International Standards Organization (ISO). Uses an analytical approach to compression called *acoustic masking.*

MPEG-2 AAC (Advanced Audio Coding)   Compression format that is approximately a 30 percent improvement over the MPEG-2 layer 3 technology (MP3), considered 100 percent better than AC-3.

MPEG-2 layer 3 technology   Compression format considered excellent for sound effects, speech, and most music. Commonly known as *MP3.*

MPEG-4 AAC with SBR (Spectral Bandwidth Replication)   The most recent coding system from MPEG that provides near-CD-quality stereo that can be transmitted over connection speeds as low as 48 Kbps.

ms   *See* millisecond

M-S microphone   *See* middle-side microphone

MTC   *See* MIDI time code

mult   *See* multiple

Multichannel Audio Digital Interface (MADI)   The standard used when interfacing multichannel digital audio.

multidirectional microphone   Microphone with more than one pickup pattern. Also called *polydirectional microphone.*

multipath   In wireless microphones, when more than one radio frequency (RF) signal from the same source arrives at the receiver's front end, creating phase mismatching.

multiple   (1) On a patch bay, jacks interconnected to each other and to no other circuit. They can be used to feed signals to and from sound sources. Also called *mults.* (2) An amplifier with several mic-level outputs to provide individual feeds, thereby eliminating the need for many. Also called a *press bridge, presidential patch,* or *press mult box.*

multiple-entry-port microphone   A mic that has more than one opening for sound waves to reach the transducer. Most of these openings are used to reject sound from the sides or back of the microphone through phase cancellation. Each port returns a different frequency range to the mic capsule out of phase with sounds reaching the front of the mic. Also called *variable-D.*™

Musical Instrument Digital Interface (MIDI)   A protocol that allows synthesizers, drum machines, sequencers, and other signal-processing devices to communicate with or control one another or both.

Music Video Interactive (MVI)   A DVD-based format marketed by Warner Music Group.

musique concrète   A recorded montage of natural sounds often electronically modified and presented as a musical composition.

MVI   *See* Music Video Interactive

mW   *See* milliwatt

narrative sound   Sound effects that add more to a scene than what is apparent and so perform an informational function. *See also* **commentative sound** and **descriptive sound.**

NC   *See* noise criteria

near-coincident miking   A stereo microphone array in which the mics are separated horizontally but the angle or space between their capsules is not more than several inches. *See also* **X-Y miking.**

near-field monitoring   Monitoring with loudspeakers placed close to the operator, usually on or just behind the console's meter bridge, to reduce interference from control room acoustics at the monitoring position. *See also* **far-field monitoring.**

noise   Any unwanted sound or signal.

noise-canceling headphone   Headphone that detects ambient noise before it reaches the ears and nullifies it by synthesizing the sound waves.

noise-canceling microphone   A microphone designed for use close to the mouth and with excellent rejection of ambient sound.

noise criteria (NC)   Contours of the levels of background noise that can be tolerated within an audio studio.

noise reducer   *See* **compander**

noise gate   An expander with a threshold that can be set to reduce or eliminate unwanted low-level sounds, such as room ambience, rumble, and leakage, without affecting the wanted sounds.

noise processor   A digital signal processor that reduces or eliminates pops, clicks, and background noises.

noise reduction coefficient (NRC)   *See* **sound absorption coefficient**

nondestructive editing   Editing that does not alter the original sound or soundfile, regardless of what editing or signal processing is affected. It changes only the pointers, not the data on the disk. *See also* **destructive editing.**

nondiegetic sound   Sound that is outside the story space, such as music underscoring. Also called *extra-sound. See also* **diegetic sound.**

nondirectional microphone   *See* **omnidirectional microphone**

nondiversity receiver   Single-antenna receiving system used with wireless microphones. *See also* **diversity reception.**

nonlinear   The property of not being linear—not having an output that varies in direct proportion to the input.

nonlinear editing   *See* **digital editing**

nonlinear editor (NLE)   A digital editor that facilitates accessing any part of an audio (or video) recording; cutting, pasting, and copying the edit; and restoring any change in the edited material to its original waveform at any time, quickly and seamlessly—all without endangering the master audio (or video).

notch filter   A filter capable of attenuating an extremely narrow bandwidth of frequencies.

NRC   *See* **sound absorption coefficient**

octave   The interval between two sounds that have a frequency ratio of 2:1.

off-mic   Not being within the optimal pickup pattern of a microphone; off-axis.

off-miking   *See* **accent miking**

Ogg   An open-source multimedia container format, comparable to MPEG program stream or QuickTime.

Ogg Vorbis   A professional audio encoding and streaming technology.

ohm (Ω)   A unit of resistance to current flow.

omnidirectional microphone   Microphone that picks up sound from all directions. Also called *nondirectional microphone.*

on-mic   Being within the optimal pickup pattern of a microphone; on-axis.

oscillator   A device that generates pure tones or sine waves.

outer ear   The portion of the ear that picks up and directs sound waves through the auditory canal to the middle ear.

output section   In a mixer and console, the section that routes the signals to a recorder or broadcast or both.

overdubbing   Recording instruments or sections of an ensemble separately. One or a few instruments are first recorded and the other voicings are added separately or in groups to the previously recorded tracks.

overload   Feeding a component or system more amplitude than it can handle and thereby causing loudness distortion.

overload distortion   *See* **loudness distortion**

overload indicator   On a console, a light-emitting diode (LED) that flashes when the input signal is approaching or has reached overload and is clipping. Also called *peak indicator.*

overroll   Recording ambience after recording narration or dialogue by letting the recorder continue to run.

overtones   Harmonics that may or may not be multiples of the fundamental. Subjective response of the ear to harmonics. Also called *inharmonic overtones.*

pad   An attenuator inserted into a component or system to reduce level.

pan pot   Short for *panoramic potentiometer.* A volume control that shifts the proportion of sound from left to right between two output buses and, hence, between the two loudspeakers necessary for reproducing a stereo image; or it shifts the proportion of sound among the six (or more) surround-sound channels, and loudspeakers, necessary for reproducing a surround-sound image.

parabolic microphone system   A system that uses a concave dish to focus reflected sound into a microphone pointed at the center of the dish.

paragraphic equalizer   An equalizer that combines the features of a parametric and a graphic equalizer.

parametric equalizer   An equalizer in which the bandwidth of a selected frequency is continuously variable.

particulate flow detection microphone A laser-based microphone, still in the experimental stage, designed to eliminate distortion.

passive loudspeaker A loudspeaker that is powered externally. *See also* **active loudspeaker.**

passive microphone mixer Combines individual inputs into one output without amplifying the signal. *See also* **active microphone mixer.**

patch bay An assembly of jacks to which are wired the inputs and the outputs of the audio components in a console and/or sound studio. Also called *patch panel.*

patch cord A short cord or cable with a plug at each end, used to route signals in a patch bay.

patch panel *See* **patch bay**

PCD *See* **protein-coated disc**

peak indicator *See* **overload indicator**

peak meter A meter designed to indicate peak loudness levels in a signal.

peak program meter (ppm) A meter designed to indicate transient peaks in the level of a signal.

percentage of modulation The percentage of an applied signal in relation to the maximum signal a sound system can handle.

perspective miking Establishing through mic-to-source distance the audio viewpoint in relation to the performers and their environment in screen space.

PFL *See* **solo**

phantom power Operating voltage supplied to a capacitor microphone by an external power source or mixer, thereby eliminating the need for batteries.

phase The time relationship between two or more sounds reaching a microphone or signals in a circuit. When this time relationship is coincident, the sounds or signals are in phase and their amplitudes are additive. When this time relationship is not coincident, the sounds or signals are out of phase and their amplitudes are subtractive.

phase reversal *See* **polarity reversal**

phase shift The phase relationship of two signals at a given time, or the phase change of a signal over an interval of time.

phasing An effect created by splitting a signal in two and time-delaying one of the signal portions, using a phase shifter.

phon A dimensionless unit of loudness level related to the ear's subjective impression of signal strength.

pickup pattern *See* **polar response pattern**

pin When the needle of the VU meter hits against the peg at the right-hand side of the red. Pinning is to be avoided because it indicates too high a loudness level and it could damage the meter.

pink noise Wideband noise that maintains constant energy per octave. *See also* **white noise.**

pitch The subjective perception of frequency—the highness or lowness of a sound.

pitch shifter A signal processor that varies the pitch of a signal. The basic parameter for pitch shifting is transposition.

plant microphone A stationary mic positioned on the set to cover action that cannot easily be picked up with a boom mic or a body mic or to provide fill sound. Also called *fixed mic.*

plug-in An add-on software tool that gives a hard-disk recording/editing system signal-processing alternatives beyond what the original system provides.

podcasting A development in Internet technology that allows users to create and distribute their own audio (and video) productions over the Web. The term *podcasting* is a combination of *pod,* referring to the iPod sound player, and *casting,* short for *broadcasting.*

podcatcher *See* **aggregator**

polarity The relative position of two signal leads—the high (+) and the low (–)—in the same circuit.

polarity reversal The control on a console that inverts the polarity of an input signal 180 degrees. Sometimes called *phase reversal.*

polar response The indication of how a loudspeaker focuses sound at the monitoring position(s).

polar response pattern The graph of a microphone's directional characteristics as seen from above. The graph indicates response over a 360-degree circumference in a series of concentric circles, each representing a 5 dB loss in level as the circles move inward toward the center. Also called *pickup pattern.*

polydirectional microphone *See* **multidirectional microphone**

pop filter Foam rubber windscreen placed inside the microphone head. Particularly effective in reducing sound from plosives and blowing. Also called *blast filter.* *See also* **windscreen.**

porous absorber A sound absorber made up of porous material whose tiny air spaces are most effective at absorbing high frequencies.

post Short for *postproduction.*

pot Short for *potentiometer. See* **fader.**

potentiometer *See* **fader**

ppm *See* **peak program meter**

precedence effect The tendency to perceive the direct and immediate repetitions of a sound as coming from the same position or direction even if the immediate repetitions coming from another direction are louder. *See also* **Haas effect** and **temporal fusion.**

predelay The amount of time between the onset of the direct sound and the appearance of the first reflections.

pre-emphasis Boosts the treble range in transmission by 6 dB per octave, starting at 2.1 kHz (in the United States) or 3.2 kHz (in Europe).

prefader listen (PFL) *See* **solo**

premix The stage in postproduction when dialogue, music, and sound effects are prepared for final mixing.

presence (1) Perception of a sound as being close and realistic. (2) Also used as a synonym for *ambience* and *room tone. See* **ambience.**

presidential patch *See* **press bridge**

press bridge An amplifier with several mic-level outputs to provide individual feeds, thereby eliminating the need for many. Also called a *multiple, presidential patch,* or *press mult box.*

press mult box *See* **press bridge**

primary frequency *See* **fundamental**

production recording Recording dialogue on the set, thereby preserving the sonic record of a production, regardless of whether the dialogue is to be rerecorded.

production source music Music that emanates from an on-screen singer or ensemble and is produced live during shooting or in postproduction.

protein-coated disc (PCD) In development, the PCD uses a theoretical high-density optical disc technology that would provide up to a 50 TB capacity.

proximity effect Increase in the bass response of some mics as the distance between the mic and its sound source is decreased. Also known as *bass tip-up.*

proximity-prone mini-mic Used for body miking; tends to add presence to close dialogue and reject background sound. *See also* **transparent mini-mic.**

psychoacoustic processor Signal processor that adds clarity, definition, overall presence, and life, or "sizzle," to recorded sound.

psychoacoustics The study of human perception of and subjective response to sound stimuli.

pure tone A single frequency devoid of harmonics and overtones.

Q A measure of the bandwidth of frequencies an equalizer affects.

quantization Converting a waveform that is infinitely variable into a finite series of discrete levels.

radio microphone *See* **wireless microphone system**

rarefaction Temporary drawing apart of vibrating molecules, causing a partial vacuum to occur. *See also* **compression (2).**

read mode Mode of operation in an automated mixdown when the console controls are operated automatically by the data previously encoded in the computer. Also called *safe mode. See also* **update mode** and **write mode.**

RealAudio Proprietary system that uses a compression method called CELP at low bit rates for speech. For music it uses the AC-3 codec developed by Dolby with higher bit rates.

real-time analyzer (RTA) A device that shows the total energy present at all audible frequencies on an instantaneous basis. *See also* **spectrum analyzer.**

recordable compact disc (CD-R) A CD format allowing users to record one time but to play back the recorded information repeatedly.

recovery time *See* **release time**

reflected sound Reflections of the direct sound that bounce off one or more surfaces before reaching the listener.

regeneration *See* **feedback**

release In the sound envelope, the time and the manner in which a sound diminishes to inaudibility.

release time The length of time it takes a compressor to return to its normal level (unity gain) after the signal has been attenuated or withdrawn. Also called *recovery time.*

remote Any broadcast done away from the studio.

remote survey   An inspection of a production location by key production and engineering personnel and the written plan they draft based on that inspection. Also called *site survey.*

rerecording   The final stage in postproduction, when the premixed tracks or stems—dialogue, music, and sound effects—are combined into stereo and surround sound and sent to the edit master.

resolution   *See* word length

resonance   Transmitting a vibration from one body to another when the frequency of the first body is exactly, or almost exactly, the natural frequency of the second body.

reverb   *See* reverberation

reverberant sound   *See* reverberation

reverberation   Multiple blended, random reflections of a sound wave after the sound source has ceased vibrating. The types of reverberation in current use are digital, convolution, plate, and acoustic chamber. Also called *reverb* and *reverberant sound.*

reverberation time   The length of time it takes a sound to die away—the time it takes a sound to decrease to one-millionth of its original intensity, or 60 dB-SPL. Also called *decay time.*

rewritable CD (CD-RW)   A CD format that can be recorded on, erased, and used again for another recording.

rhythm   The sonic time pattern.

ribbon loudspeaker   A loudspeaker that uses a ribbon as the transducer. The ribbon principle in a loudspeaker today is usually employed in the high-frequency tweeter.

ribbon microphone   A microphone with a ribbon diaphragm suspended in a magnetic field.

ride the gain   Continually adjusting controls on a console or other audio equipment to maintain a more or less constant level.

ring-off   When a dialogue line ends with the ambient ring of a room and another line begins with that ring decaying under it.

ripping   The process of copying audio (or video) data in one media form, such as CD or DVD, to a hard disk. To conserve storage space, copied data are usually encoded in a compressed format. Also called *digital audio extraction.*

room modes   *See* eigentones

room tone   Another term for *ambience.* Also called *presence. See* **ambience.**

RSS feed   A method of distributing data about a podcast, blog, or news feed to a widespread group of Internet subscribers.

RTA   *See* real-time analyzer

SAC   *See* sound absorption coefficient

SACD   *See* Super Audio Compact Disc

safe mode   *See* read mode

sample clock   *See* word clock

sampler   An audio device that records a short sound event—such as a note or a musical phrase—into computer memory. The samples can be played by triggering them with a MIDI signal from a MIDI controller or a MIDI sequencer.

sampling   (1) Examining an analog signal at regular intervals defined by the sampling frequency. (2) A process whereby a section of digital audio representing a sonic event, acoustic or electroacoustic, is stored on disk or into electronic memory.

sampling frequency   The frequency (or rate) at which an analog signal is sampled. Also called *sampling rate.*

sampling rate   *See* sampling frequency

SAN   *See* storage area network

Schoeps surround microphone system   A mic system that uses two omnidirectional capacitor capsules flush-mounted on either side of a sphere, with two bidirectional mics, one on each side of the sphere, facing front and rear.

scrubbing   In hard-disk editing, moving the play cursor through the defined region at any speed to listen to a sound being readied for editing.

SCSI   *See* Small Computer Systems Interface

segue   (1) Cutting from one effect to another with nothing in between. (2) Playing two recordings one after the other, with no announcement in between.

self-noise   The electrical noise, or hiss, an electronic device produces. Also called *equivalent noise level.*

sensitivity   (1) A measure of the voltage (dBV) a microphone produces, which indicates its efficiency. (2) The sound-pressure level directly in front of the loudspeaker, on-axis, at a given distance and produced by a given amount of power.

sequencer   An electronic device that can be programmed to store and automatically play back a repeating series of notes on an electronic musical instrument such as a synthesizer.

server   A computer dedicated to providing one or more services over a computer network, typically through a request-response routine.

SFX   *See* **sound effects**

shared system resources   Refers to the need for all parts of a video game—sound control and playback, picture display, game-play and game control, and control of various hardware components—to use simultaneously the same finite set of system resources.

shelving   Maximum boost or cut of a signal at a particular frequency that remains constant at all points beyond that frequency so the response curve resembles a shelf.

shock mount   A device that isolates a microphone from mechanical vibrations. It can be attached externally or built into a microphone.

shotgun microphone   A highly directional microphone with a tube that resembles the barrel of a rifle.

shuttling   In digital editing, moving the mouse to change the scrubbing speed. *See also* **jogging** and **scrubbing**.

signal processors   Devices used to alter some characteristic of a sound. *See also* **amplitude processor, noise processor, spectrum processor,** and **time processor**.

signal-to-noise ratio (S/N)   The ratio, expressed in decibels, of an electronic device's nominal output to its noise floor. The wider the S/N ratio, the better.

silent film   Film carrying picture only, with no sound information.

sine wave   A fundamental frequency with no harmonics or overtones. Also called *pure tone*.

single-D™ microphone   *See* **single-entry-port microphone**

single-entry-port microphone   A directional microphone that uses a single port to bring sounds from the rear of the mic to the capsule. Because these sounds from the rear reach the capsule out of phase with those that reach the front of the capsule, they are canceled. Also called *single-D™ microphone*.

single-system recording   Recording picture and sound in a film or video camera simultaneously.

site survey   *See* **remote survey**

slap back echo   The effect created when an original signal repeats as distinct echoes that decrease in level with each repetition.

slate   The part of a talkback system that feeds sound to a recording. It is used for verbal identification of the material being recorded, the take number, and other information just before each recording. *See also* **clapslate**.

Small Computer Systems Interface (SCSI)   The standard for hardware and software command language that allows two-way communication between, primarily, hard-disk and CD-ROM drives. Pronounced "scuzzy."

SMPTE time code   A reference in hours, minutes, seconds, and frames used for coding to facilitate editing and synchronization. Pronounced "sempty." Also called *longitudinal time code*.

S/N   *See* **signal-to-noise ratio**

soft cut   A term used with picture when a shot change is brief but not quite as abrupt as a cut or as deliberate as a dissolve. The effect can be used in audio for transitions that need a quick yet aesthetically graceful change.

soft knee compression   Smooth gain reduction at the start of compression. *See also* **knee** and **hard knee compression**.

soft sound effect   Does not have a defined beginning and ending and does not explicitly synchronize with the picture. *See also* **hard sound effect**.

solo   A control on a multichannel console that automatically cuts off all signals feeding the monitor system except those signals feeding through the channel that the solo control activates. Sometimes called *prefader listen (PFL)*.

Sony/Philips Digital Interface (S/PDIF)   The consumer version of the AES/EBU interface calling for an unbalanced line using phono connectors. *See also* **AES/EBU**.

sound absorption coefficient (SAC)   A measure of the sound-absorbing ability of a surface. This coefficient is defined as the fraction of incident sound absorbed by a surface. Values range from 0.01 for marble to 1.00 for the materials used in an almost acoustically dead enclosure. Also known as *noise reduction coefficient (NRC)*.

sound card   Computer hardware necessary to input, manipulate, and output audio.

sound chain   The audio components that carry a signal from its sound source to its destination.

sound design   The process of creating the overall sonic character of a production (usually in relation to picture).

sound designer   The individual responsible for a production's overall sonic complexion.

sound effects (SFX)   Anything sonic that is not speech or music.

sound envelope   Changes in the loudness of a sound over time, described as occurring in four stages: attack, initial decay, sustain, and release (ADSR).

SoundField microphone system   Four capacitor microphone capsules, shaped like a tetrahedron and enclosed in a single casing, that can be combined in various formats to reproduce sonic depth, breadth, and height.

soundfile   A sound stored in the memory of a hard-disk recorder/editor.

sound film   Film carrying both picture and sound.

sound frequency spectrum   The range of frequencies audible to human hearing: about 20 to 20,000 Hz.

sound-pressure level (dB-SPL)   A measure of the pressure of a sound wave, or sound-pressure level (SPL), expressed in decibels (dB).

soundscape   The sonic environment; any portion of the sonic environment regarded as a field for study; or abstract constructions, such as musical compositions and audio montages, particularly when considered as an environment.

sound transmission class (STC)   A rating that evaluates the effectiveness of barriers in isolating sound.

soundwalk   The exploration of a soundscape using a score as a guide. The score consists of a map, drawing the listener's attention to unusual sounds and ambiences to be heard along the way. *See also* **listening walk.**

sound wave   A vibrational disturbance that involves mechanical motion of molecules transmitting energy from one place to another.

source music   Background music from an on-screen source, such as a stereo, radio, or jukebox. It is added during postproduction.

spaced miking   Two, sometimes three, microphones spaced from several inches to several feet apart, depending on the width of the sound source and the acoustics, for stereo recording.

S/PDIF   *See* **Sony/Philips Digital Interface**

spectrum analyzer   A device that, among other things, displays the frequency response of an electrical waveform in relation to the amplitude present at all frequencies. *See also* **real-time analyzer.**

spectrum editing   Using a sonogram view of an audio file to facilitate ultrafine surgical editing.

spectrum processor   A signal processor that affects a sound's spectral range, such as equalizers, filters, and psychoacoustic processors.

speed-up pitch-shifting   Using a pitch shifter to change the timbre and the pitch of natural sounds. Also called *chipmunk effect.*

SPL   *See* **sound-pressure level**

split-band compressor   A compressor that affects an input signal independently by splitting the audio into multiple bands and then recombining the outputs of the bands into a single mono or stereo broadband signal. *See also* **broadband compressor.**

split editing   (1) Editing the same sound into two or more separate tracks to facilitate control of its length and in editing transitions. In dialogue, for example, this makes it easier to extend lines that may have been cut too short during picture editing, to overlap voices, and to carry over lines from one scene to the next. (2) A type of transition where the audio or video leads or lags a portion of the previous edit. *See* **audio-leading-video** and **video-leading-audio.**

split-track recording   Recording two separate sound sources on two separate tracks on a stereo recorder, camcorder, or disk recorder.

spotting   Going through a script or work print and deciding on the placement of music and sound effects.

spotting sheet   Indicates the music or sound-effect cue and whether it is synchronous or nonsynchronous, its in- and out-times, and its description.

squelch   In a wireless microphone system, a process of signal reception at the receiver that silences or mutes the receiver's audio output when there is no radio signal.

STC   *See* **sound transmission class**

stereo   One-dimensional sound that creates the illusion of two-dimensional sound.

stereophonic microphone   Two directional microphone capsules, one above the other, with separate outputs, encased in one housing.

stereo-to-mono compatibility   Ensuring that a recording made in stereo is reproducible in mono without spatial or spectral distortion.

sticks   *See* **clapslate**

storage area network (SAN)   Can be likened to the common flow of data in a personal computer that is shared by different kinds of storage devices. It is designed to serve a large network of users and handle sizeable data transfers among different interconnected data storage devices.

stripe coat   Magnetic film that contains two stripes of oxide coating, a wide stripe for recording single-track mono and a narrow balance stripe to ensure that the film wind on reels is smooth. *See also* **full coat.**

stochastic process Sound track development that is not deterministic; rather it is a probability-based expression of variable and predictable user actions and random elements.

subtractive equalization Attenuating, rather than boosting, frequencies to achieve equalization. *See also* **complementary equalization** and **cumulative equalization.**

Super Audio Compact Disc (SACD) Sony's proprietary extremely high-quality CD audio format intended for the audiophile market.

surround sound Multichannel sound, typically employing six or more channels, each one feeding to a separate loudspeaker that expands the dimensions of depth, thereby placing the listener more in the center of the aural image than in front of it. *See also* **5.1** and **7.1.**

sustain In the sound envelope, the period during which the sound's relative dynamics are maintained after its initial decay.

sweet spot In control room monitoring, the designated listening position, which is the optimal distance away from and between the loudspeakers.

sweetening Enhancing the sound of a recording in postproduction through signal processing and mixing.

synchronization Locking two or more devices that have microprocessor intelligence so that they operate at precisely the same rate.

system microphone Interchangeable microphone capsules of various directional patterns that attach to a common base. The base contains a power supply and a preamplifier.

system noise The inherent noise that an electronic device or a system generates.

system resources Computing power and asset (data and file) management available to a video game. System resources can be either dedicated or shared, depending on the architecture and the design of the game.

talkback Studio-address intercom system that permits communication from a control room microphone to a loudspeaker or headphones in the studio.

TB *See* **terabyte**

TD Stands for *technical director.*

tempo The speed of a sound.

temporal fusion When reflected sound reaches the ear within 10 to 30 ms of the original sound, the direct and reflected sounds are perceived as a single sound. This effect gradually disappears as the time interval between direct and reflected sounds increases from roughly 30 to 50 ms. *See also* **Haas effect** and **precedence effect.**

temporary threshold shift (TTS) A reversible desensitization in hearing that disappears in anywhere from a few hours to several days. Also called *auditory fatigue.*

terabyte (TB) 1,024 gigabytes (2^{40} bytes).

THD *See* **total harmonic distortion**

three-to-one rule A guideline used to reduce the phasing caused when a sound reaches two microphones at slightly different times. It states that no two mics should be closer to each other than three times the distance between one of them and its sound source.

three-way system loudspeaker A loudspeaker system with two crossover networks.

threshold of feeling 120 dB-SPL.

threshold of hearing The lowest sound-pressure level at which sound becomes audible to the human ear. It is the zero reference of 0 dB-SPL.

threshold of pain The sound-pressure level at which the ear begins to feel pain, about 140 dB-SPL, although levels of around 120 dB-SPL cause discomfort.

tie line Facilitates the interconnecting of outboard devices and patch bays in a control room or between studios.

timbre The unique tone quality or color of a sound.

time code address The unique SMPTE time code number that identifies each $\frac{1}{30}$ second of a recording.

time compression Shortening the time (length) of material without changing its pitch.

time expansion Increasing the time (length) of material without changing its pitch.

time processor A signal processor that affects the time interval between a signal and its repetition. The effects include reverberation and delay.

tinnitus After prolonged exposure to loud sounds, the ringing, whistling, or buzzing in the ears, even though no loud sounds are present.

TL *See* **transmission loss**

total harmonic distortion (THD) A specification that compares the output signal with the input signal and measures the level differences in harmonic frequencies between the two. THD is measured as a percentage; the lower the percentage, the better.

transducer   A device that converts one form of energy into another.

transfer   *See* **dub**

transient   A sound that begins with a sharp attack followed by a quick decay.

transient distortion   Distortion that occurs when a sound system cannot reproduce sounds that begin with sudden, explosive attacks.

transmission loss (TL)   The amount of sound reduction provided by a barrier such as a wall, floor, or ceiling.

transmitter microphone   *See* **wireless microphone system**

transparent mini-mic   Used for body miking; tends to add an open, natural sound and pick up more ambience. *See also* **proximity-prone mini-mic.**

treble   Frequency range between roughly 5,120 Hz and 20,000 Hz, the highest two octaves audible to human hearing in the sound frequency spectrum.

trim   (1) To attenuate the loudness level in a component or circuit. (2) The device on a console that attenuates the loudness level at the microphone/line input.

TTS   *See* **temporary threshold shift**

tube microphone   A capacitor microphone using a tube circuit in the preamp.

tweeter   The informal name of a loudspeaker that reproduces high frequencies. *See also* **woofer.**

two-way system loudspeaker   A loudspeaker system with one crossover network.

ultra density optical disc (UDO)   High-density optical disc format in two versions that can store up to 60 GB and 120 GB, respectively.

ultrasonic   Frequencies above the range of human hearing.

unbalanced line   A line (or circuit) with two conductors of unequal voltage.

underscore music   Nondiegetic original or library music that enhances the informational or emotional content of a scene.

underscoring   Adding background music that enhances the content of a scene by evoking a particular idea, emotion, point of view, or atmosphere.

unidirectional microphone   A microphone that picks up sound from one direction. Also called *directional microphone.*

upcut   When the board operator is late in responding to the first few utterances of a speaker, thereby missing the words or having them barely audible.

update mode   Mode of operation in an automated mixdown when an encoded control can be recorded without affecting the coding of the other controls. *See also* **read mode** and **write mode.**

upmixing   A way to handle surround sound by taking two-channel stereo and synthesizing it to multichannel pseudo-surround. *See also* **downmixing.**

upper bass   Frequency range between roughly 80 Hz and 320 Hz.

upper midrange   Frequency range between roughly 2,560 Hz and 5,120 Hz.

USB microphone   A digital microphone developed for those who want to record directly into a computer without an audio interface, such as a console, control surface, or mixer. *USB* stands for *Universal Serial Bus.*

USB microphone adapter   *See* **USB microphone converter**

USB microphone converter   Device that makes it possible to connect any dynamic or capacitor XLR microphone to a computer via USB. Also known as a *USB microphone adapter.*

V   *See* **volt**

variable-D™ microphone   *See* **multiple-entry-port microphone**

variable-frequency wireless microphone system   A wireless microphone system that can use more than one channel. Also known as *frequency-agile system. See also* **fixed-frequency wireless microphone system.**

VCA   *See* **voltage-controlled amplifier**

velocity   The speed of a sound wave: 1,130 feet per second at sea level and 70°F.

video-leading-audio   When the picture of a new scene starts before the sound of the old scene has finished. Also called *L-cut. See also* **audio-leading-video.**

virtual track   In hard-disk recording, a track that provides all the functionality of an actual track but cannot be played simultaneously with another virtual track.

VO   *See* **voice-over**

vocoder *See* voice processor

voice acting Taking the words off the page and conveying meaning, making them believable and memorable.

voice-over (VO) An announcement or narration to which other materials, such as music, sound effects, and visuals, are added.

Voice over Internet Protocol (VoIP) Technology that allows interactive video game users who have a headset and a microphone to speak with each other, give and receive instructions, and play in a team environment against others using the same technology.

voice processor A device that can enhance, modify, pitch-correct, harmonize, and change completely the sound of a voice. Also called *vocoder.*

VoIP *See* Voice over Internet Protocol

volt (V) The unit used to measure potential difference or electromotive force. The potential generated by 1 ampere of current flowing through 1 ohm of resistance.

voltage-controlled amplifier (VCA) An amplifier used to decrease level. The amount of amplification is controlled by external DC voltage.

volume control *See* fader

volume-unit (VU) meter A meter that responds to the average voltage on the line, not true volume levels. It is calibrated in volume units and percentage of modulation.

VU *See* volume-unit meter

W *See* watt

walla A nonsense word that used to be spoken by film extras to create ambient crowd sound without anything discernable actually being said.

WAN *See* wide area network

watt (W) The unit of power equal to the expenditure of 1 ampere passed through a resistance of 1 ohm for 1 second.

waveform A graphic representation of a sound's characteristic shape displayed, for example, on test equipment and hard-disk editing systems.

wavelength (λ) The length of one cycle of a sound wave. Wavelength is inversely proportional to the frequency of a sound; the higher the frequency, the shorter the wavelength.

weighting network A filter used for weighting a frequency response before measurement.

wet sound A sound with reverberation or signal processing. *See also* **dry sound**.

white noise A wideband noise that contains equal energy at each frequency. *See also* **pink noise**.

wide area network (WAN) A computer network configured for a large geographical area.

windscreen Foam rubber covering specially designed to fit over the outside of a microphone head. Used to reduce plosive and blowing sounds. *See also* **pop filter**.

wireless microphone system System consisting of a transmitter that sends a microphone signal to a receiver connected to a console or recorder. Also called *cordless, FM, radio,* and *transmitter microphone.*

woofer Informal name for a loudspeaker that produces the bass frequencies. *See also* **tweeter**.

word clock A synchronization signal that is used to control the rate at which digital audio data is converted or transmitted. Also called *sample clock* or *digital clock.*

word length Describes the potential accuracy of a particular piece of hardware or software that processes audio data. In general, the more bits that are available, the more accurate the resulting output from the data being processed. Also called *bit depth* and *resolution.*

work surface *See* control surface

worldizing Recording room sound to add the sound of that space to a dry recording or to use it to enhance or smooth ambient backgrounds that are already part of the dialogue track.

wow Starting a recorded sound before it reaches full speed.

write mode The mode of operation in an automated mixdown during which controls are adjusted conventionally and the adjustments are encoded in the computer for retrieval in read mode. *See also* **read mode** and **update mode**.

XLR connector Common male and female microphone plugs with a three-pin connector.

X-Y miking Coincident or near-coincident miking that places the microphones' diaphragms over or horizontal to one another. *See also* **coincident miking** and **near-coincident miking**.

zero crossing The point where the waveform crosses the centerline, denoting a value of zero amplitude. It divides the positive (upper) and negative (lower) parts of the waveform.

Credits

360 Systems: 12-16

Acoustic Sciences Corporation: 2-18, 2-25

Acoustical Solutions: 2-17b

ADC Telecommunications, Inc.: 4-16

AKG Acoustics: 3-23b, 3-25a, 3-27b, 3-28b, 3-29, 3-50, 3-51, 3-57b, 3-57d, 3-72d, 3-72e

Alesis: 13-19b

Alpha Audio: 2-16

AMG Electronics: 3-25b

Antares Audio Technologies: 3-19

Aphex Systems, Ltd.: 13-7

Atlas Sound: 3-63, 3-65

Audio Ease: 7-10a

Audio Services Corporation: 11-6

Audio-Technica: 3-7

beyerdynamic, Inc.: 3-3b, 3-23a, 3-69a, 8-23

James Biddle: 12-8, 20-8

Blue Microphones: 3-46

Wesley Bulla, Ph.D.: 1-18, 1-19

CEDAR Audio Ltd.: 11-12

Countryman Associates: 3-20, 3-23c, 3-24

Crown International, Inc.: 3-27a, 3-27c

Denecke, Inc.: 6-3

Digidesign: 4-22, 17-58, 20-1, 20-21

DK-Technologies, www.dk-technologies.com: 8-22

Dolby Laboratories, Inc.: 23-4

Dorrough Electronics: 4-9

DPA Microphones: 3-49, 3-57c

Earthworks, Inc.: 3-44, 3-45, 17-16, 17-39

Electro-Voice, Inc.: 3-11, 3-58, 3-60 (center left, center right), 3-69b

Esto Photographic: 12-7

Etymotic Research: 1-20

Gallery: 11-14, 15-7

Bob Ghent, "Healthy Hearing," *Mix,* March 1994, p. 153: 1-14

David Gibson, *The Art of Mixing,* 2nd ed. Vallejo, Calif.: Artistpro, 2004: 22-5, 22-6, 22-7, 22-8, 22-9, 22-10, 22-11, 22-12, 22-13, 22-14, 22-15, 22-16, 22-17

Gotham Audio Corporation: 7-11

Lynne Gross and Larry Ward, *Electronic Moviemaking,* 4th ed. Belmont, Calif.: Wadsworth Publishing, 2000: 15-8

Holophone: 3-40, 3-41

David Immer, "Phone It In," *Mix,* February 1994, p. 88: 5-18

J. L. Fisher: 3-66

JK Audio, Inc.: 13-3, 13-4, 13-6, 13-12

Bob Katz, *Mastering Audio,* 2nd ed. Boston: Focal Press, 2007, p. 47: inside back cover

Elizabeth M. Keithley, Ph.D.: 1-16

Latch Lake Music, micKing® boom stand: 3-67

Le Mobile, Inc.: 13-18

Lectrosonics: 3-52, 3-54, 3-55, 3-56

Lexicon, Inc.: 7-9

Line6: 17-56

Live Sound International: 3-53

Index

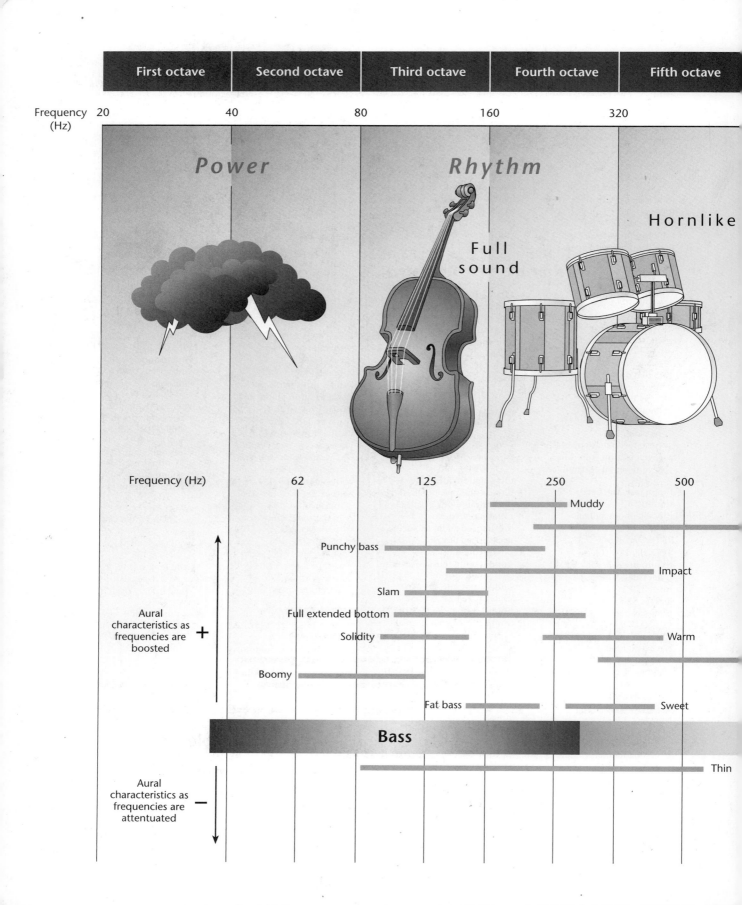